CW01271220

WAR BOWS

OSPREY
PUBLISHING

Dedication
In memory of John Waller

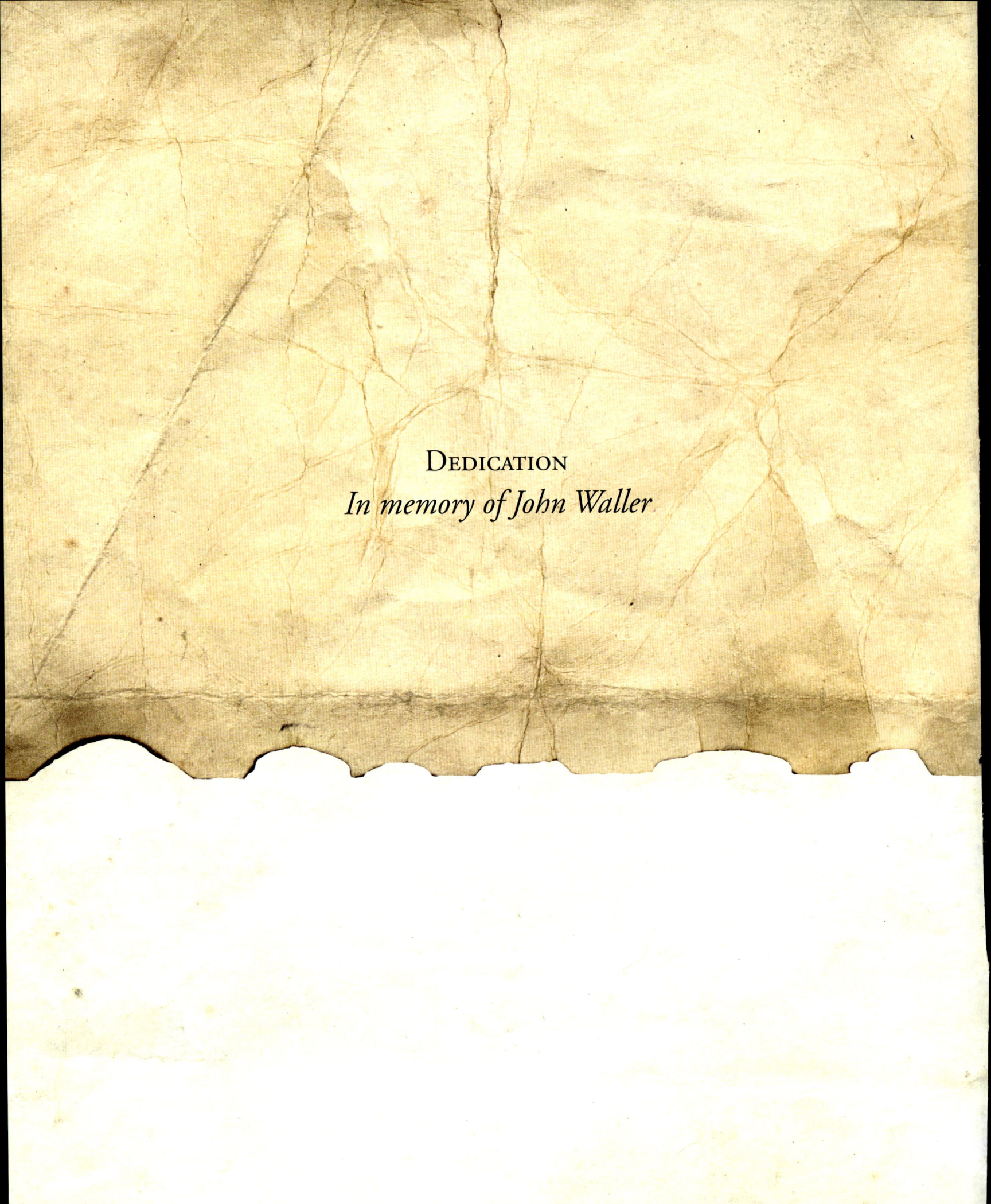

WAR BOWS

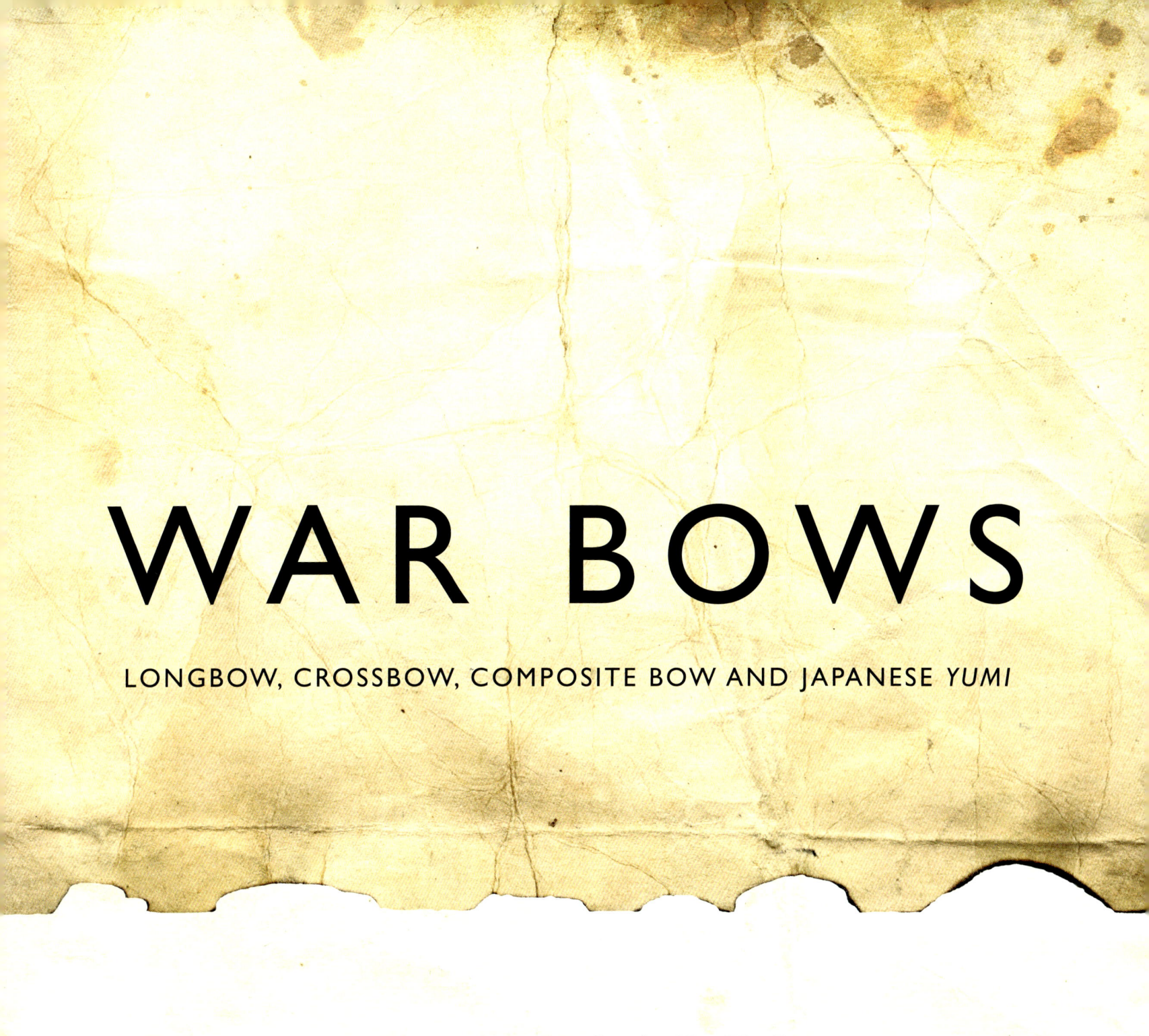

LONGBOW, CROSSBOW, COMPOSITE BOW AND JAPANESE *YUMI*

MIKE LOADES

OSPREY PUBLISHING
Bloomsbury Publishing Plc
PO Box 883, Oxford, OX1 9PL, UK
1385 Broadway, 5th Floor, New York, NY 10018, USA
E-mail: info@ospreypublishing.com
www.ospreypublishing.com

OSPREY is a trademark of Osprey Publishing Ltd

First published in Great Britain in 2019
© Mike Loades, 2019
Mike Loades has asserted his right under the Copyright, Designs and Patents Act, 1988, to be identified as Author of this work.

For legal purposes the Acknowledgements on pages 298–9 constitute an extension of this copyright page.

This edition contains material previously published in the following books by Mike Loades: WPN 43 *The Composite Bow*; WPN 30 *The Longbow*; WPN 61 *The Crossbow* (series editor Martin Pegler).

All rights reserved. No part of this publication may be reproduced or transmitted in any form or by any means, electronic or mechanical, including photocopying, recording, or any information storage or retrieval system, without prior permission in writing from the publishers.

A catalogue record for this book is available from the British Library.

ISBNs: HB 9781472825537; eBook 9781472825520; ePDF 9781472825544; XML 9781472825551

19 20 21 22 23   10 9 8 7 6 5 4 3 2 1

Index by Fionbar Lyons
Battlescenes by Peter Dennis
Originated by PDQ Digital Media Solutions, Bungay, UK
Printed in China through World Print Ltd.

Editor's note
For the most part, measurements are given using the imperial scale. Exceptions are made for energy and force, for which metric units such as the joule (J) and the newton (N) are used. The following data will help when converting between imperial and metric measurements:
When citing medieval prices and wages, references in this book are to the pre-decimal British currency of pounds, shillings and pence: 12 old pence (12d) made one shilling (1s) and 20 shillings made one pound (£1). In modern decimal currency 100 new pence make one pound. Measurements are given using the imperial scale, which has the following approximations on the metric scale:

1 mile = 1.6km
1 yard = 0.9m
1 foot = 0.3m
1 inch = 25.4mm
1lb = 0.45kg
1 gallon (UK) = 4.54 litres
100ft/sec = 30.48m/sec
1J = 0.74 foot-pound force
1N = 0.22 pound-force

Artist's note
Readers may care to note that the original paintings from which the artwork plates in this book were prepared are available for private sale. All reproduction copyright whatsoever is retained by the Publishers. All enquiries should be addressed to:
Peter Dennis, 'Fieldhead', The Park, Mansfield, Nottinghamshire NG18 2AT, UK, or email magie.h@ntlworld.com
The publishers regret that they can enter into no correspondence upon this matter.

Front cover: Ian Coote and Gary Symonds of the EWBS shooting English longbows in elevation. (Mike Loades)
Back cover: The author drawing a composite bow. (Kim Hawkins)

The below note relates to the image on page 286:
Edo period Japanese woodblock print (*nishiki-e*); ink and colour on paper: *At the Battle of Yashima in the Genpei Wars, Nasu no Yoichi Munetaka Gained Renown throughout the Land by Shooting Down a Fan as a Target (Genpei Yashima no tatakai ni Nasu no Yoichi Munetaka ōgi no mato o uchiotoshite tenka ni kōmei no zu)* by Enrōsai Shigemitsu (active *c.* 1848–54). Vertical ōban triptych 37 x 76.5 cm, Denman Waldo Ross Collection, Boston Museum of Fine Arts, 17.3209.27-9.

Osprey Publishing supports the Woodland Trust, the UK's leading woodland conservation charity.

To find out more about our authors and books visit **www.ospreypublishing.com**. Here you will find extracts, author interviews, details of forthcoming events and the option to sign up for our newsletter.

CONTENTS

Introduction	6
CHAPTER ONE: THE LONGBOW	**8**
Development: The longbow's genesis and production	12
Use: At full draw	33
Impact: Assessing the longbow	78
CHAPTER TWO: THE CROSSBOW	**88**
Development: Lock, stock and lath	92
Use: Steady, steady, steady: shoot	122
Impact: Bolts from the blue	148
CHAPTER THREE: THE COMPOSITE BOW	**156**
Development: Engineering the optimal bow	159
Use: Archery – a very martial art	185
Impact: Different bows for different blows	226
CHAPTER FOUR: THE JAPANESE *YUMI*	**234**
Development: The asymmetric bow	237
Use: The Way of the Bow and the Horse	257
Impact: The sting of the samurai	285
Epilogue	297
Acknowledgements	298
Bibliography	299
Index	305

INTRODUCTION

I began archery at the age of 9, by persuading my Latin master to form an archery club. He had no knowledge of the art but he agreed to the scheme and supervised patiently a small cadre of boys who attempted ineptly to hit the target at our weekly practice. I cannot claim to be an especially good archer but that has never diminished my passion and fascination for all things related to bows and arrows. When I was 13, I saw a beautiful recurve bow in the window of a local sports shop. I'd never seen a recurve bow before and its figured-maple riser was especially handsome. It cultivated an early awareness that bows had a beauty of form and materials, which, in addition to the thrill of shooting them, added greatly to their interest. According to the way my mother used to tell it, I pleaded with her to buy it, offering the sale of my treasured racing bicycle as a sacrifice, and by telling her 'This is not just another fad – this is going to be my life.' I still have that bow. There was certainly no well-formed plan in my mind when I asserted such precocious prescience but, as it turned out, the 13-year-old me was right. Archery has been at the centre of both my professional and private life. It became supplemented with riding and swordfighting and this triumvirate of physical skills has continuously informed and fuelled my deep interest in history. This book is another step on that journey.

I have a sentimental attachment to bows; I am utterly bewitched by them and by the joy of shooting them. I understand that draw. However, when sifting through historical evidence, it is essential to separate such feelings from the enquiry. Bows were, at various stages, important weapons, useful weapons, and even impressive weapons. However, they were never, on their own, decisive weapons nor super-weapons, nor any such nonsense. Each has to be considered within the military context in which it was used. Archers were not solo performers but part of an army. Armour worked and archery had its limitations. Somewhere within these statements is a truth that has to be teased out from beneath a smokescreen of ancient nationalistic propagandas and the tendency in some cultures to parade their particular bow as a tribal totem. Different bows existed to fulfil different needs. There is not a competition for which was the best; each was the best for its time and place. Having an understanding of that context is the key to appreciating the war bow in all its fascinating diversity.

The present work is a compilation of previously published material together with a substantial amount of new material and a number of revisions. One of many rewarding aspects about the study of historical archery is that a great deal remains to be discovered. It has been a thrill to delve into archives and mine new nuggets of evidence and, of course, it is the empirical facts that are really important. However, facts often need interpretation and that creates necessity for both hypotheses and experimentation. I have tried to make clear which is which and have adjusted where my thinking has shifted. Theories need frequent updating. Practical tests continue to shed new light on matters. We should challenge what we believe constantly. More than anything else I should like the pages that follow to be a call to further study. There is still so much to learn; in the space allotted, I can do no more that put up a few signposts.

The author, 2018. (Kim Hawkins)

INTRODUCTION

CHAPTER ONE
THE LONGBOW

In 13th-century England, the longbow began to emerge as a symbol of empowerment for the yeoman classes. Many accounts of the Robin Hood legend root him in this period. The idea that strength and skill can triumph over wealth and status is a powerful one; it is an idea that offers the hope that ordinary people can throw off the yoke of lordly oppressors. Holding more rigidly to standards of chivalric propriety and feudal hierarchy, the French nobility deplored the fact that men of inferior class, men with longbows, were able to fell expensive knights. However, to a certain breed of Englishman, the fact that this simple stick, the weapon of Everyman, was able to usurp the natural order of things made the allure of the longbow all the more compelling. The longbow has remained a very potent symbol of common justice, which is probably why it has continued to receive such romantic treatment. Longbows are also a great joy to shoot.

A late 15th-century depiction of archers in action at the battle of Crécy, 1346. They wear an assortment of sallet-style helmets; note the combinations of brigandines, mail and plate. The arrows lying on the ground are possibly an attempt by the artist to represent arrows stuck in the ground and standing upright, but the challenges of perspective may have defeated him here. (Froissart's *Chronicles*, Bibliothèque Nationale de France, Ms. Fr. 2643, f. 165v, Bibliothèque Nationale de France. Photo by: Photo12/UIG via Getty Images)

There are various definitions for the term longbow, including narrow criteria set out by the British Longbow Society (BLS) that would exclude longbows of a medieval type. The BLS, formed in 1951, exists to preserve the recreational shooting tradition of Victorian- and Edwardian-style lightweight longbows which, unlike medieval bows, have a stiff centre section. It acknowledges that the medieval style of battlefield longbow was of differing specifications and does not claim that what it defines as a longbow is of a medieval type. Medieval longbows bent 'full compass', that is with a continuous arc through the centre section; they also had no binding for the handgrip, which is only a feature of later bows. The first written reference I can find to the term 'longbow' is in a letter from Margaret Paston to her husband John, written in 1449 (Gairdner 1986: 101). At the time John Paston was embroiled in a private war with Robert Moleyns; in 1450 Moleyns sent 1,000 men to dislodge Paston from his castle at Gresham, Norfolk, and his followers subsequently attacked Margaret Paston. She had good reason to attend to the defence of her house. In her letter, Margaret urges John to get some 'crosse bowis' because the house is too low for men to shoot out with a 'long bowe'. Here 'longbow' is a term used to distinguish it from the crossbow – the longbow was both held 'longwise', not mounted 'crosswise', and it was also longer than the bow (prod) on a crossbow. Prior to this, longbows were referred to simply as 'bows'.

There is a direct correlation between the length of a simple wooden bow and the length of draw – longbows are also long. Unlike longbows, composite bows – which consist of laminations of various materials including wood, horn and sinew – are capable of taking extreme bend without breaking, and so a laminated bow or bow of composite materials can bend with a much greater arc in proportion to length than can a bow that is fashioned from a single stave of wood – known as a 'self' bow – which is the case with a longbow.

Longbows stood taller than the man who drew them because the height of the man was proportionate to the length of his arms and thus the length of his draw. A longer draw required a longer bow or the bow might break, and it was a characteristic of the medieval military longbow that the archer drew back to the ear or shoulder, a measure that sent his arrows thudding into the enemy with even greater impact. In 1590 Sir John Smythe, soldier, diplomat and author of military treatises, wrote, 'Our English bows, arrows and archers do exceed all other bows used by foreign nations, not only in thickness and strength, but also in the length and size of the arrows' (Smythe 1964: 69).

In recent years the term 'warbow' has been coined to differentiate the recreational longbow and the hunting longbow from their more powerful martial cousin. 'Warbow' is not a medieval term but it is nonetheless a very useful descriptor and I will use it intermittently in the ensuing text. However, the warbows to be discussed here are also longbows and it is that latter term, fondly familiar to me, that I will employ primarily in referring to this enigmatic weapon.

On land, the longbow had been used as a skirmish and battlefield weapon in the hands of the Anglo-Saxons and the Vikings. A line in the epic poem *Beowulf*, which may have been written as early as the 8th century AD and no later than the 11th, hints at the prevalence of battlefield archery during this early period. It speaks of the hero, Beowulf, 'who often endured the iron-tipped arrow-shower, when the dark cloud loosed by bow strings broke above the shield wall, quivering; when the eager shaft, with its feather garb, discharged its duty to the barb' (Anon 1973: 117–18). The longbow was also used by the Normans; the Norman lord Richard de Clare (1130–76), known as 'Strongbow', took several companies of Welsh archers with him for the Norman invasion of Ireland in 1169. There was nothing to distinguish the longbows of these cultures from their later medieval incarnation other than perhaps increased draw-weight for the later medieval bows.

More significantly the longbow of these earlier periods was not used in great numbers. Well into the 13th century it was still being used for campaigns in difficult terrain, but seldom in pitched battle. However, at the end of that century there was a shift in tactics, and what changed was the scale of the longbow's use. Armies now counted many thousands of archers amongst their ranks and the longbow emerged as a prominent battlefield weapon. It reached its peak of both fame and function when it was employed in massed numbers by English armies on the open battlefield during the Wars of Scottish Independence (1296–1357), the Hundred Years' War (1337–1453) and the Wars of the Roses (1455–85). As a maritime weapon, the longbow would remain of paramount importance throughout the medieval era and until the end of the 16th century, especially for the English.

Although medieval English armies used archers to a greater extent than any other nation, they did not do so exclusively. The Welsh used archers very effectively in guerrilla warfare against Edward I (r. 1272–1307) and subsequently in the service of English kings in foreign wars. The Scots fielded archers, in fewer numbers but in similar manner to the English, on the battlefield. Scottish bowmen also served with distinction in French armies during the latter part of the Hundred Years' War. During the 15th century, English archers were in high demand to fight in the armies of Burgundy, a powerful duchy that was itself at war with France. In the original publication of *The Longbow* in 2013, I concentrated solely on the longbow's use by English armies and by English navies, for it is in their service that it made its most conspicuous impact. Moreover, a greater focus was been given to its use in the campaigns of Edward III (r. 1327–77). I consider this to be the longbow's apotheosis and a source of many good examples of its versatility. However, in this extended volume I have been able to examine it a little in a broader context and acknowledge its wider use in other armies. A greater focus has been given to its use in the campaigns of Edward III (r. 1327–77). I consider this to be the longbow's apotheosis and a source of many good examples of its versatility.

Any assessment of the longbow's lethal potential must encompass an understanding of how armour developed to deal with the threat. In fact, it is mostly through the progress of armour that we can best track the development of the weapon. In appearance longbows from different eras looked much the same, but it is probable that as armour improved, the draw-weight increased. As we shall see, there was certainly an evolution in arrowhead styles, which included not only armour-attacking forms but also case-hardened points. It may be argued, however, that the most significant developments in the longbow's trajectory to iconic weapon status were changes in the recruitment and tactical deployment of the archer himself.

Archers faced a mighty and impressive foe. The most glorious, most splendid and possibly the most powerful warrior ever to put his stamp on the battlefield was the fully armoured medieval knight. He engaged the enemy by smashing into him, and it was the archer's task to stop the knight in his tracks. The bowman did not always pull it off – but when he did, he became the stuff of legend.

DEVELOPMENT: THE LONGBOW'S GENESIS AND PRODUCTION

Origins and discoveries

As a hunting weapon the longbow can be traced to the Neolithic period, which begins around 10,000 BC. Extant examples include that of Ötzi, a Stone Age hunter, whose preserved body was discovered in the Italian Alps in 1991. His yew longbow, dated to around 3,300 BC, was made from the heartwood only. Glacial refrigeration kept Ötzi's bow 'on ice' for us, but numerous longbows have been conserved by other geological caretakers, peat bogs and marine silts, which preserve organic material by creating oxygen-free environments.

In 1863, 40 longbows were discovered in a bog at Nydam in Denmark. Dating to the 4th century AD, these magnificent bows – some made of yew, some of fir – were recovered from three ship burials. The Nydam bows are in a state of almost immaculate preservation and are on display at Denmark's Nationalmuseet (National Museum) in Copenhagen. Of particular interest on two of the bows is a spike at one end – one of metal, the other of bone – suggesting an anticipation of close combat, for which the bow can be hastily converted into a pike/spear. Although relatively little is known of its use during this period, the military longbow had made its debut.

To date, no longbows from the actual medieval period have been unearthed, but there is abundant evidence for their physical form in the cache of superb mid-16th-century specimens that emerged from the Solent mud – the warbows of Henry VIII's warship the *Mary Rose*. This momentous development in our understanding of the longbow came between 1979 and 1982 with the excavation and eventual raising of part of the hull of the *Mary Rose*, which sank in 1545; of the 172 bows salvaged, 137 are fully intact. They represent the closest material resource for understanding the medieval longbow that we have to date (Hildred 2011: *passim*).

These bows proved to be of similar cross-section and length to many of the longbows that were retrieved from the Nydam ships. Fundamentally they were identical, though the draw-weights of the *Mary Rose* bows were notably heavier. Of further note is that not all the *Mary Rose* bows were of the same cross-section; some were plano-convex (D-shaped) while others were oval.

Within this narrow range of variation, the design of the longbow itself – the wooden stick – did not change very much over the centuries, but the longbow did not exist in isolation. It was part of a developed weapons system that included the archer as operator, the bow as the launch platform, the arrow as the delivery platform and many target-specific forms of arrowhead as the actual weapon. It is in these other elements that change and development are to be found. One of the main catalysts for these changes was the continual improvement in armour's defensive capability from the mid-13th century onwards, since, on the battlefield at least, armour was the principal challenge that the longbow faced. Before examining the bow itself, it is important to understand this challenge and what the longbow had to overcome to be a viable force on the medieval battlefield.

Countering the longbow: medieval armour

Any consideration of the longbow's effectiveness in battle must deal with the subject of armour. While a thorough survey of this topic would consume several volumes, there are a number of general principles that it is useful to understand.

Given average battlefield conditions, armour was reasonable proof against the weapons of the day. Had it not been, fighting men would not have gone to the expense of acquiring and wearing it. Throughout the Middle Ages, most troop types wore some form of armour and this is unlikely to have been the case if armour did not deliver adequate protection. Even at the lower end of the price range, there was a significant cost to armour relative to the means of the wearer. As well as the expense of its acquisition, armour demanded time and money for its maintenance.

There was also the inconvenience of armour. All types of armour, including full-plate armours, allowed the required range of martial movement. Nevertheless, the soldier would have been able to move more freely and more comfortably without it. Armour has always been a manageable weight, seldom exceeding around 65lb – significantly less than the standard weights carried by modern infantrymen. A 2007 Naval Research Advisory Committee report entitled 'Lightening the Load' gives the following weights for a US Marine Corps rifleman: Existence Load (landing zone – secure area), 167lb; Approach Load (20-mile march within eight hours maintaining 90 per cent combat effectiveness), 123lb; Assault Load (into the fight), 97lb. It should also be noted that the modern soldier carries the majority of this load on his/her back, whereas medieval armour distributed the load across the body.

Even so, there was a weight factor to armour, which affected comfort and fatigue and which would not have been endured without compensating advantage. In warm weather armour was unpleasantly hot and, in winter conditions, the metal conducted the cold. Ventilation was also a significant issue. With armour for the head, there was a trade-off between full protection and full peripheral vision.

Set against this premise are the legions of tests, from the backyard to the laboratory, that have demonstrated time and again the ability of arrows shot from a longbow to penetrate all kinds of armour. Many of the most compelling tests of this nature have been carried out by Mark Stretton and others of the English War Bow Society (EWBS); the results have been published in Soar 2006 (127–52), which contains two chapters written by Mark Stretton. The results of the tests are indisputable: arrows shot from powerful longbows punch through virtually everything put in front of them, and they do so to depths that would deliver mortal wounds. Such tests confirm that the longbow, at the appropriate draw-weight and with the appropriate arrowhead, was a formidable weapon. However, there are a great many factors that determine an arrow's ability to penetrate armour, and the isolated conditions of the testing ground never fully replicate the complex and chaotic circumstances of the battlefield.

Types and forms of armour varied a great deal over the centuries of the longbow's use and what follows is only a brief summary of some of the main elements the longbow confronted.

SHIELDS

The shield was the most significant item of defensive equipment against arrows. Shields were of composite structure and although some were made from adjoining panels, the core of most was formed from a single piece of wood – a German stained-glass window fragment of *c.* 1400 in the Glasgow Museum's Burrell Collection shows a shield-maker working a shield from a solid block of wood using an axe. In order to retain the curved shape, seasoned timbers were essential. European poplar and lime (also known as linden, or basswood in the USA) were the favoured woods, known both for being lightweight and easy to carve. Sycamore was another common choice; it was a little heavier, but harder.

To bolster the dense, energy-absorbing properties of the wood, shields were reinforced with multiple laminations of heavy-duty canvas, sometimes with an additional layer of parchment, which were bonded with casein glue to both surfaces of the core. Mosaic strata of horn or bone were familiar facets on jousting-shields, many of which survive. Such an additional layer on battle-shields, few of which remain to us, would have been highly effective. Most shields were finished additionally with a facing of leather, sometimes rawhide. On the reverse was a linen-covered pad, often of hair-felt, which not only buffered the shock of impact but also gave yet more depth to challenge arrow penetration.

I am not aware of any longbow testing against an authentically constructed shield but I would be fairly confident that, if properly made, the shield would be up to the task. A shield did not protect the whole body, but, held just a little way in front, it gave effective cover to a wider area than its own surface dimensions, particularly to the vital areas of chest and head. For massed troops, those behind the men of the leading rank were to a large extent shielded by those in front, and so a shield held at an angle above the head would have offered a reasonable umbrella of protection. The English chronicler Geoffrey le Baker observed that the French knights at Poitiers advanced in close formation, 'protecting their bodies with joined shields, [and] turned their faces away from the missiles. So the archers emptied their quivers in vain …' (quoted in Strickland & Hardy 2005: 237).

CUIR-BOUILLI

As a material for armour, *cuir-bouilli*, a treated, hardened form of leather that was soft and pliable before drying, was well suited to forming into shaped pieces of armour, such as those for the limbs. These shaped pieces were often reinforced with metal splints. It was also available in large sheets, something that was not usually possible with iron and steel until the latter part of the 14th century, and this made it ideal for making large, globose breastplates from a single piece. In fact, we get the term 'cuirass' from the fact that early breastplates were made from *cuir* (leather). There is discussion among historical leather-workers as to the exact nature of *cuir-bouilli* (Richardson & Beabey 1997: 94–101). Some favour boiling the leather in water, making it very hard, though perhaps a little brittle; others support the idea of impregnating it with hot beeswax. Either way, it was considered an extremely tough material and made for very useful armour.

MAIL

Perhaps the most universal metal armour of the medieval period was mail, which combined good protection with excellent flexibility. It also had the potential for repair and modification, important factors for those of lesser means. Not all mail was created equal; variations included the thickness of the wire and the diameter of the links as well as the quality of the metal. Some mail featured all the links being closed with a rivet, while other examples were composed of alternating rows of riveted and solid links. The regular assembly method attached each link to four others – two in the row above and two below. However, there is evidence for heavier, six-in-one weaves, with three in the row above and three below, which created a much denser defence. Mail tends to be especially effective in resisting cutting blows from a sword or axe. It is less useful against the punch of a bodkin-style arrow, but in order to be penetrated, the arrow needs to strike mail at a good angle at close to 90 degrees to the target surface. Even when it fails to prevent penetration, the mail continues to have some effect on an incoming arrow by absorbing a great deal of the delivery energy.

TEXTILE ARMOUR

The key to the effectiveness of medieval armour was the use of composite, layered materials; the outer skin of leather or metal was only the front line of defence, while the textile armour worn beneath provided the real stopping power. The base layer of any medieval armour was the aketon or gambeson, a stuffed and quilted knee-length coat that not only offered formidable resistance to the shock of impact but whose dense layers also obstructed penetration.

A popular form of armour among archers in the 15th century was the jack, a shorter-length coat of defence. One of several construction forms consisted of 25 or more layers of linen, plus often an outer layer of deerskin, stitched in a quilted pattern that gathered the material. This 'gathering' condensed the surface area, bunching the fibres into a denser, more impenetrable mesh, which provided excellent protection in addition to the depth of multiple layers. Textile armour, such as the jack and the gambeson, was considered to be so effective that it was often worn on its own.

Writing in 1483, the Italian traveller Dominic Mancini observed: 'the more common soldiery have more comfortable tunics that reach down below the loins and are stuffed with tow or some other soft material. They say that the softer the tunics the better do they withstand the blows of arrows and swords' (quoted in Strickland & Hardy 2005: 383).

PLATE

A major enhancement to both mail and textile armour was the coat-of-plates. This consisted of metal plates riveted to the inside of a leather or linen base, giving protection to the front, back and sides of the torso. Most well-armoured knights at Crécy would have worn coats-of-plates over mail shirts, in turn worn over gambesons or aketons. This was significant, multi-layered, composite protection.

The principle of riveting or stitching plates to a textile base was also used to good effect with the brigandine and the jack-of-plates. Here smaller plates were used and overlapped for improved resistance. These armours became increasingly common in

Mail standard or pizane, c. 1350. These were high-standing collars, offering protection to the neck and throat. The collar part extended into a mantle, which defended to just below the shoulder. Note the 4:1 assembly ratio for the mantle and a 6:1 ratio for the standing part of the collar. The yellow metal (copper alloy) is decorative. This is a good example of how the defensive properties of mail can be increased over vital areas by altering the construction. For those who could afford them or had the opportunity to loot them, mail collars like this, known either as standards or pizanes, were popular forms of armour for archers during the 14th century. They did not affect the bowman's ability to draw his bow but gave good protection against downward strikes from a cavalryman's sword. (© The Trustees of the British Museum)

Exterior view of replica coat-of-plates. Note that this construction method allows for considerable shaping of the plates and that the larger plates over the chest are prominently domed. (Photograph by kind permission of Stanislav Prošek, Mac-Armour, Czech Republic)

Interior view of replica coat-of-plates. Note that the finished armour would be worn over a combination of mail and textile armour. (Photograph by kind permission of Stanislav Prošek, Mac-Armour, Czech Republic)

the 15th century, especially for archers, because they retained the flexibility of mail but had the added stopping power of plate, which was necessary in an age when the archer more commonly confronted enemy archers in the opposing army.

For knights, the limiting factor in getting better protection for the torso had been the inability to produce large plates of iron or steel from the bloomery hearth process, hence the need to make larger structures out of smaller plates, such as the coat-of-plates. However, in the late 14th century it became possible to produce large plates of ferrous metal reliably and repeatedly (Williams 2003: 55). This technological advancement made one-piece breast- and back-plates a reality and heralded a fundamental shift in armour design.

Before the advent of solid-plate body armour, all forms of armour were flexible to some extent – they gave on impact. This meant that the energy of a blow could significantly affect the body's soft tissues, internal organs and even skeleton, as the armour flexed against the striking force, even though it might have prevented penetration. Large, shaped plates enabled rigidity. Now the body could be fully encased in a hard shell. There was still a need for some padding inside to absorb the shockwave of an impact, but much less than was required previously.

Further improvements came with the ability to harden the plates. Almost all medieval armour before the late 14th century was made of wrought iron, which could not be hardened and tempered because it contained only negligible traces of carbon. By the early 15th century, however, steel was becoming easier to produce in large amounts. An alloy of iron and a more significant amount of carbon (around 0.5–0.8 per cent), steel could be heat-treated in various ways to improve its protective qualities substantially – it could be hardened (Williams 2003: 938–39). Access to strong, tough, heat-treatable steel eventually allowed armourers to create fully arrow-proof harnesses for those who could afford them.

In the Statutes of the Armourers of Paris in 1451, the marks of Italian armourers are deciphered as meaning either *à toute épreuve* ('full-proof') or *à demi-épreuve* ('semi-proof'). The suggestion is that the semi-proof armours were tested with lever crossbows and that the full-proof ones had withstood being shot at with the more powerful windlass crossbow (Williams 2003: 924). Such a system would have given knights confidence in their equipment, though any perceived guarantee would be of small comfort if the claim proved to be false.

As well as its varying degrees of hardness and toughness, the effectiveness of plate armour was determined by its thickness and its shape. Plate armour could be thinner, and therefore also lighter, than might be expected, not only because of the strength of the metal itself, but also because of the structural integrity imparted by a strong form – a curved, dished plate being much more resistant to deformation than a flat sheet. The thickness of armour plates also varied according to the vulnerability of the different parts of the body; plates tended to be thinner on the arms and legs, and thicker on critical areas

North-west European brigandine, c. 1540–50, Royal Armouries, Leeds. This 16th-century example of a brigandine differs very little from medieval types. Note how the small overlapping plates not only articulate well but also allow for a tailored, form-fitting configuration that enhanced the wearer's range of comfortable movement, especially around the shoulders and armpits. In addition to the defensive capabilities of the plates, the mass of securing rivets and the layers of fabric also combined to augment the quality of protection. Originally the term 'brigand' referred to any foot-soldier and the armour derived its name from its ubiquitous use by such troops. (© Royal Armouries)

such as the chest and head, where a serious wound was much more likely to prove fatal. Limbs were therefore potentially more susceptible to arrow injury – but then they were also smaller, narrower targets and more likely to be in significant motion during combat.

Perhaps the most important element of plate armour's defensive capability was its ability to cause deflection. Unless an arrow strikes at an angle close to the perpendicular it is most likely to be deflected and, even if it bites, the impact will be greatly lessened according to the angle.

LEFT Great helm, c. 1350. Although early forms of the visored helm had been developed by the time of the battle of Crécy (1346), it was more common at this period for both English and French knights to wear great helms like this example. Great helms were usually worn over an open-faced bascinet, giving a double layer of metal protection to the skull. Ventilation was an issue and, in the stifling heat of battle, some knights might take their chances against arrows, trusting to their shields, and wear only their open-faced bascinet. Arrow wounds to the face are commonly reported in the chronicles. An aventail of mail attached to bascinets would protect the throat, neck and shoulders, whether or not it was worn alone or beneath a great helm. The mail tippets seen on this great helm would have added a double layer of mail protection to a vulnerable area. (Germanisches Nationalmuseum, Nuremberg/Bridgeman Images)

RIGHT This type of visored bascinet, with steep deflecting surfaces, emerged around 1370 and is typical of those worn at Agincourt (1415). Dramatic developments of form can be readily discerned from the great helm. This design offered the optimal protection to a man walking towards an onslaught of arrows. The deep snout not only encouraged arrows to be turned aside but also allowed the sights to be placed significantly further forward from the eyes than had been possible previously, so that even long, narrow bodkins seeking to snake through the narrow slits would become wedged before piercing their target. It is hard to imagine a more unnerving experience than seeing this at first hand. The position of the sights reduces the wearer's field of peripheral vision, and it is for this reason that there are secondary sights beneath the snout. These allow the wearer to look down to see the terrain below, whether he is mounted or on foot. (The Wallace Collection, London/Bridgeman Images)

HORSE-ARMOUR

Horses, though extremely vulnerable on the battlefield, were not entirely undefended – they too had armour. By the end of the 15th century, plate armour began to be available for some horses, but until then medieval horse-armour consisted of padded textile, leather and mail (Breiding 2000: *passim*). Today these perishable and recyclable materials survive only as fragments. Clear images of this type of horse-armour are rare because an outer textile covering – the cloth caparison – mostly obscured it. However, it did exist. As early as the 13th century, during the wars of Edward I, there are records of squires with armoured horses being paid 1s per day, while those with unprotected horses were paid only 8d per day (Williams 2003: 42).

Philip VI of France had two horses killed under him at Crécy (Ayton & Preston 2005: 150). Circumstantially we can deduce that Philip's mounts were taken out by English archery. All armour could fail and horse-armour was no exception, even though a king's horse might be expected to have been fully armoured. Certainly it was technically possible to build full armour for horses, and it would be a mistake to assume that all medieval cavalry were easy targets. The animal's size meant that it was a costly business to armour it, especially if remounts were to be similarly equipped, and there was probably some variation in the amount and quality of horse-armour worn. Nevertheless, most knightly horses were fully enclosed with a protective 'bard'.

A chess piece, contemporary with the first part of the Hundred Years' War and now in the Metropolitan Museum of Art in New York, shows a full mail bard for the horse. The large panels hanging over the mail are not iron or steel – at this period it was not yet possible to produce single plates of this size. More probably they represent *cuir-bouilli*, a common material for armour as discussed above. As with the rider's armour, there would have been padded textile armour beneath the mail. There appears to be some form of domed bolster of extra-thick padding on the horse's back behind the saddle – a large area vulnerable to falling arrows, though equally exposed to the fall of a sword in close combat. The shaffron covering the horse's head, including its ears, has a moulded shape, suggesting that this is intended to represent *cuir-bouilli*.

The permutations of different types of armour, its varying quality and the extent to which it was provided for man or horse are many, but tests that purport to assess the capabilities of the longbow are equally tests that evaluate the effectiveness of armour, and the question should equally be 'did we get the armour right?' as much as it is 'did we get the archery right?' I will come to such tests in due course, but first to the heart of the matter – the bow.

Ivory chess piece depicting a fully armoured horse, believed to be English, from between 1350 and 1375. (Pfeiffer Fund, 1968 © The Metropolitan Museum of Art, metmuseum.org)

Building the bow

Whether a bow would bend or break was down to delicate judgements of the bowyer's eye and his ability to decipher the instructions from the fine print of the wood's grain. For this he needed good light and in 1371 Edward III ordered that 'no bowyer of London shall work by night from henceforth, on pain of paying … for each offence half a mark'; the same order also prohibits fletchers from working after dark (Memorials). Such a law tells us that the supply of sub-standard bows was a significant problem for an army that ordered them in great quantities. In 1399, an individual named Tom Coton was appointed the Maker of the King's Bows, and was charged with inspecting the quality of bows supplied to the English national arsenal at the Tower of London (Megson 1993: 30).

WOOD FOR BOWS

Traditionally, yew has been considered the wood of choice for the construction of longbows, and yew from southern Europe, especially Italy, has been regarded as the best of all. In 1471, as the Yorkist Edward IV (r. 1461–70, 1471–83) resumed the English throne, customs tariffs levied a tax of four yew staves for every tun (cask with 252-gallon capacity) of goods imported into England from Italian merchants (Megson 1993: 54); by 1483, the year of Edward's death and the accession of his brother as Richard III (r. 1483–85), the duty had changed to ten bowstaves for every butt (cask with 126-gallon capacity) of Malmsey wine (Megson 1993: 85).

Furthermore, finished bows of any timber were regarded as an asset of national importance; accordingly, as well as import incentives there were export embargoes. In 1371, towards the end of the long reign of Edward III, 300 bows were confiscated at Southampton with a royal injunction that 'they shall not be taken out of the realm' (Megson 1993: 28). The following year an order to customs officers at Dover, which gave safe passage to a returning group of papal envoys and their retinues, declared, 'They or any of their company shall not take with them bows or arrows save two or three bows and as many sheaves of arrows, nor any armour, gold or silver in the lump, in plate or in any coined money over and above their reasonable expenses …' (CCR Ed III 1363).

A common alternative to yew was wych elm. The clergyman and chronicler Giraldus Cambrensis (Gerald of Wales) reported that the bows of the archers he encountered on his journey through Wales in 1188 were fashioned from elm (Cambrensis 1894: 371). Lord Admiral Thomas Howard, in accounting for deficiencies in some of the bow stocks supplied to the *Mary Rose* in 1513, complained that those that 'could not abide the bending' were of wych elm (quoted in Soar 2006: 12). The Anthony Roll inventory of the ship in 1546 records 250 'bows of eugh'; it makes no mention of other woods (quoted in Hildred 2011: 581). Taken together with the admiral's statement, this might lead to the supposition that any wood other than yew was not fit for service. Earlier inventories of the Tudor fleet, however, record the regular use of bows of other woods, including elm (Hildred 2011: 580).

That yew was superlative for the task and was highly esteemed at the time is beyond question, but the admiral's condemnation meant only that a particular consignment of wych elm bows, perhaps from the same supplier, were shoddy goods. I have spoken to a number of present-day archers who shoot with bows made from wych elm and they praise it universally as an excellent bow-wood. This is just as well because, for many medieval archers, their lives depended on it. Medieval longbows were fashioned from a diverse assortment of timbers.

Although Italian and Portuguese yew was the most sought-after wood for bows, there was also a brisk trade with the Polish port of Gdansk during the 14th century. Polish yew, grown in a low-lying, wet and cold climate, was not as high quality as the timber grown on warm Alpine slopes, and it was consequently less expensive. This affordability led to demand on such a scale that there was eventually significant destruction to the Polish yew forests, so much so that King Ladislaus Jagiello (r. 1386–1434) issued a proclamation in 1423, prohibiting its export. (Nadolski & Lewandowski 1990: 145 – passage translated for the author by Marcin Glinianowicz).

Joe Gibbs of the EWBS shooting a 170lb warbow made from Italian yew by bowyer Ian Coote. The staggering power of this immense bow is evident in the flex of its great limbs. Although this is an exceptionally heavy draw-weight bow, the archer himself is of relatively modest height and build. Undoubtedly he is enormously strong but his ability to draw such weights is more a matter of training and technique. (Mike Loades)

RIGHT Section of seasoned Italian yew, showing the natural bond between the creamy sapwood and the dark heartwood. Note that the grain is fairly straight, close and regular in size, which makes it ideal for building a heavy draw-weight bow. The yew tree – *taxus baccata* – grows throughout Europe, with some of the best growing conditions occurring in the Italian Alps, although Spanish and Portuguese yew were equally prized. Trees in dense plantation, competing for sunlight, grew tall and straight. Moreover, on mountainsides or in sandy soils with comparatively poor nutrition, trees grew slowly. Slow growth in even climate conditions resulted in a high-density, fine-grained wood that had the ability to store energy without failing. Modern bowyers talk about the sapwood of Italian yew as having a 'plastic' feel when being worked. Certainly it is more resistant to lifting than English or Welsh yew. This enables it to 'contain' the bow at draw, giving enhanced security against breakage and so making it the desired material for the heavier bows. (Photograph courtesy of Bowyer Magén Klomp)

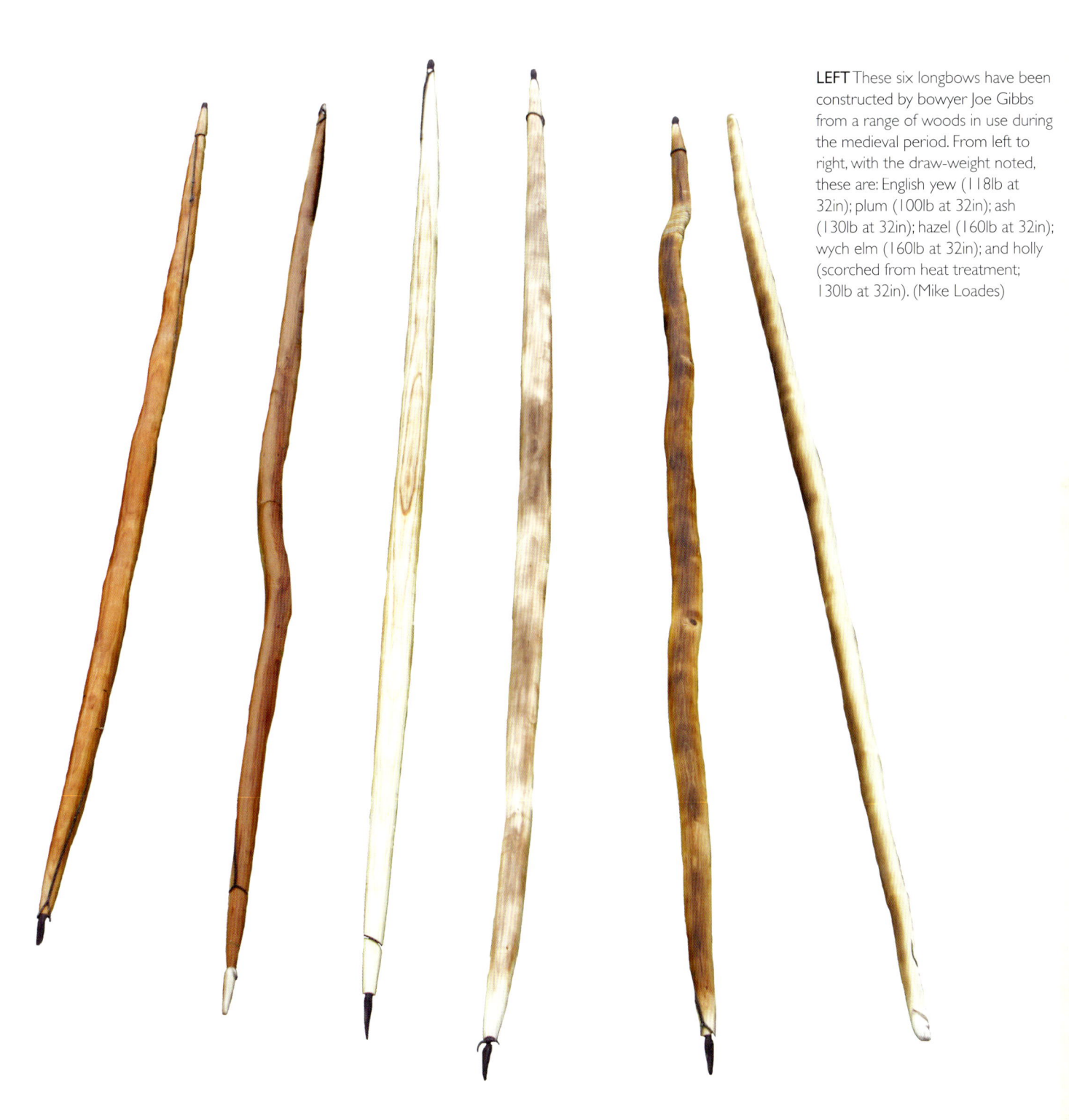

LEFT These six longbows have been constructed by bowyer Joe Gibbs from a range of woods in use during the medieval period. From left to right, with the draw-weight noted, these are: English yew (118lb at 32in); plum (100lb at 32in); ash (130lb at 32in); hazel (160lb at 32in); wych elm (160lb at 32in); and holly (scorched from heat treatment; 130lb at 32in). (Mike Loades)

THE LONGBOW

Ian Coote of the EWBS demonstrating the long draw of the medieval archer. The sole surviving complete medieval arrow found to date, the Westminster arrow, has a total length of 30½ inches. However, a tall man, such as the archer in this photograph, would require an arrow of around 32 inches. Medieval archers drew their bows back much further than modern archers do – 'Draw, archers, draw your arrows to the head!' (Shakespeare, *Richard III*, Act V Sc 3) – it was vigorous work and it required bows that would take this level of bend. (Mike Loades)

Only two years earlier, according to the 15th century Polish chronicler Jan Dlugosz, a gift of 'duobuz Anglicis arcubus' – two English longbows – was presented to King Jagiello by an English legation to the Polish court led by Gilbert de Lannoy (Vale 1996: 271). Although the bows formed only part of a present from Henry V, which also included jewels and a helm with a gold crest, it is apparent that an English longbow was a gift worthy of princes. It is perhaps also an indicator of the importance that the Polish yew trade had had in supplying Henry's armies.

DRAW-WEIGHTS

From the moment the first *Mary Rose* bows were released from the care of the Solent mud, debates have raged about the draw-weights of medieval longbows. These mighty staves suggested draw-weights far greater than had previously been imagined, although circumference is not an infallible indicator of draw-weight – I have seen 100lb bows that have a more slender girth than some 80lb bows. Much depends on the individual stave of timber. Nevertheless, the *Mary Rose* bows were monsters, and here they were in magnificent abundance.

Most modern recreational archers shoot bows in a 30lb to 40lb range and those who hunt with the bow find 70lb adequate for killing large animals such as deer. A 90lb bow used to be considered something that only rare individuals were able to manage. Now the needle has shifted and 90lb is at the lower end of the dial for today's warbow archers. There are a growing number who shoot bows over 100lb with apparent ease and a smaller but significant few shooting above 150lb. Joe Gibbs of the English War Bow Society has managed to draw and shoot a 214lb bow with a 30-inch draw (private correspondence 2018). He can shoot repeatedly with a 190lb draw-weight longbow. Shooting exceptionally heavy bows is clearly possible and there is no doubt that the heavier the bow, the harder the hit and that there is good military advantage in that. Nevertheless, I consider it unlikely that any but a rare few would find the heaviest bows practical for battle.

In 1355, the year before the battle of Poitiers, archers from Cheshire were paid 6d per day and those from other areas 3d per day (Strickland & Hardy 2005: 204). It is probable that this pay differential distinguished the regular and elite archers, and we might expect the higher-paid archers to shoot stronger bows. However, in battle they too would need to be able to shoot them for a sustained period and with great urgency. When an enemy is bearing down on you, it is not only about what weight you can pull; it is also about the number of repetitions you can manage.

Circumstantially, based on the fact that the capability of armour to defend against arrows improved so much between the mid-14th and the mid-15th centuries, we can reason that the average draw-weight of bows increased gradually throughout this period in an attempt to edge ahead in the arms race. Everyone will have his or her own opinion and, for what it is worth, mine is that battlefield bows had draw-weights of between 90lb and 120lb around the beginning of the Hundred Years' War and that these increased in the ensuing century to between 100lb and 140lb, with the majority of archers shooting bows at the lower end of these scales.

The fact that people today can shoot bows of 170lb does not necessarily signal that this was a manageable weight in battle, but it does lend credence to the notion that archers of this ability would be capable of sustained, rapid shooting with 120lb or even 140lb bows. They would be the elite, however, and by far the greater majority would be shooting bows nearer the 100lb mark. I do not doubt that super-heavy bows existed for a super-elite of archers and that they could be of use in sieges or at sea, but I question the suitability of anything over 140lb for land battle.

Even drawing a 100lb bow remains a considerable feat, and for the men who bent these bows in battle, the work rate was phenomenal. Lactic acid builds up quickly at these weights, and in a desperate fight archers would have to push through immense walls of pain in order to keep their shafts flying.

Building the longbow arrow

ARROW SUPPLY AND DEMAND

'And then the battle raged at its fiercest, and our archers notched their sharp-pointed arrows and loosed them into the enemy's flanks, keeping up the fight without pause. *And when their arrows were all used up*, seizing axes, stakes and sword.' So wrote the anonymous chronicler of *The Deeds of Henry V*, reporting how the English archers ran out of arrows at the battle of Agincourt in 1415 (quoted in Curry 2009: 36 – my emphasis). It may be true that arrow resupply to detachments on the flanks was more difficult than it would be to archers in the front of the main army, and uncorroborated observations by individual chroniclers have to be read with a measure of caution. Nevertheless, our anonymous chronicler highlights a critical issue for effective military archery – arrow supply!

In 1360, 500,000 arrows were delivered to the national arsenal at the Tower of London, making an impressive addition to the existing stocks; this followed a consignment of 850,000 arrows sent the previous year (Hardy 1992: 84). In 1417, just two years after Agincourt, an order went out for six feathers from every goose; a year later the counties had to supply 1,190,000 goose feathers to the Tower (Hardy 1992: 83). The Tower of London wasn't the only receiving depot; 11,000 arrows were dispatched to Bristol prior to the Crécy campaign in 1346 (Hardy 1992: 83), and we may imagine various other regional repositories garnering similar numbers. Other sporadic statistics hint at the scale of supply, which, naturally enough, escalates considerably both just before and just after a campaign.

Apart from the limitations of what the nation's fletchers could supply, there were considerations of logistics, ships and wagons in getting ammunition to the battlefield.

MAKING AN ARROW

First, a stave of seasoned timber is split into square blanks (**1**). Aspen (white poplar), ash and birch were the commonest types of wood used for arrow-shafts. The square blanks are worked on a shooting board (**2**), which has a rounded groove in which to rotate the blank. It is first worked with a straight plane to take off the corners and to taper a bobtail profile, which narrows towards the nock end of the arrow, giving improved aerodynamic properties.

Next, a finishing plane is used (**3**). This has a rounded blade, which shaves the blank into a cylindrical shaft. The shaft is rotated in the groove of the shooting board as it is worked (**4**). A gauge (**5**) may have been used to check that shafts were the same diameter. Crooked shafts can be heated over a flame and worked with a device like this to straighten them. The spine (stiffness) of shafts is matched by flexing them in the hands and gauging by feel. Sheaves of matched arrows need to have a similar stiffness to suit the particular draw-weight of a bow.

The shaft is then smoothed using abrasives such as sandstone and dogfish skin (**6**). Note the bobtail taper on the shaft. After being treated with oil, a slot is sawn into one end of the shaft (**7**), ready to receive the horn reinforce for the nock. A sliver of cow horn or deer antler is inserted into the groove (**8**); this will prevent the nock from splitting under pressure from the string. The nock itself is then filed at 90 degrees to the horn insert (**9**), and the end of the nock is filed to a rounded profile.

The feather for the fletching is pared away from the quill (**10**), leaving only a thin, flexible portion of quill for attachment to the shaft. Goose, swan or peacock feathers were preferred. The quill on the fletching is scraped with a knife to make it smooth and even (**11**). Glue, in this case made from rabbit hide, is heated in a gluepot and then applied to the fletching (**12**), which is then placed by eye in the correct alignment on the shaft. Although the glue holds the fletching well enough for placement, it is neither strong enough nor durable enough for shooting; the fletchings have to be bound with linen or silk thread to secure them.

This is done by teasing the barbs apart with a bodkin (13). The fletchings are then cut to shape (14) using shears or scissors; an alternative is to finish by burning a straight edge with a hot blade. The other end of the shaft is then shaved with a knife (15) to receive the head, which is first heated red-hot in order to ensure a snug fit.

Arrows destined for storage in barrels, to be kept in great military arsenals like the Tower of London, were treated with an insect-repelling compound; this was painted on between the fletchings (16). Feather mites could destroy an army's arrow supply very quickly. Tests on the *Mary Rose* arrows suggest a compound of glue, beeswax and copper sulphate was used. The copper, which shows as a green tint on the bindings, may have come from using copper gluepots, and it is uncertain whether or not the presence of copper compound was either intentional or essential.

The Westminster arrow was found in the rafters above Henry V's chantry in Westminster Abbey. A replica of the Westminster arrow was reconstructed by Mark Stretton of the EWBS (17). The original is believed to date to before 1437 and as such is the only known arrow from the medieval period in existence. Traces of a reddish compound, rather than green, still remain on the shaft. Other colours are seen in artistic depictions from the period. What is most likely is that various mixtures were used in an effort to prevent stored arrows disintegrating, and that individual fletchers had their own preferred recipes. In any event, it was yet one more process in the incredibly complex and laborious task of making a medieval war arrow.

We know from the 1513 campaign conducted by Henry VIII (r. 1509–47) that 240,000 arrows required 26 wagons (Hardy 1992: 86). Edward III took around 7,500 archers* with him on his Crécy campaign in 1346. For an archer army of this size it is likely that he required between one and two million arrows, which makes for quite a wagon train.

THE COST OF ARROWS

Medieval longbow arrows were, arguably, the most expensive form of small-arms ammunition ever devised. Arrows were counted in sheaves, with 24 to a sheaf. At various times statutes required an archer to provide a sheaf of arrows, along with his own bow, as part of his equipment when he was arrayed. In 1356 a sheaf of arrows sold for 16d; arrowheads cost 2s 6d per hundred, and may have represented an additional cost (Strickland & Hardy 2005: 21). Most regular archers were paid 3d per day (Strickland & Hardy 2005: 204), though men of elite corps and mounted archers were paid more. In other words, at this time a sheaf of arrows might cost a man the equivalent of over five days' wages, so not only did his sheaf contribute to the overall army ordnance, it also meant that the archer understood, in a very personal way, the value of each shaft he shot. It was, furthermore, an inducement for him to retrieve what shafts he could for mending at the end of a battle.

WOOD FOR ARROWS

Roger Ascham, Latin and archery tutor to Edward VI (r. 1547–53) and Elizabeth I (r. 1558–1603), wrote *Toxophilus,* the first book in English on archery, in 1545. It remains a standard work on how to shoot and is full of practical knowledge. In it he exhorts the use of ash for arrow-shafts, saying it is 'swiftest and again heavy to give a great stroke, which asp[en] will not do' (Ascham 1968: 166). He clearly understood the principle that the impact force of an arrow strike was determined by both the weight of the projectile and its speed. He lamented that the lighter, inferior aspen – known more commonly today as poplar – was in contemporary use. Samples from the 2,600 arrows recovered from the *Mary Rose* show that 77 per cent were fashioned from aspen/poplar (Hildred 2011: 674), although nine other woods have been identified.

Aspen also appears to have been the wood of choice in the previous century. In 1416, Henry V (r. 1413–22) ruled that aspen could only be used for arrows (PRME: 24: III), prohibiting by the same order its use for pattens (wooden overshoes, with a deep carved sole similar to a clog; they were in widespread popular use during the medieval period). It was a ruling that confirmed his reliance on aspen shafts for his famed archer army. In fact, the preamble to this legislation states:

> The fletchers of the city of London and elsewhere in the realm have always been accustomed to use, and still do use, a wood called aspen, and no other wood, for making arrows of all kinds ... it is probable that within a short time the same wood called aspen will be completely exhausted by the said patten-makers, to the great and perpetual detriment of archery. (PRME: 24: III)

---

* Estimates vary. Clifford Rogers (Rogers 2000: 423) calculates 7,000 foot-archers plus an unspecified percentage of his estimate of 3,500 mounted archers and hobilars. Andrew Ayton (Ayton & Preston 2005: 189) offers a more conservative 5,000 foot-archers plus an unspecified percentage of 3,500 mounted archers and hobilars. I have steered between these two.

Errant patten-makers were to be fined the princely sum of 100s. This spotlight on potential shortages of arrow-making materials gives support to the idea that damaged arrows may have been harvested from the battlefield and taken for repair.

RECOVERING AND REPAIRING ARROWS

What percentage of shot arrows survived a battle, to be gathered by the victor, is hard to estimate. Shot arrows that landed on the ground, either directly or by ricochet, were vulnerable to the crowding stamp of both feet and hooves, while those embedded in a dead comrade or opponent might easily break during attempts to extract them. Depending on where an arrow broke, it was possible to repair it, and Ascham mentions 'piecing of a shaft with brazil or holly or other heavy woods' (Ascham 1968: 168). It was an elaborate process (today called 'footing') that involved splicing with fishtail joints, and so it was unlikely to have been accomplished in a campaign camp. With his mention of more exotic woods (brazil wood came from India), Ascham is referring to a bespoke, superior-grade arrow, but it would be equally possible to piece an arrow with the same species of wood as the main shaft. We might imagine that there was some profit in gathering arrows after a battle, including those that had broken near the head. However, they would all probably need expert attention in a fletcher's workshop before they could be recycled for use.

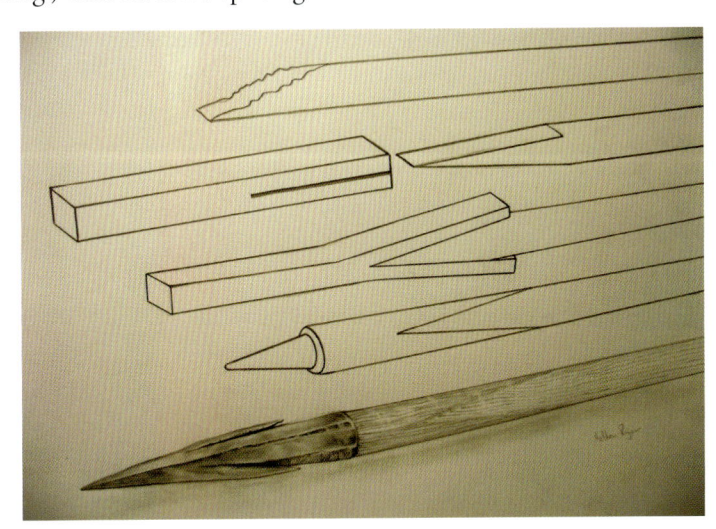

By the time of the Wars of the Roses in late 15th-century England, during which both sides used massed archers, there may have been the possibility of gathering up enemy arrows before they were trampled, but in battles such as Crécy, Poitiers and Agincourt, no such opportunity presented itself. Arrow supply remained a critical factor for an army that was reliant upon massed archers.

Stages of 'piecing' an arrow. First the broken end of the arrow is cut with precision into a wedge. A piece of new timber is sawn to receive the wedge and the two parts are spliced and glued together. The repair is then shaved to conform to the shape and size of the rest of the shaft. Before a head can be fitted, the foreshaft must be pared to receive it. (Drawing by Matthew Ryan, www.matthewryanhistoricalillustrator.com)

Making the arrowhead

Although bowyers were forbidden to work after dark, the vast industrial demand for arrowheads meant that the anvils of the arrowsmith were obliged to ring out both day and night, working only by candlelight and the glow of the forge. Aside from type diversity, there were also variations in quality. As with armour, not all arrowheads were created equal.

HARDENED POINTS

In 1356 Edward III sent out orders for 240,000 'good' arrows and 24,000 'best' arrows; the difference was that the 'best' arrows were obliged to have 'heads hard and well steeled' (quoted in Strickland & Hardy 2005: 21). It is the unique attribute of steel, even relatively low-carbon steel, that its physical properties change when it is quenched – heated to red-hot and then cooled by plunging it in a liquid – a process that makes it a much harder material. It took extra time, smiths with a particular skill and the procurement of billets of wrought iron that had an adequate level of carbon. Consequently, hardened arrowheads were more expensive, which accounted for their representing only 10 per cent of the contract. In this case it was probably only the

INCENDIARY ARROWS

Incendiary arrows were of particular use for *chevauchée* (terrorizing the countryside) and siege, facets of medieval warfare that were far more frequent than pitched battles. They were also a mainstay of naval engagements. Various kinds of fire-bearing head have been identified, but the commonest were the cage type and the bag type. The tendency for incendiary arrows to extinguish during flight is especially problematic with the cage type, and an improved solution was the bag type. For this an extra-long bodkin – it is worth bearing in mind that bodkin points 9in in length were found on the *Mary Rose* – was required to prevent the shaft from burning. It was inserted through a sausage of incendiary materials, encased in a linen bag. Various recipes exist; one from *Das Feuerwerkbuch*, written in about 1400, recommends, 'Take three pounds of saltpetre, one pound of sulphur and half a pound of charcoal and mix all well to powder. Knead the powder into a paste with brandy ... fill this bag with the paste ... finally coat it with sulphur or resin' (quoted in Anon 2001: 60).

This was in effect a mixture of gunpowder and alcohol! Gunpowder is only explosive when ignited in a confined space, otherwise it simply burns extremely fast. The ratios of carbon, saltpetre and sulphur vary according to intended use. The brandy allowed the powder to be rendered into a paste without impairing its flammability and the resin sealed it from evaporation, which was useful for storage, as well as being a combustible material in its own right. I have experimented with recipes along these lines and even though the flame appears to extinguish in flight, there is sufficient heat and spark left to re-ignite the gunpowder compound when it thuds to rest at its destination – be it ship's hull or farmer's barn. Mark Stretton has shot incendiary arrows with a similar recipe from a 140lb draw-weight bow, reaching a distance of 200yd, and the arrow has ignited in its target at the end of the flight (see Soar 2006: 149–52 for his tests with other incendiary arrow types). This was a terror weapon of considerable range.

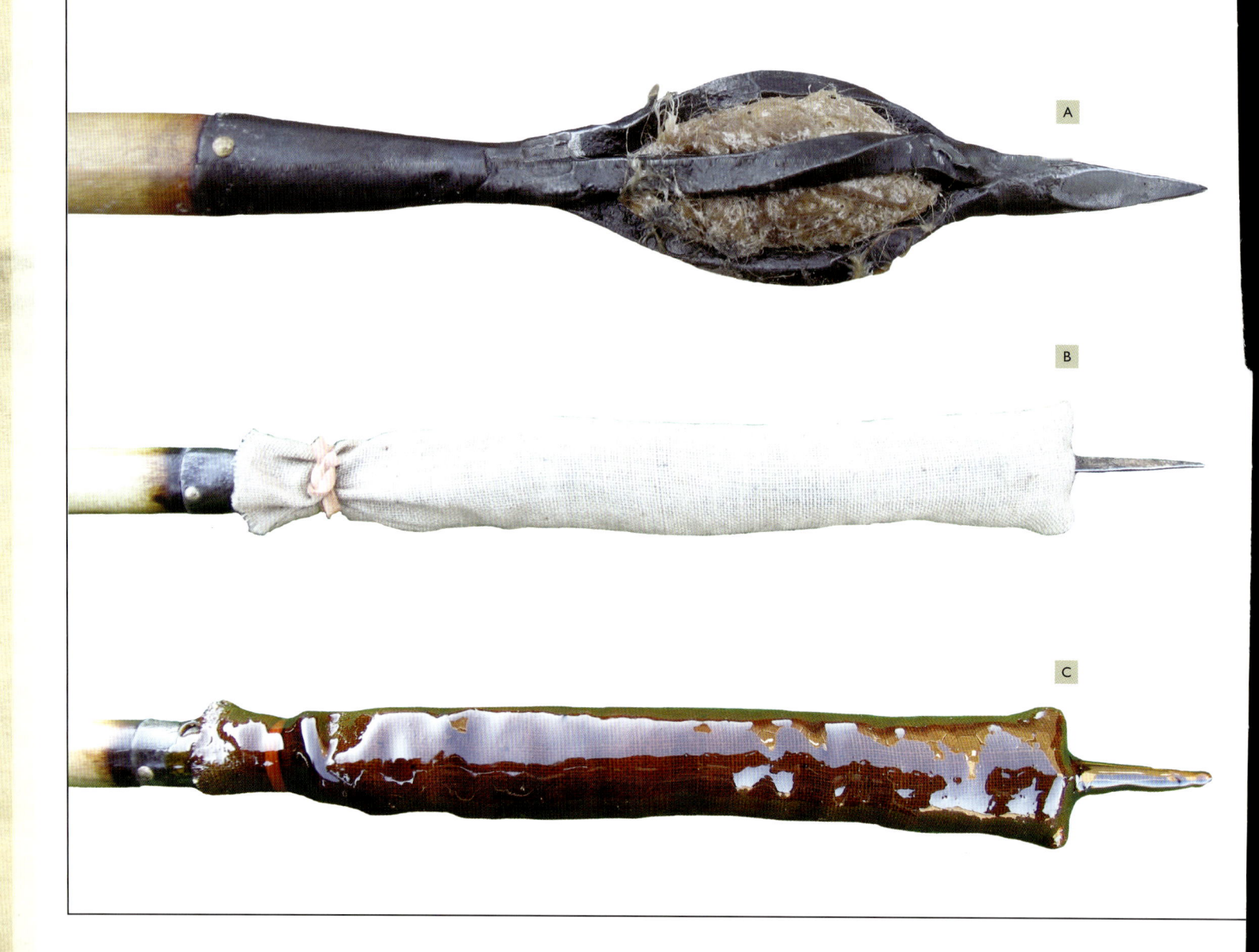

(**A**) Cage-type incendiary arrow. This type was the easiest for the archer to prepare in the field and at the moment of need. A wick of wool, hemp or tow, saturated with a flammable compound, was stuffed into the cage. The wick may already be prepared with the compound or it may be dipped in it *in situ*. Either way, the archer could travel with the wick and compound in a convenient pouch and have another pouch of push-fit cages to access if required. His quiver, however, would contain regular arrows that could be converted in an instant. (Photograph courtesy of Mark Stretton)

(**B**) Bag-type incendiary arrow. This was a more reliable incendiary arrow but it required more preparation, which needed to be done in advance. Consequently an archer would need to carry fully prepared incendiary arrows of this type with him. This picture shows the first stage of manufacture, with an extra-long bodkin arrowhead inserted through a canvas sausage of flammable paste. (Photograph courtesy of Mark Stretton)

(**C**) Bag-type incendiary arrow coated with resin. The second stage of making a bag-type incendiary arrow was to seal it with resin. The resin was itself a flammable substance but it also sealed the bag of the more combustible paste, helping to keep it from drying out completely and so becoming vulnerable to dispersing as ignited dust during flight. The resin held it together for long enough to complete the flight, when the more powerful burn of the contents then took over. (Photograph courtesy of Mark Stretton)

(**D**) Mark Stretton shooting an incendiary arrow. In an age when ships were made of wood and canvas and when wood and thatch were universal building materials both for town buildings and for barns and store-houses, the destructive potential of fire was enormous. Fire was a widely used tool of medieval warfare and archers with incendiary arrows offered an efficient way to deliver fire from a relatively safe distance. (Photograph courtesy of Mark Stretton)

Replica of an arrowhead that was found on the battle site of Towton. It has the cutting blades of the head brazed to the socket. Note that there is some splash from the brazing because an excess spill of the material spreads around in the fire when multiple heads are in production. (Arrowhead by Hector Cole; photograph by Matthew Ryan)

point of the arrowhead that was 'steeled' – that is, 'case-carburized' by reheating just the point and quenching it – but there are clues to another process.

A statute of Henry IV (r. 1399–1413) in 1405 complained of arrowsmiths supplying 'faulty' arrowheads and ordered that 'all the heads for arrows … after this time … be well boiled or brazed, and hardened at the points with steel' (Pickering 1762: 464). 'Boiled' may have been another way of saying 'quenched', since a red-hot arrowhead submerged into a quenching fluid will cause the fluid to bubble and give off steam in the manner of boiling. Alternatively, it may refer to the process of 'tempering', a necessary step after hardening to make the hardened material less brittle. Tempering requires a secondary heating. One method of tempering, used by modern gunsmiths for leaf-springs, is to boil the metal in a solution of salts that has the effect of heating it through to a uniform temperature. It is conceivable that a similar process, perhaps with animal fats, was used for arrowheads.

'Brazing' may have meant 'heated', as in 'placed on the brazier', or it could have the same meaning it has today, which is to join two pieces of metal together using brass as the welding medium. Arrowheads with traces of brazing have been found at the battlefield sites of both Crécy (1346) and Towton (1461). A possible explanation is that steel was several times more expensive than iron, so there could have been economic benefit in brazing steel points to iron sockets. Nevertheless, this union could have been achieved equally well by forge-welding the two pieces together. Being able to weld such tiny pieces undoubtedly required a high level of skill, but arrowsmith Hector Cole informs me that, having tried both methods, he finds it quicker to forge rather than to braze the parts together. Certainly, far more forged arrowheads have been unearthed archaeologically than have brazed ones. A possible advantage of brazing was that it left visible evidence of process to inspectors, but that was no guarantee that steel had been used.

Whatever the problems of interpreting the exact manufacturing methods, having hardened-steel points was highly valued and the proportion of steeled heads increased dramatically over time. Hardened-steel arrowheads had a greater chance of penetrating armour, especially if they were harder than the armour they were striking. However, full penetration need not be the only useful military objective. Swords attacked armour effectively, not with the hope of slicing through it, but by biting and getting sufficient purchase on the surface to transmit blunt trauma. An arrowhead with a hardened point had a greater potential to bite and deliver force, even when it did not penetrate, and that alone was enough to justify the extra expense. The two types designed specifically to attack plate armour were the 'short bodkin' and the 'heavy war bodkin'.

ATTACKING TEXTILE ARMOUR

A different type of arrowhead was required if the shooter hoped to penetrate textile armour, which was worn beneath plate or mail armour or on its own. The two main types for the job were the 'cutting head', or 'broadhead', and the 'long-needle bodkin'. A third alternative, a 'Type 16' following the London Museum typology, combined some aspects of a bodkin with the cutting edges of a broadhead. Type 16s were also furnished with barbs, which impeded extraction. Barbed broadheads – a very wide variety existed for hunting – are frequently depicted in manuscript illustrations of medieval battle. Although of no use against any type of metal armour, they might have been effective against textile armour or unprotected horseflesh. Mail and textile armour were both vulnerable to the long-needle bodkin.

There is no one type of arrowhead that will defeat every type of armour. A long bodkin will curl against good-quality plate armour, while a short bodkin will not penetrate multiple layers of linen. A broadhead that will cut through textile armour will not penetrate mail. Different heads evolved for a reason, namely the need for different types of head for different targets.

SELECTING ARROWS FOR THE BATTLEFIELD

So what happened on the battlefield? Are we to suppose that an archer, in the manner of a golfer, selected different shafts according to his target? Did he take a short bodkin for shooting at a knight in plate armour, yet select a long-needle bodkin for the larger target of the horse, protected by a mail-and-textile-armour bard? Did he have broadheads at the ready for any unarmoured horses and for men-at-arms wearing gambesons?

I think that such an idea is possible. It would make sense of archers in battle setting their arrows in the ground, as is often seen in art. With his arrows in front and in plain view, it would be possible for the archer to select according to the chosen target and the arrangement of two, on occasion three, different types into distinct groups – long-needle bodkins to his left, short bodkins to his right and a few Type 16s in his belt – would be a simple matter.

Unlike precious hunting broadheads, which were generally fixed to the shaft by a pin that went through holes in the socket, battlefield heads were not even glued – they were affixed solely by means of a snug push-on fit. Aside from removing a stage of manufacture, this also meant that even when an arrow was withdrawn, the arrowhead was left behind in the wound – a contaminating barb, sawing painfully at the tender lesion with the victim's every move and breath.

A short bodkin-type arrowhead said to have been found at the battle site of Crécy. Note the traces of brazing on its surface. The arrowhead was presented to its present owner by a mayor of Crécy, who had received it in the 1970s in exchange for some antique cannonballs from a gendarme, who claimed to have found it on the battlefield in the 1960s. (Private collection; photograph by kind permission of Chris Dawson)

Heavy war bodkin. This robust style of arrowhead, a slightly meatier version of the short bodkin, was developed to attack plate armour. The point is supported against turning over by the curve and angle of the sturdy ridges that are created by the four faces of the head. Arsenal inventories and procurement orders often refer to 'quarrels'. These have traditionally been presumed to be exclusively crossbow ammunition. However, since the word 'quarrel' means square, and crossbow 'quarrels' also had a square cross-section and similar appearance, it may be that references to quarrels were not necessarily related only to crossbow ammunition. In some cases it is stated specifically that they are 'quarrels for crossbows', but otherwise the term may refer to this type of four-faceted military head for use on either crossbow bolt or longbow arrow. (Arrowhead by Hector Cole; photograph by Matthew Ryan)

A B C D

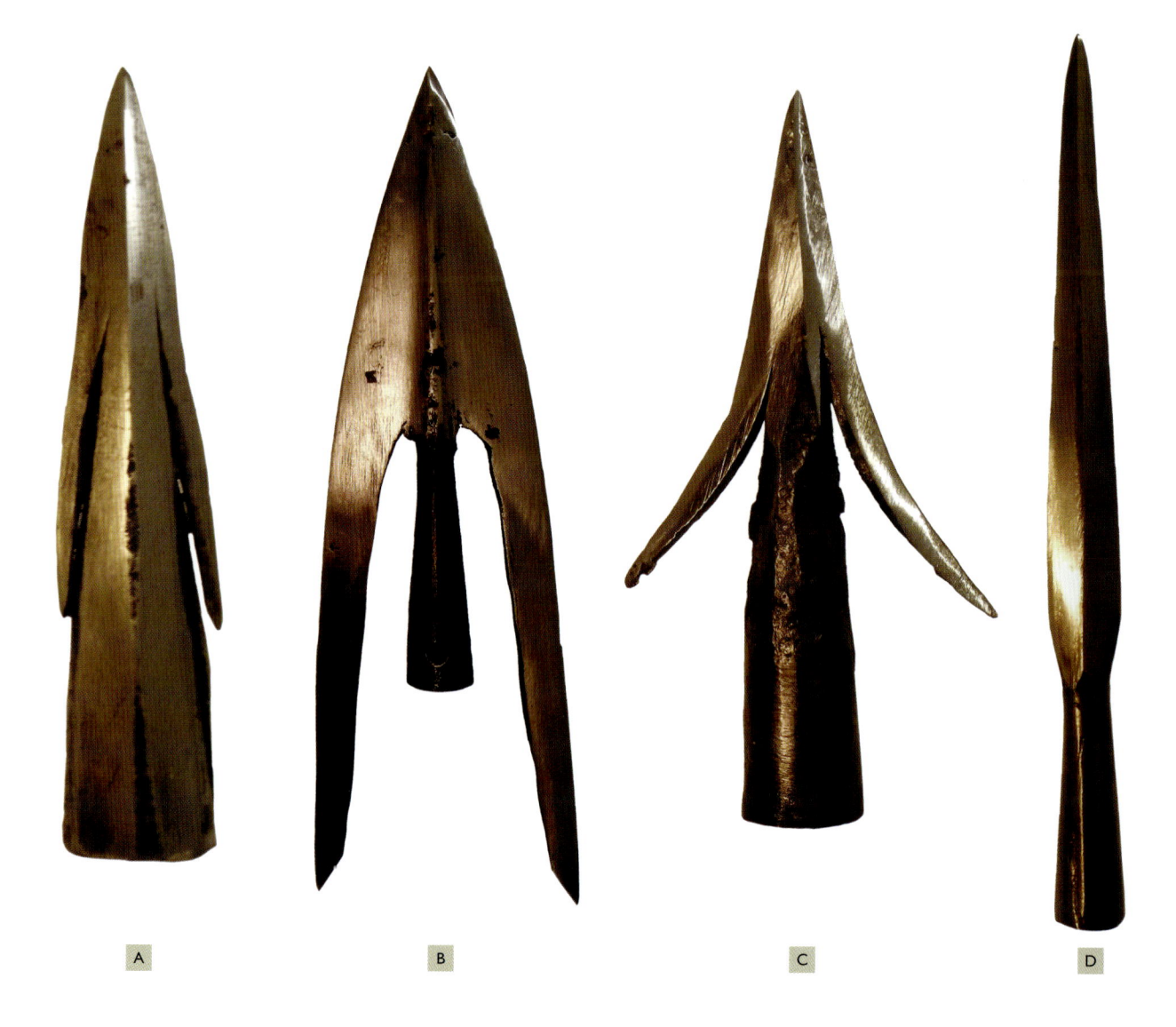

(**A**) Westminster Type 16. If the quantities that have been recovered archaeologically are any guide (and they may not be), this was possibly the arrowhead in most widespread use for medieval warfare. It combines the slender profile of a bodkin with the cutting edges and barbs of a broadhead. This particular example has been modelled on the arrowhead fitted to the arrow in Westminster Abbey – the only fully intact medieval arrow known to date. (Arrowhead by Hector Cole; photograph by Matthew Ryan)

(**B**) Swallowtail. This is a typical broadhead with large cutting blades and barbs. In a hunting context broadheads are necessary to let blood, which not only causes progressive weakness but also produces a trail that can be followed. A bodkin-style arrow into flesh is effective if it hits a vital organ, but it may not produce a wound that bleeds out – the arrow-shaft can staunch the flow. Large broadheads like this were considerably more expensive to produce than bodkins, both in the cost of materials and labour. They also required greater preparation; the blades were capable of being honed to a sharp edge. Well-sharpened broadheads offered the prospect of cutting through leather and textile, and they could be very effective against inadequately protected horseflesh. However, they would not fare well against a mail bard and certainly not against plate armour. (Arrowhead by Hector Cole; photograph by Matthew Ryan)

(**C**) Swept-out swallowtail. In this form of broadhead the blades have been drawn away from the socket to exaggerate the effect of the barbs, which prevented extraction. It is common to see this type of broadhead in medieval depictions of battle. However, it is uncertain to what extent they were actually used. It may be argued that artists sought a more visible and more sensational representation of an arrowhead for their portrayal, evoking an image of great bloodshed. Nevertheless, the sense of terror conjured by such arrowheads might have been as equally effective on campaign as it was in art. Cost may have dictated that they were used sparingly but the reputation of the hideously painful wounds these broadheads could inflict might have been of great psychological value. (Arrowhead by Hector Cole; photograph by Matthew Ryan)

(**D**) The long-needle bodkin was best suited for attacking mail and textile armour. If it managed to strike within the centre of a mail ring and at a reasonably perpendicular angle, the expanding taper of the head had the potential to force the ring to open, breaking its rivet, and to push through to some depth. It also had some of the properties of a needle when attempting to thread through textile defences. Against plate armour, however, the slender tip had a tendency to coil like ornamental scrollwork. (Arrowhead by Hector Cole; photograph by Matthew Ryan)

USE: AT FULL DRAW
The longbow in training and practice

ARCHERY AND THE LAW

On 1 June 1363, Edward III wrote to his sheriffs and commanded a

> proclamation to be made that every able bodied man on feast days [including Sundays] when he has leisure shall in his sports use bows and arrows, pellets or bolts, and shall learn and practise the art of shooting, forbidding all and singular on pain of imprisonment to attend or meddle with hurling of stones, loggats, or quoits, handball, football, club ball, cambuc, cock fighting or other vain games of no value; as the people of the realm, noble and simple, used heretofore to practise the said art in their sports, whence by God's help came forth honour to the kingdom and advantage to the king in his actions of war, and now the said art is almost wholly disused, and the people indulge in the games aforesaid and other dishonest and unthrifty games, whereby the realm is like to be kept without archers. (CCR Ed III 1363)

It was on the statute book by 1369 and it heralded a string of similar laws and recommendations for more than the next two centuries. These included, *inter alia*, statutes from Edward IV, Henry VII (r. 1485–1509), and, of course, Henry VIII, whose first statute on the matter in 1512 specified that the requirement to practise was for all men 'not lame, decrepute or maymed' under 60 years of age; in 1541, Statute 33 echoed all the old calls for men to own bows and arrows, for them to practise and to eschew unlawful games, the list of which had grown. The *Journal of the House of Commons* (Vol. 1) has an entry on 30 May 1604 that records the first reading of 'The Bill for the Maintenance of Archery, and Debarring of unlawful Games' and *The Calendar of State Papers Domestic: Charles I, 1631–3* records that on 31 August 1631 Charles I (r. 1625–49) invoked a commission that he had set up in 1628 to 'to quicken the execution of a statute of 33 Henry VIII for encouraging the use of archery'. Charles had been obliged to revoke the commission because of complaints from the counties that it was unenforceable, but it is interesting to note that the desire to promote English archery ran so late.

The basic mechanics of shooting a longbow can be taught and picked up quickly – arguably within a few hours. Some shooters are naturally good at aiming and ranging, while others need more practice. Regular practice and training are clear advantages in achieving a better aim, but good archers would be able to stay in reasonable form without having to do weekly work at the butts. The appeals for weekly practice that echo so loudly over the centuries were not because the longbow was an intrinsically difficult weapon. If you only used it for hunting or recreation, the longbow could be mastered relatively easily.

However, for it to be of use in war, there was a need for archers of exceptional strength, and that necessitated men bending-in their bows, rain or shine, for several hours every single week of the year. To be able to nock, draw to full length and, crucially, shoot rapidly under the extreme pressure of combat – facing an enemy charge – required not only a special kind of calm courage but also a muscle memory drilled to unfaltering precision and reliability, something that only came with constant practice. Drawing heavy bows is part strength and part technique. Neither alone is sufficient and both require a dedicated training regime.

The case for regular training is obvious, but those serving as military archers, or intending to do so, probably practised considerably more than once a week. For the soldier longbowman, time spent at the butts was surely a given; it did not need to be compelled by legislation.

I believe these archery laws were about more than the need for men to train. Undeniably the 1363 proclamation, and all the many others that followed it, had the effect of promoting archery, but I doubt that was either their exclusive or even their primary aim. Edward III's order was not restricted to longbow archery; practice with the sling or the crossbow ('pellets or bolts') were alternative pursuits that received equal approval. In fact, far greater emphasis was placed on what should not be done – the 'vain games of no value'. Edward does make mention of a concern that 'the realm is like to be kept without archers' but in the same year that it went into statute, 1369, the campaign army was estimated to have 3,858 longbowmen alongside 1,343 men-at-arms (Hardy 1992: 97). By that reckoning English archery was still in pretty good shape. There are hints, though, that Edward's decree should be seen in a wider social context.

On 12 June 1363, 11 days after his initial order, the king wrote to the sheriff of London urging various measures to keep the peace. These included adhering to a strict curfew, granting the power of citizens' arrest and an elaborate series of fines for aggressive behaviour. This featured such nuances as 'if he strike any man with his fist and draw no blood he shall pay 2*s*. or abide in prison eight days, and if he so draw blood he shall pay 40*d*. or abide in prison twelve days'. Innkeepers had to ensure that their guests left their weapons in their lodgings; failure to do so could result in prison. In addition, the king commanded a blanket prohibition stating 'that no man of whatsoever condition shall go armed in the city' (CCR Ed III 1363).

Such a catalogue of new laws implies a worrisome level of rowdiness and public disorder. This crime wave was fuelled in 1360 by the demobilization of thousands of fighting men after the Treaty of Brétigny, which sealed a temporary truce in the war with France. After nearly 15 years of profitable war, these men, used to violence,

TRAINING WITH THE BOW (OPPOSITE)

Archers setting up and shooting at butts (c. 1360). Butts were earth mounds that were set up in every town, village and hamlet and, by law, had to be maintained in good order. Erosion from rain and wind was minimized by the slope of the half-dome and the butts were held together by a covering of grass. As well as regularly tamping the sides into shape, maintenance involved frequent compacting of the face, and filling in the cavities created by arrow strikes. The grass would need cutting and in dry weather the butts would need to be watered. Regular Sunday practice at the butts was compulsory by law from 1363 for all men between 16 and 65. Targets, set against the backstop of the butts, were improvised and might consist of an oyster shell or a garland – a wreath of brushwood. Another popular target was the wand: a narrow stave of wood, set in front of the butt, the idea being to split it with the shot.

Inset: Shooting at the marks (c. 1500). Permanent courses were laid out in cities such as London for shooting over distances. Archers shot round these courses in groups, in the manner of golfers. They shot at designated marks set up at different distances. Each mark was identified by a distinguishing insignia on top of a wooden post, which was set in a stone plinth. In 1498 the mayor of London designated 11 acres of the city, Finsbury Fields, for archery practice. A map of the location dating to 1594 shows 194 marks, with distances ranging from 130yd to 345yd! Despite the designation of Finsbury Fields as a shooting area, it remained busy with the everyday traffic of people. Accidents happened, but the protocol was to call 'loose' if it was clear to take a safe shot and to call 'fast' (which originally meant safe) if shooting must be stopped to allow someone to pass. Playing 'fast and loose' was a dangerous game.

THE LONGBOW

Archers shooting at earth butts, from the Luttrell Psalter, c. 1320–30. In this picture we see several styles of blunt arrowhead being used, and the earth butts are pockmarked with their imprints. The butt itself acts as a backstop and the actual target here is the wreath of brushwood, known as the garland. One archer gives the impression that he may be instructing the others. I do not think that the even spread of hits is intended to indicate that these archers were bad shots, but an artistic device to convey heavy use. (The British Library, Add. MS 42130, f 147v, © The British Library/Bridgeman Images)

adventure and adrenalin, did not all step back into civilian life peaceably. Perhaps Edward's archery proclamation was intended more to regulate social conduct than it was to improve the quality of his army. If so, it may be likened to the calls for National Service as a remedy for hooligan behaviour that are still to be heard from time to time.

Whatever the motive, it seems likely that a great many of the men who trudged unwillingly to their local butts on a wet and cold Sunday morning – feckless youths, self-regarding burghers, the weak, the fearful and the frail – would have been entirely unsuited to military service and of no use in the front line. The inducement to create good, strong archers was in the decent pay they received and in the promise of reward on campaign that came with plentiful opportunities for looting.

A culture of regular archery practice must have fostered communities appreciative of shooting prowess, giving status to local men who could draw a strong bow – men who would go to the wars as heroes. It may have made some contribution to the readiness of an archer army, but it was more about discouraging dissolute activity. Roger Ascham wrote that teaching youths to use a bow not only made them shoot well, but also removed the desire for 'noughtie pastimes, as dysinge, cardinge and bowlinge' (Ascham 1968: 113). The idea that archery was a morally beneficial pursuit seems to have been deep-rooted and became an almost obligatory statement by any author on the subject.

Encouraging universal capability with the bow was not without its concerns. The Peasants' Revolt of 1381 was indicative of a society in the throes of dynamic and tumultuous transition; low-born men armed with bows were a credible military threat to the established order. In 1396, Rychardus Wedyngton (Dick Whittington), mayor of London, issued a proclamation the day before a new session of parliament, which commanded every man 'to leve his bowe and his arowys at home in hys inne' (GC). Clearly he was concerned about the possibility of civil unrest at a politically sensitive moment, and the instrument that signalled the greatest threat was the longbow. It is possible that one of the reasons the French did not arm their peasantry with the bow to the same extent that the English did is that they feared armed rebellion from the feudal underclass (Hardy 1992: 98). However, the use of massed ranks of archers in England's armies was a matter of economic expediency, and a balance had to be struck between containing lawless behaviour and having a supply of trained and armed men.

LATIMER'S EXTOLMENT OF ARCHERY

Even after the decline of the longbow as a principal military arm, there continued to be laws compelling men to train with the bow. Always alongside the injunction to practise were reminders of archery as the source of the nation's strength, and that it was an exercise that was good for you. Similar language recurred in successive statutes over the years. It was echoed in a sermon on the subject delivered by Hugh Latimer, bishop of Worcester, in 1549. Latimer railed that 'The arte of shutyng hath ben in tymes past much estcemed in this realme, it is a gyft of God, that he hath geven us to excel all other nacions wythall … but now we have taken up horynge in townes, instead of shutynge in the fyeldes' (Latimer 1832: 177). The notion that archery had fallen out of use, compared to a perceived bygone golden age, and that it was a God-given gift to Englishmen, was strikingly similar to that expressed by Edward III, 186 years earlier. Above all, the tone was moralizing rather than practical. This was in tune with the central theme of the sermon, which admonished society for its moral decrepitude.

Latimer did digress, however, with a momentary practical note, describing his own experience of archery. The good bishop, whose father was a yeoman farmer with modest landholdings, was eager to promote himself as a man of the people. He helped to cultivate that image by telling us that 'my poor father was as diligent to teach me to shute, as to learne any other thyng'; elaborating, he declared that his father 'taught me how to drawe, howe to lay my body in my Bowe, and not to draw with strength of armes, as other nacions do, but with strength of bodye' (Latimer 1832: 177), details that give us great insight into technique and which echo principles that we also read in Ascham.

Latimer added, 'I had my bowes brought me according to my age and strength, as I increased in them; so my bowes were made bigger and bigger; for men shall never shute well, excepte they be brought up in it' (Latimer 1832: 177). Here we return to a central idea of powerful bows – bows of heavy draw-weight – and the notion that such bows can only be managed by those who practise constantly.

Three replica blunts, made by Mark Wheatley, based on those depicted in the Luttrell Psalter. Note the waxed hemp twine binding set into the grooves of the example below. This may have the function of prolonging the life of the blunt head, which would be vulnerable to cracking from regular exposure to damp earth in the butts. (Photographs by Vince Beeton)

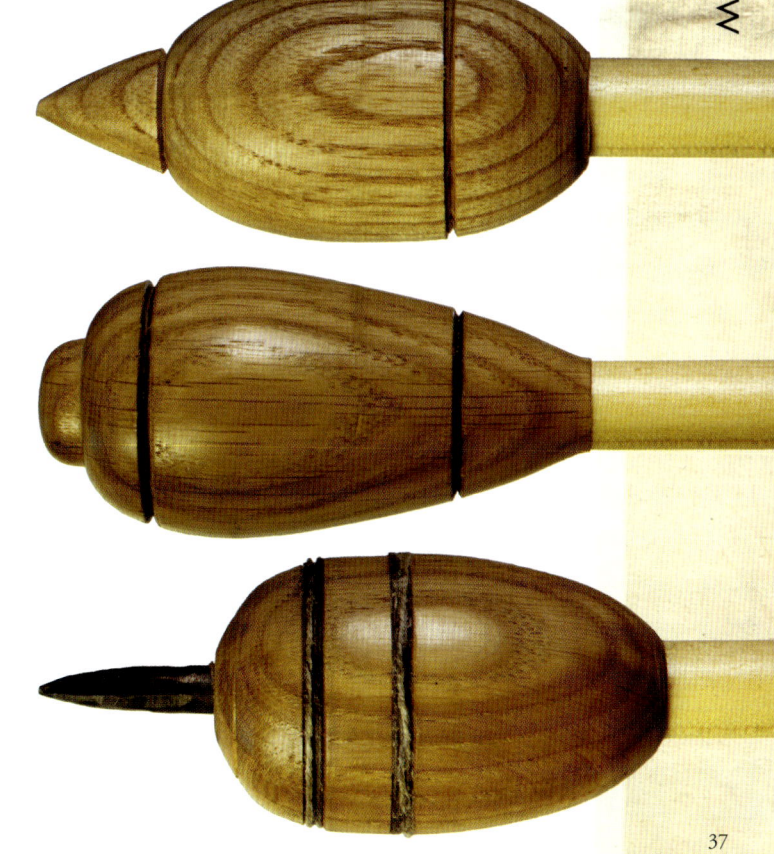

PRACTISING WITH BLUNTS AT THE BUTTS

The principal mode of archery practice was shooting at the butts. Butts were man-made earth mounds, clad with turf and given a rounded roof, so that water would run off and they would be able to stay out in all weathers. Butts had to be maintained but, given proper care, could last for years. They were permanent features in towns and villages. It is uncertain why they are called butts, but they may have developed from the practice of using a large wine butt (barrel), filled with earth, as a target. Our best image of what medieval butts looked like comes from the Luttrell Psalter. Commissioned by Sir Geoffrey Luttrell, this exquisite manuscript was illustrated between 1320 and 1330 with detailed scenes of everyday life. Among them is an image of archers practising at the butts.

One theory for the presence of blunts in the scenes depicted in the Luttrell Psalter is that because Luttrell's lands were located within the bounds of a royal forest, his tenants had to comply with forest law. Among other deterrents to poaching, such as having your greyhound's longest toes amputated

Replica bodkin arrowhead with a push-on blunt cap for shooting at the butts. It would be especially important for such caps to be bound in order to prevent them from splitting under the pressure of a heavy warbow arrow acting to drive through them. (Photographs by Vince Beeton)

(lawed), it was part of forest law that no man could carry sharp arrowheads – sharp arrows, like greyhounds, were a threat to the king's venison. How, then, could such men comply with the law to practise their archery? The answer may have been to use blunt arrowheads.

An alternative theory is of a purely practical nature. Shooting sharp arrows with a bow with a heavy draw-weight into an earth mound could have resulted in arrows burying themselves to an irretrievable depth. Large-headed blunts prevented that from happening. Blunts were also used for shooting at small game, so as not to spoil the meat, but they did not necessarily have to be separate arrows. It is possible that the blunt was a cap that fitted over an existing arrow (I am indebted to Mark Wheatley for suggesting this idea).

DISTANCE SHOOTING

Other training activities included 'roving', 'clout shooting' and 'shooting at the marks'. In roving, archers nominated natural marks in the landscape – such as dark patches of earth, leaves or twigs – as the target and shot to see who could get closest. The nearest shot called the next mark. It was a congenial pastime that involved roaming the countryside with friends.

Clout (cloth) shooting entailed shooting at a fixed distance of 240yd. The target, 18in in diameter, consisted of a canvas facing backed with coiled straw. In the centre was a wooden peg, known as the 'prick'. It was an especially esteemed feat to cleave the prick. References in contemporary sources to 'prickshafts' indicate that lighter-weight arrows were used when shooting at the clout.

This form of shooting became especially popular for shooting matches during the 16th century. In order to adjust their aim better at such distances, archers often recruited the services of a marker, who would stand dangerously close to the clout and signal whether shafts had over- or undershot or whether they had gone to the left or the right. Queen Elizabeth I was present at an unfortunate incident involving a marker in September 1569:

> Anthony Hanmer, in a shooting match … struck his own man who gave him aim, in the head with a prickshaft, in presence of a great number of gentlemen and others, whereof he is now dead. The shaft was well shot towards the mark, and his man that gave aim, desirous to see his master win, would not avoid when he was willed by crying to from both the marks, but wilfully abode at the mark, and died by his wilfulness. (CSPDEA 1871: 83)

Shooting at the marks combined the challenges of both roving and clout. Marks (wooden posts) were fixed targets at set distances, but each distance varied and the marks were laid out over a stretch of countryside that might include natural obstacles such as a stand of trees between the shooter and his mark – or the mark might sit out of direct sight, over the brow of a hill.

It may be argued that the ubiquity of these distance-shooting pursuits is evidence that the primary function of the military archer was to shoot at distant targets on the battlefield. While it is undoubtedly true that the longbow had a significant capability at long range, the mere fact that distance shooting was a popular recreational activity does not in itself prove this use in battle. Shooting an arrow in the air and watching it fly is a joyous thing to do, and as well as the exhilaration there is the challenge of competing with one's fellows to hit a distant mark. This alone would be reason enough for a culture of distance shooting, but there may also be other reasons.

The strictures for an archer to be able to shoot a certain distance were characteristic of legislation that post-dated the use of the bow as a mainstream weapon on the battlefield. Henry VIII's statute of 1542 ruled that 'no-one under 24 shall shoot at any mark of eleven score or under with any prickshaft or flight under penalty of six shillings and eight pence' (quoted in Soar, Gibbs, Jury & Stretton 2010: 194). Here it is clear that those aged under 24, those in their fighting prime, were required to be able to shoot with accuracy at a range of 220yd. Moreover, they had to do this with a heavy arrow, not the sort of lightweight arrow – 'prickshaft' – more commonly used for distance shooting. Note that the statute did not prohibit shooting at shorter ranges – it merely indicated the weight of arrow required for shooting at distance.

By 1542, battlefield archery was on the wane – though, in a last hurrah, English archers were to make a contribution to victory over the Scots at the battle of Pinkie Cleugh in 1547. Even so, the main application of the art of shooting in the Tudor period was for naval archery and, arguably, there was greater reason for naval archers to be able to shoot at distance.

Another possible reason for requiring distance-shooting ability was that it offered a visible demonstration that bowmen were shooting suitably heavy bows. Systems of measuring the power of a bow by means of draw-weight would probably have been

The stone plinth that held the wooden post for the mark known as 'Scarlet' in Finsbury Fields. It now resides in the care of the Honourable Artillery Company in Armoury House, London. (Photograph by Dave Watts)

Shooting at the popinjay. Popinjay targets took the form of wooden birds, set on spars, raised on tall masts. It is possible that the first instances of this were actual ships' masts, erected on land and stripped of extraneous paraphernalia. A popinjay is a medieval name for a type of parrot, the sort of exotic bird that would be familiar to sailors; certainly several species of parakeet, from India and Asia, were known in the Middle Ages and were depicted in bestiaries of the time. The spar could be raised and lowered, as it was for a sail, so that birds that had been knocked off could be reset easily. A ship's mast of 30–40ft was a modest target by the standards of today's popinjay shooters, who shoot to dizzying heights, but medieval ships were relatively small and that is all that was required. (Drawing by Matthew Ryan, www.matthewryanhistoricalillustrator.com)

viable with the technologies then available, but we do not know that this method was used. Although it is the system used today, it is not necessarily the best. It seems equally useful to measure the power of a bow by how far it can shoot. Setting a minimum distance with a specified weight of arrow would be one way of ensuring that bows of an appropriate power were being used.

Ascham, in referring to shooting at the 'prickes' (clout), makes the point that 'souldiours drawe quicklye in warre, for that maketh the shaft flye apace. In shooting at the prickes, hastye and quicke drawinge is neither sure nor yet comely' (Ascham 1968: 203). He is making the point that a technique seen on the battlefield is not appropriate for elegant recreation. We must not assume that the practices of the training ground always mirrored those of the battlefield precisely.

As I shall discuss, distance shooting on the battlefield needed to be used sparingly but, for centuries, the ability to shoot at distant marks had been an essential skill for archers besieging a castle or town. Being able to range accurately was of particular use when shooting at blind targets over the walls. It is my view that the military rationale for these exercises was far less to do with the archer's work on the battlefield and much more related to his tasks during sieges and at sea.

TRAINING FOR WAR AT SEA

Naval archers were an extremely important element in the defence forces of the nation. As well as needing to be able to rake the decks of enemy ships from a distance, naval archers also had to be able to shoot at targets high in the rigging. When ships grappled together, men in the crow's-nests – archers, javelin-men and men with large rocks – would assail the enemy decks with missiles; those on the decks sought to pick off those aloft. The perfect training for this was shooting at the 'popinjay'.

Popinjay shooting entailed shooting at targets, usually in the form of birds, which had been set up on tall masts. Alternatively, as was the case at Kilwinning in Scotland, where an annual popinjay contest dating to the 15th century is still held, the target could be perched on a horizontal pole that extended from the church tower. One early 14th-century depiction of popinjay shooting shows the target bird atop the sail of a windmill, an ingenious solution (Decretals f. 89r).

Shooting at the marks, clout shooting and popinjay shooting were more than mere amusements. They developed real skills with martial application, but it was at the butts that the hard work was done – shooting sheaf after sheaf of arrows, week in and week out, building archers of immense strength: the pride of the nation.

The archer

RECRUITING ENGLAND'S ARCHERS

Statutory obligations to practise may have helped to produce a reservoir of archers, but, during the ascendancy of the longbow, it was good pay and sound recruitment policies that filled the ranks of England's armies with an archer elite that was the envy of the world.

The golden age of the military longbow (*c.* 1270–*c.* 1500) was not the result of innovative weapon development. It was the consequence of gradual social change and economic expediency in England. Feudal power

> ## REGIONAL RECRUITMENT
>
> There is a persistent myth that the archer contingents of English armies were recruited almost exclusively from Wales. Certainly many Welsh archers drew their bows in the service of successive English kings, but Wales was not the only region to produce strong bowmen. Edward II (r. 1307–27) needed archers for his Scottish campaign, and a 1323 order (CCR Ed II) commanding the exchequer to raise funds for their payment records archers from various parts of the realm: Gloucester and Hereford and the Forest of Dean – 1,000; Dorset, Somerset and Wiltshire – 500; Southampton – 500; Sussex and the Weald – 500; 'Salop' (Shropshire) and Stafford – 500; Lancaster – 400; and High Peak, County Derby – 300. Edward III took archers from Norfolk, London and many other areas as well as from Wales on his Crécy campaign, and the Black Prince considered foot archers from Cheshire to be worth paying 6d a day (Wadge 2009: 103).

The archer in this photograph (Joe Gibbs) draws an extremely powerful bow, armed with a heavy war arrow. He wears good, serviceable clothing of a 15th-century style. Archers were not the lowly peasants that they are portrayed to have been in modern fiction; they were fit and strong, well equipped and relatively well paid. On the battlefield, an archer of this period would also wear armour such as a brigandine for the body, plate armour for the legs (cuisses) and a sallet for the head. He represented a fighting force to be reckoned with and each man was capable of a deadly aim. (Mike Loades)

rested on land ownership – the more land under the control of an overlord, the more knights and their retinues he could command to fight in his service. Compared to the feudal might of France, England, having less landmass, was at a disadvantage. Even before the decimation of the population by the Black Death (1348–50), feudal structures in England had begun to change more than those on the Continent, and there had long been a greater reliance on commoners as an integrated component of the national fighting force. That is not to say that the archer classes were the lowest-born peasants – far from it. They came from a variety of trades and social stations but generally not from the agricultural serfs, whose essential contribution to feudal wealth was to work the land, rather than to be absent fighting foreign wars.

Henry III's Assize of Arms of 1242 introduced compulsory bow ownership for those owning land worth more than 40s – this was the yeoman class. Bow ownership was not restricted to the better-off yeomen; those of lesser means were also encouraged to possess a bow if they were able to do so: it just was not compulsory for such men. Although such measures signified a rising recognition of the archer's military usefulness as well as his increasing social status, its purpose and that of earlier assizes was the provision of a militia for county police work, coastguard duties and the maintenance of order at home. Nevertheless, by the last quarter of the 13th century, the assizes had resulted in a substantial national arsenal of equipment, ready for the scrutiny of arrayers.

Introduced by Edward I, 'Commissions of Array' initiated the recruitment of archers on a grand scale. Not only were archers enlisted into his armies in quantity, they were selected for quality. Arrayers vetted not only an archer's shooting ability but also the standard of his equipment. It was the beginnings of creating a professional army, and obligations of feudal service were increasingly sweetened with inducements of good pay. Regular pay for an archer in Edward I's reign was 2d per day and in 1277, 100 elite archers from Macclesfield, acting as the royal guard, were each paid 4d per day (Wadge 2009: 103).

Such differential pay scales underlined a change in approach, from turning out an unskilled feudal levy towards producing a body of seasoned and proficient troops and paying them according to ability. The fact that all archers were not deemed as being equal can be further detected in the pay of archers guarding Welsh prisoners at Bristol Castle, who each received only 1d per day in 1296 (Wadge 2009: 103). These were the 'home guard' men, not the young, strong, quick-shooting men needed on a campaign.

MOUNTED ARCHERS AND MIXED RETINUES

Companies of archers were organized in groups of 20 men, each led by a vintenar – 'twentieth man' – who received double pay. Five vintenars and their men were commanded by a centenary. There was not a set rate for centenaries, though obviously they received more than lower ranks did. As with all military service there was a risk of death or injury, and, even more likely, disease. However, the rewards were enticing and a few months' military service could give a man a good start in life.

By the 1340s, foot-archers were paid 3d per day and mounted archers got 6d per day (Wadge 2009: 103). The mounted archer, who rode to battle but dismounted to fight, was to become a key player in the Hundred Years' War. His mobility had clear advantages for expeditionary forces raiding on foreign soil, ravaging the countryside, then hastening home to their ships with the plunder.

In addition to providing a rapid-strike capability on campaign, mounted archers were also useful for surprise deployment on the battlefield. At the battle of Poitiers on 19 September 1356 the English commander, Edward the Black Prince's ally, Sir Jean III de Grailly, the Captal de Buch, took a force of 60 men-at-arms and mounted archers in a wide arc around the French flank and then fell upon them from behind (Strickland & Hardy 2005: 237). It proved to be the turning point of the battle.

Muster rolls invariably counted mounted archers together with hobilars, without making a distinction as to how many of each were present. Hobilars were also 'dragoon' infantry, but they were armed with long spears or polearms, not missile weapons; they were paid at the same rate as mounted archers, however. The fact that they were always accounted for together points to a crucial interdependence.

Archers cannot stand in an open field without protection. Cavalry will too easily trample them. When not defended by stakes or a ditch or similar, archers have to be deployed among other infantry with pikes or polearms. Andrew Ayton's groundbreaking analysis of muster records (Ayton & Preston 2005: 169 etc.) has demonstrated that archers in Edward III's armies were always recruited in conjunction with men-at-arms and other troop types as part of a mixed retinue. He argues persuasively for a 'combined forces' battlefield deployment, in which the archers are not a separate bloc but have men-at-arms and spearmen/billmen deployed in among them to defend against enemy assaults. Ayton also posits convincingly that Froissart's 'herce' reference, popularly interpreted as a description of archers in a harrow formation, may in fact derive from a French word for 'hedgehog' – *hérisson* (Ayton & Preston 2005: 328). This conjures an image of archers standing alongside men armed with long spears or bills, the formation bristling like a hedgehog.

The extent to which feudal service obliged a man to fight in a king's foreign adventures, which included those in Wales and Scotland, was another matter. Arrayed troops were the financial responsibility of the counties, and by the beginning of Edward III's reign (1327) there was general agreement that if the king wanted to mobilize an army for a foreign campaign, he would have to pay for it. Funding from the royal exchequer involved taking private loans and raising taxes through parliament: challenging efforts, which put severe constraints on the military budget. The versatility of archers – useful for raiding expeditions and castle sieges as well as on the battlefield – made them a fiscally astute choice when compared to expensive men-at-arms and knights. So it was that the ranks of England's armies were increasingly swelled with brawny men who could draw a hefty bow.

The 'Knight's Yeoman' in Chaucer's *Canterbury Tales* – 'he bore a mighty bow' (Chaucer 1981: 59) – is exactly that, an archer serving as part of a knight's fighting team. Chaucer goes on to state that he was also a forester. Foresters and parkers were professional huntsmen and expert shots with the bow. As such they were keenly sought after for service in the wars, and a number of royal commands called specifically for their recruitment (Ayton & Preston 2005: 222). Hunters have never favoured long-range shots and the skill of a parker or forester would have been in dropping a deer at between 10yd and 40yd. Although doubtless able to shoot at long range, I suspect that it was their deadliness as close-range killers that was in such demand. William and John Smart, parkers from St Osyth in Essex, received royal pardons for unspecified crimes in return for fighting in the Crécy campaign in 1346 (Ayton & Preston 2005: 223).

As with armies fighting for England in later eras, the longbow contingents that accompanied successive English monarchs on campaign in the Middle Ages included more than a few criminals undertaking military service. Hundreds of royal pardons for crimes, including murder, were granted to archers during the wars in France. Of the thousands of archers recruited, hardened criminals remained a minority, but, in addition to good pay, the pardon was yet another inducement to enlist the very best bowmen in the land.

Archers were hired from many other walks of life. Richard Wadge (Wadge 2009: 243–55) tables the rank and the civilian occupations of archers recruited from London in 1337. Among them are: physician, butcher, tailor, dyer, furrier, parker, glover, chapman, barber, cook, skinner, smith, bowyer, cooper, clerk, armourer, baker and falconer. It is a random snapshot, but it reveals an illuminating cross-section of the non-military occupations of those who sought to boost their fortunes with a spell of military service.

By the end of the 14th century it had become common to sign up archers with indentures – longer-term annual contracts. Being an archer had become a profession in itself and the assurance of a year's pay made it worthwhile for a bowman to invest in a good bow, a sheaf of arrows, some armour and a horse, and to become a mounted archer. Pay of 6d a day at a time when a skilled mason earned 4d per day and an unskilled labourer only 1½d per day (Dyer 1998: 226) was a good return.

In addition to good pay were the rewards of plunder. Soldiering also offered adventure and camaraderie and the prospect of returning home a hero. It was a profession that attracted men in increasing numbers. By the time of the Wars of the Roses, the number of archers in an army was staggering. In 1471, Edward IV took steps to raise funds to pay for 14,000 archers (Megson 1993: 55).

Archers in battle, from Froissart's *Chroniques* (detail). Note short-sleeved gambeson, plate leg-harness, and ragged courtepy. The flared sleeve is probably no encumbrance to shooting, terminating, as it does, near the elbow. It has fringing which is a sign that it is wet-weather gear. The archers are also armed with swords. (Bibliothèque Nationale de France, Ms. FR. 2642, fo. 159v, © Bibliothèque Nationale de France)

The longbow on campaign

ARCHERS' GEAR

Archers had to sustain a very laborious workload, drawing back their heavy bows again and again, and so non-restrictive attire was essential. At the same time, the archer's affiliation to a particular group needed to be evident. In Edward III's armies, shire companies of archers wore identifying liveries, such as red and white for Londoners or green and white for the Welsh and Cheshire men (Ayton & Preston 2005: 186–87). We may imagine others in blue and yellow and black and a variety of parti-coloured configurations. The commonest form of archer's clothing mentioned in the records is the 'courtepy' and this is probably the garment that displayed this colourful allegiance. The courtepy has been described as a short coat or tunic (Ayton & Preston 2005: 187), but I believe it was more like a hood with a yoke extending to just below the shoulder. In *Piers Ploughman*, a narrative poem written by William Langland *c*. 1360, the hermits cut their 'copes' into 'courtepies'. A cope was a full-length cape with a hood and so, by implication, a courtepy had an integral hood. The medieval hood, with its long tail, was an ingenious piece of wet-weather clothing that functioned in the same way as fringing on buckskins or motorcycle leathers. It wicked moisture from those parts of the fabric that lay wet against the body and allowed it to run off the end. Woollen cloth, treated with extra lanolin, would offer a reasonable, though imperfect, level of rain-proofing, but hoods at least facilitated drying out quickly after a storm. Medieval art commonly shows hoods with yokes that extend to just below the shoulder. Wet weather was a constant menace to troops on campaign and so a hood was an essential piece of equipment.

An element of personal protection was also vital, however. Archers could be, and were, overrun by cavalry or men-at-arms on foot and had to engage in hand-to-hand fighting. In many instances they might also expect to be shot at by archers on the other side. During the early part of the Hundred Years' War the gambeson, a stout padded coat, augmented with a mail collar or coif and plate leg-harness, was typical equipment for an archer. By the later 15th century the jack and the brigandine supplanted the gambeson, giving both greater protection and ease of movement.

By dint of their profession, archers also needed good visibility. At the time of Crécy the archer wore a simple skullcap of iron or boiled leather, often beneath his characteristic woollen hat, the chaperon. By the late 15th century, during the Wars of the Roses for instance, when both sides used archery, some protection for the face became necessary; archers were often depicted at this period wearing sallets with visors.

We get a humbler impression of the archer's kit from the chroniclers who described the Agincourt campaign. The French chronicler Enguerrand de Monstrelet reported 'most of these archers were without armour, their hose about their knees' (Curry 2009: 160). The soldier and chronicler Jean de Wavrin, an eyewitness on the French side at Agincourt, noted that some archers were barefooted; he described their headgear as being of boiled leather or osier – made from wicker and bound with iron strapwork (quoted in Curry 2009: 160). However, the fact that the lack of armour was worthy of note serves to emphasize that normally it would have been expected. At Agincourt Henry V's army was severely weakened by dysentery, 'the bloody flux', which explains both the choice to forgo the burden of armour and the manner in which they wore their hose. Generally, however, archers were well-equipped, professional soldiers.

CARE OF THE BOW

Whatever weight or style of bow the archer carried, he needed to take care of it. Throughout the ages it has been the soldier's task to look after his weapon, and the longbow was no exception. It required regular treatment with a compound of heated 'wax, rosin and fine tallow … [which] did conserve them in all perfection against all weather of heat, frost and wet' (Smythe 1964: 69). When travelling, bows were kept in an oilskin linen bag to protect them further from weather, knocks and scrapes.

Famously sensitive to the weather was the bowstring, and legend has it that one of the reasons the English won the day at Crécy is because they had the good sense to put their bowstrings under their caps during the deluge that preceded the battle, whereas the dim Genoese crossbowmen allowed their strings to stretch. There are other reasons for the fate of the Genoese, which we shall come to, but I doubt it was their strings. Properly waxed crossbow strings should be proof enough against heavy rain and the reason the English kept their bowstrings under their hats is also probably misunderstood.

Sir John Smythe recorded that 'in times past the strings, being made of very good hemp, with a kind of water glue to resist wet and moisture … did very seldom break' (Smythe 1964: 70). These are probably the type of strings used at Crécy and, since they resisted wet, were not greatly threatened by the downpour. A greater enemy to

A PROSPEROUS ARCHER

One of the Black Prince's archers, whom we know held lands in Macclesfield, Cheshire, was William Jauderell. I have been to his grave, which is in St James' Church, Whaley Bridge, Derbyshire. The grave, prominent in the nave of the church, is marked by an engraved stone slab that reads 'William Jauderell, "the archer", died 1375'. This slab, not a contemporary marker, also lists his descendants, including his son, Roger Jauderell, who fought at Agincourt in 1415. Perhaps he shot there with his father's bow? William Jauderell was given two oak trees from the royal forest to repair his house in 1356 (Hardy 1992: 77). It would seem that the crown looked after its veterans, no doubt as a further encouragement for recruitment. The family's prosperity, evident from the status of the memorial, is easily accounted for if Jauderell, in addition to being from Cheshire, were a centenary, or at least a vintenar, and perhaps a mounted archer to boot, who then invested his earnings wisely on his return. Being an archer could be a route to great social mobility. Moreover, there were ways in which good wages could be boosted.

John Jauderell, also an archer, who fought at the battle of Poitiers in 1356, looted a valuable silver salt cellar in the aftermath, which he sold at a handsome price (Wadge 2009: 125). Looting was a very profitable business and the prospect of valuable booty was a considerable lure to men signing up for the wars. There was a great deal of portable wealth, ripe for pillage, in the towns and churches that were routinely raided on campaign, as well as what could be found in the enemy's camp after a battle. There was also money to be had from the ransom of prisoners, though the more valuable prizes, the knights, tended to be the exclusive property of their social equals. Also of great value to plunder was armour. Stripped from the corpses of the fallen it could be sold and, equally importantly, be used to equip the archer himself.

Heavy bows put immense strain on the fingers, and although a two-finger loose is often shown in medieval art, it is difficult to imagine this being possible with the heavier bows. The popular idea that the two-finger salute originated at Agincourt, as a response by English archers to the French threat to cut off those two fingers from any captured bowmen, is apocryphal. Sticking up two fingers was probably a vulgar gesture long before then. Moreover, the actual threatened penalty, according to the contemporary chronicler Jean de Wavrin, was that they 'would cut off the *three fingers* of their right hand' (Curry 2009: 155 – my emphasis). (Archer: Mark Stretton; photograph Mike Loades)

strings bonded with this soft, tacky glue* was that the glue should dry out completely and become brittle. It was probably for this reason that the English archers kept their bowstrings under their hats – a place of stable humidity that helped to keep their strings supple.

SECOND BOWS

Bows can break in shooting and rough conditions on campaign might lead to further losses, but the enormous scale of military bow production (Strickland & Hardy 2005: 24–25) suggests a provision in excess of just having replacements for breakages. I think it is possible that archers on campaign might have carried at least two bows, of different weights. In a letter to Elizabeth I in 1589, one of her courtiers, Sir Thomas Heneage, remarked, '… nor seek ether ii strings to my bowe nor ii bowes for one marke' (Cecil 1562–97: 3). It seems likely this was a saying in common use and the sense of the 'two bows' part is that he was steadfast in a single course of action, not 'hedging his bets' with alternative stratagems. Having two bows for shooting at the marks, however, could be a very useful stratagem – using the heavier bow for distant shots and the other for nearer targets. Equally, dropping down from a 130lb bow to a 100lb bow could be a valuable option as the hours of a battle progressed – and who would wish to stand in the front line without a second bow to hand? It is a detail the art does not reveal to us, but then it does not show us the essential supply chain of arrows either.

Archers out foraging for the army might require lighter bows. *Le Livre de Chasse*, a 14th-century hunting treatise, recommends that 'the bow should not be overstrong; one should be able to draw it easily without shifting one's position and to hold it unwaveringly after drawing it to enable an oncoming deer to reach the best position for the shot' (quoted in Cummins 2003: 52). There may be ambush situations for a scouting party of mounted archers that would require the service of like bows, situations where a steady aim was required. Bows of different strengths are suitable for different applications, and a glance through the London Consistory Court Wills 1492–1547 (*LCCW: passim*) reveals constant references to 'best bows', 'next bows' and 'worst bows' bequeathed to beneficiaries, confirming the common practice of multiple bow ownership in the early 16th century. I imagine it was much the same during the longbow's glory days.

CARRIAGE OF ARROWS

Two dozen arrows per man would not have been sufficient for battle and so the bulk of the stocks were issued. During a battle there must have been a lively relay of hurrying boys keeping the archer lines supplied from the carts, and not a few intemperate shouts from archers who were running low. For storage and transport, the supply arrows were kept in barrels, but the individual archer carried his personal sheaf in a linen arrow-bag. These bags had a leather separator to prevent the fletchings from crushing. The advantage of the bag, compared to the quiver, was that it could

The archer in this photograph (Joe Gibbs) mirrors the stance often seen in contemporary manuscript images. It assists in drawing the very heavy draw-weight bows. Anyone who has done any weightlifting will know that the pelvis is tilted back in a similar way for a dead-lift. In part this offers some protection to the spine, opening up the vertebrae and helping to avoid the risk of rupturing a disc, which would otherwise suffer an enormous compression load. Mainly, though, this stance enables greater power to be recruited for the draw. It connects the elastic tension of muscles and tendons throughout the back and into the legs, so that the bow is drawn with the power of the whole body, not just the arms and lateral muscles. (Mike Loades)

---

* A possible clue to the nature of this 'glue/gum' is in the heraldry of medieval Chester's Company of Stringmakers, a town guild. It featured crossed shin-bones on the shield (Soar, Gibbs, Jury & Stretton 2010: 156). Various glues and gelatins were made from the shin-bones of cattle.

be waxed and weatherproofed and pulled up so that the whole arrow was covered. It was also light. When shooting, the top of the bag could be rolled down and arrows withdrawn easily. Another version was a bag lined with a wicker frame.

It is equally common to see archers in medieval art with the arrows stuck in their belt (girdle). At first this would appear problematic; one might think that as arrows were withdrawn the consequent slackening of the girdle would allow the remaining arrows to slip through. However, Jonathan and John Waller (Waller & Waller 2010: 155–77) have demonstrated that a form of constrictor knot can be used – either a miller's knot or a marline hitch work equally well – so that as the knot loosens from the removal of arrows, it can be instantly tightened by a quick pull down on the girdle with the thumb. As a consequence the circumference of the girdle increases very slightly – just a few inches for an entire sheaf – but it remains above the hips and, more importantly, the arrows are held securely.

All of this was useful for an army on the move, but when it came to the time for archers to form up in battle order, contemporary images often depict them with their arrows staked out in the ground in front of them. Anyone who has done this will know that it can be a fiddly business, especially if the ground is dry, and it certainly anchors the archer in a fixed position. Even having to move a pace or more is an unwelcome chore. It is not the obvious choice and so there must have been good reason to do it.

One advantage was that, from this position, arrows could be more quickly taken up and fitted to the string – an arrangement that hints strongly at the importance of

LEFT Top view of an arrow-bag with wicker frame. (Mike Loades)

ABOVE Top view of an arrow-bag with spacer. (Photograph by Matthew Ryan)

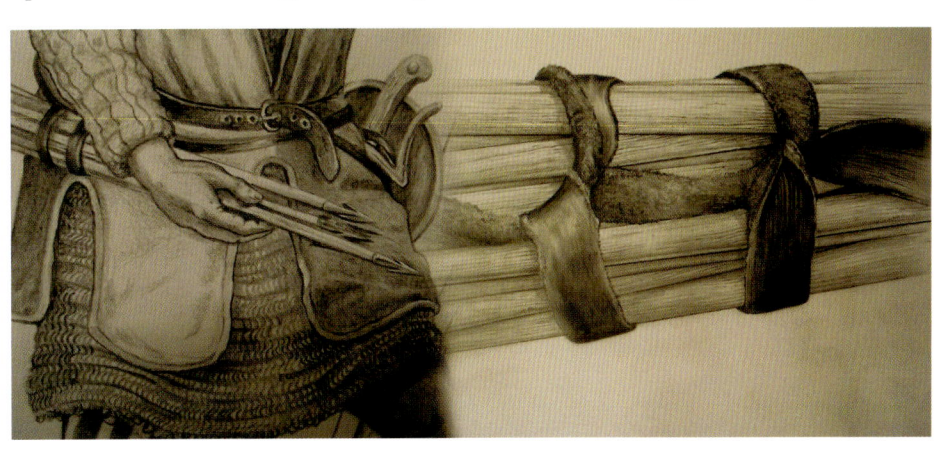

Drawing of sheaf of arrows in constrictor knot. (Drawing by Matthew Ryan, www.matthewryanhistoricalillustrator.com)

being able to shoot rapidly. A second benefit, from the point of view of enemy mortality, was that arrowheads embedded in the ground delivered the bacillae they had collected there into the wounds they created, encouraging fatal infection. Whether this was understood, or even observed, is uncertain.

The longbow's role in combat

Pitched battles were important events in medieval warfare. They were the great stages upon which chivalry's celebrities – the knights – played their dramatic parts and where reputations were made and lost. Battles were literally the theatre of war. Loss or victory could have significant political consequence, but large-scale battles were relatively infrequent occurrences; the real business of medieval warfare, the daily slog of hostilities, consisted of *chevauchée* and siege. No troops were better suited to this work than bowmen, and none more rapidly deployed than mounted archers. This is why they were recruited into English armies in such numbers. The fact that they could also render battlefield service was a bonus. Horsed archers generally accounted for a much higher proportion of the archer contingent than did foot-archers.

THE LONGBOW AS TERROR WEAPON – *CHEVAUCHÉE*

Chevauchée was the name given to a raiding campaign that swept through a swathe of the enemy's territory. The roots of the French word for horse – *cheval* – can be seen and *chevauchée* might be loosely translated as a 'raid on horseback'. It was done swiftly. In execution a *chevauchée* needed to keep momentum and not to get bogged down. Mounted archers were the ideal troops to spearhead a *chevauchée*, having the versatility to forage, scout, raid, skirmish and lay siege. Footslogging troops and a lumbering baggage train were at the centre of a march but it was the light, mounted troops who did the lion's share of destructive work, ravaging the countryside for 15–20 miles either side of the main line.

Crops were burned, houses and churches were pillaged, and people were killed and terrorized. There was considerable brutality, and often atrocity, on *chevauchée*. Edward III's troops, in an assault led by his archers, stormed the town of Caen in July 1346, rampaging through the streets in a frenzy of indiscriminate slaughter; the fighting resulted in over 5,000 deaths and most of the town being razed to the ground.

Full view of two arrow-bags. The arrow-bag on the left of the picture holds arrows separated by a leather spacer, a replica of those recovered from Henry VIII's warship, the *Mary Rose*. Although clearly unsuitable for use with broadheads, all forms of bodkin and many forms of Type 16 arrowhead can easily be withdrawn through the holes. As well as safeguarding the fletchings, this system also dampens down the clatter of arrows in transit, which was of particular advantage to mounted archers. On the right of the image is an arrow-bag with a wicker frame. Not only does this have the capacity for a greater number of arrows but the flared base is suitable for accommodating both broadheads and incendiary arrows. It is also resistant to crush, when stacked in the carts of a supply train. (Mike Loades)

CHEVAUCHÉE (OPPOSITE)

A column of mounted archers on *chevauchée*. They are part of a detachment of 1,000 men who have just raided and looted the small town in the background and are hastening away with their plunder to rejoin the main army 15 miles away. There has been a great deal of violence and killing in the town, the population have been terrorized and many buildings have been set on fire.

A vintenar is stationed by the side of the road, checking that every one of the 20 men under his command has rejoined the column. Discipline was a challenge with men exposed to drink and riot.

As well as lining their own pockets with booty, the archers have also been able to forage for the main army and have packhorses laden with foodstuffs further back in the column. Other packhorses, as seen in this picture, accompany them with vital supplies for the raid, including bags of spare arrows.

What they cannot take with them they burn. A small group of mounted archers in the middle ground are shooting incendiary arrows at a barn, which holds winter feed for livestock. This scorched-earth policy was a terror tactic intended to create discontent among the enemy's vassals, to weaken him economically by destroying his food supplies and seizing his wealth and sometimes, ultimately, to provoke him into pitched battle.

THE LONGBOW

A particular advantage of the *chevauché*e was that the vast sums of money laid out to fund the expedition could be offset with the gains to be had from plunder. The greatest prizes were the towns. Here were abundant goods and treasure to be looted; here were food, women and wine. Capturing a town enriched the king's coffers just as much as his soldiers' purses. Some towns surrendered without a fight; others did not. Medieval towns were fully enclosed behind high stone walls, having many of the defensive features of a castle; if they resisted, they had to be stormed by force.

THE LONGBOW IN SIEGE WARFARE

Town walls were not the only fortifications that could stall a *chevauchée*. Castles controlled the land, and from these secure bases mounted garrisons could pose a threat to detachments of the invading army. To ensure safe passage, castles often needed to be taken and, if so, they needed to be seized quickly. Laying siege to starve them out, undermining or building large siege engines to batter down the walls all took time. There was no time available while on *chevauchée*; it was a relentless, rapid rampage through hostile territory, making as much gain and causing as much pain as possible before the enemy could marshal the full might of his army. The quickest way to take a castle or a town was by escalade – going over the walls – and in order to accomplish an escalade, the support of archers was crucial.

Archers might begin a siege by sending incendiary arrows over the walls to fire the buildings, or they might terrorize with showers of regular arrows that put everyone in danger. Froissart's description of the siege of Tournai in 1340 records that 'the arrows shot over the crenelations [*sic*] and into the town were a marvel' (quoted in Rogers 2010: 95). In the same passage he lists six persons of note who were killed or wounded by these arrows, in many cases because, behind the perceived security of their walls, they were not wearing armour.

During an escalade, the archers' main function was to keep the walls clear so that their own men could get over on ladders. Against the escaladers the defenders might use a combination of archers or crossbowmen, men hurling down stones and spears, and men using levers to push the scaling-ladders away. For the besieging archers, picking off these targets, who were often in close proximity to one's own men, required extremely accurate shooting.

Another threat to those going over the top was presented by arrows raking along the walls from arrow-loops set in projecting towers. Arrow-loops presented to the outside in three forms – a basic vertical slit; the same with a transverse slit forming a cross; and a vertical slit with offset transverse slits. The advantage of a transverse opening was that it extended the peripheral vision of those within. However, when this was cruciform, it created a good aiming point, like crosshairs, for attacking archers to use. Offsetting the transverse elements made it very much harder to shoot through the arrow-loop from the outside. I have had several opportunities to shoot into arrow-loops at various castles, using rubber blunts so as not to damage ancient masonry. Those arrow-loops with offset horizontal apertures offer a far greater challenge.

Mounted archers were mounted to travel but dismounted for battle. However, there are occasional images in medieval art that show archers shooting from horseback. These are mostly in hunting contexts but there are some battle images. It is certainly possible to shoot a longbow from a galloping horse, as demonstrated by the author in this photograph. It would be a useful tactic for raids and skirmishes. Horsed archers were also effective in hunting down fugitives, whether it was pursuing those fleeing from a terror raid or chasing down a wanted man at home. Mounted archers were used for domestic law enforcement as well as for foreign service. (Kim Hawkins)

THE MOUNTED ARCHER'S HORSE – THE AMBLER

Mounted archers and accompanying hobilars rode a particular type of mount, a travelling horse, ideally suited to raiding warfare. These 'hobby' horses, also variously known as amblers or palfreys, had a fifth gait, called the amble (as in perambulate), whereby both legs on one side move together, followed by both legs on the other side. It is a kind of running walk. The result is an extremely fast pace, averaging 15mph, which is non-fatiguing to the horses. They can keep it up for hour after hour – compared with a canter, which they can only do for about 15 minutes before needing a lengthy walk down. An ambling gait is also extremely comfortable and non-fatiguing to the rider; he too can sustain riding at this pace for hours on end. A rider on an ambling horse experiences a gentle side-to-side rocking, as opposed to the up-and-down motion generated by other gaits, which require him to compensate with muscle-work of his own.

A number of surviving horse breeds retain the medieval ambling gene, including the Peruvian Paso Fino, the American Standardbred, the Turkish Rahven and the Icelandic horse. I once used Icelandic horses to ride from Canterbury to London and was astonished not only at how non-strenuous the ride was but also how purposeful it felt. These sturdy little horses – and all medieval horses were small by modern standards – sped along and gave a real sense of going somewhere in a hurry.

In 1417, the retinue of William de la Pole, 1st Duke of Suffolk, had four horses for each of his 90 mounted archers (Wadge 2009: 122). A plentiful supply of remounts would enable a mounted contingent to maintain an unrelenting pace for days, with all the advantages of surprise that would bring. It seems unlikely, however, that Edward III provided his mounted archers with such a high number of replacements. He had 3,500 mounted archers and hobilars for his Crécy campaign and 5,000 mounted archers for the *chevauchée* of 1359 (Strickland & Hardy 2005: 203). However, horses do go lame and fall sick, so he surely made some provision for remounts.

Archers shooting in rotation through an arrow-loop. Note that the offset transverse slits give improved peripheral visibility for the archers inside but create an optically awkward pattern, making it harder for archers outside to find an aiming point. The stonework has been left exposed on the forward arrow-loop to show its architectural construction. However, all castle interiors were originally plastered and decorated, as depicted to the left of the drawing. (Drawing by Matthew Ryan, www.matthewryanhistoricalillustrator.com)

EWBS archers (Ian Coote and Gary Symonds) shooting in elevation or 'shooting underhand' (as it is also known), because the point of aim is below the hand of the bow-arm. Shooting in the air in this way is only depicted in medieval art when the archers are shooting at defenders on the fortified walls of a castle or town. (Mike Loades)

Although every arrow may not go through, those that rattled against the edges were also effective in keeping those inside pinned down. Shooting from within towards outside targets required an archer to step into the zone where he would be vulnerable to incoming missiles. He also faced other challenges. An arrow-loop creates a potential structural weakness in a wall. In order to compensate for this, it is buttressed by an embrasure with splayed sides, which can range from between 6ft and 10ft deep. There is insufficient room for an archer to shoot within it and he must stand back within the chamber, a considerable distance from the actual opening.

A late 15th-century representation of the battle of Shrewsbury (21 July 1403). The archers are in the thick of the fighting, shooting their heavy bows at close range. During the battle both the leading protagonists from each side were shot in the face by arrows. The sixteen-year old Prince Harry (later Henry V) was wounded and his rival on the battlefield, Sir Harry 'Hotspur' Percy, was killed. The face was a primary target for archers and there are frequent accounts of arrows striking exposed faces. This is not because experienced soldiers were gazing upwards into a descending shower of arrows, but because commanders in particular may lift their visors either to give orders or to scan the battlefield for tactical information, making them vulnerable to a quick-eyed archer at close range loosing a well-aimed arrow. Philip VI of France received an arrow in the jaw at Crécy (1346), David II of Scotland was hit by two arrows in the face at Neville's Cross (1346) and Henry VI was wounded in the neck at St Albans (1455). (The British Library, Beauchamp Pageants, Cotton Julius E IV, art. 6, f. 4, © The British Library/Bridgeman Images)

Although this puts greater demands on his marksmanship, it does have another benefit. The further he stands back within the chamber, the wider the angle of shot he can achieve, creating a wider exterior killing zone.

Archers attacking a castle were generally equipped with pavises or mantlets – large freestanding shields – so that they could shelter while nocking, stepping out only briefly to shoot. Several attacking archers can train their bows onto one arrow-loop. To counter this potential rate-of-shooting advantage, I have experimented shooting in rotation with another archer from inside an arrow-loop and it works very well. As one archer steps into the operational zone to shoot, the other steps out to fit another arrow to the string. A good rhythm can be achieved, resulting in a fairly constant stream of arrows through the arrow-loop.

THE LONGBOW IN PITCHED BATTLE

Generalizations are problematic because every battle has its own unique set of circumstances. Nevertheless, one universal essential for the effective use of archery is selecting the right ground. In the world of battlefield toxophily, topography is king. Archers required prepared positions, whether they commanded the higher ground, were defended by an organized infantry or were behind a bristling array of sharpened stakes. Where they did not have at least one of these they were driven from the field. On the flat plain at Verneuil (17 August 1424), English archers were swept away by the Lombard cavalry; before they had staked the ground at Patay (18 June 1429), they were caught by French cavalry and were helpless against the ensuing charge, which mowed through their ranks and cut them down in a terrible slaughter.

Having the advantage of ground was crucial. It was a particular advantage when that entailed possession of the higher ground. Shooting down on an enemy from a position of height was not the same as launching long-distance volleys in a high parabola; it may have produced a similar hailstorm pattern, but shots at 20yd from archers atop an 8ft bank would thump home with a great deal more force than those arcing in from long range.

It is my opinion that unleashing successive flights at distant targets had to be carefully rationed. I do not contradict that it was done, but I do suggest a shift in emphasis that moves towards considering that the greater portion of the archers' work was at ranges of 50yd and closing; towards thinking of the longbow as a very effective close-range weapon, with archers in the thick of the fighting. Moreover, much of that fighting was at extreme close range – when an enemy attack was stalling at the front line, slowed by stakes or caltrops or a hedge of spears, or when the archers' companion men-at-arms were engaged in hand-to-hand struggles, still then the archers, at 10yd, at 5yd, thudded their shafts, with deliberation, into the reeling bodies of their foes.

The psychology of shooting at a recognizable human target, close enough to see his eyes and hear his screams, is quite different from launching skyward volleys into a distant mass of men. To some this may remove a romantic gloss, but anyone who doubts that these tough, muscular, war-seasoned men were anything other than deliberate and dispassionate killers has miscalculated the fierce fighting spirit of the English longbowman.

Archers shooting at an arrow-loop from outside a castle. They are protected by mantlets, freestanding wooden constructions that shielded them against arrows shot from the castle, allowing the attackers to approach to a relatively close range. The wooden construction at the top of the castle battlements is a hoarding. Its overhang allowed rocks, hot sand, etc. to be dropped onto those approaching the base of the walls. Archers were also stationed within the hoarding. (Drawing by Matthew Ryan, www.matthewryanhistoricalillustrator.com)

THE LONGBOW'S ROLE IN VICTORY

Equally important as the part it played in large-scale battles, the longbow was frequently indispensable in smaller affrays. A small group of 30 Scottish archers held the bridge at Baugé (21 March 1421), preventing the entire English army from crossing and giving the Franco-Scottish army time enough to rally and take up positions that led to its eventual victory. At Cravant (31 July 1423) English archers kept the French pinned down while the Earl of Salisbury led his men-at-arms across the River Yonne and onwards to victory. At Blanchetaque (24 August 1346), two days before the battle of Crécy, English archers were vital in giving cover to the English army as it crossed the Somme into a storm of crossbow bolts and an opposing force of 3,500 men on the French side, under the command of Godemar du Fey.

In all of these fights, preludes to larger battles, the longbow played a crucial role in setting the stage for eventual victory and was therefore as instrumental to the final outcome as anything that happened in the main battle itself. Moreover, it is difficult to separate the significance of one weapon or troop type from another in the course of a major battlefield clash. The truth is that battles are won and lost by a combination of factors and forces, and it is the marshalling and combining of all these elements that is the art of war.

In every encounter, the precise way in which archers were used and their contribution to the final outcome varied considerably. Nevertheless, Crécy stands as a textbook example of how best to use a large archer army in pitched battle. Crécy was the culmination of an immaculately planned campaign that saw Edward III launch his military bid for the crown of France. It was the beginning of the Hundred Years' War. His intelligent use of his archer arm was apparent not only in the conduct of the battle, but also in the campaign that led to the battle being fought where he wanted it. Fast-moving squadrons of mounted archers were the ideal troops to terrorize the countryside on *chevauchée*, provoking the king of France to battle. Philip VI summoned his mighty feudal host, but it was Edward's more mobile army that dictated where the battle would take place. He feigned that he had been caught on his retreat to his ships but, in fact, Crécy was a trap.

Joe Gibbs of the EWBS takes direct aim at a chosen target. (Mike Loades)

CRÉCY – THE LONGBOW'S FINEST HOUR?

The battle of Crécy began as a duel between the longbow and the crossbow. On the English side were 7,500 longbowmen; on the French side were 6,000 Genoese mercenaries, highly respected, trained and experienced troops armed with crossbows. It is a mistake to think of the crossbow as a long-range weapon, at least before the mighty windlass- or crannequin-spanned steel-prod crossbows of the late 15th century. The type of belt-and-claw-spanned composite-prod crossbows brought to the field of Crécy by the Genoese probably had an average draw-weight of 300lb, only two to three times that of the longbow. However, the string travel on a crossbow is only a fraction of the string travel on a longbow; the forces act on the projectile for a much shorter distance, delivering a lesser ballistic performance. Crossbows require additional draw-weight in order to compensate for this shortcoming.

Moreover, the stubby little twin-vaned bolt does not have anything approaching the aerodynamic properties of an arrow. Arrows really do fly; bolts do not. In any range war, the longbow is going to triumph. Crossbow bolts have a powerful initial punch but once they begin to decelerate, they lose power very quickly. Radar tests on a bolt from a 300lb crossbow conducted at Britain's Defence Academy at Shrivenham showed that it maintained almost full power for 50yd, but after 80yd had lost so much power that it could no longer be considered effective. (These tests were carried out for, though not shown in, *Weapons That Made Britain – Longbow*, a 2004 Channel 4 television programme presented by the author.)

Pushed hurriedly to the front by commanders who had yet to learn the respect due to an English bowman, and with their pavises left behind on the baggage train, the Genoese stood little chance. If they had been provided with their pavises, they might have advanced with reasonable security and engaged the English archers at an effective range for their crossbows. Unfortunately for them, however, they were forced by the impetuous, irascible and irrational French command to advance regardless (Nicolle 2000: 63). It is often assumed that the English arrows pricked them at long range, but how close they came cannot be determined accurately.

The Crécy battlefield today: a view of the bank on the eastern side of the Vallée des Clercs, looking north. This virtually sheer bank is a natural feature that existed at the time of the battle (Ayton & Preston 2005: 123). It has a 10–15ft drop and extends for over a mile. Too steep for thousands of armoured men and horses to go down, it funnelled the advancing French army on to the battlefield further along, creating crowd chaos in their ranks. It also dictated precisely where the French attack would come from and ensured that it was on a narrow front, so neutralizing their advantage in numbers. (Photograph courtesy of Andrew Ayton)

WAR BOWS

THE LONGBOW

> ## CRÉCY (PREVIOUS PAGES)
>
> The basic English formation at Crécy was the 'herecon' (hedgehog), in which men-at-arms with long spears formed a pike wall and the archers stood between them. However, at the moment depicted in this artwork there have been several French charges and the French have taken heavy casualties – these casualties are starting to form a significant obstacle at the foot of the rise occupied by the English. This enables the English archers to step forward from the protective hedgehog and form a front rank on their own.
>
> Crécy was a well-laid trap. The topography forced the French to enter the battlefield through a narrow bottleneck, minimizing the advantage of their superior numbers. It also dictated the direction of their attack, which pushed them towards strong English defensive positions where they were decimated by the combined forces of English men-at-arms, infantry and archers, who had the low evening sun at their backs. The archers had to work quickly, amid the sweat and danger of close combat.

Long-range shots would have been possible, but according to the chronicler Jean le Bel 'they came so close that the two sides shot at each other' (quoted in Rogers 2010: 132). For this to have been viable for the crossbowmen, the distance must have been less than 80yd. Furthermore, several of the chroniclers state that the Genoese were fired upon by the English guns (Nicolle 2000: 65), which also supports the idea that the engagement was relatively close. It is not certain whether the English guns at Crécy were multi-barrelled ribaudequins (short range) or vase-shaped cannon like the Loshult gun. Chroniclers report that they were slow to load and that they caused much loss (Nicolle 2000: 65), so even if they were cannon rather than ribaudequins, the circumstances suggest they were loaded with grapeshot. The barrel of the Loshult gun has signs of wear consistent with being shot with a load of small iron pieces diced from a ¾in rod, which would cause 'much loss'. Peter Vemming of Denmark's Middelaldercentret informs me that the effective range for such a load is only around 30yd (private correspondence 2012).

Either way, the Genoese were turned, only to run into the advance of the French cavalry. As the main body of French chivalry, mounted on their proud and puissant steeds, filed from the Abbeville road onto the battlefield, they encountered a steep bank where the higher ground fell sharply away to the Crécy plain. It would not have been practical for them to have entered the battlefield down this extreme slope. Moreover, they would have come across this by surprise. (I have walked the battlefield and it is invisible until you are actually at the ledge.) This dramatic topographical feature forced the French to crowd on to the battlefield further along, and as they crammed through an ever tightening bottleneck, pushed forward by the eager masses behind, they confronted the retreating Genoese.

There were a great many Genoese casualties from this clash, and the Flemish chronicler Jean le Bel recorded that 'the weak horses fell over them and the others trampled them and they tumbled over each other like pigs in a heap' (quoted in Rogers 2010: 132). More significantly, from the point of view of the English archers, the direction of the first French cavalry attack was set. This was not a last-ditch stand by a beleaguered English army; it was the perfect battleground, a site selected by reconnaissance and a trap into which the French were lured.

At the other side of the valley, the English side, lay banks and terraces that offered ideal positioning for the archers. These banks were less steep and less high than the great bank on the French side, but they provided a vantage point for shooting and helped to slow a cavalry attack. According to the writings of another chronicler, Geoffrey le Baker, the English also dug pot-holes in front of their defensive position (Ayton & Preston 2005: 336), though this is not corroborated by other chroniclers. At the top, standing shoulder to shoulder with the archers, were men-at-arms and spearmen who created a secure barrier to halt a charge and prevent the archers from being overrun. This bristling hedgehog of spears, on raised ground, is the key factor that enabled the English archers at Crécy to stand and face such overwhelming numbers of French cavalry.

I have ridden across the battlefield at Crécy and it takes about 40 seconds, galloping on the soft, loamy earth, to cover the longshot distance of 250–300yd. Damage can be done in that time by skilled archery but probably not too much to well-armoured men. However, that first French attack was stalled and slowed by the retreating Genoese and they may have been within 100yd or less of the English line before they were able to get a charge going. It is immediately after the passage describing the traffic chaos with the Genoese that le Bel recounts the havoc caused to French cavalry by the English archers: 'When the horses felt these barbed arrows (which did wonders), some would go forwards, others leapt into the air as if maddened, others balked and bucked horribly' (quoted in Ayton & Preston 2005: 132).

There is nothing here that tells us the horses were shot from a great range. Hindered by the Genoese, the French may well have been unable to charge the English from beyond bowshot, but, slowed from the front and pushed from behind, they moved forward haltingly, raggedly and slowly, becoming sitting ducks at medium to close range. This is where the problems arose with the horses.

A horse is a large target, but it also has a lot of muscle mass and only a relatively small percentage of its surface area is vulnerable to lethal wounds. Moreover, good-quality horse-armour was available at the time, though we cannot be certain of the extent to which it was used. Horses are provoked into unruly behaviour more by fear than by pain, though clearly there can be a connection between the two. Nevertheless, horses at full gallop charging towards the enemy are less likely to be deterred by the sting of arrows than those milling about in confusion. In a charge, horses have already triggered their fundamental survival mechanism, that of flight, and are moving as one in the herd. With their blood up, they would be stopped only by mechanically debilitating wounds. Horses without this impetus, on the other hand, such as those corralled and milling in the confusing crush with the Genoese, would be highly sensitive to the smart of an arrow.

The barbed arrows referred to could have been effective at cutting through textile bards, though probably challenged by mail. It is also worth noting that the chronicler does not talk about men being killed by arrows here, nor even that the horses were wounded, simply that the horses were 'maddened' by the hurt of the arrows. Whether or not an arrow penetrated the thickly padded horse-armour, a hit by a shaft from a powerful bow at near range would certainly sting.

Crucially, le Bel concludes this passage by saying that 'the English lords, who were on foot, advanced and pierced through these men' (quoted in Ayton & Preston 2005: 132). Here is a clear indication from the sources that the carnage took place close to the English front line, unless we are to imagine that dismounted English knights abandoned the safety of their lines and trudged across the heavy soil to engage the enemy 200yd away.

Once the French reached the English front, they did not just pull up, turn around and go away again. There was fighting. An attacking formation is deep – the ones at the front are pushed forward by the ones behind and cannot easily turn around. All wanted to get to the front and have their chance at glory. While the fight went on, for many minutes with each assault, and with French knights and men-at-arms engaging English knights and men-at-arms, the archers probably continued to ply their trade. This is what we see in the art. It required rapid shooting and precision shooting and was, I believe, where the archers did their main work.

Men reeling from the impact of arrows, concussed and ataxic ('punch drunk'), bruised, broken and wounded, were easy pickings for the dagger-men. Light troops, expert in martial arts, the dagger-men navigated the disorder at the front line, preying upon the archers' faltering quarry – finishing the job. As the long day wore on, the carcasses of horses and cadavers of men stacked in heaps before the English line, creating yet further obstacle to the French attack. Halted by these heaving, reeking human hedges, each successive French charge was more vulnerable than the last to the prowess of the English bowmen. Eventually the day was won for the English. It was a triumph for the men-at-arms, who had fought heroically, for the spearmen, who had held the line, and for the archers – but most of all it was a triumph for the tactical use of combined forces and the wise selection of ground.

THE LONGBOW AFTER CRÉCY

The debacle of Crécy prompted changes in the French approach. Armour improved and at many battles the French opted to dismount their horses and attack on foot. They did so at Poitiers a decade later and again, after the initial disastrous cavalry attack, at Agincourt in 1415. Much has been made of the carnage wrought by English archery upon the French cavalry at Agincourt, but the original chronicles paint a less catastrophic picture. In describing the cavalry charge by Sir Guillaume de Sauveuses with 300 lances, Monstrelet reports that 'all of them returned, save for three men-at-arms … it was their sad misfortune that their horses fell amongst the stakes'; he does concede that 'their horses had been so troubled by the arrow shot of the English archers that they could not hold control of them' (quoted in Curry 2009: 161), but this is a very different story from the annihilating arrowstorm of popular legend. There were only three dead, and these casualties occurred because their horses were skewered on the stakes and their riders' skulls cracked beneath an archer's maul. The discomfited horses undoubtedly caused problems as they jibbed and bolted back towards their own lines. However, it was the fact that the mass attack turned back into the face of advancing men, trampling their own, that created the disaster of crowd chaos – one remarkably similar to the fatal mistakes made by the French at Crécy.

Agincourt was an astonishing victory against the odds, for the few against the many, but archery played only a small part in the outcome. It was tactics and terrain, sucking mud and incompetent French command that caused the French to lose; that and the fighting pluck of the English archers. However, with their arrow supplies exhausted, it was a victory the archers won in desperate hand-to-hand fighting rather than with their bows.

Throughout the Wars of the Roses Englishman drew bow against Englishman in unprecedented numbers. Despite the din of gunpowder weapons that now blew thick palls of smoke across every battlefield, squalls of arrows continued to darken the skies. At Towton in 1461, a grim battle fought in a snowstorm, there was a brutal archery duel between Lancastrians and Yorkists. Around 28,000 men died that day, the greatest number ever in a battle on English soil, and a great many of them fell to an arrow from a longbow.

Unfortunately, we know very little about the use of archery at the battle of Bosworth (22 August 1485), although one account by the Italian chronicler Polydore Vergil states that Richard III lined up his archers in the front line 'like a most strong trench or bulwark' (quoted in Strickland & Hardy 2005: 384). The implication is that they were intended to act as the first line of defence in the event of an attack on Richard's cavalry and infantry divisions who were placed behind the long line of archers. Vergil does report an initial archery exchange between the two sides, but also records that 'whan they cam to hand strokes the matter was delt with blades' (quoted in Strickland & Hardy 2005: 386). The battle turned, of course, not on archers but on Richard's ill-fated cavalry charge. He was cut down and killed and the battle and the crown were lost.

Henry Tudor's victory at Bosworth ushered in the Tudor era. The longbow continued to be valued as a weapon for battles, but in reality its finest hour on land had passed. At sea, however, it would survive as a weapon of great significance for another hundred years.

THE LONGBOW AS A NAVAL WEAPON

In contrast to the frustrating absence of actual longbows to study from the medieval period, we are blessed when it comes to examining both the Tudor period and naval archery. Here we have the remarkable time capsule of the *Mary Rose*, whose treasures continue to further our understanding of the longbow and which, doubtless, still have secrets to reveal.

Henry VIII's great warship the *Mary Rose*, which sank in the Solent in 1545, carried 250 longbows; in fact, the *Mary Rose* was but one of a fleet of 58 ships armed with a total of 4,835 longbows (Hildred 2011: 581). Among the rest of the diverse weaponry retrieved was a broad array of incendiary devices, having sundry means of delivery from gunpowder weapons to thrown weapons, to crossbows and longbows (Hildred 2011: 520–36). Fire on a wooden ship was generally a fatal blow and one that was dreaded more than anything else.

Seven of the recovered longbows have been noted to have a distinctive profile, with a flat-sided, trapezoid section at the grip (Hildred 2011: 602). They are among the most massive bows, with the potential for greater range, and it has been suggested that this slab-sided recess may have been to accommodate a binding that would shield the bowstave from the searing heat of an incendiary arrow (Hildred 2011: 603). There would certainly be an advantage in having archers of exceptional power who could shoot these gigantic bows, sending their fiery-tailed shafts, comet-like, across the waves to bite into the timbers of the enemy's ship. However, the Tudor fleet was not short of regular arrows either: the Anthony Roll inventories 176,040 arrows for the 58 ships listed in 1546 (Hildred 2011: 581).

That archery was highly valued by the Tudor navy is evident, even though the *Mary Rose*, like other ships of the time, was also fully equipped with gunpowder weapons, from powerful cannon to arquebuses. Longbows nevertheless continued to have several distinct advantages at sea. Damp spray and gusts of wind could spoil or empty powder from the firing pan or extinguish a match, and there was a slight time delay between firing a gun and the main charge going off – a delay that could affect accuracy from a pitching and rolling deck. The longbowman, better able to compensate for such eventualities, was more reliable. He also had the advantage of a much faster rate of shooting.

THE LONGBOW IN PITCHED BATTLE – TRIUMPHS AND DISASTERS

Falkirk (22 July 1298) English archers (together with crossbowmen and slingers) prove effective against unshielded Scottish schiltrons.

Bannockburn (24 June 1314) On the second day, English archers, in an undefended position, are ridden down by a flanking cavalry action from the Scots.

Boroughbridge (16 March 1322) English archers, defended by blocs of spearmen, have a major impact against Scottish cavalry.

Dupplin Moor (10–11 August 1332) Accurate archery from the English flanks forces a crush in the centre of the Scottish ranks, causing large numbers to die from trampling.

Halidon Hill (19 July 1333) English archers shoot down onto unshielded Scottish schiltrons attempting to attack uphill.

Crécy (26 August 1346) English archers decimate unshielded Genoese crossbowmen, then keep up a continuous barrage against repeated French cavalry attacks. The English bowmen are able to hold their ground from a strong defensive position. The French, forced by the terrain to attack on a limited front, are worn down by the incessant fury of the English archery and are defeated after hours of fighting and with a high death toll amongst their nobility.

Neville's Cross (17 October 1346) English archers form on a ridge, flanked by a river on one side and a steep gully on the other. Scottish men-at-arms advance on foot with good-quality armour; they bow their heads and brace their shields against the English arrows and have initial success, although the Scottish king, David II, is wounded in the face by an arrow. A flanking action by the English archers proves effective against less well-armoured men marching behind the front lines. The Scots are routed and chased from the field.

Poitiers (19 September 1356) After an initial cavalry attack, the French dismount and their men-at-arms make a frontal assault against English archers on foot. Some chroniclers report that the English ran out of arrows. However, the English deployment of mounted archers, to assist in sweeping round the flanks and attacking the French rear, is the turning point of the battle.

Cocherel (16 May 1364) English archers, serving Charles II of Navarre, are unable to make much impact against the French men-at-arms who attacked on foot and who, according to Froissart, are 'so well armed and so strongly pavised that they took but little hurt' (Froissart 1904: 169). A French victory is subsequently achieved by a charge from reserve cavalry.

Aljubarrota (14 August 1385) Castilian–French men-at-arms are forced to attack on a narrow front, where they are hammered by a blizzard of arrows from the flanks. Archaeological excavations of the battle site have revealed a network of defensive pits and ditches to protect the contingent of Anglo-Gascon archers fighting for the Portuguese; in addition, Froissart records that the archers cut down trees to make cavalry-proof fences.

Homildon Hill (14 September 1402) English archers prevail against Scottish bowmen who hold the advantage of a defensive position at the top of the hill. It is uncertain whether or not the English advance up the hill or shoot from an adjacent vantage point; nor is the wind direction known, nor the numbers of archers involved on each side. In any circumstance it is a remarkable victory for the English longbowmen.

Shrewsbury (21 July 1403) Archers are used effectively and in large numbers on both sides. Sir Harry Percy, known as 'Hotspur', who had risen in rebellion against the reign of Henry IV, is killed by an arrow through his eye, while Prince Henry (later Henry V) is wounded by an arrow in the face; detailed accounts of its extraction indicate that it came from a more-or-less horizontal trajectory. During the medieval period, commanders were frequently obliged to raise their visors during battle in order to rally and command – this made them especially vulnerable to arrows.

Consider, then, how much more important the bow must have been before gunpowder artillery was an effective reality in naval warfare. (Guns are recorded in naval battles from as early as the battle of Sluys in 1340. However, they cannot be said to have had the range or power equivalent to those of later naval gunnery; they were more in the nature of anti-personnel, close-range weapons.) Not only was the bow a weapon of range, a weapon that could send showers of incendiary arrows to destroy an enemy vessel, it was also the key weapon in close-range ship-to-ship fighting. This was, to some extent, equally true of the crossbow, the favoured maritime weapon of other nations.

Naval battles during the Middle Ages were akin to land battles, with ships either grappling or at least closing together so their occupants could fight it out in hand-

Agincourt (25 October 1415) English archers, stationed on the edge of the funnelling tree-line, operate from the flanks to force a crush in the centre. This neutralizes the French advantage of superior numbers, compelling them to attack on a narrow front into prepared defences including sharpened stakes, archers and men-at-arms. After a failed initial cavalry charge, French knights and men-at-arms attack on foot. The French have 4,000 longbow archers and 1,500 crossbowmen in their army, but conflicts within the French command prevent their deployment. The English archers exhaust their arrow supplies but win the day after a desperate hand-to-hand struggle.

Verneuil (17 August 1424) English archers have virtually no effect against the Lombard cavalry, armed with the best-quality Milanese armour for man and horse. The English are driven from the field by a cavalry charge. Ridden down and routed, the English archers never rejoin the battle. However, the English men-at-arms rally under John of Bedford and eventually win the day.

Patay (18 June 1429) English archers are attacked by French cavalry before they can prepare a defensive position with stakes. The archers are ridden down and killed in great numbers.

Formigny (15 April 1450) An English army of around 4,300 men, under the command of Sir Thomas Kyriell and including just over 2,000 archers, takes up a defensive position behind stakes, trenches and potholes and with its rear defended by a stream and woodland. The English face a French army under Charles, Comte de Clermont comprising around 3,000 men, among whom are 1,200 mounted archers. French men-at-arms, supported by their archers, attack the English flanks but are repulsed. However, the English archers are then provoked by heavy cannon fire to move forward from their secure positions and to capture the guns. The French quickly mount a counter-attack on the exposed English archers and recapture the guns. Next, the English are hit by the arrival of French reinforcements, including another 800 French archers. The English are overwhelmed and defeated.

Towton (29 March 1461) In a snowstorm Yorkist archers, with the wind at their backs, launch the opening shots; the Lancastrian response is hampered both by a headwind and near-zero visibility, both of which affect their ability to range accurately and to see where their arrows fall – they fall short. Once the Lancastrian arrow supplies are exhausted, the Yorkist archers advance, replenishing their own arrow stocks with those of their enemy and continuing their archery barrage. With no corresponding missile response available, the Lancastrians counter-attack on foot and drive the Yorkist archers to the rear of their army. The ensuing fight is decided by hand-to-hand combat and eventually turns in favour of the Yorkists after the arrival of reinforcements led by the Duke of Norfolk.

Tewkesbury (4 May 1471) As with other Wars of the Roses battles between Lancastrians and Yorkists, archers are used to provoke the enemy into leaving a defended position. In this instance the Lancastrians hold a strong position, but Edward IV uses his superior number of archers to goad them into attack. The Lancastrians, hit by a surprise flanking attack from Yorkist spearmen who had been hiding in the woods, are then routed.

Flodden (9 September 1513) The Scots bring their archers forward in a skirmish line interspersed with swordsmen; the Scots men-at-arms are so well armoured that the English arrows have little effect. English archers do, however, decimate the ranks of the unarmoured highlander divisions. Archery plays a role but cannon and heavy infantry armed with polearms are the decisive factors.

Pinkie Cleugh (10 September 1547) Although there are several thousand archers on both sides, the battle is decided in favour of the English by combined forces of cannon, arquebuses, cavalry, infantry and naval bombardment. It proves to be the last time the longbow is fielded in significant numbers.

to-hand combat. Medieval warships were mostly adapted merchant ships, re-fitted with wooden defensive structures that were built fore and aft. Forecastles (the forecastle, or foc'sle, remains in nautical terminology) and aftcastles were sheer-sided bastions that defended against boarding. They were also elevated positions from which archers could shoot down upon the enemy decks – these cargo-carrying vessels had broad decks, which in time of war would be packed with troops, horses, munitions and supplies. A further threat to troops on the decks came from above in the form of men in the crow's-nests, who would hurl down stones, javelins, darts and pots of quicklime (a caustic powder). It was also the archers' job to tumble such men from their eyries.

Two ships, from the Decretals of Gregory IX, late 13th–early 14th century. Note the archers in the aftcastle and the use of long hand-held weapons to reach across to the enemy ship. (The British Library, Royal 10 E IV, f. 19, © The British Library/Bridgeman Images)

Men-at-arms played an important role in ship-to-ship combat, using long pikes, staffs and spears to belabour the men on the opposing decks in a preamble to boarding actions with swords drawn. When the battle was between two rival fleets, one flotilla might create a defensive barricade by roping all its ships together. This is what the French did at Sluys on 24 June 1340, in a formidable confrontation with Edward III's navy.

The battle of Sluys was the first action of the Hundred Years' War. It took place in the massive harbour estuary near the Flemish town of Sluys. This great expanse of water has now silted up and been reclaimed as land. There were approximately 200 or more ships on each side, with the French employing some 20,000 Genoese crossbowmen among their forces; the English used both longbows and crossbows (Bradbury 1985: 102). Having the advantage of the wind, the English attacked with three squadrons, keeping a fourth in reserve.

The ships on each of the wings had their decks stacked with archers who, once in range, were able to pin down the flanks of the French fleet and thus prevent them from reinforcing the centre. Advancing with the tide, Edward's centre squadron, each vessel crammed with eager boarding parties of men-at-arms, closed on the French ships, which, according to the chronicler Geoffrey le Baker, were 'like a line of castles' (quoted in Bradbury 1985: 103).

Boarding actions were the order of the day, but these were only made possible by stationing yet more archers mixed in among the men-at-arms. The secret of success in battle, at sea as on land, was the use of combined forces, with the archers creating clear bridgeheads on enemy decks for their men to board. Archers also kept hostile boarders off their own decks. It was a constant workrate, with rapid shooting crucial to stem the tide of a swarming foe. Bowmen not only had to open their chests and pull back their shoulders, drawing their heavy bows time and again: their weary legs also had to ride the motion of a constantly rolling deck in a long day of fighting that extended beyond nightfall. It was exhausting labour.

The French lines were three or four deep, and the affray became more and more like a land battle as the boarders made deeper and deeper inroads into the floating wooden citadel, with archers needing to keep up with the advance as they drove the French defenders both back and overboard. On both sides attempts to board were repulsed and renewed, reversed and regained in constant, fierce forays. Eventually, the English triumphed; the French commanders were killed and thousands of men were tipped into the sea in their armour. It was said that if fish could speak they would have been able to learn French (Bradbury 1985: 103).

Not only was this a momentous victory for Edward, who was present, and his archers – he completely destroyed the French fleet, sending in divers to bore holes in their ships (Bradbury 1985: 103) – it also meant that, for quite some time, England was safe from any threat of counter-invasion and that the coming war would be waged exclusively on French soil.

Whether toppling a javelin-man from the high rigging, firing an enemy ship with incendiary arrows, establishing a beachhead or taking a harbour fort, naval archers were reliant on the skills they had honed at the marks, at clout and at the popinjay

English longbowmen shoot at French crossbowmen in a ship battle in the Seine estuary in 1416. Note the menace from the crow's-nests, where men with large stones and javelins are a threat to the English archers. One has already been shot by an English arrow. Nevertheless, the main focus of the bowmen is shooting straight ahead and at close range to repel a boarding action. (From the Beauchamp Pageant, c. 1483–84. British Library, Cotton Julius E IV, © British Library/Bridgeman Images)

Archers covering a ship-to-shore escalade from their ships. The role of archers on ships was not restricted to fighting other vessels; they were also frequently critically important in giving cover to landing operations, such as at Cadzand in November 1337, when English bowmen drove off the French forces who sought to bar their landing (Strickland & Hardy 2005: 209). In this image we see archers shooting from their ships at the defenders of a coastal town. Many wealthy towns were fortified on the seaward side and an escalade, supported by archers, could sometimes be staged from ships sailing right up to the walls. (The British Library, Royal MS 15 E VI, f. 207, © The British Library/Bridgeman Images)

pole. When it came to supporting a boarding party, though, it was their repetitive power-shooting at the butts that was recalled. Archers were versatile troops and the medieval archer used his range of skills to shoot both at sea and on land.

THE TWILIGHT OF THE LONGBOW

Although the longbow, despite its many vociferous advocates, did not survive the Tudor period as a land weapon, it remained an essential weapon aboard ships well into the Elizabethan era. Recalling an encounter off the coast of San Francisco with a Spanish treasure ship in 1579, Sir Francis Drake's cousin John recounts that the Spanish captain refused to give up, even after a cannon shot had damaged the mizzenmast. It was not until 'an arrow shot wounded San Juan de Anton', the captain, that he struck sail and submitted (Nuttall 1914: 49). There was a precision to a longbow, even on a rolling deck, that could not be matched by the slow-firing arquebus of the time.

SLUYS (OPPOSITE)

English men-arms, supported by their archers, board a French ship. The French have formed a barricade by tying their ships together, which is why the French sails are down. The English ship has just manoeuvred alongside for a boarding action. The wooden structure at the front of the English ship is called the forecastle. These were built onto merchant ships known as 'cogs' to convert them into warships, and they were the key vantage points for the archers. Archers also combine with the mixed retinue of men-at-arms and spearmen to support the boarding action. This is similar to the way they operated on land.

The French employed Genoese crossbowmen to fulfil the same function as the English longbow archers. During a boarding action they endeavoured to keep the enemy force away from the sides of the ship, so that their own men could board. Both longbow archers and crossbowmen also shoot at the crow's-nests of the opposing ship. Here there were men armed with javelins, heavy rocks and pots of quicklime, which were hurled onto the heads of those below. A key weapon either to support or to repel boarding was the long spear, similar in length to a horseman's lance. At sea, the spearmen had the reach required to attack men at the sides of the opposing ship and on land spearmen became the archers' essential companion by creating a hedge of spears that protected archers from cavalry attacks.

THE LONGBOW

A bill of lading for the six ships returning from the Drake/Hawkins West Indies' voyage of 1595–96* – the *Defiance*, the *Garland*, the *Hope*, the *Elizabeth Bonaventure*, the *Adventure* and the *Foresight* – includes the following listings for archery-related gear: 'longe bowes'; 'bowe strings'; 'crossbows for firebaules'; 'longbowe shotte no firewourks'; 'bowstring tarslled'; 'arrows with ffirewourkes'; 'cinnset with ffirewourkes'; 'slimbowe arro for leade'; 'arrowros for longbows'; and 'chesstes for bowes and arrows'.

Most entries have an obvious meaning, though some, such as the 'slimbowe arro for leade', are harder to decipher. A translation of 'cinnset' is given in the transcription as 'crescent'; crescent-shaped arrowheads may have been a type that had use in naval engagements. Often also called 'forkers', these heads are most usually associated with hunting birds.

However, tests by Mark Stretton have shown that a crescent arrowhead also has the capacity to tear sailcloth (Soar, Gibbs, Jury & Stretton 2010: 148). Mark found that by shooting with these heads using a shallow angle at heavy canvas, he created 12in tears. Multiple shots with such arrows from a pursuing ship could have the effect of slowing down the target ship, and a high wind could cause a shredded sail to rip apart even more. The extent to which this tactic was used remains speculative.

What is more certain from the list is that incendiary arrows – 'arrows with fireworks' – continued to be an important part of the naval archer's arsenal. As an act of war, burning a ship was extremely effective; however, it was less useful if you wanted to capture a ship and her treasure as a prize. An account by Pedro Samiento de Gamboa, describing Drake's seizure of a Spanish ship at the port of Callao de Lima on 13 February 1578, gives a rare insight into the use of bows in a boarding action (Nuttall 1914: 59–60). He reports that Drake's ship, the *Golden Hinde*, entered the harbour between ten o'clock and midnight; boarding parties then transferred to the pinnace and skiff – smaller, oar-powered service vessels, used by large sailing ships for the transfer of goods and personnel either from ship to ship or from ship to shore – in order to look over the Spanish ships anchored there. After each search they cut the anchor cables. When they came to the ship of Alonso Rodriguez Baptista, the *San Cristobal*, 'they boarded her, shooting many arrows at her sailors and pilot … Alonso Rodriguez was wounded by an arrow' (Nuttall 1914: 60). This daring night-time raid resulted in Drake's capture of the ship, laden with silver; he set sail into open water before the alarm was raised on land. After two days of pursuit, the Spanish gave up. In this instance the longbow gave an advantage of stealth to the raid, providing enough time for Drake to get a head start with the wind.

The American adventures of Drake and Sir John Hawkins fuelled English interest in the New World. During the summer of 1582, arrangements were drawn up for an expedition under Sir Humphrey Gilbert to colonize American territory in the name of the Crown. Among the agreements was a stipulation that those who held land in the new colony should also be able to provide arms for its defence. It reads: 'every tenant to sixty acres of land to maintain a longbow and a sheaf of arrows together with a sword, a dagger and a wooden target [shield]' (CSPCA). The longbow featured in what must surely be the first 'assize of arms' on American soil.

Crescent arrowhead. This type of arrowhead, used for hunting birds, may also have had an application in naval warfare for ripping open enemy sails. When used for hunting, the head design delivers debilitating force to the strike without skidding off, as a blunt might, and has the potential to incapacitate wings without penetrating and making a mess of the flesh. (Arrowhead by Hector Cole; photograph by Matthew Ryan)

* Bill of lading from voyage of 1595–96, transcribed by Susan Jackson and published online by the Drake Exploration Society at http://www.indrakeswake.co.uk/Society/Research/billoflading.htm (accessed 7 December 2012).

In foreign service

FREE COMPANIES

In 1395, the chronicler Filippo Villani noted that there were archers among the English mercenaries in Italy:

> Others of them were archers, and their bows were long and of yew; they were quick and dexterous archers, and made good use of the bow. (Parks 1954: 392)

His remarks underscored the perceived value of rapid shooting in battle and confirmed that these men were using yew longbows. The archers referred to were attached to Free Companies. These independent mercenary bands offered opportunities of employment and adventure to English archers serving in foreign wars, especially during the internecine city state conflicts that ravaged the Italian peninsula in the 14th century. 'The White Company' under Sir John Hawkwood (1323–94) is perhaps the most famous of these organizations but it was one among many and formed part of a continuing tradition. As late as 1434, 100 English bowmen under the command of Sir Walter of England, were employed by the city of Venice (Parks 1954: 387). In 1375, Hawkwood's 'English Company', as it was also known, numbered 4,500 lances (1,500 cavalrymen) plus 500 archers and a body of infantry (Parks 1954: 386). Some of Hawkwood's captains of archers, fighting in the service of the city of Florence, are recorded by name as the recipients of bonuses in 1391. Their names (for the most part) have a relatable familiarity to the modern English ear: John Appleby, Richard Vince, John Wolser, Harry Brown, Richard Thornton; also Diomede Selridge, Robert Felton, John Balsam (Parks 1954: 421).

Companies of archers bent their bows in support of the main organizational unit of the Free Company, which was the *lance*. A lance comprised three mounted men, usually a knight and two men-at-arms. Lances that were unaffiliated to any particular company, known as *freelances*, could contract to the highest bidder. The lance and its associated troops formed a mixed unit that might include men-at-arms, crossbowmen, halberdiers, spearmen and archers. Lances dismounted to fight, using their cavalry 'lance' as a field weapon in the manner of a pike.

Villani offers a hint of their fighting tactics:

> Their mode of fighting in the field was almost always afoot, as they assigned their horses to their pages. Keeping themselves in almost circular formation, every two take a lance, carrying it in a manner in which one waits for a boar with a boar-spear. So bound and compact, with lowered lances they marched with slow steps towards the enemy. (Quoted in Parks 1954: 393)

We may imagine that archers, or crossbowmen, were either stationed in the middle or that they stood between the arrays of menacing lances. It was a formation that had versatility both for attack and defence.

Although Sir John Hawkwood was lionized and immortalized by his client, the city of Florence, the rough and brutish behavior of his English recruits earned them such names as *perfidi* (perfidious ones) and *sceleratissimi* (most wicked ones) (Parks 1954: 394). By contrast Scottish archers who rallied to the French flag were regarded honourably and many a Scottish archer remained in France after the conclusion of the Hundred Years' War, establishing a new home, a reasonably prosperous life and a Franco-Scottish lineage.

GARDE ÉCOSSAISE

The 'Auld Alliance' between the crowns of Scotland and France, originating during the last years of the 13th century, was for the most part a symbolic relationship. It nevertheless afforded opportunities for Scottish nobles to engage in chivalric adventures against their traditional enemy and for Scottish soldiers to gain welcome employment. In 1412 the future King Charles VII (r. 1422–61) is recorded as having a Scotsman, John Stewart, as the captain of his archers and in 1418, as Dauphin, he recruited a bodyguard of Scottish archers. On his accession to the throne four years later, he established an elite royal bodyguard, the celebrated Garde Écossaise. During the reign of Louis XI (r. 1461–83) the Garde Écossaise expanded, at first to 100 Scottish archers plus 100 French archers and finally to a total of 400 archers, 40 crossbowmen and 160 gentlemen (Strickland & Hardy 2005: 351).

Here Charles VII, portrayed as one of the Magi, is attended by his retinue of Garde Écossaise. They were a dazzling spectacle. Gilles le Bouvier, Berry King-at-Arms, described them entering Rouen in 1449:

And before them, in the first rank, were the archers of the King of France, all clad in jackets covered with gold embroidery, of the colour of red, white and green. (Quoted in Strickland & Hardy 2005: 351)

In addition to the embroidered jackets alluded to by Berry Herald, the painting shows them with panaches of red, white and green plumes. They were well armoured, having a sallet, back and breast, cuisses, greaves and sabatons. For practical reasons, their arms were without plate armour but the sleeves of a studded gambeson are evident. Also apparent is a mixture of longbowmen and spearmen indicating that they fought in herecon formation. (Adoration of the Magi, from the 'Hours of Etienne Chevalier', c.1445 (vellum), Fouquet, Jean (c.1420–80). Photo by Christophel Fine Art/UIG via Getty Images)

In 1419 a Scottish army of some 6,000 men, including a high proportion of longbow archers, was enlisted to the Dauphin's cause. They were led by John Stewart, Earl of Buchan (c. 1381–17 August 1424). Some were attached to the field army; others served as garrison troops, such as the 300 Scottish archers supplied by Sir William Douglas of Drumlanrig to the town of Yehun sur Yèvre (Strickland & Hardy 2005: 343). It was Scottish archers at the battle of Baugé (1421) who held the bridge against the English, enabling a notable French victory, and Scottish archers who bore the brunt of wrathful English vengeance after the French defeat at Verneuil (1424). It was Scottish archers who bent their bows against the English at the relief of Orléans (1429). Jeanne d'Arc had a personal guard of Scottish archers in addition to those fighting alongside the main Scottish force. She knew their value and could certainly vouch for the sting of a longbowman's arrow. At Orléans she was struck in the shoulder by an English shaft and although she retired from the field momentarily, she returned later in the day.

Among her Scottish allies was Sir Patrick Ogilvy of Auchterhouse, the sheriff of Angus, who is recorded as receiving 1,370 livres-Tournois for providing 60 men-at-arms and 300 archers for the campaign (Walsh & Williamson 2006: 2). Ogilvy was not only present at the relief of Orléans but he, and his archers, also attended King Charles VII at his subsequent coronation in Reims. French records include numerous references to the pay of Scottish archers. In an intriguing entry regarding their supply, one Jean Hubert is cited as receiving 15 livres-Tournois for:

> seven bundles of arrows which he had purchased to give to some archers from the land of Scotland, who had used up their arrows against the English. (Walsh & Williamson 2006: 4)

It is a matter of speculation where M. Hubert secured his stores, but it seems probable that there would have been an indigenous fletching industry within French-held lands. Certainly there was a robust bowmaking industry back in Scotland. Hugh Soar notes that, between 1445 and 1662, 97 bowyers are recorded as plying their trade in Edinburgh alone (Soar, Gibbs, Jury & Stretton 2010: 27).

Orléans was perhaps the high point of the Scottish contribution to the French fight, but back home in Scotland the value of longbow archery against the English had also gained favour. In 1424 the Scottish parliament passed a decree that echoed that of England's Edward III some 61 years earlier. It required all men over the age of 12 to become archers, the forsaking of football and other like games and for bowmarks to be set up in every £10 worth of land (Strickland & Hardy 2005: 351). Moreover in 1429 parliament ordered that those worth £10 were to be armed with bows, arrows, sword, buckler and knife. This compared to the 1318 Scottish Assize of Arms when the possession of a cow was qualification for having to be equipped as an archer. (Strickland & Hardy 2005: 352). Like their English counterparts, Scottish longbow archers had become relatively prosperous fellows.

Even golf receives the opprobrium of the pro-archery authorities, with an act of 1457 decrying it, as well as the ever-corrupting football, during the wappenshaws – regular musters at which men had to show that they possessed the weapons according to their station and that these were in good condition. The 1457 statute required all men to shoot at least six arrows every Sunday and those absent from the practice were fined 2d (Strickland & Hardy 2005: 353). The money was used to buy drinks for those who attended; it cannot be said that Scottish archery lacked incentive.

In this image of the Siege of Paris (1429) Joan of Arc is seen directing her longbow archers. These formed an important part of her army. On campaign Joan was accompanied by her own Garde Écossaise. (Photo by: Christophel Fine Art/UIG via Getty Images)

In 1595, James Ferguson, bow-maker to James VI of Scotland (r.1567–1625) was commanded to buy 10,000 bows and bowstaves from English suppliers (Soar, Gibbs, Jury & Stretton 2010: 28). In travelling south of the border in search of these weapons, he learned that such an arsenal was 'not available' to him. Given that tensions between the English crown and the 'auld enemy' had not abated entirely, this is perhaps unsurprising, and Ferguson had to go to Scandinavia for his purchase. However, the story demonstrates that, although gunpowder weapons had ascended to pre-eminence, military thinking in Scotland continued to uphold the importance of maintaining a strong archery tradition.

COMPAGNIE D'ORDONNANCE AND *FRANCS-ARCHERS*

In 1445, during one of those protracted lulls in the fighting that so characterized the Hundred Years' War, Charles VII of France established a standing army. Among other things it offered the ability for an immediate response to aggression rather than having to wait to rally the feudal host. The Compagnie d'Ordonnance, as it was called, had twenty companies, each consisting of 100 *lances fournies*. A *lance fournie* was a mounted unit comprising one man-at-arms, one *coustillier* (a *coustille* was a long knife/short sword from which the word 'cutlass' may derive), one page and two or three archers (the third archer was sometimes replaced with a *valet de guerre*). The Compagnie d'Ordonnance had a total force of 12,000 men of which between 4,000 and 6,000 were mounted archers. Like their English counterparts they would dismount to fight.

In his chronicle, written during the 1450s, Berry King-at-Arms observed the relative opulence of these archers, noting both their regular pay and their incentives:

> And each of the said men-at-arms had for his lance two mounted archers, armed for the most part with brigandines, armour for the legs and sallets, many of which were ornamented with silver; and at the least all of them had good jacks or haubergeons … and had their wages once a month, besides which they were allowed … to take prisoners and to ransom horses or any other cattle whatsoever, provided that, at the time, the said persons were on the side of the English. (Quoted in Strickland & Hardy 205: 354)

Charles further boosted the standing of longbow archery in France by conferring privileges on the urban fraternities of longbow archers. These have been eclipsed by the greater longevity of crossbow fraternities in Europe, some of which have survived to the present day (see page 142), but the value given to longbow archery in France during the last portion of the Hundred Years' War should not be overlooked. The fraternities encouraged practice and competition, fostering high standards and a reserve of elite archers – potential recruits for the *lances fournies*.

In addition to the archers of the ordonnance, Charles established a territorial militia called the *francs-archers* (free archers). Each parish in the kingdom was ordered to provide either an archer or a crossbowman for every (variably) 120, 80 or 50 hearths; each was to be equipped with 'a sallet, dagger, sword, bow, sheaf, jack and short coat of mail' (Strickland & Hardy 2005: 354). Both the archers in the Compagnie d'Ordonnance and the *francs-archers* received the same wage of 4 francs per month, but the ordonnance men had the edge when it came to ransom and booty.

Two thousand *francs-archers* pinned down the English garrison archers at the siege of Caen in 1450, allowing for a French victory, and as many as 4,000 did similar work at the siege of Harfleur in 1449. Louis XI increased the number of *francs-archers* to 16,000, though the divisions also contained an unspecified number of spearmen.

Despite the fact that this flowering of French archery happened behind the smokescreen of rapidly developing gunpowder weapons, there can be no doubt that it happened on a significant scale. The French had learned bitter lessons from English bowmen at Crécy, Poitiers and Agincourt and with their recruitment both of Scottish archers and of home-grown men they sought redress. The sizeable extent of French longbow archery is inconvenient to those who prefer simple tribal totems by which to understand events, but it deserves to be taken into account a great deal more than it usually is. Its failures, notably at Guinegatte (1479), may be attributed to poor organization and indiscipline rather than lack of proficiency. Perhaps its greatest success was against the English at Formigny (1450) where around 800 *francs-archers*, together with around 600 or 700 *lance fournie* archers, all under the command of Arthur de Richemont, the Constable of France, played a decisive role. Arriving late to the battle, Richemont's archers, many of whom were mounted, could be deployed swiftly. Some spearheaded a pincer movement, while others held vital bridges. The resulting victory for the French saw a final end to English occupation in Normandy.

BURGUNDY

Coinciding with the Hundred Years' War between the French and English crowns were tensions between two branches of the French royal line. On one side was the reigning Armagnac faction and on the other the competing dukes of Burgundy. Until Agincourt (1415), Burgundy set aside its differences to combat an alien foe (the English) and fought under the French banner. John the Fearless of Burgundy (r. 1404–19) was an ardent proponent of battlefield archery. He had had a notable success by using flanking archers at the battle of Othée (1408). However, despite his assurances, John did not march to Agincourt to aid the French cause. He stayed at home. This was perhaps fortunate for the English, for had he been at the battle, he may have made good use of the 4,000 French archers and 1,500 crossbowmen arrayed there. Instead they were ignored by a haughty French command and did not take part in the action.

In the wake of Agincourt, John the Fearless formulated a battle plan that aimed to learn from French miscalculations. In addition to having a rearguard of 100 archers to defend the reserve, his primary tactic was to place two sizeable divisions of archers and crossbowmen in the vanguard. Archers were literally brought to the forefront of Burgundian warfare and by the 1430s archers appeared in a ratio of 3:1 to men-at-arms in Burgundian armies (Strickland & Hardy 2005: 342).

In 1419, John the Fearless was assassinated. His son, Philip the Good (r. 1419–67) held suspicions of foul play by the French King Charles VII. This resulted in open, armed conflict between the two branches of the French royal line known as the Armagnac–Burgundian Civil War, prompting an alliance between Burgundy and England. The armies of Burgundy were renowned for strong archery. As well as the native bowmen in their ranks, they recruited large numbers of English archers; men who flocked to the fight for good pay, adventure and the chance to loose their shafts at a Frenchman.

Here a 16th-century German archer shoots a yew longbow of considerable girth. Judging by his dress, he is a gentleman of social standing. In fact it is a self-portrait of the artist, who characteristically introduced his own image into his paintings. He adopts the tilted pelvis stance of the heavy-bow shooter and we may deduce that it is a bow of significant draw-weight. Many of the details indicate that the artist is well-acquainted with archery tackle, from the leather shooting glove to the cresting on the shafts to the inclusion of a fletching compound, suggested by the darker strips between the feathers. The odd positioning of the feet is an artistic convention, indicating the artist's relationship to both within the painting and without in the studio – a foot in both worlds – but otherwise all the archery elements suggest that this is an image to be trusted. (Detail from a panel, 'Santa Croce in Jerusalem', by Hans Burgkmair the Elder in the convent of St Catherine, Augsburg, 1504. Jbarta/Wikimedia Commons/Public Domain)

THE RECURVED LONGBOW

A distinctive variation of the regular medieval longbow can be seen in many manuscript images. It was recurved at the ends. There is controversy in determining its geographical distribution and the extent of its use during the medieval period. Without the material evidence of actual bows, it is hard to be certain. Some maintain that it was exclusive to the archers in the service of Burgundy; this is based on the fact that recurved longbows are more commonly seen in Burgundian art. English archers were, of course, a mainstay of Burgundian armies during the 15th century, and so even if Burgundy were the source of this style, it may well have been adopted by some English bowmen also.

There is further debate about the method of manufacture. One theory proposes simply that staves were selected which already embodied a recurved profile. Another is that the limbs were bent into shape on a former and heat-treated to set them. (I own such a heat-treated bow. After three years the curves straightened out but they were reset and it has now lasted another six years. I still shoot it quite often. It is my favourite longbow, with a beautifully smooth action.)

The performance benefit of a recurved bow is that it has the ability for better cast – that is, it will propel the arrow further than a straight-limbed bow of equivalent draw-weight. The renowned bowyer Richard Galloway, a proponent of the ubiquity of medieval recurved longbows, calculated that recurving a bow added 20 per cent advantage to the cast (Soar, Gibbs, Jury & Stretton 2010: 38).

It seems probable that there were various regional styles to the profile and cross-section of longbows, and that the option and benefits of recurved limbs were widely known by all. Nevertheless, there is considerably more work involved in fashioning a recurved longbow. They were therefore more expensive and took longer to make, so at times of high national demand it seems more likely that it was straight-limbed bows that were produced and stacked in their thousands in the nation's arsenals.

RIGHT Modern replica of a medieval recurved longbow, made by Chris Boyton. The advantage of such a design is that the recurved shape makes the limbs work faster, the tips snapping forward like striking snakes, which in turn moves the string faster. This results in an arrow speed that would otherwise have required a bow of far greater draw-weight to initiate. Quite simply, it is a more efficient spring. (Mike Loades)

Although the first Anglo-Burgundian alliance came to an end in 1435, it was renewed with greater resolve upon the marriage of Margaret of York to Charles the Bold, who succeeded to the duchy in 1467. Just as his father, Philip the Good, had done, Charles augmented his Burgundian archers with recruits from England. In 1473 England's Edward IV sent 1,000 archers to serve under the Burgundian banner and in 1475 eight companies of mounted English archers rode in the ducal guard, and 10 companies of mounted English archers (each 100 strong) were employed by Charles in his campaigns against the Swiss in 1476 (Strickland & Hardy 2005: 363). Although the longbow was demonstrably in widespread use by other nations at this period, many in the service of Burgundy, the value of well-trained English bowmen remained at a premium. After the battle of Morat (1476) Charles's paymasters dispensed 20s to the English mounted archers but a mere 16s to mounted archers of other nations (Strickland & Hardy 2005: 363).

IN GERMAN LANDS

Whether in the service of Burgundy or 'freelancing' in Italy, the archers of other nations often included those from German lands. After all it was a German adventurer, Albert Sterz, who first commanded the White Company; Sir John Hawkwood was his successor. German mercenaries mixed with English mercenaries during the 14th and 15th centuries and many acquired proficiency with the 'English' longbow.

When the Archduke Maximilian of Austria, subsequently Maximilian I, Holy Roman Emperor (r. 1508–19), married Mary of Burgundy in 1477, a new and mighty military entity was created. During the previous several decades successive Burgundian dukes had already expanded Burgundian lands to include Luxembourg and the Low Countries and this was now matched with the Austro-Hungarian territories of the Hapsburgs.

In his idealized and fantasized autobiography, *Die Weisskunig*, Maximilian is portrayed as being an expert with every weapon of the day. Prowess with the English longbow was no exception:

> The young king taught himself, from his own impetus, to shoot with the English longbow. With this he outmatched all the Hussars at his father's court … he shot with the English longbow better with his skill than others did with their strength. (Quoted in Riesch 1995: 64)

The Hussars referred to here were Hungarian horse-archers, who would have been using the Hun composite bow with all the mechanical advantages it had. There is ambivalence to the phrase 'better with his skill than others did with their strength' because to outmatch a composite bow for range, using a similar arrow, Maximilian would have needed to have shot a longbow of considerably greater draw-weight. That he was able to do so is possible if the following passage from *Die Weisskunig* is to be believed:

> although the English are most skilful and masterly in shooting with the bow and famous above other nations and they have a lot of strong men among them, no English or other man came close to Maximilian in shooting more forcefully with the longbow. He once shot a wooden shaft, which had no iron tip, through a board of larchwood, being very hard and three-fingers thick. (Quoted in Riesch 1995: 65)

Here Maximilian exhibits his usual hubris, but also tips his cap at the high reputation of English bowmen. These are men he knew well from their service in Burgundian armies. Again in *Die Weisskunig* he references how he spent time with them:

> After the king had taken the land of Burgundy there came a lot of English mercenaries to him and these could shoot very well with the longbow. Maximilian was a keen archer and so it happened that he often practised with the bow in his free time and with him were his English mercenaries that shot with the bow too. In such leisure time he learned from them the English language. (Quoted in Riesch 1995: 65)

I dare say that many of the phrases he learned from rough-hewn English archers may have seemed indelicate within refined court circles. Maximilian is a paradox, both a military modernizer and the preserver of traditional fighting arts. In restructuring the armies of the Holy Roman Empire, he placed enormous emphasis on gunpowder weapons. However, he also introduced the longbow, doubtless inspired by the utility of his English archer comrades. The principal troops of Maximilian's new army were the Landsknechte – massed infantry armed mostly with with harquebus and pike – and it was into these ranks that he recruited longbowmen. Early firearms were not always reliable, especially in wet or windy weather. As well as greater reliability, the longbow had greater range and, in skilled

OPPOSITE A landsknecht archer. These brawny men had the reputation of being able to shoot massive and powerful bows. Although the sizes, of both bow and arrows, depicted here are clearly fanciful and exaggerated, Landsknechte did shoot arrows of much greater length than other nations; around 39 inches. It is unclear what the perceived advantage of this may have been. Arrows were carried, with the heads upwards, in a distinctive deer-skin or boar-skin quiver, known as a *Rauchköcher*, which can be seen here on the ground. (Image from 'Archery in Renaissance Germany' *Journal of the Society of Archer-Antiquaries*, 38 (1995) 63–7. Courtesy of Holger Riesch) hands, accuracy. It could also be shot more rapidly. Woodcuts in *Die Weisskunig* show groups of archers mostly on the flanks of pike blocks. These were relatively small contingents compared to the many thousands of archers employed by English armies in earlier decades. Nevertheless, they were possibly useful as dependable, fast-shooting safeguards to defend against flanking actions. An indication of the ratios of troop types is given in Maximilian's preparation for the defence of the Netherlands in 1511, where he arrayed 1,000 mounted men-at-arms, 9,000 foot soldiers and 1,000 archers (Riesch 1995: 66). It was a significant number of archers and there can be little doubt that a tradition of German longbow archery can be claimed. The longbow was finally decommissioned as a military weapon in the reforms of Maximilian's grandson Charles V (r. 1516–56).

IMPACT: ASSESSING THE LONGBOW

Elevation shooting and range

There is no image in medieval art that depicts archers on a battlefield shooting up into the air, 'in elevation'. When bowmen are shown attacking a castle, there is abundant imagery of archers leaning back from the waist and angling their bows upwards, but you never see this in a battlefield context. It is also true to say that many contemporary depictions of battles represent both armies, and that the empty space in between has clearly been condensed for better picture composition. Even so, it would still have been possible for artists to show archers leaning back and shooting in the air, if this were the more familiar action. This is not to say that shooting in elevation could not be done on the battlefield, nor even to say that it was not done. It is simply to point out that although this is a familiar and iconic image from Hollywood, it is not an image from the medieval period.

Extreme ranges (approaching 300yd) were possible for a war arrow,* though 200–250yd was probably more typical. We also know there was a culture of distance shooting during the Middle Ages, at clout, at the marks and roving. Undoubtedly all this long-range shooting had practical applications in siege and naval warfare, but it does not automatically follow that shooting repeated volleys at distance on the battlefield was the best military use of the weapon, nor that it was the universal practice. The potential for long-range shooting is not in question and we can be reasonably sure that it was used, but the regularity with which it was employed, the extent to which it characterized the archer's main activity on the battlefield and the percentage of his shafts spent in long-range flight all merit closer examination.

In the same passage in which he attests to the power of the Welsh bow, with tales of it being able to penetrate an oak door four fingers thick and pinning a knight's legs to his saddle through his leg armour,** the 12th- and 13th-century chronicler Giraldus Cambrensis stated that the bows used by the Welsh were 'not calculated to shoot an arrow a great distance but to inflict very severe wounds in a close fight' (Cambrensis 1894: 371). A bow capable of such penetrative feats would clearly have had the ability to shoot an arrow a very great distance. I interpret the chronicler's words to mean that the Welsh archers strategized (calculated) to shoot at close ranges, even though their bows were capable of shooting further. It does not necessarily make military sense to shoot at long range just because you can. I believe that this is exactly the view being put forward by Sir John Smythe in 1590, when he writes, in a marginal note:

> If musketeers may give effectual volleys twenty-four scores off (as is fondly reported), then some number of archers being chosen that could with their flights shoot twenty-four and twenty scores (as there be many that can) may by the same reason give volleys

---

* Joe Gibbs of the EWBS has shot a heavy livery arrow a distance of 306yd. Livery arrow is the name given to replicas of those found on the *Mary Rose*. They weigh around 2¼oz. The fletchings are a little over 7in long. The shaft is ½in at the shoulder with a bobtail taper towards the nock. These are very substantial arrows with considerable weight and drag compared to the type of arrows used by modern archers. The record was attained in 2012 and still stands at the time of writing. It was shot using a 170lb bow of Italian yew made by Ian Coote.

** At the time, 1191, this would be mail chausses, and the story is that having had one leg shot through and pinned to the saddle by an arrow, the knight wheeled his horse around, only to receive a second arrow, which nailed the other leg in the same fashion.

of flights at their enemies eighteen scores off, which both the one and the other are mockeries to be thought of, because there is no weapon in the field effectual to a convenient and certain distance. (Smythe 1964: 62)

Range and deceleration

Range is a key factor that affects the force with which an arrow strikes. From the moment an arrow leaves the bow, there are forces of drag, which begin to slow it down. In 2003 I had the chance to gather some data on this. It was for the *Weapons That Made Britain* television programme (Channel 4, 2004) and the tests were conducted by the UK Defence Academy at Shrivenham, Oxfordshire, in collaboration with Dr Alan Williams, Visiting Research Fellow at Reading University and consultant to the Wallace Collection. An arrow, shot by Mark Stretton from a 150lb bow, was tracked by Doppler radar in order to measure its rate of deceleration. The deceleration was significant, slowing from 170ft/sec as it left the bow to 137ft/sec after just 0.8 of a second in flight. A 300lb draw-weight crossbow was also tested. The fast punch of the crossbow meant that initially the bolt suffered very little drop in acceleration. It then decelerated dramatically after approximately 80yd.

Frustratingly, the test did not tell us all we needed to know because the radar lost contact with the arrow before it began its descent – a malfunction that could not be corrected on the day. Clearly there would be a significant pick-up in speed as the falling arrow came under the forces of gravity. Even so, this is unlikely to have been as great as the maximum speed achieved for the first 20yd or so of its flight.

The physics of arrow flight are complex and affected by many factors, which there is not space here to pursue further. I simply flag up some of the issues for consideration. However, it seems reasonable to suppose that the longbow was at its most powerful and effective at ranges up to 40–50yd, and that there was then a diminished capability until around 120yd, when parabolic shots received the assistance of gravity – albeit these are not quite as effective as shots at the closer ranges.

Volley-shooting

Although the word 'volley' may be used as a synonym for flight or salvo, simply implying a number of arrows being shot together, the phrase 'volley-shooting' has the more specific meaning of entire contingents shooting at once with coordinated timing. If three out of ten archers shoot more or less together, it could be called a volley. It is in that sense of the word that I have used it throughout this text. With thousands of archers in an army, there can be massed flights of arrows in the air at any one moment.

The tactic of volley-shooting, however, would require all ten archers to shoot at exactly the same moment, and that is quite a different matter. This meme, beloved by the silver screen, seems implausible in practice. It may be possible with small groups of men, say ten or even 20, but it becomes exponentially more difficult to coordinate larger blocs.

Visual signals seem unlikely; it is inadvisable to stand in front of a line of bowmen. Shouted commands would not be heard above the clamour of battle by any beyond the immediate area. Musical cues from trumpets or drums may have been possible, but they would also be an announcement to the enemy that a volley was about to be shot and so prompt them to take cover with their shields.

Any potential advantage of saturating a zone in the enemy ranks with a shower of shafts would be muted by the recipients' ability to defend against it and then to advance with impunity until the next volley was trumpeted.

At Agincourt, the commander of the archers, Sir Thomas Erpingham, was said to call 'Nestroque' as a signal for his men to shoot. Various theories have been advanced as to the meaning of this, but the one I favour is the one proposed by Hugh Soar (Soar, Gibbs, Jury & Stretton 2010: 5). He deduces that it is a contraction of the phrase '*menée* strike' and thus was an order to the trumpets to strike up (sound) the *menée*. The *menée* was one of a number of named medieval hunting calls; it was the one that signalled that the hounds were in full flight in pursuit of their quarry and doubtless sent a chilling message to the enemy as well as an order to the archers.

Following such an inaugural fanfare it is conceivable that the first shots would come more or less all at once, but heavy bows cannot be held at full draw awaiting the readiness of others; with thousands of archers, all with a different rhythm of nocking and drawing, subsequent flights would be unlikely to be synchronized. Certainly coordinated volley-shooting would be nonsensical at close ranges, when everything is happening very quickly. Archers needed to react to immediate threats and had no time to wait for commands. Even if possible, at longer ranges the use of volley-shooting would have been of questionable military advantage. Ranging accurately – especially against a moving target – requires intuitive timing that is not conducive to being marshalled by a bugle. Moreover, a tactic of 'shoot-at-will' would create less predictable patterns of onslaught that would be more unnerving to an enemy. In any event it was the arrows shot from closer ranges that had the most effect.

The arrowstorm – a reinterpretation

Very often, medieval chroniclers used precipitation metaphors to describe the density of arrows from thousands of archers – an arrowstorm. They likened it to hail and snow and rain; they said it blotted out the sun. Leaving aside the fact that a blizzard can be a horizontal event, one must allow a certain amount of poetic licence to those invoking poetic metaphor. In a similar vein Enguerrand de Monstrelet, a chronicler of the battle of Agincourt, wrote 'the French began to bow their heads so that the arrow fire [*sic*] would not penetrate the visors of their helmets' (quoted in Curry 2009: 160). This surely suggests the arrows were coming straight at the French! In fact, much of what the chroniclers reported with regard to arrowstorms could have been as true of a mass volley at 50yd as it would have been at 200yd. Even relatively near-range volleys may still be considered to have been hitting at 'a distance'; the chroniclers, alas, did not specify at what distance.

I consider it likely that shooting in a parabolic arc limited the odds of success. Although it offered depth to the salvo, the exposed target zone of each man was greatly limited by the physical presence of the ranks in front and shields were an effective means of ensuring that where gaps occurred, they were well defended. Certainly there would be casualties, but shooting in an arc did not offer a good percentage chance of success for those husbanding precious resources.

In contrast, shooting with a trajectory nearer to the horizontal would have allowed more targeted and more robust hits, causing great disruption as enemy men and horses fell in the path of those behind. When archers were used to shoot from the flanks, they could bring about significant problems of crowd chaos by targeting those on the edges of the attacking army, forcing a concentration of men towards the centre. Shooting into the centre with arcing volleys would have the opposite effect.

Arrow stocks – a key factor in battle

Apart from the clear advantages of accuracy and impact, the issue that must have most concerned the massed archer companies of the 14th and 15th centuries was the question of arrow stocks. Medieval war arrows were a sophisticated and elaborate form of ammunition, which could not be made readily by an army on campaign. It was serious news for the chamberlain of Chester to discover in 1356 that 'no arrows can be obtained from England because the king … has taken for his use all the arrows that can be found' (quoted in Hardy 1992: 84). On the one hand this tells us that the king took a lot of arrows with him on campaign, but on the other it reminds us that arrow stocks were a finite commodity.

I have discussed the scale of arrow procurement earlier, and, although we cannot be certain of the numbers, between one and two million is probably a generous guess for an expedition such as Edward III's Crécy adventure. Of course, not all of these shafts would have been available to the archers for the main battle. Commanders needed to ration their arrows, especially when on a foreign campaign. A good amount would have been used in the skirmishes and raids that occupied six weeks of relentlessly aggressive *chevauchée* prior to the battle, and ideally some stocks would have been held back to cover any hope of retreat in the event of an indecisive result on the battlefield.

Moreover, it is probable that a certain percentage was unusable. There are numerous warnings of dire consequences for those who supplied sub-standard arrows – such as in Edward III's 1369 order for 1,000 sheaves of arrows, which carried the sanction that 'unless the said sheaves be made of seasoned wood … the king will cause the sheriffs … to be arrested and imprisoned, their lands, goods and chattels to be seized' (CCR Ed III 1369). In addition to this penalty for those responsible for the procurement, the fletchers themselves were threatened with a punishment that 'shall be a terror to others' (CCR Ed III 1369). Such harsh measures indicate a significant problem with faulty goods – unseasoned, green-wood arrows that appeared good enough on delivery but warped subsequently, a flaw not discovered until they were unpacked from their barrel on campaign.

As a discussion point, let us say that Edward had one million arrows available for the main battle at Crécy (Robert Hardy (Hardy 1992: 83) suggests a more conservative figure of just half a million). If we suppose that the majority of bows were in the 100–120lb range, it seems reasonable to estimate a rate of shooting of eight arrows per minute.* Estimates for the number of archers vary but if we take a mean figure of around 7,500, then there is the potential for the archer corps to shoot 60,000 arrows a minute. It is obvious that no archer could sustain this rate of shooting with a heavy bow minute after minute, but the mathematics tells us that only just over 16 minutes of shooting at that rate is available to the army before stocks run out, irrespective of how those minutes are spread out during the course of the battle.

---

* I can shoot 12 arrows per minute with a 70lb bow and there are others who can shoot faster. However, this is not with the heavy warbow. It therefore seems wiser to take a more conservative number. Mark Stretton of the EWBS can shoot ten per minute with a 140lb bow, but would not be able to shoot 20 in two minutes (private correspondence). He regards six per minute more achievable for consecutive minutes with such a bow, but if we consider that the average bow would be of a lower weight, then it is probably reasonable to propose a rate of shooting under pressure of eight arrows per minute.

At Crécy, initial volleys were expended into the unshielded Genoese crossbowmen and the remaining stocks had to be husbanded to repel the French attacks. According to some authorities the French attacked 15 or 16 times (Hardy 1992: 73). We can be sure that each assault lasted more than a minute and so, quite quickly, the arithmetic becomes challenging. When the pounding hooves of the enemy charge are massing within yards of your front line it is surely no time to ration supplies, so commanders had to conserve their resources when they could by limiting the use of distance volleys.

Arrow stocks were not the only element to be used sparingly. Even the strongest archer could not keep up the work rate of shooting rapidly with a heavy bow for very long. Archers would need to have been ready to repel an attack when it came to close quarters with an unrelenting, pounding barrage of shafts. Expending energy on more speculative targets at longer ranges risked exhaustion for when it really counted.

Whether or not the French actually did attack 15 times at Crécy does not change this argument. As far as the English knew, they may have attacked less but, equally possibly, they may have attacked more; the battle may have lasted longer. There could have been another battle to come. In calculating both the stamina of the archers and the provision of arrows, a commander needed to be sure that every shot would count. Even if there were two million arrows available at Crécy, which I strongly doubt, the need to be prudent with them would have been just as great. The statistics and particulars will be different for every battle, but despite a wide range of variables, the principle remains the same.

The battle of Crécy from Froissart's *Chroniques*, c. 1470–75 (detail). Although this 15th-century image is anachronistic for Crécy, note that arrows are placed in the ground, the archers are well armoured, they shoot recurved longbows and they are in the midst of the fighting. (Bibliothèque Nationale de France, MS Français 2799, fol. 223, © Bibliothèque Nationale de France)

The longbow's effectiveness against armour

It is beyond the scope of this present work to catalogue, analyse and disentangle the results of all the dozens of penetration tests that have been carried out over the years. Without question, the longbow is capable of delivering arrows with sufficient force to pierce most types of armour in ideal conditions. What is less certain is the odds of these ideal conditions presenting in the random chaos of battle. Describing an arrowstorm at the battle of Agincourt, the Benedictine chronicler Thomas Walsingham recorded that 'many of the French fell, pierced with arrows, here fifty, there sixty' (quoted in Curry 2009: 52). Given such writers' propensity to exaggerate, these seem trifling numbers.

Arguably the most crucial factor in determining penetration is the angle of strike. Tests against static, perpendicular, flat sheets of metal or other target material are informative because they show what effect an arrow would have if it struck at an angle of exactly 90 degrees to the surface. They show the potential of an arrow to penetrate. What they do not show is the probability of how many arrows would strike at this angle, which is affected by the deflective nature of armour's curves, the fact that a man in battle would be in a state of constant motion, the influence of wind at long range and archer's paradox – a term used to describe the action of an arrow bending around a bow at the moment of release – at short range.

Arrows that strike at angles other than perpendicular to the target usually fail to penetrate. That is, in part, because some of the force arising from an arrow hitting goes along the line of the armour and not through it. It is also because an arrow is flexible and the force that is not along the line of the arrow will cause it to bend. When an arrow strikes at 90 degrees and does not bend, then the whole mass of the arrow is aligned behind the point and so there is a high force as all the mass is being slowed down at once. However, if the arrow bends on impact, then some of the mass of the arrow will try to continue forward with its momentum, causing the arrow to bend even more, which will result in a lower force being transmitted to the target.

Many tests set up the target armour against a rigid stand that allows for no movement on impact. Bearing in mind that an arrow strike from a heavy bow has the potential to lift a man off his feet – the equivalent of being hit by a sledgehammer – the energy absorbed by a moving body's response to the hit needs to be factored in. Countering that is the opposite effect of a body moving at speed, such as on a galloping horse, towards the arrow strike (see Soar, Gibbs, Jury & Stretton 2010: 140–43 for some interesting tests conducted by Mark Stretton using fast-moving oncoming targets on ziplines). These are important variables.

Other variables include the draw-weight of the bow, the range of the shot, the weight of the arrow, the type of arrowhead, whether or not the arrowhead is hardened steel, and, of course, the quality of the armour, which can vary enormously. Not all armour was the best quality; nor were all arrows shot from the most powerful bows, nor with the best-quality arrows, nor with exactly the right type of arrowhead for their destined target. The battlefield was an inconsistent environment.

Penetration testing has become the Holy Grail for assessing the effectiveness of the longbow in war. This narrow focus has been useful as far as it goes, though tests against household objects or re-enactment-grade armour do not really count and the appropriate quality and combinations of metal and textile armour are seldom incorporated. Testing mail in isolation from an authentically constructed aketon, for instance, is irrelevant.

I have long thought, however, that the real merit of the longbow in battle does not rely on penetration alone; non-penetrating strikes were also effective and a great deal more common. Certainly, men were wounded and killed by arrows piercing the body; armour on occasion failed. Moreover, a man may not be completely protected by armour, either by choice – sacrificing full protection for the advantages of comfort and mobility – or because he could not afford it. Visors were raised to get a better view or catch a breath; there were moments of rashness and vulnerability. Generally speaking, though, armour was reasonable proof against the weapons of the day.

If the longbow really did have the ability to puncture with certainty all medieval armour, English armies would have had the capacity to annihilate 100 per cent of their foes on the battlefield in very short order, and that did not happen. A generally accepted number of French men-at-arms killed at Crécy is 2,200 (Ayton & Preston 2005: 333). It was a genealogical catastrophe that gave the military aristocracy of France a crushing blow, the hammerhead of which was English archery. However, it was not total destruction. According to Froissart there were 20,000 French men-at-arms at the battle, though the more conservative Richard Wynkeley estimated only 12,000 (Ayton & Preston 2005: 269). Even if we take the lower number, we can see that a high percentage of men survived the arrowstorms. Seemingly, in most cases, shields and armours were adequate to the task.

However, penetration need not be the true measure of an arrow's military effectiveness. In fact, it may not even have been the principal purpose of battlefield

Sample of textile armour made by Deborah Lee. Note that the stitching pattern has gathered the layers together in such a way that the density of the fibre mass has been intensified. This is the specimen that was used for tests measuring the effects of blunt trauma from a non-penetrating arrow strike. (Photograph by Tobias Capwell)

archery. There must have been reason for recruiting well-paid archer armies in so many thousands, more than just working the percentages against the odds of armour penetration.

My belief is that the main function of massed archers was to deliver a consistent barrage of hits; even though few would penetrate, all would strike with a significant blunt-trauma force, landing a debilitating onslaught of heavyweight blows – blows that would soften up and weaken an enemy, sapping his stamina and will. The ability to deliver repeated hits, consistently and unwaveringly, may have been a greater contribution to military success than scoring a random number of kills.

Blunt force as a battle-winner

In 2011 I had the opportunity to carry out some blunt-force tests. Once again it was for a television programme: *Going Medieval* for H2 Channel, USA. I recruited the help of Mark Stretton and Joe Gibbs of the EWBS, who each shot 140lb bows, and Dr Matthew Pain, Senior Lecturer in Sports Biomechanics and Motor Control, Loughborough University, who set up a device to measure impact. A martial-arts mannequin was used as the mount. It had a weighted base, allowing the dummy to move when struck. The weight corresponded approximately to that of a man, creating a similar inertia. A custom force plate (CFP) measuring about 6in by 8in was affixed to the chest area. This CFP consisted of four three-component ICP 260A01 force

Screen-grab from the slow-motion camera recording blunt-force impacts. Note that this arrow is bending slightly on impact, which is already beginning to dissipate some of the force of the blow. An arrow hitting at a perfect 90 degrees, and which does not bend, will have the whole mass of the arrow aligned behind the point, thus creating a strike of greater impact. (Photograph courtesy Dr Matthew Pain)

transducers sandwiched between a pair of 2in-thick metal plates. Layered on the surface was ½in of modelling plasticine. Over this we suspended a sample of textile armour, consisting of 25 layers of linen with a deerskin top layer, and on top of this we placed a replica of a riveted mail shirt.

The archers stood approximately 10yd away and shot livery arrows shod with short bodkins from 140lb yew warbows. As anticipated, the mail was defeated by many of the arrows, but even at this extreme close range and using the upper possibility of draw-weights, none of the arrows fully penetrated the textile armour. We knew that if the archers had used long bodkins, this type of armour could have been penetrated at this distance, but that was not the purpose of the test. Arrowhead selection was informed by our objective of determining a measure of blunt trauma in the event that the armour did its job.

One of the more surprising outcomes of the test was that even though both distance and equipment were constant, impact forces varied considerably from 60lb to 300lb, with the vast majority of hits being between 160lb and 250lb. Of the several dozen arrows shot, the 300lb reading was a one-off extreme peak, but the shock of receiving such a hit can be compared to wearing a bulletproof vest and being hit by a .44 Magnum round! This is a measurement of the impulse/momentum – the thudding, stopping feeling that someone would experience on the receiving end of such a hit. However, the analogy should not be taken too far: the energy delivered by this arrow was only around 100 joules, whereas the energy for the lowest end for a

Magnum is around 1,000 joules.* It should also be noted that the vast majority of arrow strikes in a battle would be at a greater distance and most bows would likely be of lesser draw-weights. We were testing the extremes.

Nevertheless, the test did highlight what I consider to be the key role of the longbow on the battlefield – to thump the enemy with very heavy hits. It was a bonus when a shaft penetrated, whatever the percentage chances of that may be, but nearly all shafts can be counted upon to hit. That was the fight. That was the battle – relentlessly striking the foe with powerful blows. It did not matter, within certain parameters, that the force of the blows varied in intensity, either because of the angle of strike or the draw-weight of the bow; even the lighter, but still strong, strikes would have taken their toll cumulatively. Archers were engaged in a slugging match; arrows were steel-clad fists with a considerable reach. It was attritional warfare, wearing the enemy down with hard strikes. In such a contest the power of the hits was important. Heavier bows and closer ranges were better, but the knockout punch was not everything. Of equal importance was the frequency of the hits, dependent upon both the rate of shooting and the number of archers.

The really big hits would rock a man and, before the advent of rigid plate armour, they could cause flexible armour to deform into the body, causing damage to internal organs. For the man-at-arms facing such a bruising attack, having a developed muscle-mass, especially around the abdomen and the neck, was as essential a protective layer as the armour itself. It was about being able to take the hits and it was about stamina.

For the archer, too, it was about strength and endurance. Repeatedly shooting heavy bows was arduous, back-straining, muscle-cramping, sweat-inducing toil. At range the longbowman occasionally had the opportunity to gall and goad standing troops, provoking them into abandoning their positions, but at whatever we consider to be the optimum range to begin shooting, the enemy ultimately closed quite quickly. That was when the archer's work was needed most and for the longest time – fighting at close range and hitting the enemy as hard as possible with targeted arrows.

Archers required a defended position – be that terrain, obstacles or a hedge of spears – without which they were extremely vulnerable. However, even a defended position needs to be actively defended and when the enemy attacked, the archer could not slack. He must set to his strenuous task without pause. If overrun, or if arrow supplies were exhausted, archers were expected to engage in hand-to-hand fighting. They were adaptable soldiers.

The longbow was an easily portable and powerful weapon that had a considerable impact on the medieval battlefield and even more so at sea and on campaign. Indeed, the longbow's greatest advantage was its versatility – its suitability for use in a wide range of military operations. However, it was not a magic stick and it was not infallible. Terrain and tactics had to be right for it to be effective and the arms race between the longbow and ever improving forms of armour was close-run, with neither side edging far ahead but rather maintaining a constant state of precarious balance.

Although there have been enormous advances during the past few decades, I believe that our full understanding of the longbow and the way in which it was used in medieval warfare remains incomplete. This, of course, fuels the endless fascination that many have for the subject. Personally, I would like to see future tests focusing more on 'rate of shooting' with heavy bows rather than on extreme range, and tests

---

* Private correspondence with Dr M. Pain.

that concentrate more on trying to replicate the full array of medieval armour more accurately. We also need to find a way to simulate the constantly varying and random angles that targets present during battle, and we need always to keep open minds.

CONCLUSION

As the 16th century gave way to the 17th, the longbow disappeared entirely from military use. The English victories over the Scots at Flodden (1513) and Pinkie Cleugh (1547) were the last major land battles in which it played a significant part, and Drake's voyages saw its final use at sea. Gunpowder weapons got better, though the longbow still had many advantages and, over the years, its many ardent proponents. In 1625, prior to the English Civil War, William Neade proposed a system of training men with a bow-and-pike combination. His 'double-armed man' had a pike strapped to his bow, creating a defensive hedge against cavalry while allowing the same man to be an active shooter. Charles I was a supporter of the scheme and it had some initial traction before being eclipsed by the onset of war.

In 1798, with the threat of an invasion of Britain by French forces under Napoleon, another British military tactician, R. O. Mason, wrote a tract called *Pro Aris et Focis*, which was illustrated with various drill exercises for the archer/pikeman. Mason, too, argued that the bow was a superior weapon to the musket. However, perhaps the most articulate advocate for the reintroduction of the military longbow was Benjamin Franklin, though his recommendations ran contrary to the military thinking of the times; neither was there an adequate national resource of bowyers, fletchers or trained bowmen.

Nevertheless, in a letter to General Charles Lee in 1776, at the outset of the American Revolutionary War, Franklin proposed that longbows be standard issue for the Continental Army. His idea was prompted by a shortage of gunpowder, but he set out an argument that remained as true then as it had been the day the world shook to the first gunshot. Among his most important points were the facts that 'an archer can discharge four arrows in the time of charging and discharging one bullet' and 'that his object is not taken from his view by the smoke of his own side' (Franklin 1882: 170). I can do no better than close this brief study with another quotation from Franklin. He wrote that longbows were 'good weapons, not wisely laid aside' (Franklin 1882: 170).

CHAPTER TWO
THE CROSSBOW

The crossbow has long enjoyed a popular cachet for dastardly cunning and villainy. It was the subject of two papal bans (in 1096 and in 1139). These incurred a penalty of excommunication, excepting for its use against infidels. Anna Komnene, the Byzantine princess who left an eyewitness account of the First Crusade (1095–99), concluded that the crossbow was a diabolical mechanism, describing it as 'verily a devilish invention' (Komnene 2009: 282). In England a national love-affair with the longbow, enduring to the present day, has tended to eclipse the military importance of the crossbow in the popular imagination.

A trilogy of crossbow attacks on English kings in the 12th century further feed an unwarranted notion that it is somehow an underhand weapon. While hunting in the New Forest, William II Rufus (r. 1087–1100) was killed by a crossbow bolt; an assassin's blow conferring an association of

A superb replica, made by Andreas Bichler, of a composite-lathed crossbow belonging to Count Ulrich V of Württemberg (1413–80). The original crossbow is in the collections of the Metropolitan Museum of Art, New York. This replica has a hornbeam tiller and the inlaid plates have been made from ibex horn and bone (the bone substitutes for the original ivory). Missing from the museum piece are the string and stirrup, both of which have been incorporated into the working replica. Note the ridge on the stirrup. This was a common feature that allowed for a relatively narrow (and therefore lighter) gauge of metal while maintaining functional rigidity. The double-layer covering of painted birch bark for the lath is also largely missing from the original but two small fragments remain to give a clue to part of the decorative scheme. These fragments reveal a dense pattern of light spots on a black ground. In this masterful rendering of how the original may have appeared, Herr Bichler has given us a glimpse of the vibrant splendour of such high-status crossbows. The verse painted onto the zigzag relief on the cheek piece is a rhyming Latin prayer to the Virgin Mary and also includes the date, 1460, of the bow's manufacture. A verse from the Gospel of Luke appears on the opposite side. Other decoration includes the heraldic achievements of the count and his third wife, Margaret of Savoy, various floral motifs and a cryptic inscription in Hebrew letters on the underside. Despite the elaborate array of painted, inlaid and carved decoration on three of the surfaces, the top surface is relatively unadorned so as not to distract the shooter. (Photograph: Andreas Bichler)

perfidy to the weapon. His son Henry I (r. 1100–35) narrowly escaped a bolt shot by his illegitimate daughter Juliana in her failed attempt at both patricide and regicide. In 1199, in France, the English king Richard I (r. 1189–99) died as a result of gangrene occasioned by a crossbow bolt in the shoulder at the siege of Châlus Castle. The sniper, famously equipped with a lowly frying-pan as a shield, was a commoner by the name of Peter Basilius. His action, carrying the apparent stain of being unchivalrous, was another blemish on the reputation of the crossbow.

Such a legacy is undeserved. Chivalry was a code of behaviour among nobles of equal status – it did not extend to other ranks, nor did it restrict the use of the most capable weapons for the combat at hand. The papal bans were never taken very seriously, intended as they were to curtail the endemic internecine violence among fellow European knights rather than to ostracize the crossbow itself. Crossbows were ever a high-status hunting arm for the nobility and remained prestigious weapons in general use throughout the medieval period.

Although not new to history, the crossbow had been absent from the European battlefield until its appearance at the end of the 10th century. A few were suspicious of these seemingly new-fangled contraptions, but reactionary voices were quickly drowned out by the louder clamour for military advantage. Prior to the longbow's dominance in 14th-century English armies, the crossbow was considered by far the more useful weapon. Moreover, both in continental Europe and in England, the crossbow was the weapon of choice for defending castles and fortified towns from the late 11th to the mid-15th centuries. After that the ubiquity of the crossbow began to fade, increasingly obscured behind a pall of gunpowder.

An abiding modern perception is that the crossbow is a weapon of superior technological sophistication and of greater power than the longbow. Though it undoubtedly incorporated some mechanical ingenuity, attributions to its power have been overstated. Very powerful, steel-lathed crossbows did evolve in the 15th century, but during the time of its greatest supremacy on the battlefield – roughly from 1100 to 1250 – the crossbow packed a more modest punch. Its martial merits hinged not on its power, but on other factors. These included ease of use, comparatively inexpensive ammunition and the ability to hold a bow at full span for a sustained period, waiting to seize the optimal moment for a shot. This latter element was of particular benefit in siege warfare, both for attack and defence, and also at sea. For the hunter, too, the crossbow's chief advantage was that it could remain spanned and ready to shoot. It offered stillness and imperceptible movement at the moment of shooting, reducing the risk of startling an animal before the bolt struck home.

This study focuses primarily on the military crossbow of the European Middle Ages and Renaissance, though I have also presented what I consider to be necessary historical and global context with the inclusion of a few crossbows from the East and the Ancient World. In introducing the European crossbow, there is an inevitable English bias to much of the discussion, partly because this undertaking is in English and partly because the crossbow in English armies has been too often neglected in favour of its more fêted cousin, the longbow. There is a need to redress that balance.

In a work of this size, it is impossible to also cover the many other variants of the crossbow that occur in places such as Africa and South-East Asia. Nor is it possible to examine the equally interesting stonebow – a variant of the crossbow that featured a double string with a pouch. This propelled either a stone or a clay pellet, used primarily for shooting birds.

TERMINOLOGY

It is necessary at times to distinguish between regular hand-held bows and crossbows. The Close Rolls of Edward II (CCR Ed II) include several references to the term hand-bow in order to make the distinction, as do documents as late as the 17th century. I shall follow that practice here and also use the term regular to indicate hand-bows as opposed to crossbows.

An arbalist is an alternative name for a crossbowman or, sometimes, a crossbow-maker. When spelled 'arbalest', some dictionaries assign the meaning to be the crossbow itself. The distinction is one of little difference, since both are derived from erratic medieval spelling and the intended meaning is best gauged from context.

Arrow, bolt and quarrel are all commonly used terms for the projectile, though 'quarrel' is specific to a type of military bolt fitted with a distinctive octahedron head.

The attachment of the lath to the tiller was by means of a cord or leather binding known as a bridle. The term 'bridle' may also be used to describe the cord loop fastened to a cranequin.

Also known as a rack or a cric, a cranequin is a spanning device whereby the turning handle operates on a ratchet bar via toothed gear wheels.

A false string is a bowstring that is longer than the correctly fitting string proper. It fits, without strain, onto a second set of nocks at the terminals of the limbs, enabling them to be bent sufficiently to allow the string proper to be put in place. It is more widely known today as a bastard string, but 'false string' is the idiom used in medieval documents.

Lath refers to the bow of a crossbow. During the last century the word prod entered everyday speech as an alternative term. As W. F. Paterson explains, however, this usage originated from a 19th-century mistranscription of the word *rodd* in a list of crossbow effects from an inventory of Henry VIII's possessions in 1547 (Paterson 1990: 28). Paterson recommends that the only correct terms are either lath or bow. I shall follow his guidance.

Lock is the name given to the release mechanism. This includes the catch for the string, sears, the trigger lever and the housing.

Power-stroke is the distance of string travel from the strung, resting position of the string to its location at full draw. The length of the lath has a direct bearing on how far the string can be retracted. The shorter the lath, the shorter the power-stroke and thus the less time and distance is available for the forces to act upon the projectile.

Spanning and bending are both terms for the action of pulling back the bowstring to full-draw.

Stock is the wooden stock onto which the bow is mounted. It is also known by the more common medieval name tiller. Either term is correct.

Even after they were obsolete on the battlefield, crossbows continued to develop with improved locks, differently shaped stocks and powerful laths. Hunting crossbows and target crossbows remained popular throughout the 16th, 17th and 18th centuries. These are the crossbows that mostly populate our national museums. They include glorious specimens, fine works of art; princely arms of the highest order. However, these were not the soldier's weapon. That has left a more ghostly mark, to be glimpsed at only in the dusty pages of inventories and ordnances and with faint glimmers in manuscript art. It is that weapon which is the primary concern in the brief survey that follows.

DEVELOPMENT: LOCK, STOCK AND LATH
Crossbows in the ancient world

CHINESE CROSSBOWS

Archaeological finds of locks made from cast bronze announce the appearance of the crossbow in China around 650 BC, during the Spring and Autumn period (771–476 BC). Since crossbow locks may also be manufactured from organic materials – bone or wood – the crossbow may have existed prior to this period but, to date, there is no evidence for it.

The extent to which the string could be drawn back was a significant advantage in the design of the Chinese crossbow, compared to the European variety. A greater distance of string travel enabled more work to be done, so that more potential energy was stored in the bent bow. It also transferred energy to the arrow for longer – a longer barrel on a gun confers a similar benefit. It took around 20 inches to draw a Chinese crossbow string from its resting position to hook it behind the trigger catch. By contrast, on a European crossbow the power-stroke was typically only 4–5 inches. In part this longer power-stroke was made possible by the design of the Chinese lock, allowing it to locate at the tail-end of the tiller. The long horizontal lever on European crossbows necessitated placing the string-catch much further forward.

Longer power-strokes were also achievable owing to the style of bow. As early as the Warring States period (475–221 BC), it was common to arm the Chinese crossbow with a horn-and-sinew composite lath in the style of a standard recurve hand-bow. In fact, because the regular hand-bows of the period were relatively short, Chinese crossbows could be fitted with them without adaptation. Compared to the shorter and stockier laths of European crossbows, these bows could be pulled back much further without fear of breaking. Similarly, a carriage-spring-style lath made from bamboo strips, also in common use, had a far longer limb-length: draw-length ratio than any European counterpart.

The disassembled parts of a Chinese crossbow – lock, stock and lath. Note that the composite lath has the shape and proportions of a regular hand-bow. In fact, in many cases, it was a normal hand-bow. Bows, perhaps captured from an enemy, which had in the past been shot by hand, could be pressed into service for use by relatively unskilled troops, simply by lashing them to wooden tillers fitted with mass-produced bronze locks. Two transverse wooden wedges provided a brace against which to tension the lashing cords. Converting hand-bows to crossbows necessarily produced crossbows of lower draw-weights, less than 150lb, which was towards the upper end for regular bows. Bows with a heavier draw-weight had to be specially made for the crossbow. With the longer power-stroke of the Chinese crossbow, however, even lower-weight bows offered a useful military performance, especially when used en masse. (Kim Hawkins)

Early Chinese crossbows were spanned by sitting on the ground, bracing the feet against the bow and pulling the string back with both hands. Subsequently, during the Ming Dynasty (1365–1644) the crossbowman used a cord in the manner of a stirrup in order to span his weapon while standing. For the average recruit – a peasant on a low-protein diet – either spanning method probably limited the power of these bows to less than 250lb draw-weight and many were likely a good deal lighter than this, particularly since most were repurposed hand-bows. During the Han Dynasty (206 BC–AD 220), however, it was claimed that a few elite troops were capable of bending crossbows by the hands-and-feet method with a draw-weight in excess of 750lb (Selby 2000: 172). This seems to stretch credulity not only for the power of the shooters, but also for the capacity of the lock. Whether or not a few men possessed such Herculean might we may never know. Nevertheless, the principle advantage of the crossbow was that it required little training and it could be used to equip tens of thousands of relatively low-grade troops. For reasons of stamina and to gain the advantages of rapid shooting, crossbows with lower draw-weights had a more broadly useful military application.

The discovery in 2015 of a nearly intact crossbow in pit 1 of the Terracotta Army at Xi'an revealed a recurve composite lath measuring around 57 inches. A sizeable bow, it was found together with a pair of curved pieces of wood, each with three holes. These were *tepeliks* (see Loades 2016: 27) – wooden formers – that were tied to the bow to guard against any twist and to preserve the even curve of each limb during storage or travel, but removed for action. To date, 288 crossbow mechanisms have been excavated from pit 1. It is notable that these others were not complete with bows. Crossbow locks were mass-produced items, which were inexpensive and readily available. By contrast, the sinologist and practising archer Stephen Selby has calculated that it

ABOVE Consisting of several moving parts, the lock of a Chinese crossbow had a short, vertical trigger lever, which could be operated by one or two fingers. This contrasted with the long, horizontal trigger lever required to release the rolling-nut on European crossbows. Once the workings were assembled, the lock housing was easily slotted into a recess in the tiller and secured with two bronze rods. This replica was built by Yang Fuxi. (Kim Hawkins)

LEFT Once the workings were assembled, the lock housing was easily slotted into a recess in the tiller and secured with two bronze rods. Note the sighting-pin, which served double duty by also acting as a cocking-lever to reset the lock. Incised markings at the rear of the sighting-pin calibrated the elevation of the shot. (Kim Hawkins)

BOTTOM An advantage that the Chinese crossbow enjoyed over its European counterpart was that the design of its lock permitted a significantly longer power-stroke. Chinese crossbows spanned approximately 26 inches from the front of the tiller to the nut, compared to approximately 10 inches for a European crossbow. European crossbows would require many times the amount of power in order to match performance. (Kim Hawkins)

would have taken approximately 3,261 man-years of labour to equip all 1,087 terracotta crossbowmen with composite bows for their weapons (Selby 2000: 170).

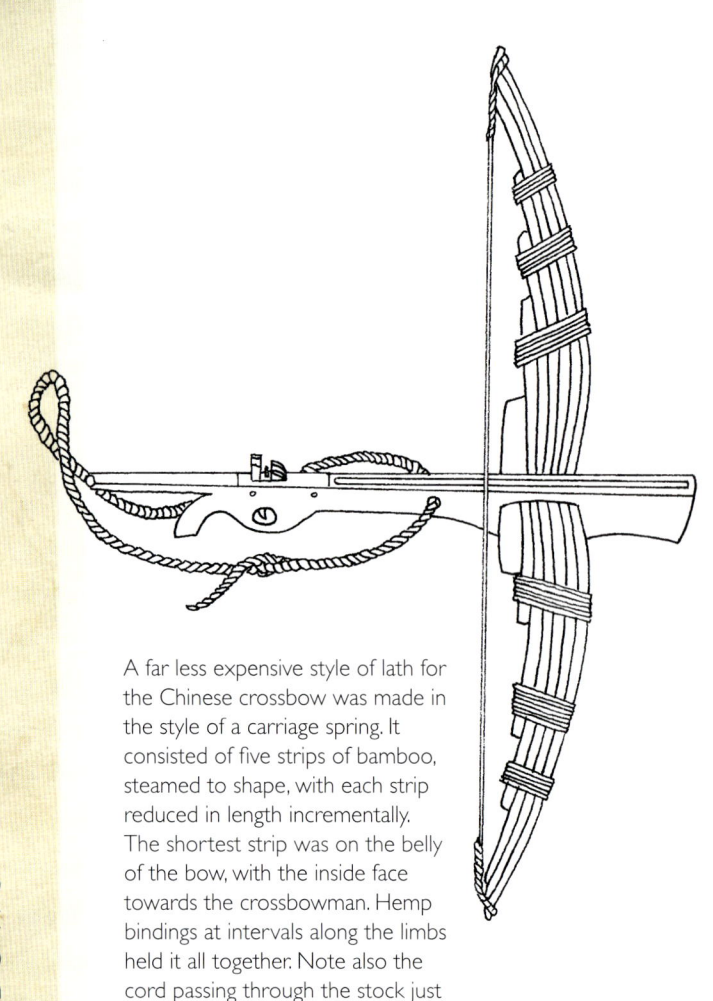

After the Qin Dynasty (221–206 BC), the crossbow remained in use in China but, in contrast to the development path of the European crossbow, it became less sophisticated, less expensive and much quicker to produce. Instead of using composite laths, the Chinese substituted multiple bamboo strips. Often these were weapons of lesser power, requiring poisoned arrows to make them effective.

The Chinese repeating crossbow – which transliterates from the Chinese as the *chu ko nu* – was capable of shooting successive bolts from a magazine by means of the continuous operation of a lever. It was, for the most part, a low-cost peasants' weapon, constructed using mulberry wood. Laths were sometimes also fashioned from mulberry and sometimes built with several strips of bamboo. These unglued strips were held in place by the bowstring, which passed through holes at each end of the lath. Wedges held the centre securely in the stock. Most magazines held ten bolts, though there are instances of larger types carrying 12 or 15 bolts. The *chu ko nu* varied in size. Some versions, equipped with twin magazines and twin bolt grooves, were able to shoot two darts simultaneously.

One tradition for the origin of the *chu ko nu* gives its name as the homophonic *zhuge nu* and claims that it was invented by the Chinese military strategist Zhuge Liang (AD 181–234). Even so, there is archaeological evidence for the *chu ko nu* as early as the late Warring States period and it may have existed even earlier than that.

In order to minimize the risk of a jam, bolts were not fletched, allowing them to sit in the magazine with parallel alignment. The absence of fletchings resulted in relatively erratic flight over distance, but the *chu ko nu* was not sufficiently powerful to perform well over great distances, and this was not its purpose. It was a short-range weapon that had the advantage of putting numbers of arrows into the air rapidly. In theory it could be shot as quickly as a person could move the handle to and fro. In practice, though, doing this leads not only to jams but to an extremely jerky action, in turn creating an erratic aim. It is essential to use smooth, rhythmic strokes that maintain the weapon in a relatively still position. The string was subject to a great deal of abrasion when in continuous use. For this reason, it was reinforced with a finely sanded piece of split goose quill slotted over the centre section.

After shooting its initial salvos during the Warring States period, the *chu ko nu* seems to disappear from the record until the Ming Dynasty. A Chinese encyclopaedia

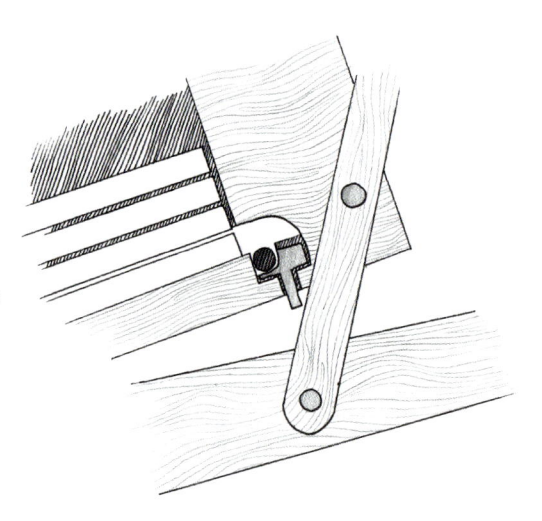

A far less expensive style of lath for the Chinese crossbow was made in the style of a carriage spring. It consisted of five strips of bamboo, steamed to shape, with each strip reduced in length incrementally. The shortest strip was on the belly of the bow, with the inside face towards the crossbowman. Hemp bindings at intervals along the limbs held it all together. Note also the cord passing through the stock just behind the lath, which served double duty. It was both a lanyard that enabled the crossbow to be carried over the shoulder on the march and also a proto-stirrup that allowed the bow to be hand-spanned with the crossbowman standing fully upright. (David Joseph Wright)

The key to the repeating crossbow being able to cycle shots is this T-shaped peg. It hangs freely in the string groove. When the string is engaged it drops down, allowing the string to locate. At the end of the lever pull, the magazine is brought flush with the stock, forcing the T-peg upwards and so pushing the string out of its groove to release the shot. (David Joseph Wright) from the Qing Dynasty (1644–1912), the *Guin Tushu Jicheng*, declares that 'The Zhuge Nu is a handy little weapon that even the Confucian scholar [i.e. a weakling] or palace women can use in self-defence' (Peter Dekker 2017: private correspondence). This underlines its role as the 'home protection crossbow', by which name it was also known. The source goes on to state that:

> It fires weakly so you have to tip the darts with poison. Once the darts are tipped with 'tiger-killing poison', you can shoot it at a horse or a man and as long as you draw blood, your adversary will die immediately. The draw-back to the weapon is its very limited range.

Whether used by peasants defending their village against marauding hordes of horsemen in the Warring States period or in urban guerrilla warfare as late as the Boxer Rebellion (1899–1901), tiger-killing poison, most probably compounded from aconite, gave the *chu ko nu* a lethal advantage. Repeating crossbows without poison darts were popular for harvesting wildfowl. When a skilled stalker could get close enough to a raft of ducks, these speedy weapons could be used to shoot at multiple targets as they took flight.

In addition to the lightweight hand-held types, much larger versions of the *chu ko nu* also appeared during the Ming Dynasty. These featured immensely powerful composite laths, often requiring a two-man crew to operate them. Shot from the ramparts of fortresses or the gunwales of ships, the larger weapons had to be mounted

Two views of an original Chinese repeating crossbow from the salerooms of Mandarin Mansion. It dates to the early 20th century, but its design remains unchanged since the earliest incarnations in the 3rd century BC. The double bamboo bow has a draw-weight estimated at above 70lb. At the forward cycle of the lever, the notch in the magazine housing engaged the string. As soon as the string went behind the notch, it created sufficient clearance for gravity to cause one of the unfletched bolts in the magazine to drop onto the bolt channel. When the lever was pulled back, both string and magazine were brought to full draw. During this cycle the tail-end of the magazine travels up and over in an arc, pivoting on transverse pins through the lever handle. There is a small, free-moving, T-shaped peg that hangs through a hole in the magazine beneath the string notch. When the lever is brought back fully, the magazine makes contact with the stock and this peg automatically pushes the string up, releasing it from the notch. The bolt is shot and the lever moves forward in a continuous cycle to reload. In operation, the T-bar at the end of the stock rests against the hip, the left hand holds beneath the stock, and the right hand shuttles the lever. (Images courtesy of Peter Dekker at Mandarin Mansion: Antique Arms and Armor)

A multiple-bolt, single-bow, siege crossbow. Mounted on a shooting table, this version has an immensely long lath that appears to be of composite, recurve construction. Some varieties, from at least the 2nd century BC, had the capacity to shoot several bolts at once. Multiple-shot crossbows had a broad stock with the relevant number of parallel bolt grooves; usually seven. Fanning out from the centre, each one was a few inches shorter than its neighbour. One account from AD 950 describes a 'rapid dragon engine', whereby several multiple-bolt crossbows were linked together with one central release (Turnbull 2001: 14). (Japan Archive/Stephen Turnbull)

During the Song Dynasty (960–1279), both the double-lath (**RIGHT**) and the triple-lath crossbow (**FAR RIGHT**) made an appearance. All the laths are of stout, recurve, horn-and-sinew composite construction, with each acting upon the other by means of a continuous string that is secured at the end of the forward lath and then loops over the curled tips of the secondary (and tertiary) laths. A recent reconstruction by Lukas Novotny of a triple-bow version demonstrated that the system only works if the reversed bow is linked to the others by means of a pulley. Although no pulleys are shown in contemporary illustrations, Justin Ma has translated text adjacent to the image of such a bow in the *Wujing Zongyao* (an 11th century military manual) which makes reference to a pulley (private correspondence 2018). Locks were proportionately larger versions of the standard lock in cast bronze used for the standard Chinese crossbow and both are spanned by means of a bench-mounted windlass. These immensely powerful artillery pieces had no equivalent in the Western world, though they did migrate to parts of South-East Asia, where they were used, mounted on the backs of elephants! (Japan Archive/Stephen Turnbull)

onto some form of support. Woodblock images from the Imjin War between Japan and Korea (1592–98) show the great *chu ko nu* being deployed at sea to rake the decks of an enemy ship prior to a boarding action.

Similar to the European 'great-crossbow' (see below), the Chinese deployed an outsize weapon of immense proportions. A text from the early 4th century BC, concerning the warlord Mo Zi, refers to crossbows built on a four-wheeled framework, standing 8 feet high and requiring a crew of ten men (Turnbull 2001: 13). Supposedly, the missiles for this colossus were 10 feet in length, projecting 3 feet in front of the stock, and were attached to a line so that they could be retrieved. We might surmise that there is some exaggeration in this account, but there can be no doubt that very large crossbows existed.

GREEK CROSSBOWS

The crossbow of the Ancient Greeks was an ingenious weapon that incorporated a slider mechanism to draw back the string. It was known as the *gastraphetes* (belly-shooter) because the shooter leant partially into the device with his belly in order to push the slider back. Heron of Alexandria documented the first surviving explanation of how the *gastraphetes* worked in the 1st century AD, following the now-lost record of Ctesibus in the 3rd century BC. It is a detailed account, including a drawing, which allows for reasonably accurate modern reconstruction. No other visual record occurs in Greek art. Opinion is divided regarding the date of the *gastraphetes'* invention, though it may have been as early as the 5th century BC.

A modern replica of a *gastraphetes* made by Leo Todeschini. The bow has been fabricated from modern materials, but it conforms to the shape and proportions suggested by Heron of Alexandria's drawing. In use, the slider is brought forward until the claw at the front of the trigger block engages the string. The front end of the slider is then braced against the ground. Note the two bronze strips of ratchet teeth positioned either side of the tiller. Once a significant strain was engaged, pawls attached to the trigger block engaged with these teeth to hold the tension. Thereby the string could be pushed back in gradual, controlled increments. (Tod Todeschini of Tod's Worshop Ltd)

Like the Chinese crossbow, the *gastraphetes* employed a full-size composite bow, made in the same style as the hand-bow of the time. It had an exceptionally long draw-length. Maximum draw-weights can only be estimated, but an upper limit of around 120lb seems probable. Other Greek and Roman artillery – *ballistae* and the like – mimicked the slider with a pawl-and-ratchet system. Although *ballistae* are frequently likened to 'giant crossbows', it is incorrect to do so. They do not have bows but rather two separated and independent arms that are powered by twisted skeins of sinew; they operate with torsion power; a bow employs tension power.

ROMAN CROSSBOWS

To date, the only contemporary accounts of the *arcuballista* – the Roman crossbow – appear in the pages of *De re militaris*, written by Vegetius in the late 4th century AD. Drawing on a miscellany of earlier sources, Vegetius makes frustratingly vague references. He writes at one stage about crossbowmen lining up with other artillerymen (using torsion machines) in line of battle and at another about both *sagittarii* (regular archers) and *arcuballistarii* (crossbowmen) working together on siege towers to clear the ramparts of defenders. These are flickering glimpses, however; he gives little indication of the extent to which the *arcuballista* was used in warfare, or of the numbers of troops in a legion who might have been armed with it.

Fortunately, two Gallo-Roman carved reliefs in France, at Salignac and Saint-Marcel, offer tantalizing glimpses of the form. In both cases it is clear that the crossbow is being carried in a hunting context. Consistent in both carvings are three elements: a composite lath, a square stock and a distinctive shape to the butt. It is also apparent from the Salignac example that the draw-length is longer than that of later medieval crossbows. It shot a longer arrow and both carvings show a quiver suitable for longer arrows. In this regard it was similar both to Chinese and to Greek antecedents and different from medieval crossbows. In practical trials, the positioning of the trigger, the shape of the handgrip and the balance of the weapon suggested that it was shot from the hip. It was most natural to shoot it in roughly the same position as it was held for spanning, making it quick and ergonomic to use.

Employing a replica made by Leo Todeschini, Steve Senior of The Hoplite Association demonstrates how the *gastraphetes* is spanned by leaning into it and pushing the slider against the ground. Bows of military power may need to be braced against a more solid surface in order to avoid the slider embedding. The rocky terrain of the Eastern Mediterranean would have provided adequate resistance, however. (Steve Senior of The Hoplite Association UK)

Inset: Detail of the trigger block for a *gastraphetes*. Made from bronze, the block sits at the back end of the slider. Note that the claw has engaged the string and has been locked into place by a lever, which also acts as the trigger. Before the bow is spanned the pawls will be flipped to be forward-facing, so that they engage the ratchet teeth. (Steve Senior of The Hoplite Association UK)

An interpretation of the *arcuballista*, built by Leo Todeschini. The length of the composite lath is around 39 inches and the string can be drawn back around 16 inches to engage with the nut, allowing 22-inch arrows to be shot. Although difficult to discern in this photograph, there is a shallow bolt groove running along the top of the tiller. The shape of the trigger lever is speculative, but the return curl at the end aids one-handed operation, which could make such a weapon suitable for horsemen. A composite lath would be very light and the shape of the handle suggests the possibility of one-handed use. The length of the lever is determined by the closeness of the nut to the tail-end of the tiller. To hold the lath in place, wedges have been used instead of a cord bridle and the front of the tiller has been reinforced with two ash pegs because the stresses would otherwise be too great. (Tod Todeschini of Tod's Workshop Ltd)

The release mechanism is not clear on the carvings, but it looks as if it may be a rolling-nut, as found on later crossbows. In 1893, archaeologists digging at Southgrove Farm (Burbage, Wiltshire) unearthed a rolling-nut made from bone. From the context of the find site it was dated to the Roman period. The invention of the rolling-nut was a breakthrough that had an immense impact on the development of the crossbow.

No mechanical spanning device is shown in the sculptural evidence, suggesting a bow of relatively light draw-weight. In tests with a replica, Leo Todeschini used a bow with a 45lb draw-weight. He experimented by placing the rounded end of the tiller against his lower stomach and drawing the string back with both hands. He found this to be both comfortable and efficient. With the 45lb bow he shot the 22-inch arrows a distance of over 100yd. Such power may be adequate for hunting small game but of little military application. One idea, suggested by the dome at the base of the tiller, would be to have a thick, moulded-leather cup incorporated into a leather belt to aid spanning. Locating the dome into the cup would spread the load and prevent the tiller from slipping. With such a system, draw-weights in excess of 130lb may have been achievable.

The European medieval crossbow

THE LOCK

The challenge for a crossbow lock is to be able to overcome the friction generated by the taut string of a spanned bow pulling against it. The more powerful the bow, the greater the friction. Imagine a stout post embedded in the ground. A rope passes around the post and is held in tension at either end by two strong friends standing in front of the post and leaning back with all their might. Try to knock the rope up and off the post with your hand. Provided that your friends are strong enough, they should be able to generate sufficient friction against the post that you are unable to dislodge the rope. The ability to overcome these forces is determined by the design of the crossbow lock and trigger.

The vast majority of crossbows employed some form of rolling-nut as the release catch. These were mostly made of bone or antler, lightweight materials that spun with little inertia. Rolling-nuts sat in a precisely carved recess in the stock, known as a saddle. On release, the nut rotated freely within the saddle. When the string was engaged, the front of the nut pushed against the front of the saddle. A bone veneer lined the forward end of the saddle, strengthening it and reducing friction. There was no axle for the nut; tremendous forces were at work and a narrow axle would have bent. The centre hole did not provide the axis for spin, but rather facilitated a means for retaining the nut. In order to prevent the nut from jumping out at the moment of shooting or when being carried, a band of cords passed through the centre hole and bound around the outside of the tiller.

In the collections of the Metropolitan Museum of Art, New York are fragments of a rolling-nut that were excavated at Montfort Castle in Palestine and which date to before that castle's destruction in 1271. The nut was fashioned from staghorn and shows traces of iron reinforcement. There is considerable stress on the nut when the bow is spanned and some examples had a metal pin inserted into each finger of the claw to strengthen it. Most also had a plate of metal on the underside of the nut, where it engaged with the sear of the trigger.

Various, more complex, systems were developed during the 16th century and beyond for both target and hunting crossbows. These entailed a separate sear interacting between the trigger lever and the nut. Resetting them involved a short cord that hung outside the body of the tiller. Later, even more complex mechanisms made an appearance, some having two cords for setting multiple sears. Such intricate devices were not ideal for military service and are beyond the scope of this present work.

A series of images showing a replica of a rolling-nut made from antler by Leo Todeschini. The claw of the nut is bifurcated creating two 'fingers'. The gap between these allows the insertion of the bolt so that its tail-end sits flush against the string. On the underside of the nut is a little notch into which the sear of the trigger catches, preventing rotation until the trigger is released. Note the little iron plate at the point of maximum friction, protecting the antler from wear and providing a smooth, hard surface for the trigger-sear both to hold against and to disengage from. (Tod Todeschini of Tod's Workshop Ltd)

RIGHT Example of the 'rising peg' system. The drawn string hooked into a transverse slot in the stock of the crossbow and the trigger lever operated a wooden peg that pushed up from beneath the string to release it above the slot. A significant drawback is the limited ability of the rising peg to overcome powerful loads. It is therefore restricted to bows of relatively light draw-weight. Nevertheless, its simplicity and ease of manufacture made it a popular choice for poachers and for members of the mob at times of civil unrest. (David Joseph Wright)

FAR RIGHT The trigger for the early-medieval crossbow had the benefit of great simplicity. A Z-shaped lever engaged the nut directly. It pivoted on a pin, with the sear end considerably shorter than the longer lever end. The greater weight of the lever end tended to hold the sear end in place, but for added security a horn, and later steel, spring was added. (David Joseph Wright)

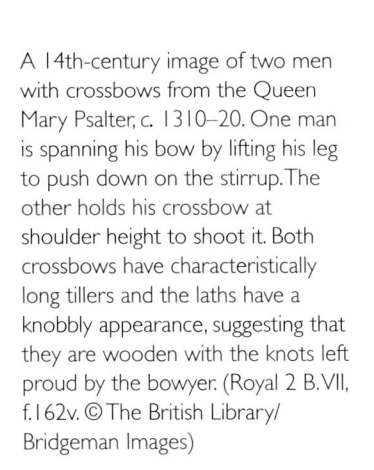

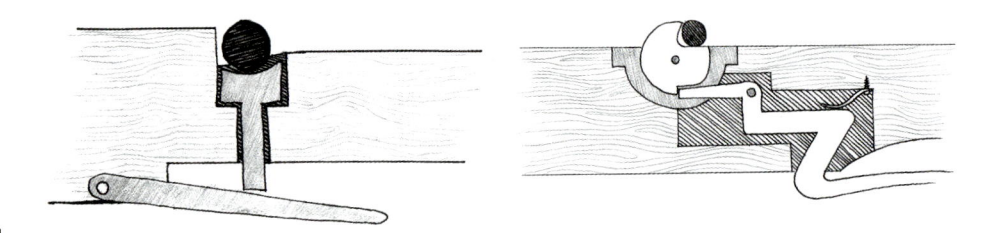

THE TILLER

In order to withstand the repeated strains of a powerful bow at full span, the tiller had to be tough. Single billets of wood were fashioned with gradual curves and robust proportions. Fruitwoods were popular choices, especially pear and cherry; hornbeam, hawthorn, walnut and maple also appear with regularity. As well as displaying attractive figure – that is the patterning on the finished surface – what these woods all have in common is the potential for interlocking grain. Interlocking grain occurs when spiral-grained trees alternate their annual direction of growth. It is highly resistant to splitting, obviously an advantage for a crossbow tiller, but it also makes the timber harder to work for the crossbow-maker. Most crossbows were also reinforced with an iron pin, set vertically through the front of the tiller.

The weapon historian Josef Alm quotes a reference in Burgundian accounts from 1384 to 'a complete crossbow in the Genoese fashion with iron bands' (Alm 1994: 25). He goes on to explain that these bands were for reinforcement of the stock on either side of the lock. Clearly, such buttressing suggests bows of enormous power. As a more decorative alternative to metal, the sides of the tiller, known as the cheeks, were often strengthened with plates of bone or antler.

While munition crossbows were mostly left plain, those made for wealthy patrons had highly decorated stocks. Full or partial veneers, using either cowhorn or staghorn, were common. Staghorn in particular lent itself to bold relief carving. Alternatively, either material could be used for elaborate inlay, often creating figurative scenes of great intricacy. Brass nails or brass bands might sometimes be added for additional opulent accent and colour was occasionally introduced with painted features. The crossbow could be both functional and a work of art. Even relatively unadorned specimens were given a veneer of polished bone or antler along the top of the tiller,

A 14th-century image of two men with crossbows from the Queen Mary Psalter, c. 1310–20. One man is spanning his bow by lifting his leg to push down on the stirrup. The other holds his crossbow at shoulder height to shoot it. Both crossbows have characteristically long tillers and the laths have a knobbly appearance, suggesting that they are wooden with the knots left proud by the bowyer. (Royal 2 B.VII, f.162v. © The British Library/Bridgeman Images)

where the string passed, so as to minimize friction. The lath was set into the tiller at an angle a little forward of 90 degrees to ensure the string did not abrade too much.

In the late-medieval period a notched ridge was fitted on top of the butt-end of some tillers. This enabled the shooter, whose fingers operated the trigger lever on the underside, to place his thumb in calibrated positions and to use his thumb knuckle as a sighting aid.

The length of tillers varied. To some extent this was determined by the spanning device. With a windlass, for instance, it was ergonomic for the centre of the winding handles to sit just above waist height, whereas with the cranequin the winding could be more easily managed with a shorter stock. Shorter stocks also offered easier portability and were especially convenient for the man on horseback.

WOODEN LATHS

Despite the fact that composite-bow technology was in use during the Roman era and that there is evidence for its continued employment in the West during the Viking era, and despite a proliferation of images (particularly in the Utrecht Psalter) showing the composite bow in use in Europe in the 9th century AD, early medieval European crossbows were fitted with wooden laths.

Writing between 1180 and 1190, Murḍā al-Tarsūsī, who dedicated a treatise on weapons to Saladin, stated, 'The crossbow … is fitted with a simple bow without horn or sinew … It should be of yew of the best kind that grows … After yew comes wild olive wood, of which there are two varieties, one imported from North Africa, the other from Yemen' (quoted in Paterson 1990: 35). Yew is not surprising and olive wood is interesting, but what is most striking about this statement is that it both acknowledges the existence of composite bows and also declares that they were not used for crossbows.

The engineering of the composite bow for crossbows involved an entirely different stacking arrangement of the materials than was the practice with regular hand-bows. At the time Murḍā al-Tarsūsī was writing, this was an advance that had not yet been developed. Until the very end of the 12th century and possibly not until the 13th century, all European crossbows had wooden laths.

Assessing proportions from art, combined with measurements from the few medieval wooden crossbow laths that have survived, indicates that 4 feet was a common size, though some seem to have been shorter. For any given length of limb there is a limit to the draw-weight attainable for a wooden bow. According to the bowyer Chris Boyton (private correspondence 2017), the maximum draw-weight for a wooden bow, with a span of 4 feet, would probably be around 200lb, and less for shorter bows. At this size a crossbow may be designated a 'great-crossbow' (see below) and so the 200lb estimation is at the extreme upper limit of the scale for a standard crossbow of maximum length. When considering these draw-weights it is important to bear in mind that, unlike a longbow where an archer drawing to the ear will have a draw-length of 30–31 inches, the crossbow has a power-stroke of only

A wooden bow for a crossbow found in 1931 during excavations at Berkhamsted Castle, England, and believed to date to the 13th century. It measures 49 inches. It is a powerful and hefty lath with a stout, deep 'D' section and may be considered to be the lath of a great-crossbow. For obvious reasons few wooden laths survive, but they continued in extensive use throughout the medieval period. (© The Trustees of the British Museum)

Here we see a man sitting to span his crossbow by placing his feet on the bow, in the manner described by Anna Komnene approximately 200 years earlier. The artist has not drawn in the tiller of the bow, either because the image was incomplete or because of technical challenges. There can be little doubt, however, that this represents a crossbow and a style of spanning it that endured, despite advances in other spanning technologies. The strain on his face is evident. He is shooting a style of blunt arrowhead that is widely depicted in this manuscript. It is useful both for hunting and for target practice at earth butts. See the first section of this book on the longbow for a wider analysis of these heads. (Add 42130 f.54r: border detail from the Luttrell Psalter, c.1325–35. (British Library, London Bridgeman Images)

In this image of Parisians stocking the city's arsenal, it seems clear that the laths are wooden. Most significantly we see that they carry bundles of spare laths. On the one hand this highlights a disadvantage of wooden laths – that they are prone to breakage – but it equally illustrates the advantage of wooden laths, which is that they can be produced economically en masse and are readily replaceable. (Royal 20 C VII f.132. British Library, London Bridgeman Images)

around 4–5 inches. Moreover, if we assume that the bow must be spanned several times a minute, repeatedly, for it to be effective on the battlefield, then perhaps a draw-weight of 150lb might be more typical for the average soldier. Spanning devices had yet to appear.

Anna Komnene tells us how the early crossbows were spanned: '[It] has to be stretched by lying almost on one's back; each foot is pressed against the half-circles of the bow and the two hands tug at the bow (string), pulling it with all one's strength towards the body' (Komnene 2009: 282). While a strong man could lean his back into perhaps 250lb with this technique, there remains the mechanical limitation of tillering a short wooden bow above a certain weight without the risk of it breaking.

Surviving wooden-bowed crossbows from the medieval period are extremely rare – those not used for firewood have rotted away – and this can give a misleading impression of their prevalence. They were used extensively throughout the period. Compared to composite bows, wooden bows were simple, quick and economic to manufacture, with readily available materials. They could be produced in considerable numbers and, for both battlefield and garrison troops, they were adequate for the task and required relatively little maintenance in the field. For these reasons, wooden-bowed crossbows remained in general use long after the introduction of composite bows. Guy Wilson (former Master of the Royal Armouries and an eminent crossbow scholar) offers the following summary from primary sources:

In 1418 the town of Blois had within its armoury crossbows with bows made of Portuguese yew. When the victorious Henry V of England had France at his mercy in 1421 and ordered an inventory to be taken of the arms available in Paris and elsewhere, among the many crossbows found were ten large windlass and ten smaller crossbows, all with bows made of Portuguese yew, as well as five large bows made of something called 'Flemish wood' that may have been Prussian yew. In 1436 22 large wooden crossbows were bought from a Spanish merchant for the Duke of Burgundy; and it was not until 1461 that the town of Tournai replaced its wooden crossbows with steel ones.

(Wilson 2007: 322)

In his survey of European crossbows, Josef Alm cites a Burgundian inventory from 1362 which lists 189 crossbows with composite bows and 382 crossbows with wooden bows (Alm 1994: 25). He goes on to refer to an order of 7,000 bow-staves of yew to be supplied to the Grand Master of the Teutonic Order for the making of crossbow laths in 1396 (Alm 1994: 27). Furthermore, Burgundian military accounts include crossbows with yew bows for the years 1433, 1437 and 1442 (Alm 1994: 34).

The wooden bow of this crossbow is believed to date to the 13th or 14th century. Both the tiller and the iron fittings are 19th-century substitutions and so no guide to age or style. Originally, the wooden bow would have been cradled in the fork of a tiller with a strip of leather and bound into place with cords. Also, the metal of the stirrup would not have attached with direct contact to the wooden bow. The bow itself is a magnificent example, however, and, like the Berkhamsted bow, the knots in the wood have been left proud on the back, producing a characteristically knobbly appearance. The bow measures 45.5 inches. (© CSG CIC Glasgow Museums and Libraries Collections, www.csgimages.org.uk)

The historian Sir Ralph Payne-Gallwey, in his 1903 magnum opus on the subject, records a translation from a mid-14th-century poem by David-ap-Gwilym, which commences with the following couplet: 'And thou crossbowman true and good / Thou shooter with the faultless wood' (Payne-Gallwey 1981: 6). It offers a suggestion of wooden-bowed crossbows by a contemporary witness. Another, more specific, 14th-century reference dates to 1346, the year of the battle of Crécy: 'Robert Arblaster and Simon Russell were ordered to cut down yew trees in the manor of Easthampstead to make cross-bows' (Cal Pat: 9). It is worth noting the etymological connection between the name Arblaster and the word for a crossbow-maker or crossbowman (arbalist). We also see that, at a time when there had been great demands on stocks of premium timber for Edward III's French adventure, home-grown yew was deemed perfectly suitable for crossbows. Nevertheless, as with longbows, Italian yew was especially desirable. Two Genoese merchants were issued a writ in September 1390 for dodging the customs tariffs on '35 tuns of malmsey and 288 staves for crossbows' they had taken to London for sale (CCR Rich II). No less in demand were Iberian supplies, as indicated in the following requisition for 400 yew staves to make crossbows in 1284:

> To Peter de la Mare, constable of Bristol castle. Order to cause to be provided four hundred staves (*baculos*) of Spanish yew to make cross-bows, four hundred nuts (*nuces*), four hundred keys, four hundred 'stirrups' (*stripodia*), a hundred baldricks (*baudreas*), twenty pieces of whalebone (*balena*), a thousand bow-strings (*nervis*), a hundred thousand quarrels for cross-bows for two feet, and a hundred thousand quarrels for cross-bows for one foot, and to cause them to be carried to Kaernarvan, there to be delivered to Master Richard de Abindon, the king's chamberlain there. (CCR Ed I 1284)

Baleen is a cartilage-like material that is made of keratin, a primary constituent of horn. Plates of baleen are situated in the mouths of various species of whale. Bristles attach to these plates to act as a filter when feeding. It is a stiff, strong and springy material. Although known popularly as whalebone, it is not bone. Baleen, from the whale's palate, was used for centuries to back bows in Inuit culture and I suspect that was its intended purpose here. Backing a wooden bow with parchment or similar material by attaching a strip to the back of the bow with a strong adhesive remains a common practice among traditional archers. It relieves the tension stresses on the back of the bow and prevents fibres from lifting, making it less likely to break and rendering it more efficient to shoot. With its inherent elastic properties, baleen would make a superior material for the task and probably also boost performance. It cannot be stated for certain that this is why baleen appears in a list of crossbow-making materials, but it is a possibility. If I am right, then it may be that the baleen was for backing all 400 staves, or it may have been reserved for patching old bows that were showing signs of weakness, thus keeping them going a little longer.

Either way, baleen-backed wooden bows may have been an intermediate technology between wooden bows and true composite bows made with horn. It is possible that baleen-backed bows were able to exceed the typical draw-weight of a simple wooden bow. As with the longbow, small pieces of horn were sometimes used to reinforce the nocks of the more powerful wooden-lathed crossbows.

Taybughā al-Ashrafī al-Baklamishī al-Yūnanī, author of *Kitāb ghunyat at-tullāb fī ma'rifat ramy an-nushshāb* (*Essential Archery for Beginners*) c.1500, noted that for naval operations the most useful type of crossbow is one with a lath made from yew. It is perhaps obvious that wooden bows would be less sensitive to the wet conditions of maritime warfare than a composite bow would be, but he adds interest to the observation by telling us that 'The limb of this weapon should be made of two opposing staves' (quoted in Latham & Paterson 1970: 8).

Wooden bows may also be made by laminating two staves together, either of different woods or the same, and this would seem to be the intended meaning here. Manuscript art sometimes shows differently coloured strata on a bow, which may be an indication of laminate construction. A laminated lath would be more robust, resilient to everyday knocks and bumps, than a true self-bow would be, and would be less prone to breakage. While laminate construction did not, of itself, produce greater power, its dependability might encourage confidence in risking higher draw-weights.

Both wooden bows and composite bows had a limit to how long they remained serviceable in storage, especially if they had seen prior use. Good maintenance was essential. Accounts from the privy wardrobe at the Tower of London in 1353 describe: '4 small crossbows with composite bows, worn out, 59 old and worn out wooden normal crossbows, 4 of which were broken' (Richardson 2016: 150). Here the use of the word 'normal' associated with wooden bows is intriguing. Does it suggest that crossbows with wooden laths represented the mainstream? Despite their commonality, wooden-lathed crossbows were not necessarily considered lower-status weapons because the same entry goes on to inform us that the Tower inventory included '86 new ones with wooden bows, one for the king's personal use' (Richardson 2016: 150).

An ordinance from Germany in 1382 specified a crossbow with 'a bow of yew' to be delivered to the Holy Roman Emperor for a hunting expedition (Alm 1994: 27). In 1553 William Rothwell, keeper of the privy wardrobe at the Tower of London, ordered 200 wooden bow-staves for crossbows at a cost of 26s 8d per hundred – that is 3¼d each. This was exactly the same price he paid for longbow staves. Once fashioned into working bows these same crossbow staves were valued at 6s 8d each. The cost compared favourably with that of composite bows, which the same account records at 20s each (Richardson 2016: 151). Improved technology carried a significant premium.

COMPOSITE AND HORN LATHS

Although more costly, composite-bow technology offered two distinct advantages over the wooden bow; shorter limbs and more power. With bow lengths ranging typically between 23 and 36 inches, composite bows were much less cumbersome than their wooden antecedents; easier to handle on both battlefield and rampart and far more discreet to manage on the hunting field. The materials and construction design enabled the manufacture of bows with draw-weights that could range from 200lb to 600lb. These greater weights demanded spanning mechanisms with mechanical advantage and these developed in tandem as the strength of bows increased.

The composite bow delivered its power with greater efficiency, so that even a 200lb composite bow was able to shoot a bolt with greater force than could the equivalent weight of wooden bow. A further benefit of the composite bow was that it was more reliable, less prone to shattering than either the wooden bow or the steel bow.

Methods of constructing composite bows for crossbows were wholly different from the way in which composite hand-bows were made (see Loades 2016: 22–26). The breakthrough came in redesigning the composite structure from a simple linear lamination of materials (as was the case with hand-bows) to assembling a complex matrix, which concentrated the power into a shorter, stockier limb and magnified it by having multiple strata of horn. This innovation appears at some point at the end of the 12th or beginning of the 13th centuries, most probably originating in the Middle East, more than 2,500 years after the appearance of hand-bows made with

TOP Section of a composite lath from a 15th-century crossbow. Note that this specimen has no wooden core. It has two rows of cattle horn, the strips mixed in both size and pigmentation, and wedge-shaped strips of horn at the outer edges in place of the more usual wooden support. The whole is wrapped in sinew, built up into many layers on the back of the bow. (Kim Hawkins)

BOTTOM Section of a composite lath from a 15th-century Swiss or German crossbow. The catalogue listing identifies the components as baleen, horn and tendon (sinew) with an outer covering of birch bark. The species of wood at the core has not been identified, but is probably beech. Note the precision-grooved surfaces of both the horn and the wooden billets. These create interlocking toothed parts which give a secure foundation for an adhesive bond and which resist slipping. (Metropolitan Museum of Art, www.metmuseum.org)

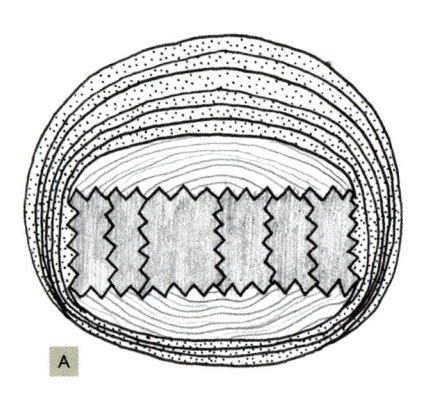

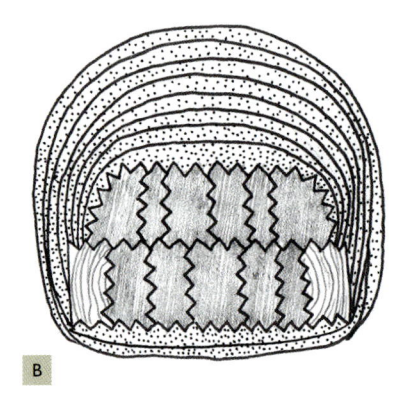

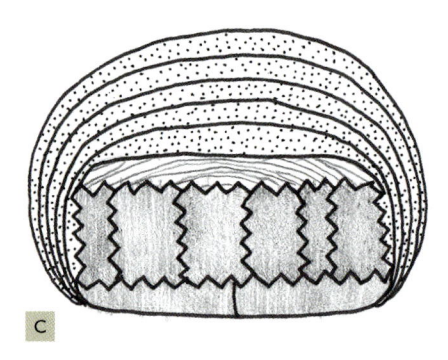

Three variations on the internal construction of a composite lath. One (**A**) has a single layer of horn strips as the core, held in place above and below by wooden billets. The whole is wrapped in sinew. The second example (**B**) has two layers of horn strips, steadied only on the lower row by wooden strips at the sides. It too is covered in multiple layers of sinew. The third example (**C**) is a plan for the cross-section of the Novotny bow (below). It has a central wooden core – beech – identified by wood-grain-style lines; layers of sinew, indicated by the dotted section; and both vertical and horizontal strips of horn, the shaded section. (David Joseph Wright)

wood, horn and sinew. To all intents and purposes the composite bow for the crossbow was an entirely new invention. Surviving specimens (already in a broken state) in both public and private collections have been sawn to produce clean cross-section views, revealing that a wide variety of construction schemes were employed.

Horn was the key material; it was the source of most of the power, and contemporary references referred to these bows as horn-bows. While water-buffalo horn was most prized for the composite hand-bow, composite bows for the European crossbow were more usually built with either cattle or goat horn, materials that were more readily available. Ibex horn was especially favoured.

Bundles of different-sized horn strips were stacked in two layers with each strip fused to its neighbour on both abutting planes. Prior to assembly each length of horn was prepared by using a toothed scraper to cut precision parallel grooves on its surfaces. Bonded together with powerful hide-glue, each piece interlocked with its fellow. The grooves not only offered a larger surface for adhesion but also counteracted the potential for slipping.

Baleen also featured in some composite bows. Three pieces of baleen were itemized in a comprehensive list of components for the making of 40 composite laths for crossbows in 1345, commissioned by the Tower Armoury (Richardson 2016: 147). It is difficult to determine the extent to which baleen was used in bow manufacture because, in its desiccated form, it has the appearance of dried sinew. Equally hard to discern are its mechanical advantages. Baleen had neither the springiness of horn nor the tensile strength of sinew.

The horn nucleus was encased in layers of sinew, with many extra layers built up on the back of the bow. It was the horn, naturally resistant to compression, which generated the most stored energy when the bow was bent. It was the sinew that held everything together, however. Made from dried animal tendons, soaked in fish-glue, the sinew also contributed an amount of elastic energy to this complex spring.

A third component was wood, but the extent to which it was employed varied from substantial to barely present. There were several different arrangements for the placing of the wood within the matrix, ranging from a robust wooden core to thin strips either side of the horn centre. In some bows, a wooden strip ran either above or below the

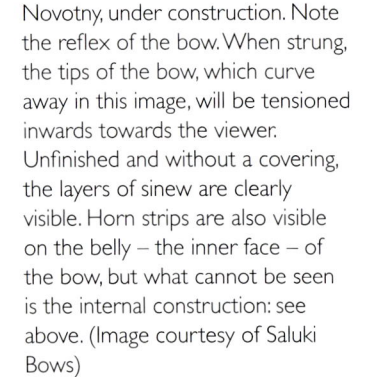

Composite-bow lath, built by Lukas Novotny, under construction. Note the reflex of the bow. When strung, the tips of the bow, which curve away in this image, will be tensioned inwards towards the viewer. Unfinished and without a covering, the layers of sinew are clearly visible. Horn strips are also visible on the belly – the inner face – of the bow, but what cannot be seen is the internal construction: see above. (Image courtesy of Saluki Bows)

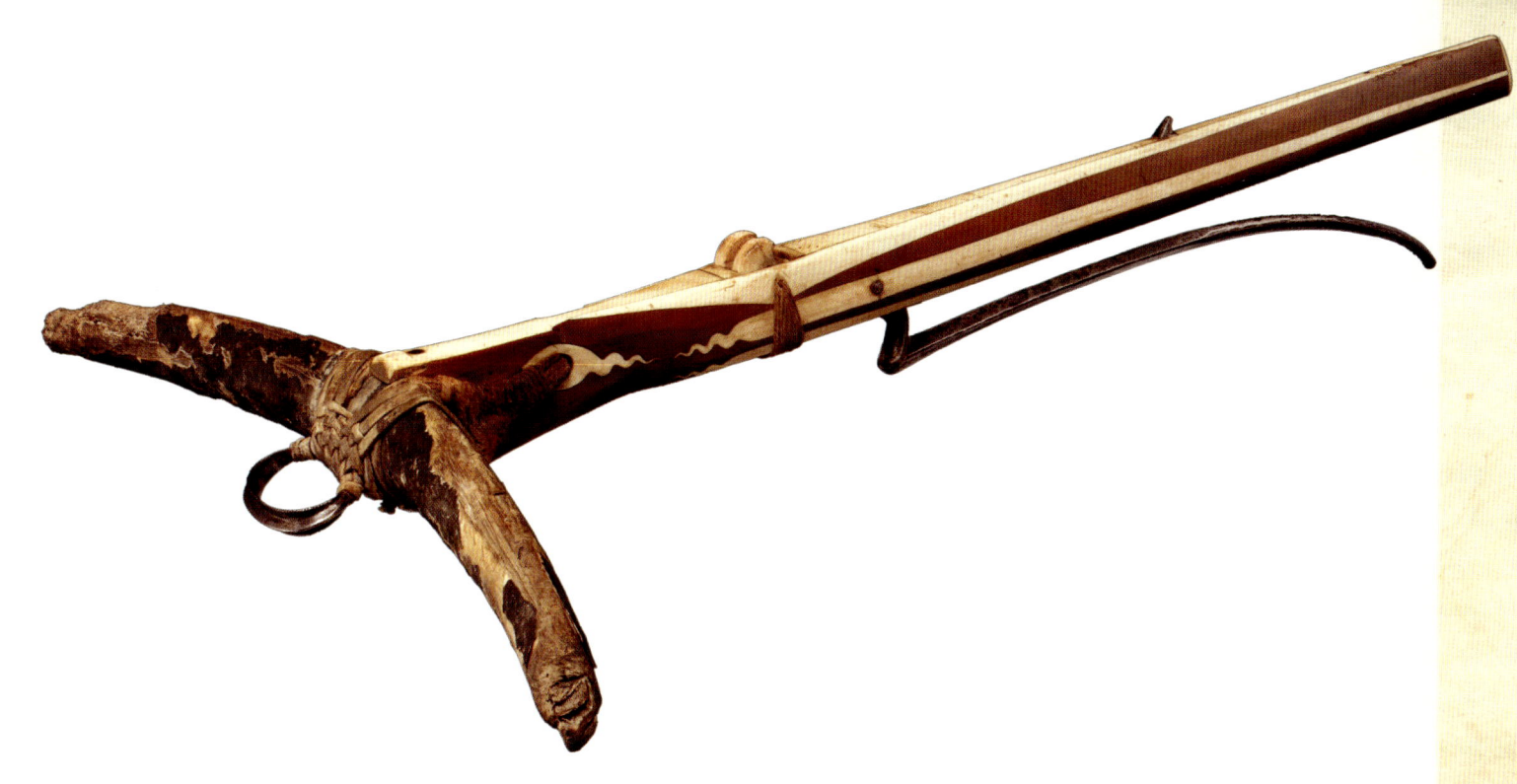

This unstrung composite bow, possibly Austrian c.1425–75, shows a large degree of reflex with the limbs at rest. Imagining such stout springs drawn back to the strung position, let alone to full draw, conjures up a sense of this bow's considerable power. Length 37.6 inches; width 29.8 inches; weight 8lb 12oz. In this case the bow has traces of birch bark as its outer layer. Covering materials varied widely and also offered a range of decorative options. They were usually applied in two layers; for instance, a layer of leather topped with an outer skin of parchment. Parchment, vellum, paper, linen, leather and bark were all used as wrappings and all presented a canvas that invited painted embellishment. Parchment, the most common material for the outer layer, was often decorated to simulate snakeskin. Actual snakeskin was also fashionable, viper skin being especially popular. Another commonly used material, particularly in England, was dogfish skin. Whatever the outer layer of the bow, it remained prudent always to carry it with an additional waterproof cover. Crossbows with composite bows continued to find favour on the hunting field long after the development of high-powered steel laths. European nobility are depicted using them throughout both the 15th and 16th centuries, particularly in Northern Europe where the cold weather of the hunting season could cause steel crossbows to shatter – an alarming prospect! (Bashford Dean Memorial Collection, Metropolitan Museum of Art, www.metmuseum.org)

horn. Compared to the greater forces of horn and sinew, this wooden component probably didn't add anything to the elasticity of the bow. It was there to counteract the potential for the horn cluster to shift or twist. During the manufacturing process it could provide a skeleton on which to build the muscles of horn and the tendons of the sinew, lining everything up while the slow-curing glues set. It offered stability.

Traditional bow-woods such as yew or elm were useful, but the most common timber seems to have been beech. Beech responds extremely well to steaming, which may have a particular advantage for the crossbow lath. To augment the power of composite materials, some bows were made with a prominent reflex, that is to say, the limbs curved away from the shooter in the bow's unstrung state. Steam-bent lengths of wood may have been especially useful in establishing the geometry of a reflex bow. Even so, there is evidence that reflex laths were sometimes made without the stability of a wooden framework. All horns have a natural curve and certainly the long sweeping curve of ibex horn seems especially suited to creating reflex laths, requiring only a modicum of steaming to coax their arcs into symmetrical bends.

Damp conditions had the potential to be deleterious to the glues that were the essential bond between the laminations of a composite structure. In order to protect them from the weather, composite bows were covered and sealed with a varnish.

A 15th-century crossbow with a steel lath (A1032) in the Wallace Collection, London. The lath has been blackened, then covered with gilded parchment and painted with red floral motifs. It is held in the tiller by a bridle of hemp cord. By the late 15th century it became increasingly common to mount steel laths in their tillers with metal bow irons. At the fore-end, a gilt-iron hanging ring has been attached with interlaced leather strapping. The entire tiller has been veneered with panels of polished antler, adorned with spectacular figurative relief carvings. These have been enlivened with a girdle of painted coats-of-arms, whose colourful display stands out against the almost white background of the carved panels. The additional weight of steel-lathed crossbows compared unfavourably to the composite bow; one of a number of reasons why high-status hunters continued to prefer the lightweight, portable elegance of the older technology. Moreover, the heavier the lath, the greater the amount of the bow's potential energy required to move it. Therefore, steel bows had to be of proportionally higher draw-weights than their composite or wooden counterparts in order to counter this inertia. However, the capacity for steel laths with exceptionally high power to be produced meant that they could outperform this minor limitation by a considerable margin. (The Wallace Collection, London/Bridgeman Images)

STEEL LATHS

The earliest mention of a steel crossbow lath appears in 1316, listed in an inventory of goods stolen from Mathilda of Brabant (1268–1329); it was gilded (Breiding 2013: 30). Most probably it was a low-powered prototype with a certain novelty value. Manufacturing a shootable steel lath of low poundage was one thing, but forging one with colossal power was quite another. Experiments with steel bows continued throughout the 14th century, but it was only when they began to exceed the draw-weights possible with composite bows that they began to usurp the military dominance of the older style. Eventually, by the end of the 14th century, it became possible to fabricate steel laths of staggeringly high draw-weights. Slightly in excess of 1,500lb was possible for the larger bows, though most would have been less than this. Even so, at 750lb steel bows offered a significant improvement to the maximum 600lb possible with a composite bow (most were less).

By the end of the first quarter of the 15th century, steel became a more common material for crossbow laths. The durability of steel compared to wood or horn has meant that museum collections have a disproportionate number of surviving specimens. However, the truth is that wooden or composite bows were never entirely replaced by steel laths, at least not until the 17th century, when they became ubiquitous for both hunting and target crossbows.

DETERRING RUST

Rust was to be greatly feared with a steel lath; any weakness and the bow could break under strain. Given the high draw-weights of steel bows, such a breakage would have been a violent event. Consequently, various measures were employed to deter rust. One simple measure was to paint the lath, but more advanced techniques involved blackening the steel by heat treatment. As with composite bows, steel laths were also covered with leather or other material, though this ran the risk of rust developing undetected. All crossbows could be given extra protection for travelling by slipping them into a waterproof case made from waxed leather or canvas. This covered either the entire crossbow or, often, just the strung lath. In 1239 the Constable of Chester paid 5s for canvas to cover the king's crossbows (Blackmore 1971: 181).

A curiosity of surviving steel laths is that they are sometimes adorned with small silk pom-poms. These cluster around the bridle and sometimes also appear on each extremity of the bow-limbs as well as on the trigger lever. Surviving examples can be seen on many hunting crossbows in museums. The hunting context is perhaps a clue. It may be that these pom-poms were a form of camouflage, breaking up the lines of the crossbow's silhouette. It is also a possibility that they acted in the manner of buckskin fringing, wicking and guttering rain away so that it didn't pool and precipitate rust, especially where it could not be seen under the bridle.

Replica 15th-century crossbow by Leo Todeschini. Note that the steel lath has been fitted with safety cords. Steel bows were often covered with leather or other material, not only to protect against rust but also to minimize the risk of flying steel splinters if the bow shattered. Steel bows were prone to fracture with or without rust. An alternative method of containing these airborne shards was to bind the lath with safety cords. A braided cord was glued to the front of the bow and this was held securely in place with a series of whip bindings at intervals of several inches. (Tod Todeschini of Tod's Workshop Ltd)

Significant advances in the production of iron and steel occurred during the 14th century, not only prompting major improvements in the quality of armour but also unleashing the potential of steel to make a powerful spring. A greater understanding of heat treatment, judging the colour of steel in the forge before quenching at exactly the right moment, enabled smiths to manipulate molecular structures with enormous sophistication. For crossbow laths, historical blacksmith Hector Cole recommends a uniform orange heat and quenching in brine or vegetable oil before flash-tempering in the fire (private correspondence 2017).

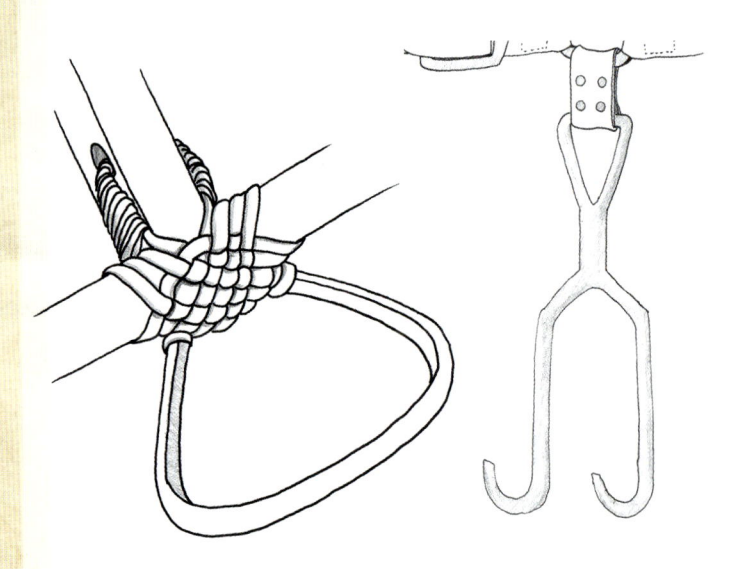

ABOVE The stirrup was usually lashed to the front of the tiller using an elaborate interlace of leather strapping. This contrasted with the hemp cords that were used for the bridle holding the lath in place. (David Joseph Wright)

ABOVE RIGHT Belt-and-claw. This example shows a twin hook to the claw. An advantage of the twin hook was that the fork of the claws could locate on the tiller to ensure that it was placed centrally on the string. In use, the belt-and-claw enabled the crossbowman to ready his bow from a fully standing position and to substitute the power of his arms for that of his leg and, to some extent, his back, thereby using stronger muscles that would make the work less fatiguing. (David Joseph Wright)

Also during the 14th century it became possible to produce cleaner steels with higher carbon contents. Clean steels contain a minimum of slag inclusions, that is, the porridge of silica and elemental impurities that are part of the mix when blooms of iron are smelted from the ore in the first stages of steel production. If left present, these impurities create weak spots where the steel would fracture under stress. The art of the smith in forging a lath for a crossbow was to create a piece of metal that was tempered to possess both strength and elasticity and also to be as homogeneous as possible. Furthermore, shaping the lath to have a profile that tapered towards the tips, with symmetrical precision on both limbs, ensured an even distribution of strain throughout the bow when in use.

Although it took considerable skill to forge a steel lath, it was a far quicker process than manufacturing a composite prod, which required not only rare skills but also months of drying times for the all-important glues at various stages of construction. Steel laths could be hammered out in a matter of a few hours and were bow ready as soon as they had cooled from the final temper. They were made from a single, readily available, recyclable material. When produced on a large scale, steel laths were far less costly than composite bows.

Flanders was a traditional centre for crossbow manufacture throughout the Middle Ages and beyond. Among the many entries for 'crossbow thread' (which was presumably hemp cord for crossbow strings and bridles) shown on bills of lading from 16th-century Antwerp is a listing for '100 lbs of crossbow laths' (LPB). Trading by weight only makes sense with regard to steel laths. Cost presumably related to the amount of metal being sold rather than the quantity of laths – heavier draw-weight bows would have required thicker laths. One assumes that laths were of fairly uniform quality, unless they were blanks and yet to be tempered.

Gilles le Bouvier, a French chronicler, did not trust steel bows in the cold and, in 1455, extolled the virtues of the composite bow for snowier climes: 'These people [Bavarians] are good crossbowmen on horseback and on foot, and shoot with crossbows of horn and sinew, which are good and strong and do not break when they are frozen, for the colder it is the stronger they are' (quoted in Payne-Gallwey 1981: 64). Steel-lathed crossbows never replaced either wooden or composite laths entirely, but they did become the most universal type during the final half-century of that weapon's useful military service – a period when they competed with the fire and fury of gunpowder weapons.

Spanning aids

THE STIRRUP

As noted previously, early crossbows were spanned by sitting and placing both feet on the bow. A solution to this sedentary inconvenience was the introduction of the stirrup at some point in the 12th century, which allowed the shooter to remain standing while performing the same procedure. In the West, the stirrup was fashioned from iron, but both Mamluk crossbows and some Chinese crossbows were fitted with stirrups made from cord.

German sources in the 14th century distinguish between the stirrup crossbow (*Steigreifarmbrust*) and the 'back' crossbow (*Ruckarmbrust*): 'In 1307 and 1308, ten back crossbows (*balistas dorsales*) and ten foot-loop crossbows were purchased for the city of Hamburg' (Alm 1994: 26). One speculative explanation for the difference is that, when hand-spanning, the stirrup/foot-loop crossbow was bent by using one's arms to pull back the string and that it was only when equipped with a belt-and-claw that the arbalist really put his back into it. Another possibility is that the back-crossbow was spanned by sitting and placing both feet on the bow. It seems certain that this practice continued beyond the introduction of the stirrup, as the fellow in the margins of the Luttrell Psalter (page 102) confirms.

Neither the goat's foot lever nor the cranequin required the assistance of a stirrup, and bows intended for use with these devices were equipped with a hanging-ring instead of a stirrup. Crossbows were stored, whether in castle guardrooms or great state arsenals, by hanging them by either the stirrup or the hanging-ring.

THE BELT-AND-CLAW SYSTEM

Consisting of an iron hook attached to an adjustable strip of leather that hung vertically from a waist-belt, the belt-and-claw system is first mentioned in the work of Murḍā al-Tarsūsī *c.*1180. In English medieval accounts it was referred to as a baldric. The baldric was the simplest of spanning aids and its use continued for military crossbows until the very end of the 15th century, despite the introduction of other, more powerful contraptions. Not only was the belt-and-claw easy and relatively quick to operate, it was significantly less expensive to produce.

There was a limitation to the draw-weight the belt-and-claw could assist. I suspect that most bows used with this system were around 150lb draw-weight, though 200lb might have been possible for strong men. An important factor would be how long the crossbowmen were expected to maintain a constant work rate. For most munition-grade crossbows, the belt-and-claw remained the standard system throughout the medieval period.

BELOW LEFT A replica of a single-hook belt-and-claw system made by Leo Todeschini. It required particular attention to ensure that it was placed precisely in the centre of the string, but single hooks were nevertheless in widespread use. (Tod Todeschini of Tod's Workshop Ltd)

BELOW This glum monk demonstrates one of the two spanning methods used with the belt-and-claw system. First the bow was lifted and the string hooked onto the claw, then the arbalist raised one foot, placed it in the stirrup and pushed down to retract the string until it engaged with the nut. This technique, with a raised foot pushing down, is observable in numerous contemporary representations. Seemingly, the medieval arbalist required the assured stability of a flamingo. However, other examples in art show less agile crossbowmen with the stirrup planted firmly on the ground. They are bending over and lifting with their arms and back. (Add 42130 f.56r: border detail from the Luttrell Psalter, *c.*1325–35. British Library, London Bridgeman Images)

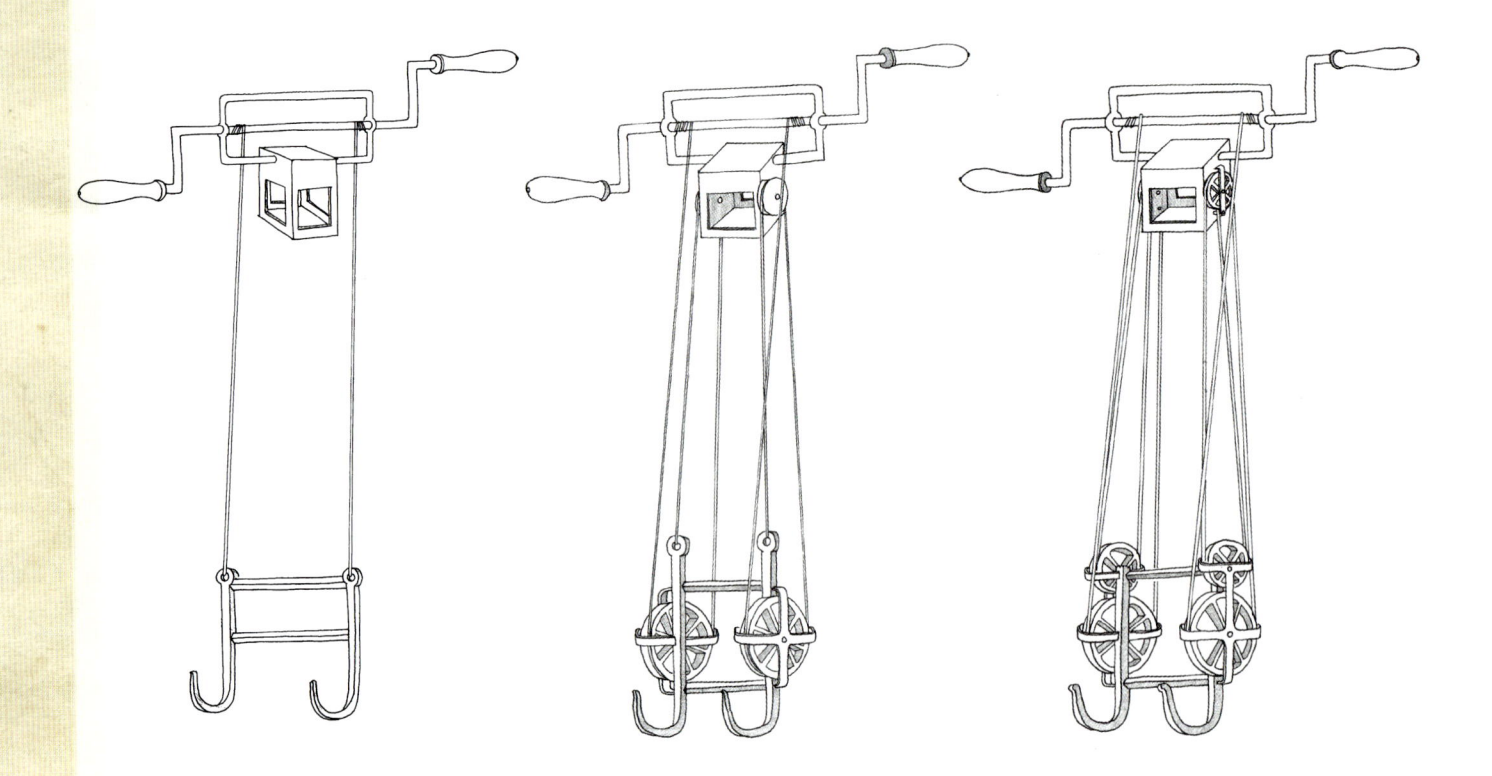

At left is a simple windlass that delivers a power advantage of approximately 10:1. The windlass in the centre is augmented by a single pulley block, delivering a power advantage of roughly 30:1. The windlass on the right has an additional pulley block, which generates a massive power advantage of around 45:1. (David Joseph Wright)

THE WINDLASS

The windlass, or winch, was the heavy-lifting workhorse of medieval artillery and it manifested in a number of forms. With the advent of composite laths, higher draw-weights became possible. It was the windlass that enabled the development of these more powerful weapons and for that to continue into the next generation of high-powered steel laths.

First appearing at some point in the 13th century, the early windlass was a simple capstan without pulleys. A box-like metal cap fitted to the butt of the tiller. Attached to this cap was a frame, housing the capstan and the winding handles. Cords extended to the hooking tackle. In operation the arbalist steadied the bow on the ground by means of the stirrup and wound the handles. Once the bow was spanned he had to reverse the winding by a few turns to create enough slack to disengage the hooks.

Once it became possible to make bows of extreme power, after the development of steel bows, the primary form of the windlass was boosted with additional pulleys. The more pulleys, the greater the length of cord and the greater the potential for entanglements when this winding gear was laid on the ground between loading procedures. The windlass crossbowman had to be both methodical and adept at handling his tackle. There was a knack to it and modern tests have shown that a reasonably practised person can manage to load and shoot a bolt in a fraction above 30 seconds. Rather than saying two bolts a minute, it might be safer to suggest eight bolts in five minutes for the most powerful crossbows.

In order to situate the winding gear at an ergonomic height for the arbalist, windlass crossbows had longer tillers. This, together with the windlass itself, made them bulky and awkward, far more suited to the static conditions of a siege than to the battlefield. Although superseded by the more sophisticated and far more powerful cranequin, the windlass crossbow continued to see service. A 1523 inventory of the goods of Lord Mounteagle included two windlasses for crossbows (LPFD Hen VIII 3).

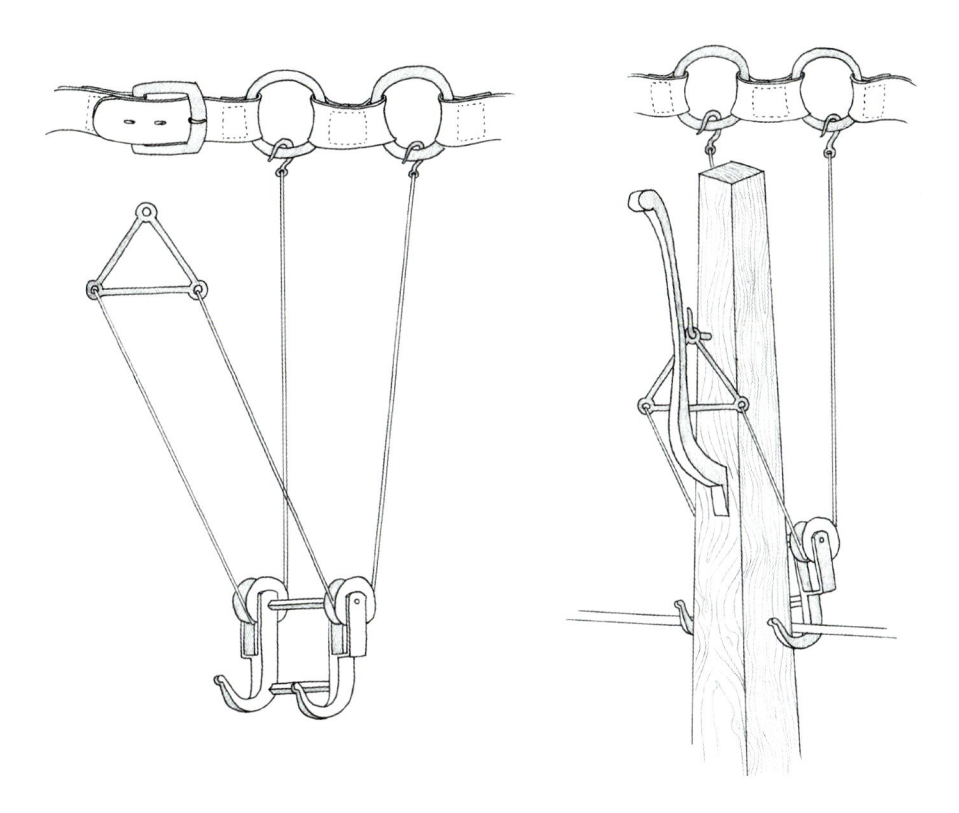

The cord-and-pulley. These drawings show a twin-hooked pulley block. Some examples had just a single pulley with a single hook. One end of the cord was attached to a waist-belt and the other had a ring, which slipped onto a hook fixed to the underside of the crossbow's tiller. Running along the cord was the pulley fitted with the hook(s). By bending his knees, the arbalist was able to lower himself a little to engage the string with the pulley-hook(s). Straightening his legs by standing up spanned the bow, with the pulley delivering a 2:1 power advantage. (David Joseph Wright)

THE CORD-AND-PULLEY SYSTEM

A simpler, and much quicker, device, which also offered the mechanical advantage of a pulley, was the cord-and-pulley system, which came into use in the early 15th century, possibly a decade or so earlier. Although it looks to be the probable antecedent of the windlass, current evidence suggests that it appeared later.

By the measure of other devices such as the windlass or the cranequin, the cord-and-pulley system did not offer a huge power advantage. Even so, at a ratio of 2:1 it did enable a man to use a 300lb bow with relative ease and frequency. Slower than the belt-and-claw but quicker than other mechanical systems, it was a useful, inexpensive and lightweight apparatus suitable for medium-weight bows. According to Alm, the 'Sampson belt', as he calls it, was particularly popular in Sweden during the 15th century (Alm 1994: 41).

Crossbows spanned in this manner are depicted in *The Martyrdom of Saint Sebastian* by Antonio del Pollaiuolo, c.1432–98 (National Gallery, London) and it is clear that their bows are not fitted with stirrups. With one hand on the end of the tiller, they steady their weapons by stepping over the bow with one foot, cradling the lath between the heel of the forward leg and the shin of the rear leg. In this instance they are using a single cord with a single pulley and hook.

THE GAFFLE

Bending levers, known originally as gaffles, took various forms, both fixed and hinged. The alternative nomenclature – goat's foot lever – derived its name from the curve of the lever arms that resembled the hind legs of a goat. With a mechanical advantage of 5:1, these benders were powerful tools that were also quick to use. Modern experiments conducted by Leo Todeschini have demonstrated that it is possible to shoot five bolts a minute using this device on a crossbow of 300lb draw-weight.

Gaffles do not seem to be represented in art before the middle of the 14th century but are well known thereafter, remaining in use throughout the 15th century,

Gaffle or goat's foot lever, late 15th or early 16th century. The surfaces of each lever are decorated with simple punched designs. There is also decorative file work on the bridge and the grapple. Note the hook attachment for carrying it on a belt. When the device is folded, the suspension hook swivels 90 degrees both to secure the ends of the twin levers and to orientate the carrying hook for its purpose. Length extended: 19.6 inches; width 2.8 inches; weight 25oz. The claw hooked over the string and the terminals of the curved fork braced against stout pins that protruded either side of the crossbow tiller. When the hinged lever arm was pulled towards the butt of the stock, the fork acted against the pins, applying the leverage required to draw back the string. The gaffle delivered a mechanical advantage of around 5:1. (Metropolitan Museum of Art, www.metmuseum.org)

especially for hunting bows and for mounted crossbowmen. Despite their efficiency, gaffles were not employed extensively on the battlefield during the 14th century; the less-expensive belt-and-claw system continued to dominate. Gaffles did, however, gain favour in defending fortifications, offering greater speed than the windlass and greater mechanical assistance than the belt-and-claw.

A variation, which enabled the arbalist to exert greater force, featured a curved 'T' at the terminus of the lever. This was braced against the crossbowman's thigh, allowing him to grasp the tiller of his bow with both hands and pull using his back and arms. Examples are rare, though there is one in the Berne Historical Museum. Instances of its use can be seen in Italian art, for which reason it is sometimes known as the Italian type.

THE CRANEQUIN

According to W. F. Paterson, the earliest record of a cranequin is in 1373 (Paterson 1990: 51) and its use reaches a peak during the 15th and 16th centuries. Utilizing gear wheels cut with engineering precision, the cranequin was the most powerful of all crossbow-spanning devices. It was also the most sophisticated and expensive. It had other names, the rack or the cric, and there were regional variations. The 'German winder' had teeth cut into the side of the ratchet bar with the gearbox mounted on top, so that the handle turned parallel to the lath of the crossbow, whereas the 'French winder' or 'Spanish winder' was mounted in such a way that the handle turned at right angles to the lath, parallel to the tiller.

When a cranequin in the collections of the Metropolitan Museum of Art, New York was tested on a crossbow of 1,090lb, it required only 7.5lb force applied to the handle in order to draw the bow – a mechanical advantage of 145:1 (Paterson 1990: 52).

A fine example of a high-status cranequin. Both the gear casing and the ratchet bar have been etched and gilded. Note the hook for carrying the device on a belt. Cranequins enjoyed particular prestige, not only because they gave unrivalled mechanical advantage but also because they represented state-of-the-art precision engineering. The cranequin consisted of a geared winding block that travelled along a toothed ratchet bar. A claw to engage the string was located at one end of the ratchet bar and a thick cord bridle was attached to the winding block. This bridle slipped over the end of the tiller to be arrested by protruding pins on either side; thus as the mechanism was wound it moved the ratchet bar to retract the string. (The Wallace Collection, London/Bridgeman Images)

The complex gearing on individual cranequins varied considerably, but it seems probable that 145:1 is at the upper end of what was achievable.

Despite its clear advantages, the cranequin was relatively slow to use and somewhat heavy to carry around. It was even rather noisy, though this did not reduce its popularity among high-status hunters. Of course, if you were of sufficiently high status, you had someone else to do the winding for you.

Not only did the cranequin carry the prestige of great expense and the cachet of cutting-edge technology, its large metal surfaces lent themselves to elaborate artistic embellishment. Many cranequins were exquisite works of art, featuring pierced, punched, chiselled, filed, etched and gilded decoration. More utilitarian examples existed for use by regular troops. Nevertheless, it is generally true to say that the cranequin came into existence at a time when the crossbow's military usefulness was already in decline. Cranequins were to be seen more often in the hunting field or at the shooting ground than on the battlefield.

THE SCREW

Though depictions are rare in medieval art, the screw or 'vice' is mentioned frequently in 14th-century documents. Below is a selection of entries extracted from the records of the privy wardrobe at the Tower of London:

> 4 one-foot composite crossbows and one of wood with screw mechanism (1330)
> 2 old screw winders for the crossbows (1330)
> 32 crossbows in another batch, two of them screw crossbows (1340)
> 14 composite bows with screws (1353)
> 12 screw crossbows (1553)
> 3 screw winders for crossbows (1360)
> seven screw crossbows and of these three large (1360)
> 7 screw crossbows and 3 additional screws for crossbows (1364)
> 1 great composite screw crossbow with a length of 6 feet (1375) (Richardson 2016: 144–153)

From these listings it appears that the screw mechanism was used as a device for crossbows of a standard size as well as for great-crossbows. From its frequent appearance in inventories, it would seem that the screw was in greater use than is portrayed in art.

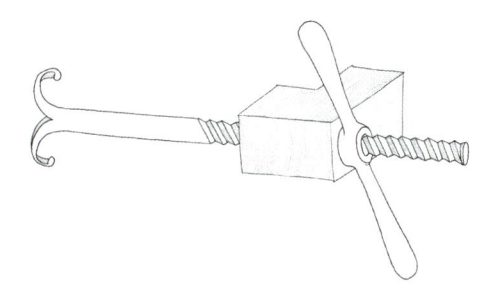

Known as the vice in medieval documents, the screw could be either a detachable mechanism (as illustrated here) or incorporated into the bow itself. A housing fitted over the end of the tiller. Through this passed a threaded rod, which had a claw at one end to catch over the bowstring and a handwheel at the other end. As the handwheel was turned, engaging the thread of the screw within the housing, the rod retracted, drawing back the string. Once the string was located behind the nut, the handwheel was spun in the opposite direction, allowing the claw and rod to be removed. (David Joseph Wright)

The amount of mechanical advantage offered by the screw mechanism depended on the pitch of the thread. This would have varied and, without surviving examples, is difficult to determine. Presumably it was of adequate assistance, albeit fairly slow. Where inventories list 'screw winders' it is hard to know if this is an alternative descriptor for the entire screw mechanism or whether they are referring to the handwheels as separate elements. Certainly the length of the arms on these handwheels would be a factor in creating mechanical advantage, particularly on versions for the great-crossbow, where the longer arms, usually four, acted as significant levers.

Other types of crossbow

THE GREAT-CROSSBOW

Great-crossbows were outsize versions of the standard crossbow. Jean Liebel, who to date has written the only work dedicated to the subject, tracks their genesis to the early 11th century (Liebel 1998: 25). Great-crossbows continued in universal use

One of two great-crossbows depicted in Walter de Milemete's manual of military instruction, *De nobilitatibus, sapientiis, et prudentiis regum*, created for the young Edward III in 1326. This version sits on a tensioning table and is operated by a large windlass, manned by two men. The other version was spanned by means of a vice. With the bow at full draw, one man offers the protection of his shield to the shooter. Note the knobbly appearance of the bow, indicating that it is a wooden lath. Despite its evident power, the limitation of the great-crossbow is illustrated here by the adjacent image of a standard crossbow. This exhibits both its greater versatility in being able to shoot down at extreme angles and its convenient portability. (MS 92, fol. 70v. Image courtesy of the Governing Body of Christ Church, Oxford)

SPANNING, c.1400 (OPPOSITE)

By 1400 a range of mechanical spanning devices was available, allowing bows of greater power to be developed. The windlass (top left) first appeared as early as the 13th century. The number of pulleys varied. This one, with a single set of wheels, generated a power advantage of 30:1. Here it is being used to span a composite lath of around 600lb draw-weight. The cord-and-pulley (top right) was a much later development than the windlass, only appearing at the beginning of the 15th century. It offered a power advantage of 2:1. Here it is being used to span a composite lath of around 200lb draw-weight. The gaffle, or goat's foot lever (lower left), was known from the mid-14th century, but did not occur frequently until the 15th century. It gave a power advantage of 5:1. Here it is being used to span a composite-lath of 300lb draw-weight. The cranequin (centre right), the most powerful of all spanning mechanisms, was developed during the last quarter of the 14th century. Some versions had the potential for a 145:1 power advantage. Here it is being used to span the new technology of the steel lath, with a draw-weight of 800lb.

THE CROSSBOW

ONE-FOOT AND TWO-FOOT CROSSBOWS

There are frequent mentions in contemporary sources of 'one-foot crossbows' (*arbalistae ad unum pedem*) and 'two-foot crossbows' (*arbalistae ad duos pedes*). According to W. F. Paterson (Paterson 1990: 38), who follows the thinking of earlier authors such as Payne-Gallwey, this distinction related to the width of the stirrup, with the two-foot versions able to accommodate two feet instead of one. A problem with this analysis is that no images in contemporary art show two feet together in a stirrup and common sense dictates that such a stance would cause a standing crossbowman to lose his balance during spanning, occasioning much mirth among his enemies.

Primary sources often cite two-foot crossbows with specific reference to crossbows spanned with a windlass. An order for crossbows and other armaments to be procured for the defence of Porchester Castle in 1326 reads: '100 crossbows with windlass (*de turno*) for two feet, 200 cross-bows for one foot, with baldrics (*baldredis*)' (CCR Ed II). Here, and in many other instances, there is a clear distinction between the two-foot crossbows, requiring the power of a windlass, and the one-foot crossbows, which were for use with baldrics, that is to say, the belt-and-claw system. The association of a windlass with a two-foot crossbow certainly confounds any idea that the term related to the older practice of lying on one's back to span the bow with both feet on the lath. Nevertheless, we have to be cautious when interpreting references to 'windlass' crossbows, unless there is other context. It may be that the author intended a 'great-crossbow' (a crossbow of 'two-feet') or it may be that the reference was to a normal-sized 'one-foot' crossbow, powerful enough to require a windlass. The designations 'great-crossbow' and 'two-foot crossbow' refer only to size. It remained possible to have a 'one-foot crossbow' spanned by the type of portable windlass tackle described previously. The term 'windlass', in the context of a great-crossbow, referred to a similar winding mechanism incorporated into a spanning bench.

Wooden, horn and steel laths are all mentioned in the records for bows of either type, so materials were not a determining factor for the 'foot' taxonomy. There was, however, a price distinction. In 1305, in England, the cost of a one-foot crossbow was 3s 6d compared to 5s for a two-foot crossbow and 8s for a three-foot crossbow (Blackmore 1971: 183, 362n). To date this is the only known reference to a three-foot crossbow, and it suggests a classification according to size, with larger, more powerful crossbows being, as we would expect, more expensive. Currently, the most widely believed explanation proposes that the terms indicate a distinction between a crossbow of standard size that shoots a bolt of 'one foot' in length and a 'great-crossbow' that shoots a 'two-foot' bolt (Liebel 1998: 24). This theory includes the persuasive argument that there was a benefit in standardizing the size of ammunition for crossbows, notwithstanding that there was some size differentiation, even between crossbows of a similar type. The head of a crossbow bolt or quarrel protrudes in front of the crossbow itself. This not only allows the shaft to sit flat, but also avoids any damage that an iron head might cause to the surface of the bow. Crossbow ammunition is therefore not a critical fit. It would also be a simple matter for the individual crossbowman to make a small adjustment of a half-inch or so for optimal balance. Having two basic categories of quarrel size makes complete sense for mass procurement, with more outsize versions being by bespoke order. Relatively few records specify requisitions for quarrels according to type (either according to the 'foot' classification or for windlass crossbows); the vast majority of orders are non-specific with regard to size (Wilson 2007: 317). The presumption is that, unless otherwise stated, the order would be for one-foot crossbows. Certainly, one-foot crossbows were invariably ordered in greater numbers than were two-foot crossbows. For instance, an order to the sheriffs of London in 1288 enjoined them to send 'forty good cross-bows for one foot and four cross-bows for two feet' (CCR Ed I 1288) to the constable of Bristol Castle. Four decades later, in 1328, the sheriffs of London were ordered to send '100 foot-crossbows, and 20 crossbows with windlasses' (CCR Ed III) to Portsmouth. Expense was doubtless part of the calculation, but one-foot crossbows could be spanned and shot much more speedily and used in a more versatile set of circumstances. The great-crossbow was a specialist weapon.

until at least the mid-15th century, especially for the defence of castles, towns and cities. Though used primarily as rampart bows, great-crossbows were also employed by besieging armies for attack.

Liebel catalogued a number of known specimens, giving measurements for the length of their laths as: 5 feet 3 inches, 5 feet 9 inches, 6 feet 1 inch, 6 feet 2 inches and 6 feet 6 inches (Liebel 1998: 25). The varying sizes within this small sample are consistent with the range of sizes for great-crossbows that appear in art. While substantially larger than standard crossbows, their modest measurements contrast starkly with those of Leonardo da Vinci's drawings for the design of 'great-crossbows', which had lath measurements of 27 feet 6 inches and 82 feet respectively (Liebel 1998: 25). These were clearly outside the normal range and it is unlikely that such massive bows were ever made.

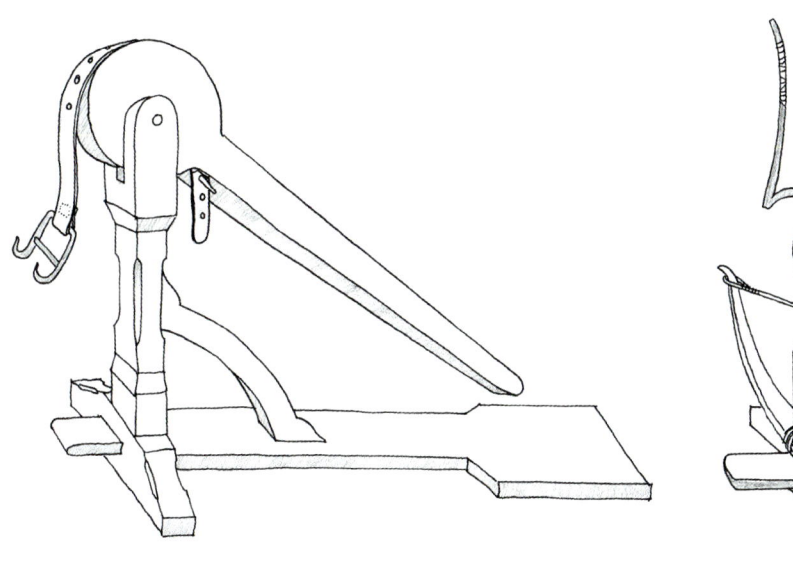

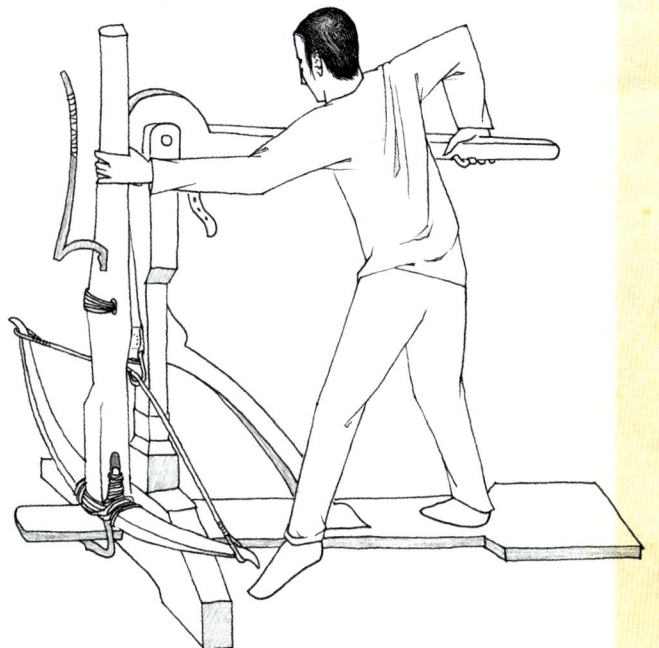

Some great-crossbows had steel laths, such as the twelve 'great-crossbows of steel' stationed at Orléans in 1419 and 1427 (Liebel 1998: 35). The majority of great-crossbows had either wooden or horn laths, however. At this large scale, the difference in weight between steel and either wood or horn was significant. The choice between wood and horn was determined largely by cost. Composite laths were superior, but more expensive. In 1313, in Artois, in the same transaction for two crossbows of equal size, the horn-bowed crossbow was priced at 2 livres, whereas one with a wooden lath cost only 1 livre (Liebel 1998: 24).

Listed in 14th-century accounts of the Tower Armoury are numerous mentions of *hancepes* in connection with spanning larger crossbows (Richardson 2016: 145). It is a term that does not occur elsewhere but it is strikingly similar to the word *haussepied*, which appears regularly in French records and has been identified as a spanning stand (Liebel 1998: 43). Documents in Latin use either *ausepearum* or *auceprem* in the same context. In 1358, in a dramatic departure from the policies of earlier pontiffs, Pope Innocent VI (r. 1352–62) ordered '30 auceprems' for spanning the great-crossbows that defended his castle at Avignon (Liebel 1998: 48). Spanning stands (*hancepes*) were notably less expensive than the more complex, screw-threaded vice mechanism. Tower records from 1353 record the cost of a *hancepes* at 5s compared to 13s 4d for a vice for a great-crossbow (Richardson 2016: 151).

An inventory from 1445, recording armaments for the defence of Dijon, lists various great-crossbows (*grosses arbalestes*) with bows of yew. One was described as '"*une vielle arbaleste gemelle*" – an old twin crossbow' (Alm 1994: 37). Alm suggests

ABOVE LEFT A spanning stand or *hancepes*. An alternative to mounting a great-crossbow on a tensioning bench or trestle was to use a 'spanning stand' and to then rest the great-crossbow on a small bench for shooting. The strap was adjustable in order to accommodate bows of differing sizes. Such a system had the benefit of greater portability within the confined passages and stairways of a fortification and it was very quick in operation. (David Joseph Wright)

ABOVE How the spanning stand was used. One man could use it, although especially powerful crossbows may have needed two men on the lever. The spanning stand offers an even faster rate of shooting when two crossbows are made available to a two-man team: one man spans, while the other shoots. (David Joseph Wright)

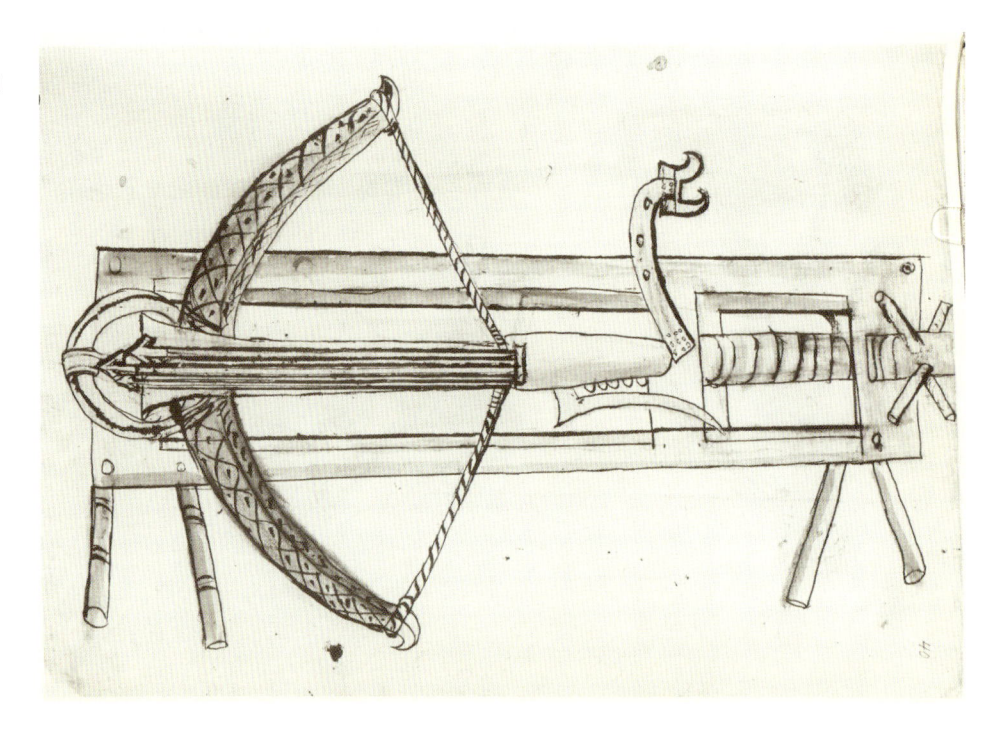

Great-crossbow (for three bolts), mounted on a bench and tensioned by means of a vice. In 1353 Robin of York and other engineers of London supplied 11 screw-threaded mechanisms at 13s 4d each, specifically for great-crossbows (Richardson 2016: 151). The vice or screw was a common apparatus for great-crossbows and, depending on the pitch of the thread, it allowed great-crossbows of considerable power to be spanned by one man, albeit slowly. (Bayerische Staatsbibliothek München, Clm 197,I, fol. 40r)

that it was designed to shoot two bolts simultaneously, whereas Liebel considers these 'twin-crossbows' were fitted with two laths (Liebel 1998: 55). Twin-crossbows are also referenced at Metz in 1402 (Liebel 1998: 36). By the 15th century, gunpowder artillery had begun to usurp the long-range role of the great-crossbow, though it is of note that a 1505 inventory of the Hôtel de Ville in Paris counted '48 great steel crossbows' and '5 great crossbows of yew' among its armaments (Liebel 1998: 56).

THE LATCHET

During the 16th century, small crossbows of moderate power – seldom more than 200lb – were developed for specific use by horsemen. Known as latchets, they had an inbuilt spanning lever making them simple and fast to span, an action that could be accomplished while holding the reins and the lightweight tiller with one hand and operating the spanning lever with the other. A thumb-trigger was mounted on top of the tiller, making it possible to shoot one-handed.

Two views of a replica 16th-century latchet built by Leo Todeschini. The inbuilt spanning lever lifts to enable the grapple to catch the string and the bow is fully prepared by pulling the lever back to locate within the tiller. The thumb-trigger on top is sprung and so automatically resets after shooting. Its power is limited not so much by what was possible for a small steel lath, but rather by the short length of string travel. Even so, it could be effective when shot at close range by a horseman. The lath on this example is 13.5 inches wide. (Tod Todeschini of Tod's Workshop Ltd)

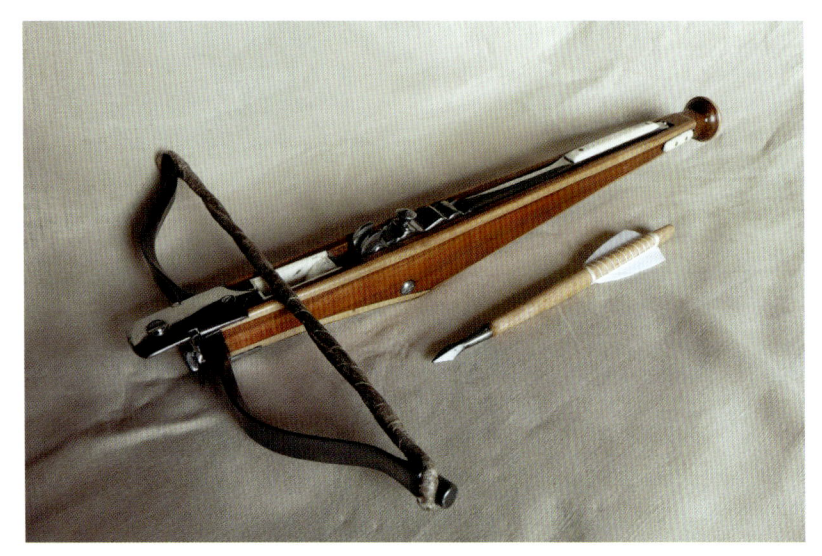

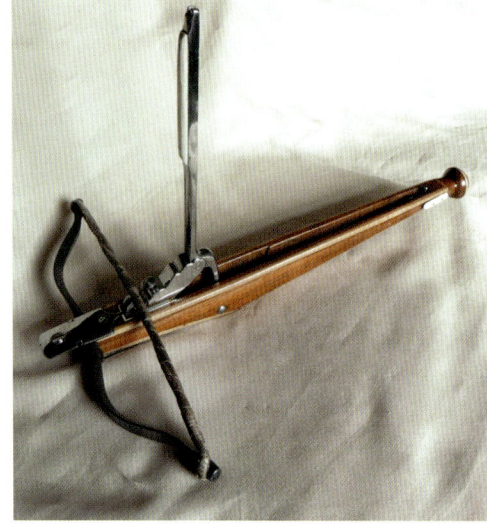

In the borderlands between Scotland and England, this weapon was known as the 'latch', and was among the arsenal carried by the Border Reivers. During the 16th century these hard-riding marauders were considered among the finest light cavalry in Europe, in addition to their more nefarious reputation as robbers and rustlers. A latch was not only a useful weapon of stealth on a cattle raid, it was also a dependable back-up to the – not always reliable – wheel-lock pistols that the Reivers carried. Latchets also served as easy-to-use personal defence weapons, for folk of modest means wishing to protect their homes.

THE BALESTRINO

Balestrino means 'small crossbow' in Italian and is the only historical name we have for these tiny bows that first appeared in Spain and Italy during the 16th century. They are also popularly known as the 'assassin's crossbow', but this is a modern term. *Ballestrini* were more powerful than their size would suggest. All were fabricated entirely in steel and spanned by an integral screw mechanism that operated a sliding trigger block. In the same way that a screw-jack for a car can lift enormous weight for little effort, these screw-operated contraptions were able to function with a steel lath in excess of 300lb, albeit it had a very short power-stroke – less than a couple of inches. Surviving examples are rare, but to give an idea of scale there is a 16th-century original in the Metropolitan Museum of Art, New York that measures just 11.5 inches in length with a lath of 8.6 inches. Compact and easily concealed, quiet and packing enough punch to pierce an unarmoured man at close range, these little weapons were clearly suitable for the dark work of the assassin, especially if used with poisoned bolts. To date, no accounts of their use in this context have come to light, however, and modern scholars consider it more likely that they were novelty items for the wealthy to play with – toys. Who can doubt the fun of them?

Made by Leo Todeschini, this small crossbow is based on an amalgam of designs from several surviving examples. This powerful little bow (320lb) is spanned with an integral screw mechanism, which functions in conjunction with a sliding block. In this case the turning handle is a cylinder but another common style was for the winder to be in the shape of a winged clock-key. A thumb-trigger is set on top. Length 10.8 inches, lath 8.8 inches. The form of the bolt is speculative, but for a short-range weapon like this, it makes sense to use a heavier bolt. The additional weight of the steel fore-shaft would make an infinitesimal difference to the speed of the bolt at close range, but the extra mass would impart greater impact to the target. (Tod Todeschini of Tod's Workshop Ltd)

USE: STEADY, STEADY, STEADY: SHOOT
The crossbow in China

CROSSBOWS AND CHARIOTS

When men first strained their backs pulling crossbow strings on the battlefield, it was chiefly in order to use their crossbows as anti-chariot weapons. The development of precision bronze casting in China had enabled the mass-production of crossbow locks, which in turn had led to the recruitment and equipping of mass armies on a scale never seen before. China's first emperor, Qin Shi Huang (259–210 BC), deployed rough regiments of crossbowmen in colossal numbers against the chariot squadrons of his enemy's nobility.

Shooting a regular bow took years of training. It was an art. With the invention of a sophisticated lock mechanism, however, you could fit a bow to a stock – you could make a crossbow – and a man could be taught to shoot a crossbow in a matter of minutes. Speedy training together with a ready supply of crossbows led to the recruitment of mass armies. Tens of thousands of peasants were pressed into military service. Against such impenetrable masses and such an intense barrage of missiles, the chariot was increasingly ineffective. Crossbows, together with the more agile horse-archer, were the chariot's nemesis and by *c*. 250 BC the chariot bells had fallen silent on China's battlefields. Before then, however, during the latter part of the Qin Dynasty, the crossbow had begun also to replace the hand-bow as the weapon of the chariot-archer.

Crossbows took longer to load than hand-bows and could not achieve the same rate of shooting. Rapid shooting techniques with the hand-bow, combined with the hit-and-run dash of a galloping chariot, gave the early chariot-archer considerable battlefield versatility. By contrast, shooting crossbows on the move would have been an inefficient use of the chariot. It could be done, but the team would exert more effort and cover too great a distance between individual shots. Although we do not have precise documentary evidence, it seems more likely that the crossbow was used from static chariots. A chariot still offered the advantage of mobility to deploy quickly on the battlefield, but I suspect that chariots were laagered into standing formations once in position. In support of this idea the archaeological record shows an increase in the length of associated *ji* (halberds) coinciding with the use of the crossbow by chariot warriors.

Chinese chariot crews were composed of three men: a driver, an archer and a *rongyou*. The latter was really a mounted infantryman, charged with the defence of the chariot in hand-to-hand combat. He was armed with a *ji*. In the earlier period this was no more than 8 feet in length and could be wielded from the chariot platform. However, at the time when the crossbow supplanted the hand-bow on chariots, archaeological finds show a vastly increased length in the *ji* – ranging to as much as 14 feet. It is awkward and impractical to use a polearm of this size from the platform. Consequently, I believe it was intended that the *rongyou* dismounted to lead the defence of his chariot in a fixed position. In addition to the *rongyou*, 25 running infantry accompanied each chariot. When in static formation, chariots could be vulnerable to an onrush of enemy cavalry. Arraying support infantry with a bristling porcupine of long *ji* was a solution to such a threat and allowed Chinese chariots to be effective shooting platforms for the crossbow.

In the *Romance of Wu an Yue*, written in the 1st century AD, Chen Yin describes the fundamentals of shooting the crossbow:

LEFT The rail of a Qin Dynasty chariot is around knee height. When standing with flexed knees as is necessary to balance on a moving chariot, it is perfectly possible to stand and shoot, either on the move or with the chariot at a standstill. However, the low rail invites the archer to kneel and to steady himself with one knee against the top rail and the foot of his other leg against the uprights. In this position he has a clear shot over the heads of the horses and yet minimizes himself as a target. (Photograph by Han Zhang)

RIGHT The biggest challenge of using a crossbow on a Chinese chariot is that of spanning. Qin Dynasty crossbows were comparatively large and had to be spanned by bracing the lath against the feet. By contrast the space on a chariot platform, which accommodated three people (driver, crossbowman, *rongyou*), was extremely compact. One possibility, as demonstrated here by the author, was for the *rongyou* to act as a loader and to sit with his feet hanging from the back. In this way he could span the bow and pass it to the crossbowman. It is a system that would have worked whether deployed in a static position or on the move. (Photograph by Han Zhang)

> The basic form of all shooting is: the body is as erect as if it were held in a wooden frame; the head relaxed like a pebble rolling in the stream; the left foot aligned with the target; the right foot at right angles to the target; the left hand as if glued to the grip; right arm as if cradling a baby; you raise the crossbow towards the enemy; draw your concentration together as you inhale and then shoot in coordination with your breathing so that the whole series of actions is in harmony. Your inner mind is settled and all conscious thoughts must be driven out. There must be absolute separation of those parts which move from those which don't: the right hand pulls the trigger and the left hand never reacts, as if one body were controlled by totally different impulses set at opposing extremes. (Quoted in Selby 2000: 160)

On the one hand this description evokes the highest principles of aristocratic martial arts, such as empty-mindedness; yet on the other hand the context makes it clear that this is prosaic instruction for the masses. Qin's Terracotta Army contains a large number of crossbowmen, all of whom assume a posture exactly as described by Chen Yin.

A Ming Dynasty (1368–1644) crossbowman in action. Crossbowmen like this are often depicted in rotating ranks of three – spanning, advancing and shooting. The lath is inexpensively made from bound bamboo strips and it is spanned by hand, using the carrying lanyard as a stirrup. Simplicity of both manufacture and operation made it ideally suited for use by massed troops. Although use of the crossbow had begun to decline for the main army at this period, it was still used in great numbers by local auxiliaries. The Ming period saw a divergence of crossbow forms. The bamboo-strip construction method adapted easily to a wide variety of sizes and strengths and working replica great-crossbows of the period have been made using as many as 20 strips of bamboo for the lath. The Miao, a mountain people from Southern China, were also famous for their great-crossbows, in their case fitted with massive wooden laths. Spanned by hand, these took three people to draw the string back, each bracing a foot on the lath. By contrast the standard five-strip bamboo lath, hand-spanned by one man, was relatively weak, its advantage being that it could be deployed in large numbers and shot in volleys. (David Joseph Wright)

VOLLEY-SHOOTING

A singular advantage of the crossbow is that once spanned it can be held far longer before shooting than is possible with a powerful hand-bow – although there is some trade-off between holding it spanned for too long and the lath beginning to lose power, especially with wooden bows. Not only did this ability confer clear advantages upon both the hunter and the sniper, it also gave rise to the possibility of volley-shooting. An early example of this was recorded in Sima Qian's account of the battle of Maling (342 BC). Sun Bin placed 10,000 crossbowmen in concealed positions either side of a defile. Their instructions were to 'shoot together if you see a fire lit' (quoted in Selby 2000: 171). The enemy, under Pang Juan, arrived at the pass at twilight. Sun Bin had stripped a tree of its bark, laid it on the road and written 'Pang Juan will perish under this tree' on the white wood. Straining to read the message, Pang Juan had torches lit. Instantly Sun Bin's crossbowmen unleashed a devastating volley, resulting in victory.

In the *Tai bai yin jing*, a Tang Dynasty (AD 618–907) military manual from 759, there is a drawing illustrating a drill for volley-shooting by rotating ranks of crossbowmen. The front-line rank of 'shooting crossbowmen' cycles with a second rank of 'loading crossbowmen'. Drummers are shown, commanding the actions to a regimented beat. Writing half a century later, in the *Tong dian* (AD 802), the scholar Du You explained that, 'They take turns, revolving and returning, so that once they've loaded they exit [to the outer ranks] and once they've shot they enter [to within the formation]. In this way the sound of the crossbow will not cease and the enemy will not harm us' (quoted in Andrade 2016: 150).

By the 11th century, just as the military crossbow was becoming established in Europe, Chinese tacticians had introduced a third rank of 'advancing' crossbows to the rotation in between the loaders and the shooters. This three-rank system endured to at least the end of the Ming Dynasty. In 1621 Cheng Chongdou, a student of the Shaolin Temple, wrote that

> The ancients used ten thousand crossbows shooting in concert to win victories over enemies … The first hundred men, which is to say the 'shooting crossbows' shoot. After they are done they retire to the rear, at which the second hundred men, the 'advancing crossbows', move to the fore and themselves become 'shooting crossbows' … and in this way they revolve and take turns firing in a constant stream. (Quoted in Andrade 2016: 155)

Cheng advocated volley-shooting for use in Ming armies and also that crossbowmen should be trained in the use of either the lance or the sword for close-quarter defence. It must be obvious that drilling troops for volley-shooting is the most useful way to employ massed crossbowmen on the battlefield. Unfortunately, there is a lack of evidence to support such an idea on European battlefields. That is not to say that such tactics were not used, merely that we do not know they were. We know even less of the crossbow's use by Greece and Rome.

Japanese crossbows

The crossbow – *ōyumi* – was certainly used by the Japanese in battle during the Heian period (AD 794–1185) but seems to have been withdrawn from use as a military arm thereafter. No early Japanese crossbows have survived, but it seems probable that they were of Chinese design. Each 50-man company was assigned two *ōyumi* (Turnbull 1998: 128). This may indicate that they were quite large, 'great-crossbow'-type field pieces. One account says that 'even tens of thousands of barbarians cannot bear up to the arrows of one machine' (quoted in Turnbull 1998: 128), which may be suggestive of the use of repeating crossbows. Certainly it would seem that the crossbows used by the Japanese at this period were mechanically sophisticated. There were frequent bulletins calling for experienced crossbow operators to teach conscripts and in AD 914 Miyoshi Kiyotsura (847–918) complained that 'those named do not yet even know of the existence of the weapon called the *ōyumi*, still less how to use the strings and bowstrings' (quoted in Turnbull 1998: 128).

Given the *ōyumi*'s suitability for naval warfare, and the preponderance of naval engagements in Japan's civil wars, it seems most probable that it found employment on board ships, despite the absence of images on art. Its resurgence as a high-status hunting weapon in the 19th century probably had more to do with European influences than indigenous ones. Nevertheless, these later bows with their multi-leaf laths were clearly in a tradition of earlier Chinese bows. That understanding of how a crossbow was made had not been lost.

The crossbow in Europe

The crossbow in Europe seems to disappear from the record after the end of the Western Roman Empire in the 5th century AD, not reappearing until sometime in the 10th century. Crossbow use is recorded by the French chronicler Richerus at the siege of Senlis in 949 and again at the siege of Verdun in 984 (Blackmore 1971: 175). It seems unlikely that it would have fallen out of use entirely for 500 years but, perhaps used only by the stealthy hands of poachers, it has left no trace during the intervening time. The earliest archaeological find to date is the remains of an 11th-century crossbow found at Lake Paladru, north-west of Grenoble. It is small (20 inches in length). During the 11th century occasional flickers of the crossbow's existence occur in the record – William of Poitiers (d. 1090) affirms their presence at the battle of Hastings (1066) and William Rufus was killed by a crossbow bolt in 1100. By the early 12th century,

An extremely rare and exquisite example of a Japanese crossbow. Although this is a 19th-century hunting weapon, far removed from the *ōyumi*'s battlefield heyday in the Heian period, it exhibits a continuation of early Chinese design influence with its multiple-lath construction. It has three laths made from baleen and held together by a binding of thin cord around the centre and two iron clamps at either side. The tiller is of persimmon wood. On either side it has prominent grooves for the fingers. Attached underneath the tiller is a recess that carries four bolts. The nut is of brass, operated by a trigger of buffalo horn through a series of intermediate components pivoted on ivory pins through the stock. Behind the nut is a recess for a lift-up sight of black horn, part of which remains. On the left face of the stock are two Tokugawa *mon* (family crest) in gold and red lacquer; on the right face there are three. (© Royal Armouries) however, the crossbow had entered general use as a mainstream battlefield weapon. The first flood of information, from both Arab and Western sources, comes to light during the Crusades to the Holy Land, where it was used by all sides.

MEN OF THE CROSSBOW

The troubadour Ambroise, who gave a poetic account of the Third Crusade (1189–92), wrote after the battle of Arsuf (1191), 'That day our excellent crossbowmen fought nobly and did service yeoman' (quoted in Strickland & Hardy 2005: 106). Arsuf was one of several victories for Richard I of England (r. 1189–99), as commander of the Frankish forces. He was an ardent proponent of the crossbow. Famously, arriving by ship to raise the siege at Jaffa (1192), he leapt into the surf at the head of his men and waded ashore, shooting his crossbow as he did so. Richard relied heavily on specialist crossbowmen, *ballestriarii*, from Genoa and Pisa for his victories in the Holy Land. For his subsequent campaigns in France, he imported recruits from Syria, including Peter de Tanentonne and Martin of Nazareth and their companies of crossbowmen (Strickland & Hardy 2005: 115). It seems likely that this contingent was among the first to bring the composite bow to Europe. In 1205, Peter the Saracen was sent to Northampton to make and repair crossbows at a wage of 6d per day. It is probable that he too was a maker of the new-fangled composite laths. Sixpence was also the daily wage for 'Turpin the *arbilistarius*' sent on Prince John's Irish campaign of 1184–85; Strickland suggests he may be the same Turpin who received a land grant in France from Richard I in 1190 (Strickland & Hardy 2005: 115). It was certainly common for crossbowmen to achieve elevated status. William le Breton recounted that Richard's one-time friend and later bitter rival Philip II Augustus, king of France (r. 1180–1222), rewarded his crossbowmen handsomely and that he 'enriched them with manors, goods and money' (quoted in Strickland & Hardy 2005: 115). Richard's younger brother John (r. 1199–1216) accorded his crossbowmen similar value; he endowed them with lands and pensions and ranked them immediately after the

JAFFA, 5 AUGUST 1192 (OPPOSITE)

Having relieved the town of Jaffa after a spectacular amphibious landing, the crusader forces under Richard Coeur de Lion were faced with a major land battle against Saladin's larger army. Saladin's forces consisted of an estimated 7,000 light cavalry, many of whom were horse-archers. Richard's forces numbered just 50–60 knights and around 2,000 infantry. A large proportion of these were Genoese and Pisan crossbowmen; the remainder were spearmen.

The spearmen were drawn up in defensive formation, kneeling and with the butts of their spears dug in to present a glinting porcupine of spearheads at the height of a horse's chest. More than half the knights dismounted to command sections of this shield-wall and to hold the men steady. Behind and in between the spearmen were the crossbowmen. They worked in pairs – a loader and a shooter – so as to maintain a constant barrage of bolts against the enemy. Hammered into the rocky ground in front of them was a field of iron tent-pegs, causing certain crippling injury to any horse that stepped on them. It is an inviolable rule of military archery that archers, especially crossbowmen, can only operate successfully in well-defended positions.

Saladin's horsemen were unable to close and wheeled about in successive attacks. Each time the efforts of his horse-archers were outmatched by Richard's crossbowmen, who relentlessly hauled back their strings to send bolt after bolt thudding into the vulnerable cavalry. Lancers and swordsmen could not get within arm's reach.

After much slaughter, Saladin's forces held back and Richard led a counter-attack with his crossbowmen at the head of the line, shooting as they advanced. The crusaders had fewer than ten mounted men and yet Saladin's mighty army of horsemen was driven from the field. It was a remarkable victory for the crossbow and the final battle of the Third Crusade (1189–92).

THE CROSSBOW

A reconstruction of a wooden crossbow by Andreas Bichler representing a type from c.1200. The lath is made of ash with a backing layer of sinew. It has a draw-weight of around 80lb. For all the many improvements that were made to crossbows over the centuries – composite laths, steel laths and various spanning devices – the simple wooden bow was the one that was the most used in warfare. This example is fitted with a stirrup to assist with spanning. Before the stirrup was introduced at some point in the late 12th century, however, crossbows otherwise identical to this had to be spanned by the crossbowman, or a companion loader, sitting on the ground and bracing the lath against his feet while he pulled back with both hands. This, without the stirrup, is the type of bow that Richard I's *ballestriarii* would have used during the English king's campaigns in the Holy Land. (Photograph: Andreas Bichler)

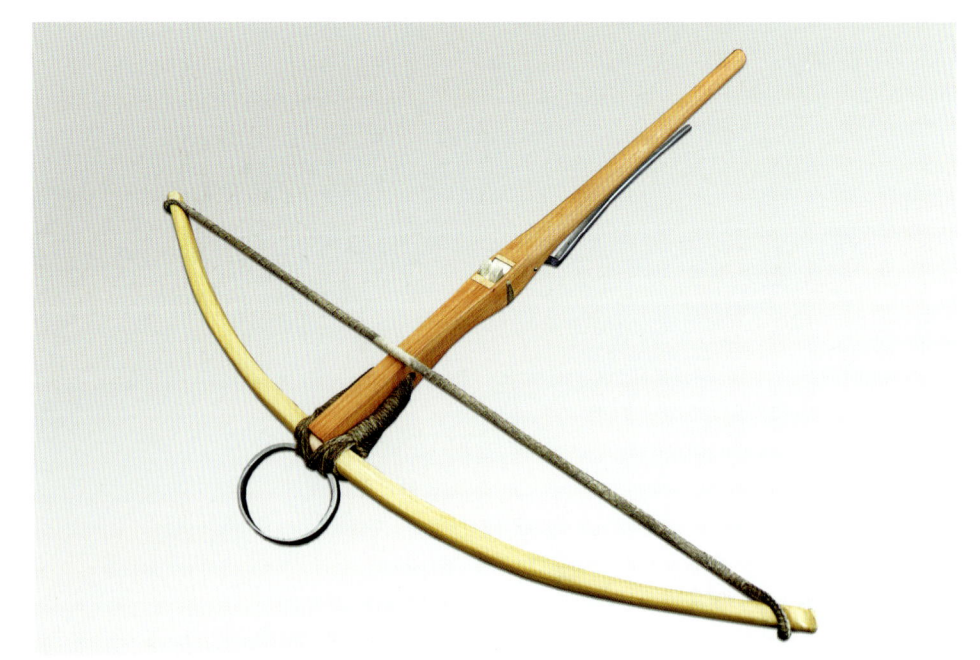

knights. Higher-ranking crossbowmen in service on his campaign in Normandy (1202–04) received an astonishing 4s per day (Powicke 1960: 225).

When the crusading baton passed to other European monarchs they too set great store by crossbowmen. Some 4,000 crossbowmen served on the Fifth Crusade (1217–21) and Louis IX of France took 5,000 crossbowmen to Egypt during the Seventh Crusade (1248–54). The great Templar castle at Saphet was garrisoned in 1260 with 50 knights and 300 crossbowmen (Strickland & Hardy 2005: 114). Mercenary crossbowmen were in constant demand for European armies throughout the medieval period. In 1215 both mercenaries and crossbowmen featured in the provisions of Magna Carta imposed on King John, 'And immediately after concluding peace we will remove alien knights, crossbowmen, serjeants and mercenary soldiers' (quoted in Carpenter 1996: 11).

Such conditions related to the limitation of royal martial power and John's reliance on foreign mercenaries rather than irrational prejudice against the weapon itself. Notwithstanding the curtailments of Magna Carta, Henry III of England (r. 1216–72) and his regent William Marshall continued to employ foreign crossbowmen in the service of the English crown, favouring recruits from Gascony. Others were recruited from Anjou, Poitou, Flanders, Brittany, Spain and Portugal, as well from several Italian city-states. They were all professional soldiers, worthy of their high reputation. Henry III maintained a retinue of 20 crossbowmen for his personal protection and he considered the crossbow to be of such importance that, in 1255, he instructed his sheriffs to ensure that all *cruce-signati* (those pledged to go on crusade) practised with it on a regular basis (Tyerman 1988: 168).

Henry III's son, Edward I (r. 1272–1307) deployed an elite force of Gascon crossbowmen in his Welsh campaign of 1282–83 (Strickland & Hardy 2005: 114). Although Edward I recruited unprecedented numbers of longbowmen for his Scottish campaigns, he did not neglect the crossbow. He sent significant numbers of crossbowmen to Scotland and, in 1295, ordered London to send 500 crossbowmen for the defence of the coast. Also in 1295 was the battle of Maes Moydog, an engagement in which Edward I's close friend, William de Beauchamp, Earl of Warwick, triumphed over Welsh forces. He used a combination of archers and crossbowmen, together with his cavalry, to rout the army of Madog ap Llywelyn. Notably, he placed one crossbowman in between every two cavalrymen (Bradbury 1985: 84). By using combined forces Warwick was able to break the Welsh squares of spearmen. Standing just a short way off, cavalry could be quick to exploit the gaps in the line created by bolts thudding into the lightly armoured infantry.

By the 13th century, feudal tenure, that is holding land in exchange for service, extended to crossbowmen. John de Cordebof held land in Mendlesham, Suffolk 'by sergeanty of staying with his crossbow in the army for forty days at his own cost', and William le Areblaster held four carucates (about 120 acres) 'by crossbow service and doing guard at York castle in time of war for forty days at his own cost, and if longer at the king's cost, and conducting the king's treasure through the country at the king's cost' (quoted in Bradbury 1985: 79). Forty days was the standard term for feudal service. After that the crown had to raise cash to pay its armies, as it did also when recruiting for foreign adventures. Feudal service was only for duties at home.

Domestic recruitment of crossbowmen continued long after the ascendancy of the longbow. In November 1314, a few months after the English defeat at Bannockburn, the north of England was deemed to be in peril. Consequently, the cities of York, Lincoln, Northampton and London were ordered to supply crossbowmen 'armed with aketons [padded coats], coats of mail or bascinets of plate at the king's expense' (Powicke 1962: 142). The requirement for them to turn out as well-armoured infantry suggests that they could be expected to make a stand in the field, as well as to garrison towns and castles.

Although it is difficult to evaluate the worth of rates of pay, especially as they occur in changing economies from one period to another, we can discern the relative value of crossbowmen compared to other troops. It is universally the case that crossbowmen were paid well and at a higher rate than longbowmen. The economics of fielding large contingents of longbowmen was one of the reasons they were so beloved of impoverished English kings. In the mid-14th century, at a time when a longbow archer received 3d per day and a mounted (longbow) archer received 6d a day, a crossbowman was paid 8d per day – the same as a man-at-arms on foot (Bell, Curry, King & Simpkin 2013: 190). Although sailors and garrison troops could be provided with crossbows by the crown, the soldier on campaign was more likely to own his own weapon. A significant capital investment was required to command these higher wages.

According to a 1381 inventory of his goods, a London grocer, one Richard Toky, owned not only a crossbow but also four hand-bows, arrows, bolts and armour (Bradbury 1985: 175). He may have possessed both his crossbow and his hand-bows for hunting, but it is equally possible that he owned them because he boosted his income occasionally by short-term enlistments in military campaigns, sometimes as an archer and sometimes as a crossbowman. It all depended on what the job market at the time required.

CROSSBOWMEN IN THE 15TH CENTURY

The universities of Southampton and Reading have produced an online resource (http://www.medievalsoldier.org) that provides a searchable database, derived from muster rolls and counter rolls, of medieval soldiery serving in late-medieval English armies. A search for crossbowmen revealed the following breakdown of postings between 1415 and 1450.

After the English victory at Agincourt (1415), many French towns came under English occupation and by far the majority of crossbowmen on the rolls – 55 per cent – were recruited for garrison duty. Urban defences were a crossbowman's main

SHOOTING THE CROSSBOW ON HORSEBACK

The Museum of the Han Dynasty (206 BC–AD 220) in Xuzhou, China, contains a carved stone image of a horseman spanning his crossbow (he also has a severed head hanging from the saddle) and the Nan Yang museum has a painting of a Han Dynasty horseman, carrying his crossbow over his shoulder, riding as an escort to a dignitary being driven in a chariot. To date these are the earliest known references to the crossbow being used from horseback.

In Arrian's *Ars tactica*, a treatise on Roman cavalry tactics written in about AD 136, there is mention of 'missiles shot not from a bow but from a machine' (quoted in Hyland 1993: 76). Given that the context is for this 'machine' to be operated on horseback, it seems most probable that Arrian is referring to the *arcuballista* – the Roman crossbow. It is listed among other mounted weapon skills to be performed at the gallop. Unfortunately, no evidence exists elsewhere to indicate the prevalence of this use. Curiously, perhaps the earliest depiction of the crossbow during the medieval period is of a rider, at full gallop, carrying a spanned crossbow in one hand. It is remarkably similar in style to the *arcuballista* type. This image, a detail from a Catalan manuscript, *The Four Horsemen of the Apocalypse*, now in the Cathedral Library, Burgo de Osma, Spain, dates to 1086. Even so, crossbow cavalry, as distinct from dragoon-style mounted crossbowmen, remain elusive in the historical record, despite numerous depictions of crossbowmen shooting from their horses in the hunting field throughout the medieval period.

It is certainly possible to shoot a crossbow from horseback. I have done so, both stationary and at full gallop. The trick, when in motion, is to keep the bolt in place by holding its tail with the tip of your thumb over the nut – the tail protrudes a fraction above the claw of the nut and a light pressure is all that is required. An alternative method is to use a bolt-retaining clip, but this slows loading, undesirable in a military context. The more pressing problem is the business of spanning.

Emperor Maximilian I (r. 1493–1519) was especially keen on hunting dangerous game with the crossbow from horseback. For such risky undertakings a powerful bow was required, and for heavy draw-weight bows, a cranequin was the only option for the mounted man. Hung from either the saddle or the belt, the cranequin was elementary for a rider to manage provided that the horse stood reasonably still. Many examples in 15th- and 16th-century art show cranequins being used by hunters on horseback. For martial purposes, however, the cranequin was frustratingly slow. Lighter to carry and quicker to use, albeit less powerful, was the goat's foot lever or gaffle.

Asserting his preference for crossbows over pistols for mounted men – pistoliers were prone to spill the powder when trying to load their pieces on a fidgety horse – Sir John Smythe, writing in 1590, recommended that mounted arbalists be equipped with gaffles: 'For all the crossbowers on horseback ... I would they should have crossbows of two pound and a half of the best sort, with crooked gaffles hanging at their strong girdles after the manner of Germany, that they might on horseback bend their crossbows the more easily and readily, with four-and-twenty quarrels in a case' (Smythe 1964: 113).

Whether his 'two pound and a half' was an error of penmanship or a shorthand expression of the day, it seems reasonable to interpret it as a draw-weight of 250lb, which would be consistent with using a gaffle. He goes on to say that he advises his crossbowmen be mounted upon 'good cold geldings' (Smythe 1964: 113). That is to say horses of a very steady (cold-blood) temperament, suited for transport and for the business of spanning and shooting a crossbow but not for the dash of the battlefield. The artist Albrecht Dürer (1471–1528) shows a mercenary soldier armed with a crossbow on just such a horse. Perhaps in compensation for his workaday mount, the soldier wears puff and slash clothing over his breastplate and displays a crossbow bolt in his feathered bonnet for additional debonair dash. Images of similar – though less ostentatiously dressed – troops are common in numerous *Hausbücher*. *Hausbücher* (housebooks), popular in German lands during the 15th century, were books of drawings that recorded everyday life, especially military retinues. They often depict mounted crossbowmen forming part of a lance – a military unit of the 14th and 15th centuries, comprising a small band of differing troop types in support of a knight. Among them were halberdiers, archers and, usually, a crossbowman. All were mounted to travel together, though most fought dismounted. Mounted crossbowmen in the *Hausbücher* are shown with gaffles, but these did not appear until the 14th century. What, then, of Gerard Tusard in the early 12th century – how might he have spanned his bow in the saddle?

A clue comes from a Mamluk manuscript. Taybughā describes using the belt-and-claw method from horseback:

> The drawing-claw should have two hooks. What the archer does is slip the drawing-strap over his left shoulder ... placing the claw beneath his right armpit close to the nipple. When he wishes to shoot he takes the reins in his left hand and the bow in his right and sets the string in the hooks, keeping the stock right in between them. He then bends forward in a stooping position until the front half of his right foot is in the stirrup [of the crossbow]. The archer now stands in his stirrups [of the saddle], as he draws the string at its centre point until it catches in the nut ... This done, he bends over forward, removes his foot from the bow and lifting the crossbow off the hook, transfers it to his left hand and holds it along with his reins. He nocks his bolts with his right hand and shoots in the usual way to destroy the enemy. (Latham & Paterson 1970: 85–86)

With this, Taybughā offers a system that could be utilized from the back of a galloping horse. Those who doubt the possibility of spanning by this method at speed should consider that some Ottoman archery treatises describe archers unstringing and then restringing their powerful composite bows from the saddle at the gallop (Loades 2016: 46); by comparison, bending the crossbow was a lesser feat. More importantly Taybughā makes it clear that the intended use for his mounted spanning method was in battle. He further notes that even a 'slightly-built archer' can shoot a crossbow of considerable draw-weight and that it can be used 'after only a few days' practice' (Latham & Paterson 1970: 85–86).

Smythe reinforces the idea that crossbowmen should be able to both shoot and span their weapon on a moving horse: 'Both archers and crossbowers, I would have to be well practiced that they might know how to discharge their arrows and quarrels galloping along the hand and in all other motions of their horses, and the crossbowers to bend again with great readiness' (Smythe 1964: 114). Note that the phrase 'hand-gallop' remains in use today and denotes a speed faster than a canter, though not quite a flat-out gallop. Smythe capped this advocacy with 'I come to conclude that crossbowers on horseback used by many foreign nations of great antiquity … do far exceed and excel all weapons of fire on horseback' (Smythe 1964: 115). It is important to note that Smythe was not necessarily observing contemporary practice, rather suggesting what he thought would be improvements to it.

BOTTOM LEFT A Mamluk military treatise, the *Kitāb al-mahzūn ǧāmiʿ al-funūn* (c.1470), shows a crossbowman shooting his weapon at full gallop. Note the extremely long tiller, couched under the arm in the manner of a lance and giving greater stability and counterbalance to the crossbow in motion. Long tillers are also seen in contemporary depictions of Arab infantry crossbowmen. A long tiller allows for the trigger lever to be set further back – note the position of the trigger hand – which in turn allows for the nut to be set further back, delivering a longer power-stroke. The rider retains the reins in his left hand while shooting. There is no indication of a spanning aid other than a stirrup, so the bow was presumably of relatively light draw-weight. It is a simple matter to hand-span from the saddle using a stirrup crossbow, given a bow of manageable power. (Bibliothèque Nationale de France, Paris)

BELOW A mounted crossbowman shooting over his shoulder, from Hans Talhoffer's 1459 *Fechtbuch* (MS Thott 290.20), illustrated by Michel Rotwyler. This technique permits a far more direct shot at a pursuer than would be possible from turning in the saddle and also allows the rider to manage his reins. Both this and a second image of a mounted crossbowman in the manuscript portray the combatants in civilian dress, suggesting that this was one of the many weapon configurations for the judicial combats popular in German lands at the time. In his 1467 *Fechtbuch*, Talhoffer shows the mounted crossbowman pitted against a mounted man with a heavy lance. He illustrates how, having shot his bolt at the lancer, the crossbowman may use his weapon to parry and lift the oncoming lance to one side. (Hans Talhoffer/Wikimedia Commons/Public Domain)

ARBALIST ARMOUR

Replicas of three types of helmet commonly worn by European crossbowmen. These are known variously as war hats, iron hats, kettle hats and *chapeaux de fer*. Two examples – one dating from the 13th century (**A**) and the other from the 14th century (**B**) – are based on wall paintings in Austria, while an example from the 15th century (**C**) is modelled on types seen in Burgundian art. Crossbowmen were always extremely well armoured, and – as demonstrated by (**C**) – they could sometimes be quite resplendent. These helmets are all brightly burnished, but it was also common to paint iron hats in the livery colours of the crossbowman's company. Painted armour was in regular use during the 12th and 13th centuries, serving not only as an identifier but also as a protection against rust. In addition to his crossbow and his war hat, the crossbowman had to provide serviceable armour. In earlier periods this consisted of a stout aketon (padded coat) and mail. By the second half of the 15th century he might also have had to provide plate armour. It is an advantage of the crossbow that it can be operated by a fully armoured man. Crossbowmen were heavy infantry and the expense of their equipment was one of the reasons they could command relatively high wages. Broad-brimmed helmets such as these were a distinctive element of the crossbowman's accoutrements. The crossbowman could shoot his weapon in such headgear without obstruction, something that would not have been possible for the longbowman. The broad brim gave protection to the face and throat when bending over to span and also when shooting the crossbow with the head tilted slightly downwards, sighting along the tiller. War hats were well suited to siege operations, an aspect of warfare in which crossbowmen excelled. When approaching walls, they shielded against stones and missiles raining down from above. (**A** and **B**: Andreas Bichler; **C**: Jason Daub)

workplace. Great towns such as Rouen even gave the specific patrol location – town, castle or gates. In the case of Poissy, it was the bridge that required guarding. A further 7 per cent were posted on city watch with all the policing duties that implied. Just over 5 per cent served in either the personal retinue of a knight or were on escort duty for great nobles. Roughly 13 per cent were listed as rendering field service for a siege and 3 per cent did not have their duties recorded.

Naval service accounted for the remaining 17 per cent. This was divided between 'naval expeditions', 'keeping of the sea' and 'naval sieges'. Port towns were prime targets for attacks by crossbowmen aboard ships.

Further analysis by the authors of this study has demonstrated that many soldiers served as different troop types over time (Bell, Curry, King & Simpkin 2013: 191). For instance, Raymond de Lor served as a gunner in 1442, but did duty as a crossbowman at Rouen in 1446. He also served as an archer on two other occasions. Similarly, one John Paskyn began his military career as an archer in the retinue of Lord Willoughby and then served as a crossbowman under Sir John Fastolf before returning to Lord Willoughby's ranks as a man-at-arms. In English armies, at least, versatility was a key asset, with men taking up the crossbow when that was the weapon most apt for the mission. Whether a man's primary expertise was as an archer, a halberdier or a gunner, the crossbow's ease of use made it available to anyone seeking military employment.

Nevertheless, the profession of crossbowman was pursued more earnestly and more single-mindedly by troops from mainland Europe, where the weapon enjoyed a higher status. Doubtless the levels of proficiency – accuracy and speed – of 'career' crossbowmen exceeded the capabilities of more occasional recruits. The English army rolls are populated conspicuously with crossbowmen from Portugal, Genoa and Flanders as well as those from home.

MOUNTED CROSSBOWMEN

In exchange for his sergeantry (land grant for feudal service), Henry I (r. 1100–35) obliged Gerard Tusard 'to find one Archer on horseback for the King's service, also a crossbow for him to shoot with, and to maintain him 40 days in the King's army at his own cost, whenever the King went into Wales' (THCN: 326). Here the term 'Archer on horseback' is clearly used to mean a mounted crossbowman. Mounted crossbowmen could be deployed more speedily than infantry. They could be sent quickly to garrison a captured stronghold, they could patrol with a law-and-order function and they could provide flank protection to travelling retinues.

Many thousands of mounted crossbowmen were recruited by crusading armies, providing an essential screening function to the columns of knights that were vulnerable to the harassing attacks of horse-archers and light infantry. However, like mounted (longbow) archers, these were dragoon troops. Dismounting for battle was the defining characteristic of mounted archers, in contradistinction to horse-archers who shot from the saddle at the gallop. Mounted crossbowmen operated in a similar way to mounted archers, dismounting to fight, though it is probable that, on occasion, they also shot their bows from the saddle.

Mounted crossbowmen were remunerated handsomely. In the 12th century, those in the pay of Philip II Augustus, king of France (r. 1180–1222) received 48–54d per day compared to the 12–18d paid to the infantry crossbowman (Strickland & Hardy 2005: 115). This variation in pay may indicate not only rank according to experience but also to the number of horses the mounted crossbowmen brought into service.

In a unit of 84 mounted crossbowmen in the service of King John of England in 1200, 26 had three horses each, 52 had two horses each and seven had one horse each (Strickland & Hardy 2005: 115). Mounted crossbowmen were especially suitable for escort duty. As late as 1515, at the battle of Marignano, Francis I, king of France (r. 1515–47), had 200 mounted crossbowmen serving as his bodyguard (Payne-Gallwey 1903: 48).

The crossbow in the siege

There can be little doubt that, whatever its battlefield successes, the crossbow's most natural habitat was on the ramparts, whether they be town wall or castle. Fortifications gave security to the time-consuming business of spanning and the crossbowman was only briefly vulnerable for the split second his shot was taken. The period of the crossbow's ascendancy coincided with the evolution of the medieval castle; each had a symbiotic relationship with the other.

In his chronicle *Flores historiarum*, Roger of Wendover (d. 1236) tells of the fate of many crossbowmen who fought on the losing side at the siege of Rochester Castle in 1215. The castle had been held against King John by a force of rebel barons, but after a protracted siege, the royal forces prevailed: 'All the soldiers, except the crossbowmen, he gave up to his own soldiers to be ransomed; and some of the crossbowmen, who had slain many of his knights and soldiers during the siege, he ordered to be hung' (Wendover 1849: 339). Such retribution, singling out crossbowmen for the ultimate penalty, underlines both the importance and the effectiveness of crossbowmen in a defended position. In later centuries Henry V (r. 1413–22) made a similar exception at the siege of Rouen (1419). Despite offering clemency to the majority of the defenders, he singled out Alain Blanchard, the leader of the crossbowmen, for execution (Bradbury 1985: 307).

Matthew Paris (*c*.1200–59) added a marginal note in his chronicle telling the story of a crossbowman in the service of William of Alberney. They had seen King John riding to inspect the siege defences and the crossbowman enquired of his master whether or not he should shoot. Alberney replied, 'No, no; far be it for us villein, to cause the death of the Lord's anointed' (Wendover 1849: 339). Given the fate of John's elder brother, this is possibly a romantic fiction intended to convey a reassuring sense of divine order at a time of turmoil. Nevertheless, it speaks to the use of the crossbow as a fearsome sniper's weapon.

Crossbowmen again played a central role at the siege of Lincoln (1217). Prince Louis (1187–1226), later King Louis VIII of France (r. 1223–26), had landed in England and claimed the English crown. He had support from English barons and

CROSSBOWMEN MANNING THE HOARDING (OPPOSITE)

Crossbowmen in action during the siege of a castle, *c*.1200. Castle ramparts and towers – as well as some town walls – were augmented by a wooden gallery, called a hoarding. This provided a platform overhanging the walls. Apertures in the floor could be used to drop stones onto the heads of attackers trying to work at the base of the walls with picks or to ascend with ladders. The low ceiling and confined conditions made the hoarding especially suitable for use by crossbowmen, who could move quickly around the walls to any trouble-spot that required manning. Here the crossbowmen work in teams of two, so that while one is shooting, the other is spanning his weapon. Both wooden-lathed and composite-lathed crossbows are in use and both are spanned by the belt-and-claw method.

THE CROSSBOW

THE PAVISE

Crossbows took time to span and, on the battlefield, crossbowmen were immensely vulnerable to the missiles of the enemy. During the 14th century a type of very large shield, called a pavise, was developed. It is believed to have originated in Pavia, one of many Italian city-states renowned for the prowess of its crossbowmen. This Pavian shield gave protection to a kneeling or crouching man while he was spanning his crossbow. Exposure was minimal when he levelled his weapon above the top edge to shoot. A distinctive feature of pavise design was a raised central panel. The corrugated shape provided rigidity to the design, thus allowing lightweight materials to be used in its construction. It also shelved slightly at the top edge to create a rest for the crossbow when shooting and provided a recess at the back to allow a prop to be stowed neatly away for carriage. Crossbowmen had to carry their pavises into position on the field, which they did by hoisting them onto their backs with a pair of straps. The gutter of the central ridge bridged the spine, so that the shield sat comfortably. Even so, pavises were too cumbersome for infantry to carry on a long march and too large for mounted crossbowmen to shoulder when on horseback. Pavises were usually transported on the baggage train.

Genoese crossbowmen at the battle of Crécy (1346) were forced onto the field without their pavises by their impatient French paymasters. Their pavises were on a baggage train that had become stalled at the back of the main French army. Once they came into range of the English longbowmen, the Genoese crossbowmen were defenceless and outranged. It is little wonder that they took the prudent military decision to retreat from that position, despite the hot-headed haranguing of their French commanders. There is an old story that they fled because their strings had suffered in the downpour that preceded the battle. It is nonsense. Well-waxed strings are impervious to the effects of damp. Sir Ralph Payne-Gallwey, writing in 1903, claims to have sunk a strung crossbow in a tank of water for a day and a night and observed no difference in the tautness of the string (Payne-Gallwey 1903: 5).

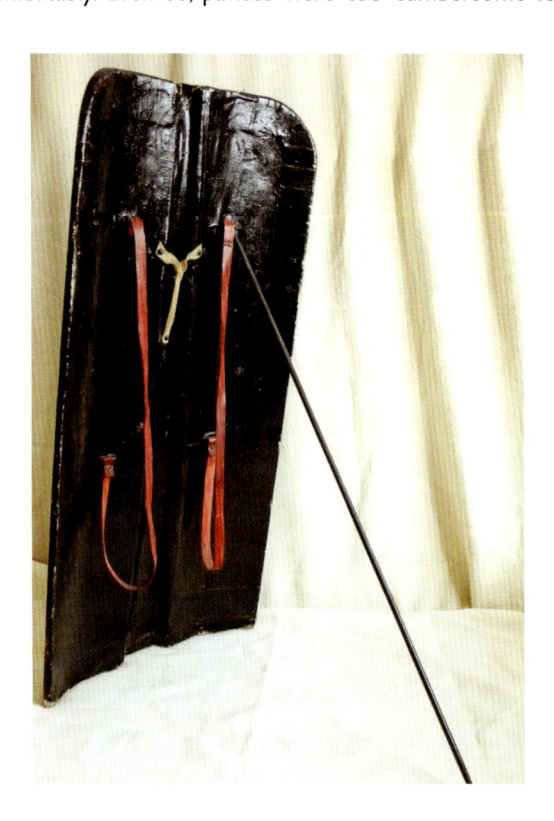

Two views of a replica pavise constructed using narrow-gauge boards of linden (lime). The boards were dowelled and glued together. Linden was a traditional wood for shields because it is both light and strong. Even so, in panel form, it required additional strengthening. A linen canvas, soaked in rabbit-skin glue, was laid over the boards. As it dried, the canvas shrank and so tied all the boards tightly together, enhancing the overall structural strength. The shape of the central ridge created additional rigidity. For decorated pavises like this, several layers of gesso (a mixture of glue and plaster) were applied, smoothed and painted, before being sealed with a shellac varnish. Pavises were often wondrous examples of medieval art and many splendid examples survive. Coats-of-arms of the town and heraldic displays of guild affiliations were common and some, like this example, were also adorned with fine-art paintings worthy of an altarpiece. On the back is a pair of shoulder straps and a handgrip. Traditionally, handgrips were made from a bull's pizzle. (Pavise built and photographed by Alex Kay, Sir John Paston's Household)

had laid siege to Lincoln Castle. William Marshall, regent to the young King Henry III, assembled an army consisting of, among others, 406 knights and 317 crossbowmen. They marched on Lincoln to raise the siege. Roger of Wendover tells us that 'The crossbowmen all the time kept in advance of the army' (Wendover 1849: 393). This insight into march formation hints that, in the event of encountering the enemy, the crossbowmen would create a forward screen, holding ground while the rest of the army organized. Once efforts to raise the siege were under way, crossbowmen were again in the vanguard:

> Falkes de Breaute entered the castle with the company of troops under his command, and with the crossbowmen, and stationed them on the roofs of the buildings and on the ramparts, whence they discharged their deadly weapons against the chargers of the barons, levelling horses and riders together to the earth … At length, by means of the crossbowmen, by whose skill the horses of the barons were mown down and killed like pigs, the party of the barons was greatly weakened. (Wendover 1849: 394–95)

When shooting a crossbow in depression – that is, tilting it downwards to aim – the same procedure as shooting it from horseback applied. In order to prevent the bolt from slipping off, it was kept in place by applying a light pressure on its tail with the thumb. Crossbows were not only suitable for shooting down at attackers and up at defenders; they were also ideal for use on belfries (mobile siege towers). Although belfries could be, and were, employed to send troops over the walls, their principal function was to give cover to workings at ground level. These might be either a ram or mining operations. Crossbowmen on the upper levels were well positioned to keep defenders at bay, enemy troops who might otherwise be leaning over the ramparts to drop stones or shoot down with crossbows. Belfries, enormous and perilously top-heavy structures on wheels, were manoeuvred into position with ponderous progress. One account from the Second Crusade (1147–49) describes a tower moving just 90 feet in one day (Bradbury 1985: 249). Such a sluggish advance required good missile defences against those who would rush to topple it.

Crossbows were sometimes used by spies to send intelligence messages to the enemy. During the siege of Rhodes in 1522, Apella Renata shot a message to the besieging Turks with his crossbow. He was hanged and quartered. Blasco Diaz was put to the rack for a similar use of his crossbow. Unable to walk, he had to be carried to his execution (Bradbury 1985: 317).

The late-medieval author Christine de Pizan (1364–1430) recorded detailed lists of the armaments necessary to defend a castle or town against a siege. Although many of her recommendations were copied from the pages of a 5th-century Roman writer on military matters – Vegetius – her references to gunpowder weapons and to various types of crossbow are unmistakably contemporary. Notwithstanding that she does not mention the size of the place to be defended, her emphasis on a wide range of crossbow types is revealing. She recommended 'three large crossbows on wheels, provided with the necessary arrows … twenty-four good crossbows well equipped, six others on wooden bases … twelve score crossbows with hooks … twelve machines for bending crossbows' (Pizan 1999: 111). The twelve score (240) crossbows with hooks were obviously belt-and-claw bows, signalling the importance of such weapons in great number. The three large crossbows on wheels and the six on wooden bases must surely have been great-crossbows, though the precise nature of the 24 'good crossbows' is uncertain. The 'twelve machines for bending crossbows' could refer to large spanning stands or perhaps windlasses. It may be that these were for the 24 'good crossbows', indicating two bows for each of the 'machines'. There is a great deal of sense in having one man spanning one bow while his fellow shoots the other.

Crossbows being shot downwards from towers and ramparts have a clear range advantage compared to those of the besiegers, who are shooting upwards. Even so, the standard, hand-held crossbow should be considered a relatively short-range weapon, most effective at distances less than 100yd and even more effective at very close range. When the ladders are against the walls and the rams are at the gate, when the belfry trundles into range or when men smash through the hoardings and onto the wall-walks, then the crossbowmen of the garrison must run to their posts, hurry up winding stairs and along narrow walkways, to stem the tide of an enemy attack. Then their portable weapons can perform much service. For most of the long hours, days and weeks of a siege, however, the enemy busies himself with activities beyond ordinary range. To harass him here the garrison must possess great-crossbows.

GREAT-CROSSBOWS

Great-crossbows were most usually placed on the top of towers, partly in order to give them greater range and partly because, on a tower, they could be turned to cover more angles than would be possible in an embrasure. Some castles, such as Krak des Chevaliers in Syria, did feature embrasures large enough to accommodate a great-crossbow on a spanning bench, but these are the exceptions to the rule. The primary task of a great-crossbow was to be able to strike at distant targets and this was better accomplished from a position of height. This also made it less vulnerable to counter-attack. It is sometimes difficult to discern from the records when a great-crossbow is being referred to, particularly where the only clue is that it is spanned by a 'windlass'. Not all crossbows spanned by a windlass were great-crossbows, but the context, including cost and quantity, can be a useful indicator.

In 1209, during the Albigensian Crusade (1209–29), Simon de Montfort deployed 'balestas tornessas' on the tower of the Château Narbonnais so that he could shoot over the walls of the town of Toulouse, which were no more than 100yd away. During the *reconquista* of the Balearic Isles, James the Conqueror, King of Aragon (r. 1213–76),

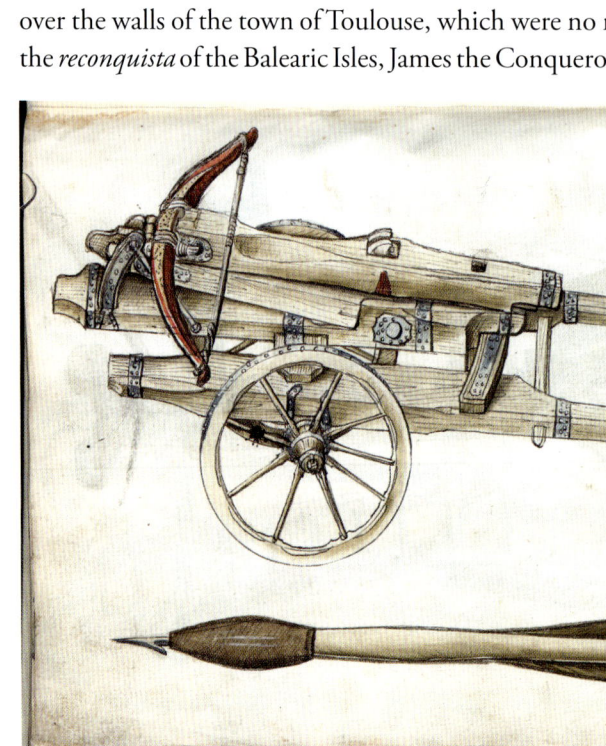

A great-crossbow mounted on a wheeled carriage, appearing in *Das Feuerwerksbuch* of Martin Merz, 1473 (Cgm 599, fol. 35v). Also illustrated, though not to scale, is an incendiary bolt armed with a single-barbed head. The expense and physical inconvenience of the great-crossbow is rewarded with its greater range and ability to carry a much heavier missile. This can have no larger pay-off than in the delivery of incendiary ammunition, especially when targeting fortifications that have flammable buildings within. The crossbow has the capacity to be adjusted for both elevation and line with calibrated precision and can be wheeled into position easily. At first sight the bow appears to be without a spanning mechanism, but on the previous page of the manuscript there is a depiction of a large cranequin with a square-section lug extending on the underside of the gearbox. Note the square hole on top of the tiller behind the nut; this was clearly intended to receive the lug on the cranequin. (Bayerische Staatsbibliothek München)

sent for a powerful 'windlass crossbow' at the siege of Majorca in 1229. He requested it specifically for use against the enemy's counter-mine operations. One imagines it, set on a low bench, at the opening where the enemy tunnel intercepted James's workings. Even if a suicide squad of men had been coerced to lead the attack, their certain deaths would have blocked the tunnel long enough for the great-crossbow to be reloaded. It was a considerable deterrent.

Christine de Pizan asserted that six windlass crossbows were required in a town or castle under siege, and 30 to attack one (quoted in Liebel 1998: 38). When attacking a fortification, these valuable machines had to be installed behind good defences. Great-crossbows could not be moved easily if attacked. Whereas the crossbowman in the field relied on his portable pavise, the soldier laying siege required something more substantial – a mantlet. Mantlets were relatively large, freestanding structures that defended against projectiles and provided a solid barrier against marauding sorties. Osier wickerwork was a common construction medium; it was lightweight and adequate against arrows. Wooden mantlets, made with sturdy boards, offered greater protection, but were heavier and more cumbersome to manoeuvre. On occasion both wicker and wooden mantlets were fitted with wheels, affording them some mobility. More elaborate structures, L-shapes for instance, were capable of sheltering several men and a great-crossbow. It all added to the logistics of fielding these larger weapons. In the Black Prince's Spanish campaigns, which culminated at the battle of Nájera in 1367, he took windlass crossbows on 'carts and carriages' (Liebel 1998: 38); they were clearly larger than a man could carry.

Whether employed in open battle or during a siege, great-crossbows had a terrifying ability to target a leader. During the siege of Paris in 1429, Joan of Arc was struck in the thigh by a bolt from a 'hausspied' crossbow, that is a great-crossbow bent on a spanning stand (Liebel 1998: 42). She recovered from her wound, suggesting the large bolt only grazed her. No matter how effective great-crossbows could be at picking off individuals, though, there can be little doubt that their most devastating use was as delivery systems for incendiary ammunition. Medieval recipes for

CASTLE SIEGE, c.1300 (OVERLEAF)

Defence of the castle is being directed by the wife of the castellan because he is away fighting elsewhere. The besieging army has fielded a screen of crossbowmen behind various types of mantlet, some wicker, some wooden. An incendiary bolt has been placed onto a great-crossbow. It is targeting a large L-shaped wooden mantlet behind which are crossbowmen, ready to give cover to a unit who are running in to attempt an escalade of the lower ramparts. A vice-style spanning bench is being reset, ready to span the great-crossbow again after it has been shot. A soldier lifts a box behind the great-crossbow, containing a variety of bolt heads for it; another man is taking shafts for these from the barrel. It was more common, however – especially for standard crossbows – for bolts to be already fitted with their heads and packed in barrels. Re-supply of these could be winched up to the tower by the treadwheel crane.

A wooden chest in front of the great-crossbow contains incendiary bolts for the great-crossbow.

Standard crossbowmen are in support of the great-crossbow on the tower. Some still use wooden-lathed crossbows, while others have more powerful, and more expensive, composite-lathed crossbows. Both use the speedier belt-and-claw spanning method when preparing to repel an attack. From the high point of the tower, they have the advantage of range.

The besiegers, behind their mantlets, span their powerful bows with a simple windlass mechanism. It is slower, but they need the extra range, have the protection of their barricades and do not need to respond as quickly as the castle's defenders may have to once the enemy has ladders at their walls.

WAR BOWS

140

THE CROSSBOW

incendiary arrows abound and there is some discussion of this earlier in this book. Medieval towns were crammed with timber-framed buildings, many with thatched roofs, nested together in a huddle of narrow streets. They were immensely vulnerable to fire. Great-crossbows were able to deliver it with precision.

Bolts, booze and brotherhood

Guilds, companies and fraternities of crossbowmen flourished in parts of mainland Europe throughout the Middle Ages and thereafter, many surviving to the present day. In Flanders and Northern France, in Swiss and German lands and in many Italian city-states, crossbows were elevated almost to a cult status. These shooting societies were founded, in the words of one 15th-century charter, 'for the security, guard and defence' of the towns (Crombie 2016: 21). The Brussels Guild, founded in 1213, has some claim to be the oldest, but since most charters refer to existing custom and practice, many may be older than that. The strata of society that enlisted to be crossbowmen were similar to those for longbow archers – a broad cross-section of tradesmen – although the crossbow guilds also attracted extremely wealthy burghers to their membership and received the patronage of nobles and princes. Crossbow shooting conferred status.

Shooting guilds were as much a part of civic society as they were an adjunct to military organization. Often wearing the livery of their patron, all classes of men met, feasted, drank and shot together on an equal footing. Privileges, which included the right to bear arms, tax exemptions and the prospect of making useful social connections, were among the inducements for recruitment. Members of the Saint Sebastian archery guild in Lille were immune from prosecution for accidental death – a great boon to the more festively inclined arbalist. In most societies, membership was for life, which meant that veterans enjoyed both public esteem and the comradeship of their peers after their years of active service. Most importantly, brothers that were wounded or who fell ill might expect financial support from their fellow members.

The requirements of membership were good character, proficiency at shooting and the ownership of a serviceable crossbow. The guild in Lille specified that a new member should have a crossbow worth £3 and 'other arms needed for the exercise of the bow' within six weeks of joining; Bruges also demanded the provision of costly crossbows valued at £3, whereas in Arras, a 16s crossbow was deemed good enough (Crombie 2016: 65). This cost discrepancy may relate not only to the quality of the bow but also to the 'other arms needed'. A powerful bow requiring the adjunct of an expensive cranequin would clearly cost a lot more than a wooden-lathed bow that could be spanned with a belt-and-claw. For instance, in 1452, a yew crossbow was purchased by the aldermen of Compiègne for a mere 12s. 'A suitable bow' is all that was required for the crossbowmen of Douai in 1383, but in 1499 it was indicated that they had the choice between one with a wood lath or one with a metal lath (Crombie 2016: 65).

As well as providing their weapons, novitiates had to make cash payments to enter a guild or fraternity. The 1442 charter for the Lille guild required them to pay '24 shillings for the profit of the guild' and '12 shillings for drinking in a recreational assembly on the day of their entry'. A further 12s had to be deposited 'which will cover drinking for the confreres who carry the body' as an essential funeral expense (quoted in Crombie 2016: 65–66).

Detail from a Book of Hours c.1530 (MS II 158, fol. 11v), attributed to Simon Bening. Here, members of a crossbow fraternity gather at their shooting ground. The shooters wear a sumptuous livery, tailored from an abundance of expensive cloth, proclaiming the status of both their town and their guild. A gentleman of great importance watches them, together with other wealthy burghers. Windlasses are required to span the powerful bows and a servant is shown acting as a loader. Such immensely stout laths can only be of composite construction. It is of note that they are bound with security cords, in the manner of steel laths. In this case the bindings would help to prevent the horn delaminating from the sinew, a considerable risk with such short and powerful laths in such an acute arc. The small brick edifice with the grille is for the protection of a scorer. To the left of the picture is one of the target houses. Targets were situated at each end of the range, so that when the shooters had shot one way they would walk to the targets and then turn and shoot the other way. There would be a second scorer's shelter at the opposite end. He would either call out the hits or signal them with a flag. (Royal Library of Belgium. All rights reserved)

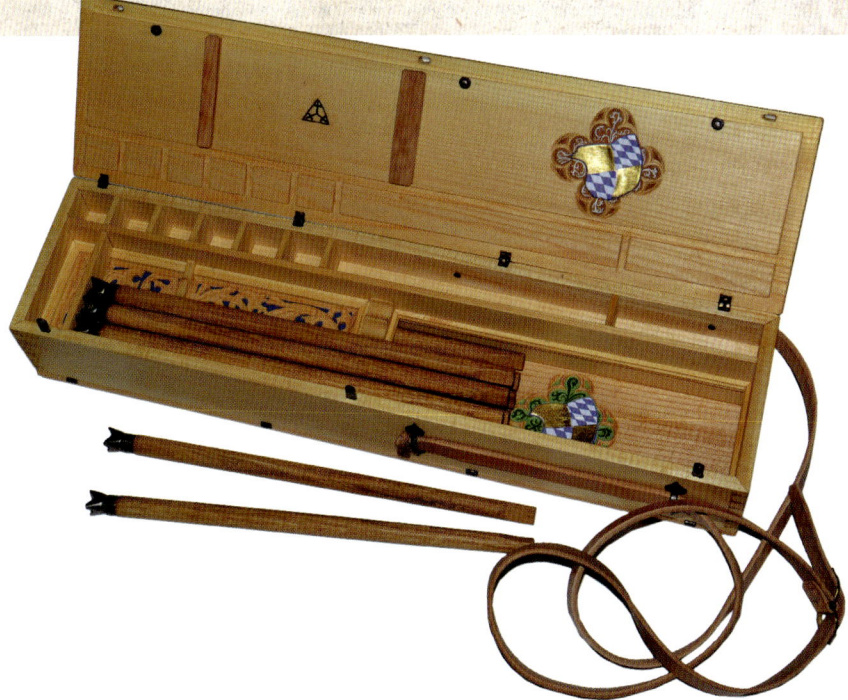

Replica coronel-headed bolts and box, made by Andreas Bichler. This type of bolt was also used for small game, for the popinjay and for other shooting games. The fellows of European crossbow fraternities carried their prized bolts in decorated boxes that were also emblazoned with heraldic emblems. Competition bolts would be finely tuned, weighted and balanced, for a particular crossbow. Individual bolts were identifiable at a contest because the shooter would write his name onto the shaft with a quill pen. (Photograph: Andreas Bichler)

THE CROSSBOW

A   B   C

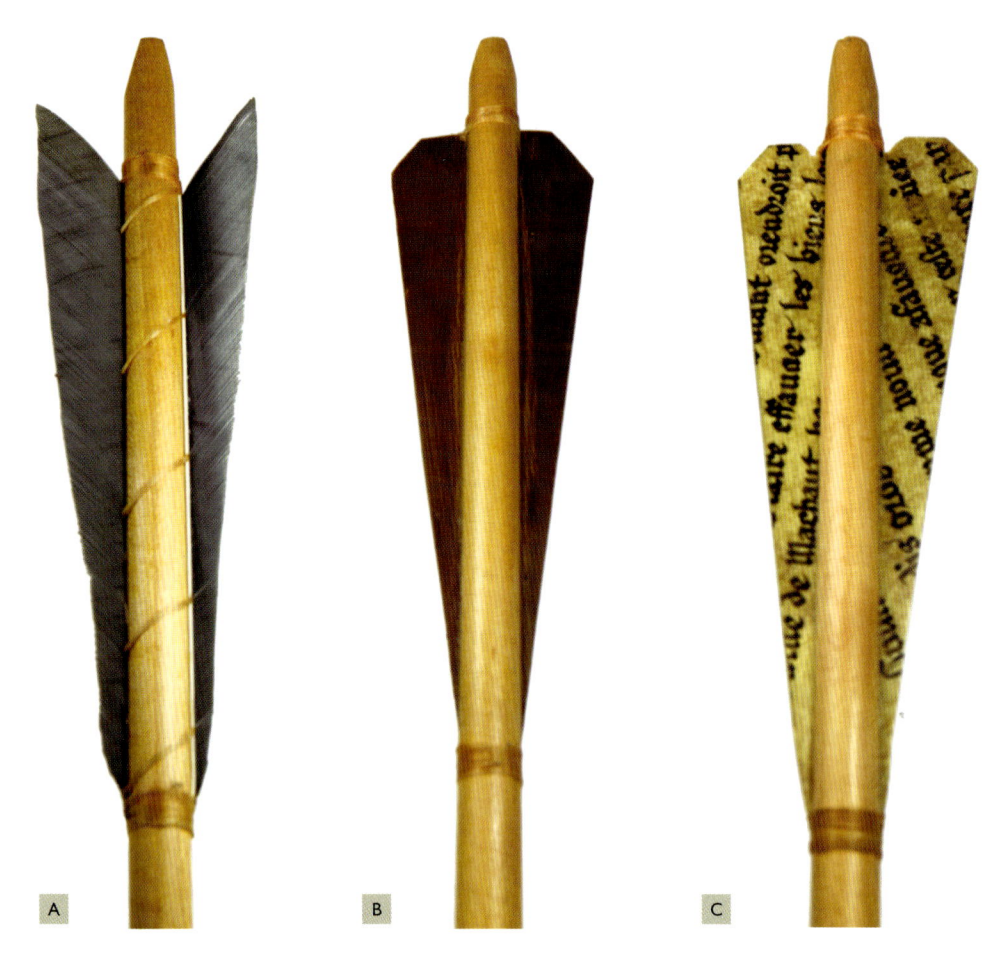

Some examples of common fletching materials for crossbow bolts: feather (**A**), leather (**B**) and parchment (**C**). Old manuscript parchment was frequently cut up and recycled for this purpose. A shallow groove was scored into the shaft in order to receive the base of the fletching. Here, the feather-fletched example uses goose feather, which was the most usual type used. Around 1355, however, the Tower Armoury specified an issue of nearly 1,920 quarrels fletched with hawk feathers (Richardson 2016: 151). (Kim Hawkins)

Aside from initial membership dues, shooting fraternities were funded from the town's coffers and in addition to an annual grant of money, there was also an annual grant of wine. Some shooting societies, particularly those in Burgundian lands, included longbow archers as well as crossbowmen and the wine grants give an insight into the hierarchies involved. The town accounts for Lille record that in 1437, the greater crossbowmen received '18 lots of wine' (roughly 8 gallons) and the lesser crossbowmen received '12 lots of wine'. By contrast the greater archers received '12 lots' and the lesser archers '9 lots' (Crombie 2016: 129). Clearly, crossbowmen were considered to be of higher status.

As mercantile towns prospered during the Middle Ages, the more they attended to their own security with town walls. Imposing walls were embodiments of civic pride and identity. In a similar fashion the guardians of these walls, the crossbow societies, became representatives of the town's image. Being properly attired was of importance. Shooting guilds in Flanders, a cloth-producing region, were granted generous amounts of cloth by the town so that the guildsmen could dress in extravagant finery. German guilds were thriftier, bestowing only a grant of trousers or money for trousers (*Hosengeld*). As a further enhancement to a town's prestige, the crossbow guilds of Europe provided impressive spectacle. Shooting competitions were held on a grand scale, with invitations sent far and wide. A great deal of emphasis was placed on procession and theatrical tableaux. In typical form, the 1498 invitation to the Ghent contests included the phrase 'the noble game of the crossbow (which) is above and before all other games in morality and nobility' (quoted in Crombie 2016: 178). How attitudes had changed since the papal injunctions of the 11th century.

Well-groomed, permanent shooting grounds were the venues for weekly shooting practice, but the town square was the more usual location for invitational matches in which regional towns assembled to compete, sometimes for as long as a month. For the annual popinjay shoots, a tall mast was erected and wooden birds were placed on transverse spars. These were shot at with heavy blunts in the hope of dislodging them from their high perches. It is my belief that the popinjay began as a practice for naval warfare (see page 140). For crossbow shooters masts of tremendous height, 90 feet and greater, were employed. The majority of the matches, however, were at targets horizontal to the shooters. Lots were drawn to decide who would shoot first. In Tournai in 1455, according to guild records, the shooting order was announced with intricate fanfare:

> A portable meadow had been installed in the town hall. Complete with bushes and flowers made from wax, and in the meadow stood wax female figures representing the companies in attendance. To the heads of these female figures were attached missals bearing the names of the cities and towns which had sent companies to the contests. A beautiful young girl dressed in a bright red tunic embroidered with the emblem of the Tournai crossbowmen stood beside the meadow. The girl held a little rod in her hand which she used to touch each of the wax figures in turn. (Quoted in Crombie 2016: 214)

Such splendour was eclipsed in 1498 with the Antwerp contingent's entrance to the Ghent games. This included over 1,300 people, 50 pageant carts and an elephant (it is uncertain whether this was a live elephant or a wooden one pulled by ropes). At the same event, Oudenarde's entrance involved 130 wagons, trumpeters, fair maidens and a procession of horses. Philip the Fair as Duke of Burgundy (r. 1482–1506) led the contingent from Bruges and on another occasion Anthony, the Great Bastard of Burgundy led the contingent from Lille. These were very grand occasions.

The importance of crossbow shooting was also acknowledged in Tudor England. In 1537, Henry VIII (r. 1509–47) granted a charter to the 'Fraternity or Guild of Artillery of Longbows, Crossbows and Handguns'. This became subsequently the Honourable Artillery Company, now recognized as the oldest regiment in the British Army. Its original charter established it for the 'maintenance of the science and feat of shooting in longbows, crossbows and handguns', giving equal status to all three shooting arts.

A replica of a crossbow blunt with a horn cap. Blunts were chiefly employed in shooting games such as the popinjay. They were also used for hunting smaller animals, especially waterfowl. Unlike metal-headed bolts, blunts did not sink and could be retrieved by a dog. In 1576 Elizabeth I's physician John Keys, who adopted the fashionable affectation of Latinizing his name to Johannes Caius, wrote a book on dogs called *Of Englishe Dogges*. In the chapter on water spaniels he notes that 'we use them also to bring us our boultes and our arrowes out of the water' (Caius 2005: 17). Konrad Keyser, in his work *Bellifortis* (1405), proposed insertions into the hollowed-out shafts of blunt bolts that had magical properties. In one formula he recommended axle-grease and the yoke of an egg and in another the heart of a bat. He claimed these would ensure infallible aim (Blackmore 1971: 195). (Kim Hawkins)

A standard medieval quarrel (replica, made by Hector Cole). It has a quartet of faces on each side, making it a slightly flattened octahedron. At the shaft end, the octahedron merges into a cylindrical socket. The four faces nearest the tip are only one-third of the length of the four faces nearest the cylinder of the socket. Quarrels were a universal style of head for the military crossbow. Their distinctive shape ensured immense rigidity, supporting the delivery of energy behind the point. Quarrels were not needle-sharp, but were sufficiently pointed to gain purchase on armour. Two of the outside edges had a relatively sharp cutting profile. Broadheads, while widely used from crossbows in the hunting field, were only used occasionally in warfare. (Kim Hawkins)

A common form of crossbow quiver had a distinctive flare at the base. In this example of an original piece, the wooden case was covered with hair-on hide. Although the hair has disappeared with age, the hide can be identified as badger. The two-tone effect of a badger-hide would have given a decorative variation to the more usual boarskin. (Bashford Dean Memorial Collection, Metropolitan Museum of Art, www.metmuseum.org)

Supply: bolts and quarrels

Although it seems most probable that there were standard sizes for crossbow ammunition (12-inch shafts for the one-foot crossbows and 24-inch shafts for the two-foot or great-crossbows), there were, nevertheless, diverse materials and methods for fletching. Fletching, the attachment of vanes, stops the projectile from turning tail over tip by creating drag at the tail-end. A fletcher both fashioned the shaft and fitted the fletching. In contrast to the three vanes used on a longbow arrow, a bolt or quarrel only required two. This allowed the bolt to sit flush on the tiller. Materials for bolt fletching included wood, feather, parchment, leather, horn and metal. A total of 2,200 copper-fletched quarrels for crossbows with windlasses were purchased for the English crown's Scottish campaign in 1307 (Liebel 1998: 36). Copper seems a surprisingly expensive choice, but this is by no means the only mention of its use. For the most part it seems that quarrels were ordered and supplied as complete units, with the heads already fitted to the shaft. Even so, Tower Armoury records from 1378, inter alia, refer to 4,760 quarrels with heads and 14,950 quarrels without heads (Richardson 2016: 152).

In 1421, two cases of '*gross traits viretons*' for the great-crossbow called 'Ortie' were inventoried at Blois Castle (Liebel 1998: 36). Ortie belonged to the duke of Orléans. Viretons, also known as vires, were fletched helically. This imparted spin to the flight with the prospect of a stabilizing effect. They seem to have been especially favoured for the large bolts shot from great-crossbows. Late-14th-century accounts for the town arsenal in Bologna record '300 vires with an iron head for great-crossbows partly fletched with horn' (quoted in Liebel 1998: 36). Christine de Pizan itemized 24,000 spinning arrows, 12,000 of them for longer distances (Pizan 1999: 111). Viretons were more expensive. Charles ffoulkes cites an order from 1419 stating the cost at 8s a dozen, compared to 4s a dozen for standard bolts (ffoulkes 1912: 64). A 1543 packing list that includes some rather dapper hunting gear for Henry VIII, itemized the following, 'Four canvas bags for pheasants. Shoes, black velvet quartered, Spanish leather. 2 crossbows, and 16 forked arrows. 2 vyrall bolts' (LPFD Hen VIII 14). The 16 forked arrows are exactly what we would expect for hunting ammunition, especially when hunting pheasant and a 'vyrall bolt' must surely be the same as a vireton. It is difficult to determine why there were only two out of a provision of 18, but perhaps they were intended for longer-range shots.

The crossbow at sea

Taybughā offered his perspective on the usefulness of the crossbow at sea: 'My own view is that in the manoeuvres of mounted combat, in the desert, and on expeditions the hand bow is a better and more serviceable weapon, whereas in fortresses and sieges, and ships greater power and advantage will be derived from the crossbow' (quoted in Latham & Paterson 1970: 9). In 1241 a law was passed in Denmark (Jutland) that the helmsman on every naval vessel should have, in addition to other weapons, 'a crossbow with three dozen bolts and a man who can shoot with it if he cannot do so himself' (Alm 1994: 23). In the mid-14th century, the accounts of Thomas de Snetesham, Clerk of the (English) King's ships, reveal that despite the popularity of the longbow, crossbows were still considered essential for war at sea. During 1338–39, 256 one-foot crossbows were ordered for the fleet. This compared with 241 longbows. Perhaps more telling was the requirement for 2,496 one-foot quarrels and an astonishing 30,844 two-foot quarrels (Wadge 2007: 159). These last were presumably to provision a large number of great-crossbows that already existed in the fleet. Although longbow-armed infantry would be aboard expeditionary vessels in some numbers, it seems reasonable to suppose that the demand for so many crossbows was to arm the sailors themselves with weapons that they could master with little training.

Arguably, the defining naval engagement of the medieval period was the battle of Sluys (1340). It is covered in some detail in the section on the longbow earlier in this book. Even so, it is worth reiterating here that the French had an estimated 20,000 Genoese crossbowmen aboard their ships and that the English force also included large numbers of crossbowmen alongside their more celebrated brothers-in-arms, shooting longbows. The contemporary chronicler Geoffrey le Baker refers to 'an iron shower of bolts from crossbows' during the action (quoted in Bradbury 1985: 102). The cogs of the period, with their augmented defences such as wooden castles, provided ideal conditions for crossbowmen to operate. They could shelter behind stout timbers while loading and then rake the enemy's decks from positions of high advantage. Moreover, as le Baker implies, the fact that a crossbow can be held at full span for a period of time, meant that the crossbowmen could not only time their shots with the swell – they could also shoot in volleys. As well as standard crossbows, most probably those spanned by means of a belt-and-claw, there is evidence for great-crossbows present at Sluys. Liebel cites a reference to a '*ban a tender grosse arbalete*' (a bench for tensioning a great-crossbow) being loaded aboard a ship that set sail for Sluys in 1340. The longer range of the great-crossbow had obvious benefits at sea; not least its capacity for shooting incendiary bolts.

In 1239 the Emperor Frederick II ordered all his ship's captains to have on board 'three good windlass crossbows' (quoted in Liebel 1998: 38); and in about 1400 the admiral of France ordered that should his fleet find themselves in the presence of enemy ships, they should 'greet them with powerful windlass crossbows' (quoted in Liebel 1998: 39). An order from 1441 commands the captains of Genoese ships to carry 28 windlass crossbows on board and 14 windlasses for spanning them (Liebel 1998: 39). This suggests a two-man team, a loader and a shooter, with two crossbows for each spanning device.

Replica bolts and quiver by Andreas Bichler. This boarskin quiver has been ornamented with carved bone plates. Wild boar were a prized quarry for the crossbow hunter and the totemic use of the animal's hide for quivers was almost universal. Crossbow bolts were always carried heads-up, affording the most ergonomic movement when taking one and setting it in place. It also allowed the shooter, who may have a variety of heads in his quiver, to distinguish them by feel. On other occasions bolts were carried tucked into a belt. This was a practice that had dire consequences for a somewhat boisterous widow by the name of Desiderata. Legal records from Sussex in 1276 recount how she accosted William de Stanegate while he was walking along the road with his crossbow slung over his shoulder. She enquired if he was in pursuit of lawbreakers and bantered that she would be a match for three such as him. Stretching her arm across his neck and sticking her leg behind his, she bowled him over. Stumbling as she did so, she fell upon him and was pierced through the heart by a crossbow bolt tucked into his belt. She died instantly and the verdict was death by misadventure (Bradbury 1985: 78). (Photograph: Andreas Bichler)

IMPACT: BOLTS FROM THE BLUE

The term 'crossbow' cannot be taken to mean a single weapon type and there can be no blanket assessment of its impact. To quantify the impact of 'a crossbow' would be as meaningless as quantifying the impact of 'a gun' without specifying whether it is a musket, a pistol or a high-powered rifle. Crossbow is a generic, collective term describing a wide variety of weapons with a wide range of capabilities. Each of these has to be assessed according to the precise type and within the context of the armour and battle tactics of the day. Compared to the longbow, little experimental work has been done on crossbows in the modern age and we have to rely more on anecdote.

An entry in *The Warring States Papers* states:

> the hardest bows and most powerful crossbows in the world all come from Han. The bows named 'Xizi', 'Shaofu', 'Shili' and 'Qulai' all have a range of more than six hundred paces. Your Han troops all use their feet to pull their crossbows and when

THE KING'S QUARRELER

In determining the cost-effectiveness of any projectile weapon system, the logistics of ammunition procurement are far more important than the cost of the weapons themselves. Quarrels were clearly produced on an industrial scale. Christine de Pizan, in her recommendations for siege preparation, itemized 200,000 quarrels and 1,000 large bolts for provisioning 300 standard crossbows and 30 great-crossbows (Pizan 1999: 121). Between 1344 and 1351, a period when longbow use was at its zenith in English armies, the Tower Armoury issued 103 crossbows and 37,095 quarrels (Richardson 2016: 149). It may be argued that an advantage the crossbow held over the longbow was that quarrels were less complex and therefore less expensive to produce. In either case large stocks had to be held in a nation's arsenals; in time of war supplies could be exhausted rapidly, far more rapidly than it was possible to produce them.

St Briavels Castle in the Royal Forest of Dean, nestled near the English/Welsh border in Gloucestershire, was a major centre for the manufacture of quarrels. At some point during the 1220s Edward I's father, Henry III, sent the smiths William and John de Malemort, together with their fletcher William, to establish a factory there. According to the *Calendar of Liberate Rolls* of Henry III (1226–40) they were paid at the following daily rates: William 7½d, John 6½d and William the fletcher 5½d (Storey 1998: 177). Given that the crown provided all the materials, together with a house and forge and bellows, it is difficult to ascertain the actual cost of the quarrels. In any event, these were high wages by the standards of the day; a skilled carpenter at this period might only get 2d per day.

It seems probable that William de Malemort was John's father, and that he died shortly after the venture began, because by the 1230s only John de Malemort is mentioned in the records. Between 1241 and 1245, John's atelier produced an astonishing 266,000 quarrels (Storey 1998: 177). St Briavels was only one of a number of manufacturing centres and production on this scale offers an insight into the prevalence of crossbow use in England during the 13th century. By the 1250s John de Malemort was contracted to produce 25,000 quarrels per year for a fee of 25 marks (Storey 1998: 177), which works out at roughly 13d per day for a six-day week. If he had no other costs, then the King's Quarreler was a wealthy man. In 1257 he received double the fee and was expected to produce 50,000 quarrels.

Henry III's son, Edward I, was an even greater patron of his 'great arsenal' at St Briavels. In March 1277, four months before the launch of Edward I's expedition into Wales, there is record of a staggering quantity of quarrels needed to supply his army: 'Order to cause to be made at St. Briavells with all speed 200,000 quarrels, whereof 150,000 shall be for crossbows of one foot and 50,000 for crossbows of two feet, as the king wills that quarrels shall be made and kept there for his use' (CCR Ed I 1277). Clearly, such large-scale production on a tight deadline would be beyond the capacity of one man, and Malemort must have employed a substantial workforce. It may be that he had to pay other workers from his handsome fee. Even orders placed at times of less extravagant military ambition were of a scale to be too much for any individual, such as this requisition in October 1293: 'To John Butetourt, constable of the castle of St. Briavells. Order to cause to be prepared without delay six thousand quarrels, whereof three thousand shall be for two feet [crossbows] and the remainder for one foot, and to deliver them to Richard de Bosco, constable of Corf castle, for the munition of the same' (CCR Ed I 1293).

St Briavels was ideally situated in an area abundant with the raw materials necessary for the manufacture of quarrels. Quarrel heads required iron ore and this ran in rich seams throughout the area. Copious amounts of charcoal were they shoot. Not a shot in one hundred fails in effect: they pierce the chest of any enemy who is far off and the heart of any who is near. (Quoted in Selby 2000: 172)

It was a requirement of Han troops to be able to span a crossbow with a draw-weight of 168lb and it is perhaps reasonable to suppose that this is a likely median draw-weight for the crossbows used by crusading armies, crossbows that were described by Anna Komnene as being spanned in like fashion. In attesting the impact of the crossbow, Komnene does not shrink from hyperbole:

the missiles do not rebound when they hit a target; in fact they pierce a shield, cut through a heavy iron breastplate and resume their flight on the far side, so irresistible and violent is the discharge. An arrow of this type has been known to go straight through a bronze statue, and when shot at the wall of a very great town, its point either protruded from the inner side or buried itself in the wall and disappeared altogether … The unfortunate man who is struck by it dies without feeling anything, so strong is the force of the blow. (Komnene 2009: 283)

---

needed to smelt and forge the ore. Charcoal is a very timber-intensive product and the woodmen of the forest would have had their work cut out supplying the voracious demands of the charcoal-burners. Dense with oak and beech, with their bountiful yield of acorns and mast, the Forest of Dean offered excellent pannage for pigs. Pigs also played a part in the production of quarrel heads – lard was a preferred material for quenching. Quenching is when the red-hot metal is plunged into a cooling medium, in this case lard, in order to cool it at a controlled rate, so affecting the molecular structure and inducing hardness. By quenching in lard, the quarrels were also given some protection against rust. Large batches of bolts required a great deal of fletching and goose feathers seem the most likely material for St Briavels' bolts. Great skeins of geese are drawn to the wetlands of the Severn Estuary and so there was a plentiful, local supply. Numerous fast-flowing brooks and streams, tributaries of the mighty Severn and Wye rivers, powered an array of water-mills in the region. Bran, which is the husks separated from the flour, was a by-product of milling and quarrels were packed into either chests or barrels of bran. It may be that these are the origin of the Christmas bran-tub, since it was chance whether the crossbowmen filled his quiver with high-quality shafts or whether the bran concealed second-rate goods.

Mass production on such an industrial scale involved the skills of miners, charcoal-burners, smiths, woodmen, fletchers and coopers as well as labour for packing and transport. It is a matter of speculation how many were employed by John de Malemort, but to be ready by July 1277, before Edward I's punitive expedition into Wales, they would have needed to produce approximately 1,500 quarrels per day to meet the March order of 200,000. That is considerably more than the 100–200 quarrels a day that were required when the Malemorts first set up shop for the Crown. Master arrowsmith Hector Cole calculates that the smiths would be able to hammer out a quarrel head in six minutes (private correspondence 2017). Note, however, that would not be every six minutes of an hour – there were forges to maintain and billets of iron to be sorted and forged into blanks before the actual arrowsmithing commenced, as well as some necessary breaks from the relentless pounding. Working in 12-hour shifts, day and night, they could achieve a phenomenal output, but the King's Quarreler required a small army of artisans, probably working with some semblance of an assembly line.

The Forest of Dean was a royal forest and permission had to be granted to fell oaks, beeches, ash and chestnuts. It seems that beech was the timber of choice for quarrel shafts. A royal directive of 1278 instructs the constable of St Briavels: 'Order to cause John de Malemert to have in the forest of Dene two beech-trees for shafts (*flecchas*) for quarrels and two oak-trees to make two chests for the king's use to place the said quarrels in' (CCR Ed I 1278). Edward I's order for 40 crossbows from the sheriff of London was issued on the same day in April 1288 as requisitions for 5,000 quarrels each from the sheriff of Gloucester and the constable of St Briavels. The order continued: 'To the constable of Bristol castle. Order to receive the aforesaid crossbows and quarrels, and to cause them to be carried to Kermerdin [Carmarthen], there to be delivered to the constable of the castle' (CCR Ed I 1288). The date coincides with a great deal of rebuilding at Carmarthen and it may be that the armaments were fresh stock for when it was to be regarrisoned. We cannot know whether or not they augmented an existing arsenal, but it is tempting to speculate that the ratio of consignments represented a typical allocation of quarrels per crossbow. If so, then each crossbow had a supply of 125 quarrels – a resource that would need careful husbandry in the event of a siege.

Although it is plausible that a bolt could embed itself in mud-brick walls or even pierce a hollow bronze statue, it must be remembered that the weapons she is describing are the early wooden-lathed versions of the crossbow, with possibly 100–175lb draw-weight and a power-stroke of 6–7 inches, and that their ability to penetrate armour at anything other than extreme close range seems doubtful. Wooden-lathed crossbows were in exclusive use until about 1200 and remained in common use thereafter, despite the availability of composite bows and subsequently steel bows. To date, however, they have largely been ignored by experimental archaeologists and we do not have data for either their performance or for the maximum poundage achievable in their manufacture.

At long range

In 1901 Sir Ralph Payne-Gallwey shot a crossbow bolt across the Menai Straits – a distance of around 450yd (Payne-Gallwey 1981: 14). For this test he used an antique steel lath, which he believed to have been made in Genoa in about 1500. He measured its draw-weight at 1,200lb. The distance he achieved is consistent with the following account from the 16th century. An anonymous correspondent, writing to Lord Walsingham in 1588, during the height of that prolonged summer of naval skirmishing between the English fleet and the Spanish Armada, urged 'the re-introduction of the bow, the crossbow, and the steel bow, as weapons terrible and unused by the enemy. The bow, our natural weapon, good at home but naught abroad; the crossbow flieth far and striketh forcibly, but above all the steel bow, which flieth 20 score [400] yards, and can be discharged twice as fast as the crossbow' (CSPD Eliz I: 520). It is noteworthy that the correspondent emphasizes the distinction between the steel bow and the standard (presumably composite) crossbow. Although steel laths existed from as early as the 15th century, they remained a relatively rare and cutting-edge technology. The sheer quantity of steel-lathed crossbows from later centuries that survive in our museums can give a false impression of the medieval inventory. Although 1,200lb is probably twice the draw-weight that would be possible for the short limbs of a standard composite-lathed crossbow, it is an achievable weight for the longer-limbed great-crossbow with a composite lath.

Great-crossbows

In 2015, Andreas Bichler built and tested a great-crossbow with a draw-weight of 1,276.48lb, comparable to that used by Payne-Gallwey. Bichler's bow is of composite construction, however, based closely on an original in the Schweizerischen Landesmuseum, Zurich. He calculated that it had a draw force of 5,680N at a draw-length (from lath to nut) of 14.7 inches and that the tensioned bow stored nearly 1,277J of energy. Different bolts were used, ranging between 5.4oz and 12.2oz. Measured through a chronograph, these were shot at velocities between 173.60ft/sec and 222.96ft/sec. The 12oz bolt produced a projectile energy of 487.79J, almost equal to the muzzle energy of a 9mm Luger pistol (Sensfelder 2016: 101). At a distance of 26yd, the quarrel head penetrated a 1.7-inch board of spruce, emerging on the other side by over an inch. The bolt did not pass through. Although not tested for range, it seems likely that Bichler's crossbow would match the distance achieved by Payne-Gallwey.

Reconstruction by Andreas Bichler of a great-crossbow on a windlass-style spanning bench, typical of late 14th- and early 15th-century types. The crossbow is a copy of AG 2570 in the Schweizerischen Landesmuseum and the spanning bench is a copy of one in Castle Sion, Switzerland. Unstrung, the distance between the inner nocks is 59 inches and the length of the tiller is 50 inches. The overall weight is 23lb and the draw-weight is 1,276.48lb! It has been fitted with a 'bastard' or 'false' string in order to bend the lath so that it can receive the standard string. In use, it would either have a prop at the front end of the spanning bench or be removed from the bench and mounted on the castle wall for shooting. When shot it recoils dramatically! (Photograph: Andreas Bichler)

Crossbows of the same genus may vary considerably in draw-weight and so we should be cautious when ascribing range and impact potential to a particular class of crossbow. Jean Liebel calculates a more modest range, around 275yd, for great-crossbows, but he makes the point that accuracy may be challenging at long ranges and that long-range shooting was mostly for harassing effect, as when, in 1347, the captain of Bioule ordered his crossbowmen to shoot first with 'the windlass crossbows that shoot further' (quoted in Liebel 1998: 42). As with all military bows, far more important than ultimate range was the potential to deliver force with the strike. Liebel cites an account of the defence of Dijon in 1431 that speaks of great-crossbows capable of 'buckling plate armour' (quoted in Liebel 1998: 41).

At short range

The crossbow bolt is heavier than a longbow arrow. It is also much shorter and thicker and so is subject to more drag, slowing it down at a faster rate. This loss of velocity translates to a loss in kinetic energy and consequently the force with which the bolt strikes its target. In 2003, tests were conducted at the UK Defence Academy, Shrivenham, as part of a television programme I was presenting about the longbow. We wanted to compare the deceleration of a longbow arrow from a 150lb bow with that of a bolt from a steel-lathed 300lb crossbow, measured with Doppler radar. As I have noted earlier, the radar malfunctioned on the day and the results were not conclusive, but the following was observable. The longbow arrow, a heavy livery arrow, began to decelerate early in its flight but continued to fly for around 200yd.

A composite lath for a great-crossbow placed alongside a standard-sized crossbow to show the difference in scale between these two weapons. Both replicas were made by Andreas Bichler. The standard crossbow is a reconstruction of one in the collections of the Landesmuseum, Linz (C 805) and the great-crossbow lath is a reconstruction of an example (AG 2570) in the collections of the Schweizerischen Landesmuseum, Zurich, pictured here before it received its covering of decorated birch bark. (Photograph: Andreas Bichler)

By comparison the crossbow bolt lost very little initial velocity, having a higher-energy launch, but once it started to decelerate, after approximately 60yd, it did so rapidly, losing any military effectiveness despite continuing to travel another 30yd or so.

There is an image from the *History of the Northern Peoples* by Olaus Magnus (1553) that shows crossbowmen shooting at cavalry. Lines of arbalists hold the butt of their crossbows at the hip and are shooting at 45 degrees, raining bolts in a parabolic arc (see Alm 1994: 53). They are using a type of bolt, common in Sweden, that has a tanged iron head at least half as long as the overall shaft. Those that have missed their mark create an anti-cavalry spiked field, akin to caltrops. For the most part, however, the crossbow was used as an aimed weapon, holding steady to take out a particular target at relatively close range. In such circumstances, considerations of arrow supply and the optimal range for delivering adequate force with the strike come into play. It was clearly part of the function of the great-crossbow to be able to shoot at greater distances, but for the standard munition, hand-held crossbow, having the capacity to shoot at distance did not mean that long-range shooting was the preferred tactic. Far better to use that power at closer range and to hit the enemy harder.

The heyday of the crossbow as a battlefield arm had passed before the twin technologies of geared cranequins and powerful steel laths transformed the utility weapon of the 12th, 13th and 14th centuries into the potent force it was to become. Until then, the hand-held crossbow was a weapon of only medium power and equal emphasis was placed on speed of loading. The belt-and-claw system remained in general use long after more powerful mechanisms were introduced, which limited the draw-weight a man could manage.

In W. F. Paterson's authoritative study of the crossbow, he states that 'Doubling the draw-weight of a bow, or crossbow, does not result in doubling the discharge velocity nor the range. At best it will only be increased by one quarter and it is likely to be less. What is of more importance is that a greater draw-weight enables a heavier bolt to be shot without loss of range' (Paterson 1990: 31). Range, to the extent that you can fight an enemy 20–60yd away, is obviously a key element for projectile weapons. What is most important, however, is that you can strike hard. As discussed in the longbow chapter, the effectiveness of projectile weapons depends not so much on whether armour is penetrated, but rather the level of injury inflicted by blunt force trauma (see pages 84–7). Similar arguments apply to the crossbow.

With the exception of the specialized longer-range capabilities of the great-crossbow, I would argue that the standard, munition medieval crossbow was intended for relatively close-range use. Early-medieval crossbows were effective battlefield weapons, when used en masse and at short range. It was only during the final decades of the 15th century, when cranequin-spanned crossbows entered general use, that longer-range sniping became a reality. By then, handgonnes had begun to assume the role of close-range artillery and the crossbow, as a military weapon, was already in decline.

Armour

Considerations of the crossbow's penetrative power must be evaluated with a full understanding of both the type of armour worn and the type and power of the crossbow in use against it. For a brief survey of some styles of medieval armour see the longbow section above.

During the siege of Acre (1189–91), a crossbow bolt, shot by a Saracen defender, penetrated the three-layered defences of a Frankish sergeant. It went through the mail coif, the mail hauberk beneath it and the padded aketon beneath that. Even so, the man's life was saved by a charm that hung around his neck (Bradbury 1992: 124). Even when a bolt struck home, it did not guarantee certain death. During the siege of Valencia (1238), James the Conqueror was struck in the forehead by a bolt from a crossbow. Although it pierced deeply, he broke off the shaft and witnesses recounted how the blood ran down his face, which he brushed off with a laugh so as not to frighten his army. On returning to his tent, however, his eyes became so swollen that he could not see. Miraculously, James survived the blow, reigning for another 38 years.

Henry VIII's ambassador to the French court, Sir John Wallop, recorded the following incident involving a crossbow in 1543:

A Chinese repeating crossbow, probably dating to the early 20th century. These weapons, essentially unchanged from their original incarnation, remained in use in China until at least the 1950s. This version, having a double magazine and double bolt grooves, shoots two bolts simultaneously. In all other respects it operated identically to the single-magazine weapon illustrated on page 95. (Bath Royal Literary and Scientific Institution Collection)

ARMOUR PROOFING

It is the primary function of armour to protect its wearer, as best it can, from the weapons of the day. Armour was developed to defend against a variety of attacks, from longbow arrows to lance strikes or sword blows. Nevertheless, there is a parallel graph that may be drawn between the improving metallurgy of plate armour and the increased power of the crossbow, arising from changes in lath technology and spanning devices. There are three elements that offer protection: gauge, shape and hardness. Using thicker-gauge steel added undesirable weight and so, provided that its effectiveness could be demonstrated, lighter armour was preferred. Hardness, created by the alchemical wizardry of the armourer, judging heats and quenches, cannot be seen by the purchaser, however. From the 14th century onwards, it became common practice for armourers to show that their wares were crossbow-proof by shooting a bolt at close range to create a dimple – a proof-mark.

Previously, mail armour was proofed using a sword or axe and by means of a blow called the *estramaçon*. With the greater threat posed by ever-more-powerful crossbows, however, a crossbow shot became the more usual benchmark of proof. Regulations in 1347 required the wardens of the Heaumers Company of London to oversee proofing, 'also that helmetry and other arms forged by the hammer ... shall not from henceforth in any way be offered for sale privily or openly until they have been assayed by the aforesaid wardens and marked with their marks' (quoted in ffoulkes 1912: 65).

In some instances, a piece of armour may be marked fully proof, in others merely semi-proof. A clue to the distinction is to be found in the 1448 Statutes of the Armuriers Fourbisseurs d'Angers. They state that in order to be fully proofed, an armour must be tested with a windlass crossbow (*arbaleste à tilloles*). Pieces that passed the standard were stamped with two assayer's marks. Semi-proof armours only had to withstand a shot from a belt-and-claw crossbow (*arbaleste à croc*) and were awarded only a single assayer's mark (ffoulkes 1912: 65). Although we get a general idea from this, many variables remain uncertain. At what range were the tests conducted? What type of head was fitted to the bolt? Most importantly, exactly how powerful was the bow? Undoubtedly, a range of different standards existed. An order dating to 1378 in Angers refers specifically to viretons for use when proofing, implying that these helically vaned bolts struck with more force (ffoulkes 1912: 64). A document in the municipal archives of Orléans, dating to 1416, refers to arrows for proofing that have the heads dipped in wax (ffoulkes 1912: 64). It may have been believed that this helped in reducing the effects of deflection, but the merits of this are yet to be tested empirically with modern scientific methods. Moreover, notwithstanding the oversight of the guilds, the proofer was also often the seller and there must have been all manner of ruses to flatter the outcome.

On Saturday afternoon three footmen of the garrison of Arde, returning home from Guisnes, met and quarrelled with two Englishmen coming from Anderne, who, seeing they were two to three and one of the Frenchmen had a crossbow bent, retired; and therewith the Frenchmen cried Tue, Tue, and shot a quarrel at one of them, striking him into the body. He plucked it out and ran furiously to the Frenchmen, of whom he wounded and overcame two with a halbert and the third ran away. That night the Englishman who was shot died, and two days after, the Frenchman that shot him. (LPFD Hen VIII 18)

While the report is vague about precisely where the bolt struck – it seems likely that it was the torso (probably a gut wound, which occasioned the poor fellow's death some hours later) – it is notable that the victim was not only able to pull it out, but to also run and fight with conspicuous valour immediately after he was struck. Of equal note is that his foe was patrolling with his crossbow spanned.

CONCLUSION

Until the advent of viable breech-loading guns in the 19th century, the crossbow remained a superior arm for hunting, notably among European noble elites. Crossbows also continued in service as sporting weapons at the shooting grounds of the European guilds. On the battlefield, the crossbow remained more formidable than gunpowder weapons for some time. As the power of crossbows improved, however, so too did the quality and hardness of armour. For the crossbow to remain relevant on the battlefield, it had to be fielded in its latest manifestation – steel laths, spanned with cranequins or windlasses. Both the steel and the spanning device were an added weight burden for the soldier. Moreover, by 1482 a steel-lathed crossbow cost 6s 8d, which was twice the cost of a handgun (Williams 2003: 49). Furthermore, the cost of gunpowder was falling – and it was significantly less expensive to produce lead balls, which were also recyclable, than it was to manufacture bolts. The crossbow had disappeared from the battlefield by the early 16th century, seeing only occasional use thereafter. Even so, crossbows have continued to be employed by special forces to the present day, used not only as a weapon of stealth but also to deploy zip lines and grappling hooks. One 19th-century example, now in the Imperial War Museum, London, was used to propel hand grenades from the trenches during World War I (1914–18).

Medieval crossbows have, to date, received comparatively little attention from English authors. It is hoped that this brief survey will stimulate more research and motivate the practical experimentation needed to assess more thoroughly the crossbow's military effectiveness, especially for types with wooden and composite laths. During the Middle Ages, crossbows and longbows co-existed; the same men enlisted at times as crossbowmen and at other times as archers. It cannot be said that one weapon was superior to the other; they simply had different, often complementary functions. Archer-historians would do well to embrace the study of both types of bow and to consider them as equal actors on the same stage.

A 16th-century hunting crossbow (A1037) in The Wallace Collection, London. The stock has been elaborately ornamented with incised plates of antler on both the top and bottom. Both sides feature intricate inlaid designs, depicting a hunting scene and augmented with foliage and dot decoration. Note the cords securing the nut. This crossbow has also been fitted with a horn bolt-retaining clip. These clips prevented the bolt from slipping off when angling the bow in either elevation or depression. Holding the bolt in place with a clip was useful for a hunter manoeuvring into position with a spanned bow and also for the mounted crossbowman. Such bolt-retaining clips did not appear until c.1500. Prior to that the arbalist simply placed his thumb, very lightly, over the tail of the bolt to hold it in place while he shot. The steel bow, which is a replacement from the original, has been blackened to discourage rust as well as to remove its glint for hunting. It has been fitted with silk pom-poms. (The Wallace Collection, London/ Bridgeman Images)

CHAPTER THREE
THE COMPOSITE BOW

Shooting a composite bow with traditional techniques is a dynamic and thrilling form of archery. It is done with flair, punch and attack. It is done standing, kneeling, walking, running; it is done from the platform of thundering chariots and from the back of galloping horses. The materials – wood, horn, sinew – sing in the hand; their oscillations are in tune with the body. Composite bows are smooth to draw, both because of their cleverly engineered designs and because of the perfect elasticity of these components. A true horn-and-sinew composite bow is a superior bow.

Across the epochs and empires of the Eastern and Near Eastern world, composite bows have appeared in a diverse array of sculptural forms – beautiful shapes that change dramatically through the various stages of being strung and drawn. To protect the component materials from the weather, composite bows often had coverings of either bark or leather; they were then

This quartet of composite bows in Peter Dekker's collection illustrates just some of its diverse forms. From top down: Korean bow, Mughal crab bow, Ottoman war bow, Qing bow (note that the string bridges are missing on this specimen). These bows vary considerably both in size and shape and were designed to shoot a correspondingly diverse range of arrows, varying in weight, dimension and style of arrowhead. Some bows, such as the Korean bow, were built for speed and distance, shooting light arrows rapidly, while others, such as the Qing bow, were engineered to deliver a very long, heavy arrow. To the Manchu (Qing Dynasty), heavyweight punch and accuracy were more important than either rate of shooting or great distance. (Photograph courtesy of Peter Dekker)

The main driver for different bow designs was the type of arrow they were intended to launch. To illustrate the extremes of arrow design that have informed the requirements of bow design, this image shows a replica Qing arrow (manufactured by Jaap Koppedrayer) alongside a Turkish flight arrow (author's collection). (Kim Hawkins)

frequently painted with opulent decoration before being sealed with a lacquer. Composite bows were not only highly efficient weapons, they were also exquisite works of art.

According to the *Encyclopaedia of Archery* a composite bow is 'composed of three or more layers of dissimilar materials' (Paterson 1984: 38). This distinguishes it from a self bow, which is one that is made from a single homogeneous material, such as a wooden bow from yew or elm, and a laminated bow, which Paterson, a respected authority, defines as 'a bow constructed from several layers of basically similar materials' (Paterson 1984: 73). The Japanese *yumi* is constructed from laminations of bamboo and deciduous wood (usually *haze* wood) and is therefore classed as a laminated bow. Discussion of its bold proportions, asymmetric elegance and gracious curves will be found in the final part of this book, for it is not a true composite bow.

A bow is a spring. Bending the limbs stores elastic potential energy, which is then released when the bow is shot. The heavier the draw-weight of the bow, the more energy is generated. However, the efficiency of composite-bow materials and design meant that less effort had to be expended for a performance equivalent to that of a self or laminated bow. An English longbow, for example, would need to be of significantly higher draw-weight to launch an arrow of the same weight and dimensions at the same speed.

Composite bows were high-status weapons – they were expensive. Manufacture required highly developed skills and took a long time. The glues used to bond the sinew and horn were slow to dry, and a composite bow was at least several months in the making. In fact, there is a correlation between how long a bow was left to dry and set in a pre-stressed shape before moving to the next stage of manufacture and the resultant power of that bow. The strongest bows took one or even two years to produce, and that gave them considerable value.

Despite their expense, composite bows were used in large numbers, both by regiments of infantry archers and massed troops of horse-archers. Even so, this widespread employment did nothing to diminish the high standing of the composite bow among warrior elites – it remained the aristocratic weapon of choice.

Medieval treatises on *furūsiyya* – the Arabic knightly arts of war – extol the use of the bow on horseback as the most noble of skills. There are also surviving manuscripts from various Chinese dynasties, Ottoman Turkey, India and Persia, among others, which offer practical instruction for both infantry- and horse-archers. Their existence is an indicator that the upper echelons of the composite-bow-archer class were, in large part, educated and literate. It is not until 1545, with the publication of Roger Ascham's *Toxophilus*, that an equivalent work was available in the West.

Arabs, Assyrians, Avars, Chinese, Egyptians, Hittites, Huns, Koreans, Magyars, Mongols, Mughals, Parthians, Persians, Scythians, Tartars and Turks are among the chief peoples to have used and venerated the composite bow. There are others, spanning both time and continent, and all jostle for attention. In this brief survey it is only possible to touch on a few themes and to sample just some of the practices and archery lore from such a span of cultures. I hope, though, that it will be enough to stimulate the reader into further study of this most fascinating and bewitching of arms.

DEVELOPMENT: ENGINEERING THE OPTIMAL BOW

Geometry

There are two essential elements to a composite bow – the geometry and the materials. To begin with the geometry: bow-limbs that bend away from the archer are known as reflex and those that bend towards the archer are known as deflex. A combination of reflex and deflex is called a recurve. Composite bows appear in a variety of forms but they are all, to a greater or lesser extent, recurve bows. There is a trade-off of benefits between reflex and deflex, and the search for the perfect bow led to an extraordinary diversity in bow designs.

One distinct advantage of a recurve bow is that the design, combined with the powerfully elastic properties of the materials, induces the limbs to return with an accelerating velocity; this in turn transfers into arrow speed. To deliver an equivalent performance with a non-recurve self-bow would require a heavier draw-weight. Secondly, a recurve design requires less work from the archer to draw the bow to its full extent. When drawing a bow, the ends of the bow (the *kasan* and *bash* sections and, where present, the *siyahs*) do not bend, but rather act as levers. With a relatively straight-limbed bow such as the longbow, for example, there comes a point where the tips pass an optimal angle and no longer offer mechanical advantage to bending the limbs. At this point the archer perceives an increase in the effort required to draw the bow, a phenomenon known as stacking. It feels harder to pull, yet there has been no actual increase in either power or draw-weight. Once the tips cease to act as levers, the archer is in effect trying to stretch the limbs rather than to bend them. By changing the angle of the energy transfer, the recurve limbs of a composite bow, acting like crowbars, permit the archer to draw a bow of comparable draw-weight for significantly less muscular exertion.

Contact recurve bows, having long *siyahs* that sweep away from the archer, offered an additional advantage to the archer – 'let-off'. Although he had to push through an initial resistance at the commencement of the draw, as the levers reached the appropriate angle, he would feel a distinct let-off in draw-weight. This in turn enabled

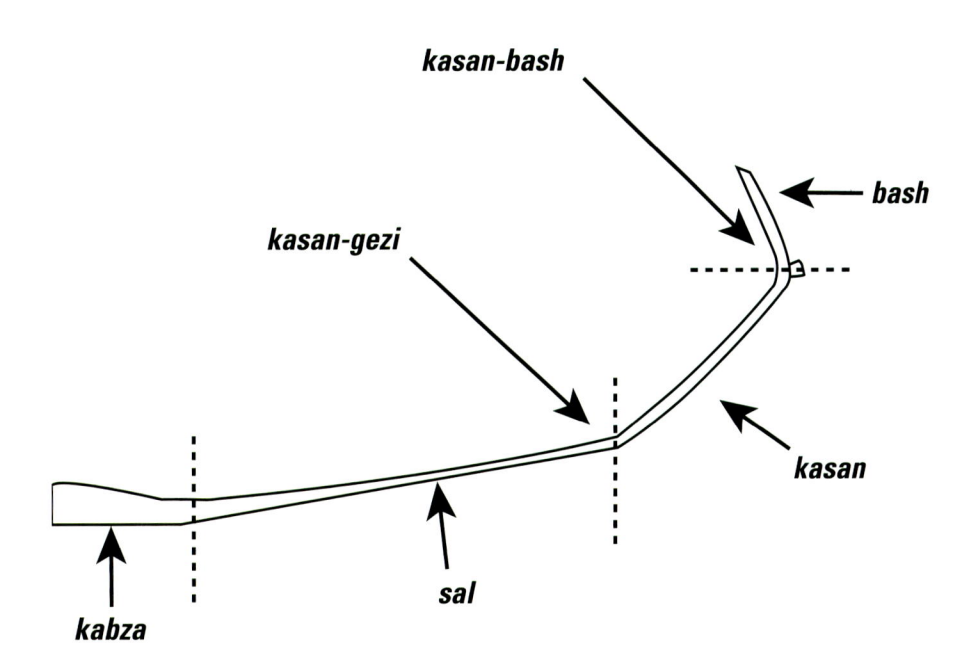

Parts of the bow were named, in their respective languages, by all the cultures that used the composite bow. Because bows from the Ottoman Empire were the ones most familiar to English-speaking antiquarians, an orthodoxy arose, in English, to use Turkish terminology when discussing composite-bow design. The term *kabza* refers to the grip; the *sal* is the primary bending section and the *kasan* is the stiff section of the limb, usually ridged for strength, which embodies the recurve. The *kasan-gezi* is the angled join between the *sal* and the *kasan*; this is the juncture at which recurvature begins. The *bash* is an angled static tip that acts as a lever, usually of solid wood; the *kasan-bash* is the angled join between the *kasan* and the *bash*. An exception to this is the word *siyah*, which is of Arabic extraction. *Siyah* is equivalent to *bash* but is applied, by English speakers, to the non-bending lever extensions to a bow when they are of notable length, irrespective of which civilization the bow comes from. (Drawing by Robert J. Molineaux)

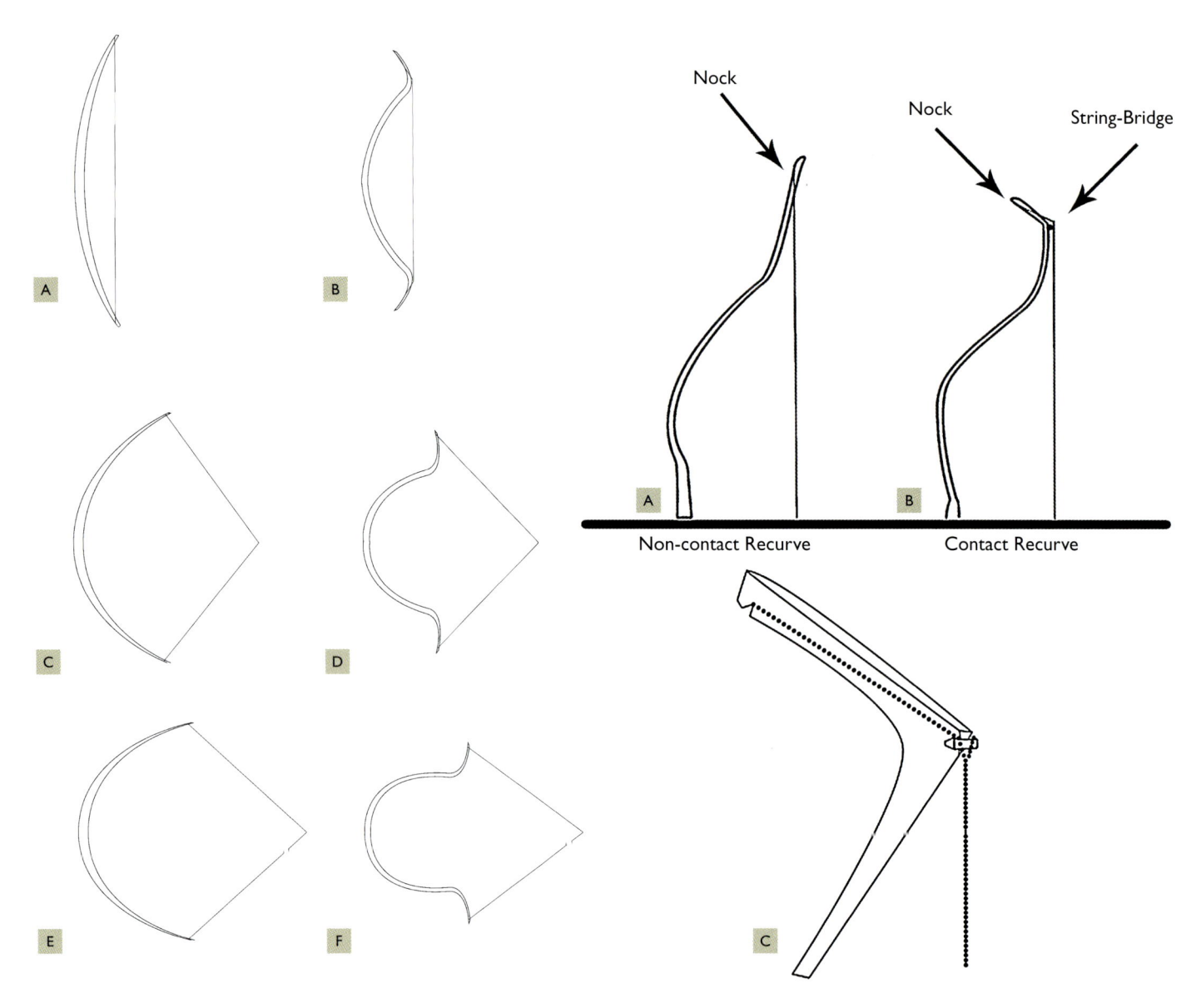

ABOVE LEFT Here we see a mechanical difference between a straight-limbed bow (**A**) and a recurve bow (**B**) Centre left we see a straight-limbed bow drawn to its optimal point for bending (**C**). This is the limit of this bow's mechanical efficiency, although it is not necessarily at full draw. Centre right, we see a recurve bow drawn to an equivalent length (**D**). Here the limbs retain considerable potential for bending beyond this point and the *siyahs* are about to come into play to assist that further bend. Bottom left, we see the straight-limbed bow pulled beyond its optimal bending curve (**E**) where the limbs are now being stretched rather than bent. Bottom right, we see the recurve bow drawn to an equivalent length (**F**) where the rigid *siyahs* continue to work as levers to lessen the work required to flex the bending section, demonstrating both the greater efficiency and the longer draw of the recurve design. (Drawings by Robert J. Molineaux)

ABOVE RIGHT One further aspect of geometry to be noted is the distinction between non-contact (**A**) and contact (**B**) recurve bows. On some bow designs, particularly those with highly reflexed *siyahs* – that is, pointing away from the archer – the string comes into contact with the bow at the upper end in the resting position and if left unmodified, it would have a tendency to slip off. Obviously, there is a requirement for the string to form a taut and straight line. The remedy was to affix a block, usually of horn, wood or bone at the junction between *kasan* and *siyah*. This was known as a string bridge (**C**) or string pad, depending on its prominence. On a Qing bow, for instance, the bridge needed to be quite large, whereas on a Turkish or Korean bow only a small pad was required to seat the string correctly. (Drawing by Robert J. Molineaux)

him to hold at full draw for longer. The downside of this design was that with beefed-up *siyahs* and string bridges, there was an addition of mass to the limb: mass that required energy to shift, energy that would otherwise have been transferred to the arrow. With a non-contact recurve bow, there remained some degree of lever advantage, and because the angle was more torsionally stable, the *siyahs* could be made thinner and lighter, which enabled a more efficient energy transfer to the arrow. Every design modification in the composite bow's many manifestations had both advantages and consequences.

Origins

The discovery of the advantages offered by a recurve design may have coincided with the early adoption of composite materials. Adding a sinew backing to strengthen a wooden bow seems the most likely first step; sinew's value as a strong and elastic material was well understood by early peoples. Many Native American bows were made with wood and a sinew backing alone. Compared to wood fibres, sinew fibres have a greater capacity to stretch before breaking, and the back of a bow (the part facing away from the archer) stretches the fibres a great deal on bending. Moreover, the sinew is applied wet in an adhesive solution and it shrinks as it dries. This shrinkage compresses the wood fibres so that they in turn are also more resilient to being pulled apart under tension. As the drying sinew shrinks, it also pulls the tips of the bow away from the archer and creates a basic reflex design.

Sinew-backed bows with their higher tolerance of tensile failure enabled shorter bows to be made. This was especially useful in areas where long billets of suitably elastic bow-woods (such as yew or elm) were not available. Even where such woods were available – the North American West Coast, for instance – shorter, sinew-backed bows were widely used, possibly because hunters seeking concealment in low brush preferred them and because they offered greater power and general toughness.

Simple composites of wood and sinew produced very serviceable bows, but the next step was to enhance the power of the limbs by adding horn. Shorter bows were particularly suited to this improvement because continuous strips of horn, whether from water buffalo, bighorn sheep or mountain goats, are limited in size. The inherent 'springiness' of horn, especially its ability to store energy under compression, made it the ideal material to complement the tensile strength of sinew. However, the essential advance that enabled the genesis of true composite bows was the discovery of the right types of glue. Only hide and fish glues have the strength and pliability to bond the sinew, and the horn, to a wooden core. The elasticity of these glues also contributes

The author with his replica of a Klamath Valley Native American bow, which has a magnificent piece of yew at its core. Built by Robert Molineaux, it was based on finds from the Klamath River Valley. Note how the sinew backing has pulled the limbs into reflex. The sinew has been painted to seal it from the damaging effects of moisture. Unstrung, it is only 40 inches from nock to nock, but its broad limbs and the sinew backing allow it to be drawn without breaking. It packs a punch of around 50lb, even though it can only be drawn to about 20 inches. A shorter draw is common with many aboriginal cultures. Expert stalking skills enabled the hunter to get extremely close to his prey and a short draw minimized movement so as not to startle the animal. (Kim Hawkins)

to the overall spring and resilience of composite bows. (Exceptionally, some Inuit bows have the sinew bound to the wooden core with an elaborate knot system because of the difficulties of manufacturing appropriate glues in extremely cold temperatures.)

Although the wooden core remained important to hold the bow in shape, in particular resisting torque, and although it continued to assist in the delivery of elastic power, its main function was to act as a framework for the shape of the bow. With everything held in place by multiple layers of sinew, the wooden core was able to take on elaborate shapes created by a series of joins. It could therefore be used to build engineered geometries that would optimize the potential energy created by the horn, the sinew and the wood when under strain.

Typology of composite bows

The diversity of historical composite-bow designs is vast, and space only permits a brief summary of some of the more predominant types.

THE SCYTHIAN BOW

The Scythian bow lays claim to be one of the earliest types of fully composite bow, and it remained in use for many centuries. It is an extraordinary and elaborate construction of opposing curves that was once thought to be the product of artists' fanciful imaginations. During the first decade of the 21st century, however, archaeologists unearthed a number of bows, including one almost completely intact example, from graves in the Yanghai cemetery, Xinjiang, China. This magnificent bow is approximately 3,000 years old and reveals the same sinewy contours of a type of bow represented widely in Greek art. It was a Scythian bow.

In 2009 a magnificent working replica of the Yanghai bow was constructed by Adam Karpowicz. It was based on measurements and analysis by Stephen Selby, who had inspected the original at first hand. The bow possessed a central core formed by a continuous strip of horn in each limb, sandwiched between laths of wood, each approximately 6 inches in length and spliced to its fellow. The laminated core has a triangular cross-section, with the apex facing the belly of the bow. Fillets of wood were then applied to build out the bow along its length, creating a slightly more rounded cross-section before applying the sinew layer to the back of the bow. The whole was then wrapped in sinew and covered with a protective layer of birch bark. Among excavated samples there is some variation to the internal construction methodology, but all have a closely similar overall length and external shape.

It has not to date been possible to verify the precise type of wood or horn used in the original, though the wood is believed to have been tamarisk. Water buffalo horn was used for building the replica, but Selby and Karpowicz have speculated that it may have been the natural curl of the horn from the Siberian ibex that endowed the Scythian bow with its idiosyncratic shape (Selby & Karpowicz 2010: 94–102). If this is so, as seems probable, it begs the question as to whether the highly complex form of the Scythian bow was informed entirely by mechanical principles, or whether there was some belief in the shamanic power of the ibex. Certainly the ibex, along

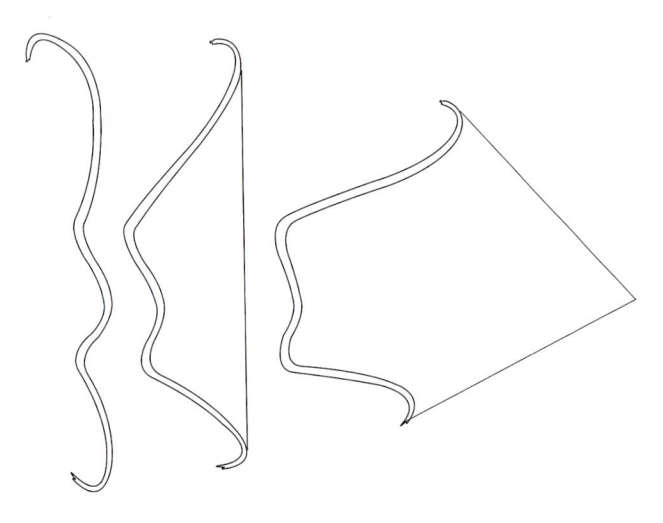

No other bow embodies both extremes of reflex and deflex to quite the same extent as the Scythian bow. According to the Greek historian Herodotus (5th century BC) the Scythians were a nomadic people, originating in the North Caucasus, Crimea and Black Sea regions. By the early centuries AD, the designation of Scythian ethnicity had become both broad and vague, encompassing a variety of peoples who inhabited the Pontic–Caspian Steppe. Celebrated as expert horse-archers with composite bows, the Scythians spread their influence – and their bows – even further afield. They reached west as far as the Danube, Indo-Scythians populated the Punjab region of north-west India and, to the east, their material artefacts have been found in areas of China adjacent to the silk routes. (Drawing by Robert J. Molineaux)

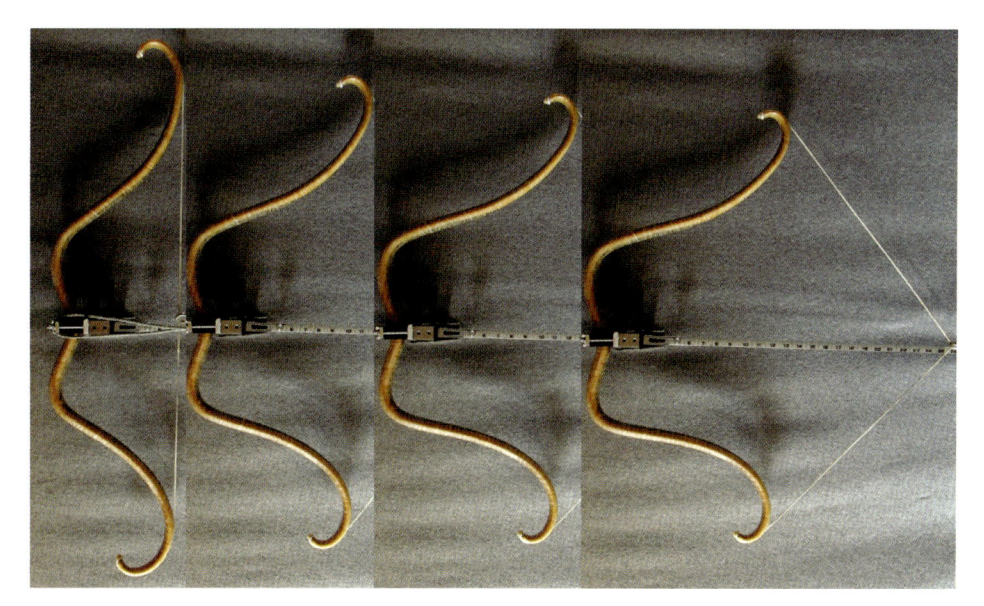

Replica Scythian bow, by Adam Karpowicz, showing the dramatic changes in profile as the bow is drawn. It has a draw-weight of 120lb at 28 inches. This shorter draw of the Scythian bow is often seen in art. However, arrows found alongside the original bow measured between 30 and 31 inches, indicating the possibility of a longer draw. Selby and Karpowicz calculate that the range of draw-weights for the Scythian bow would probably fall between 80lb and 140lb, comparable to estimates for other types of composite bow (Selby & Karpowicz 2010: 94–102). When considering draw-weights, it should be noted that the Scythian bow was also the bow of the 'Amazons', those celebrated warrior women who so terrified the Ancient Greeks with their horse-archery skills. Though undoubtedly a match for any man with their riding, shooting and ferocity, it may be that they used bows with draw-weights at the lower end of the scale. However, for the horse-archer, who can ride close to his target, this would not be a disadvantage. (Photograph courtesy of Adam Karpowicz)

with the sturgeon (from which the best possible glue can be made for bonding the sinew) is prevalent in Scythian art, and it may have been thought that a weapon that embodied its mighty horns in some way took on some of its power. For further examination of Scythian archery and the author's experience using replica equipment, see pages 217–225.

THE ANGULAR BOW

It is possible that the Scythian style was the first type of composite bow, but there is another contender. In contrast to the sinuous serpentine curvature of the Scythian bow is the stark, linear geometry of the angular bow. Developed in the Ancient Near East, this is the type of bow that is represented universally in art from Mesopotamia to Anatolia and, most significantly, evidenced in surviving specimens of actual bows, notably those from the tomb of Tutankhamun. It is generally accepted that the angular bow was introduced into Egypt by the Hyksos at some point during the 17th century BC. The Hyksos probably originated from somewhere in the Levant. The angular bow became the bow of choice for Egyptians, Hittites and Assyrians and many others in the region. It was the universal bow for the chariot-archer and, with the Assyrians, transferred to be the arm of the horse-archer. As an infantry weapon it was employed both on the battlefield and in siege warfare.

At first glance, viewed when strung but not yet drawn, the angular bow appears to be a most unlikely shape for a bow. The steep angle at the centre gives the impression that the bow is already starting to break. However, it is in fact an excellent bow. Neither the horn nor the sinew have joins at the apex of the angle – both run in continuous strips through the angle in laminated overlays. Moreover, the grip comes under relatively little load when the entire bow is flexing.

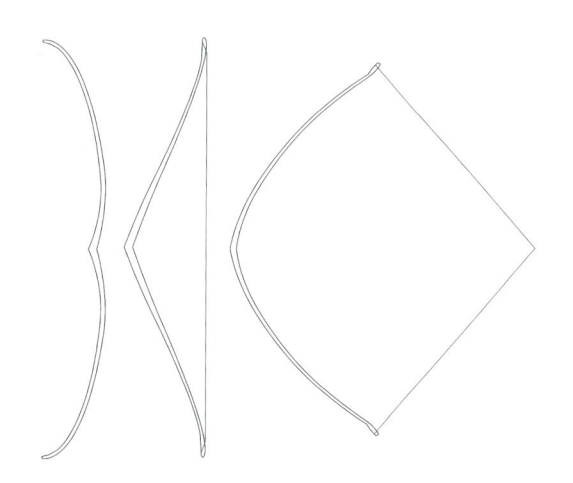

In its unstrung mode, the angular bow resembles a very flattened 'W'; note the very pronounced deflex angle at the grip. When the angular bow is strung, the limbs assume the familiar triangular shape seen in art of the region, though it should be noted that there is more curve in the limbs and reflex at the tips than some of the cruder representations in art would suggest. When the angular bow is drawn fully, a little bit of archery magic occurs as the bow morphs yet again, forming a perfect crescent. The acute deflex angle at the grip facilitates the extremely long draw – the draw-hand reaching to the right shoulder – that we see in art depicting these bows. There are advantages to a long draw, just as there are to a longer barrel on a gun – the propelling force of the string acts on the arrow for a more sustained period. (Drawing by Robert J. Molineaux)

THE COMPOSITE BOW

163

This replica angular bow, in the author's collection, was made by Lukas Novotny of Saluki Bow. The birch bark covering protects the sinew from the elements. It is a fast and powerful bow. Exceptionally light in the hand, despite its 75lb draw-weight, it is easy to manoeuvre. I have shot it on foot, from chariots and from horseback. Angular bows have especially narrow limbs, less than an inch wide before the bark wrap is applied, which means that they are vulnerable to torsion. When I first took delivery of my angular bow, I had a number of alarming moments as it sprung out of my hand. It turned itself inside out when attempting to string it or loosing it. It did this with a mighty and terrifying force! The problem was that I didn't have the bracing height set correctly. Bracing height is the distance between the centre of the string and the centre of the bow when strung in the resting position. Small adjustments can be made by twisting the string to shorten or lengthen it. Angular bows require a higher-than-average bracing height in order to hold the limbs under the correct tension to be stable. It was in an attempt to redress this stability problem that these bows have such an accentuated deflex at the grip; it helps to direct the limbs to bend in the correct alignment. (Kim Hawkins)

The bow of the Achaemenid Persians combined the simple lines of the angular bow with the sinuous elegance of the Scythian bow. Sufficiently reflexed to offer exceptionally high-speed limb return with elongated tips that provided efficient leverage for a powerful draw and sufficiently deflexed at the grip section to accommodate a long draw, this was a beautifully designed bow. (Drawing by Robert J. Molineaux)

THE ACHAEMENID BOW

The Achaemenid Empire, known also as the First Persian Empire (*c.*550–330 BC), was founded by Cyrus the Great and became the largest empire in the Ancient World. It employed masses of infantry archers in its armies, the scourge of the Greek city-states. This is the bow of the famed 'Immortals', a select force of 10,000 men who served as elite infantry on the battlefield and also as the Imperial Guard. It was also a bow that was put to good use by horse-archers.

THE TURKISH BOW

Under Ottoman rule, archery was practised in every city, town and village, archery literature abounded and archers of merit were held in the highest esteem. This was so in other composite-bow cultures, but perhaps nowhere was archery quite as venerated as it was in the realms of the Ottoman Turks. Being able to shoot the furthest distance became a national obsession, and they took bow design to new frontiers. There were two main types of Ottoman Turkish bow – the *hilal kuram* bow and the *tekne kuram* bow. Each shape achieves a different goal by varying the length of the limbs, adjusting the curve and setting the stiffness of the *kasan-gezi*.

Hilal kuram bows were designed for flight-shooting – an activity that enjoyed great popularity as an aristocratic sport in Ottoman Turkey and which was concerned solely with the distance an arrow can be shot – and had the ability to cast very light arrows a very great distance. I own two, both made by the master bowyer Lukas Novotny. This is not a novice bow, though I was a novice when I acquired mine. Suffice to say that when things go wrong, as they do with such a virtuoso instrument, the epithet 'temperamental' is not exclusive to the bow. Even so, I find these bows astonishingly beautiful; they have taught me a great deal, and I enjoy shooting them immensely. As I draw them, I never cease to be thrilled by their dramatic changes in shape and the extraordinary power of such a feather-light object.

In addition to these two main types, there were other Turkish bows, including one called the *kepade*, which was a light draw-weight, slightly reflexed bow, used exclusively for practising form. It had a padded section on the string and the tyro used it with a three-finger draw for conditioning. Mustafa Kani, a Turkish master who wrote a treatise on archery in 1847, commands the novice to be able to draw it 500 times in succession without tiring. As if this were not daunting enough, he adds 'it is altogether advantageous if he can draw it 30,000 times' (quoted in Klopsteg 1987: 111). Further, Kani stipulates that all archers, whatever their level of experience and no matter how busy they are with other matters, should draw the practice bow 66 times every morning upon rising throughout their lives. (66 is a number of religious significance to Muslims.)

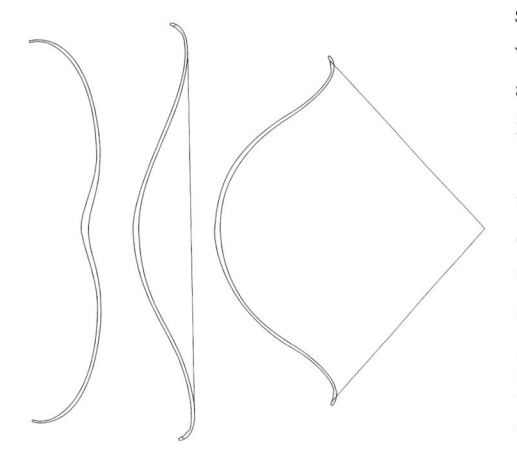

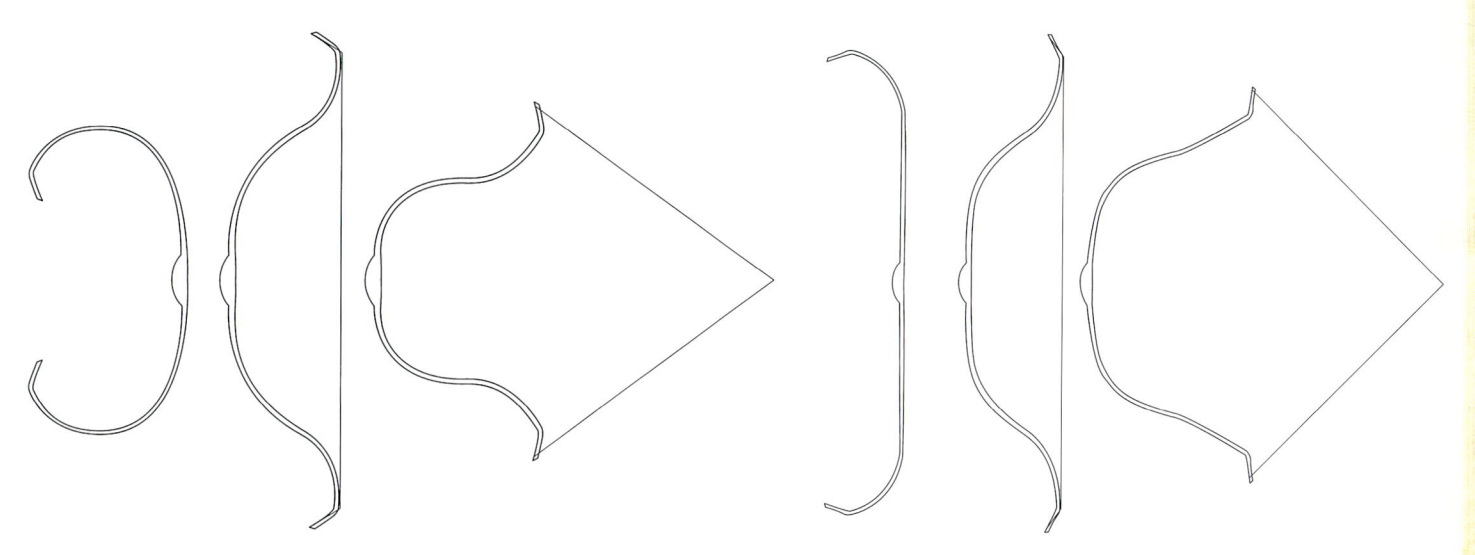

ABOVE LEFT The *hilal kuram* or 'crescent moon shape' bow is short with slender limbs, and is extremely reflexed – characteristics that reduce its mass, enhancing the speed of limb return – but at the cost of making it less stable. By having a long, continuous transition between the *sal* and the *kasan* sections, which remained stiff in all stages of the bend, the *hilal kuram* bow bent in an arc closer to the central grip than was common in other bows. This increased the bow's mechanical efficiency but further reduced its stability. The result is a bow that can be temperamental but with a cast that is unparalleled. (Drawing by Robert J. Molineaux)

ABOVE RIGHT The *tekne kuram* or 'boat shape' bow was designed for both warfare and target archery. Wider-limbed and less reflexed than the *hilal kuram* bow, the *tekne kuram*, most importantly, had a moderately bendable *kasan-gezi*. This subtle and supple flex in the *kasan-gezi* offered advantages to a bow that had to withstand the rigours of campaign, albeit at the expense of some mechanical efficiency. It made the bow more stable and much less likely to turn inside out. Moreover, *tekne kuram* bows could, if necessary, be left strung for extended periods of time, because the stresses were distributed over wider and longer limbs. (Drawing by Robert J. Molineaux)

The explosive power of the Turkish bow is evident in these two images of *hilal kuram* bows, both made by Lukas Novotny. Note the extreme reversal of the curve of the limbs from the resting to the strung state. Tremendous forces are at work here. (Kim Hawkins)

The back and sides of Turkish bows, where the sinew was exposed, were covered with fine leather and sealed with varnish, usually sandarac. This not only protected the sinew from the warping effects of moisture but it also provided a reasonably rugged outer skin to withstand the knocks and bumps of military life. These leather facings also provided a canvas for the most exquisitely painted and gilded arabesque decoration. When combined with similar ornament on the highly polished surface of the horn belly, this created bows of exceptional beauty.

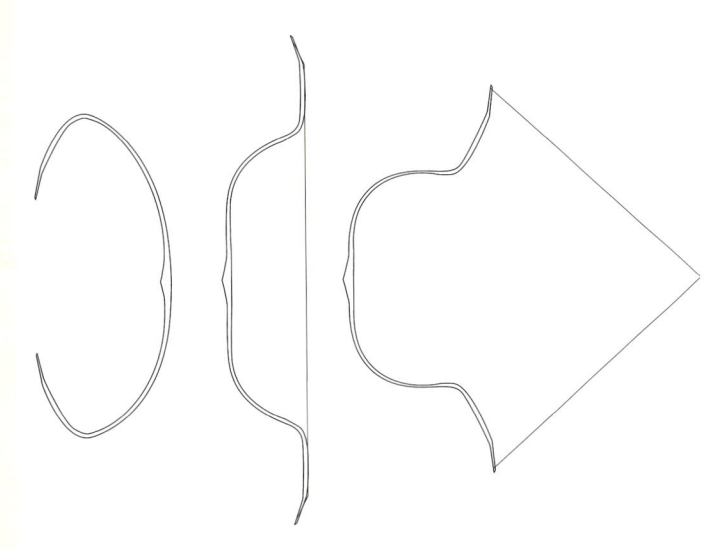

THE MUGHAL CRAB BOW

Closely allied to the Turkish *hilal kuram* is the *kaman* or crab bow of Mughal India. This remarkable bow took recurve design and the properties of composite materials to the extreme. In some examples the tips, in the unstrung state, curl so acutely towards the centre that they overlap, resembling the pincers of a crab.

Unlike the *hilal kuram*, however, the limbs of the crab bow are wide, allowing the bow to be left strung for extended periods of time. This was often desirable because the process of stringing and unstringing such a bow could be both exhausting and somewhat perilous. The broader limbs also meant that it didn't quite have the ultimate performance of its slender Turkish cousin.

THE INDO-PERSIAN BOW

Widely used both on the battlefield and in the chase was the Indo-Persian bow. Unlike Ottoman bows, which were typically built with a three-piece wooden core construction, Indo-Persian bows usually consist of a five- or even seven-part wooden core. Their simpler, elegant external form masks an intricate level of engineering within. Moreover, the breathtaking magnificence of their painted and gilded surface decoration is a match for even the finest Ottoman bow. While Ottoman bows are decorated exclusively in intricate scrolling and floral patterns, Indo-Persian bows often feature delightful figurative painting.

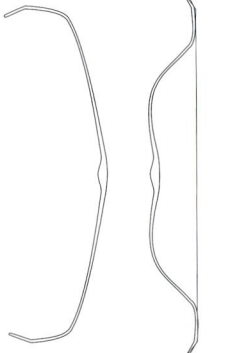

THE CRIMEAN TATAR BOW

Even though they were substantially longer, Crimean Tatar bows were constructed using methods closely similar to those used to manufacture Ottoman Turkish bows. The Crimean Tatars were an integral part of the Ottoman military, and Ottoman bowyers regularly produced their native style of bows to satisfy military demand in that region. Crimean Tatar bows had long working limbs and, often, a deeply reflexed grip. The transition into the *kasan* at the *kasan-gezi* was much less acute than in shorter bows, and the *kasan* itself takes up less of the bow's length proportionally when compared to Ottoman bows.

Crab bows place an enormous amount of reflex into the bow's *kasan-gezi* and a small amount in the transition between the *kasan* and *bash*. Both of these reflex points are then left completely stiff and non-flexible, forcing the entire bend in to the working limbs alone. The result is a bow that at full draw pushes the ends of the working limbs past the point of being parallel to each other! (Drawing by Robert J. Molineaux)

ABOVE The working sections of the Indo-Persian bow are wider and longer than those of Ottoman war bows, while the *kasan* and *bash* sections are shorter. This results in a stable bow that is fast and also capable of delivering a heavier war arrow than its Ottoman counterpart. (Drawing by Robert J. Molineaux)

RIGHT An Indo-Persian bow in the collections of the Pitt Rivers Museum, Oxford. Note the broad limbs. The back of the bow has been exquisitely painted with scenes from the hunt. (1936.76.1 © Pitt Rivers Museum, University of Oxford)

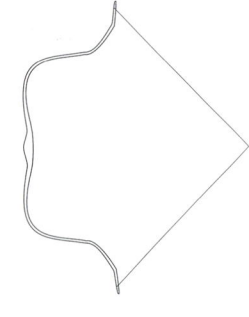

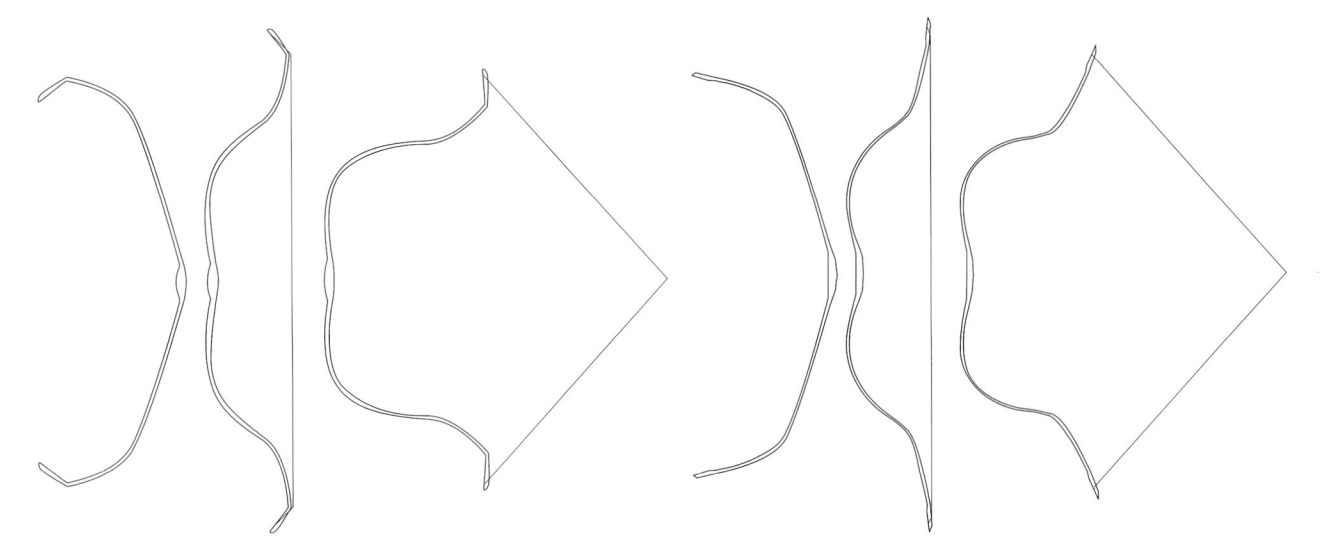

LEFT Most significantly, the Crimean Tatar bow possesses *siyahs*. Similar to the *bash*, in that they are a non-bending tip to the bow, *siyahs* are much longer wooden extensions adjoining the *kasan*. They accentuate the mechanical assistance given to the archer in pulling back the limbs; they are levers. In particular, they facilitate the use of a long draw and a heavy draw-weight. The Crimean Tatar bow was well suited to shooting a lengthy war-arrow of considerable mass. (Drawing by Robert J. Molineaux)

RIGHT The Hun bow is a powerful, robust, medium-sized bow with long *siyahs*. Although it is most associated with the area that is now Hungary and it achieved its greatest military distinction in the marauding armies of Attila, it should perhaps be considered more of a pan-Eurasian bow, as its geographical dispersal was very wide. It is essentially an old Turkic steppe design that may lay claim to being one of the longest in continuous use. (Drawing by Robert J. Molineaux)

THE MAGYAR/HUN BOW

The principal materials of composite bows – horn, wood, sinew – decompose readily. Consequently, there is a scarcity of excavated evidence for most types of composite bow. Exceptions to this are the bows of the Huns and Magyars – twin branches of what may be broadly thought of as the same peoples. Their bows used plates of bone as side panels to stiffen both the grip and the *siyahs*, and bone survives very well in almost any soil condition. It was the practice of these peoples to bury a warrior with his bow laid across his chest. Numerous graves, from Siberia to Western Europe, have been unearthed with the bone plates *in situ* and intact. This has enabled precise and reliable calculations to be made for the size and shape of the original bows. The *siyahs* on a Hun bow were angled to correct twist in the working limbs. Although not the most efficient of composite bows, this type was among the most user-friendly and received widespread use with peoples living a rugged outdoor life.

The asymmetric Hun bow has the upper limb longer than the lower limb – a feature it shares with the Japanese *yumi*. (Drawing by Robert J. Molineaux)

THE ASYMMETRIC HUN BOW

A variation of the regular Hunnic bow, which also had the grip and *siyahs* stiffened with bone plates, was one with asymmetric configuration. The mechanical benefits of asymmetric design are hotly debated among bowyers, but the arguments are too lengthy and technical to consider here. One theory is that it was a way of providing a bow with considerable draw-length and power – a long bow – while maintaining the lower limb as short as possible for convenient use on horseback.

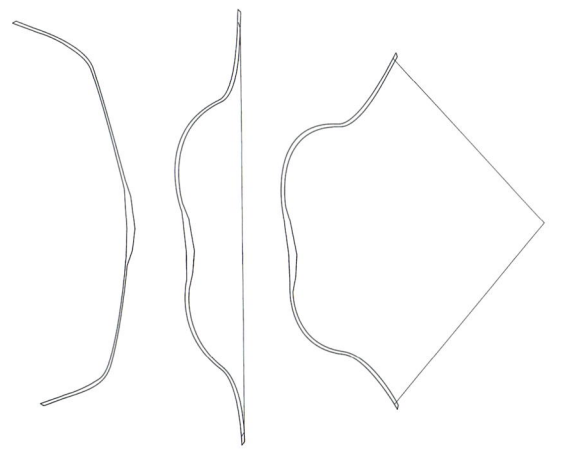

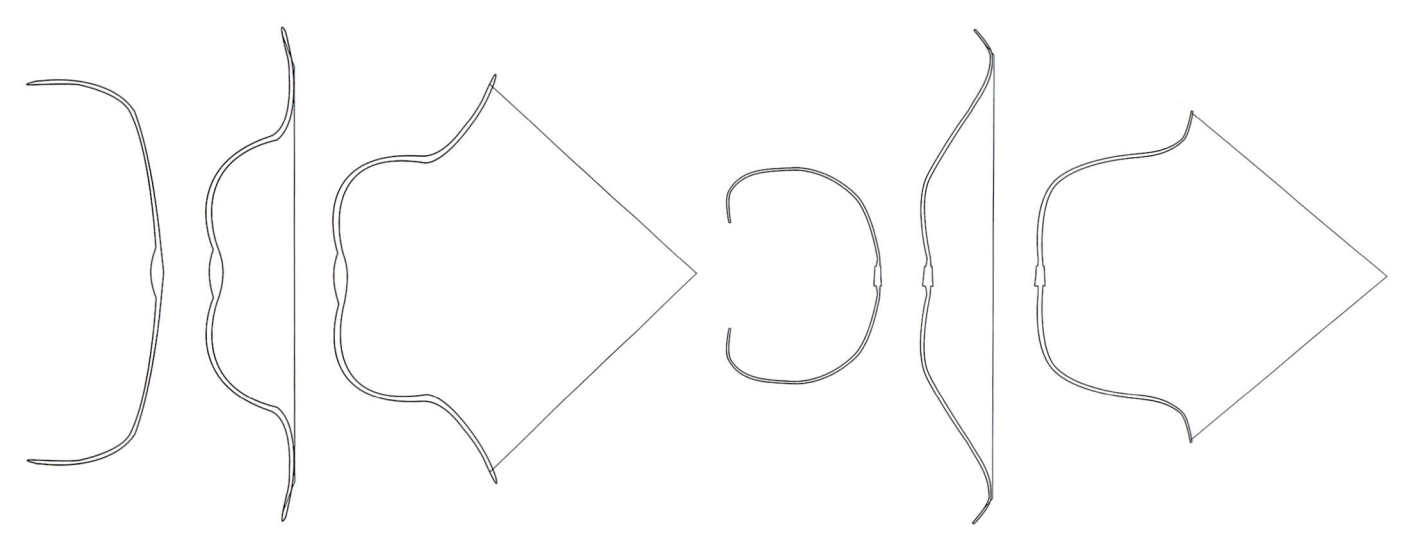

LEFT The drawing here represents a bow of the Genghis Khan (Conquest) period. It is based upon a bow found, still strung, in a cave at Tsagaan Khad, Mongolia, dated to the 14th century, and upon bows depicted in contemporary paintings. Images in art show bows that were relatively short with broad limbs. They had long, sweeping *siyahs* and a prominent semi-triangular *kasan* section that provided the necessary structural strength between the accelerating forward angle of the nocks and the acute reflex of the bending limbs. The Tsagaan Khad bow showed traces of delicate decoration with red, black and yellow pigment, gold leaf, and birch bark inlays. It also possessed a red silk string. The bows that are in common use in Mongolia today are in fact a slightly smaller variant of the Qing bow. They are not bows that would have been familiar to Genghis Khan or his successors in the 13th century. (Drawing by Robert J. Molineaux)

RIGHT Similar in many ways to the Ottoman flight bow, the Korean bow was designed for extreme performance. Examples of older Korean war bows show that the limbs were originally wider, offering the necessary stability for a battlefield weapon. (Drawing by Robert J. Molineaux)

THE MONGOLIAN BOW

By the 17th century the Mongols had all but abandoned use of the bow in warfare. Their principal adversaries, the Manchu (Chinese Qing Dynasty, 1644–1912), were the last major culture to continue the use of the bow as a mainstream weapon. It was only after the fall of the Dzungar Khanate (1758) that the bow, in the form of the Qing bow, was reintroduced into Mongolian martial culture.

THE KOREAN BOW

The Choson Dynasty dominated the Korean peninsula for five centuries (1392–1897), and archery flourished under its influence, achieving both a military and cultural high status. The Korean bow is a very fast bow that embodies an astounding amount of spring and elasticity, resulting in phenomenal cast. Its very narrow, fine limbs and its high degree of reflex render it prone to twisting and reversing, however, and it requires constant and expert tuning and maintenance.

THE MING BOW

Archery was valued very highly indeed in the military culture of the Ming Dynasty (1368–1644); it played a central role on the battlefield, in the hunt and in the lavish military spectacles of the Ming court. To date, there has been no excavated example of a Ming bow, nor have any survived in collections. Nevertheless, there is no shortage of references in art, giving a clear idea of the various forms in common use. Moreover Gao Ying, writing in 1637 in his treatise *The Way of Archery*, fills in the gaps with detailed accounts of materials and construction techniques. He also cautions: 'When people these days choose bows, they pay attention to whether the outside is shiny and pretty. They do not realize the most critical element of the bow is the core, followed by the tips, then the horn, the sinew and lastly the glue' (quoted in Tian & Ma 2015: 75).

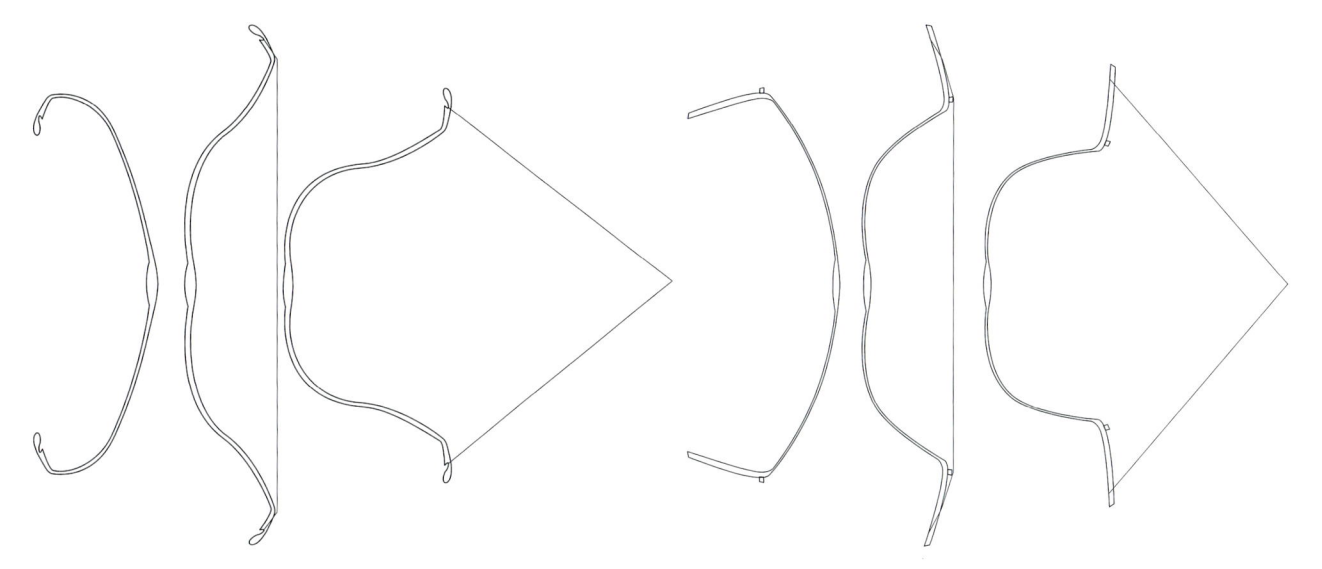

LEFT While most bowyers use a tree wood for the core, the builders of Ming bows favoured seasoned bamboo, and Gao Ying goes into considerable detail about the various stages of preparation that are necessary for this material. He also specifies where the best horn, sinew and glues are to be obtained and recommends mulberry for the *siyahs* (Tian & Ma 2015: 75–77). (Drawing by Robert J. Molineaux)

RIGHT The Qing bow's large proportions were designed to propel an especially heavy arrow to deliver a thumping blow that, at short range, would more than match the impact of a musket ball. In order to do this the Qing bow was fitted with long *siyahs*, tremendously powerful levers that abutted to the bending section of the limbs at an extreme angle and via a short but very stout *kasan*, which provided an entirely stiff transition between the *siyah* and the bending limb. This configuration offered the capacity for an exceptionally long draw – Manchu archers drew all the way back to the point of the right shoulder – and very powerful draw-weights. (Drawing by Robert J. Molineaux)

THE QING BOW

The Qing or Manchu bow is the longest and most massive of all composite-bow types. It is a very impressive bow indeed. Qing bows favoured mulberry, or similar wood, as the core; bamboo cores were considered inferior. The Qing Dynasty (1644–1912), known also as the Manchu Dynasty, coincided with the age of firearms and the use of the musket on the battlefield. Yet, for these fierce warriors from Manchuria, the bow retained a pre-eminent role both as an infantry and a cavalry weapon.

The Qing bow sits at the opposite end of the spectrum from the Turkish flight bow. It was the optimal design for shooting the heaviest and longest of arrows and delivering them with a hefty thump of kinetic energy. It was a bow for the power shot, rather than the rapid shot. Despite its great size, it was managed adroitly by Manchu horse-archers both on the battlefield and in the hunt and Manchu infantry archers were agile and nimble, often shooting on the move.

One sub-type of Qing bows that are of special interest are 'strength bows', sometimes known as 'numbered bows'. Larger than usual, these were broad-limbed bows of extra-heavy draw-weight, braced with a thick ox-gut string. Many, though not all, examples bore a wax seal stamped with a number. The number testified to the

An 18th-century Qing bow in the collections of the Royal Armouries, Leeds. Remarkably, it is still able to be strung. It weighs 2lb 4oz and, when strung, measures 64.7 inches. Note the long *siyahs* and the staghorn string bridges. The back is covered with birch bark and the grip with cork. (© Royal Armouries)

draw-weight of the bow, so that a No. 1 bow, for instance, had a draw-weight of just over 156lb and a No. 2 bow drew 130lb. Draw-weights did not necessarily descend uniformly with the bow's number, however, and there are references to some bows having a draw-weight as heavy as 240lb.

'Strength bows' were used during the archery component of a military examination to test a candidate's ability for drawing a heavy bow. They were never used for shooting arrows, merely as a measurement of an archer's might. The cadet extended his left arm and, holding the string with all four fingers, demonstrated, if he could, a full draw. He was obliged to perform the action three times. Such feats of strength were also accompanied by tests of shooting ability using regular bows.

Materials and manufacture

MATERIALS

The *Tale of Aquat*, an Ugaritic text from the 14th century BC and originating from what is now Syria, has the following lines:

I vow yew trees of Lebanon
I vow sinews from wild oxen;
I vow horns from mountain goats
Tendons from the hocks of a bull
I vow from a cane-forest reeds:
Give these to Kothar wa-Khasis
He'll make a bow for thee (Quoted in Pritchard 2011: 139)

Maple was considered the best wood for building the core of the bow. Note the straight grain, which helps to deter the bow from twisting. Maple was also favoured because it takes glue very well and both the lamination of the horn to the wood and the joins of the wooden core itself were dependent on the strength of adhesive bonds. (Mike Loades)

It is a list of ingredients for a composite bow and its companion arrows. The precise species of materials varied according to region and period, but all composite bows consisted of wood, horn, sinew and glue with either a bark or leather casing.

In general, maple has been the wood of choice for making the core, though there are mentions of yew in some Turkish texts. Not only does maple have a fine, straight grain and good elastic properties, it also bonds securely with adhesives: 'Maple accepts glue exceedingly well, and is one of the best-gluing of all cabinet woods' (Klopsteg 1987: 41). For the finest bows the tree has to be felled when growth is dormant, and a single bole of maple produces sufficient timber for only two bows (Klopsteg 1987: 42).

Horn from the water buffalo. This is the most widely used horn for composite bows, able to withstand compression and to store and release energy to an exceptional degree. Other types of horn can be used, though bovine horn tends to delaminate too easily. The horn is applied as a single continuous piece to each limb of the bow. It is sawn from the horn in longitudinal strips. These strips are steamed to soften them and, for uniformity, sometimes clamped against a flat iron bar while drying, in order to remove the curl. (Mike Loades)

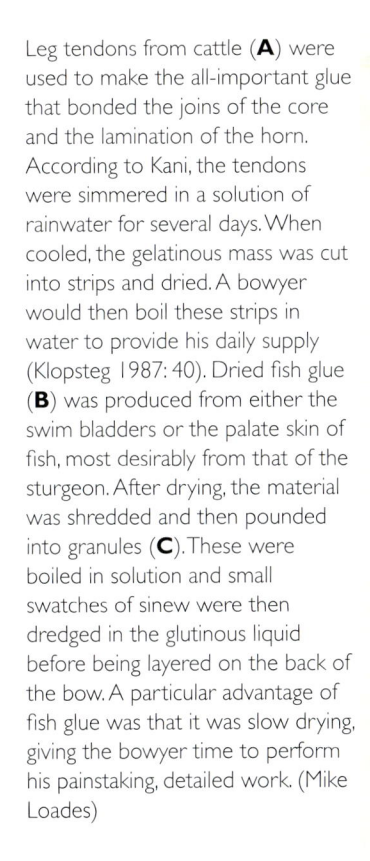

The broad, long tendons that extend along a quadruped's spine are known colloquially as 'backstrap tendon' and are usually sourced from cattle. They not only deconstruct readily into fine strands of sinew, but also produce especially long and strong fibres, which are ideal for applying to the back of the bow. After being hammered on a wooden block the sinew is worked by hand. Gradually, it is reduced to finer and finer fibres, which can then be combed and laid into neat bunches ready for applying to the bow. (Mike Loades)

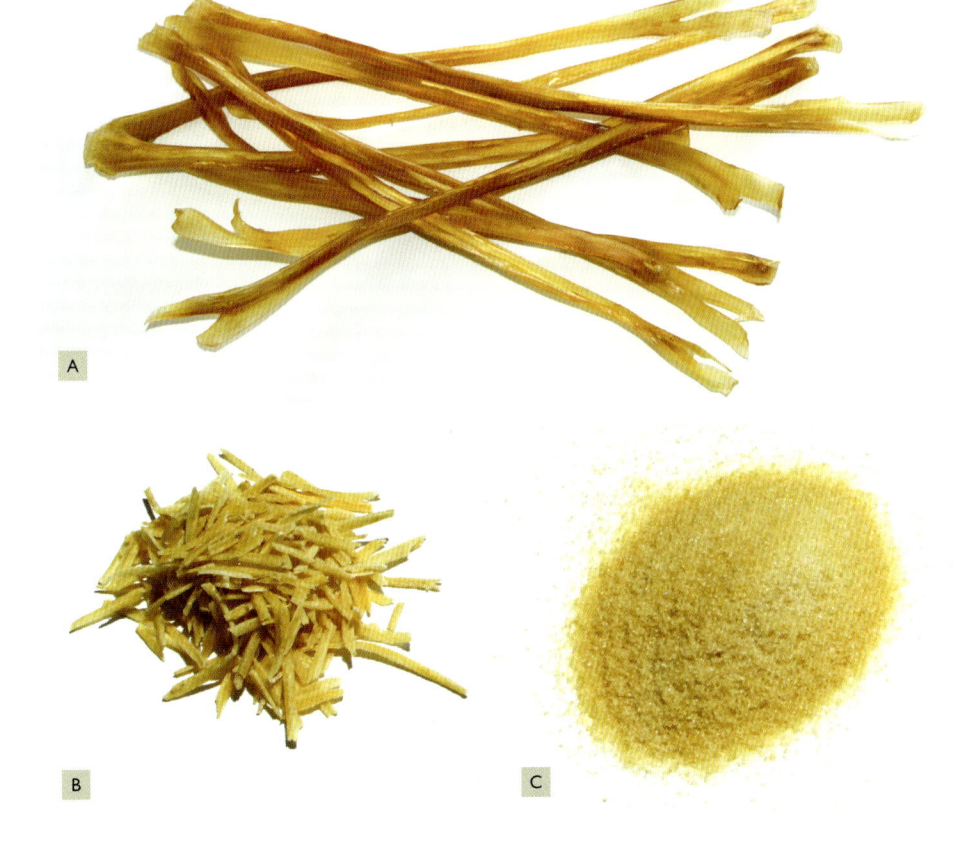

Leg tendons from cattle (**A**) were used to make the all-important glue that bonded the joins of the core and the lamination of the horn. According to Kani, the tendons were simmered in a solution of rainwater for several days. When cooled, the gelatinous mass was cut into strips and dried. A bowyer would then boil these strips in water to provide his daily supply (Klopsteg 1987: 40). Dried fish glue (**B**) was produced from either the swim bladders or the palate skin of fish, most desirably from that of the sturgeon. After drying, the material was shredded and then pounded into granules (**C**). These were boiled in solution and small swatches of sinew were then dredged in the glutinous liquid before being layered on the back of the bow. A particular advantage of fish glue was that it was slow drying, giving the bowyer time to perform his painstaking, detailed work. (Mike Loades)

BUILDING A BOW

Once the materials have been prepared, the bowyer begins by making the wooden core (**1**). Billets of maple are steam-bent to create the all-important reflex of the bending section. Once set, these are joined to the other parts of the bow, which have been meticulously shaped with saw, chisel and file. Tendon glue and precision joints ensure the structural integrity of the wooden core. High-stress zones, such as the *kasan* and the *bash*, may also be reinforced with inserts of horn.

After the glue has dried, the wooden core is scraped and sanded into a smooth finished shape (**2**). Note the engineered strength of the *kasan* profile, which manages the stress of transferring the levered power from the *bash* into the reflex resistance of the *sal*. Both the core and the strips of horn to be applied to its belly are shaped to form a convex surface on one side of the wood that will seat snugly into a corresponding concave gutter on the horn. This concave/convex shaping also provides structural strength in the same way that a retractable steel tape measure is stiffened by its shape.

Both surfaces are also scraped using a tool called a *tashin* – a bowyer's scraper (**3**). This scores parallel, corrugated lines on both the wooden core and the horn strip that attaches to it. These grooves not only increase the surface area for the glue, but also increase resistance to sideways slip.

Tendon glue is then applied to affix a strip of horn to each limb, building the muscles of the bow. The lamination is held under pressure while it dries by means of a helically wound cord applied with a tool called a *tendyek* (**4**). This tensioning tool enables the bowyer to create both a strong and even pressure with every turn. A cord is then tied between the nocks and tensioned with a peg. This holds the bow under reflex tension while drying and manipulates the limbs into alignment. The bow is then placed in a conditioning box.

Today, the conditioning box is an insulated container warmed by heat lamps (**5**), but it was formerly a felt-lined wooden box that was placed into a baking oven. Bows and bow parts were placed in an environment of steady warmth either while drying in manufacture or prior to tuning manipulation during their working life. In this example the conditioning box houses a pair of steam-bent strips of maple setting into their reflex shape while being clamped to formers. There is also a full core that has received its horn layers and is being left to dry – note the spiral of rope holding the lamination under pressure throughout its length.

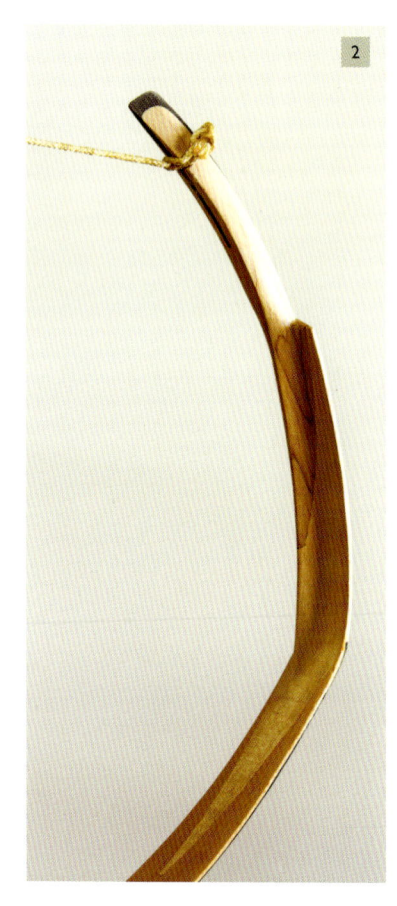

When ready – and the longer it can be left to dry the better – a rasp is used to shape the horn on the back of the bow, tapering it into a smooth union with the core and determining an even thickness, according to desired draw-weight, along its length. Next the entire core is coaxed into a more finished shape with drawknife, rasp and abrasive papers. At the very centre of the bow, where the two plates of horn meet, is a narrow gap (**6**). A small sliver of bone, called a *chelik*, is inserted into this. It has no real practical function but it possesses a mystic significance.

The core is then ready to receive the sinew. This will both augment the power of the bow and also make it tough and resilient. Small bundles of prepared sinew are soaked in fish glue and laid carefully onto the back of the bow (**7**). The sticky bundles of fibre have been dredged in a bath of gelatinous fish glue. Every strand must run straight; any snaking may cause twist in the finished bow. It is a critical and difficult task; it is an art. Much of it is accomplished with the bowyer's skilled and patient fingers but he also has a special tool, the *sinir kalemi* (**8**). Its teeth can be used to comb the sinew, its back can be used to smooth and flatten and the little hook is invaluable to tease out any snags. Made of brass and placed in a jar of water between applications, it resists becoming clogged with adhesive.

Strong bows require several layers of sinew, and each layer requires a drying time of several weeks. With each stage, the bowyer makes adjustments to the curvature and alignment of the limbs. Once the final layer of sinew has dried and the entire bow has been shaped and smoothed with abrasives, it is then tied, in extreme reflex, into a pretzel shape to season (**9**). Kani recommends that the best bows should be left in this state for about a year (Klopsteg 1987: 49). (All photos courtesy of Mike Loades)

Tepeliks tied to a previously unstrung bow. There is not only considerable resistance in reversing the extreme curve of the pretzel; it is also important that, at their first bending, the limbs suffer no twist. *Tepeliks* not only offer a pivot for leverage, they also provide a uniform curve, training the bow to its future bending pattern. (Mike Loades)

Though Hun bows famously use the horn of Hungarian grey cattle (*Bos taurus*), the most universal horn used in the making of the composite bow was that of the water buffalo (*Bubalus bubalis*). This was readily available throughout the parts of the world that adopted the composite bow. One might think of the horn as the muscles of the bow and the wooden core as its skeleton. To extend this analogy, we must also think of the work done by the tendons in an animal body, and this is exactly the role provided by sinew in the composite bow. It is what holds it all together under tremendous strain and it also lends a great deal of elastic power to the flex and return of the limbs.

Animal sinew, when hammered and combed to reduce it to fine fibre strands, has phenomenal tensile strength. According to Klopsteg, reporting on a 19th-century Turkish work by Mustafa Kani, the best sinew came from the Achilles' tendon of cattle (Klopsteg 1987: 42). However, many present-day bowyers prefer the broader, longer and more fibrous backstrap tendon from cattle or deer, as well as tendon from the ostrich.

The wood, the horn and the sinew all have to be held together by adhesives that remain secure under enormous stresses and are able to flex, stretch and contract without cracking. It is impossible to overstate the importance of the discovery of the correct glues in the development of the composite bow. Leg tendons were, and are still, used for making the glue that was used both to join the sections of the wooden core and also to bond the horn to that core. Hide glue was an acknowledged alternative, but tendon glue was the strongest. However, the application of the sinew required a different genus of adhesive – fish glue.

TUNING AND STRINGING THE BOW

When released from its constraints the bow, now firmly set in an acute reflex, requires assistance to reverse the arc so that it can be strung. This is achieved with the aid of shaped wooden blocks, called *tepeliks*. The *tepeliks* tie to the bow, holding it in a semi-strung position while the fibres relax, before the bowyer puts a string on it for the first time.

Strings could be made from silk, but the anonymous author of *Arab Archery*, a 15th-century Arab treatise, recommends that the best strings should be made from 'the hide of a lean camel which has gone hungry through the winter and therefore has become emaciated', adding that in winter 'it should be rubbed with a fine polishing stone; then treated with a mixture of fox fat and yellow beeswax melted together' (Faris & Elmer 1945: 95). Strings were also made from goat hide, intestines or sinew. I have tested a sinew bowstring, well-waxed with beeswax, by soaking it in a tub of water for 24 hours. There was no indication of stretching and it shot perfectly well immediately afterwards.

Once strung, there then begins a wrestling match. The bowyer tunes the bow by bending it over his knees and by twisting and flexing it between his powerful hands. He adjusts the limbs correctively and holds them in position for a few minutes, encouraging them to take a new set. Working by eye, he alters any tendency a limb may have for torsion and he balances the tiller – by pushing an amount of curve from one limb, he induces correspondingly more curve in the other. It is strenuous work. Occasionally he will make slight adjustments by removing a bit of material with a scraper or smoothing with abrasives. He gradually pulls the bow to longer and longer draw-lengths, making careful adjustments every time he pulls it back another few inches. In some cases the bow may have to go back into the conditioning box to soften it prior to more strenuous manipulation. It is then shot repeatedly over days. With each arrow it is checked, corrected and tuned. When it is finally tamed, a protective leather covering can be glued over the sinew and the bow is handed to an archer. It remains a living thing, however, and that archer needs to know how to care for it and how to keep it fine-tuned.

MAINTENANCE

There is a common misconception that composite bows were not popular in Western Europe because their performance would have been too adversely affected by the damp climate. However, when properly sealed, they thrived not only in the considerably wetter climes of Asia; composite bows, in the form of the bows for crossbows, proliferated throughout Europe. Social factors, military culture and economics were the reasons that composite bows did not see wider use in the West, not climate. Having said that, composite bows do require constant expert care and attention. They need to be shaded from direct sunlight just as much as they need to be kept warm and dry. Extreme changes in temperature can cause distortion or reduce performance.

Taybughā al-Ashrafī al-Baklamishī al-Yūnanī, author of *Kitāb ghunyat al-tullāb fī ma'rifat ramy an-nushshāb* (*Essential Archery for Beginners*) c.1500, advises that when on campaign 'an archer should never neglect his bow for a single moment, and in extremes of temperature he should inspect it day and night, hour by hour, and not let it out of his mind even if he is sure that it is stable and true'. He continues, 'when the weather is cold, his best policy is to put the bow inside his clothes and warm it with his body. When going to bed at night, he should also keep the bow inside his clothes to protect it against the damp' (quoted in Latham & Paterson 1970: 94).

For more extreme twists, misalignments and tiller adjustments, Taybughā directs the archer to warm his bow gently by a fire before applying corrective pressures (Latham & Paterson 1970: 94). In *The Way of Archery* (1637), Gao Ying suggests that heating a bow over a fire before shooting is normal practice. This was presumably the case in colder climes (Tian & Ma 2015: 77). When yet more serious modifications are required, Taybughā recommends fixing the warmed bow into a rigid structure – some kind of mould or jig – which may be similar to the *tepeliks* used for the initial stringing of a new bow (Latham & Paterson 1970: 100). Such workshop hardware would presumably be stowed in the baggage train rather than carried by individual archers, but Taybughā clearly considered it part of every archer's remit to be able to undertake a sophisticated level of bow maintenance. Apart from their prowess at hitting the mark, this ability to maintain such a nuanced and expensive weapon is something that set these elite bowmen apart from other troops.

Although composite bows can remain strung for considerably longer than longbows without undue detriment, they do need to be unstrung and allowed to relax

A superb example of a steel bow in dazzling condition, showing how impressive these bows could look when given a high polish. It has a distinctively set-back grip, covered in black leather. The limbs curve acutely where they extend from the grip but then flow in a gentle sweep towards the tips. The tips have been ornamented with finely modelled finials in silvered copper, representing a black-buck antelope. (Private Collection. Photograph by Runjeet Singh)

regularly or else they lose power. Images in art tend to show archers with only one bow but it is inconceivable that an archer depending on a composite bow in time of war would carry less than two. He must always have one strung in readiness for ambush or other surprise action and the second must rest in its unstrung state, preserving its power.

Of equal importance to care for the bow was maintenance of the bowstring, and 'having a second string to your bow' was an essential provision. According to one 16th-century Persian archery treatise, silk bowstrings should be changed every 40 days, or sooner if a lot of arrows have been shot (Khorasani 2013: 90).

The steel bows of India

A DIFFERENT TYPE OF RECURVE BOW

Although not made from composite materials, steel bows were made with a recurve form in the image of the composite bow and so, although they are a distinct sub-type, they most logically fall within this taxonomy.

During the 18th and 19th centuries, bows made entirely of steel were produced on an industrial scale in India. Crossbows, of course, had been made with steel laths in Europe since the 15th century but there was such hefty mass to these thick-limbed bows that they had to be made exponentially more powerful to overcome the inertia, more powerful than would be feasible for a hand bow. Indian steel bows were of finer construction. The idea that a strip of metal can make a useful spring is a commonplace notion today, but to make an effective steel bow requires extremely sophisticated steel technology. With their elegant curves, suggestive of the profile of recurve composite bows, the steel bows of India were relatively lightweight, having broad but slender limbs. These bows have been found in great number, rack upon rack, stocking the arsenals of local potentates throughout the country. Steel bows, as munition arms, were unique to India and what is more, they were exclusively military bows – war bows.

The Indian sub-continent was home to a galaxy of superb composite bows from the Mughal crab bow to the Sind *chahar-kham* (four-cornered bow). These were superior bows to even the best performing steel bow, but they had significant drawbacks for a rajput wishing to stockpile arms against some unknown future threat. They took a long time to make, they were very expensive and they were unreliable for long-term storage in a hot and humid climate. Composite bows required constant care from a knowledgeable owner and could not be left for years on end in a moist atmosphere where they might twist or delaminate. Provided that they were protected from rust with a coating of grease, steel bows risked no such deterioration. Similarly, wooden bows, which India also produced in a variety of highly effective forms, might be prone to warp in the steam-chamber that was an Indian arsenal during the monsoon season. Individual, personal bows can be cared for in a way that those conscripted to lay in ranks upon shelves cannot. G. N. Pant in his book *Indian Archery* cites correspondence he received from the ever-reliable W. F. Paterson regarding steel bows:

> My own observations and experience show that most steel bows are inferior in performance to the composite. However, composite bows are liable to distortion ... From this point of view the steel bow was more reliable and never needed such attention. It would therefore have an appeal to the horseman for relatively short range use, even if it was relatively less efficient. (Pant 1978: 120)

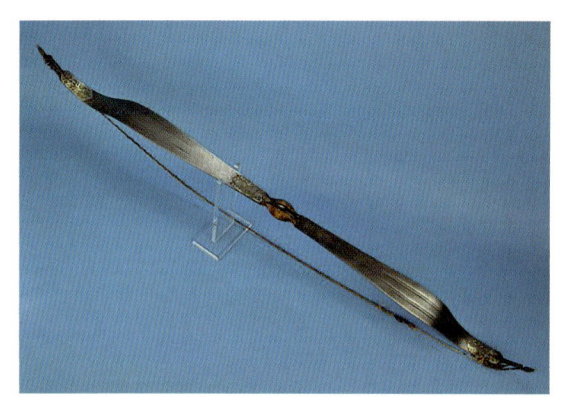

Three views of an Indian steel bow from the 18th or 19th centuries. The broad limbs are of a common form, curling gently away from the grip and then curving steeply towards the tips, which are augmented with *siyah*s. Note the distinctive wooden handgrip that was formerly covered with red velvet. Note also the thickness of the bow limbs at this point, suggesting that this was a bow of considerable power. There is bold incised decoration at the tips, which are also relatively sturdy. The grooves on the upper part of the limb may be of mechanical as well as aesthetic benefit. Grooves or fullers could offer both strength and the removal of material for lightness. Most significantly, they may militate against the possibility of the limbs twisting, which is the bane of the composite bow. (Private Collection. Photograph by Runjeet Singh)

HIGH-STATUS BOWS

Steel bows offered an answer to the problems of bulk storage in arsenals and doubtless many were of plain design, as befitted munition arms. However, it seems probable that steel bows were conceived first as technological showpieces, as so many surviving examples have been decorated and embellished with a prestigious flourish, worthy of any nobleman or maharaja. Not only that, but steel bows existed long before their appearance in quantity in the nation's armouries.

In the Furusiyaa Art Foundation Collection in Vaduz, Liechtenstein, there exists a steel bow from 15th century Iran. It is an unusually early example. A steel bow belonging to the Mughal Emperor Shah Jahan (1628–58) is displayed at the Dogrā Art Gallery, Jammu, India. It has a wooden grip and the steel limbs are decorated in gold, bearing an inscription, which translates as 'this bow is the embellishment of the hand of Shāh Jahān' (quoted in Pant 1978: 121). It was clearly a bow of considerable status.

High-end steel bows were decorated in a number of ways, from simple incised patterns to *koftgari*, a technique in which a pattern is laid on the surface of the steel by hammering gold or silver wire into an incised area. Some, such as those in the Royal Collection at Sandringham House in Norfolk, have a blued finish with a floral design damascened in gold. An 18th-century example in the Wallace Collection in London (Cat no: 2299) has a fully gilt grip and the limbs have been decorated in narrow bands of gold *koftgari* floral scrolls introducing Persian characters. The inclusion of Persian script on many bows has led to the frequent classification of steel bows as Indo-Persian. Certainly Persian craftsmen worked extensively at the Mughal courts in India, and the shared martial and material cultures are difficult to separate. It is also probable that the most exquisite examples of steel bows were valued in Iran just as they were in India. However, current evidence suggests that production was exclusive to India and it is only in India that we find steel bows in widespread use, appearing often as the weapons of horse-archers in Mughal miniatures as well as being produced in great quantity as munition arms.

Hyderabad and the surrounding area was an especially important centre for the production of steel bows. In Bidari, north of Hyderabad, steel bows were made with a particular form of decoration called *bidri*. This steel bow has been decorated in this fashion. The surface was treated with copper sulfate, turning it black. This was then incised with a hard stylus to outline the patterns. Gold and silver wire were hammered into the incised grooves. (Image courtesy of Stefan Domoney of www.ashokaarts.com)

BELOW A 19th century Indian steel bow in the author's collection. It was very common for steel bows to be made in 'take-apart' form. Note the bold thread on the uppermost limb. It is unlikely that being able to disassemble a bow in this manner had any significant benefit from a storage point of view and it seems more likely that it had advantages at the manufacturing stage. (Kim Hawkins)

BELOW RIGHT The bow in its assembled state. The surface of this bow is incised with intricate patterns, which have been accented with small rosettes of gold *koftgari*. The limbs curl gently away from the grip and then take extreme curves towards the tips, to which are attached *siyah*s of a notable length. (Kim Hawkins)

INDIAN STEEL

Steel enjoyed an exalted status in India, especially among the Akali Nihangs from the Punjab region, and steel weapons of any type were particularly desirable. That it became possible to render the composite bow form in steel was not only a technological achievement, it was an aesthetic triumph.

India has always been at the forefront of iron and steel technology. The Iron Age began there around 1,000 BC, several centuries before it did in other parts of the world, and there are indications of sporadic iron working even earlier than that. Most importantly, crucible steels were being manufactured in India from at least 200 BC. There has been insufficient analysis of surviving steel bows to determine whether or not they were all made from a crucible steel, but it is probable that they were. A crucible steel is one that is made in a sealed ceramic container, called a crucible, in a process whereby the metal is taken to a fully molten state. In its purely liquid form, the impurities float to the top and can be isolated. This produces an exceptionally clean steel. By contrast, iron and steel produced using the European bloomery hearth method contains what is known as slag – comprising silicates and other impurities. In the bloomery method, iron particles are extracted from the iron ore (rock) by means of a heat-induced chemical reaction known as smelting. The metal is never heated sufficiently for it to become molten and it therefore retains an amount of non-ferrous material. These slag inclusions create weaknesses in the steel, whereas a clean crucible steel is much less prone to breakage. In Europe cast iron did not become possible until the late 15th century and crucible steels were not produced there until the 18th century, nearly 2,000 years after they were first produced in India!

Not only is it likely that all Indian steel bows were manufactured from crucible steel, it is most probable that they were made from *wootz,* which is a type of crucible steel. All *wootz* is crucible steel; however, not all crucible steels are *wootz*. Once a cake of clean steel is produced in the crucible, it can then be thermo-cycled (a process of heating, slow cooling and reheating that re-organizes the molecular structure) which, when done correctly, creates *wootz* steel. It is an art. A particular advantage of *wootz* steel is that it is composed of spheridized carbides. This means that there are fewer internal stresses in a bar of *wootz* when bending because rounded surfaces are acting on one another. *Wootz* would undoubtedly be a superior metal for a bow.

Wootz Damascus is a term that is applied to *wootz* steels that exhibit a particular surface pattern. It is valued highly for its beauty, but the pattern is also an indicator that the steel is in fact genuine *wootz*. *Wootz* can exist, and be equally mechanically sound, without the pattern, but the pattern gives an outward stamp of authenticity.

Although no known steel bows survive from before the 15th century, there are references to them from as early as the first millennium AD. The *Agni Purana* and *Vishnudharmottara Purana* are Sanskrit poems which both refer to steel being one of several materials for making a bow; the others, of course, are wood and horn (Pant 1987: 118). Interestingly, the *Agni Purana* also notes that steel bows were usually made in parts (ie take-apart) and were inlaid with gold.

DRAW-WEIGHT

It is extremely difficult to estimate what the average draw-weight would have been for steel bows. An original example in my possession has lost its temper (springiness) and it would require heat treatment to restore its original spring. This is not possible because the surface has been decorated with a sprinkling of little gold rosettes and these would be lost if the limbs were heated. The first responsibility has to be to conserve the object. I have, nevertheless, tried drawing an Indian steel bow belonging to a friend. I did so cautiously and using a spring balance to measure the draw. We felt too nervous to take it, responsibly, beyond a 26-inch draw, where it was starting to stack. At that length it measured 45 pounds. It is reasonable to calculate between 3 and 4 pounds per inch for the end of the draw, so at 30 inches this bow may come in at between 57 and 61 pounds. This seems a fair estimate for these weapons. In his article 'Steel Bows from India' (Elmy 1969: 17), Douglas Elmy reports that Dr Robert Elmer (1877–1951) owned an Indian steel bow with an estimated draw weight of 60lb and that it shot between 97 and 137yd, depending on the weight of arrow used. Such ranges are more than adequate for close combat situations and certainly indicate a power that would be sufficient for a horse-archer shooting at close range. Of course the draw-weight of the bow is only part of the equation when seeking an appreciation of its power. What counts is the speed of the limb return and this is affected every bit as much by the properties of the material and the geometry of the bow as it is by sheer draw-weight. The current perception is that these steel bows would have been relatively slow, but the work really hasn't been done on them. Accumulating performance data on quality replicas of steel bows is a field of enquiry yet to be explored.

The loss of temper, in other words the springiness of the steel, as has been the fate of the bow in my possession, is a problem that is counter-intuitive to the argument that these bows were produced for their durability in long-term storage. Douglas Elmy (Elmy 1969: 17) reports that he has seen several steel bows with narrow strips of reinforcing steel riveted to both back and belly to boost performance. For munition bows, without inlaid decoration to be destroyed, it may have been a routine matter to take them back to the forge to be re-tempered. However, a lot probably depended on the quality of the smithing in the first place, and the best bows have probably retained their temper, undiminished by either time or use.

I have alluded to the fact that the limbs of these steel bows 'imitate' those of composite bows. This is true to the

An exquisite thumb ring in *wootz* with *koftgari* decoration, attesting to the Indian love of steel. It is believed to have been made in Hyderabad in the 17th or early 18th century. (Ph. Missillier Collection. Photo Runjeet Singh)

An Iranian man trains with the *kabbadeh* chain and bow. It is swung rhythmically from side to side and conditions all the muscles in the arms, shoulders and back that are used in archery. (Photo by Eric LAFFORGUE/Gamma-Rapho via Getty Images)

extent that the limbs are recurved. However, the precise shapes are unique to steel bows and do not mirror exactly any particular composite bow. In fact, there is a tendency for most examples to have an extreme curve at each of the upper ends of the limbs that would not be possible with composite materials. Steel bows have their own distinctive forms.

TRAINING BOWS

Entirely unrelated to Indian steel bows, but nonetheless of bow form and made of steel, is a piece of apparatus used in traditional Iranian gymnasium exercises called the *kabbadeh*. The bow part is of thick and heavy steel; it does not bend but merely acts as a bow-shaped weight to condition the bow arm and shoulder. A chain, in place of a string, hangs loosely on the bow, but when fully extended is long enough to simulate the full-draw position. This chain is weighted with heavy metal discs that also act as jangling cymbals. In a martial training regime known as *zoorkhaneh*, the *kabbadeh* is held high above the head and rhythmically swung from one side to the other, working dynamically to strengthen all the muscles of the arms and back that are used in the shooting of a bow. *Zoorkhaneh* routines, which also include strength training with massive wooden clubs and heavy shields, are accompanied by chants and drums. The ringing of the string-weights adds to the cacophony.

THE MODERN STEEL BOW

In the late 1950s/early 1960s, it was very fashionable for archers to use a steel bow. A British company, Accles and Pollock (who also pioneered tubular steel shafts for golf clubs some decades earlier) produced a take-apart bow in tubular steel. It was exceptionally lightweight and portable – ideal for commando use – and was hailed as having a very fast limb action. Mostly, though, it was modern. V. R. Dikshitar in his book *War in Ancient India* (1948) comments on the uptake of steel bows during the Mughal period: 'Steel was the new invention and the old things were cast aside for the new' (quoted in Elmy 1969: 15).

He perhaps exaggerated the extent to which the steel bow replaced the composite bow; the latter's superior performance ensured that it remained of premium value to a Mughal warrior. Nevertheless, his observation has a ring of truth. Military men are often drawn to what appears to be brand-new technology, even if its performance doesn't always outperform the existing systems – how else could the early gun have superseded the longbow? The drawback of the tubular steel bow was that it was impossible to detect whether or not the inside had succumbed to any corrosion. Rust in the interior of the tube made these bows susceptible, without warning, to dangerous and explosive fracture. So although the tubular construction created very lightweight limbs with a high return velocity, it compromised severely the ability to keep these bows for any length of time. This was in stark contrast to the storage capabilities of the Indian steel bow. These were an entirely different species.

A great many of the steel bows of India survive in museums and private collections. They remain largely in pristine condition – I suspect that many remain shootable. They are glorious weapons that cry out for further study.

The development of shooting techniques

THE THUMB-DRAW

Alongside the mechanical developments of the bow came developments in the way the bow was drawn and loosed. For the composite bow, methods of drawing with the thumb were almost universal, although we see faint clues here and there of other techniques.

A thumb-draw is quite different from the so-called 'Mediterranean draw' of Western Europe, which hooks three (sometimes two) fingers around the string. This latter draw was used by longbowmen and remains the standard method today for archers with all types of bow. In the thumb-draw, usually accomplished with the aid of a thumb-ring, the string sits close to the crease of the thumb, which is folded around the string and secured in place by various combinations of the fingers.

The author of *Arab Archery* makes disparaging mention – 'a corrupt draw, used by the ignorant' – of a draw used by some Greeks who employed all four fingers on the string but no thumb (Faris & Elmer 1945: 45). Greek art certainly shows a number of methods. He also observes that: 'the Slavs have a peculiar draw which consists of locking the little finger, the ring finger and the middle finger on the string, holding the index finger outstretched along the arrow and completely ignoring the thumb ... They also make for their fingers *finger-tips* of gold, silver, copper and iron' (Faris & Elmer 1945: 45). This reference is reminiscent of a photograph from a private collection that appears in *Saracen Archery* (Latham & Paterson 1970: 136) of a pair

Lukas Novotny demonstrates a typical lock with a thumb-ring. *Arab Archery* (Faris & Elmer 1945: 43) gives six variations of lock for the thumb-draw, and there are yet others to be observed in the art of various cultures. (Mike Loades)

Modern illustration, based on an example in a private collection, of Phoenician finger-tips made from gold. The holes around the bases imply that they were sewn onto a leather glove. To date their precise application remains an intriguing and unsolved puzzle. Conjecturally it seems probable that they were used on the tips of fingers acting in support of a thumb-draw. The thumb would be locked either with the index finger or, in the case of the Sassanian draw, with the middle finger, and the tips of the next two digits would have a supportive role touching the string but not wrapped around it. Edward Morse, writing in 1885, gave a description of a style he saw demonstrated by young Japanese, who 'drew the string back with the thumb and interlocked fingers as already described and assisted the drawing back of the string with the tips of the second and third fingers' (Morse 1885: 19). (Drawing by David Joseph Wright)

of gold finger-tips that are purported to be Phoenician from the 5th century BC. Whatever the truth regarding the use of these idiosyncratic thimbles and other lesser known systems, there can be little doubt that some form of thumb-release was the norm for most users of the composite bow throughout history.

There are advantages to using the thumb to draw, whether with leather tab, glove or solid thumb-ring. One is that it makes it a great deal easier to hold a nocked arrow in place against the bow while moving; this is of significance because composite bows were used by a variety of archers who shot while in vigorous motion – from chariot-archers, to horse-archers, to skirmishing infantry. All benefited by having more secure control of the arrow immediately prior to shooting.

In the three-finger draw, the fingers rotate the string clockwise, and it is partly for this reason that the arrow is placed against the left-hand side of the bow. To keep it in place the archer must keep the directional twist on the string and if necessary give the bow a slight diagonal tilt (known as canting the bow). However, when dealing with the bone-shaking bumps and bounces of a galloping chariot or the high-speed dash of a spirited horse, keeping the arrow against the bow becomes more challenging. With the thumb-draw, which places the arrow on the right-hand side of the bow, the index finger holds the arrow in place, however erratic the motion.

A further factor determining on which side of the bow the arrow should rest is the tendency of an arrow to flex as it is pushed forward by the string – aka archer's paradox. It bends around the bow as it leaves and, depending on whether the string has a clockwise twist (finger release) or an anti-clockwise twist (thumb-draw) it clears the bow more cleanly from the appropriate side.

Compared to a three-finger draw, the thumb occupies a smaller surface area of the string, resulting in less friction and a faster, cleaner release, transferring more energy to the arrow. This is especially true when used with a solid thumb-ring. Here the string of even the heaviest bow sits on the tiniest ledge of a smooth, hard surface. Most importantly, the thumb-draw facilitates a faster loading speed. A right-handed archer wears his quiver on the right hip; from here an arrow can be drawn and placed on the right-hand side of the bow in the most ergonomic fashion. The thumb-draw also enabled a technique for rapid shooting that involved holding arrows in either the bow-hand or the string-hand.

Lukas Novotny demonstrating how the lock of the thumb-draw holds the arrow securely against the bow at all stages of the draw. The thumb-release, which gives the string an anti-clockwise rotation, is better served by placing the arrow on the right-hand side of the bow. This results in the index finger of the string-hand being positioned to apply a locating pressure to the arrow. (Mike Loades)

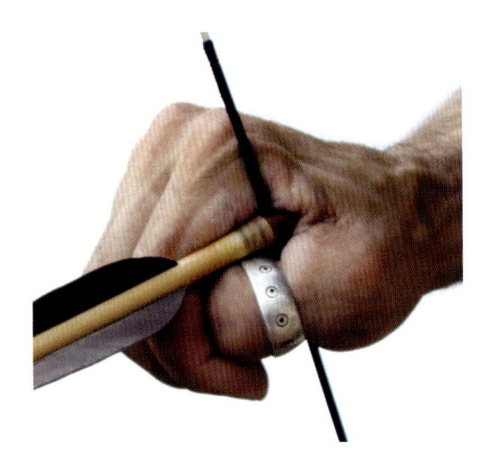

THE THUMB-TAB

It is apparent from art that the Egyptians, the Assyrians, the Hittites and others who used the angular bow did so by means of some style of thumb-release. To date no physical evidence of solid thumb-rings or shooting gloves has been discovered, but there is a clue that leather thumb-tabs may have been employed. That clue is what I consider to be a misidentified object in the collections of the Metropolitan Museum of Art, New York. Excavated at Thebes during 1926–27, it has been catalogued as an archer's wrist-guard and was found, still tied to the archer's wrist, in a mass grave of 59 soldiers. However, the dimensions – a fraction over 2 inches from top to bottom – suggest that it is absurdly small to be an effective wrist-guard. Both the shape and size are consistent with it being a thumb-guard.

The burial is dated to the reign of the Pharaoh Senwosret I (r. 1971–26 BC), which is around 300 years prior to the arrival of the Hyksos. We may therefore deduce that the thumb-draw was in use in Egypt prior to the adoption of the composite bow. Moreover, it seems most probable that leather thumb-tabs remained in use into the age of the angular bow.

THE BOW-HAND RING

An image (see page 207) of the Assyrian king Ashurbanipal, shooting from horseback, reveals a broad ring around the base of his bow-hand thumb. He is at full draw and presses his vertically held thumb against the bow to hold the arrow securely prior to shooting, stabilizing it as he gallops and aims. The narrowness of the angular bow enables this use of the bow-hand thumb. At the moment of shooting the thumb opens a fraction to allow unimpeded passage of the shaft. It is then that the thumb becomes the arrow-shelf, and this is where the ring comes into play.

In the Korean archery tradition it is common for a ring, made from a variety of materials, to be worn on the bow-hand thumb; it is known as the *san ji geun*, which translates as 'brace ring' (Koppedrayer 2002: 32). A bow-hand ring can occasionally be glimpsed in the art of other composite-bow cultures, and I suspect it was more widely used than representations would suggest.

THE SASSANIAN SHOOTING GLOVE

An unusual form of lock appears in Sassanian art (AD 224–651), showing both the index finger and sometimes also the little finger extended. Only the back of the hand can be seen and the position of the thumb, middle and ring fingers is obscured. It is entirely possible that this draw was a two-finger draw, using only the middle and ring fingers. However, the slightly pronated wrist, evident in most of the art, is more consistent with it being a form of thumb-draw.

THUMB-RING TECHNIQUES

Shooting with the thumb-draw is an arcane art and when used with a solid thumb-ring, the technique becomes even more nuanced. It is significantly more difficult to learn than the

Replica of an Egyptian thumb-tab based on an example in the Metropolitan Museum of Art, New York. Made and tested by the author, it was found to work well. The curious little nipple at the apex of the tab was puzzling at first, but made sense in practical trials. It served as a locator between the base of the index and middle fingers, ensuring a consistent position and preventing the tab from slipping. (Kim Hawkins)

A bow-hand ring. With the thumb-draw, in which the arrow passes on the right-hand side of the bow, the base of the bow-hand thumb acts as an arrow-shelf. It is perfectly possible to shoot arrows over the bare hand, especially when the sharp quill ends are pared down and secured to the shaft by means of a silk binding, but the smooth shelf offered by a simple ring worn on the bow-hand thumb is an advantage, both for comfort and consistency. I use one made from leather and find it a boon – especially when using unbound, glued-on fletchings, which can otherwise lift and skewer the hand. (Kim Hawkins) three-finger draw and beginners all too frequently quit early on, finding it too difficult. Shooting the composite bow in an authentic manner is a sophisticated martial art. A solid thumb-ring creates the archery equivalent of the hair-trigger. The entire weight of the draw is held on an extremely narrow surface, and the slightest inconsistency in angles and alignments can cause the string to slip from the ring prematurely. It is a wonderful teacher and yet also an unforgiving taskmaster; errors frequently cause pain to either thumb or index finger. With each increase in draw-weight there is less tolerance for error and the reproving lash of the string becomes even harsher. Eventually, consistency is drilled into the archer's form and the reward of a fast, clean release is immense.

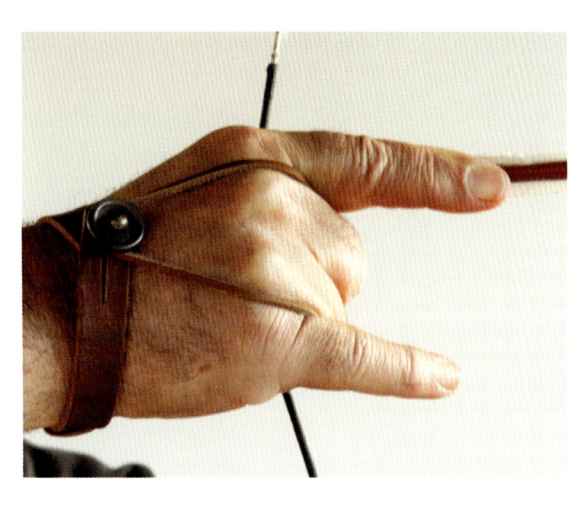

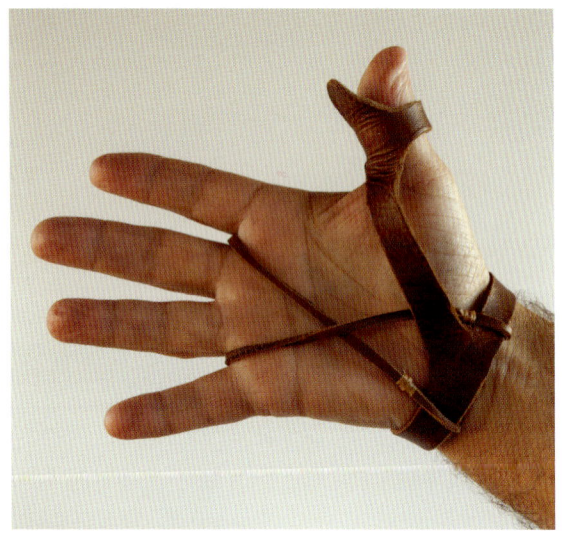

Closely allied to the draw with the thumb-ring is the push with the bow-hand and consequent follow-through, known as the *khatrah*. Taybughā teaches: 'What the archer should do is to dip the bow sharply from the grip in such a way that at the moment the string is loosed he would appear to give his arrow a push with the string. The action must be strongly executed and come from the wrist-joint like the punch of a man in anger' (quoted in Latham & Paterson 1970: 68).

In numerous manuscript images, archers who have just shot display this characteristic forward-cocked wrist. Taybughā counsels that it is a great fault to anticipate the action, which would result in a dropped bow-arm, and equally poor form to mimic it after the event. It should be the outcome of correct shooting style, emphasizing the push with the left arm in equal measure to the pull with the right. According to Taybughā, 'the movement increases both cast and range' (quoted in Latham & Paterson 1970: 68).

A possible interpretation of the construction and method of use for a Sassanian shooting glove, demonstrated by the author. The cross-strapping holds a thumb-tab securely in place. The tip of the thumb braces against the ring finger and is then locked by the middle finger. It is of note that in some styles of Japanese archery the index finger is extended along the shaft of the arrow in a similar manner. The purpose of extending the little finger is not clear and, in some depictions, it is folded. (Kim Hawkins)

Similar follow-throughs are advocated by various old masters, including that of allowing the bow to spin a half-rotation to the left on release – a technique still greatly valued by Japanese *kyūdō* archers. The essence is that these movements of the bow should be a natural consequence of a clean release, not something to fake for display.

The Chinese general and writer on military matters Tang Jingchuan (1507–60) recommended a similar procedure but with a lot of unnecessary flourish, suggesting the 'bow tip painted the ground' and the 'draw hand snapped back with the palm upturned slightly' (quoted in Tian & Ma 2015: 140). Such affectation was roundly condemned by Gao Ying some decades later. He scoffed that 'Youngsters love this flowery style of release, but they fail to recognize its faults' (quoted in Tian & Ma 2015: 140).

As the composite bow developed and diversified, so too did schools of thought for optimal shooting styles. The steady shot of the long-range sniper, target-shooter or hunter required nuances in technique that differed from the demands of the horse-archer, galloping at high speed and with only seconds to let fly as many arrows as possible while operating at an effective range. For him, the snap and push of the *khatrah* aided both his performance and his instinctive aiming ability. To my mind a properly executed *khatrah* is an exciting, decisive, attacking style of shooting that only adds to the thrill of using this powerful weapon.

USE: ARCHERY – A VERY MARTIAL ART
The chariot-archer

During the Zhou Dynasty (*c*.1046–256 BC) the Chinese used chariot archery extensively. However, for the purposes of this discussion, I confine my observations to the early chariot cultures of the Near East and their use of the angular bow.

Angular bows were employed by infantry archers, horse-archers and chariot-archers, but it was as the weapon of the chariot-archer that this early form of the composite bow made its most dramatic and consequential entry onto the battlefields of antiquity. It was a principal weapon of Egyptians, Hittites, Assyrians and other military cultures of the Ancient Near East. Compared to wooden bows, the shorter limb length of the angular bow offered a distinct advantage when managing a bow in the cramped space of the chariot platform. The archer stood next to a driver and needed to be able to shoot in all directions.

For exhibition shooting, however, it was usual for the archer to ride solo with the reins tied around his waist. There is an account of the Pharaoh Amenhotep II (r. 1427–1401 BC) shooting arrows at a copper ingot target from his galloping chariot:

> he entered into his northern garden and found that there had been set up for him four targets of Asiatic copper of one palm in their thickness, with 20 cubits between one post and its fellow. Then His Majesty appeared in a chariot like Montu [the Egyptian god of war] in his power. He grasped his bow and gripped four arrows at the same time. So he rode northward, shooting at them (Pritchard 1969: 244)

This reference to grasping four arrows at the same time suggests the early use of speed-shooting techniques with the composite bow; arrows held in the bow-hand ready to be nocked in rapid succession. A cubit is reckoned to be around 20 inches (less by some calculations), which means that Amenhotep's targets were approximately 11yd

In battle, a driver accompanied the chariot-archer. I have driven chariots on the plains of Troy (Hisarlik) and the sands of Giza and common to both these arid landscapes were the clouds of dust generated by pounding hooves and spinning wheels. Chariots creaked and rattled onto ancient battlefields by the several thousand. Such squalling squadrons would have whipped up dust storms of great magnitude – in places reducing visibility to a few feet. Here, the author is the archer in a replica Egyptian chariot (built by Robert Hurford) carrying a replica angular bow (built by Lukas Novotny). The bow remains outside the perimeter of the confined space of the chariot body at all times. I have shot an angular bow from a number of Egyptian, Hittite and Assyrian chariot replicas; the space is very tight indeed. Quivers were mounted externally to the vehicle and placed with ergonomic convenience for the archer. With this arrangement the arrow pulls into place on the right-hand side of the bow; the correct side for shooting an arrow by means of a thumb-draw. (Photograph by Robert Hurford)

THE SOLID THUMB-RING

The ultimate, and most widely used, method for engaging the thumb-draw was with a solid thumb-ring. These provided, in effect, a trigger mechanism for the bow. Made of stone and cylindrical in form (**A**), the earliest archer's rings so far discovered have been excavated in north-eastern China and date to between 4700 BC and 2920 BC (Koppedrayer 2002: 19). Cylindrical rings are especially associated with China and Tibet, but they were not universal in all periods. Their most conspicuous ubiquity was during the Qing Dynasty (1644–1912) – the age of the Manchu and their mighty bows. I have a number, which I have picked up in street markets in China, and they feel strong and secure to shoot with. The cylindrical ring overlapped the crease of the joint, so that the thumb remained straighter than it did with a lipped ring. The thumb could still bend a little, owing to the concave bevel at the top of the ring, and this secured the ring from flying off. The lower portion of the ring, which had string contact, was convex. It was locked into place by the index finger at the tip of the thumb, rather than over it.

One advantage of the cylindrical ring for the military archer was that it always maintained the correct alignment, unlike the lipped ring. With the lipped ring there was the possibility, especially during intensive action, that it could rotate and misalign – a moment lost, a shot missed – before the archer could quickly twist it back into position.

The lipped ring consisted of a narrow band that sat just below the knuckle at the back of the hand and rose at an angle so that the ledge or groove of the ring was situated across the thumb crease on the inside of the hand. Extending from this little shelf was the lip, also known as the 'shield', which protected the thumb pad from the strike of the string on release.

On most lipped rings, it was the ledge at the base of the ring that retained the string (**B**); note how slim this ledge is and consider that the entire draw-weight of the bow is held by it. It offers an exceptionally clean and fast release. An alternative arrangement involved a groove near the base of the shield, to locate the string (**C**). Fit was critical – a ring that flew off the thumb in battle was both an inconvenience and an embarrassment. The oval aperture of the ring was placed onto the thumb with the shield to one side; it was then rotated so that the shield sat against the pad of the thumb. A properly fitted ring will stay in position and will neither rotate, nor slide down during use – such a ring is a prize beyond value and an archer will likely try many rings before he finds the right one. Several styles of Chinese lipped rings, especially from the Ming Dynasty, had a V-shaped notch at the base to accommodate the protuberance of flesh created when the thumb bends; a replica is shown here (**D**).

Another variant of the thumb-ring, common in China during the Warring States period (475–221 BC) but also noted occasionally on Turkish rings, was the spur ring (**E**), a lipped ring with a curved projection to one side. In use, the curve of this spur cradled the shaft immediately in front of the nock, and, with a bulbous nock, acted to hold the arrow in place by pushing it back against the string in the line of draw (**F**). This contrasted with the usual manner of holding the arrow in place securely, which was by means of lateral pressure from the index finger. It is an easy fault to exert too much pressure, thus distorting the lie of the string, and it may be to address this problem that the spur ring was developed. It offered an opposing lateral pressure to counter that of the index finger. Relying primarily on backward pressure and neutralizing any lateral pressure would have been especially advantageous when using arrows with shallow nocks – such arrows were commonplace. Surprisingly, despite their evident ingenuity, spur rings never achieved widespread use.

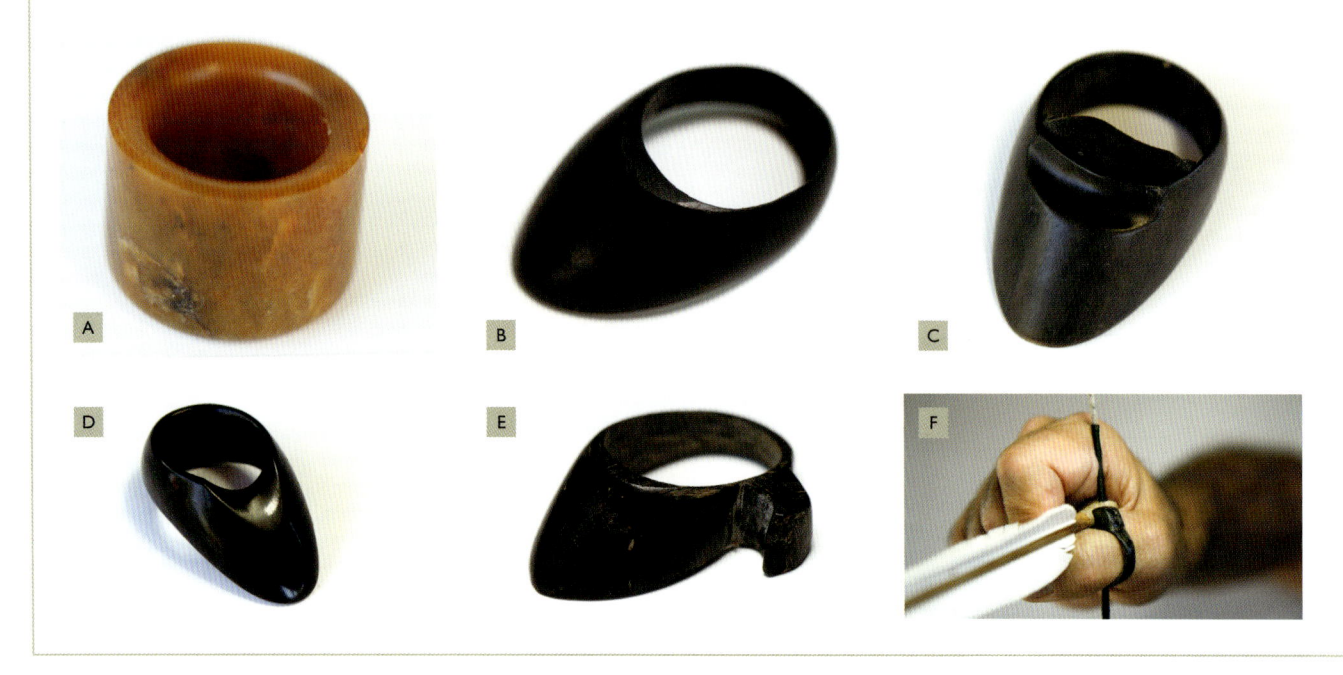

In Korean archery there were two distinct styles of thumb-ring. The *sugakji* (**G**), known as the male ring, was not really a thumb-ring at all in the conventional sense, but rather a release-aid that was worn on the thumb. The thumb inserted into the ring and the prong, secured by the index finger, hooked over the string. It acted as a latch to hold, draw and release. The *amgakji* (**H**), known as the female ring, was similar to other lipped rings from elsewhere, though the shield tended to be longer on Korean rings; a replica in the author's collection is shown here.

Thumb-rings were made from various materials including horn, bone, ivory, antler, hardwoods, several types of stone – especially jade – and metals including iron, bronze, brass or silver. There is considerable variation in the size of rings and some materials tend to be bulkier than others. Everyone had their preferences, but silver rings (**I**) – a replica in the author's collection is shown here – enjoyed particular favour. A metal ring can be made with finer proportions and yet still be mechanically strong. For use on horseback, where the ability to reload rapidly was a key component, a smaller, daintier ring interfered much less with the nimble dexterity of the thumb, index finger and middle finger – the active digits for speed-nocking techniques.

Some, but not all, rings employed a thin leather insert, called a *kulak* (**C** and **I**). This both refined the fit and created greater friction against the thumb to thwart rotation or slipping in the heat of action. The lower portion of the *kulak*, a tiny tab known as the *kash*, extends beyond the ledge. It provides a flat surface behind the string so that any bulges of flesh, created by flexing the thumb, do not get pinched between the string and the ledge of the ring.

Archer's rings became high-status ornaments, attesting not only to the wearer's good taste and wealth, but also to his warrior standing. Indian portraiture of maharajas and other high-ranking nobility, both Hindu and Muslim, frequently shows that the ring has been reversed when worn in a non-military context – the shield sits on the back of the thumb. It has been suggested (Koppedrayer 2002: 32) that this was a symbol of peaceful intent – that the wearer simultaneously proclaimed his prowess as an archer, while indicating that he was not about to shoot anyone at that moment.

The materials from which thumb-rings were made invited elaborate decoration. A Persian thumb-ring made of white jade with a floral design created by an inlay of pink and green tourmaline and gold outline is shown here (**J**); it dates from between the 17th and 19th centuries. Thumb-rings could be carved, incised, inset with gold or silver wire and embedded with fine jewels. On occasion a ring might become so embellished with surface adornment that it was no longer suitable for its intended purpose. Such rings were worn at court solely as jewellery. A particular feature of Qing Dynasty rings is that they were usually carried in exquisitely ornate cases, made from appliquéd silk, intricately carved wood, ivory or jade, and during the Zhou Dynasty there were protocols at formal gatherings that ritualized the putting on of the thumb-ring (Koppedrayer 2002: 26).

Even after the introduction of other materials to make solid thumb-rings, leather remained in widespread use for defending the thumb (**K**). The author of *Arab Archery* is a proponent of the virtues of leather thumb-rings, considering that they offer sensitivity similar to shooting with a bare thumb. He advises that they be made with medium thickness leather and lined with fine leather, adding that they should be indented with a groove for the string (Faris & Elmer 1945: 123). I shot with a leather ring for some time before acting on the advice to incise a groove for the string. I found it immensely useful to be able quickly to feel a correct and consistent alignment for the string. (All photos courtesy Kim Hawkins except **G** and **J**, courtesy Museum of Anthropology, University of Missouri)

apart. If we assume, as surely we must, that he was galloping his chariot, then this represented a very impressive rate of shooting. Equally impressive was the power of the shots. Copper ingots used as targets were traditionally in the shape of hides. These were standard trade commodities, harking back to a time when animal hides had been trading currency. The regular size was probably an inch or less thick and the 'one palm' thickness suggests that Amenhotep's targets may have consisted of multiple copper sheets placed back to back.

Such shooting displays, with the reins tied around the waist, were customary demonstrations for pharaohs affirming their martial prowess. I have tried this and found that, for the forward shot, it was possible to adjust and maintain the direction of the horses by slight movements of the torso. However, to turn and shoot to the side or to the rear required twisting at the waist to an extent that caused the horses to veer. With targets set up at an approximately 45-degree angle to a straight track, the forward shot was achievable – it being a slight diagonal from the line of travel, rather than directly over the horses' heads.

In battle, each chariot had its *peherer* (runner), armed with a spear. His duties might range from adjusting harness, changing over a horse team or clearing obstacles to replenishing arrow supplies, marshalling captives or repelling boarders in a skirmish. The stamina and swiftness of today's long-distance runners is evidence enough that it would be possible for elite men to maintain contact with the vehicle in most circumstances. At times they might also ride on the chariot and act as a shield-bearer, but such discussions threaten to divert from the main theme. There can be little doubt, though, that the *peherer* would have been of considerable support, and in defensive positions these spearmen might deploy with the archers to form a protective hedge.

When going up against formed infantry a chariot would be too vulnerable if it ran parallel to the front line, even with armoured horses. In my view it would have been more likely that chariots attacked, in troops of ten, in a wheeling charge. I envisage parallel troops attacking at a slight angle towards the enemy front line to give the

CHARIOT BATTLE BETWEEN EGYPTIANS AND HITTITES (OPPOSITE)

A pall of thick dust generated by the stampede of horses and the spin of wheels has created very limited visibility. Chariot-to-chariot warfare may be analogous to the aerial dogfights of World War II, with an enemy suddenly appearing out of the clouds, and it was the job of the driver to position the archer for maximum advantage. We may imagine a constant swirling, skidding and jockeying for position as drivers manoeuvred their teams not only defensively but also to avail the archer of his best shot. Engagement in the optimal position might only last for a few seconds and the ability to shoot rapidly was of great advantage.

Although it is entirely possible to shoot from either side of the chariot – switching places with the driver is an easy two-step dance – images in art and the configuration of quivers on surviving Egyptian chariots suggest that the archer stood predominantly to the left of the driver. This contrasts with Chinese chariot-archers, who stood to the right of the driver (Selby 2000: 144). The latter positioning seems more expedient because the resulting angles between driver and archer would allow the archer to come to full draw without risk of knocking the driver with his elbow.

Horses must surely have been primary targets in such encounters, but light, flexible scale armour, constructed from pieces of hardened rawhide sewn to a multi-layered fabric base, offered reasonable protection to large areas. Similar armour, with either leather or bronze scales, was worn to defend the torsos of the archers and drivers who could afford it. Thick leather sidings to the chariot body offered the occupants a good defence from the waist down.

Even when his vehicle was immobilized, the chariot-archer, provided that he remained relatively unscathed, could still undertake a useful role in the battle by sniping from behind the wreckage.

THE COMPOSITE BOW

189

Detail of the platform on a replica Egyptian chariot (built by Robert Hurford). Widths for Egyptian chariots varied between 36 inches and 43 inches. From front to back, the woven-rawhide, sprung platform was around 20 inches or less. In order to stabilize, when shooting forwards or to the side from a jolting vehicle at high speed, it helps to brace the right foot on the bar that forms the rear of the platform frame and lean the left hip into the front rail. When shooting to the rear, the archer simply turns and leans against the side. The narrow depth of these platforms enables these braced positions without compromising a vertical stance. (Mike Loades)

archers a clear shot without shooting directly over the team ahead. When they neared the enemy line they would turn sharply, minimizing the time they presented their vulnerable flanks, and continue in a loop. It may be no coincidence that this configuration corresponds to the elongated oval of a Roman chariot-racing circuit; echoes of the ancient chariot attack pattern? The archer would have been able to shoot continuously on both the approach and the withdrawal and to repeat this manoeuvre over and over again. *Peherers* stationed at the home end of the circuit would have been able to re-supply with armfuls of arrows. They would also have had no more than a 200yd dash to run in with a replacement horse team.

Certainly these tactics of attack and retreat are those identified as the tactics of the chariot-archer's successor – the horse-archer.

The horse-archer: origins

It was the Assyrians who transferred the skills of the chariot-archer to those of the horse-archer in combat. At some point around the 9th century BC they deployed horse-archers, shooting angular bows, in battle. Curiously, Assyrian reliefs of the time show pairs of riders, one an archer and the other a horseman alongside, holding the reins of the archer's horse. It evokes the companion bond that must have been established between a chariot-driver and his archer. Both are riding bareback with just a saddle-cloth. I have done this, in a pot-holed, rock-strewn gully in Turkey, with a companion riding alongside and taking the reins of my horse. Surrendering control of one's horse in this way is deeply unnerving, and although I managed to shoot and hit the target, I could perceive no benefit to having a co-rider. Soon enough such an idea was abandoned and the horse-archer proper thundered onto the ancient battlefield.

It is possible that nomadic steppe peoples developed the idea of shooting their bows from horseback even earlier than this, and that these two strands of development were independent, but archaeology has yet to yield a definitive verdict. Either way, the composite bow in the hands of the horse-archer created a new breed of warrior – one who was to dominate the battlefields of the Eastern World for many centuries to come. The power of the composite bow combined with the speed and mobility of the horse created a new force in warfare – one that had the ability to establish empires.

SADDLES, STIRRUPS AND THE RISE OF THE HORSE-ARCHER

It is perfectly possible to shoot a bow from a horse while riding bareback. I do so at the gallop as part of my regular practice, and many Native American tribes – most notably the Comanche – were accustomed to shooting bareback both for war and hunting, although by the 19th century they also used various forms of saddle-pad and saddle.

There have been many horse-archer cultures – among them Assyrians, Scythians and Parthians – who shot their bows from horseback using either saddle-pads or saddles without the additional aid of stirrups. A saddle and stirrups, or lack of, is not a determining factor to being able to shoot a bow from horseback. That is not to say that a saddle does not make a difference; it does. It helps with stability and, more importantly, it is the rigid saddletree that allows for the suspension of stirrups. Stirrups are a considerable aid to the archer, making it possible for him to change his posture on the horse. With stirrups he can stand slightly and lean a little forward, enlisting his knees to be the fulcrum of suspension, while still supporting some of his weight on his feet. He rises to separate himself from the motions of the horse in order to achieve a smoother shot.

Although various proto-stirrup systems, such as toe loops and a single stirrup to aid mounting, pre-date the development of paired stirrups, it was this latter that was of significance to the archer. The breakthrough was made during the latter part of the 5th century AD by the Xiongnu, a people originating to the west of China and generally thought to have been the antecedents of the Huns – they were a horse-archer people.

I would further suggest that a major advantage of stirrups is that they facilitate the use of heavier bows from horseback. For any man's given strength, he is able to shoot a heavier bow from the ground than he is from horseback. A strong man can shoot a much heavier bow from horseback than can a weakling from the ground, of course, and because of such individual variation it is impossible to ascribe precise values to a comparison. Nevertheless, there remains a general principle that the infantry archer is able to draw a heavier bow than the mounted man because he employs his whole body to do so.

The characteristic stance of the heavy bow shooter, whether he be an English longbowman or a Manchu archer with his great composite bow, is with flexed knees and an angled torso that tilts the pelvis, in the manner of a weightlifter, to both protect the spine from vertebral compression and to recruit all the muscles, including those of the legs, into the power of the draw. Conversely, a man sitting on a horse with his seat in contact with the saddle has to rely on his upper body strength alone. Now mighty men have great upper-body strength and undoubtedly strong bows were in use on horseback before the stirrup appeared, but the archer's strength was not fully optimized when seated, thus limiting his full potential.

A modern drawing of a detail from the north wall at Abu Simbel. It is the earliest known depiction (to date) of an archer on horseback. Dating to around 1264 BC, this image existed several hundred years before the emergence of horse-archers as a force on the battlefield. Armed with an angular composite bow, the rider is probably a messenger; it is difficult to know if he carries the bow for dismounted defence, or whether it was shot from horseback. Note his position, the so-called 'donkey seat'. Riding bareback, he is perched on the hindquarters of the horse. Representations in art of the earliest riders invariably depict them in this manner, possibly because horses had not yet been bred with sufficient bone and muscle to carry a man in a more forward position. It is a less secure position from which to ride and shoot. (Illustration by David Joseph Wright)

HORSES AND THE HORSE-ARCHER

There were two distinct types of horse that gave rise to different horse-archer traditions – the steppe pony and the Turkoman/Arab horse.

From the broad swathe of grassland plains – the steppe – which stretched, broken only by the Altai Mountains, across Eurasia from China, through Mongolia, Kazakhstan and Ukraine to its outposts on the Pannonian Plain of Hungary, came the steppe pony. These large-headed, squat, shaggy horses carried the Mongol horde to create the largest contiguous empire the world has ever seen, and Attila and his Huns rode into Europe on steeds of a similar stamp.

Men would travel with a string of horses, sleeping in the saddle. Additional horses simply ran with the herd. The Archdeacon Thomas of Split (13th century), describing the Mongol host, wrote, 'However many horses a man possesses, they are so trained that they follow him like dogs' (quoted in Jankovich 1971: 65). Riders would switch horses to spare the animals fatigue, but they remained mounted constantly. It meant that an army on the move never had to stop. *The Secret History of the Mongols*, written anonymously a few years after the death of Genghis Khan in 1227, cites one of his orders regarding the treatment of horses on the march: 'Bridles will not be worn on the march – the horses are to have their mouths free' (quoted in Jankovich 1971: 64). These hardy little horses could sustain themselves from the rough grazing they found on the way. There was no need for wagons to carry supplies of oats, hay and other fodder, as required for other types of military mount. No farriers were needed for their tough unshod hooves. Such lumbering logistics did not slow the inexorable advance of a nomad army.

Furthermore, these horses were naturally inclined to the fifth gait – a type of very fast walk known as the amble, previously described in the longbow chapter. It provided an exceptionally smooth ride that was less tiring for the rider. Moreover, it was a gait that the horse could sustain for many miles, hour after hour, maintaining speeds between 10 and 15 miles per hour.

Steppe ponies were equally capable of galloping for short bursts in a battle but it was their ability to keep going, without pause, day after day, which earned a reputation for surprise attack. A Mongol army that was estimated, by scouts, to be days away, might suddenly arrive the following dawn. In action these little horses were effective, but they lacked the élan and excitement of horses from the desert.

In complete contrast, the hard-rock deserts of Turkmenistan and Kazakhstan, in the foothills of the Altai, gave rise to the Turkoman horse – a fiery whirlwind of equine fury, a smooth-coated, hot-blooded animal with a warrior's heart. This area was the homeland of the Oghuz and other Turkish tribes before they migrated to create the Seljuq Empire in the 11th century. They brought these courageous horses with them. Today the breed is considered extinct, though it lives on in the form of the Akhal-Teké, an equally tough, fast and spirited horse of immense stamina. These horses were high-maintenance beasts, however, often fed on diets that might include mutton fat, chicken, barley, raisins and dates – a quartermaster's nightmare.

From the sands of Arabia emerged the spirited, snorting hauteur of the Arab horse, with its fine bones, characteristic small head and dished face; it too was a sleek and slender speed machine. Alike in both appearance and temperament to the Turkoman, the Arab horse also required considerably more care and logistic support and was fed on a similar diet.

In combat both the Arab and the Turkoman possessed unequalled boldness, dash and pace. Companies of horse-archers could appear from nowhere in an instant, strike, disappear and reappear, and they could outpace anyone reckless enough to attempt pursuit. They were the ultimate masters of hit-and-run tactics on the battlefield, of encirclement, and were the scourge of the marching column.

The more slender build of these desert breeds was conducive to greater flexibility in the saddle for the horse-archer, who could turn and angle his shots forwards, back, up, down and to the opposite side of the horse's neck with greater ease and agility. These majestic horses brought excitement, verve and flair to the business of the horse-archer and he cultivated it into an art.

ABOVE The author demonstrating the forward shot from horseback. A horse-archer rises to shoot. In this way he achieves relative stillness and minimizes the vibrations and bounce from the horse's movement that might affect the shot, his knees acting as a suspension system. In this position he also assumes a semi-standing posture, with a tilted pelvis, which is broadly similar to the stance of an infantry archer shooting a heavy draw-weight bow. Not only is the spine protected from compression injury, but the archer is also able to engage the muscles of his core and his legs into supporting the draw; conversely, the seated man can only draw with his arms. (Kim Hawkins)

Few people today shoot bows of a realistic military weight and so this image of the archer with his tilted pelvis, though common in art, often seems strange to modern eyes, more used to observing recreational archers shooting bows of modest weights (below 70lb). It was nevertheless, historically, the stance of the power shooter. By rising in the stirrups and angling forward, the horse-archer mimicked closely the posture of the infantry archer drawing a heavy bow. There was some slight loss of power because an amount was diverted into maintaining balance on the moving horse, but stirrups enabled the archer to harness significantly more of his total body strength into the draw than would have been possible otherwise. For example – the following figures are notional and the ratios speculative – a man who can draw a 100lb bow on the ground may well be able to draw an 80lb bow on horseback with stirrups, but may only manage a 60lb bow without stirrups.

There were other benefits to stirrups – such as ease in mounting taller horses, lessening the fatigue of long-distance riding, enabling a ridden horse to jump higher obstacles, and aiding stability for impact combat (a job done fairly well previously by the four-horned saddle) – but by far the greatest contribution of the stirrup was as an aid to the horse-archer.

The horse-archer prepares for war

The art and literature of the composite bow gives scant information on the precise use of this weapon in war, but it is rich with examples of how it was used for courtly entertainment, as public display and in competition and training. It is from these glimpses of what was possible, what was done, that we must extrapolate its deployment on the battlefield.

THE QABAQ

Arguably the most spectacular and demanding skill for the horse-archer was to shoot at the *qabaq*. *Qabaq* means 'gourd', and gourd-shooting was an extremely popular form of training, competition and exhibition for horse-archers throughout the Middle East and Persia.

Actual gourds were the most common form of target, though for higher-status events these were substituted with an artificial gourd constructed from a precious metal such as gold or silver; it remained possible to penetrate it with an arrow. In the modern incarnation of *qabaq*, a metal plate is used and shot at with blunt arrows, hits being registered acoustically.

Another variation was to have birds in a cage atop the pole. The objective was not to shoot the birds themselves, but rather to release them by the arrow striking some form of latch. A more challenging alternative was to have birds tethered to the mast by cords. In order to set them free the archer had to cut the cords with a crescent-headed arrow. This was theatre.

It is an old confusion to think that shooting at aerial targets on masts is practice for shooting birds. More probably, *qabaq* originated as a practice for horse-archers riding the perimeter of fortified towns or castles and shooting up at defenders. Such actions are portrayed in art. Nevertheless, it was as a means of displaying martial prowess that shooting at the *qabaq* found most favour.

Taybughā sounded a word of caution to the gourd-shooter, whose gaze was perforce focused on his elevated target, saying that he 'should beware of his horse bumping into the mast and … keep a man's arm's length between his horse and the mast' (quoted in

Latham & Paterson 1970: 76). Such a narrow margin exacted both highly skilled horsemanship and shooting: the shorter the distance between rider and mast, the more the shot was admired. The risks of such a tactic were evident from the fact that Taybughā also reported that His Excellency Azdamur, the Viceroy of Tripoli (in Syria), riding before a crowd of applauding onlookers, took his attention away from his horse, with the consequence that they collided with the mast. Both the viceroy and his horse were killed (Latham & Paterson 1970: 76).

Perhaps with this incident in mind, Taybughā offered an alternative method of practice for this feat, which was to mark a circle on the ground. The idea was that if the archer shot sufficiently vertically as he passed the mark, the arrow would land in the circle, by which time one's horse would have sped its rider to a safe distance – not an exercise to be attempted with a horse that is not sufficiently forward-going!

THE *FURŪSIYYA* TRACK

A rare example of target arrangements for the practice of horse-archery is contained in a 14th-century military manual, *Münyetü 'l-Ġuzāt* (*Wish of the Warriors of the Faith*), which describes the stages of progression that a horse-archer should undergo:

This copy of a detail from a manuscript miniature (Hazine 1523 f138a) in Istanbul's Topkapi Palace Museum depicts Sultan Murad II (r. 1421–11 and 1446–51) shooting the *qabaq*. In this exercise a gourd was placed on top of a mast approximately 25 feet tall and archers, riding by at a fierce gallop, endeavoured to pierce it with their arrows. It was a thrilling exercise, with the archer often positioned at extreme angles alongside the horse's neck in order to achieve a direct line of vertical shot parallel to the pole. Hits could be achieved at shallower angles, either approaching or going away from the target, but it was the true vertical shot that won the most acclaim. (Illustration by David Joseph Wright)

> When you wish to start shooting arrows on horseback while riding, you should take a weak bow and arrow(s) which are good for this skill. Then erect five barcas [targets] that are following each other. The distance between each of them should be forty arshins. Then take five arrows, ride your horse fast and shoot these one after the other. When you become good at shooting at these, make the distance between them thirty arshins. Every time reduce (the distance between the barcas) like that, until the distance is seven steps. (Öztopçu 1986: 199)

An *arshin* equates to around 28 inches, so 40 *arshins* equals approximately 31yd. That is the approximate distance between targets for some modern horse-archery courses. I can hit all the targets with that distance between them, even on a very fast horse. Reducing that distance incrementally is one thing, but taking it down to seven steps between targets defies the imagination. The author goes on to humble us further:

> When you also become skillful at this, try to shoot fast. This [seven-step distance] is the limit in this practice. Then erect them in another way, that is to say, three barcas on your left side and opposite to them two barcas on your right side. Then ride fast, come and shoot first at the ones that are on your left side and then at the ones that are on your right, if you can. When you become skillful also at this, take a strong bow and shoot with it in the same way that you had done with a weak bow. Once you have perfected your accurate shooting, from then on you will shoot accurately everywhere, that is to say, in the time of war, while shooting deer and in the hippodromes. From then on you will not be afraid of shooting arrows. (Öztopçu 1986: 199)

Not only does the master require faster shooting and quicker riding, he demands the ability to shoot on either side of the horse. Then, lest the student should become conceited with his abilities, he is told to discard the weak 'starter' bow he was advised to begin with and take up a bow with a heavy draw-weight. Draw-weight makes an immense difference to the ability to shoot rapidly. It is comparatively easy to do so with a lightweight bow, but shooting at speed necessitates not only a fast nocking technique but also the ability to pull the string back to full draw very quickly – there is no time for a gradual draw. To do so without injury calls for both flawless technique and immense strength and anything less than full draw diminishes the military effectiveness of the shot. In the final passage of this section, the bar is raised even higher:

> Then erect ten barcas, five of them on your left and five of them on your right in various places. The distance between each of them should be in accordance with the limit that we had mentioned earlier. Take ten arrows that are suitable for this practice. Hold five of them together with the grip (of the bow) and insert (the other) five between the fingers of your right hand. When you finish shooting the arrows that were between your fingers, take the arrows next to the grip and insert them between your fingers, then shoot them as before. These arrows should be thin, so that they will fit between your fingers while you shoot. (Öztopçu 1986: 200)

Here he is advocating a larger than usual in-hand arsenal by employing both the bow-hand and the draw-hand to hold arrows. To be able to shoot this fast, with a heavy bow, and at targets on either side is simply astonishing.

THE OTTOMAN TRACK

A 17th-century Ottoman manual of military horsemanship, the *Kitab-ı Makbûl der-Hâl-i Huyûl*, describes elaborate mounted exercises that incorporated the use of the bow together with the sword, the mace and the shield, giving us insight into the dynamic, multi-weapon virtuosity of the horse-archer and his capabilities on the battlefield. My thanks to Gökmen Altinkulp for information on this manuscript, which is not currently available in English translation.

All the drills required the archer to be ambidextrous, making alternate runs of the track shooting to the right with the bow in the right hand and then shooting to the left with the bow in the left hand; for some of the more advanced exercises, the bow had to be switched mid-course. The archer was also required to maintain constant contact with the reins by means of a small finger loop attached to the reins by a lanyard, which he held in his bow-hand.

Of particular note was the deployment of the *kalkan* (shield) while shooting. Suspended by a strap, the shield had to be shifted nimbly from shoulder to shoulder according to which hand held the bow. For a right-handed-shot (bow in left hand) to a target on the left, the shield had to be on the right shoulder, and vice versa. There was much emphasis placed on the ability to swiftly switch bow and *kalkan* between runs.

Nearly 20 different drills are described, ranging from simple three-shot runs, drawing arrows from the quiver, to courses that demanded an arrow be shot both going towards and going away from each target. For this doubling attack, hitting each target with a one–two shot, it was recommended that additional arrows were carried in the string-hand.

More complex exercises required a combination of archery and strikes with the sword. In one example the archer is instructed to unsheath the sword, hang it from the right arm, take three arrows, nock one and put the other two between the fingers of the string-hand. *At the gallop*, he is then required to shoot forwards into the first target; then shoot behind himself to the same target; shoot the third arrow at the

A modern copy of the track plan illustrated in the *Kitab-ı Makbûl der-Hâl-i Huyûl*. It depicts a broad, straight track, around 8yd wide and 190yd in length. In the original manuscript distances are given in bow-lengths (a bow-length approximates to 3 feet 5 inches). To the left of the track are three archery targets set on posts, roughly 60yd apart. These also have secondary targets, in the form of rope circlets placed on sand mounds, at the foot of the posts. Additionally, to the left there is a *qabaq* target. The penultimate target on this side is a post-mounted target set further back from the track. To the right of the track, for left-handed shots, are also three archery targets on posts with secondary targets on sand mounds at their bases. A fourth post-mounted target is set back further from the track between the first and second archery targets. Also to the right of the track are three targets (possibly gourds) for either the sword or the mace. One is placed on a knee-high mound of sand; the other two, set on poles, are waist-high to a mounted man. (Illustration by David Joseph Wright)

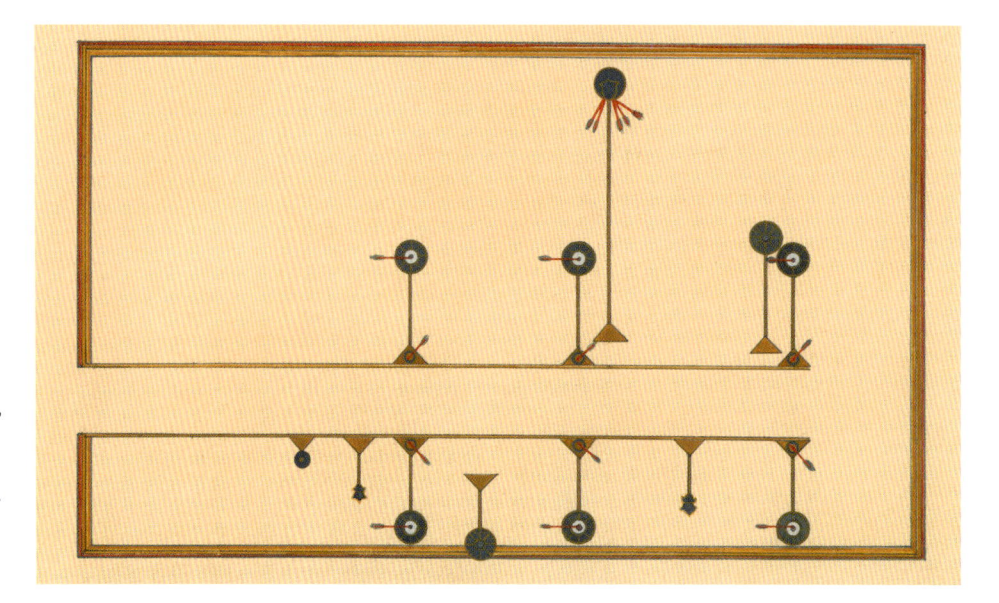

qabaq target; cut at the next sword target, sheath the sword; then shoot at the next target. For another run, which focused on the low sand-mound targets, the archer was not permitted to nock the arrow until after he had passed the target. Some courses required all three sword targets to be struck in addition to archery shots. Likewise, the mace was incorporated to attack the sword targets. One run required setting the mace on the first sand-pile, shooting the bow on approach, picking up the mace, twirling it three times, striking a target with it, then shooting at the *qabaq*, then drawing the sword and cutting a target to the right.

Even more extreme feats were summoned for archers who could shoot at a target on the approach, then – while still at full gallop – unstring and restring their bow, cut at a

TRAINING FOR HORSE-ARCHERY (OPPOSITE)

Here, an Ottoman horse-archer trains according to a system set out in a 14th-century *furūsiyya* manual – *Münyetü'l-Ġuzāt* – now in the Topkapi Palace Museum, Istanbul. He has an arrow on the string and is at full draw. Two arrows have been shot and he retains a further two in his draw-hand. An additional five arrows are held in the bow-hand, making ten in all for the prescribed course. The targets, constructed from sand-filled wicker baskets with a cloth facing, have been placed both to the left and the right of the track. The distance between each target has been reduced from the 31yd suggested for beginners to a barely believable 'seven steps', which the manual requires for the best archers.

The text specifies the arrangement for carrying arrows in each hand, and recommends that they are thin. It is plain that the more slender the arrowshaft, the greater the number that can be comfortably held in the hand, and such speed-shooting techniques are limited to lighter arrows. However, it is probable that arrow-carriage with this number of in-hand arrows was reserved for the display ground and the competition track. It was less suitable for the battlefield.

For a right-handed archer, shooting at the targets on the right-hand side is especially challenging. He has the option to switch the bow to his right hand but must otherwise take the bow over the horse's neck. A shorter bow is an advantage in doing this. Simply twisting at the waist is not enough to set up for the shot. The elbow of the string-hand needs to be aligned with the bow-arm and for this to happen in the saddle, the archer must rise and pivot and also adjust the position of his legs, requiring an athletic agility.

Under Ottoman rule large areas, specifically for archery, were established in many cities. Known as *ok meydani* (arrow places), these massive arenas were for training, for competition and for lavish public display. The *ok meidan* was where infantry archers would hold contests in flight-shooting and target-shooting, as well as being a place for the horse-archer to practise and perform. Together with their trainers and staff, the top archers – professional athletes and martial artists – were accommodated within the purlieu of the grounds. Archery was held in very high regard and the best archers enjoyed considerable celebrity.

THE COMPOSITE BOW

A COURT SPECTACLE

On 21 July 1582, Queen Elizabeth I's ambassador to the Ottoman court, William Harborne, witnessed an elaborate military tattoo in Constantinople. According to his account of the event, 100 horsemen gave a demonstration of martial skills, which included *qabaq* shooting and other feats with the bow:

> A very long mast with a golden ball at the top of it was planted in the middle of the Hippodrome, and on one side and the other in a straight line were planted two rows of trenchers [wooden plates] with a little blank in the middle, on rods six quarte high from the ground, and over against them was extended on the ground a log of wood representing a man. These marks were laid in order a good hand-cast apart.
>
> The horseman rode straight for them, and at the beginning of the course drew his sword, aimed a blow at the log, at once replaced his sword, shot an arrow at the ball on the mast, and at once taking another from his quiver shot it at the other mark, almost as the course was ending. This was done by all, always in one course.
>
> Then they ran with their arrows only, shooting the first at the first mark, and taking another smartly shot at the mast, and then did the same at the last mark, always at full speed, and returned to do the same feats with the left hand.
>
> Then some ran with shields, shooting the arrow with the right hand and holding the shield in the left, and then put the shield in the right and shot with the left, doing all this at unbroken speed.
>
> Others, with sword and arrow, shifting the sword to the right hand and the left, did marvellous things.
>
> Others after shooting their arrows, drew their swords, and rising from their horses touched the ground with one foot, struck a blow and remounted instantly with much dexterity, aimed a second arrow at the mark at the end of their course, doing it to right and left alike; and certainly very few shots went astray, some having in one course hit all the marks except the ball …
>
> Very good were those shots when riding one after another they turned, looking backwards, and shot the arrow behind them, hitting the mark to the great marvel of everyone. (CSPF 1909: 170–88)

Harborne was at pains to point out that everything was done 'at full speed' and his report went on to describe equestrian acrobatics and the throwing of javelins. What marvellous theatre it must have been, and a drama that emphasized not only the archery skills of the horse-archer but also his proficiency with other weapons. Ability with the bow was the most esteemed, but expertise with the shield and the sword carried almost equal regard.

Javelins, usually in a case of three, were commonly carried by Turkish, Persian and Mamluk horse-archers as additional missiles and, although not a feature of the display that Harborne witnessed, aptitude with the lance was almost always a part of the horse-archer's martial repertoire. Whether Hunnic, Mongol, Tatar or Chinese, whether Mamluk *fāris*, Persian or Turkish, almost all horse-archers also carried the lasso as a battlefield weapon – with echoes of their nomadic herding origin. Not only was it used to haul a man from his horse; it was a primary tool for the taking of prisoners. The horse-archer was an extremely versatile warrior, one for whom training was a daily exercise.

BELOW When the Turkish bow was in use, the grip, which was often highly decorated, was covered with a wrap of waxed linen called a *mushamma*. This narrow bandage, wound on spirally, also enabled the size and shape of the grip to be customized precisely to the archer's hand. An alternative to the traditional *mushamma* was to bind the grip with a strip of leather, protecting the grip against tarnish from the hand and abrasion from the arrow. (Kim Hawkins)

BOTTOM A view of a replica *hilal kuram* bow built by Lukas Novotny, showing the *bash*, which is the non-bending 'lever' at the tip of the bow. Note that the sinew layers on the back of the bow are covered with leather and the horn on the belly of the bow is polished and left uncovered. Both are decorated with gold paint. (Kim Hawkins)

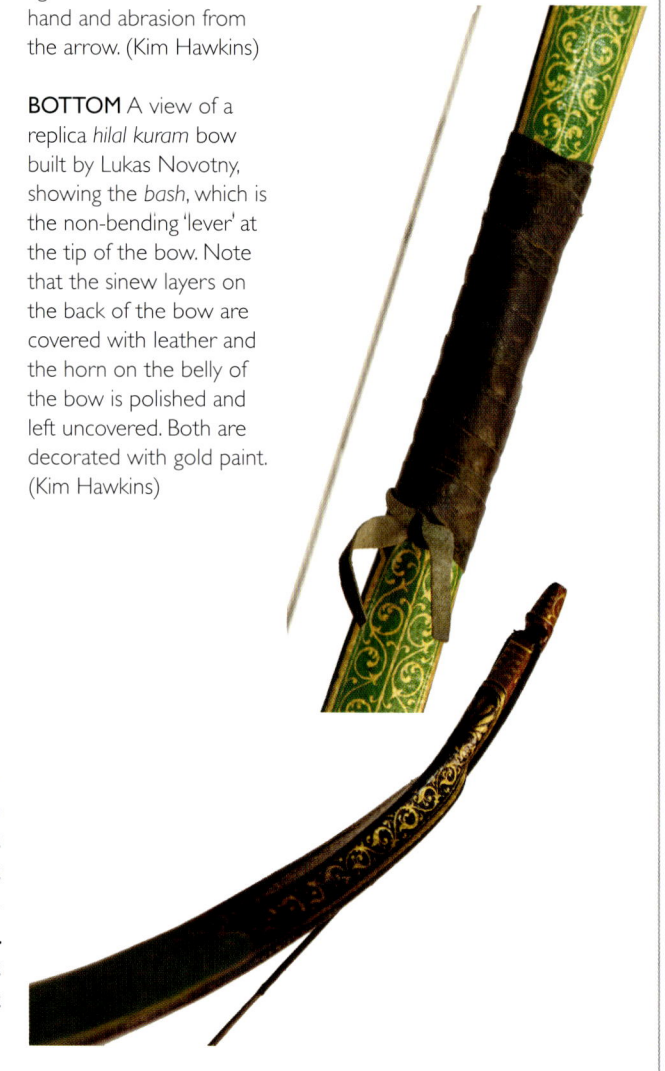

sword target, followed by a shot at the *qabaq* and finally slice a gourd in two with their sword. By comparison, leaning out of the saddle at the gallop to collect one's arrows from a sand-pile at the start of the run (another recommended exercise) was relatively elementary.

The constant switching from sword to bow to mace and the swapping of the shield from one shoulder to the other demonstrated tremendous versatility – it was the epitome of martial flow. Moreover, the culture of flamboyance and panache that these exercises promoted surely transferred to the battlefield. Bearing witness to such outstanding skills must have been daunting to the average soldier – the horse-archer was a formidable and glamorous foe. When contests exhibiting this level of skill, flourish and excitement were held at the *ok meidan*, they drew large crowds of enthusiastic onlookers. They celebrated the art of the horse-archer and elevated his status in society.

THE MANCHU TRACK

As late as the 19th century, a Chinese Jesuit priest, Étienne Zie, recorded details of an ongoing tradition of horse-archery trials in Qing Dynasty China. These proceedings were a component of formal military examinations. Eager to perpetuate the proud heritage of nomadic fighting arts, the Manchu emperors had long promoted horse-archer skills in the army. It helped to forge a distinct Manchurian identity and to rally the fighting spirit of the horse-archer class with a sense of exceptionalism.

Zie recounts that the elementary-level examination for the military required the candidate to ride a course which commenced with a curving section into the straight, and to shoot at three targets. The archer started out with both a bow and a single arrow in his left hand, and carried a further two arrows stowed in his belt. In these respects the exercise resembles the present-day Korean three-shot course, as contested in international competition.

It differed greatly, however, with regard to the distance between the targets and the necessity for rapid shooting. The modern track is 90yd, with just 30yd between targets. The best archers on the fastest horses do this, and hit all three marks, in around 7 seconds; others take as long as 9 seconds. By *furūsiyya* standards – shooting at ten targets placed a mere 7yd apart, on horses of equivalent speed – the modern track would appear leisurely. However, the Manchu elementary track was an even less hurried excursion. It extended a massive 335yd, with targets placed almost 100yd apart. The most common form of target was the 'heaven-man-and-earth target', which consisted of a rolled rattan mat, standing 8 feet high, wrapped in white paper and marked with three circles. Two small pennants fluttered on top to indicate wind direction, though this was of negligible significance given that the targets were placed just 6 feet from the outer edge of the low, earth embankment that flanked the track (Selby 2000: 355).

It would seem that there was a different emphasis for the novice Qing horse-archer than for the elite *fāris* at the height of his skills. Being able to shoot successive arrows quickly was not a requirement; neither was being able to shoot a great distance. This really was beginner's stuff, although the targets were probably fairly narrow columns (their diameter is not recorded) and so flashing by on a quick horse required careful timing to land the shot. Amusingly, Zie adds that 'the local hotheads always try to grab the arrows in full flight, resulting in varying degrees of injury' (Selby 2000: 351). We might deduce that, for this to be even remotely possible, the cadets were using lightweight bows, as recommended in the early stages of training by all archery cultures.

> ## AMBIDEXTROUS ARCHERS
>
> There is a passage in the Bible, referring to a cadre of elite warriors in the service of King David (r. 1010–970 BC), which states that they could 'shoot arrows with the left hand or the right' (1 Chronicles 12: 1–7). Both the account of the entertainment witnessed by William Harborne in Constantinople and the exercise from the *Kitab-ı Makbûl der-Hâl-i Huyûl* required shots not only to the left but also to the right. Both sources are specific in reporting that the archers switched their bows from hand to hand accordingly.
>
> It is quite awkward for a right-handed archer to shoot on the right-hand side of the horse. It can be done – indeed it was done – but there is just one fairly narrow forward angle that anatomy will allow in this attitude. The ability to switch the bow to the opposite hand makes it possible to shoot at all angles, which clearly has a military advantage.
>
> Chinese archery literature contains a number of references to the desirability for horse-archers to be able to shoot with both left and right hands. In *The Archery Manual of Li Chengfen* the old master declares, 'If you want to learn horseback archery you have to learn to shoot with either hand, you have to shoot ambidextrously before you can achieve anything' (quoted in Selby 2000: 305–06). He goes on to say that you're in trouble if the enemy comes at you from the wrong side.
>
> Several portraits of warrior nobles from Mughal India depict them with an archer's ring on each thumb (Koppedrayer 2002: 32), suggesting that they were proficient at shooting a bow with either hand. It is an idea supported in a Sanskrit treatise on Dhanurveda (the art and science of archery) written by Vasistha in the 17th century, but drawing from much earlier teachings, which also advocated the necessity of being able to shoot with either hand (Ray 2014: 28).
>
> In recent years I taught myself to shoot left-handed. Although it was awkward at first, it quickly became easier and I achieved similar accuracy (and inaccuracy) to my right-handed shooting. Although I cannot yet pull an equally heavy bow left-handed, there is no reason why that wouldn't be attainable with training. Being able to shoot with either hand is both enjoyable and empowering.

Manchus who were born into banner households (hereditary military families) were trained in archery and horsemanship from an early age; few bannermen were required to take these entry-level tests. The elementary military examinations were primarily a route for other Chinese, of a non-military background, to enter or to advance in the Qing army. Since these candidates were not destined to be high-calibre troops, lightweight bows were appropriate for their expected abilities. Commanders frequently complained about the poor quality of troops enlisted via this system. Elite Manchu horse-archers were more likely to display their proficiency in the hunting field and to shoot powerful bows.

MOGU

In Korea, horse-archers trained not only by shooting at targets along a track but also by taking part in an exciting hunt-related contest called *mogu*. The *mogu* was a large wickerwork ball, about 3 feet in diameter, covered in canvas. It was towed by means of a rope behind a galloping lead horse. Horse-archers rode after it in competing pairs. Their blunt arrows, having been dipped in some form of dye, registered hits with splotches of their respective colour. Though appearing more like a rehearsal for hunting, pursuit games like this were of equal value to the military archer.

EXHIBITION SHOTS

In *Arab Archery* a variety of challenging shots are listed, from shooting out the flames of candles to a boomerang shot, which involved shooting an arrow, nocked and fletched at each end with four feathers and having a lead weight inserted at one end only. Perhaps the most ambitious was to be performed from the back of a galloping horse. For this shot, the archer took a blunt wooden arrow, flared at the end but with no head, and shot it at a sword planted in the ground. The objective was to split the arrow (Faris & Elmer 1945: 134–38).

The horse-archer: angles of shot

The most convenient and usual shots for the right-handed horse-archer were either to shoot forwards to the left of the horse's neck or directly to the left-hand side. These provided good attack opportunities for either approaching or moving along an enemy line. Ambidextrous ability allowed for these positions to be reversed when countering mounted assailants engaging from the opposite side. This still left a number of angles unexploited, however, and two specialized shots bridged the gap.

THE PARTHIAN SHOT

This iconic shooting stance of the horse-archer, in which he turns in the saddle to shoot over his shoulder, has been traditionally ascribed to Parthian origins. The identical shot is evident in art from all cultures, however, including those that pre-date the Parthians; it is seen on Assyrian wall-reliefs, for instance. The Parthian shot is universal to all horse-archer traditions and is as old as horse-archery itself.

An extreme version of the Parthian shot is described in *Arab Archery*, where the archer is enjoined to turn in the saddle with sufficient rotation to shoot to the right of his horse's tail and to aim his arrows at the hoof-prints left by his horse in virgin ground. Its author tells us phlegmatically that such a shot is 'useful in the event that you are followed by a lion … which might hang on to your mount. A shot would disentangle the beast' (Faris & Elmer 1945: 136).

The author demonstrating the Parthian shot – a shot that is synonymous with horse-archer tactics. It involves the archer turning in the saddle to shoot behind. Chiefly, it was used in a feigned retreat that had succeeded in drawing pursuit from enemy cavalry. However, it could also be used in a regular assault against blocks of infantry. The archer shot forwards as he galloped towards a formation. If a column of horse-archers approached at a slight diagonal, then all archers would have the ability to shoot successive shots diagonally forwards from their horses, raking along the enemy line. They could then wheel away on the opposite diagonal and continue to shoot 'Parthian shots' for a distance equal to their approach. (Kim Hawkins)

WAR BOWS

202

THE COMPOSITE BOW

PARTHIAN HORSE-ARCHERS ATTACK A DISRUPTED LINE OF ROMAN LEGIONARIES (PREVIOUS PAGES)

Although this image is not intended to represent the battle of Carrhae (53 BC) specifically, it draws on aspects of that notable engagement, which saw horse-archers deployed to very great effect. Shortly before the moment depicted, the Romans have formed a *testudo* (tortoise) formation as a defence against continuous assaults from horse-archers. In response, the Parthians have sent in their heavy armoured cavalry – the *cataphracts*. Some of these crack troops and their horses have been struck and skewered by *pila* (javelins) as they drew near. Their corpses litter the Roman front line. A majority of *cataphracts* have managed to crash through, however, disrupting the Roman formation and creating chaos. As they smashed into the shields with their well-armoured horses, they thrust to left and right with their thick spears, using powerful two-handed stabs. They rode through, on and away.

Reeling from the shock of this steel-clad juggernaut, the Romans – mangled, bloody and broken – have attempted to pick themselves up and to reform. At that moment, however, the instant of this image, a tornado of Parthian horse-archers bursts through the thick clouds of dust generated by thousands of clattering hooves on the desert rock. Staying out of reach of the Roman *pila*, which were short-range weapons, the Parthian horse-archers launch wheeling attacks to exploit the Romans' disarray. Injured, scrambling, jostling and without clear commands, the Romans are unable to order their shields quickly enough. This leaves them exposed to arrows more than usual. Aimed shafts find their marks in necks, faces, arms and legs.

Like the Parthian horse-archer portrayed on a stone relief now in the Museum of Islamic Art, Berlin (see page 206), these horse-archers carry spare arrows in their bow-hands. This enables them to shoot extremely rapidly, delivering a burst of arrows as they gallop in and away from their unfortunate quarry. The Parthian shot was as effective in a frontal assault on a line like this, as it was when turning to shoot pursuers in a feinted retreat. It allowed the archer to keep shooting for every second that he was in bowshot of the enemy.

JARMAKI

The *jarmaki* required the archer to shoot with his draw-hand behind the head. It enabled a very tight, downwards shot, adjacent to the horse, allowing the archer to shoot at targets that were otherwise unreachable. On the battlefield it may have been used to dispatch fallen foes as the archer rode by during the rout. In the hunt it had the potential to shoot an animal that had been overtaken in pursuit or an animal, such as a lion, that was itself about to pounce at the hindquarters of the horse.

The author demonstrating the *jarmaki*. In his treatise on archery, written in the 14th century, Taybughā described an unusual shooting position, which he called the *jarmaki*. It required the archer to 'bring his right hand up and over his head, tuck his head beneath his right wrist so that his hand rests in the nape of his neck' (quoted in Latham & Paterson 1970: 82). What initially sounds like a challenging contortion becomes reasonably easy to accomplish if, at approximately half-draw, one rotates the bow-arm to be palm uppermost and simultaneously swings the draw-hand behind the neck. Completion of the draw is executed by pushing down with the bow, rather than pulling back with the string. (Kim Hawkins)

Taybughā also commended the *jarmaki* shot for the infantry archer shooting down from fortifications; it facilitated a shot angle to the base of the wall while minimizing the archer's need to lean over and expose himself to danger. He further proposed the technique for shooting at an enemy hiding in a well (Latham & Paterson 1970: 137).

SPEED-SHOOTING

William of Tyre observed in his chronicles of the Crusades that 'The Saracen cavalry ... began to shoot thicker and faster than one could believe possible' (quoted in Smail 1995: 76). Being able to shoot successive arrows in rapid bursts was fundamental to the tactics of many horse-archers, who could be in contact with their target for only a few seconds at a time.

There were two main challenges to being able to shoot quickly; the first was the ability to come to full draw. Qi Jiguang (17th century) advised, 'When you teach mounted archery tell them: "You should ride like the wind ... reach full draw and release quickly"' (quoted in Tian & Ma 2015: 123). Gao Ying agreed with him, noting that failing to reach full draw was a common fault (Tian & Ma 2015:123). With a powerful bow it takes time to draw the string to the ear; it requires every muscle in the body, and such effort is usually engaged gradually. However, on a quick horse there is no time and the draw cannot be compromised or the archer will miss his mark. The real power requirement for a horse-archer is not just that of being able to draw a heavy bow, but in being able to draw it fully in an instant, without tearing or straining muscles.

The second skill to be mastered was the ability to place an arrow on the string in the blink of an eye. Impressively rapid nocking – taking shafts directly from the quiver – was possible, but it did not match the speed of holding a second or third arrow in the hand. *Arab Archery* relates four methods for in-hand shooting (Faris & Elmer 1945: 151–53).

The first was to hold several arrows by the nocks with the three outer fingers of the string-hand folded into the palm – the thumb and index finger were used both to locate the arrow on the string and also to draw and shoot. It seems a precarious grasp, possibly not suitable for the battlefield, but many modern horse-archers achieve remarkable speeds using this method.

An alternative, according to our authority, was to hold the nocks of the arrows between each divide of two fingers, with the arrows extending from the back of the hand. For nine arrows, three arrows in each divide were suggested. Apart from the fact that it is not explained how one then locks the thumb with the index finger for the draw, there is the issue of arrows wagging furiously, and dislodging, when the archer is in motion.

Thirdly, another draw-hand technique is a method whereby the archer holds the arrows midway on the shaft, with the nocks towards the elbow. I have used this system both from chariots and horseback and, with reed-slim shafts, feel comfortable holding several in the hand securely. It is quite an easy method to master.

A tombstone in the Landesmuseum, Mainz. According to the inscription, it represents a horse-archer named Maris, son of Casitus. Maris, along with his brothers, Masicates and Tigranus, served in a squadron of Parthians and Arabs in the pay of Imperial Rome. Maris sports a fistful of shafts in his bow-hand. Note also the figure on the ground, distributing handfuls of arrows. It suggests a system in which a swirling loop of horsemen, attacking a position, would circle back towards their own lines and pass, still at the gallop, a supply station, where they would grab another clutch of shafts. (© GDKE-Landesmuseum Mainz (Ursula Rudischer))

A carving of a Parthian horseman. Note that he carries several arrows in his bow-hand. It is also notable that, despite the fact he rides without stirrups, he is nevertheless angling his torso forward and assuming a posture very similar to that of heavy bow shooters and of horse-archers who use their stirrups to take this position. (© bpk/Museum für Islamische Kunst, SMB /Georg Niedermeiser)

Finally, *Arab Archery* refers to the technique of holding arrows in the bow-hand and instantly dismisses it because 'it renders the grip weak' (quoted in Faris & Elmer 1945: 153). This system was also described by Qi Jiguang: 'When you are on horseback, you should hold three arrows. You should hold two of them together with the handle and have one arrow already nocked' (quoted in Tian & Ma 2015: 122). Gao Ying disagreed with his teaching. He too maintained that holding arrows in the bow-hand rendered the grip unsteady.

This was not a view shared by everyone. An overwhelming majority of images in art that depict in-hand arrows show them in the bow-hand, not the string-hand. An Assyrian wall-relief from Nimrud (*c*. 865 BC) and now in the British Museum depicts an archer on the battlements holding a pair of arrows in his bow-hand and, as already noted, there is an account of the Pharaoh Amenhotep II holding four arrows in this manner.

In the 12th century, Mardi ibn Ali al-Tarsusi, who wrote an important military manual for Saladin, advised: 'If you wish to shoot and have a sword, drop the sword from your right hand, seize the wrist loop and slide it up the forearm. Hold the bow and three arrows in your left hand' (quoted in Nicolle 1994: 52). Clearly, it is easier to manage a sword hanging from your right arm while shooting, if the action of taking the next arrow involves no more than a relatively horizontal back-and-forth movement of the string-hand to reach for arrows from the bow-hand, rather than dropping it vertically behind to take arrows from the quiver.

Moreover, we have the testimony of the *Münyetüʾl-Ġuzāt*, which is clear that the archer can shoot with five arrows in his bow-hand as well as his string-hand. Bow-hand carriage is a system favoured by many horse-archers today, including myself. It is fast and it is secure, ideal for competitive and display shooting with relatively lightweight bows. Even so, both the author of *Arab Archery* and Gao Ying had a point – carrying arrows in the bow-hand was a system that had the potential to weaken the grip.

Arab Archery refers to Al-Tabari achieving a burst of 15 successive arrows. Even with the shafts distributed between both hands, this would be too many for a strong bow. Such cumbersome numbers would undoubtedly unsteady the grip. Three in the bow-hand is the maximum for me with lightweight bows (under 60lb), but if a heavier bow were to be used, there would need to be fewer in-hand arrows. With the notable exception of the archer in the Bayeux Tapestry who is carrying four arrows in his bow-hand, the evidence of art is that two or three arrows were the most ever carried in this fashion into combat. It is a number that can be accommodated without compromising the ability for a correct grip. Larger numbers of arrows were carried in-hand on occasion, such as for exhibition shooting, when a lighter draw-weight bow could be used but, for the battlefield, two or three sufficed.

Apart from considerations of grip, there was no necessity for more. A fast-galloping horse covers a considerable distance in a few seconds, and two or three arrows in a sequence of burst-shooting at a particular target before passing it would have been optimal. A further small cluster of arrows could then be drawn swiftly from the quiver.

It is technically possible to hold very large numbers of arrows in the bow-hand, as is the practice among some modern horse-archery enthusiasts, who can manage as many as twelve shafts threaded between their fingers. It is clever and impressive stuff, useful for multiple shots from a slow horse in a competition or for an entertainment display, but of limited military application. Setting up with anything other than a simple clutch of three requires time-consuming and careful digital arrangement that is not compatible with battlefield urgency.

Furthermore, horse-archers were versatile troops, equally adept with sword and mace. The demands of the battlefield might change in an instant and they needed to be able to switch from bow to sidearm in a breath; to be able to take up the reins and draw a sword without the fuss of dropping an excess of valuable ammunition. Retrieving the reins remains possible with only one or two arrows in the bow-hand (which is also the rein hand) but not with a bouquet of shafts. With regard to the string-hand (which is also the sword hand), it was more prudent, on the battlefield, to leave that unencumbered.

Details of a wall-relief depicting the Assyrian King Ashurbanipal hunting. Note the ring on the thumb of the bow-hand, serving as an arrow-shelf. Ashurbanipal rides bareback, save for a textured saddle-cloth. He does not rise to shoot. He is taking a difficult shot on the off-side of the horse. Both he and his attendant are wearing shoulder-quivers and the attendant has a pair of arrows at the ready to pass to his master, indicative that the archer might hold an additional arrow in-hand in order to be able to make a rapid second shot at his prey. Similar images showing him hunting on foot also include an attendant passing him a pair of arrows. (Werner Forman)

Infantry archers: training and practice

Even for the infantry archer, shooting the composite bow required a range of shooting techniques and modes. Vasistha, in his *Dhanurveda Samhita*, offers high praise to the archer who can pierce two wooden balls thrown into the air at the same time. He generously gave the option for the archer either to pierce both with one shot, or to be fast enough to get a single shot off at each (Ray 2014: 41). Although this may seem an improbable feat for the average archer, it highlighted the importance of training to be able to hit moving targets. Vasistha went on to decree that archery on foot should also be practised while running; this underlined the fact that, during combat, the archer himself may be on the move.

For the Qing military examinations candidates were required to shoot at six roughly man-size targets. Originally these targets were placed at 135yd – quite a distance for a heavy Manchu arrow. After 1693 the distance was reduced to 84yd and eventually, after 1760, to 50yd.

There was also a seventh target – a leather ball, lacquered bright red. This was set in a mound of earth. In his eyewitness account Étienne Zie compares it to a pumpkin standing around 2 feet tall and about 1 foot in diameter. He doesn't say,

Justin Ma (co-author of *The Way of Archery*) demonstrating the immaculate and elegant form of Gao Ying's teachings, aligning the skeleton in the optimal manner for mechanical efficiency, and thus reducing the stresses on muscle and tendon. Ancient teachings in all archery cultures placed emphasis on perfecting form before either increasing the draw-weight of the bow or shooting at faraway targets. (Mike Loades)

Ice-skating Manchu archers are depicted during a performance for the Qianlong emperor (r. 1735–96) during Chinese New Year on Houhai Lake in Beijing. Ice-skating divisions of archers were deployed in northern campaigns because they could move swiftly over frozen rivers. The figure under the arch is shooting up at the target suspended from the arch with a shot that combines elements of the *qabac* with the Parthian shot. (Image courtesy of The Palace Museum, Beijing)

but I would guess that it was filled with seeds or grains to give it some weight. This was an exercise in delivering 'thump'. Zie notes that 'the candidate not only has to touch the ball; he must knock it out of the supporting hummock' (Selby 2000: 353).

We are not told the distance for the ball shot, but Zie does mention that to accomplish this feat, the archer used a hefty arrow armed with a leather blunt some 2½ inches in diameter. That is a heavy missile that could only have been delivered with the requisite force from a reasonably heavy bow. Qualification depended on only three of the seven targets being hit.

A Safavid Persian treatise, *Jāme al-Hadāyat fi Elm al-Romāyat* (*The Complete Guide Concerning the Science of Archery*), written around 1575, advocated being able to shoot both standing and sitting (kneeling): 'When sitting, one keeps the sole of the right foot flat on the ground as is natural and keeps the right knee erect. He kneels on the left knee and sits on the heel of the left foot' (Khorasani 2013: 79). Such practices were useful for the front rank of an in-depth formation of archers, or in topography where it benefited the archer to stay low to the ground or remain concealed behind a natural feature.

Arab Archery describes the practice of shooting blindfolded in the direction of a sound (Faris & Elmer 1945: 134), a technique also recommended by Vasistha, who explained that an assistant throws stones at a bronze vessel to create the target acoustic (Ray 2014: 43). Such ability obviously had its advantages in the event of a night raid, though it was perhaps of equal risk to friend and foe.

More prosaically, archery training began with a close-range target, a lightweight bow and the perfection of form. Close-range targets in all cultures were similar – from the Turkish *torba* to the Chinese *gaozhen*. Consisting of either densely packed wood-shavings in a sack or tightly bundled straw, they were barrel-shaped and shot end-on, receiving arrows shot from only a few feet away. The angle that an arrow struck the target revealed faults in the form of the release – a clean loose would result in the arrow sticking in perpendicular to the target. Technique had to be perfected before stepping outside to aim at more distant targets.

Targets were even more varied than the types of composite bow that existed. In many instances the target was no more than a mound of earth or a block of clay, softened with water prior to shooting. These wet-clay targets could be shot with either sharps or blunts. More elaborate were panniers of sand or coils of straw, covered with a painted canvas. A particularly distinctive type of Ottoman target was a stuffed leather bag called a *puta*. All these butts were devised to permit the practice of accurate shooting. Another type of target, known as a *darb*, was used to test penetration.

Different cultures placed varying emphasis on the size and the penetrability of targets. In Turkey and in Persia, chief among the archery arts was the quest to shoot for the longest-possible range. An ultimate demonstration of the power of the composite bow, this exercise was known as flight-shooting.

Turkish targets. The puta (**A**) is made from leather and stuffed with cottonseeds. The curious pear shape probably represented the face-on profile of a man on a horse, with the swell of the lower half suggesting the form of a man's legs astride the animal. These targets manifested in several sizes, but the largest approximated to the size of a man. When suspended from a wooden frame, with the top of the target above the ground to the height of a mounted man, it offered target practice at approaching cavalry. Intended to be shot at long range, this example has bells affixed to it to let a distant shooter know that he had struck. The precise scoring system is not known, but clearly there were zones for both man and horse, which may have scored differently. Darb targets served to demonstrate the penetrating power of the bow. These ranged from polished metal plates in frames (like mirrors) that were held up by nervous servants, to ploughshares, bells and blocks of wood. These examples in Istanbul's Military Museum show a pierced bell (**B**), a ploughshare that has been penetrated (**C**) and a very dense log of wood that was shot by Hasib Ziya in 1719 (**D**). (Images courtesy of the Military Museum, Harbiye-Istanbul)

Flight-shooting

On 9 July 1794 the Secretary to the Turkish Ambassador to London, Mahmud Effendi, impressed onlookers gathered in a field behind Bedford Square by shooting an arrow a distance of 482yd (Heath 1971: 79). We are not told in which direction the shot was made, but it is tempting to think that the arrow may have landed within the footprint of what is now the British Museum, which lies adjacent. The spectators included members of the Royal Toxophilite Society, and Effendi – who had been made an honorary member of the society in 1794 – complained to them that the grounds were too restricted for what he would consider a long shot. The area had a number of established buildings and was not entirely open space. Effendi was merely demonstrating the techniques of the flight-shooter, not claiming his shot to be any great distance by Turkish standards. The bow and arrow used on the occasion are preserved in the society's collection at Archer's Hall in Buckinghamshire.

Just a few years later, in 1798, the Sultan Selim III drove an arrow into the ground at a distance of 972yd (Heath 1971: 79). That was more like it. By the 18th century, flight-shooting had become a Turkish passion – some would say obsession. In order to achieve these impressive distances, special equipment was used. First the bows were of tremendous power, but more significantly, special arrows and techniques were employed.

Arrows needed to be as light and aerodynamic as possible. Flight arrows were much shorter than regular arrows. This reduced their overall mass, meaning they required less energy to propel them, and also minimized the amount of air resistance that they encountered. These diminutive, needle-like shafts required a special piece of

Replica flight arrows in the author's collection. Flight arrows were constructed to be as light and slender as possible in order to minimize the slowing effects of friction and drag. The thinner you make an arrow, however, the more you reduce its 'spine' – its stiffness. An arrow of insufficient spine will not stand in a heavy bow; it will break. In order to counteract this, flight arrows were barrelled – made thicker in the centre and tapered towards the ends. This profile increased the stiffness of the shaft, while making it as light as possible. The middle arrow is feather-fletched and the bottom arrow is parchment-fletched. These tiny vanes provide the necessary stability at the cost of minimal drag. The top arrow is an *abrish*, used in practice. (Today, an arrow with this arrangement is called a 'flu-flu', after the onomatopoeic 'floo-hoo', a word employed by the Seminole Indians to describe a very broad-fletched arrow used for hunting small game at close quarters; Maurice Thompson recorded its use (Thompson 1878: 202).) The spiral fletching of the *abrish* created drag, causing it to fly slower and for less distance. This not only made it easier to recover but, most importantly, observers were able to track its flight pattern and advise the archer of any refinements he should make to his technique. (Kim Hawkins)

A *sipur*. This device, strapped to the wrist of the bow-hand and separate from the bow, acts as an arrow-shelf. It extends to within the bow and allows an 'overdraw' – that is to say, a short arrow may be taken to full draw by allowing it to be pulled back to within the radius of the bow's arc. It is used in flight-shooting. The *Münyetü 'l-Ġuzāt* extols the virtues of shooting with such a device: 'This is a good skill to shoot at the people in high fortresses and the people who are far away and for many other things. Because an arrow like this travels a long distance; it travels about one thousand arshins [roughly 775yd] and even more, they say' (Öztopçu 1986: 198). Vasistha commented that arrows shot with the *nalika* (a similar device used in India) 'can be shot a great distance from a high place and are especially useful in siege craft' (Ray 2014: 21). (Image courtesy of the Military Museum, Harbiye-Istanbul)

equipment in order to shoot them – a *sipur*. Such tiny projectiles, fitted with minimal fletching, were capable of being shot over a vast distance and obviously required a clear landscape in order to be able to find them. Today, the world flight-shooting championships are held on the salt flats of Utah, for obvious reasons.

Following the Turkish conquest of Constantinople in 1453, an archer's guild was formed in the city. It established a famous shooting ground called the *ok meidan*. Kani mentions numerous other cities throughout the Islamic world where similar shooting grounds existed. These included Mecca, Alexandria, Damascus, Gallipoli, Belgrade, Baghdad and Cairo (Klopsteg 1987: 107). At the *ok meidan*, spectators would enjoy all manner of archery events, shaded in luxurious tents and lounging on sumptuous cushions. The chief attraction, however, was always flight-shooting. In parts of Turkey, particularly Istanbul, exquisitely carved stone pillars that were erected to mark shots of significant distance may still be seen today.

THE COMPOSITE BOW IN WESTERN EUROPE

In a sequence depicting the Norman attack at the battle of Hastings (1066), the Bayeux Tapestry represents a number of infantry archers in Duke William's army using composite bows. A group of four is shown in the main panel in support of charging cavalry and a further 23 appear in the lower border. The bows have been portrayed crudely, but they are short and there is enough suggestion of the signature recurve shape to be confident with this identification. In a separate section, the tapestry illustrates a horse-archer, amid other cavalry, pressing home the rout.

The infantry archers are shown shooting with a chest-draw and, for the most part, doing so while running forwards in the attack. Their recruitment and presence has not been chronicled, but there were strong links between the Norman/Norse world and the Varangians. The Varangians formed an eastern branch of Viking expansion and settlement, centred upon Kiev, where they would have encountered the composite bow. Furthermore, crack Varangian troops served as the bodyguard of the Byzantine Emperor in Constantinople. Harald Hardrada, who invaded the north of England a few days prior to William's landings in the south, was formerly a commander of the Varangian Guard, and it is possible that he recruited some elite archers from the East to support this adventure. If so, it is not inconceivable that, following his defeat at Stamford Bridge (1066), these soldiers of fortune might have raced south and gained employment with Duke William.

It is equally possible that they were homegrown troops. Carolingian art, from the late 8th century to the end of the 10th century, is plentifully populated with images of archers shooting composite bows. Between the 8th and 10th centuries the Franks, with whom the Normans assimilated, had waged frequent wars on their eastern borders against the Avars and Magyars. These fierce horse-archers introduced them to the composite bow and it appears that, up until the Norman invasion of England, the composite bow was well established and widely used by the warrior class in Western Europe. Archaeologically, the bone laths that buttressed the grip and *siyahs* of Hunnic-type bows have been found extensively throughout Western Europe and Scandinavia.

This detail from the Bayeux Tapestry shows infantry archers using composite bows with a characteristic recurve shape. Note that one of the archers wears a shoulder-quiver, while the others wear belt-quivers. One archer is holding four arrows in his bow-hand. All the archers are shooting while running. (Photo by DeAgostini/Getty Images)

There were four classes of members in the Constantinople Guild: 'the Seniors', 'the 900s', 'the 1000s' and 'the 1100s'. These numbers represented the distance, measured in *gez* (100 gez = 68 yards), that had been attained by a particular class of archer (Klopsteg 1987: 107). In yards we might call them the 610yd men, the 680yd men and the 750yd men. There were also 820yd men ('the 1200s'), but they were of such exceptional ability that they apparently didn't warrant an officially assigned class of their own. Doubtless such rare beings enjoyed celebrity by dint of their individual name rather than by mere guild qualification. An archer continually had to prove his ability to shoot at a designated distance: failure to do so meant that he was downgraded.

Earlier, in the longbow section of the book, I posited that a possible reason for Henry VIII's injunctions for archers to be able to shoot a certain distance (280yd) was not necessarily because great range was required on the battlefield, but because it was a way of measuring an archer's ability to draw a bow of adequate military power. Today we calibrate bows according to draw-weight, but doing so according to their ability to propel an arrow of known weight a certain distance seems an equally good measure. Moreover, it combines this with an indication of the archer's ability to deliver the full power of his bow with good shooting technique.

Arrow types

A bewildering array of arrows was shot from the composite bow. They carried many different styles of arrowhead and displayed diverse forms of shaft, nock and fletching. Space does not permit a comprehensive study, but some of the more ingenious and unusual varieties call out to be mentioned.

Rocket arrows pre-date and are distinct from incendiary arrows. Shortly after the invention of gunpowder in the 9th century AD, the Chinese launched firework-like rockets by means of an arrow. The arrow provided the propulsion to direct the missile, with reasonable accuracy, towards a target area. Before the end of its flight the fuse of the rocket ignited, and the resulting firecracker dance of flame, smoke and noise caused terrified panic among enemy horses. If it was to ignite in the air, where it created maximum impact and confusion, a rocket arrow had to be shot neither too early, nor too late. I have shot a replica of one of these contraptions and they demand very careful timing!

Incendiary arrows had obvious advantages for naval warfare in an age of wooden ships, and for besiegers wishing to fire a town. Various types existed, ranging from the Korean *hwajeon*, which consisted of rolled linen and paper impregnated with a black-powder compound and coated with resin, to a tar-soaked, straw-and-cotton ball inserted into a fire-basket arrow as advocated by the author of *Arab Archery* (Faris & Elmer 1945: 134) That author also goes on to cite a mixture of otter fat, wax, black sulphur, cherry seeds and a tree resin similar to myrrh that was kneaded together with balsam oil. It received an additive of quicklime. Once dry, the hardened paste was ground into granules. Apparently, this amalgam required no pre-ignition, but burst into flames as it travelled through the air.

Arguably, the most impressive type of incendiary arrow was that described by Taybughā (Latham & Paterson 1970: 140). It involved draining an egg and filling it

Arrows with whistling heads were a particular feature of Chinese archery. These examples dating to the Han Dynasty are made from iron. Wood, bone and horn were also common materials. Primarily they served to flush game in the hunting field. They were also used for battlefield communication, as signalling arrows. An early written reference occurs in the *Annals of Sima Qian* (c.109 BC): 'Miedun then made whistling arrows and drilled his troops in their use' (Liao Wanzhen 1999). In the din of battle shouted commands were often futile, and valuable time could be lost in relaying messages from a commander to individual troop captains. Seizing the optimal moment to strike was as important as deciding where to strike. A commander could direct a troop by shooting a whistling arrow at precisely where he wished a strike to land. Its shrill pitch could be distinguished from the roar, stamp and clash of battle. Used in particular with cavalry, a whistle signal produced an instant response at the moment of a commander's decision. An enhancement was to use a whistle and incendiary arrow combination, producing both an audible and a visual signal. (Photograph courtesy of the Dunhuang Museum)

with naphtha. This – now-flammable – egg was inserted into the wide, open end of a cone mounted at the fore-end of the arrow. Prior to introducing the egg, a red-hot iron pellet was located in the narrow neck of the cone. The angle of the cone was such that the egg could not come into direct contact with the iron pellet in the resting position, provided that the device was held at an upward angle. The arrow, unfletched, was tied to the string by its nock and steadied at the forward end by a loop around the grip of the bow. When shot, the blunt head of the arrow acted as a ram, pushing through the cone, forcing the pellet into the egg and igniting it. At the same time it launched the egg as a ball of fire. Taybughā alludes to it being used at the siege of Acre – probably the second siege in 1291, in which Baybars al-Bunduqdari fielded multiple batteries of trebuchets (Latham & Paterson 1970: 143). A common defence against trebuchet barrage was to suspend thick bales of cotton over targeted areas to buffer the shock; incendiary arrows were an ideal means of countering these great cushions.

Seeking ways to render shot arrows unusable to the enemy was a common challenge. In his account of the siege of Adrianople (AD 378), Ammianus Marcellinus describes a simple measure – severed binding. This allowed arrows to be doctored in such a way as to render them useless to an enemy: 'So an order was given that the thongs binding the arrowheads to the shafts should be partially cut through before shooting. This did not affect them in flight, and if they found their mark they were as effective as ever but if they missed they at once fell to pieces' (Marcellinus 1986: 441). The type of arrowheads being used here were fitted into the shaft by means of a tang. In order to keep a tanged arrow securely in place, the end of the shaft was bound tightly with thread.

TOP LEFT Unique to the use of the composite bow in India was an iron arrow, called the *naraca*; this antique example is in the author's collection. The skill in its manufacture is extraordinary. There is no perceivable join and yet the shaft swells towards the nock, which has been made to resemble a bulbous nock. Only the arrowhead, with razor-sharp edges, has been forge-welded in place. Once it had cut through, there would be almost no friction generating resistance to the heavy but fine, bodkin-like shaft. An iron arrow was heavier than a wooden arrow and so also delivered considerable kinetic energy. Moreover, its slender shaft could stitch through a body as effortlessly as a needle. Vasistha advises that the *naraca* requires five feathers to stabilize it, and also notes that only strong and skilled archers could use it (Ray 2014: 21). Clearly, the *naraca* necessitated a bow with a heavy draw-weight to launch it. (Kim Hawkins)

BELOW Although some short arrows could be shot with a *sipur*, darts (less than half the length of a normal arrow) required a more elaborate apparatus – an arrow-guide, known variously as a *mijrat* or *navek*. Here, Dodo Tanyer demonstrates the use of a replica *navek*. The wooden guide, which has two holes drilled at the nock end, is tied to the string, so that it is retained after the shot. On release, the string moves both arrow and guide forward until the string comes to rest; the arrow then travels along the guide before exiting and continuing its flight. An amount of energy is lost owing to the mass and friction of the guide, though much of this is compensated for because the smaller arrow has less air resistance to overcome. Short arrows were commonly used during sieges to avoid supplying the enemy with standard ammunition. (Photograph courtesy of Cemal Hünal)

ARROWHEADS

Although there are literally hundreds of different styles of arrowhead used with the composite bow, three are among the most common.

The bodkin-style head (**A**) was intended primarily for attacking metal armour; the four-sided head is slender but, having curved edges, is very tough structurally.

Slight variations on the lozenge-shaped head (**B** and **C**) occurred in all cultures where the composite bow flourished, and it was the most common type used for war, possessing the optimal angles of cutting edge for attacking leather armour. The two examples here also show the two systems for fitting an arrowhead to the shaft. Arrowheads were either fabricated with a tang that inserted into the arrow (**B**), or made with a tapered socket that fitted over the shaft (**C**). Tanged arrowheads were ideal for bamboo arrows, but were also widely used on wooden shafts. Heating the tang until red hot and using it to bore a hole in the shaft created a tight custom fit. The shaft, whether bamboo or wood, was then tightly bound with thread to maintain compression.

The barbed arrowhead (**D**) was especially suitable for attacking unarmoured horses. Penetration would lead to extensive bleeding. The barbs prevented it from being dislodged easily, so that it would wag in the wound and cause havoc-creating pain for the poor animal. Slender barbed arrowheads were also slight enough and sharp enough to have some impact against poor-quality armour at close range.

The crescent-headed arrow (**E**) was common in all cultures and generally considered to be for shooting small game or birds. There is an intriguing passage in Vasistha's *Dhanurveda Samhita*, however, that refers to the 'two bladed arrow with the little curved fist' shooting enemy arrows out of the air, going on to state that 'If the archer cuts off the enemy's arrows with the help of his own arrows, then he will be proclaimed as "arrow breaker"' (Ray 2014: 40). If such a feat were possible, it probably depended upon the archer being stationed a little forward and on the flanks of his own army and shooting across the line.

First appearing during the Bronze Age and common throughout the Ancient World, the trilobate arrowhead (**F**) consisted of three blades. Although they offered a greater challenge to manufacture than a normal double-bladed broadhead, these nasty little points were a source of terror on the battlefield. It was especially difficult to staunch the flow of blood from a trilobate arrowhead, because it created what surgeons today refer to as a star wound – it was significantly more difficult to stitch together the resulting multiple flaps of skin.

The Manchu plum-needle arrow (**G**) was the most widely used form of arrowhead for Qing warfare. The sharp cutting edges of the head, made from folded steel, taper into a sturdy shank. This gave both weight and minimal resistance to allow penetration to a fatal depth. Extending from the shank on the example shown here is a tang that embeds into the bamboo shaft, which is bound at this point with a cherry-bark wrap to prevent splitting. (All photos courtesy Kim Hawkins)

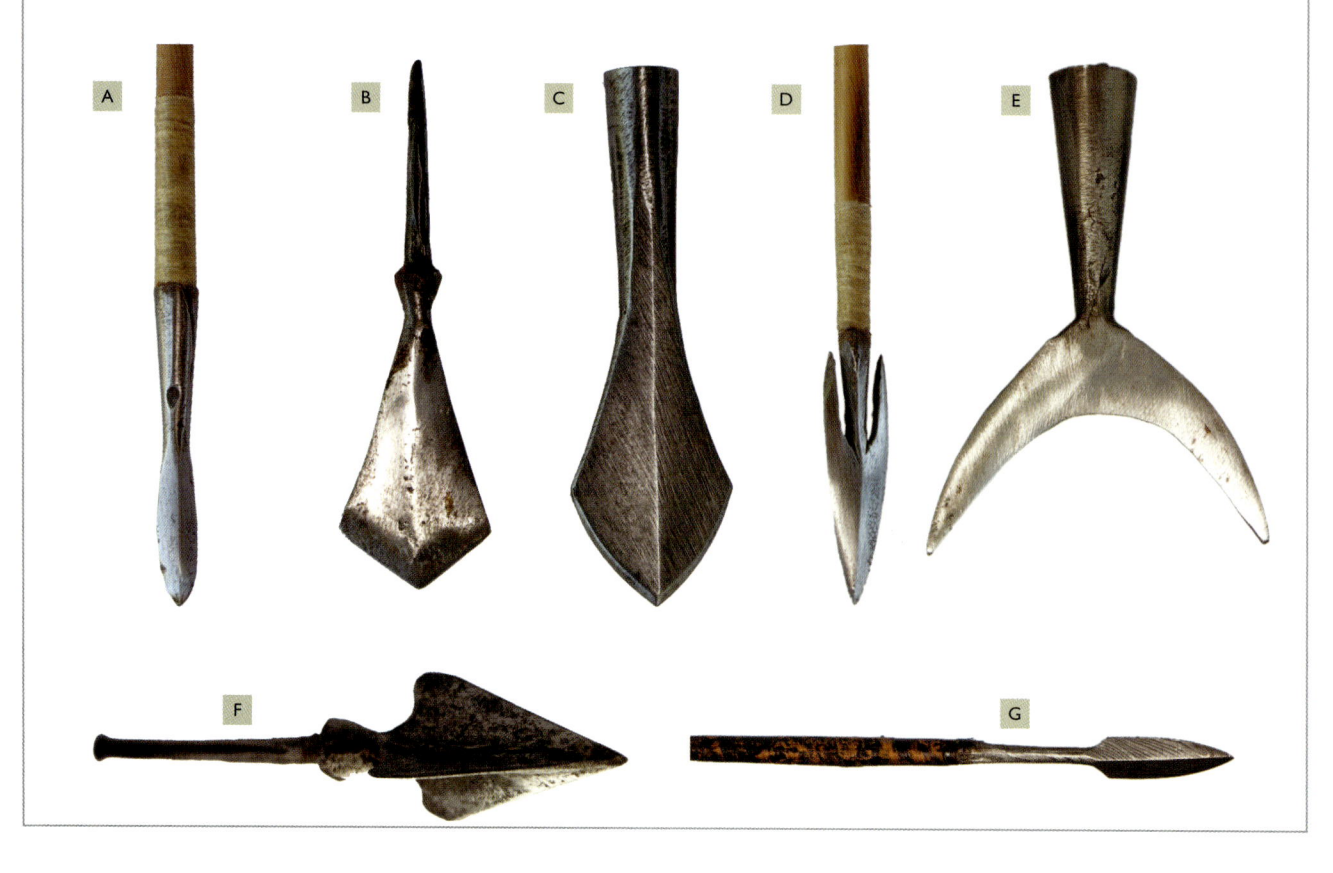

SHAFTS, NOCKS AND FLETCHINGS

Arrowshafts were either of wood – birch was the most common choice – bamboo or river cane. Lightweight bamboo or cane shafts could be given more weight, and thus deliver more wallop, by being fitted with a wooden foreshaft (**A**); the examples shown here are replica Egyptian arrows made by Edward McEwen. Note the different types of bronze arrowhead, which have been mounted on the acacia-wood foreshafts. These foreshafts also provided a strong union at the junction with the arrowhead. If the arrow snapped here on impact, which arrows were prone to do on very light shafts, it reduced the energy delivered to the target. Maintaining the weight and directional force of the arrowshaft behind the head enhanced the power of the punch. The bottom arrow of the four is fitted only with a foreshaft of sharpened ebony; against unarmoured opponents or for hunting small game, such arrows were as effective as those with a metal head.

Nocks were very often bulbous. This not only made them strong but also exaggerated the feel of the nock in the fingers, and that was an advantage when orienting the notch to the string with blind-nocking techniques – essential for speed-shooting. On wooden arrows a bulbous nock was usually made by laminating shaped slivers of either hardwood or horn to the sides of the shaft at the nock (**B**). The whole was then bound with sinew or other strong thread and glued. When dry, the notch of the nock was cut to bisect both the wood and the binding. Bulbous nocks could also be produced by taking a larger shaft and carving them before reducing the main length of the arrow to the required diameter. This was a highly skilled process that might also involve shaping the shaft to be either bob-tailed or barrelled. For bamboo or cane shafts, bulbous nocks were carved as separate pieces from a different material such as wood, horn, ivory or bone.

A particular problem in siege warfare was that when shooting into fortifications, the attacking force inadvertently replenished a supply of ammunition that the defenders might otherwise exhaust. The opposite case was equally true. One solution was the use of the nockless arrow, requiring a specific device fitted to the string to enable them to be shot (**C**). Taybughā recommended the *julbah*, a tubular contrivance into which the coned end of the arrow inserted (Latham & Paterson 1970: 139); the arrow could not be shot back without the enemy possessing a similar device. The author of *Arab Archery* suggested a *birun* – a ring fitted with a spike – that was also attached to the string. A hole was bored in the end of the arrow and this located onto the spike (Faris & Elmer 1945: 133).

Another type shot using a *julbah* was the razor-nock arrow (**D**). In the frenzy of battle an enemy might retrieve such an arrow and attempt to shoot it back. If he did not notice the concealed blade (polished here to highlight it for photography) it had the capacity to cut the bowstring, with the consequent potential to destroy the bow. I have also shot this type of arrow successfully, protecting the string with a piece of stout quill. A quill is an item that an archer might have about his person, and is therefore an expedient measure if the hidden blade has been detected.

A chief function of Manchu archery was to deliver a massive whack of kinetic energy at short range; shown here (**E**) is the ray-skin-covered nock of a high-status Manchu arrow built by Jaap Koppedrayer. Larger, longer fletchings helped to stabilize the heavy arrow quickly after leaving the bow, so that it could be accurate at closer distances. However, because these fletchings were longer than the brace-height of a bow, there was a risk of the feathers becoming dishevelled during the drawing process. Consequently, an archer needed to hold the arrow on the string by the nock alone, for a moment of pre-draw to clear the feathers beyond the bow limbs, before he could settle the shaft against the side of the bow. The rough surface provided by the ray-skin assisted in the secure handling of these heavy arrows during this process, especially when in motion on horseback. It also served to reinforce the nock, which was done by other bindings when ray-skin was not available. (All photos courtesy Kim Hawkins)

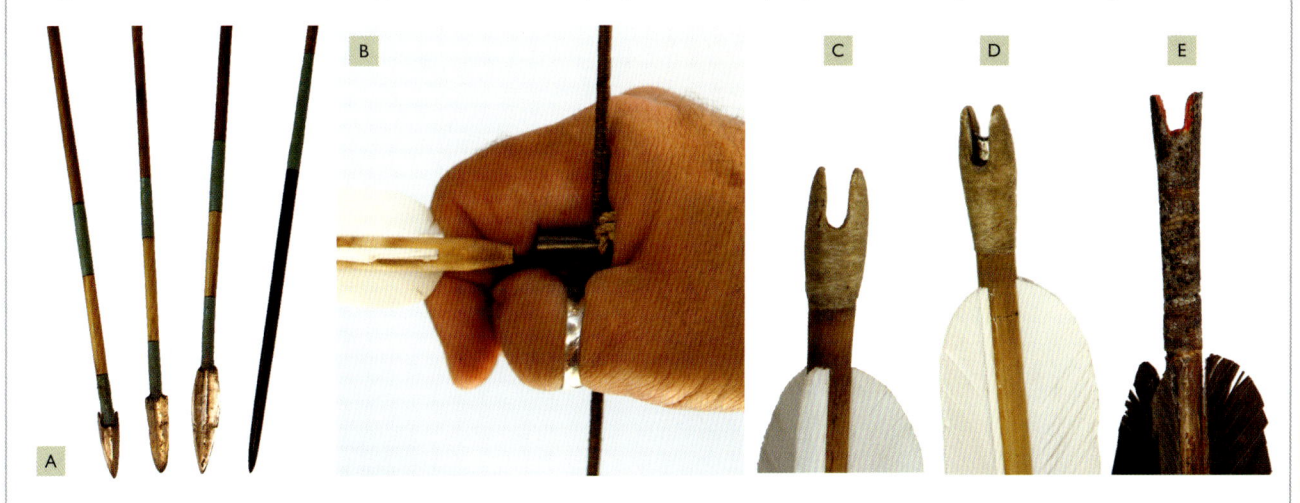

RIGHT 19th-century Manchu quiver in a private collection. Although the cross-straps at the front are a later Mongolian/Tibetan influence, the proportions and organization of this quiver are otherwise reminiscent of a Manchu type. The large bows of the Manchu required correspondingly large arrows, and these needed to be stabilized by large fletchings. Manchu quivers allowed the shafts to be fanned, keeping individual arrows spaced to prevent crushing. A sheet of felt was folded into several tight layers and arrows were wedged securely between the folds. The felt held the arrows sufficiently tightly, even for a galloping horseman, to allow for the quiver to be very short. A short quiver enabled a very fast draw. Additionally, Manchu quivers were fitted with pockets that hinged to the rear and slits that created compartments at the front (here substituted by the cross-straps). Both the rear pockets and the front compartments accommodated arrows with a different head from those in the main partition. These may be any number of specialty arrowheads either for hunting or for war. It was an ingenious system. Similar types were common in Mongolia, Tibet and Korea. (Photograph courtesy of Peter Dekker)

FAR RIGHT This replica made by Zack Djurika shows the Hungarian style of closed quiver. In this instance the quiver has been constructed from bent laths of spilt bamboo and a thin, but very tough, skin of boiled rawhide. It is light but crush-resistant. Arrows were carried with the feathers located at the lower, flared end of the case. Many Chinese, Mongol, Ottoman, Tatar and Persian quivers were also of a similar type, consisting of a stiff leather casing that flared at the base and tapered to a slight waist, 6–7 inches below the top. (Kim Hawkins)

The use of poison arrows seems to be universal to all composite-bow cultures. Each had their own recipes, usually a cocktail of various plants, but one example from Persia involved the bones of a dead cow, buffalo or jackass. These were steeped in a porridge of jackass urine and dung for a period of time, until the bones 'became fat and poisonous' (Khorasani 2013: 59). These toxic bones were then carved into arrowheads. A sliver of bone was likely to remain in the body, even if the victim was able to remove the arrow.

Arrow carriage

Styles of quiver were as wide-ranging as types of bow. Images in art of Achaemenid Persians depict outsize shoulder-quivers, capped with a lid and capable of carrying more than a couple of dozen arrows. The author of *Arab Archery* also describes a type of shoulder-quiver, stating that it should hold between 25 and 30 arrows, although he adds that 'One should not, however, limit himself to that number in battle, but should carry others stuck in his boots up to the feathers and others stuck in his belt' (Faris & Elmer 1945: 155).

In the Bayeux Tapestry one of the composite-bow infantry archers in Duke William's invasion force is shown wearing a shoulder-quiver, although the other

26 wear quivers slung from the waist-belt (see page 211). Nevertheless, a majority of quivers used with the composite bow were worn on the hip. Some quivers were deep, reaching up to the feathers, to prevent arrows falling out during vigorous movement. Others were extremely short, enclosing no more than the lower third of an arrow. Folds of felt lining these quivers enabled the arrows to be held securely. Shorter quivers were favoured by horse-archers in particular because they enabled arrows to be withdrawn much more quickly and ergonomically than from a deeper quiver.

Many composite-bow cultures employed closed quivers, which were usually augmented with a leather flap or cover at the opening. The principal advantage of these closed quivers was to protect the arrows from the elements when on campaign. In use they also offered the opportunity for an archer to select a particular type of arrowhead by feel. The design is such that it is easy to feel the heads and withdraw them without any risk of the hand being pricked by the top of the arrow – even at the flat-out gallop. Any unwelcome rattle from carrying arrows in so solid a receptacle can easily be overcome by inserting a sheepskin plug at the mouth – I have tried such a device and it is no hindrance to drawing shafts swiftly and smoothly.

The 14th-century Mamluk training manual *Nihāyat al-suʾl wa l-umniyya fi taʿlīm aʿmal al-furūsiyya* suggested an additional use for these drum-taut containers. It advised that anyone wishing to ascertain the proximity of an enemy should 'place it on the ground and lay your head against it, and thus you can hear the sound of hooves or of feet' (quoted in Nicolle 2001: 47).

Loading a closed quiver had its challenges, if the feathers were not to be ruffled. The solution, as seen in art, was to encase the fletched ends of a cluster of arrows in a silk bag. This enabled the entire sheaf to be inserted without damage. Individual arrows drew from this silk wrap without resistance or damage. We may imagine that resupply sheaves of arrows, carried by pack animals, were already parcelled in these linings, and that they could be put in place as quickly as a magazine of rifle cartridges.

More thoughts on Scythian archery

I was privileged to present a paper on Scythian warfare at a conference at the British Museum to coincide with their exhibition on the Scythians in 2017. During that time, I was able to see first-hand a number of objects on loan from other museums. This prompted me to make some replica objects with which to experiment. What follows are thoughts arising from that enquiry.

A Turkish bow from the 16th or 17th century with its bow-case and matching quiver. Both the bow-case and quiver have been fabricated in leather and covered with red velvet featuring silver relief embroidery and with silver sequins. Both were suspended from a belt at the archer's waist, of equal use to the infantry and to the horse-archer. For a right-handed archer the *gorytos* was worn on the left hip and the quiver sat on the right hip. The *gorytos* might carry some additional arrows. Bow-cases and quivers were frequently made en suite and with showy materials – exotic animal skins; fine velvets; damask silks encrusted with rich embroidery or richly tooled fine leathers. In Arabia, Turkey and Persia were to be found quivers of brightly coloured leather, faced entirely with an intricate tracery of metal – usually silver – fretwork. Even on relatively everyday campaign quivers, it was usual, in most cultures, to adorn them with a liberal scattering of metal furnishings cast in gold, silver or bronze. These resplendent and gorgeous accoutrements, 'military bling', indicted both the status and swagger of the wearer and the great value he placed on archery. (© Staatliche Kunstsammlungen, Dresden, Jürgen Karpinski)

WAR BOWS

BELOW RIGHT A rare Scythian bow in extraordinarily good condition dated to the 5th to 3rd centuries BC. Unstrung it spans 44 inches, which by composite bow standards is not an unusually short bow. The sinew layers are visible and there are traces that show that it was originally covered in birch bark. (Image courtesy of Hermann Historica GmbH, Munich)

TOP RIGHT Parts of the wooden and horn core laid out before assembly and the application of sinew. This layout, produced by Jason Beever, gives an idea of the complexity of these bows. Such elaborate construction shows an advanced appreciation of mechanical principles that must surely have been intended to produce bows of military effectiveness. (Image courtesy of Jason Beever)

FAR RIGHT A small gold plaque depicting two Scythian archers back-to-back from the Kul'Oba burial mound near Kerch. They have extremely short bows and are either only partially drawn or are using a very short draw. This iconic piece is widely published and helps to foster a belief that the Scythians had small bows. The piece is a mere 3¼ inches in height. It was originally part of a larger set that would have been stitched onto a garment as decoration. (© The Trustees of the British Museum)

THE BOW

There is a trend in Scythian art for their bows to seem quite miniscule. This has led to the supposition that they were that small in reality. It is an assumption that needs to be viewed with caution. Certainly the length of a bow has a direct correlation with the possible length of the draw, and the popular presumption of tiny bows has led to a corresponding belief that the Scythians used short arrows. Neither of these ideas are supported by the archaeology. Many Scythian arrows have been found that are in the 30–31 inches range and the few bows or fragments of bows discovered are comparable to the shorter types of composite bow from other cultures, which nevertheless are capable of being drawn to the ear. Certainly the mechanics of the Scythian design work very well with a bow of around 45 inches (strung). The American bowmaker Jason Beever has produced a lot of replica Scythian bows, using traditional materials. His bows, typically 45 inches in length, have been measured at 85lb at 32 inches and 103lb at 34 inches, illustrating that both the materials and the geometry of the Scythian bow are capable both of a long draw and of delivering a military draw-weight. There is nothing inherent in the design that would limit making reasonably sized, powerful bows.

Why then might they be portrayed so often as smaller bows in art? We may hypothesize. An especially iconic piece is the little gold plaque unearthed at Kul'Oba (below). It is an intricate piece of cast gold and there may be mechanical limitations with this medium in producing bows of greater size; the limbs might be far too fragile and snap off. We also see the image of smaller bows in some, though by no means all, painted art. In these circumstances it may be that the bow is purely emblematic, there to signify that the subject is an archer. It is an identifier but, as an object, has less status than the human it defines and is therefore rendered at a lesser scale. There may be other conjectures. What is certain is that there are inconsistencies of size in art depicting Scythian bows but, to date, the archaeological evidence is fairly consistent.

Gold drinking vessel from Kul'Oba – a 4th-century BC Scythian burial mound (*kurgan*) in the Crimea. The mode of suspension for the *gorytos* is shown clearly. It sits on the left hip. The figures on the vessel represent a Scythian creation myth concerning a challenge to string a strong bow. Here we see one of the contestants suffering from a broken tooth, where the bow presumably struck him in the face, and on the adjacent panel another is having a shattered shinbone bandaged. The author has a broken wrist as a result of a wrestling match with a powerful bow that he lost whilst trying to string it, and understands at first hand the hazards involved. Composite bows take skill to string and the heavier the bow the harder it is. The slightest twist and the bow wrenches out of the hand and delivers a reprimanding strike to the errant archer. (The State Hermitage Museum, St Petersburg. Photograph © The State Hermitage Museum. Photo by Vlademir Terebenin)

The Scythian bow is the most complex design of all composite bows, not only in its extremely recurved profile but also in its cross section. This was a highly engineered bow, manufactured with painstaking craftmanship; it would make no sense for it to be other than a high-powered weapon of significant draw-weight.

THE *GORYTOS*

The *gorytos* is the Greek name given to the distinctive bow-case/quiver combination used by Scythian archers. After detailing the Scythian method for scalping and tanning the skin – these macabre trophies were hung as a 'hand-towels' from the horse harness – Herodotus (5th century BC) reported that: 'Many too take off the skin, nails and all, from their dead enemies' right hands and make coverings for their quivers' (Herodotus 2013: 618).

Recent tests, using ZooMS and SEM technology, on ten *gorytoi* found in a burial site in Southern Ukraine have shown that one example was indeed manufactured from flayed human skin. Herodotus' grisly claim has been proven true!*

Aside from the use of such gruesome materials, many *gorytoi* were embellished with a highly ornamented faceplate, usually in gold, such as the splendid example found in the Macedonian tombs at Vergina from the later part of the 4th century BC. Whether on horseback or on foot, Scythian archers are portrayed in art wearing the *gorytos* on a belt at the left hip. It faces rearward and is suspended by a single strap.

In all other cultures the quiver is set on the right hip, from which arrows can be drawn easily with the right hand. The positioning of the Scythian *gorytos* on the left hip begs the question of how the archer drew his arrows. Suggestions range from reaching behind the back, to turning the *gorytos* to face forwards, to drawing arrows with the bow-hand. In order to assess the merits of these propositions, the author made an approximate reconstruction. The capacity of the arrow compartment was

---

* From the paper 'Testing Herodotus' by Dr Luke Spindler, Dr Margareta Gleba, Dr Marina Daragan and Professor Matthew Collins, delivered to a conference at the British Museum – Scythians and Other Early Eurasian Nomads – on 29 October 2017.

Author wearing a replica *gorytos*. Not only does the *gorytos* balance well for the horse-archer, it is equally suited for the infantry archer. The single strap allows for small adjustments by sliding it along the belt. When running on foot the important thing is to keep the lower leading edge further forward than the extension of the leg; in this way there is no risk of entanglement. It can be nudged a little forward if extreme motion is anticipated, or nudged a little back for an optimum shooting position. (Kim Hawkins)

made to a generous size because many grave finds have suggested several dozen arrows were carried. This had the consequence, as the quiver was emptied, of creating a great ratting din with the remaining arrows, which was both annoying and distracting. A simple solution was to stuff the quiver with hay, though if broadheads had been used, I am sure that grass-seeds would have been equally effective.

Whilst possible to reach behind to take arrows, the author found this to be relatively slow and slightly awkward on horseback. The idea of turning the *gorytos* was not viable because it quickly returned itself to its natural orientation. Besides, having the arrows facing forward creates an unnecessary hazard to the horseman, who would be porcupined in the face were he to fall. Of course, brave men would not shrink from the dangers of the battlefield, but nor are they likely to design their kit to cause such easy jeopardy.

When wearing a replica *gorytos*, the author was immediately aware of how well it balanced. Whether with or without the bow and as the weight changed when arrows were used, the angle of suspension barely registered any alteration. The broad single strap, about one third from the top, balanced it precisely. A clue that suggests an ability to finesse that balance even further may be in an account of Scythian practices credited to the 3rd century BC historian Phylarchus. He related that Scythian braves would put stones in their quivers – black stones for a bad day and white stones for a good day. Clearly it wouldn't take too many days, of either eventuality, before the quiver became unduly heavy, which makes the anecdote slightly suspect. On the other hand, the story may indicate the existence of a practical custom of balancing a quiver with small stones that subsequently acquired a mythology. It seems a plausible idea.

The author found that by far the easiest and most intuitive way to draw arrows from the *gorytos* was to take them with the bow hand. The cutaway at the front of the quiver lines up precisely to where one's hand falls and equates to exactly the optimum position on the shaft to take it. It is a very swift and easy matter, with bow in hand, to use the thumb together with the index and middle fingers to withdraw an arrow, which then sits on the right-hand side of the bow. The right hand then takes the nock and positions it on the string. With just a little practice this becomes an extremely smooth, flowing and ergonomic action.

THUMB DRAW

The equipment informs us how it is best used and the practical trials make it clear that the above is the obvious method for withdrawing arrows from the *gorytos*. That, in so doing, the arrow is positioned on the right-hand side of the bow gives a strong suggestion that the Scythians shot with a thumb release of some sort. The argument against this is that, archeologically, no thumb-rings have been found to date. Absence of evidence is not evidence of absence and it is equally true that no finger protectors have been found to support the idea of a three-finger loose. Much of the art is inconclusive, though in some instances it appears to show a version of the thumb-draw whereby the string passes between the index and middle fingers. Like anything unfamiliar, it feels awkward at first, but I have tried it and it can be done. A thumb draw makes the most practical sense for those engaged in horse-archery, for reasons outlined in previous pages. Scythian thumb rings may have been made from leather that may have decayed or a solid example may yet be found. Either way, it seems probable that the design would have been similar to the Sarmatian ring unearthed in recent years in what were once Scythian lands.

As previously indicated, it is of paramount importance for a horse-archer to be able to shoot with either hand. Drawing and nocking the arrow for the ambidextrous archer is an easy operation with the *gorytos*; the archer simply holds the bow in his right hand and can withdraw from the quiver with his left in the usual way.

SCYTHIAN ARCHERS IN ATHENS

There are a few Athenian images purporting to represent Scythians that have caused confusion regarding the operation of the *gorytos* because they show it suspended by a baldric and facing forward. However, these images were created by Athenian artists representing Scythians as 'exotic' foreigners and are unreliable for detail. Indeed, the artists may never have seen either a Scythian bow or a *gorytos*. Although the images are beautifully executed, they represent fantasy 'dress-up'. They are bogus historical images from the same mould that we use to create inauthentic images in print and film today. To an Athenian, the Scythians were often figures of fun.

In the 5th century BC, 'Scythian archers' formed a proto-police force in Athens. At first 'archers' seem an unlikely choice to impose civil order – arrows flying through the streets doesn't sound like a good idea. It is probable, however, that the word 'archer' was used to describe these Scythians as a signifier of their ethnic type, rather than suggesting that they literally carried bows in the streets. Greek literature is full of references to these 'archers' beating people and hog-tying

Replica bronze Sarmatian thumb-ring, made by Custom Thumb Rings. Dated to around 100 AD, the original was discovered by archaeologists in Ukraine in 2015. It is the earliest known solid ring to have been unearthed outside China. The Sarmatians are generally considered to be descended from the Scythians and it seems highly probable that they would have used a similar style of ring. It incorporates an eye for a lanyard. Practical trials indicate that this either attached to the base of the thumb (a few strands of sinew would suffice) or that a cord attached to a separate wrist strap. The most notable feature of this style of ring is the very short shield. In using a replica, the author found this to be especially beneficial, giving unencumbered 'finger-feel', for rapid nocking techniques that are ideal for horse-archery. (Kim Hawkins)

Athenian plate representing a Scythian archer. This image and one or two other similar images present a problem. At first glance, it supports the idea that the Scythians turned their quivers to be forward-facing in use. This appeals to confirmation bias for those who imagine it too difficult for a right-handed archer to draw arrows from a rear-facing quiver on the left hip. However, this image is suspect. The clothing seems impossibly tight, not only for the fabrics of the day but also compared to the loose-fitting Scythian dress we see in other depictions. He wears Persian headwear, not a Scythian hat, and the *gorytos* he is wearing not only appears the wrong shape for the bow he is holding but, hanging from a baldric unsecured by a belt, it would flap around most annoyingly. It seems that what we see here is a caricature, a pantomime rendition of an exotic on a souvenir plate. The Scythian quiver system works and it works very well indeed. It is represented hanging rearwards in the vast majority of art depicting Scythians. When made correctly, the Scythian *gorytos* is not reversible. (© The Trustees of The British Museum)

(**A**) Scythian bronze arrowheads from Arzhan 2, Southern Siberia, dating from the 7th century BC. Some are tanged and others socketed. Many are trilobate. The horn blunt is most probably for hunting birds or small game. A distinctive feature on a number of surviving Scythian arrowheads is that they have a neat hole in the blade, as can be seen here in the second column, third arrowhead down. It has been suggested that this is a fault in the casting but, in the view of the author, it is more likely that these holes were created deliberately in order to plug the arrowhead with a poisonous paste. (The State Hermitage Museum, St Petersburg. Photograph © The State Hermitage Museum. Photo by Vlademir Terebenin)

(**B**) Trilobate Scythian arrowheads from Arzhan 2, second half of the 7th century BC. Exquisitely decorated with yellow metal inlaid into iron and illustrative of the very high status of Scythian military archery. (The State Hermitage Museum, St Petersburg. Photograph © The State Hermitage Museum. Photo by Vlademir Terebenin)

(**C**) Replica Scythian arrowhead showing an example with the single barb. (Kim Hawkins)

them; there are no references to them shooting their bows. Archaeology reveals that Scythian archers carried a short horse-whip with a wooden handle – it is identical to the whips carried by Cossack police in Russia, the same whip that lashed out at the Bolsheviks in 1918 and the same whip that was used against protestors at the Sochi Olympics in 2014. Not only are these whips tools of chastisement but by holding the lash against the base of the handle, they become tools of arrest; wrapped either around the neck or the hands, and using the wooden handle to exert leverage, they lend a particular urgency to the phrase 'come along with me, sir'. In Athens, Scythians were largely despised and laughed at for their country accents. Aristophanes frequently lampooned them in his plays. It is in this spirit that they are represented by Athenian artists, who made up their idea of what their archery gear looked like – giving them a bow and arrow because they were called 'archers', not because they actually carried bows.

ARROWS

Although iron was also used for Scythian arrowheads, a large number were cast in bronze. Philip of Macedon (r. 359–36 BC) once threatened to enter Scythian lands on the pretext of setting up a bronze statue of Hercules. The Scythian King Ateas announced that if Philip attempted this, then Scythian warriors would seize it and melt the bronze into arrowheads. Scythian arrowheads took various forms. Many have a distinctive single barb on one side. A second type, a high proportion of those so far discovered, were trilobate. These create what surgeons term a 'star wound', which is more difficult to sew together than two linear flaps of skin. Consequently, there is a greater risk of the victim bleeding out and also the greater the terror at receiving such a wound. In addition, many of the blades on these trilobate heads were set with a propeller twist, causing the arrow to spin and thus have greater aerodynamic efficiency.

Scythian arowheads varied in size but many are very tiny indeed and so would not fit onto a shaft of a size that would stand in a bow of military power. It therefore seems reasonable to assume that they used foreshafts, that is, short sections of hardwood, which were inserted into the main shaft. An additional advantage of a foreshaft, whether for hunting or for warfare, is that the foreshaft can be sacrificed, whilst the main body of the arrow may be saved for re-use. Regular arrows may break when trying to retrieve them from a victim, especially if embedded with a barbed head. Foreshafts also add weight and therefore energy to the strike. The fact that they separate from the main shaft and remain in the body makes them especially useful for delivering poisoned arrows. Foreshafts are most usually associated with cultures using river cane or bamboo arrows. However, it is equally possible to mount a foreshaft into a solid wooden shaft; a hole is drilled to receive a corresponding peg. Archaeological evidence to date suggests that the Scythians made their arrows from birch and that they used a foreshaft system.

SCYTHICON

The 4th-century BC Greek work *On Marvellous Things Heard* by pseudo-Aristotle states that:

> the Scythian poison, in which that people dips its arrows, is procured from the viper. The Scythians … take them, and allow them to putrefy for some days. But when the whole mass has become sufficiently rotten, they pour human blood into a little pot, and after covering it with a lid, bury it in a dunghill. And when this likewise has putrefied, they mix the sediment, which is of a watery nature, with the corrupted blood of the viper, and thus make it a deadly poison. (Barnes 1995: 1294)

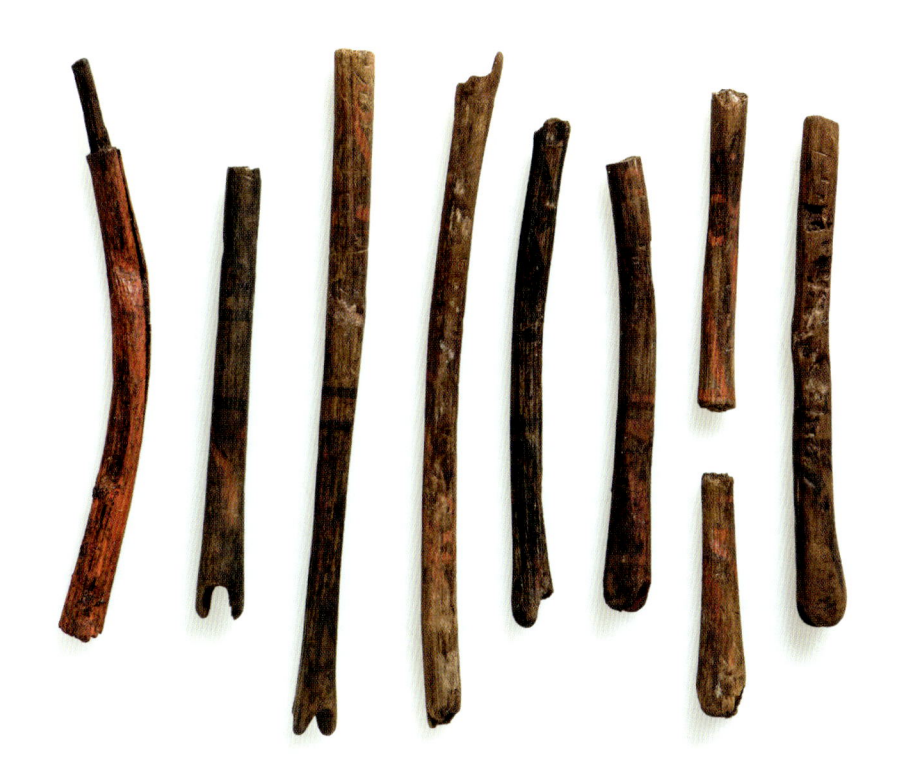

Fragments of painted arrow shafts from the burial mound at Pazyryk 3, southern Siberia, from the 7th century BC. The shafts are of birch and have been painted. Cinnabar red is dominant because it is a pigment that survives better over time. However, traces of white, black and blue pigment are also evident. The paint may be protective against the elements, it may be decorative and it may indicate personal livery. All these aspects may be true; it may also be a means of identifying arrow type. On some, zig-zag and diamond patterns can be discerned, like the markings on a snake; perhaps this is an indication of a poisoned arrow. While some show the nock end, the specimen on the left has a neatly fashioned dowelled end. This is almost certainly a foreshaft. It could be inserted into either a cane shaft or a birch shaft that has been drilled with a corresponding hole. (The State Hermitage Museum, St Petersburg. Photograph © The State Hermitage Museum. Photo by Vlademir Terebenin)

ABOVE The author's reconstruction of a Scythian saddle under construction. From the tomb evidence, the bolsters at the corners are given some rigidity with wooden arches. The pads are stuffed with sheep's wool. A felt saddle cloth is tacked to the underside with a few stitches, making the whole thing a single entity. (Kim Hawkins)

ABOVE RIGHT The author's reconstruction of a Scythian saddle *in situ*. Note that the two padded panels in the centre are joined by a single layer of leather. This was a significant improvement on a simple pad saddle, which cushioned the seat for the rider but still put weight on the horse's spine. With this design, there is the beginnings of a gullet, which provides some space over the equine spine. Secured with a single surcingle, it is remarkably light and folds in two, making it wonderfully portable, ideal for a nomad warrior grabbing a horse from the herd. (Kim Hawkins)

RIGHT A Scythian horse archer figurine from the 4th–5th century BC. He is shown sitting in the 'chair seat' with bent legs hooked into the bolsters. It may be that this position is how they rode, but, in the author's experience, it is extremely difficult and counter-intuitive to do and so may simply be an artist's interpretation of how the equipment is used, perhaps an observation of relaxed riders walking along rather than the fury of battle.

In AD 9, the Roman poet Ovid was exiled to Tomis, a town by the Black Sea. His vivid description of the locals – the Sarmatian descendants of the Scythians – tells of a fierce horse-archer people whose signature weapon was the poisoned arrow:

> Great hordes of them and their Sarmatian cousins
> Canter to and fro along the rough roads
> Everyone with bow and quiverful of
> Arrows yellow-nibbed and vile with venom. (Quoted in Williams 1998: 46)

Ovid's poetic phrasing conjures the psychological dread of poisoned shafts.

SCYTHIANS AS HORSE-ARCHERS

Although the Scythians are also known as infantry archers, they were first and foremost horse-archers and an essential piece of horse-archery kit is the saddle. Saddles in remarkable condition have been preserved in the tombs, and in order to explore the practicalities of these, the author made a reconstruction based on the information given from the very well recorded reconstruction of the saddle from Pazyryk Barrow 3 that was created under the guidance of Dr Elena Stepenova of the State Hermitage

Museum, St Petersburg. The Scythian saddle is of ingenious design, having four raised bolsters, one at each corner. This suggests the possibility that the Scythians, despite not yet having the stirrup, may have raised themselves in the saddle to shoot. The author found by experience that it is indeed possible to lean into the forward bolsters and raise the rider's seat from the saddle. This has the distinct advantage of isolating the rider from the bounce of the horse and is the foundation of high-performance horse-archery. It is certainly possible to sit down on the saddle and to shoot whilst bouncing along. A number of modern horse-archers do this with a degree of success. However, the best rise to shoot and I think it is most probable that the Scythians did the same. Certainly, with their saddles, it was possible. Against this idea are depictions in art which show Scythians sitting on their horses in the so-called chair seat. It is evidence that cannot be ignored but the inferences from art must be set against the dynamic posture that is enabled by the Scythian saddle design. Although the 'legs-up' position of the chair seat can offer a temporarily comfortable change of position when riding without stirrups at a gentle pace, it is an awkward position for the horse-archer at full gallop. Given that the bolsters on the Scythian saddle encourage a raised, forward posture when shooting and that this is the optimum position for shooting, it seems most probable that the Scythian saddle developed specifically to facilitate this. It transformed the abilities of the horse-archer and was arguably a more significant development in horse equipment than that of the stirrup many centuries later.

THE PARTHIANS

The Scythians spread their influence, and briefly their presence, into Iran. They left behind a martial heritage, particularly that of the horse-archer, which was reflected in the indigenous Parthian culture from the 3rd century BC onwards. In particular, the type of saddle that was used by the Parthians was a four-horn saddle without stirrups. It owed much to the Scythian saddle and it was subsequently adopted by the cavalry of Rome.

ABOVE Replica of four-horn Parthian-style saddle. The derivation from the Scythian saddle is clear, with the bolsters having evolved into pronounced and sturdy horns. (Kim Hawkins).

LEFT The author shooting from a Parthian-style saddle. Note that there are no stirrups. Nevertheless, the forward horns enable the rider to lean forward and so elevate his seat from the bounce of the horse's motion at the moment of shooting. It is a stable position and the knees may be used as shock-absorbers in the same way that they are when riding with stirrups. It requires a level of riding fitness that the 'stirrupped' saddle does not, but to young Parthian warriors, that was no detriment. The rear horns prevent the rider from slipping backwards in the saddle and would also enable him to sit into an impact from a lance. (Kim Hawkins)

IMPACT: DIFFERENT BOWS FOR DIFFERENT BLOWS

Recalling his experiences at the battle of Arsuf (1189), Saladin's biographer, Ibn Shaddād, wrote: 'I saw foot soldiers with as many as ten arrows in their backs, who marched on just as usual without breaking rank' (quoted in Verbruggen 1997: 235). The Byzantine princess Anna Komnene, writing half a century earlier, reported an incident in which 'the arrow did not fly in vain from his hand, but pierced through the long shield and cleft its way through the corselet of mail so that arm and side were pinned together' (Komnene 2009: 288). These testimonies – one hailing the effectiveness of armour, the other a salute to the potency of the bow – are apt to leave us confused. There are many other instances of conflicting accounts. Advocates for the superiority of the one over the other can select texts at will to advance whatever argument they are predisposed to favour.

The composite bow was not a universally standard weapon, however. There was an enormous disparity in draw-weights, in arrow types, in armour styles and in tactical applications. Variations in any one of these elements could affect the outcome, and thus evidence which at first seems contradictory, can be reconciled if we understand it to be describing a variety of entirely different circumstances and intentions.

There are different military benefits to being able to shoot quickly compared to being able to shoot powerfully. Although seasoned with biased and boastful exaggeration, the contrast between strong shooting and quick shooting was recorded in an account of the Persian wars by the Roman writer Procopius in the 6th century AD:

> For while their missiles were incomparably more frequent, since the Persians are almost all bowmen and they learn to make their shots much more rapidly than any other men, still the bows which sent the arrows were weak and not very tightly strung, so that their missiles, hitting a corselet, perhaps, or helmet or shield of a Roman warrior, were broken off and had no power to hurt the man who was hit. The Roman bowmen are always slower indeed, but inasmuch as their bows are extremely stiff and very tightly strung, and one might add that they are handled by stronger men, they easily slay much greater numbers of those they hit than do the Persians, for no armour proves an obstacle to the force of their arrows. (Procopius 2007: 169–70)

Draw-weights

It was an aspiration of early Chinese military archers to be able to penetrate seven layers of leather – this was the thickness of a helmet where it was densest, by the ear (Selby 2000: 132) – and shooting powerful bows remained central to Chinese archery culture right up to the end of the Manchu era. As late as 1934 George Cameron Stone, who had been to China some years earlier, observed that 'Bows of 150 pounds are by no means rare in China … The bows that I saw in Peking … were huge, about six feet long strung, with a cross section at the handle of nearly two square inches. They were said to have a pull of about 200 pounds and looked it' (Stone 1961: 134). Not only did the Manchu use the composite bow to a later date than other cultures, they also kept meticulous records, and it is from these that we can glean some insight into the range of draw-weights that were employed, a spectrum that most probably applies equally to the bows of other cultures.

Official documents from 1736, when archery was still a highly valued battlefield skill in China, record detailed test results for the 3,200 men of the elite Hangzhou banner corps. A relatively small group – 80 men – proved their capacity to use bows between 147lb and 173lb. However, the majority – 2,200 men – shot bows in a range between 80lb and 133lb. Lower down the field were 920 bannermen, who were only able to manage bows of 67lb draw-weight or less (Dekker 2012: 103). How much less is not specified, but I would presume there would be nobody shooting less than 60lb. More than two-thirds were in the 80lb to 133lb range. By today's general archery standards these were strong shooters, but there is nothing astonishing about their abilities – many historical archers today shoot bows above 100lb draw-weight and a much larger number can manage bows above 80lb draw-weight. These are not people of superhuman strength; they have simply applied themselves to training in the appropriate techniques for shooting heavy bows, which are quite different from those employed for recreational archery.

There was a distinction between the maximum weight a soldier was able to draw, holding it steady without shake, and the weight he was able to shoot with effectively. The data quoted above is derived from shooting tests in which candidates had to drive their arrows into a target. In military examinations all bannermen were additionally required to draw, but not shoot, 160lb as proof of their strength. Gao Ying advised shooting half the poundage an individual could pull. This fits well with the Manchu statistics, showing that most archers could shoot 80lb or more. What the Manchu data reveals more than anything else, however, is that there was a very wide diversity in draw-weight capability, and that even shooting 60lb and over was within an acceptable range.

In 1727 the Chinese emperor railed against a trend among younger men to advance to heavier and heavier draw-weight bows too quickly and to get injured in the process, considering them to be overambitious: 'If there are those who wish to learn how to use a hard bow, they should practice naturally, gradually increasing the strength of the bow ... Besides, using a hard bow on horseback is difficult, so what is the advantage? A bow that is of strength six [80lb] or greater is enough' (quoted in Elliott 2001: 180). Here is an extremely valuable guide as to the sort of draw-weights that we might expect from a horse-archer, and an acknowledgement that it is harder to draw a heavy bow from the saddle than it is on foot. With this in mind, and also taking into account the acceptability, just nine years later, of archers shooting bows in the 60lb bracket, it would be reasonable to deduce that the average horse-archer, across all cultures, probably drew a bow within the 60lb to 80lb range.

The more spectacular draw-weights were reserved for infantry archers. Even among these brawny bowmen, the 80lb to 130lb grade, the main cadre of Hangzhou bannermen, would seem the most plausible spectrum. Then, as now, there would have been men of exceptional ability – quite a few of them, but exceptional even so – and it was they who drew the most powerful bows: over 130lb on horseback and up to 200lb on foot. These are the men and the bows that achieved the feats of legends, the men who drove arrows deep into wooden blocks and who had the ability to pierce through a shield, a mail coat and an arm, as Anna Komnene described.

The English war bow archer Joe Gibbs, at full draw with a Crimean Tatar-style bow made by Adam Karpowicz. It has a 180lb draw-weight at 31 inches. Joe is using a Mediterranean three-finger draw because that is what he is familiar with, but he demonstrates even so that men with the right training could shoot bows of such immense power. Joe is of modest stature, though obviously fit and well-muscled. He reports that once the *siyah*s came into play, after about 18 inches, the bow became significantly easier to draw and that there was no stacking. At the time of writing he had only shot it on a couple of occasions, but in a comparison test with an English longbow of identical draw-weight, the Crimean Tatar bow shot further. He used the same arrow (2.1oz with 7-inch fletchings) for both shots. Weather conditions were adverse for achieving a long-distance shot, especially with such a heavy missile, but the arrow from the English longbow made 298yd, whereas from the composite bow, it reached 320yd. (Photograph by Kirsty Gibbs)

Arrows and armour

In addition to the wide range of draw-weights used, there was wide variation in arrow types and the armours designed to defeat them. Less-well-off troops might have nothing more than a felt or padded coat – good enough against the cudgelling blows of a mace or even a strike from a sword, but only of small benefit against arrows, even those tipped with bone rather than iron. Marauding bands of horse-archers – the Xiongnu, the Avars, the Huns, the Tatars, the Mongols – who, as well as facing armies in the field, terrorized unarmoured villagers in waves of territorial expansion, frequently used arrowheads fashioned from bone. Bodkin-shaped bone arrowheads can be surprisingly effective and I have witnessed them, shot from modest-weight bows, punching through a replica plywood shield. However, when the need arose, all these armies also had a variety of highly effective arrowheads forged from iron.

Marco Polo reported that 'Every [Mongol] is ordered to carry into battle sixty arrows, thirty smaller ones for piercing and thirty larger with broad heads for discharging at close quarters' (quoted in Turnbull 2003: 47). Some 60 years earlier, Giovanni da Pian del Carpine – author of the *Ystoria Mongalorum* and papal legate to the Great Khan – observed that 'When they come in sight of the enemy they attack at once, each

Replica of Egyptian scale armour made by Todd Feinman. This was constructed from rawhide scales, coloured with milk paint and sealed with shellac. The scales have been sewn with cord to six layers of gathered linen. A further 12 layers of linen were stitched together to form the type of under-armour backing that was likely to have been worn. Each scale overlaps not only vertically but also horizontally, so that at any point an arrow hits, it is obstructed by three layers. Moreover, the nature of the scale assembly over a multi-layered fabric backing produces a repelling spring-like effect on contact. (Kim Hawkins)

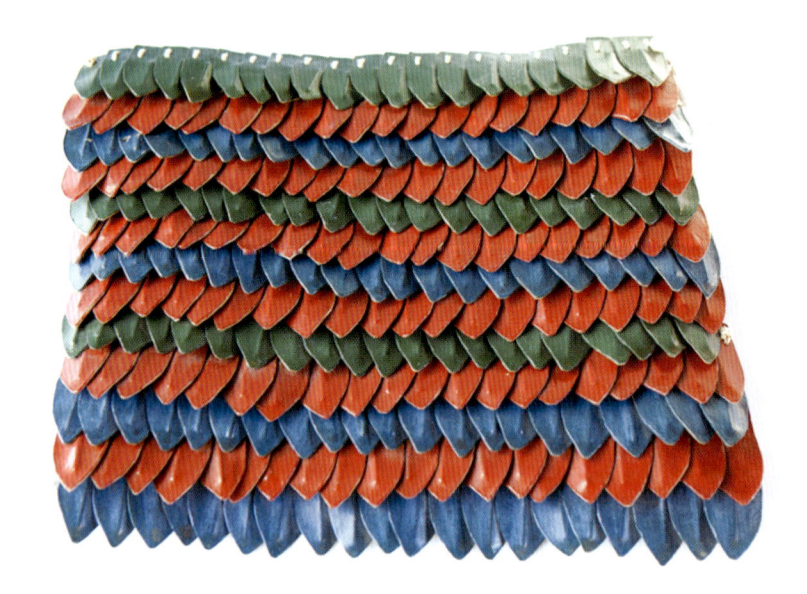

MANCHU INFANTRY ARCHERS (OPPOSITE)

Manchu infantry archers attacking the distinctive tower fortifications of a village during the Jinchuan wars. During the Qing Dynasty (1644–1911) Chinese forces fought two wars against the Jinchuan tribes of Sichuan province, the first in 1747–49 and the second during 1770–76, which led to a final conquest of the region by the Qing. Although the Manchu also used muskets, they continued to rely heavily on the bow even at this late date; it was innate to their military culture. Archery was promoted heavily in the army as an affirmation of Manchurian martial heritage. The rebellious Jinchuan tribes lived in inaccessible, mountainous country. With its stealth and lightweight portability, the bow was ideally suited to these campaigns, which involved sniping, ambush and raid.

Images in art depicting the fighting typically show this type of guerrilla skirmish, with archers shooting on the move or shielded by features in the landscape as they prepare to storm the citadels. Incendiary arrows were especially useful to set conflagrations within the towers and to flush out those taking refuge. Once the Jinchuan were out in the open, fleet-footed in their natural environment, there was an advantage in having fast-moving, hard-hitting bowmen who could hunt them down before they could disappear into the landscape. By comparison, musketeers were too slow.

THE COMPOSITE BOW

A fragment of late Tang Dynasty (AD 618–907) lamellar armour from Miran in China, consisting of thick rectangular scales made of carved leather lacquered in black and red. Lamellar armour is constructed with small plates of either leather or metal laced together. Leather lamellar armour found particular favour in Mongolia and China, though it was also used by other composite-bow cultures. (© The Trustees of the British Museum)

one shooting three or four arrows at their adversaries' (quoted in Turnbull 2003: 48). This sounds very much like a description of burst-shooting tactics, of galloping in and letting fly as many arrows as possible in the few seconds available at reasonable range (60–20yd) during a wheeling charge at the enemy's line; perhaps shooting the smaller arrows from further away and saving a broadhead for the moment of greatest proximity. Of course, the optimal arrow for the task depended on an enemy's armour, and the composite bow was challenged by many sophisticated armour designs.

A common form of armour in the Ancient World was constructed by overlapping small scales of either hardened leather or metal (bronze or iron). These were stitched onto several layers of linen backing. I had a replica of an Egyptian-style scale armour built, based on an example from the tomb of Tutankhamun. I tested it at ten paces against my 75lb draw-weight angular bow, shooting a bronze arrowhead, mounted on a bamboo shaft, with an acacia foreshaft. It made a perceptible mark, but bounced off with no hint of penetration. Lightweight armour of this sort was equally suitable for the protection of chariot horses, but it would probably have been no match for the Pharaoh Amenhotep II and his mighty bow who, from his chariot, shot at copper targets one palm – around 4 inches – thick. His chronicler reported that 'It was really a deed which had never been done nor heard of by report: shooting at a target of copper an arrow which came out and dropped to the ground' (quoted in Pritchard 1969: 244). Allowing for a certain amount of pandering to Pharaonic vanity, such stories are a useful benchmark for defining what was extraordinary and unusual. It may be that such a feat was possible, but the point about it is that it was exceptional, not normal. Of greater interest to the student of the bow is what was commonplace and that, I would suggest, is that armour worked reasonably well against archery – though not infallibly, of course.

Armour of great ingenuity was developed to keep its wearer as safe as possible. A medieval Persian set of instructions for making a leather *josan/jawshan* – a body armour of rectangular plates laced together – details depilating camel hides in a solution of milk and soda and then cutting the leather into the appropriately shaped plates. When dry, four layers of a special glue compound were applied to the surface of each plate, allowing drying time between each coat. This 'glue' included granules of red copper and crushed corundite (emery), as well as two other substances that have not yet been identified by translators (Nicolle 2002: 179). It seems reasonable to assume that the unidentified ingredients provided the adhesive solution to bind the materials and apply the coating. Furthermore, it seems probable that such composite layering of leather, metal and rock would create shock-absorbing and surface-hardened armour, capable of repelling arrows from all but the strongest bows.

Few armours gave protection against arrows to the same extent as a *kazaghand*, a multi-layered armoured coat that was worn throughout the Near East and Persia by those who could afford it, and also adopted by some European crusaders. In a slide of pronunciation, the *kazaghand* became known as the *jazerant* as it emigrated to the backs of crusading knights. If the men that Ibn Shaddād witnessed with arrows sticking in them after the battle of Arsuf were in fact dismounted knights wearing the *jazerant*, the story becomes more credible without downplaying the considerable power of the Saracens' bows.

This is especially so if we consider that the 'porcupining' of these poor fellows was most probably inflicted by horse-archers, men who were shooting bows that were perhaps in the 60lb to 80lb range. Moreover, their deployment had been directed to disrupt and annoy, a tactic requiring fistfuls of slender, lightweight arrows that could be loosed with repetitive bursts of speed-shooting. There should be no surprise if a combination of relatively light bows and arrows against a supreme model of armour resulted in superficial damage and few fatalities. Even so, it would not follow that the archery had not achieved its intended goal – if that goal was to harass. As I noted earlier in the longbow chapter, modern analysts tend to be preoccupied with penetration, considering it the sole gauge of an archer's effectiveness. It is a false measure.

Tactical impact

The effectiveness of military archery has to be assessed according to its intended purpose: whether it is to kill or wound enemy combatants with powerful shots that either penetrate or cause catastrophic blunt-trauma in a battle of attrition, or whether it is to harass, unnerve, control and contain the movements of enemy forces with incessant showers of arrows. Wallop and saturation require different approaches with both tactics and equipment. Each should be weighed on a separate scale.

There is a correlation between the power of a bow and the ability to shoot it rapidly. Moreover, the selection of arrow type was informed not only by the armour of an opponent but also by the style of shooting – rapid burst-shooting tactics required slimmer, lighter arrows, not only for their ease in management but also because an archer could carry them in greater numbers. Snipers and those in siege situations were advantaged when shooting especially powerful bows with thumping, heavy arrows. Infantry archers shooting en masse at range required heavy bows in order to make the distance. (See my observations on the military expedients of long-range shooting and husbanding arrow stocks in the earlier discussion of the longbow.) They equally had use for heavy bows when shooting at relatively close targets, when the intention was to make every arrow count with a knockout punch – this was the military thinking of the Manchu. Rate of shooting was of lesser importance in these instances because the archers were either in a defended position, behind walls or pavises, or because the sheer numbers of a large archer contingent generated a sufficiently impressive volume of shafts. However, infantry archers deployed as skirmishers, shooting rapidly and on the move, were better served with slightly lighter bows and lighter arrows.

Similarly, horse-archers shot lighter bows – compared to those of strongbow infantry. All bows had to be of a useful military weight, of course, but as we have seen this covered a very wide range. A horse-archer can ride reasonably close to his target and so can to a large extent compensate for lower poundage – a 70lb or 80lb bow could still deliver an arrow with an impressive whack at 20, 30 or 40yd. Persistent harassment by horse-archers, the psychological equivalent to a constant artillery barrage, ground away at an enemy's resolve and put him on edge. It wearied him. Not every arrow had to kill; it simply had to be a threat and an irritant, and to pack a sufficient degree of painful punch. Moreover, such assaults could be executed with relatively little risk to the attacking force, and they could be sustained for days.

Whether or not there was a heavy casualty rate, one of the most effective aspects of military archery was that it could enable one army to keep opposing regiments pinned in position: it offered control of the battlefield. This was particularly so with the use of horse-archers. A common tactic during the Crusades, as well as other

Developed primarily to withstand arrow strikes, the *jazerant* was a complex, layered defence; this replica section was made by Nicholas Checksfield. A single garment, it was worn over a shirt and from the inside out consisted of: a rabbit skin *gambeson*, made of stitched-together, hair-on rabbit pelts (rabbit is an especially dense but lightweight pelt) sandwiched between layers of thick linen; a full-length coat of riveted mail covering the arms and extending to below the knees; a second, outer *gambeson* that was tightly stuffed with silk waste; a half-length coat of riveted mail; and an outer covering of brocade silk. The entire armour was riveted through with pigtail rivets, which gathered together all the layers into quilted pockets. This quilting effect made all the materials – pelt, linens, mail, stuffing – considerably denser and less penetrable. There would also have been another layer of linen on the inside to cover the coils of the pigtail rivets. *Jazerants* opened at the front, so that they could be donned quickly, in the manner of an overcoat. The skirts were divided front and back, so that the horseman could wear it in the saddle. (Photographs courtesy of Deborah Lee)

conflicts, was to shoot at the horses. Armour for horses was available with varying degrees of completeness, but horses nevertheless remained larger and more vulnerable targets than their well-armoured riders. Moreover, even seasoned warhorses could be distressed and panicked by the sting and terror of an arrowstorm. Anna Komnene recalls an incident when a troop of horse-archers were sent against the Norman military leader Bohemond's cavalry: 'they rained down arrows on their mounts and thus created a scene of chaos for the riders' (Komnene 2009: 143). The tactic was used here in the context of pursuit – to keep driving an enemy off without engaging him in direct contact. Horse-archers, and other light cavalry, were also of considerable value in the rout, in sealing a victory.

In *Taktika*, a book of military tactics written by the Byzantine Emperor Leo VI (r. 886–912), he advised his archers to shoot at the horses of the Arabs because it would put them to flight: 'They will do this for two reasons, namely because of their desire to save their horses, which are highly prized, and not easily procured, and because they want to save themselves as well through saving the horses' (quoted in Dennis 2010: 129). Even so, a successor emperor – Nikephoros II Phokas (r. 963–69) – cautioned that if Arab horsemen were driven off, it would be a mistake to pursue them; they were somewhat fleeter than Bohemond's cavalry: 'When pursued they are not overtaken and, aided by the speed of their horses, they quickly counter-attack and strike against our men. It does no good at all to go chasing after them' (quoted in Dennis 1985: 104).

The effectiveness of the horse-archer was inextricably connected not only to the power of his bow but also to the celerity and stamina of his horse. In pitched battle, horse-archers were used very effectively both for encirclement, flanking manoeuvres, what the Mongols termed the *tulughma*, and for a constant stream of attacks. When the Magyars and the Patzinaks raised their challenge to the Byzantine Empire, the Arab historian al-Masʿūdī gave a detailed account of their tactics during a campaign in 934:

> The engagement began with the horsemen of the right wing attacking the main battle of the Byzantines, showering it with arrows, and taking up a new position on the left. Then they of the left wing likewise advanced and shot against the Byzantine main battle, changing over to the right side of the line. So the mounted bands kept wheeling across the Byzantine front, grinding away at it like millstones. (Quoted in Jankovich 1971: 103)

This fluidity characterized a fundamental difference in military thinking between East and West; between fighting from entrenched, defended positions and the mobility of the horse-archer. Even when mounted, European knights formed moving walls, as fixed in formation as any fortress, relying on impact for effect. They had to make contact to engage an enemy. However, the horse-archer was able to strike at distance, always able to elude direct contact unless it was on his own terms; unless he had softened an enemy sufficiently. Moreover, he was able to remain continuously mobile, forever changing the direction and timing of his attack on both the battlefield and the march. It gave him a versatility and adaptability unmatched by any other type of combatant.

There can be no doubt that the composite bow, in its myriad manifestations, has also been a highly effective weapon for the infantry archer – both on the battlefield and in siege warfare. It was in the hands of the horse-archer, however, that it has had its most lasting impact.

CONCLUSION

The study of the composite bow, once solely the preserve of a few gentlemen antiquarians, is now enjoying considerable popularity. This coincides with a deepening interest in traditional and historical archery in general. A growing band of skilled artisans are practising the arts of the composite bowyer. Replica bows, built from genuine horn and sinew, are available to purchase more than ever before. Some archers are conditioning themselves to shoot bows of historical poundage, and shooting with a thumb-ring has become an increasingly familiar sight at archery ranges. All this sets the stage for much-needed empirical experimentation to understand more about how these bows were used and what they were capable of achieving. There are now many useful independent websites, but the Asian Traditional Archery Research Network (ATARN) is the central body through which all meaningful online research is disseminated.

Strongly linked to the resurgence of interest in making and shooting the composite bow is the growth in popularity of horse-archery, both as a competitive sport and as a pure martial art. In some countries, namely those having a strong horse-archer heritage, it has become a statement of cultural identity, with practitioners often dressing in traditional garb and using only the bow of that culture. In places without a national tradition, horse-archers shoot an assortment of bow forms, including modern hybrid styles, and in a variety of attire. Archery with the composite bow is a living art and the best are beginning to shoot with the power, the speed and the accuracy of horse-archers from the past.

Today's horse-archers develop a connection to their horse, to their bow and to themselves that a warrior from the steppes would have understood and that a noble *fāris* would have admired. Study of the composite bow is a gateway to learning about a diverse gamut of peoples and historical periods; a study of infinite fascination and reward. When so much historical study is nationalistic in character, this extraordinary, beautiful weapon opens new horizons for cross-cultural knowledge and discovery.

CHAPTER FOUR
THE JAPANESE YUMI

Kyūjutsu (the art of archery) is the Japanese martial art of using the bow. *Kyūjutsu*, not *kenjutsu* (the art of the sword), was the principal and defining martial skill of the samurai class during the greater part of their military hegemony. *Yumiya no michi* (the way of the bow and arrow) and *kyūba no michi* (the way of the bow and the horse) were phrases that defined a samurai's calling. Until the very late 16th century, the bow, not the sword was the symbol of the professional warrior in Japan. From the mid-Heian period (AD 794–1185) to the end of the Muromachi period (1333–1573) the samurai of feudal Japan were first and foremost archers; more specifically they were horse-archers. Their bow was the *yumi* – the Japanese longbow – and it had a distinctly different shape and construction from the bows of other cultures. The samurai horse-archer, *yumi* in hand, attacked head-on, unleashing a burst of arrows from his galloping steed; he was brave, skilful

RIGHT A woodcut c. 1811–1830 depicting the warriors Kumagai Naozane and Taira no Atsumori in full battle regalia. (Library of Congress, Washington)

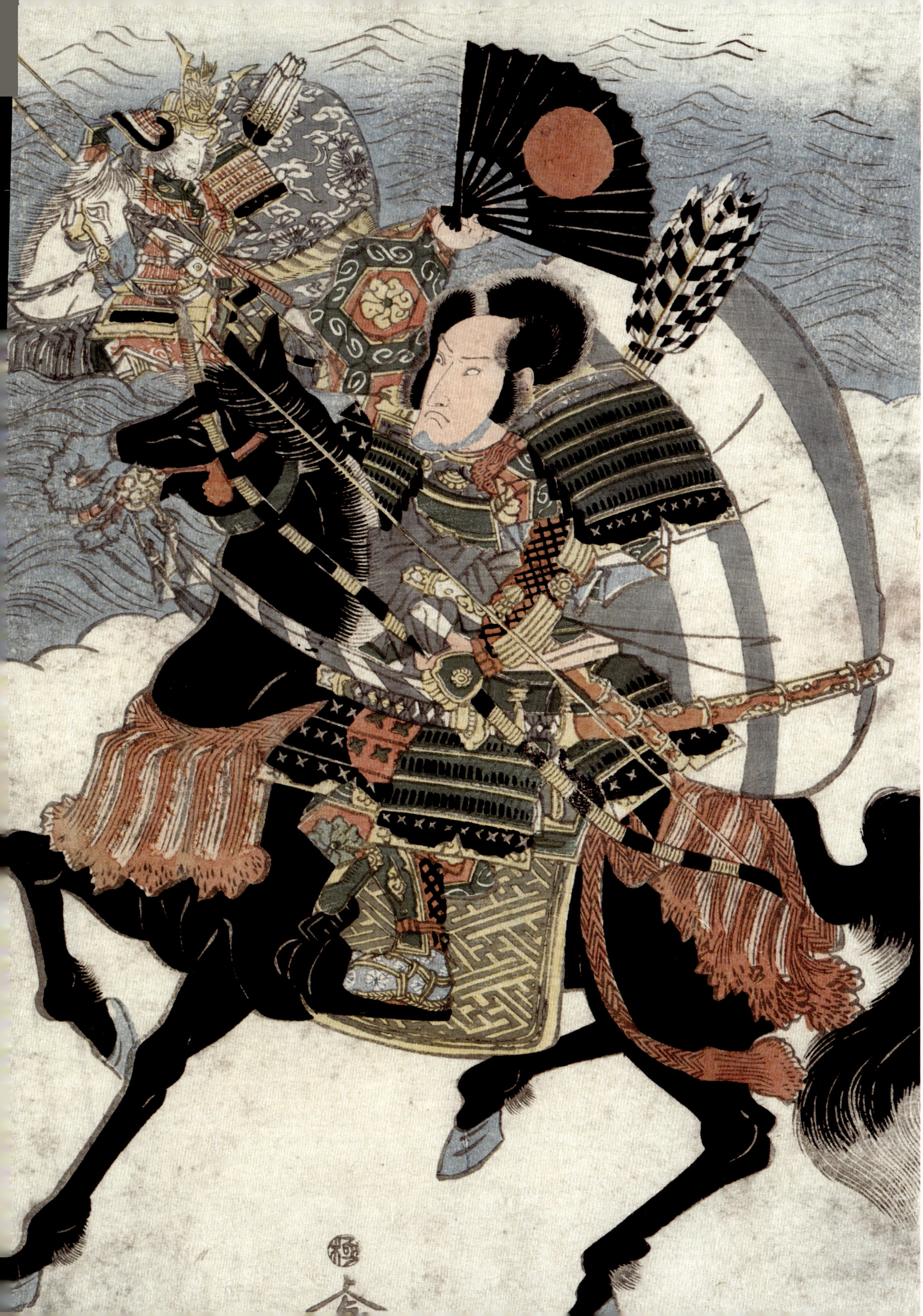
極

Himezori (princess curve)

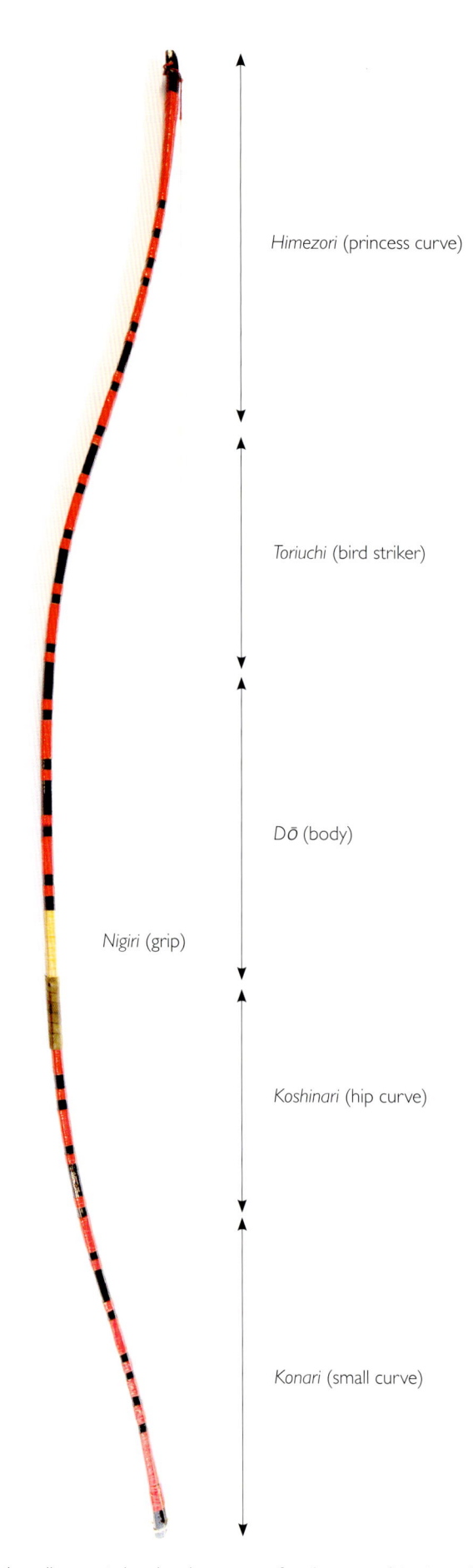

Toriuchi (bird striker)

Dō (body)

Nigiri (grip)

Koshinari (hip curve)

Konari (small curve)

A replica *yumi*, showing the names of each curve of the bow. (Kim Hawkins)

and magnificent. His time of prime importance on the battlefield was during the late Heian and Kamakura (1185–1333) eras and much of this brief study focuses on this period. Nevertheless, the *yumi* continues to be of such significance in Japanese culture that its later manifestations in sport and ceremony cannot be ignored. Indeed, the continuing tradition of these rituals can sometimes offer clues to the *yumi*'s martial past. For this reason, *kyūdō*, 'the way of the bow', and the ways of the horse-archer in ceremonies such as *yabusame*, are touched upon in order to put the long legacy of the *yumi* in context.

It was only under the influence of Tokugawa Ieyasu (r.1603–05) that the sword and sword-related rituals began to eclipse the bow. Nevertheless, despite the emerging cult of the *katana*, the bow remained of great importance. Many archery rituals were refined and became embedded in Japanese martial culture during Japan's prolonged period of self-imposed withdrawal from the world. *Sakoku* (closed country) is the name given to the unique Japanese experience of isolation. During the 1630s, Tokugawa Iemitsu (r. 1604–51) issued a number of proclamations that resulted in Japan closing its doors. Nobody was allowed in and no Japanese could travel out. This remained the case for over 200 years until 1853, when Commodore Matthew Perry, commanding the United States fleet known as the 'Black Ships', forced Japan to re-open its doors with 'gunboat diplomacy'. *Sakoku* was a period of unprecedented peace and, counter-intuitively, a period in which the samurai flourished and nurtured their martial traditions. Without the theatre of the battlefield, systemized martial display became a way of proclaiming class identity.

A significant legacy of Toyotomi Hideyoshi (1585–91) was the rigid categorization of the Japanese class system. Under his edicts it became law that only the samurai could bear arms. This, combined with *sakoku*, led to circumstances in which there was neither social mobility within the country, nor the influences of the wider world without. Traditional martial skills were kept alive in remote and aloof isolation and no longer informed by battlefield experience. To some extent they were embalmed with such formality and ritual that they would be unrecognizable to a samurai who fought with his bow and his horse, winning fame and glory in dashing encounters during the Gempei War (1180–85) but the essence of *yumiya no michi* remained, and it exists to this day in Japan's unique and magnificent archery heritage.

DEVELOPMENT: THE ASYMMETRIC BOW

The *yumi*

ASYMMETRY

The *yumi* is distinctive for its length, graceful curves and its asymmetry. No discussion of the construction of the Japanese bow can begin without addressing the issue of asymmetry. The upper limb of a Japanese bow is two-thirds the overall length. Combined with its sinuous curvatures, this asymmetry created a bow of extraordinary elegance. Indeed, it may be that considerations of beauty were a key factor in influencing the preference for asymmetry. *Fukinsei* (asymmetry) is a recurring theme in Japanese aesthetics. Another aesthetic concept that is valued in Japan relates to objects bearing the signature of the natural world. The most basic form of a bow is a springy sapling, its natural taper being much thicker at one end than at the other. To balance the force of the limbs, such a bow must be held with the grip placed considerably lower than centre. It could be perceived from this that the *yumi* exhibits the shape of a bow in its most natural, unfashioned and primitive state.

An image of a hunter with an asymmetrical bow appears on a *dokatu* (a type of ceremonial bell) dating to the Yayoi period (250 BC–AD 330). A 3rd-century AD Chinese text, the *Gishi Wajin-den*, records that the people of the islands of Japan use 'a wooden bow with upper and lower limbs of different lengths' (quoted in Onuma & DeProspero 1993: 38). The Japanese were not alone in favouring asymmetric bows. Most composite bows have slight asymmetry. Others, such as some Scythian bows and some Hun bows, had a more pronounced asymmetry. However, the very high degree of asymmetry found on the *yumi* was unique to Japanese bows. As far as practical considerations go, a longer upper limb enabled a longer draw that could only otherwise be achieved by making the entire bow longer. In Japanese archery, the draw is long. Maintaining a relatively short lower limb was not only advantageous on horseback, it was also useful for the infantry archer who may wish to shoot whilst kneeling. Kneeling archers allowed for standing archers behind them; they also presented a smaller target to the enemy and, in ambush, were able to position themselves in concealed locations. For the horse-archer, the ability to pass the bow easily across the horse's neck to shoot on either side was of great benefit. In battle he had to be able to shoot on all sides. However, asymmetric bows predate the use of the bow on horseback and so that seems unlikely as the originating reason for their shape. A more likely practical reason is that the asymmetric design delivers less hand shock. As the limbs spring forward upon release, the shock waves from each travel towards the middle, colliding in a centre-grip bow to where the hand holds the bow. An asymmetric bow avoids this harmonic interference and an expertly balanced *yumi* is extremely smooth to shoot.

Another theory, advanced by Graham Ashton in volume 55 of *The Journal of the Society of Archer-Antiquaries* (2003), is that the asymmetry facilitates a 'strong wrist' position. In both karate and iaido, he argues, there is great emphasis placed on maintaining a straight and therefore strong wrist, able to project energy. He has calculated that with the wrist held straight from the arm, a rod passing through the hand sits at 65 degrees to the horizontal. This angle occurs naturally lower down

A 19th-century *yumi*, unstrung. It is lacquered black and bound with rattan that has been lacquered red. The grip is wrapped in doeskin. The overall length of the bow is 7 feet 1¼ inches. The length from the upper nock to the grip is 4 feet 5 inches. It weighs 1lb 13oz. (© Royal Armouries)

the bow. Thus at full draw, the asymmetric design balances the *yumi* when held with this straight grip. It is called the *tenouchi*.

EARLY BOWS

The earliest Japanese bows were self bows – that is to say, they were made from a single piece of wood. Two types of wood are associated with these first *yumi*. One is *azusa*, the Japanese cherry birch. '*Azusa-yumi*' is also the name given to a specific type of sacred bow. There is a continuing tradition to enshrine 59 *azusa-yumi* at the Ise Grand Shrine; 29 are lacquered in vermilion and 30 in black. They are replaced every 20 years. According to legend, the Emperor Jimmu (r. 660–585 BC), mythologized as Japan's first human ruler, possessed a bow made from *azusa* wood. This bow was able to dispel evil simply by plucking its string. By custom, many noble families display a single pair of these sacred bows in their homes (one vermilion, one black). They are referred to as *Gokaho-yumi* – 'Great Family Treasures'.

However, for practical *yumi*s, catalpa wood seems to have been the more usual timber. It had natural springiness and was receptive to shaping by means of steam bending. According to the *Shaho Sambu Sho*, written in 1689, 'in ancient times the bow was made by steaming the material' (quoted in Grayson *JSAA* Vol. 6: 28). The wooden form of the Japanese bow, known as the *maruki-yumi*, was in use from at least the 5th century AD, possibly earlier, to the 9th century AD. It was a longbow, approximately 6 feet in length with a slightly squashed oval cross-section, and it was asymmetrical.

Building the *yumi*

CROSS-SECTIONS

Almost certainly influenced by Chinese composite bows, which were used widely at the Japanese court between the 4th and 9th centuries AD, the traditional Japanese *yumi* was eventually incarnated as a two-piece lamination at some point in the 9th century. The simple wooden bow was backed with a strip of bamboo. In subsequent centuries, different and far more complex configurations of lamination evolved. Each development offered a greater mechanical advantage; each gave more spring for any given amount of effort to draw back the string.

PREPARING THE BAMBOO

The method of preparing bamboo for bow-making is an age-old tradition that is still continued to this day. It begins in the dense bamboo forests where the culms are carefully selected and cut.

Straight specimens with thick walls are preferred. Also important is the distance between the nodes as this affects the harmonics and thus the smoothness of the limb return. When harvesting, the node spacing is measured against a benchmark strip. Cut bamboo poles are taken away and stored vertically to dry. After a year the culms are split to create strips. These strips are laid horizontally on racks to season under the sun for another year. Then, in the third year of seasoning, the strips are placed in a heat chamber. This brings the wax to the surface for a lustrous shine, which is aesthetically desirable for a bow with a plain bamboo finish. Although bows for war were protected by lacquer

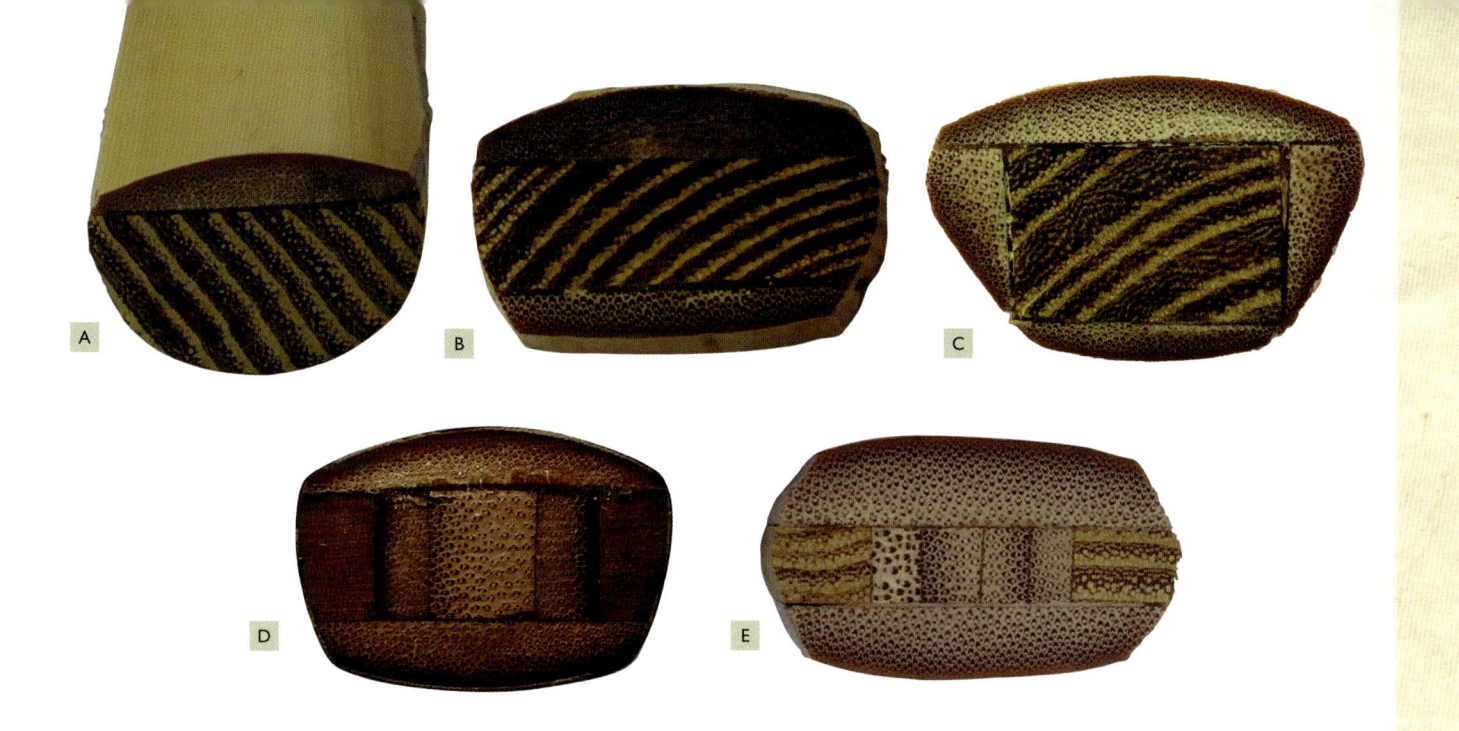

Cross-sections of different construction styles. Note the honeycomb cellular structure of bamboo. Where bamboo acts as a core material, it is first tempered by heating. The wooden strips are *haze* (wax-wood). The black lines between the laminations are glue. (**A**) *Fusetake* (9th–10th century) Two-piece: wood on belly / bamboo on back. Note that at this period the *yumi* retained the rounded, oval cross-section of the original wooden bow. (**B**) *Sanmaeuchi* (12th–13th century) Three-piece: wooden core with bamboo on back and belly. Here we see the transition into a more rectangular cross-section. (**C**) *Shihodake* (14th–15th century) Box construction: single strip wooden core encased by bamboo on all four sides. This was a major change in construction, moving from simple linear laminations to one with cross-lamination. (**D**) *Sanbonhigo* (mid-16th century). A three-piece core of bamboo strips with wood strips at the sides and bamboo facings on the back and the belly. (**E**) *Yohonhigo* (early 17th century). A four-piece bamboo core, with bamboo on back and belly and haze wood on the side. By this period the *yumi* was already transforming from a primary weapon of war to an instrument of ritualized spiritual practice. In a subsequent form, *gohonhigo*, the core laminations were increased to five. (Cross-sections made by and photographs courtesy of Jaap Koppedrayer)

and bindings, which covered the surface, they still benefited from the heat chamber treatment. It gave a clean, even surface with no bumps that was ideal for the application of smooth layers of lacquer.

When fully seasoned, the strips are fashioned so that the inside face is made flat, suitable for lamination. It is shaved with a drawknife and then smoothed with a plane. Making it perfectly flat and even was and remains an art. Each strip is also tapered towards the tips. Gauging the correct and even taper for multiple strips that would eventually work in conjunction requires an expert eye. Next, the inside face of each strip is grooved to hold the all-important glue.

In the final stage of preparation, the strips are laid horizontally in the rafters of a smokehouse. Originally this was done in the roofs of kitchens. The smoke treatment gives a distinctive colour to the bamboo but, more importantly, it dries it out, making it much lighter. Lighter limbs ensure a faster limb return, which makes the bow more efficient. The smoking achieves this whilst at the same time making the strips more resilient and durable. Smoked bamboo is an altogether tougher material.

PREPARING THE WOOD

Of equal importance to the bamboo is the wood used for the core. The timber of choice was *haze*, known in the west as wax-wood. It has both resilience and spring. There has been a popular misconception that mulberry wood was used, but the esteemed maker of Japanese bows in the US, Jaap Koppedrayer, considers it unsuitable and believes the

OPPOSITE A *maruki-yumi* made from catalpa wood. This example has been designated an 'important cultural property', just one grade down from being a 'national treasure'. It is from the Nara period and has been dated to the 8th century AD. Its length is 6 feet and it is clearly asymmetrical. There are also hints, softened with time, of the reflex and deflex curves that characterize later, laminated *yumi*. This fine specimen attests that the traditional form of the *yumi* was fully established by this early date. (Image courtesy of Tokyo National Museum)

ABOVE A stand of *madake* bamboo with workers taking a break during the bamboo harvest. *Madake* is the premium species of bamboo for bow-making as it has characteristically thick walls. Culms are at the optimum size for wall thickness at 3 to 4 years old. Weaker, thin-walled *henon* bamboo can be used for very light, recreational bows today, but for a military bow of any power, only *madake* was used. Harvesting is in December, when the sap is down. This means fewer damaging insects and shorter drying time. (Photograph courtesy of Tony McNicol Photography)

ABOVE CENTRE Using bamboo with the appropriate node spacing is very important. Here a benchmark strip is being used to gauge the selection of a specimen. (Photograph courtesy of Tony McNicol)

ABOVE RIGHT Here the *yumi*-maker is using a plane to fashion a strip of bamboo. Drawknives, planes and scrapers were employed in this delicate stage, where each strip was shaved to ensure that the thickness was even, so that the strip bent consistently throughout its length. It required immense judgement from the *yumi*-maker, who gauged the thickness according to how strong he wished to make the bow. He also had to balance the taper towards the tips. (Photograph courtesy of Tony McNicol Photography)

confusion arose because the colour of *haze* and mulberry wood is very similar. *Haze* continues to be the preferred timber for traditional bowyers in Japan today. It is also used in the manufacture of martial arts weapons such as the *bō* staff and it is the traditional material for spear shafts. Similar properties of consistency are required for a 6-foot fighting staff as they are for a 6-foot or 7-foot lamination strip for a bow. The grain is reliably straight and long, making it difficult to splinter. *Haze* is also extremely flexible, tough and durable, with a natural springiness that is an obvious quality for a bow. It is also lighter in weight than other woods with similar characteristics and so is a good choice for minimal mass in the limbs. Strips of *haze* are planed flat and tapered towards the tips to match the taper on the companion bamboo strips. As with the bamboo, the surface is incised with shallow channels in order to better receive the glue.

ASSEMBLY

The first phase of assembling the *yumi* was to lay the strips together in whichever configuration was the style of the period (see cross-sections on previous page). Shaping the distinctive curves came later. Full-length strips were used for the core and the back of the bow, but the bamboo strip for the belly was cut shorter. Adjacent to the tips, about 6 inches from the top and about 4½ inches from the bottom, the bamboo was substituted with stiffer pieces of haze wood. Simply butted against the main belly strip of bamboo, these wooden reinforcements had the effect of stiffening the sections by the nocks. They acted in a similar way to static tips on a composite bow, working as levers to bend the bow.

Prior to assembly, the contact faces of all the strips were coated with glue, applied swiftly with the index finger. Most bow-making workshops had their own secrets for small variations to the glue's composition. Rice-glues may have been used in some ateliers but, traditionally and predominantly, Japanese bows were made with deer-hide glue. Unlike the fish-glues used for composite bow-making, deer-hide glues set almost instantaneously, at least within a few minutes. This clearly posed a problem when trying to assemble complex laminations. The answer was to apply the glue to each strip of both bamboo and haze wood and to allow it dry fully. The matrix of dry strips was then assembled and held in place by wrapping a manila cord tightly around the bundle in a criss-cross fashion.

Japanese *haze* (wax-wood) logs stacked for seasoning. Keitarō Yokoyama, a highly-regarded *yumi*-maker in Japan, who adheres to traditional practices, seasons his *haze* for a minimum of 20 years and for his best bows is still using stocks put aside by his grandfather. In turn he is beginning to season *haze* logs for his grandson. After seasoning, the logs are sawn into planks and then strips of the heartwood, which is better at storing energy in compression, are prepared for the core. One of the properties that makes wax-wood so suitable for bow-making is that it has a consistently long and straight grain. Therefore, a strip as long as a bow can be fabricated that has perfectly parallel grain from top to bottom. This makes the limbs less susceptible to twist. (Photograph courtesy of Keitarō Yokoyama)

TEACHING THE CURVES

When the time came to give the bow its shape, it was placed, section by section, in a steam tent to soften the glue. This gave a few valuable minutes to work that segment. It was only after this procedure that the glue was activated and the laminations adhered to each other. Training the limbs to their distinctive curves was a process of spectacular metamorphosis. Bamboo wedges were tapped in between the turns of the cord holding the laminations together. They were inserted on the outside of the required bend. When all were in place, the *yumi* took on the appearance of a bizarre spinal skeleton belonging to some mythical creature. Using his hands and feet, the bowyer pulled the section he was working on into the desired curve and then quickly hammered the wedges in further to lock in the shape, while the glue dried again. It was important to work quickly and it was the bowyer's skill to determine how far each wedge must be tapped and thus the degree of curve it created. When I asked Jaap Koppedrayer, a renowned maker of Japanese bows in the US, how heavy the mallet strike should be, he replied that it must be done 'with authority'!

The bow was left for 2–3 days in order to dry completely before both the wedges and the cord were removed. Using a series of scrapers and planes, the *yumi* was then cleaned and smoothed and shaped. Edges were rounded and the nocks were carved. At this stage it began to look like the finished bow, but the curves, although bending in the right directions, remained relatively shallow. They had to be 'taught' the right degree of bend, and these bends all had to be balanced with one another. To train it to flex correctly, the *yumi* was stretched in a special bow-bench. When repeatedly manipulated in a particular direction, the materials acquired a memory. Once the serpentine of reflex and deflex had been established to the bowyer's satisfaction, he braced the *yumi* with a thick string. It was then left strung for a week to learn the bend. Only after this stage was it shot for the first time.

A normal, thinner string was fitted and there followed an intense period of shooting and adjusting. Limbs were flexed and twisted by hand to tweak the performance, only rarely being returned to the bow-bench for more rigorous encouragement. Special shaping blocks, called *yumigata-kyōseiki*, were sometimes required to refine the torque of the bow when this affected the lie of the string. If not cared for properly, the *yumi* has a tendency to lose its curves. All bows behave slightly

(A) Bamboo is characterized by its nodes – the circumferential swellings seen at intervals along the culm, from which branches and leaves stem. When assembling strips for lamination, laths of bamboo had to be very carefully matched for node placement. Node spacing on the belly (which compresses) and the back (which comes under tension) had to be calculated precisely so that the bend functioned correctly. Variations of where on the bow deflex and reflex occurred also have to be taken into account. (Photograph courtesy of Keitarō Yokoyama)

(B, C) Detail of *yumi* assembly, upper tip. On the belly side of the bow (the side that faces the archer), the upper and lower tips are made stiffer and stronger by making them thicker and by substituting a strip of wood in place of the bamboo strip for the last several inches. The length of this reinforcement is made in proportion to the asymmetry of the bow; thus it is longer at the upper tip. Stiffening the tips encourages them to work as levers to pull the bow into shape. (Photograph courtesy of Jaap Koppedrayer)

(D) Keitarō Yokoyama tapping the wedges in to form the curves. Holding the desired shape, which he judges carefully by eye, in position with his foot and right hand, Yokoyama uses a wooden mallet to tap the wedges home. He works quickly to accomplish the task before the glue sets. (Photograph courtesy of Tony McNicol Photography

(E) Bamboo wedges. These are shaped roughly, with a point at one end and a flat top where the mallet strikes the other. (Photograph courtesy of Jaap Koppedrayer)

(F) A *yumi* under construction. Wedges have been tapped into the cord binding, exerting pressure to coax the bow to bend in five key places. They are located on the outside of the bends. After inserting the wedges a little way, the bowyer uses both hands and feet to pull each curve of the *yumi* into its desired shape. Then he quickly hammers in the wedges so that it will hold that shape while the glue sets firm. (Photograph courtesy of Jaap Koppedrayer)

(G) A detail of the 'princess curve' at the top of the bow. The pressure exerted by the wedges is evident, pulling the laminations into shape from each side. (Photograph courtesy of Jaap Koppedrayer)

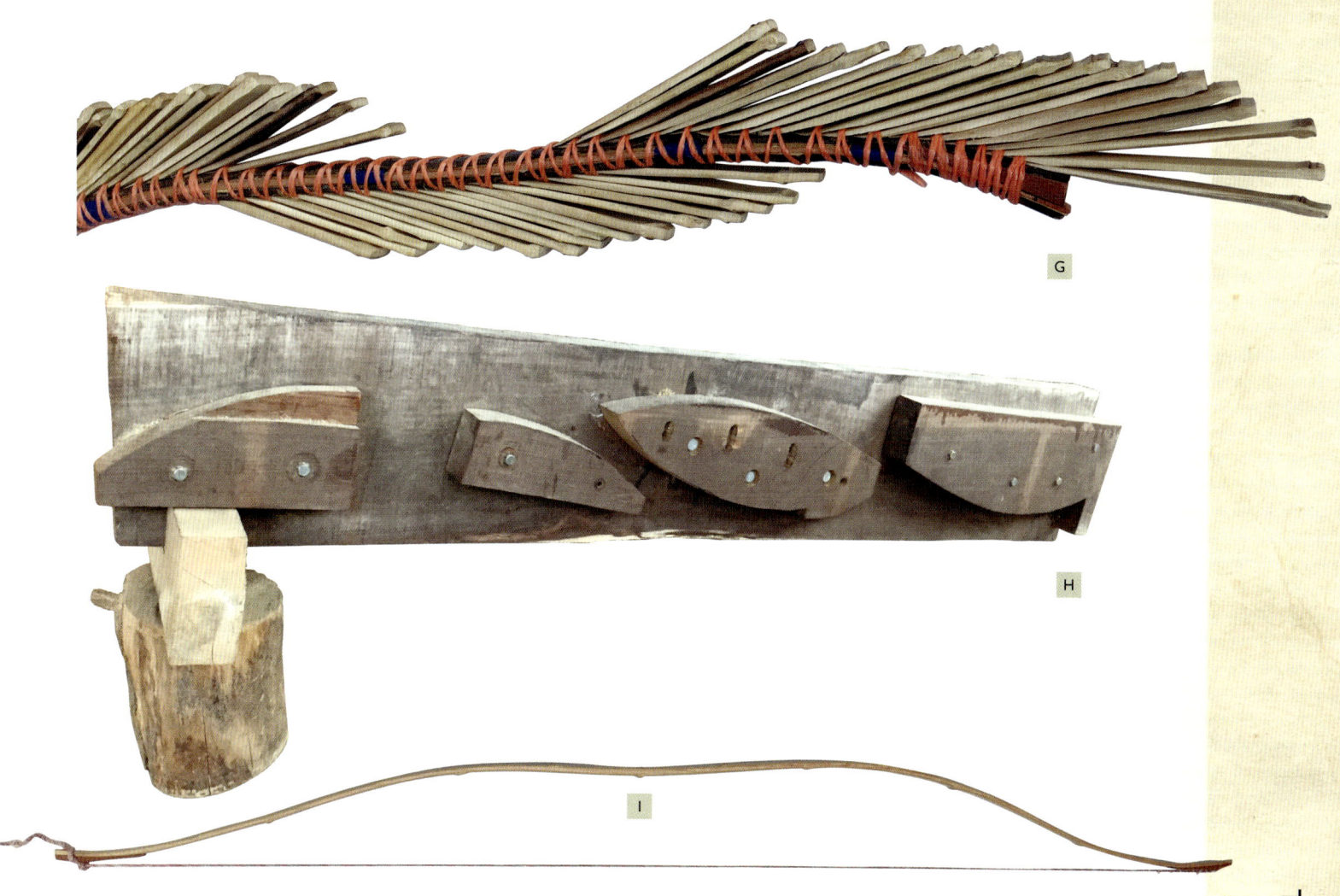

(H) A *haridai* – a bowmaker's shaping bench. A series of wooden formers, attached to the side of the bench, align to create the shape of the *yumi*. Eventually, the entire bow can be set within these blocks. At first, however, different juxtapositions are used as leverage points to persuade the limbs to take the right bends, section by section. The bowyer threads a section between two blocks and flexes it over and over again, warming the fibres of both the wood and bamboo, and teaching it the direction of bend it will finally hold. First he sets the curve that is second from the top, then the second from the bottom. Next he bends the third from the top, followed by the uppermost curve and finally the long curve at the bottom. Every *yumi*-maker has his own signature shape and style and so makes his own *haridai*. No two *haridai* are identical. (Photograph courtesy of Jaap Koppedrayer)

(I) A *yumi* with the string on for the first time. This is the same bow shown in (F) where it was freshly glued and festooned with wedges. An especially thick string is used for the first stringing because there may be additional strains from a bow that is not yet fully tuned. These have the potential to break the string, with deleterious effects on the young bow. It is left strung and untouched for a week. The thick training string, is reusable on other new bows and a finer, faster string will be substituted for the final adjustments. (Photograph courtesy of Jaap Koppedrayer)

differently and the archer had to know his bow. He had to be aware of temperature and humidity; he had to know when to leave it strung and when to unstring it. He had to know when to adjust the string knot to ensure the correct brace height. He had to take great care of his string and he had to be sure to warm the fibres of his bow by repeatedly flexing the limbs before shooting. Mostly the archer was able to correct the bend by applying pressure at a given point, but occasionally he had to resort to heat treatment. A samurai archer not only had to shoot well; he also had to be a bow technician. Like English longbows and like composite bows, the *yumi* of the samurai was a living thing.

(J) A *tsuru*, or shooting string, for a *yumi*, and its string-holder, known as a *tsurumaki*. Strings were constructed with hemp fibres and a pine-resin and cedar-oil mixture called *kusune*. This enabled strong strings to be made relatively thinly, resulting in fast shooting. Obviously the heavier the bow, the thicker the string required, and military bows needed many more fibres than the exceptionally fine strings that span modern lightweight *yumi*s. *Kusune* also provided a protective coating to the string, sealing it from the elements – bowstrings could be damaged equally by spells of very arid weather (common in Japanese winters) as well as by the more familiar wet conditions.

Japanese hemp and resin strings were similar to English longbow strings, which were made from hemp and glue (see pages 44–6). Both had a tendency to kink, which weakened them at that point. To avoid this, spare strings for the *yumi* were wound on a circular *tsurumaki*, made from rattan (the English solution had been to coil their strings beneath their caps). A reinforced nocking area (*nakajigake*), equivalent to the serving on European bows, extended for four or five inches and was created by wrapping a flattened length of hemp, impregnated with *kusune*, around the string. Glue might also be added to keep it in place. It was gauged for a snug fit with the arrow nock and to sit comfortably in a groove on the glove. The *tsurumaki* was suspended from the belt at the left hip. (Kim Hawkins)

(K) A *waraji* and a lump of *kusune*. This small pad, made of hemp or rice straw, was used to either apply fresh *kusune* to the string or just to generate enough friction to melt any *kusune* already on the string and to redistribute it by working it into the fibres. *Kusune* is a mixture of tree resin and cedar oil. A *waraji* was fashioned by the Japanese art of *mizuhiki* (knotwork) in the form of a miniature samurai sandal. The Japanese word for these sandals is 'waraji' and it is because of its resemblance that the little *kusune* pad acquired this nickname. (Kim Hawkins)

(L) *Yumigata-kyōseiki* – shaping blocks. In addition to losing the correct shape of its reflex and deflex curves, the *yumi* could be prone to twist, which these blocks were used to correct. *Yumigata-kyōseiki* were made in different sizes to fit at different points along the length of the bow. The large one is placed opposite the arrow-pass at the widest juncture between bow and string and the smaller ones are located near the tips. (Photograph courtesy of Jaap Koppedrayer)

(M) A bow being adjusted with a *yumigata-kyōseiki*. The twine around the nock is to prevent the string slipping off altogether. The string should lie a little to the right of centre. If it deviated from the proper line, it could be corrected by using these wooden formers to hold bow and string in correct alignment until the limbs adjusted to the new set. Throughout the bow's life there may be a need to use these blocks periodically in order to keep it shooting correctly. (Photograph courtesy of Jaap Koppedrayer)

LACQUERING AND BINDING

Once the bow had been trained and was shooting correctly, it was sealed with multiple coats of tough lacquer. This both strengthened the *yumi* and protected it from Japan's damp climate. Prior to applying the lacquer, the shiny outer skin of the bamboo had to be removed to ensure adhesion. In some instances, for additional durability, the bow was wrapped with fine silk thread before the lacquer was applied. These were soldiers' bows that had to withstand the rigours of the battlefield.

The lacquer, known as *urushi*, was made from the sap of the Japanese sumac tree (*toxicodendron vernicifluum*). Care was required in handling this sap as it contains allergenic compounds that cause severe and painful skin rashes. Traditionally sap was harvested from 10-year-old sumac trees by making a number of horizontal incisions on the trunk. After several stages of pouring it through paper filters, the amber liquid was mixed with a pigment to give it colour. It was then applied to the bow with a brush. A strong lacquer skin required several coats of *urushi*. Each one has to be cured. Hardening was triggered by a chemical reaction, set off by a particular set of temperatures and humidity. After 24 hours in a chamber with 80 per cent humidity and maintained at a steady 75 degrees Fahrenheit, the lacquer polymerised to a tough and hard finish. An *urushi*-covered bow possessed a decorative sheen that was extremely pleasing to the eye, and the many layers of semi-translucent lacquer give an enigmatic sense of depth to the material.

Further protection was given to the bow by rattan bindings. These originated as bindings to hold the laminated strips of bamboo together, especially if a lesser quality glue had been used; they had practical necessity. They also acted as useful buffers against the knocks and scrapes to which a warrior's bow would inevitably be subjected. According to Feliks Hof, the bow most commonly used for war was the *nurigometo no yumi*, which was lacquered black-brown and had rattan wrappings that were lacquered the same (Hof 2002: 31). However, Japanese art tends to show samurai with *yumi*s that have bindings of contrasting colours. For decorative variation the rattan was sometimes left a natural wheat colour and at other times lacquered red or blue.

Following the codification and systemization of Japanese archery practices that began in the early Edo period (1603–1868), status was ascribed to the number of bindings. Further nuances of rank could be interpreted from the patterns made possible by different arrangements of broad and narrow sections of binding. Yet more designations could be inferred from the colour of the lacquer. *Shigeto-yumi* is the generic name for any lacquered bow with rattan bindings, and the present-day practitioner of *kyūdō* would be deemed presumptuous to shoot with such bow. A *shigeto-yumi* is reserved for archers of high status within the schools. However, at the time when the *yumi* was a principal weapon of war, such niceties didn't apply. Images of samurai in art show them all with colourful and heavily bound bows. It is probable that there was a livery system with certain colours and patterns designating clans and/or individual squadrons. Whether or not this was the case, the practical benefits of both lacquer and binding were adopted universally.

SUPERSTITION AND CUSTOM

After lacquering, an invocation to a deity, inscribed on fine paper, was usually placed beneath the handgrip. This was covered with silk, which in turn was wrapped with a spirally wound strip of leather to create the handgrip (*nigiri*). For most high-status samurai the *nigiri* was black, violet being the exclusive preserve of the shōgun.

WAR BOWS

THE JAPANESE YUMI

BATTLE OF MIZUSHIMA, 17 NOVEMBER 1183 (PREVIOUS PAGES)

Mizushima was a naval encounter during the Gempei War. Minamoto no Yoshinaka had sent an expeditionary force by sea to take the strategically important stronghold of Yashima on nearby Shikoku island. The Minamoto fleet sailed through the narrow straits between Shikoku and the tiny island of Mizushima; it was here that the ships of the Taira confronted them.

In this scene, the Taira ships in the background have been lashed together to form a boom, blocking the Minamoto fleet from reaching Yashima. Additional fighting platforms have been created by connecting the ships with planks, and archers stationed here unleash an unrelenting deluge of arrows onto the Minamoto ships.

Some of the Minamoto troops have made it to the shore, but are pursued by Taira samurai who have plunged their horses fully equipped into the foaming sea and ride up the beach shooting. According to the *Heike Monogatari*:

> the Heike [Taira] had brought their horses with them in the ships, and as they approached the shore they pushed them off into the water to swim to the beach. Since they were ready accoutred, as soon as they found a foothold the riders clambered into their saddles and rode them with a mighty splashing through the shallows to the shore, and 500 horsemen, led by Noto no kami Noritsune, precipitated themselves on the Genji [Minamoto], who ... fled headlong in confused panic. (Quoted in Turnbull 1998: 203)

In order to keep the bow-hand dry the archer used a powder (*fudeko*) made from fine wood-ash, although such a refinement was probably eschewed on the battlefield.

To this day it is considered bad luck to lean a *yumi* against a tree because it is thought the tree will drain its energy. Moreover, when propped at rest anywhere it is considered disrespectful to stand the *yumi* upside down. It displays an equal lack of respect to step over a *yumi*. Touching another person's *yumi* without their permission remains a serious breach of etiquette, and even when permission has been granted, it is bad form to touch the grip. To what extent these protocols evolved after 1600 and to what extent they were observed during the height of the *yumi*'s military career is difficult to discern.

It was a widespread belief that the sound emitted from a plucked bowstring had magical powers, capable of summoning good spirits or driving away evil ones. During the Heian period (794–1185) official 'bow-twangers' performed at royal births, at exorcisms and when the emperor entered the bath! In addition to its power in the spirit world, the note from a bowstring had the ability to cure disease. When the emperor Horikawa (r. 1087–1107) fell ill, Minamoto Yoshiie cured him with 'three demon-killing twangs of his bow' (Hurst 1998: 108). Up to the present day, miniature bows (*hamayumi*) and miniature arrows (*hamaya*) are sold at shrines as good-luck charms.

TYPES OF JAPANESE BOW

Present-day *yumi*s are classified by name according to different bow lengths. They range from 'short' bows (*tsumari*) that are 7 feet through regular bows (*namisun*) at around 7 feet 3 inches to long bows (*nobi*) ranging from 7 feet 5 inches to 8 feet. The requirement for greater length relates to both the archer's height and the length of his/her draw (*yazuka*). A demand for exceptionally long *yumi*s has been a consequence of the spread in popularity of *kyūdō* to longer-limbed populations in the West during the past several decades. It may also be attributed to a probable increase in the height of present-day Japanese compared to their ancestors in the 13th century. Another factor that may have contributed to the emergence of especially long *yumi*s is a cultural emphasis on exaggerating the *yumi*'s most distinguishing characteristic, which is its length. By the scale represented in art, however, it seems unlikely that fighting *yumi*s reached quite this stature. The term *daikyū* applied to bows at the longer end of the spectrum, but at precisely what length a *yumi* became a *daikyū* is difficult to ascertain. Within limited parameters, samurai archers used a range of bow lengths, according to their own physical stature and depending on the circumstances for their use. During the *yumi*'s supremacy on the battlefield, it seems reasonable to assume that the overall length was seldom more than between 6 feet and 6 feet 8 inches. A *daikyū* may have been a few inches more than that.

Although to the untutored eye most *yumi*s look the same, there can be subtle differences in the amount of curve given to each section. All *yumi*s have the same four principal curves: 'the princess curve' (*himezori*) at the top, 'the bird-striker' (*toriuchi*) below that, 'the hip curve' (*koshinari*) immediately below the grip and 'the small curve' (*konari*) towards the base. Giving a different degree of bend or length to different curves affected how the bow shot and behaved. Different schools of shooting favoured different styles of bow. Some claimed that one form delivered a more natural *yugaeri* – a rotation of the bow upon release (see page 260) – whilst others preferred a certain type for shooting at distance (*enteki*). A type known as the *satsumanari* was considered best for penetrating shots (Hoff 2002: 33). One is tempted to think this would be the bow most suited to battle. However, as with so much else concerning Japanese archery, these classifications are not recorded until the 17th century. They are likely to have some ancestry and it is probable that different schools of thought prevailed favouring different forms of bow, but we must be careful not to ascribe too much meaning from the evolved systems of *kyūdō* to the war bows of the samurai.

HANKYŪ

A variation on the standard *yumi* was a shorter bow known either as the *hankyū* (half-bow) or the *tankyū* (short bow). When encountered prior to the Edo period, *hankyū* and *tankyū* are alternative terms for foreign bows – that is, the shorter composite bows from China, Korea and Mongolia. Subsequently, during the long span of the Edo period, in addition to more formalized practices, a variety of archery amusements developed. These 'games' required shorter bows, especially for indoor shooting. Such bows were made on the model of the *yumi*, and the old term *hankyū* was redefined to apply to these recreational bows. Shortening the length of a *yumi* to as much as half reduced the maximum draw considerably – very different from the long draw of the *yumi*, which is pulled back to the outside of the right shoulder. Although it is possible for a short bow to be a functioning bow whilst maintaining the distinctive *yumi* shape, such bows could only be produced at relatively light draw-weights, ideal for the shooting salon. They were made from laminations of bamboo only, without a wooden core, and it is very doubtful whether such bows were ever 'war bows'.

There is a popular misconception that the samurai used such bows to arm the peasants, arming them to recruit them in their armies whilst limiting their power in the event that they should rebel. Apart from the nonsensical logic of this theory, there is no evidence for it. Another thought is that the more compact *hankyū* was of use when fighting on foot in hill country or in dense woodland, or when overrunning a fortress in a siege or in taking a city and fighting in the streets. In certain situations, there may have been a requirement to favour slightly shorter bows. However, a shorter *yumi* is not necessarily a *hankyū*; it is just a shorter *yumi*. Many examples of recreational *hankyū*s have survived and may be found quite often in auction houses and antique emporia. Mostly they are from the 18th and 19th centuries. They are genuine specimens, but they are not examples of a type known during the age of the fighting samurai.

KAGO-HANKYŪ – THE PALANQUIN BOW

The *kago-hankyū* was an especially short bow, spanning no more than two feet when strung and having recurved limbs made from tough, springy baleen. Known also as the *rimankyū*, it was supposedly invented by Hayashi Riman of Kii province, a *daimyō* who lived at some point during the early Edo period. The primary purpose of the *kago-hankyū* was as a self-defence weapon for persons travelling by palanquin. A palanquin was a high-status conveyance consisting of a small, enclosed box, suspended from a pole, which was carried by a number of bearers. The acutely confined quarters in which the single occupant knelt restricted the size of bow that could be managed. Long, processional journeys by palanquin were a common occurrence during the Edo period for both nobles (*daimyō*s) and their senior officials. Ponderous pedestrian progress made them an easy target for either brigands or rebels and such a cramped situation made it essential to have a short bow, with an equally short draw. Despite its small size, the *kago-hankyū* was adequately powerful at close range and, should an assailant break open the cabin of a palanquin, close range was the only option. It was an effective defence against being hauled out, robbed, killed or subjected to ignominy.

Ammunition and accoutrements

YA

As with everything else associated with a Japanese warrior's kit, the arrow (*ya*) may be an object of beauty as well as of practical worth. Bamboo was the universal material for arrow-shafts. In abundant supply and requiring relatively little preparation, it was perfect for the job. Nodes had to be smoothed and quality shafts could be given some taper, but the basic shaft was simply grown – already in the shape of an arrow! Carved wooden nocks had to be inserted and, of course, fletchings added. Eagles' wing feathers were the best and the most prestigious, but other feathers were in common use. These included, in descending order of importance, copper pheasant, crane, hawk and snipe feathers.

One of the beneficial characteristics of bamboo arrows is that 'spine' is not as critical as it is for wooden shafts. 'Spine' describes the whippiness or flexibility of an arrow-shaft and it is generally important to match this to the bow. The heavier the bow, the stiffer the spine required. A good fletcher is able to match spine simply by the feel of flexing shafts in his hands, and although there was a great deal of tolerance when it came to selecting bamboo shafts for a certain bow, all archers would want to have any particular set of arrows as closely matched as possible.

Many surviving examples of samurai arrows have lacquered shafts and it is probable that this was a universal practice for war arrows. Lacquering, albeit time-consuming and expensive, offered several important benefits. Despite the innate strength of bamboo, lacquering made it stronger. Most importantly it sealed the shaft from the damaging effects of Japan's wet climate, particularly over the nodes, which were porous. Lacquer also made the shaft heavier. The business of battlefield archery is

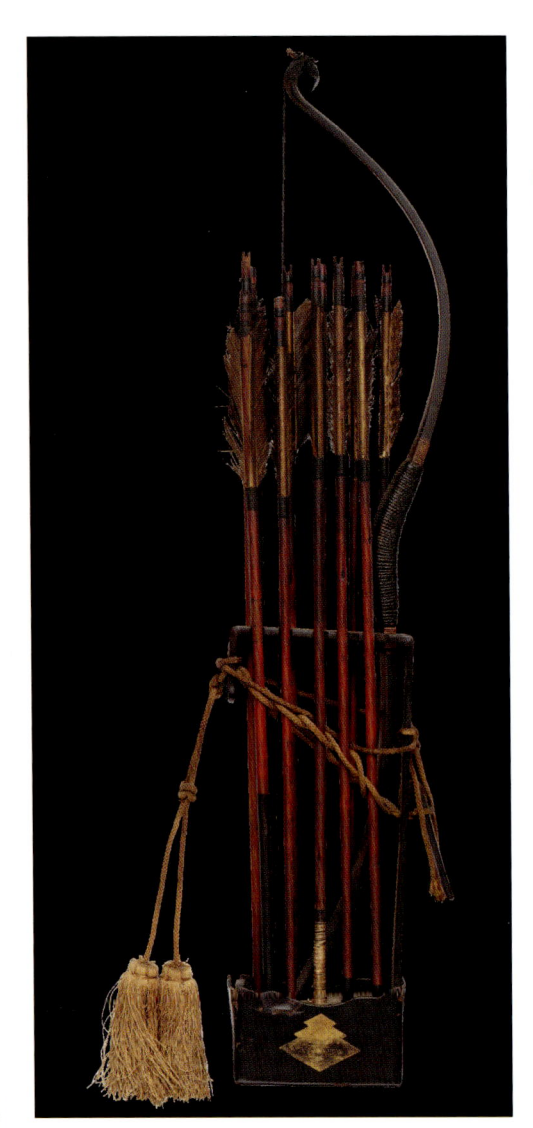

Palanquin bow, 18th century. The bow, made from baleen, fits into a lacquered carrying frame, and 11 arrows are slotted in alongside it. The arrows are constructed from dark red bamboo, and most of them have gilding between the fletchings. Six of them retain their small armour-piercing heads, whilst another has a small broadhead pierced with a heart shape. The base of the case is decorated with a triple overlapping diamond *mon* (family crest) in gold. (© Royal Armouries)

about delivering force to the target. The energy of that force is a combination of both the speed of the arrow and its weight. A heavier arrow had military advantage, though it required a bow of military draw-weight to send it thudding home.

YANONE

Although arrowheads (*yanone*) appear in dozens of different individual forms, they fall into two main categories – 'functional arrowheads', intended for war or hunting, and 'ornamental arrowheads', created for ritual offerings, decoration and ceremony. Many of the ornamental types were exquisite works of art, prized and collected in their own day as much as they are now.

Broadheads, called *yanagi-ha* (willow leaf), were favoured for this work because they provided a large 'canvas' on which to incise various 'lace-like' patterns. Although highly decorative, these leaf-shaped heads were equally functional for either battle or hunting and a samurai would carry a single decorated *yanagi-ha* in his quiver as his symbolic 'last arrow'. The best examples were made from *tamahagane*, that is, the highest-quality Japanese steel, also used for swordmaking. Like a sword-blade, these premium arrowheads featured a *hamon*. This is a distinct band of harder steel, able to be made sharper, which appears adjacent to the edge. It was valued not only for its utility but also for its decorative beauty. Different hardnesses of steel, having different microstructures, appear as contrasting patterns. *Hamon*s could be straight (*suguha*) or created in a variety of undulating patterns (*midare*), each with a specific name. Today swordsmiths create the *hamon* by painting layers of clay onto the blade at the tempering stage before heating and quenching it. By retarding the cooling rate where the clay is thicker, the metal remains softer. In this way the arrowhead is given a tough, resilient core that will not shatter on impact but is armed with razor-sharp edges of harder steel. There was an older method to the clay process, which is not fully understood; however, the result was the same, as it produced arrowheads with a *hamon*.

Arrowheads of artistic merit were signed by the maker, and arrowsmiths were often as celebrated as swordsmiths. In fact, it was not unusual for swordsmiths to also make arrowheads. One of the most famous arrowsmiths was Umetada Myōju (1558–1632). He also made *tsuba*s (the discs that act as guards on Japanese swords). Both mediums lent themselves to incorporating intricate cut-out features. Pierced, open-work patterns were created using punches, fine-toothed saws and small files. Popular themes included *sakura* (cherry blossom) and *inome* (boar's eye) as well as the representation of family crests (*mon*). More rarely, the cut-out might incorporate either a human or animal figure or a landscape scene. When this was the case, the work could be chiselled and chased with remarkable detail and great artistry. The finest examples were sometimes inlaid and embellished with accents of gold. Unlike the surgically effective *yanagi-ha* leaf-shaped blades, some other ornamental arrowheads were curiously shaped, defying their supposed purpose as weapons to either cut or puncture. There were arrowheads in the shape of stars and some that resembled the *jumonji-yari*, a type of Japanese spear with three blades. These could have no other use than for ceremony and symbolism.

Battlefield arrowheads, like their western counterparts, could be classified simply as either pointed, bodkin-style, heads (*togari-ya*) or broadheads (*yanagi-ha*). A particular sub-type of *yanagi-ha* was called the *watakushi*, the 'flesh-tearer'. It had long barbs, sweeping down close to the blade, similar to a European swallowtail head.

(A) Arrowhead with plum-blossom piercing, 19th century. This broadhead style was principally used for hunting, though it could also be of service on the battlefield. This example has been incised with decoration. Elaborately fashioned heads were used principally for ceremony, but wealthy samurai might also have hunting and war-heads pierced in this manner. (© Royal Armouries)

(B) Exquisite example of a ceremonial broadhead. This arrowhead is dated 1645 and signed by Umetada Motoshige (died 1675), a member of the Umetada school of swordsmiths, *tsuba* makers and iron chisellers. Large arrowheads, pierced and elaborately chiselled with landscapes, birds, flowers, dragons and Buddhist divinities were created to be admired for the beauty of their metalwork and design. The head measures 4½ inches long and 2¼ inches at its widest. (Metropolitan Museum of Art, www.metmuseum.org.uk)

(C) *Karimata*. This forked style of arrowhead was very common and was used both for hunting, sport and war. It appeared in many different sizes. (© Royal Armouries)

(D) A range of different *togari-ya* (pointed arrows). Those with the more bodkin-shaped heads were also known as *yoroi-doshi* (armour-piercing) arrows. These are the type most used on the battlefield (Image courtesy of Hermann Historica GmbH, Munich)

(E) Two examples of *togari-ya*. Like all Japanese arrows, these have a tang that fits into the bamboo shaft, rather than the socket of most European arrows. Note the actual head is closely similar to many medieval European bodkins in terms of size, cross-section and elongated form. (© Royal Armouries)

(F) OPPOSITE An example of a war arrow (*sōya* or *shuraya*) from the late 17th century. Note that the shaft has been selected for its taper and is stouter, heavier and stronger at the front end. To prevent the shaft from splitting where it receives the tanged arrowhead, it has been reinforced with silk binding and then sealed with black *urushi* lacquer. War arrows were characteristically 'shadow painted' with bands of black lacquer over the nodes, as is the case here. Applying the lacquer by brush and with the subtle feathered-edge look was extremely time-consuming. This lacquering had the practical value of preventing moisture from penetrating. It also gave the shafts a most menacing, warlike appearance. (Photograph courtesy of Jaap Koppedrayer)

With regard to the ornateness of even everyday versions, the following observation was made at a meeting of The Japan Society in 1904. When an enquirer challenged the utility of so much intricate work, the chairman responded:

> You have probably overlooked the intensely artistic nature of the Japanese; he would think of the artistic satisfaction of the person being hit by the arrow, which would be a consolation in his last moments. (Quoted in an article by W. F. Patterson, *JSAA* Vol. 14 1971:19)

What is certainly true is that the status of one's assassin did matter greatly and that arrows with finely wrought arrowheads were signifiers of high status.

EBIRAS
Ebira is the Japanese word for quiver. There are two principal types – open quivers and closed quivers. The simplest was the *yadzutsu-ebira,* a type of closed quiver. It was a tube, a cylindrical arrow-case used for target arrows. Usually around 3½ inches in diameter, it was the means by which arrows were transported to the shooting ground, and remains in use for that purpose to this day. High status versions often comprised a bamboo tube smoothed, lacquered and decorated with gold or silver foil and topped off with a laquerwork cap. *Yadzutsu-ebira* could be very elegant indeed.

In essence the *yadzutsu* was a single length of bamboo with the internal diaphragms hollowed out and was thus, in this simple form, an inexpensive and secure way to store military supplies. We might imagine them during the medieval period, carrying stocks of arrows that were fletched but not yet fitted with their points; tanged arrowheads could easily be inserted after archers had received their shafts. Bamboo tubes were ideal for stacking both in storehouses and on carts.

A far more elaborate style of closed quiver was the *utsubo-ebira*, with its characteristic elongated hourglass shape. *Utsubo*s could be fashioned as exquisite works of art. Superior *utsubo*s were made by applying lacquer to a papier-mâché base and ornamenting with gilt. Others were made with rattan and these too could be pleasingly decorative.

Utsubo-style quivers are considered to be principally for arrow carriage between destinations. However, they might be worn and used as functional quivers. They could either be worn at the side with the aperture for arrow retrieval uppermost, or they could be strapped across the back with the opening facing downwards. Although they do not offer the quick draw of a *kari-ebira* (see page 255), drawing downwards from the *utsubo* would have been quick enough in most hunting situations. Moreover, it was important for the hunter to keep his arrows dry, as well as to guard them against entanglement in rough country. Whilst surviving images in art tend to show hunters in open country with the *kari-ebira*, the evident practical advantages of the *utsubo* design are difficult to ignore. *Utsubo*s also look very similar to the closed quivers of China and other composite bow cultures, which further suggests they were a practical shooting quiver for the mounted man, not just for the transportation of recreational or ceremonial shafts.

Of the open quiver types, the *shiko-ebira* had a limited capacity and was used mostly for either ceremonial or recreational shooting, though it might also have been of service to the hunter. However, it was the *kari-ebira* that was the war-quiver of the samurai, par excellence. This had considerable capacity and it facilitated the fastest draw, whether for horse-archers or for those shooting on foot. Japanese arrows were longer than those of other nations and in a fight they were too slow to withdraw from a deep quiver such as the *utsubo*. For battlefield archery, especially for horse-archery,

(A) A 19th-century *utsubo-ebira*. The elaborate shape has been constructed with wood and papier-mâché. It has been sealed with multiple layers of black lacquer and decorated with two red lacquer bands and a red lacquer *mon*. It has been lacquered with gold on the inside. A gilded leather pouch, attached to the inside of the lid, carries a spare bowstring. At the base of the *utsubo* is an eyeleted hole, which allows for drainage in the event that wet arrows needed to be carried. Within are eight war-arrows fitted with willow-leaf heads. (© Royal Armouries)

(B) An 18th-century *utsubo-ebira*. The top portion consists of a wood and papier-mâché frame decorated with red lacquer and emblazoned with two gilt *mon*. The frame on the lower portion has been covered with boar-skin, suggesting perhaps that this *utsubo* was intended to carry hunting arrows. Apart from its bragging splendour, announcing the wearer's status at a hunt gathering, an *utsubo* like this was immensely practical for keeping arrows dry. It also protected them from getting snagged, broken or damaged when hunting or travelling in woodland areas. (Museum of Anthropology, University of Missouri)

(C) An 18th-century *shiko-ebira*, a variety of open quiver distinguished by its small size. At the base of an upright wooden strut is a shallow leather box in which the arrowheads rested. Affixed to the top of the strut is a transverse bracket, which seats the shafts of ten arrows, five on each side. These are secured by a cord. Arrows are drawn by lifting the arrowhead from the box and then pulling the shaft down through the cord. Integral to the wooden back support was a slot that permitted the quiver to be hooked onto a belt. The arrows have been fletched with eagle feathers and have been fitted with blunt heads for shooting at knock-down targets in the shooting house. (© Royal Armouries) arrows had to be taken from the quiver at lightning speed. Like all thumb-release archers, the Japanese located their arrow on the right-hand side of the bow. Sitting just behind the right hip, the *kari-ebira* was extremely ergonomic to use. The archer grasped the arrow near its head and, first lifting it out of the box, pulled it down and forward, delivering the arrow to its position on the bow in a fluid sweep of the arm.

A *kari-ebira* consisted of a short wooden or iron box, subdivided with thin wooden panels in horizontal rows – similar to a letter rack. Soft material within these compartments held arrows in place securely. Some *kari-ebira*s were able to hold as many as two dozen arrows. An arched frame, of either bamboo or iron, was attached to the back of the box, its thin, lightweight structure braced by a lattice of cords. In order to prevent the arrows, top-heavy in the extremely short quiver, from toppling over, a retaining-cord was tied to the back-frame and looped just below the fletchings. It was an easy matter to pull a shaft down through this. In order to hold arrows more securely when travelling, the retaining-cord could be tightened.

YUGAKE

Like the composite bow, the Japanese bow was shot by means of a thumb draw. However, instead of a thumb-ring, the samurai used a special shooting glove called a *yugake*, made from deerskin. Sometimes a sliver of either wood or horn was stitched into the thumb as a reinforcement. Unlike shooting with a thumb-ring, the thumb was not hooked around the string but rather only slightly crooked. A secure hold on the string was achieved by a slight counter-clockwise rotation of the forearm. With the ultra-lightweight bows used in *kyūdō* today, there is no need to even slightly bend the thumb – it is held straight. Present-day *kyūdōka* use a special rosin, called *giriko*, which helps to prevent the string from slipping. This is carried in a small horn powder-flask attached to the *tsurumaki*. However, the patient procedures of the *kyūdōjō* are unlikely to have found favour in the haste of the battlefield and it is implausible that a straight thumb could hold a bow of 100lb draw-weight or more. A cotton under-glove (*shitagake*) was worn to protect the deerskin, which would otherwise become stiff and spoiled with sweat. The *yugake* was a prized personal possession and, if properly cared for, could last for generations. It was common for a *yugake* to be handed down from father to son.

Various types of *yugake* evolved after the 15th century, having extra-stiff thumbs that assisted in holding a longer, more mindful, draw for shooting at static targets. A *yugake* with significantly more padding overall was developed as a response to the physical challenges of sustained shooting at the Sanjūsangendō temple competiton in Kyoto (see page 282) and it is this style that has influenced the thick gloves used today. However, these heavy padded gloves with bulbous thumbs would not have suited a samurai in battle. He required a far more flexible glove so that he could not only shoot his bow but also transfer to a secure grip on his sword, should the need arise, at a moment's notice. He wore a glove of the same lightweight deerskin on his bridle hand.

ARM GUARDS

An arm-guard, known as a *tomo*, existed during the Heian period (794–1185). It was made from either deer-hide or sometimes bear-hide. The *tomo* seems to have gone out of use by the beginning of the Kamakura period (1185) (Newman 2016: 313, note 6). The notion, often cited, that it acted in a similar way to an English 'bracer', to protect against the string striking the arm, doesn't seem plausible, despite the fact that there are poetic references to the sound of the string against the *tomo*. Using the thumb-draw with the *yumi* means placing the arrow on the right-hand side of the bow. Provided that

A 19th-century *kari-ebira*, the style of quiver used by samurai warriors in battle. The main body has been constructed with sheet iron that has been lacquered black. On the inside it has been furnished with a letter-rack arrangement of thin, flexible leaves of wood. These hold the arrowheads securely. Rattan-covered iron wire forms the back and side supports, which have been braced with a green silk cord. Textured black leather, gilded at the edges and for the *mon*, covers the box. On the base of the cover is a hole for water drainage surrounded by an ornate eyelet. (© Royal Armouries)

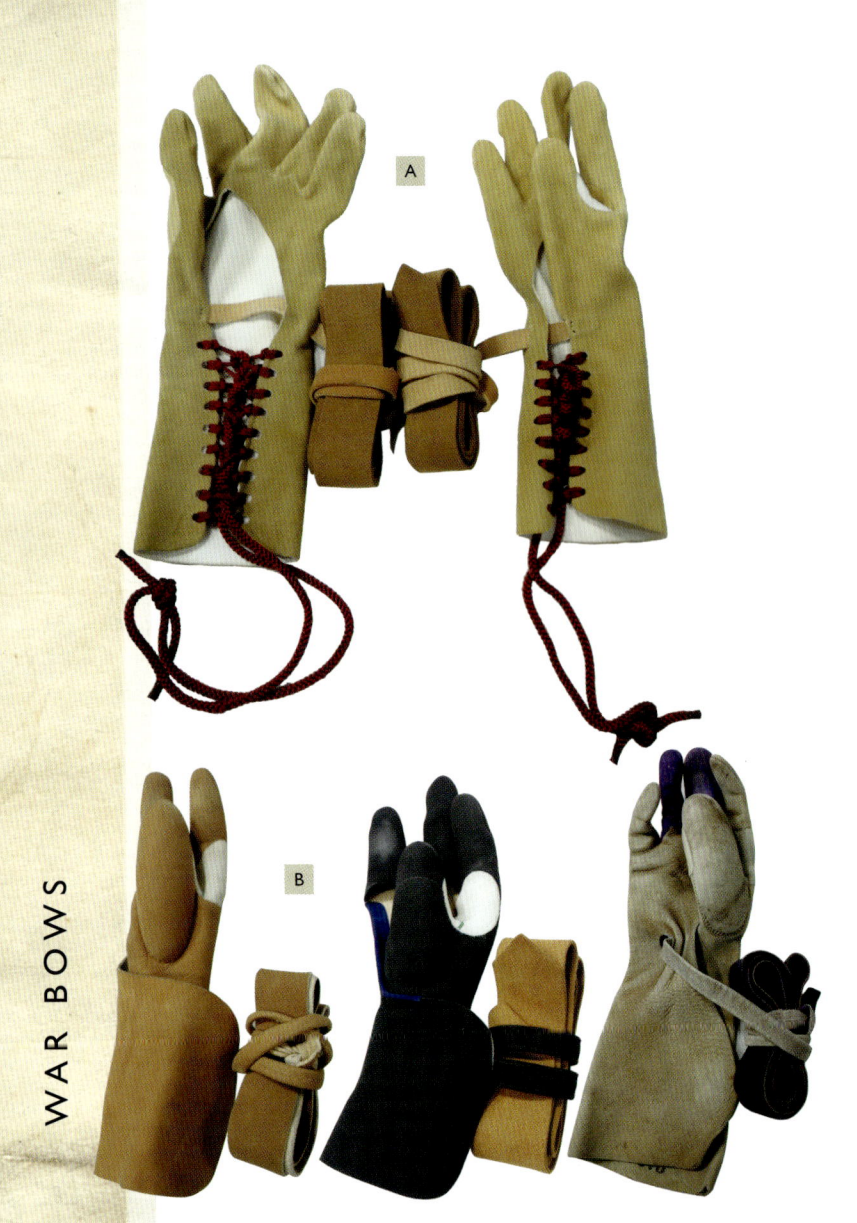

(**A**) A pair of gloves, *kishagake*, used for *yabusame*. These represent the type of gloves worn by a samurai in battle. Made from soft deerskin, they are light and flexible. The right-hand shooting glove has a slight reinforcement to the thumb but still remains very pliable. Unlike present-day, bulkier versions of the *yugake*, a thinner glove allowed the warrior to use his sword or other weapons, when the situation demanded. Moreover, in the heat of battle an archer would need to shoot rapidly, requiring nimble dexterity for speed nocking. A samurai had no need of the enhanced support offered by the more substantial forms of the *yugake* used today for *kyūdō*. His was a different task. (Image courtesy of Ogasawara-ryū)

(**B**) Different forms of the *yugake* used in *kyūdō*. From left to right: a *mitsugake*, a *yotsugake* and a *morogake*. All three types are thick, padded and stiff. After the development of these heavier gloves, variations were introduced that covered a reduced number of digits. Irrespective of the number of digits, they all provide support to both the thumb and the wrist, enabling the archer to hold the string at full draw for a sustained period of contemplation. Different *ryū* have their preferences, so that the Ogasawara-ryū will almost exclusively use the *morogake* and Heki-ryū favour the mitsugake. A principal impetus for the development of these thicker shooting gloves, and in particular the *yotsugake*, were the range and endurance shooting contests held at Sanjūsangendō temple (see page 282). (Image courtesy of Ogasawara-ryū)

the bow is held and shot correctly, arm-protection is generally not required when the arrow is shot on the right-hand side of the bow; the angles preclude its usefulness. Most probably, the *tomo*, rather than guarding the inside of the arm, was intended to ensure that the string didn't catch on loose sleeves. *Yabusame* participants, riding in Kamakura-era hunting attire, wear an *igote*, which, having the form of an over-sleeve rather than a traditional bracer, does precisely that.

A panoply of accoutrements used in *yabusame*. Note the saddles (*kura*), which are similar to both Chinese and Mongolian horse-archer saddles, and the stirrups (*abumi*), which are uniquely and distinctively Japanese. The saddle, finished in white hide and with trappings in orange cord, sits on a *mokuba*, a wooden horse for training. The reins, as is usual, are constructed from fabric. Two *yumis*, showing different patterns of rattan binding, are in a stand behind the *mokuba*. In front is a *kari-ebira*, holding the type of *kabura-ya* arrows used for *yabusame*. Behind them, leaning against a stand, is a range of differently sized *hikime* (ceremonial whistling arrows) each designated for particular ceremonies. To the right of the picture is a samurai armour. (Image courtesy of Ogasawara-ryū)

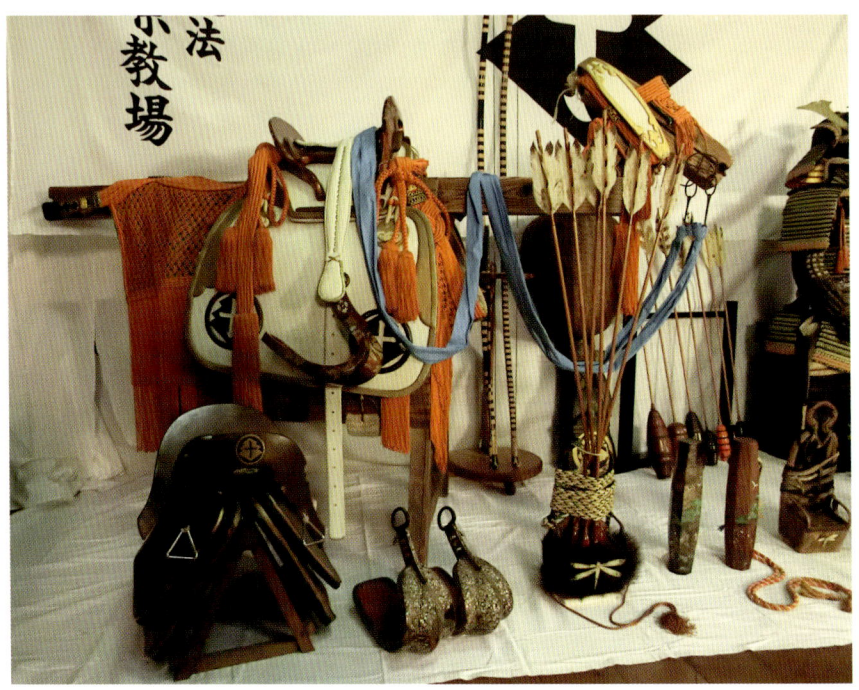

USE: THE WAY OF THE BOW AND THE HORSE

From the earliest times, great store was set in the practice of archery. An entry in the *Nihon Shoki* (Japanese chronicle written in the 8th century) records an Imperial command for the year 68: 'orders were given to the Mayors of the Right and Left Divisions of the capital and to the Governors of the 30 provinces to build places for the practice of archery' (quoted in Aston 2008: 393). Archery requires constant practice and any culture that gives value to military archery will have deep-rooted and codified shooting systems. When archers also form the social and military elite, as was the case with the samurai, then their archery education will be elevated to an art and endowed with mystique. Being able to shoot with good form was seen as a sign of good character and archery was one of the six accomplishments (*rikugei*) expected of a gentleman. This was a concept imported originally from the mainland (China) and one that has resonance also with European ideals of the Renaissance man. The six accomplishments were mathematics, music, calligraphy, etiquette, horsemanship and archery. Note that archery is the only martial skill in this list; there is no mention of swordsmanship. Given its pedigree, it is unsurprising that Japanese archery is so imbued with courtly formality.

Over time, different techniques and practices developed. These were passed down to future generations by the establishment of different *ryūha* – schools. To this day the different *ryūha* command fierce loyalty and carry status according to their history and their connection to ancient power. A *ryū* is more than a 'school' in the sense of disseminating mere physical instruction; it incorporates equally a spiritual path. Rituals of *yumi*-shooting occur in both Shinto and Buddhist ceremonies and many practise *kyūdō* as a means of developing spiritual insight. However, the notion that Japanese archery is a pathway of 'Zen Buddhism', as proposed by the German author Eugene Herrigal (*Zen and the Art of Archery*, 1948) is considered by Japanese practitioners to be very wide of the mark. Japanese archery undoubtedly has a spiritual dimension, but it is first and foremost a practical art, a warrior's art.

Kisha

Japanese archery is divided into two main branches: military archery, known as *busha*, and ceremonial archery, known as *reisha*. These in turn have other sub-classifications, principally foot-archery (*hosha*) and equestrian archery (*kisha*). Being an effective horse-archer was the defining skill of the samurai. His path was *kyūba no michi*, (the way of the bow and the horse). *Kisha* is the collective name for both ceremonial and competitive horse-archery events, which include *yabusame*, *kasagake* and *inuōmono*. It is through the lens of these continuing traditions that we can best glimpse the capabilities of the samurai horse-archer in battle.

Although shooting the bow from a moving horse (*umayumi*) was the characteristic skill of the samurai, horse-archery is referred to in Japan long before the samurai's existence. In the *Nihon Shoki*, there is a tale of the Emperor Yūryaku (r. 456–79) who hatched a treacherous scheme to be rid of Prince Oshiha:

'Along with the Imperial Prince, I wish in the first month of winter, when the sky is cloudy and the cold wind blows keenly, to go for an excursion in the moors, where we may somewhat divert our minds by *running archery*.' The Imperial Prince Ichinobe no Oshiha accordingly followed the hunt. Hereupon the Emperor Ohohatsuse drew his bow and, putting his horse to a gallop, called out falsely, saying, 'There is a wild boar!', and shot the Imperial Prince Ichinobe no Oshiha dead. (quoted in Aston 2008: 336)

Aston's footnote makes it clear that his literal translation 'running archery' refers to the practice of horse-archery. Hunting wild boar with bows from horseback was an aristocratic pursuit at an early date and the emperor's ability to slay his victim by shooting him from his galloping horse is a clear indicator that such skills had their use in war.

In the *Shaho Sambu Sho*, a treatise on archery written in Kyoto in 1689 by Asano Masachika, there is a reference to hunting with bows from horseback as a training exercise.

For the purpose of practicing horse-archery, several archers (Kashiwara, Hiki, Miura, Chiba) hunted deer in the grass plain on August 20th in the third year of Kenkyu on the order for the Shogun. Sometimes they made deer-shaped targets of wood. (Quoted in Grayson *JSAA* Vol. 6: 28)

'In the third year of Kenkyu' is 1192, during the reign of the first shōgun, Minamoto no Yoritomo. He did much to promote the skills of horse-archery among his warriors. This event was called *kusajishi* and it was usually contested between two teams of five. The use of wooden deer-shaped targets, presumably set up over an area of the grass plains, suggests a most wonderful mounted field course – zig-zagging, shooting at varying distances, shooting on all sides – the perfect training for battle. Whether such an activity was familiar to Asano in the 17th century is difficult to determine. He would however have been familiar with *yabusame*, which too has a strong connection with Minamoto no Yoritomo.

Kiyomoto Ogasawara, a direct descendent of the founder of the Ogasawara-ryū, at full gallop and at full draw. His family have presided over this style of *yabusame* since the 12th century. He rides with panache, precision, pluck and piety. His attire, most distinguishable by the dappled deerskin chaps, is a traditional hunting costume from the Kamakura period. It was during this era that *yabusame* came to prominence. (Photograph courtesy of Ogasawara-ryū)

YABUSAME

A resplendently attired archer intones, with increasing volume, the haunting chant of '*in-yo-i, in-yo-i*', as he gallops with power and purpose along a narrow track, shooting arrows into three successive targets. This is *yabusame* and it is perhaps the most majestic and thrilling sight in all of archery. As each target, a square wooden panel mounted on a bamboo pole, is struck with the hardwood bulb of a *kabura-ya* arrow, it shatters, delivering a resounding crack and a dramatic shower of splinters, to the great delight of a cheering crowd. It is theatre, it is sport and it is art. Perhaps more than anything else, however, it is ritual, a profoundly spiritual Shinto ceremony executed with punctilious decorum and solemnity.

The straight track, fenced with a rail on either side, is 230yd long and the three targets are spaced around 65yd apart. Each target is staked 6yd from the centre of the track at a height of 6 feet. There is great honour in performing *yabusame* on very fast horses and riders gallop the length of the track, shooting at each target successively, at a furious pace. One of the essential skills is being able to nock an arrow quickly. If the rider fumbles and his shot is too late, etiquette dictates that he drops the arrow from his string and takes another from his quiver before the next target. Carrying his arrows in a *kari-ebira*, the archer reaches behind his back and with an initial lift to free the *karimata* head from the sandwich leaves of the quiver, he then pulls it down and forward onto the bow. As each arrow is nocked, the archer intones '*in-yo-i, in-yo-i*', signifying darkness and light (*yin* and *yang*). Starting with a low tone before the first target, not only does the archer's voice rise in pitch with each shot, but the chant is also extended in duration as successive targets are passed. In addition to its ritual significance, the call encourages an in-breath with the '*in*' and an out-breath with the '*yo*'. Remembering to breathe is important in order to maintain a calm flow during moments of intense pressure. At the *yabusame* events held at the prestigious Nikkō Tōshōgū shrine, riders train all year to be granted just one single run. It is high stakes, testing character as much as skill. A rider who is permitted to take part in *yabusame* is called an *ite*. He must undergo a prolonged and strict training regimen. Only an *ite* of the highest calibre is entrusted with continuing the tradition.

Around 50 annual *yabusame* events continue to be held at shrines throughout Japan and *yabusame* is an important aspect of Japanese cultural heritage. In addition, there are highly competitive tournaments at other venues. At shrine events, however, the focus is more on the act of riding and shooting as a religious dedication. This combines with ceremonies that invoke the benevolence of the Shinto gods. Among the rituals that precede the runs on horseback is the *Tenchōchikyū no Shiki* (the ceremony of heaven and earth). In this ritual the principal *ite* rides three counter-clockwise circles, followed by two clockwise circles; he then draws his bow, first aiming at the sky and then at the ground. Prior to the Tokugawa period, the associated prayers asked for the health and good fortune in battle for the warrior. Today this ceremony invokes the gods to bring peace, health and abundance to the people.

A *kaburaya* (turnip-head arrow) fitted with a *karimata* head. This style of arrow is typically used for *yabusame*. The *karimata* (V-shaped head) fits securely between the leaves of a *kari-ebira* quiver. The turnip-shaped whistling head was made from either wood, horn or bone, cut with flutes to make a shrill whistle in flight. On occasions when a *kaburaya* is used without the *karimata*, the additional arrows are carried in the belt (*obi*) of the rider. In either case, the heavy bulb of the *kaburaya* splinters the wooden target boards with a resounding crack. (© Royal Armouries)

Kiyomoto Ogasawara has loosed his arrow, which shatters the target made from *hinoki* (Japanese cedar wood). The shards from these broken boards are valued as good-luck charms and are distributed to onlookers. Note the position of the bow, which has rotated partially in the archer's hand. It has not, however, rotated to the extent of full *yugaeri*. This would have placed the string on the outside of the arm. *Yugaeri* and partial *yugaeri* are nuanced technical aspects of shooting and a signature flourish of masters of the art. Full *yugaeri*, used universally in *kyūdō*, is unlikely to have been employed in the heat and haste of battle. Nevertheless, it is probable that a small rotation, a natural consequence of shooting, was encouraged because this turned the bow away from the path of the arrow. It eliminated, or at least reduced, archer's paradox. Ergonomically, for the rapid shooting that was demanded in battle, movements had to be minimized. In *yabusame* the correct form is to use partial *yugaeri* on the first two targets and then to deliver a full *yugaeri* upon shooting the last target. In this image, the rider has just shot the second target. (Image courtesy of Ogasawara-ryū)

TACHISUKASHI

Tachisukashi is a style of riding that evolved specifically for the courtly refinements of *yabusame*. It is a highly stylized mode of riding in which, by standing in the stirrups, the seat is lifted a paper-width above the saddle. This, combined with a posture of turned-out knees, resulted in only the heels having contact with the horse. In pre-Edo period art, riders are represented with their entire foot resting on the soleplate of the stirrup, with the consequence that the inside leg is in contact with the horse. However, in the *tachisukashi* style, the rider pinches the outer raised rim of the stirrup between his large and second toes and the foot sits at an angle diagonally across the stirrup so that only the heel is touching the horse. This opened the hips and turned out the knees in a posture that mimicked the stance taken by an archer shooting on the ground. In theory it isolates the archer, leaving him unaffected by the motion of the horse, while he takes his shot. Minimizing bounce combined a perception of dignity with sound shooting mechanics. Poised just above the saddle, the very best seem to hover with minimal vertical motion. Character, courage and an immense amount of skill are required to ride a galloping horse in this stylized way. It is a statement of elite warrior prowess. Being on the back of a high-spirited, fast horse is no reason not to shoot a bow in the precise, courtly manner instructed in the *dojo*. Practitioners claim that the horse can be controlled both directionally and for pace by subtle shifts of weight. Correct *yabusame* technique demands that the horse is moved to the left side of the track for each shot and then to the right side for nocking the next arrow, tracking a diagonal zig-zag course. Controlling a horse by adjusting one's weight is a principle of advanced equitation everywhere, but in other cultures it requires the supplement of full leg contact. *Tachisukashi* is distinct from all other equestrian doctrines and would seem to have limitations on the rider's ability to manage his horse in other than the most controlled circumstances. Riding a serpentine course within a straight, railed track is one thing, but being able to manage a horse effectively amidst the turmoil of a battlefield must surely require contact with the entire leg. The full potential and versatility of the *tachisukashi* style has yet to be demonstrated in the modern age beyond the single, straight run between the rails of the *yabusame* track. Problems of isolating the archer from the motion of the horse when shooting were solved in other horse-archer cultures by rising from the knees and using them as natural shock-absorbers. In doing so the rider leant forward. This forward lean required an even steeper angle when turning in the saddle to shoot behind (the Parthian shot). It is clear from art that the samurai shot at all angles in battle; it is equally clear that shooting a Parthian shot would be extremely unstable with the *tachisukashi* style. In *yabusame*, the archer only has to shoot at a target in direct line with his left shoulder. When shooting at angles that require twisting and leaning forward in the saddle, such as shooting on the off-side, considerable support may be given by the saddle. It is notable that the Japanese saddle is very similar in form to those of other horse-archer cultures.

Yabusame dates to at least the 12th century. In its earliest forms the *ite* had two runs, one in each direction of the track. He shot at three elevated targets on the outward run (as he does today) and then, on a return run, shot at small targets set close to the ground. These low-angle targets were made from clay and measured just 3½ inches in diameter! A story in the *Azuma kagami* (a chronicle of the Kamakura Shōgunate, written *c.* 1266) describes such an event in 1187. According to the chronicle, the Shōgun Minamoto no Yoritomo commanded a captured Taira warrior, Suwa Morizumi, to prove his skill on a *yabusame* course. The event took place at the Tsurugaoka Hachiman shrine. On his outward run, despite having to ride an ill-tempered horse, Morizumi managed to hit all three of the high wooden targets and on the return run he shattered all three of the little clay targets. Yoritomo then bade him set off on a third run with the objective of shooting the little pegs that held the high targets in place. Although fearful for his life, Morizumi remained focused and succeeded in hitting all three pegs. It was an extraordinary feat. Yoritomo rewarded him with his freedom and honoured him by taking him into his service (Hurst 1998: 118). Claiming its antecedence from this event, a *yabusame* festival is held each year at the Tsurugaoka Hachiman shrine on 16 September. Although the tradition has not been unbroken, it is considered one of the most prestigious festivals, with participation limited to only three riders. Like the high-status *yabusame* festival at the Nikkō Tōshōgū shrine, the Tsurugaoka Hachiman shrine event is regulated by the Ogasawara-ryū.

The history of *yabusame* is inextricably linked with the histories of the Ogasawara-ryū and the Takeda-ryū, the two schools that continue the traditions of samurai horse-archery to this day. Although the Takeda school can claim a longer ancestry (it is believed to have been founded by Minamoto no Yoshiari (845–97) in the 9th century), the Ogasawara school can claim greater continuity. Its founder, Ogasawara Nagakiyo (1162–1242), was the archery instructor at the court of Minamoto no Yoritomo, called there in 1186, a year before the *yabusame* challenge faced by Suwa Morizumi – an ordeal that must have been conducted under Nagakiyo's watchful gaze. The Ogasawara-ryū has a connection to *yabusame* from this time to the present day and continues to be administered by the Ogasawara family, direct descendants of Ogasawara Nagakiyo. There were occasional periods when *yabusame* fell out of favour, such as during civil wars, but the Ogasawara-ryū was always concerned with the teaching of archery.

During the reign of the Emperor Go-Daigo (1288–1339) the Ogasawara teachings were inscribed into a treatise called the *Shūshin-ron*. This family code remains the bedrock of Ogasawara instruction today (Ogasawara 2014: 10). Central to that code is etiquette – the proper way to behave and the correct way to perform actions. This is applied to every nuanced detail of form and equal emphasis is placed on both the body mechanics and the appropriate state of mind for every action. The Ogasawara-ryū remained prominent at court during both the Muromachi and Edo periods. After the Meiji Restoration in 1868, it continued to retain Imperial influence and in 1880 the school opened its doors to the public. Thereafter the Ogasawara family decreed that it was forbidden to earn a livelihood from these teachings and to this day the tradition is continued on a voluntary basis. They do this to ensure that they are never influenced by commercial considerations to increase attendance and that they can remain faithful to the principles embodied in the *Shūshin-ron* (Ogasawara 2014: 40).

Although it is conducted with strict formality and considered a sacred ritual, *yabusame* retains a joyful and celebratory energy, especially among the crowds. However, I suspect that the crowd-pleasing antics displayed by one *ite* on the occasion of General Grant's visit to Japan in 1879 were not entirely in keeping with the protocols of a sacred rite. Grant was witness to both a *yabusame* and *inuōmono* demonstration and a newspaper account of the former reported: 'The last rider won well-earned applause by brandishing his arrow in his hand until the target seemed to have been passed, when suddenly its very centre was found to have been pierced!' (*The Japan Mail*, 2 September 1879).

That such circus-tricks were possible is a humbling insight into the level of proficiency that is likely to have been achievable by the best of the samurai.

KASAGAKE

Like *yabusame*, *kasagake* is an ancient form of courtly horse-archery that involves shooting targets along a track from a galloping horse. However, the course is considerably more varied. Some targets are situated at shoulder height, while others are at ground level, and others are on the opposite side of the track. These all required different shooting angles. For the *yundeyoko*, the archer shot directly to his left at shoulder height, as in *yabusame*. The *yundesugai* shot required the archer to shoot at a ground target on the left hand side. It is a difficult shot for the *yumi*, and the *ite* has to get the angle just right if the bow is not to touch the horse. Most challenging of all was the *metesugai*, which necessitated a difficult twist of the body and lifting the bow to the other side of the horse in order to shoot at a target on the right-hand side. The demands of these different shooting positions replicated the requirements of the battlefield more closely than *yabusame*. Even though the back-shot (or Parthian shot as it is also known) was not used in *kasagake*, it is nevertheless represented in samurai art as something that was done.

The word '*kasagake*' translates as 'hat-shooting'. According to one legend the practice originated when the Emperor Jimmu (r. 660–585 BC), mythologized as Japan's first emperor, used his hat as a target. Others claim that the practice began in the reign of Minamoto no Yoritomo, the first shōgun of the Kamakura Shōgunate. Several types of Japanese reed hats lent themselves as impromptu targets. Most especially, the *ayaigasa*, which is from the Kamakura era, offers both an inner and outer target zone. When used as targets, these hats were sometimes covered in a mud render. Baked dry in the sun, this offered a dramatically explosive effect when struck, registering the hit. Whatever their millinary derivation, *kasagake* targets evolved and diversified and several different types of *kasagake* completion were developed. One popular option for the target was a circular wooden board, which was covered with a dome of leather and stuffed with cotton, wool or straw. It was marked with either two

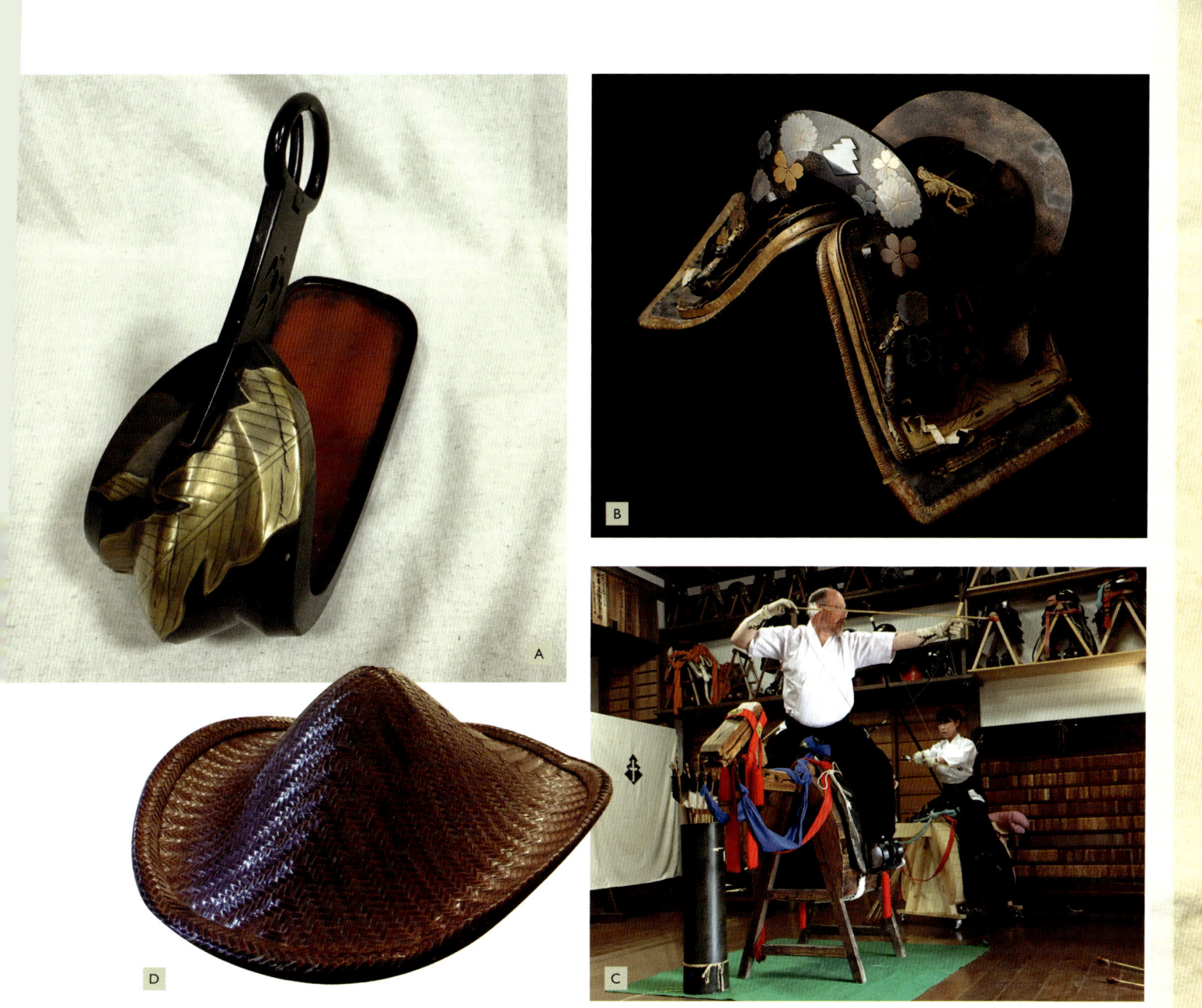

(A) A *shitanaga abumi*, Japanese stirrup, made from iron, which has been lacquered in black and red and inlaid with brass decoration. In the 5th century, the earliest forms of stirrup in Japan had a simple metal hoop with a flat bottom, similar to all stirrups. This evolved into the *tsubo-abumi*, which had enclosed iron toecaps, similar in shape to a Dutch clog. Stirrups, like the one featured here were not developed until the end of the 12th century. They then endured to the end of the samurai era. *Shitanaga abumi* had a sole-plate that extended from toe to heel. It retained an element of the toecap but the sides were left entirely open. One obvious advantage of this design is that, unlike stirrups from other cultures, an unhorsed rider ran no risk of being dragged with a foot caught in the stirrup. The exceptional weight of these stirrups gives them an added stability for riding in the *tachisukashi* style. (Image courtesy of Ogasawara-ryū)

(B) Edo-period saddle in the collections of the Ogasawara-ryū. The artistic magnificence of this piece is an indication of the high regard given to the samurai horse-archer. At the front is a raised panel (pommel), which can give support to the archer in certain shooting positions. It also provides protection to the warrior's groin against strikes from spear, sword or arrow. (Image courtesy of Ogasawara-ryū)

(C) Training for *yabusame* on the *mokuba*, a wooden horse accoutred with the correct saddle and stirrups. Here Tim Macmillan is practising in the *kyūdōjō* of the Ogasawara-ryū. He is one of a very few non-Japanese to be invited by the Ogasawara-ryū to ride as an *ite*. Having been a participant at the pre-eminent *yabusame* festival at the Nikkō Tōshōgū shrine since 2003, Tim was inducted fully into the Ogasawara-ryū in 2016. This means that he may now ride in any *yabusame* festival held under Ogasawara auspices. Note the riding position, with the knees turned out, which is unique to *yabusame*. (Photograph: Maria Peterson)

(D) A *kishagasa*. This type of stiff, broad-brimmed, lacquered reed hat formed part of the Kamakura traditional hunting attire and is one of two styles worn by Yabusame *ite*. A consequence of wearing such headgear is that the *ite* must draw at an angle away from the face to ensure the string does not snag the brim. This requires a wider draw than that practised by the *kyūdō* archer and a 'floating anchor', that is, an anchor-point that does not touch the face or body, making consistency harder to achieve. A samurai's helmet had a very broad neck guard that extended a good way from the face and necessitated a similar draw. (Photograph by Tim Macmillan) or three scoring zones. These pad-targets were suspended by cords within bamboo frames and shot at with blunts. Phlegmatic track officials sat hazardously close to the targets in order to adjudicate and annotate the precise scores.

In 2004, under the auspices of the Takeda-ryū, the Kamigamo shrine in Kyoto re-introduced an annual *kasagake* event, evoking a tradition at the shrine originating in the 13th century. In its present-day incarnation, female riders compete on equal terms with the male riders. It is a religious occasion, with purification rituals and prayers and including rites common to *yabusame* such as the Heaven and Earth ceremony. For the most part, *kasagake* is a serious ceremonial event. However, there are also recreational and competitive forms that are run on a much more informal basis.

INUŌMONO

Inuōmono was a form of horse-archery in which participants shot blunt, padded arrows at live dogs. Though such an activity is deeply shocking to modern sensibilities, it is nonetheless an important facet of Japanese archery heritage. *Inuōmono* was at the height of its popularity during the Kamakura and Muromachi periods, with its earliest mention dating to 1207 (Guttman & Thompson 2001: 50). Early forms also included *ushiōmono*, which involved shooting at cattle. In 1341, Ogasawara Sadamune presented an archery treatise – *Inuōmono Mokuabumi* – to his pupil, the Shōgun Ashikaga Takauji (r. 1338–58). In it he emphasized the importance of *inuōmono* as the paramount exercise for training warriors (Hurst 1998: 120). From a purely military training point of view, it offered the advantages of having to shoot at multiple and varying angles, at moving, unpredictable targets and at high speed. This was all very different to the measured distances and consistent angles of *yabusame*.

Inuōmono took place in an arena formed by two concentric circles of straw rope. From art it appears that these ropes had a girth of over 2 feet in diameter although in the below image the rope seems significantly thinner. Within each cordon the ground was covered with sand – a different colour for the inner and outer circle. In the outer circle stood riders awaiting their turn. They presumably also acted as wardens to keep the poor target animal from fleeing the circus – either by shouts or shots.

A print showing three portraits of *kasagake* riders. As with *yabusame*, they wear the traditional hunting attire of the Kamakura period, including the traditional *ayaigasa* hat. Note the distinctive type of horse they are riding. Today most *yabusame* and *kasagake* riders use modern European breeds. However, there are several breeds native to Japan. This image is most probably representing a *kiso*, a type of horse ridden by the samurai. (Kim Hawkins)

A painting by Yōshū Chikanobu (1838–1912) depicting *inuōmono* – dog shooting. (Metropolitan Museum of Art, www.metmuseum.org)

KASAGAKE FORMS

A traditional *kasagake* track (*saguri*) is approximately 120yd long with wooden or bamboo rails (*rachi*) situated on either side. In order to facilitate a clean shot, there is usually a break in the rail opposite a target. Some historical images show no rails at all and the track can also be curved. Riders must gallop the full length of the track and usually have ten runs.

Tōkasagake **(single shot)** This is a single-shot course with a 22-inch diameter target set no closer than 12½yd from the track and sometimes as distant as 25yd. The target is situated roughly halfway along the track.

Kokasagake **(short range)** Breakable targets, made from thin panels of wood, are set close to the ground on short bamboo poles. These shatter when struck with an arrow armed with a hefty wooden blunt. The boards range from 10 to 20 inches square and are placed a little over 6 feet from the rail. It demands the low-angle *yundesugai* shot.

Kuji kasagake **(by lots)** This is a competitive team event, of the type still held at the Kamigamo shrine. Ten riders draw lots to determine pairings and the five pairs then compete, using the aggregate score of each team to register the highest number of hits. Both *tōkasagake* and *kokasagake* courses are run.

Hasamimono **(everyday objects)** This form was for purely recreation or entertainment. *Ōgi* (hand-held fans) or other suitable objects were attached to bamboo poles at various heights and at an arbitrary distance from the track. *Hasamimono* was not exclusive to *kasagake*. Archers on foot also used improvised targets. *Hasamimono* could range from setting up an impromptu target at home to an elaborate display of trick-shooting for court entertainment.

Tanabata kasagake **(7-shot *kasagake*)** *Tanabata*, also known as the 'star festival', celebrates the mythology of two astral lovers, separated for eternity by the Milky Way, but who can meet once a year on the seventh day of the seventh month. It is a day to make wishes. Archers either have seven runs at a single target or shoot at a succession of seven targets.

Hyakuban kasagake **(100-shot *kasagake*)** This is a form of prayer ritual and the archer has to shoot 100 times. It stands to reason that in order to accomplish this as a continuous exercise at a single target, the archer would need a change of several horses.

In many contests it was customary for three teams of 12 riders to compete, each team being stationed in the outer zone while a single team member took his turn at shooting. Each competitor entered the arena at the gallop and a handler then released a dog for him to shoot at. Arrows were slightly larger than the standard *kabura-ya*. They were also padded and lacquered black. Points were allocated according to where the arrow hit and certain parts of the anatomy were prohibited zones. Even presuming that very lightweight bows and heavily padded arrows were used, there must have been a great deal of suffering on the part of the dogs, severe wounding and occasional fatalities. It was standard for each of the three teams to ride against 10 dogs in each of five rounds (Guttman & Thompson 2001: 51). This meant that no less than 150 dogs were required for a single tournament. These dogs were bred especially for the task. White dogs were favoured, possibly because a marking ink was used on the arrowheads to show where the hit landed.

Ogasawara Mochinaga (1396–1462) was, like his great-grandfather Ogasawara Sadamune, tutor to the Shōgun. He also wrote about *inuōmono* – he devoted five volumes to the study! A match was judged as much, if not more, on form and comportment as it was on hits. There were many variations of the standard course and some accounts suggest multiple riders all acting at once to pursue a dog within a much larger arena. Former US president and civil war general Ulysses S. Grant attended a presentation of both *yabusame* and *inuōmono* when visiting Tokyo in 1879. However, according to the *Japan Mail* (2 September 1879) the latter event was listed as '24 horsemen with bows and arrows hunting a sham dog'. This fortnightly, Yokohama-based, English-language newspaper, distributed in Europe and the United States, also gave an account of what transpired. After explaining that the 'usual' practice was to shoot at live canines, its report continued:

> On Monday drags were used, and much fun arose from the attempts of the crowd of horsemen to overtake and shoot the drag, which was drawn by one of their number at full gallop across the field.

It is apparent from this that the principal event was akin to the Korean sport of *mogu*, where a large ball (stretched fabric over a wicker frame) is towed behind a horse. Riders compete for hits using blunt arrows dipped in identifying paint. Furthermore, this would suggest that *mogu* originated as a substitute for a Korean form of *inuōmono*.

Seeing 24 riders galloping and shooting, whilst competing to edge each other out of the way to gain an optimal shooting position, must have been a thrilling sight. Sadly, such splendid entertainment was marred by a concluding match in which, according to the *Japan Mail*:

> One black dog was, however, let loose and he seemed to be an old stager at the game, for in spite of several palpable hits from the blunted arrows, he gave good sport in doubling through the crowd of pursuers until, tired out, he was allowed to rejoin his keeper and go to kennel.

BATTLE OF KURIKARA, 2 JUNE 1183 (OPPOSITE)

In this key conflict of the Gempei War, the armies of the Taira and Minamoto clans had come together on the gentle slopes of a broad valley at the foot of the Kurikara mountain pass. Minamoto no Yoshinaka, who occupied the higher ground, had the inferior force and had already tricked the Taira into believing they faced greater numbers by unfurling 30 white banners on Kurosaka Hill, which caused the Taira to pause and deliberate. Meanwhile, Yoshinaka sent one unit on a wide arc to attack the Taira in the rear, and dispatched three units to hide in ambush at the foot of the pass. His challenge was how to hold the Taira in place while these deployments were completed; the answer was to initiate ritual combat – *ikki uchi*.

Minamoto no Yoshinaka first sent forward 15 men to challenge an equal number of equal status Taira samurai. Each pair in turn spurred towards each other, shooting screeching *kabura-ya* (whistling arrows) from the saddle. Next it was 30 men, then 50 and then 100. Only once this was done did the samurai finally draw swords to engage in hand-to-hand fighting. The delaying tactic worked: a little before sunset, the Minamoto forces smashed into the Taira rear, driving them forward into the pincers of the concealed men, many of whom were archers. The Taira were driven towards the narrow mountain pass with its sheer-sided rocky precipices. Finally, Yoshinaka's men drove a herd of terrified oxen, lighted torches tied to their horns, after the fleeing Taira, knocking them off the ledges of the narrow mountain path and to their deaths below.

In this scene we see the formal archery duel which began hostilities. A Minamoto warrior gallops toward his opponent, preparing to loose a *kabura-ya*. He carries a *kari-ebira* quiver and is raising himself on his stirrups to provide a more stable shooting platform. Behind him, the other participants await their turn to demonstrate their valour and prowess with the bow.

THE JAPANESE YUMI

Despite the fact that, as a concession to Western opinion, *inuōmono* had been banned in 1862, it appears to have made an unfortunate comeback on this occasion. Grant is said to have expressed displeasure at the practice. The last recorded performance was in 1881 at a residence of the Shimazu clan (Guttman & Thompson 2001: 52). It is now illegal.

The horse-archer in war

In contrast to the elegance, courtliness and spirituality of later samurai martial displays, a narrative scroll from the Heian period, the *Obusuma Saburō Ekotoba,* tells of the life of an especially brutish samurai. It reveals a base attitude to archery practice. Obusuma Saburō's residence was a well-known hangout for an unsavoury band of military men. There he encouraged a culture of barbarous cruelty, calling for a constant supply of freshly decapitated heads to decorate his compound and urging his household to use passers-by as target practice:

> Hunt for heads and hang them on the fence of the horse-yard! Keep it up … Go after the *shugenja* (mountain monks), or the beggars passing in front of the gate … and chase them down! Shoot them with kabura arrows. (Quoted in Ikegami 1995: 65)

By any standards, Obusuma was a thug, but there can be no doubt that such brutality extended to the battlefield. Samurai warfare had its share of ambushes and surprise attacks, of night-raids and civilian atrocities. There has always been an

Woodblock print by Utagawa Yoshikazu depicting the battle of Kawanakajima (1561). Note that several horse-archers are turned in their saddles, shooting behind them. Although this particular painting was executed in 1857, the image of archers shooting whilst turned in their saddles is common in art of the samurai period. In order to be effective on the battlefield, the horse-archer needed to be able to shoot at multiple angles from the horse. (Library of Congress)

SIGNALS AND MESSAGES

In addition to their use for ritual challenges, for ceremony and for various *kisha* events, whistling arrows could be used on the battlefield to signal troop movements. An arrow with a piercingly shrill tone shot in the direction of part of an enemy's position announced not only when to charge but also showed the direction of that action. Moreover, a whistling arrow might be the command to disengage and regroup. Little is known of any precise instructions they might signify, but they certainly had the potential to be of use in ordering fast-moving cavalry. They could be equally effective in signalling where to attack during a siege.

A whistling arrow played a decisive role during the siege of Hiuchi in 1183. Hiuchi was a rudimentary wooden stockade set on rocky crags, but the Minamoto commander, Yoshinaka, had improved its defences by building a dam to create a moat. Thus he was able to hold out against the Taira even though he had inferior forces, at least until a traitor in the Minamoto camp sent a message arrow to the Taira, informing them how to breach the dam and drain the moat. This they did and the Hiuchi stockade fell (Turnbull 1998: 201). It cannot be said for certain whether or not this treacherous shaft was armed with a whistling head, but it seems most likely. A random arrow arriving unannounced could easily be ignored.

An observation about the etiquette of sending message arrows appears in the *Shaho Sambu Sho*. In answer to the student's question, 'What about the message arrow?', the master replies:

> There is no certain way for that. The writing however should be courteous. The names of the sender and the recipient should be correctly described. The paper used should be very light. (Quoted in Grayson *JSAA* Vol. 6: 28)

apparent contradiction between the honour ideals espoused by an elite cadre of fighting men and the realities of war. As it was for the chivalrous knight in medieval Europe, so it was for the samurai in medieval Japan. Understanding either chivalry or *bushidō* requires both the barbarism of man and the nobility of man to be held in equal balance and an acknowledgement that each was only ever intended to apply to warriors of the same class. Even so, the samurai horse-archer was above all else a man of honour, an adherent of the samurai code – *bushidō*.

IKKI UCHI

Ikki uchi was ritual mounted single combat, an ancestral tradition that offered a samurai the chance for glory, for his name to be lauded in epic verse, for a heroic moment or a noble death. It was how a proud samurai most wished to wage war; it was correct. During the Heian and early Kamakura period it was customary for a samurai to issue a formal challenge to an opponent of equal rank by shooting a *kaburaya* (whistling arrow) at him; every samurai carried at least one whistling arrow in his war quiver. It is not clear whether the arrow had to strike home or simply pass nearby for the challenge to be official. Either way, the next stage was to ride at each other and shoot from the saddle. Holding one's nerve to take a close shot offered a greater chance of success for both accuracy and impact. However, a skilled archer, who could hit his mark from further away, might fell his enemy before the other had a chance to let loose his arrow. It was a high-speed game of 'chicken' and it was conducted in full view of one's comrades. This was all about fame and glory.

Two *kyūdōka*s shooting at the Kashima Shrine *kyūdōjō*. The shooting house (*shajō*), which is otherwise fully enclosed and covered, opens up on one side. Archers shoot across the courtyard (*yamichi*) at targets set into a bank of black sand (*azuchi*). This is sheltered by a target house (*matoba*). The target centres are 30yd away from the shooting line. (Photograph by Maria Peterson)

SQUADRONS

Surviving traditions do much to inform about the manner and capabilities of the individual horse-archer. However, it should be noted that a majority of battlefield images in art depict horse-archers on the battlefield operating in concert, in squadrons. Groups of six or more riders are commonly seen galloping together as they approach an enemy. For the squadron to be effective going forward, it needed to fan out in such a way that at least the first two or three ranks of riders had a clean forward shot. As the squadron wheeled past enemy lines, then it almost certainly ordered into line, so that all could loose lateral shots. Of course, once in the swirl and mayhem of close combat each horse-archer had to manoeuvre for position and pick his shots. Horsemanship was the paramount skill in this situation, and the archer also had to take care not to put his comrades at risk if he were to miss. It was a highly skilled way to wage battle. Although there is only circumstantial evidence, such as images on art of archers turned in the saddle to shoot behind, it seems probable that the samurai horse-archer also operated in a similar fashion to those of other cultures, namely by using tactics of feigned retreat such as luring an adversary to break ranks and pursue and then turning on him. Where such images occur, they do so not as individuals but as small squadrons all executing the same move.

Hosha

Hosha is ground archery. The bow was used on the battlefield in the hands of both samurai infantry and *ashigaru* alike. Different circumstances called for different tactics. As will be discussed, there is much about Japanese archery that has become either formalized or sanctified. However, there was also an informal side and a decidedly non-spiritual side. For instance, it was common, among the nobility of the Heian period, to gamble on the outcome of archery matches. *Noriyumi* (betting-bow) competitions were held, away from court, in their private domains. Here nobles either placed bets between each other, wagering on the winner, or there was a prize to be won. Such events were contested keenly by men who trained to use the bow in war.

Alongside the martial tradition, the spiritual significance of the bow played its part in court ritual even before the rise of the samurai. By the 7th century, in a practice borrowed from the mainland, a ceremonial performance of archery skills was held at court during the first lunar month of the year. At some stage elements of competition were introduced and visiting dignitaries sometimes took part in these contests. Records show that delegations from at least two of the three Korean kingdoms competed at a New Year archery match held at the Japanese court in Nara, those from Silla in 715 and those from Parhae in 740 (Hurst 1998: 109). They shot at a large target faced with three concentric circles. Awards were given, but not as prizes to the highest score, rather as tokens of participation. Bolts of cloth were the traditional gift and these were allocated according to status, a greater quantity being given to the more senior bowmen.

Over the centuries, ground archery developed as court ceremony, competitive sport and a martial skill for the battlefield. All of these influences combined in the evolution of *kyūdō*.

KYŪDŌ

The form of Japanese archery most widely practised and most well known in the present day is *kyūdō*. *Kyūdō* means 'the way of archery' in contradistinction to *kyūjutsu*, which means 'the art of archery'. In some ways it is a distinction of little difference, as both are concerned with shooting a bow. However, *kyūjutsu* is the traditional martial art of archery as used in war and *kyūdō* is a formalized archery practice rooted in Buddhist philosophy. To observe a *kyūdō* practitioner shooting with precise, elegant and mindful movements is to witness both an aesthetic ideal and spiritual serenity. It is spell-bindingly beautiful, it quiets the mind and it soothes the soul. At its heart, however, it has a greater connection to the manner of military archery in feudal Japan than do the techniques of a present-day target archer, with either a longbow or a recurve bow, to his/her respective antecedents.

Kyūdō is a distillation of many teachings from many different *ryūha*. The old schools such as the Ogasawara-ryū had equal influence on the development of ground archery and horse-archery and they still have their own distinct teachings for *kyūdō*, although these are often focused on ceremonial drills. Another school that had significant influence is the Heki-ryū. According to tradition, Heki Danjō Masatsugu came to prominence as the archery instructor to Yoshida Shigekata (1463–1543) and his son, Yoshida Shigemasa (1485–1596). He advocated a new approach to shooting, which he called '*Hi, Kan, Chū*' (Fly, Pierce, Centre). It caught the imagination of the age. Scholars disagree about the details of his life, which have been scantly recorded. However, Heki-ryū has given rise to around a dozen other *ryūha*, each different but each also claiming common ground with the original teachings. Heki-ryū survives today as one of the main influences on *kyūdō*. Since its origins date only to the end of the 15th century, it is considered one of the 'New Schools' compared to the 'Old Schools' of Takeda, Ogasawara and others. Some branches of the Heki-ryū continue to practise techniques of battlefield archery, including rapid nocking techniques.

However, more familiar to the modern observer are the slow movements of the *kyūdōka* (a person who practices *kyūdō*) and there is a popular tendency to dismiss this as having neither semblance nor relevance to the samurai *yumiya no michi* (the way of the bow and arrow), and its application on the battlefield. Undeniably the archer must shoot quickly in battle. However, an archer who can shoot quickly and accurately must train slowly; he must isolate each small element of his technique and refine it to the perfect form and build it into his muscle memory. Such is the training of a warrior. The deliberately slow and meticulous execution of each stage of preparing for and shooting an arrow may seem of no apparent use on a battlefield, but it embodies the essence of what a warrior must do to train; he then takes it to the next step of becoming faster at it.

In *kyūdō* there are eight stages of shooting a single arrow. Individual stages may incorporate a number of separate actions, each with its own name. Collectively the eight major stages are known as the *hassetsu*. Small differences manifest depending on whether the archer is an adherent of the *bushakei* style, which developed from foot-archery traditions, or an adherent of the *kishakei* style of the horse-archer. The first stage is setting the feet, (1) *ashibumi*, followed by adjusting the overall posture of the body, (2) *dozukuri*, a stage that also includes nocking an arrow to the string. Readying the bow is called (3) *yugamae*, a procedure that includes placing the thumb on the string at the correct angle (*torikake*) and holding the bow with the correct grip (*tenouchi*) – both critical steps. The distinctive act of raising the bow high above the head is called (4) *uchiokoshi*. It is a style that is mirrored to some extent in other horse-archery cultures, because this is the best position from which to draw the bow when on horseback. When performed at ceremonial pace, it may look stylized but it is also extremely practical. (5) *Hikiwake* is a two-step stage for drawing the bow and (6) *kai* is a final stage before releasing. It is partly physical and partly spiritual, a highly nuanced hold incorporating aspects of breathing. (7) *Hanare* is the release, which includes the *yugaeri* (a rotation of the bow in the hand). Although it may not have been ergonomic for a samurai in battle to allow full rotation, a certain amount is beneficial to offset the archer's paradox and help the arrow fly straight. (8) *Zanshin* is the follow-through, a moment of calm after the shot and the lowering of the bow.

The teachings of the Ogasawara-ryū are concerned not only with shooting a bow but also with everyday actions: 'This is movement that eliminates futility, contains beauty, is effective, and natural' (Ogasawara 2014: 58). Although elements of courtly and ceremonial elegance are apparent in *kyūdō*, its essence is one of ergonomic efficiency; it is concerned with the best way of doing things. That approach is the approach of the true warrior. The general principle of perfecting form by slow, repetitious, consistent movements is central to martial ability. In order to be fast, in order to be instinctive, every muscle must be rehearsed and every motion refined to its most efficient. For the battlefield, of course, everything has to be speeded up, but I suspect there would be a lot in the training of a samurai archer that a present-day *kyūdō* practitioner would recognize.

Setting speed aside, among the other discernible differences is the *ashibumi* posture. A samurai is unlikely to have his feet fixed in this way in combat. An infantry

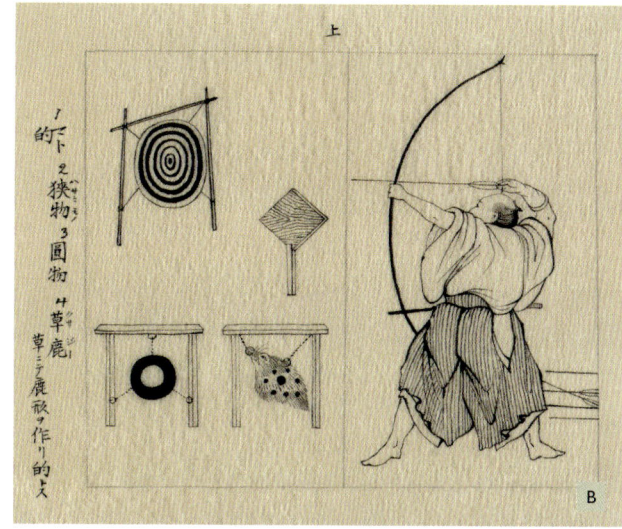

(A) Maria Peterson, founder of the Redwood Kyudojo in California. Note how the second arrow is held in the string-hand, grasped with the ring and little fingers. (Kim Hawkins)

(B) An assortment of targets. (Ink on paper, 1878). The most common device was to suspend a target within a frame. Here, among others, are the concentric rings of the *kasumi mato* and also the board as used in *yabusame*. For *kyūdō*, targets are set with their centre at 10½ inches above ground level. The reason for this is thought to be to train archers to shoot well at a kneeling foe. When deploying kneeling and standing archers together, it was the kneeling archers who were in front. If the defending army shot only at the standing archers, the kneeling archers could advance unscathed. It was therefore vital to concentrate their aim on the kneeling rank (Onuma & De Prospero: 60). (Library of Congress)

(C) *Makiwara*. This type of straw target is used at very close range, generally a bow-length away, for form practice. Even at only a few feet distance, form faults can be diagnosed by the angle at which the arrow hits. Stalks of straw are laid endwise and bound tightly. This gives a good arrow stop, even from strong bows at close range. Japanese art from the feudal period sometimes shows *makiwaras* that have the straw packed tightly in a barrel – this has a strong resonance with the butts in English archery. (Image courtesy of Ogasawara-ryū)

(D) *Kasumi mato*. This is the standard target face for *kyūdō*. The differently sized concentric rings give it a slightly ethereal optical quality, which is why it is commonly known as the 'mist target' (not because of the obvious bad pun)! As with all *kyūdō* targets, it is a sheet of paper pasted onto a bamboo cylinder called a *matowaku*. This standard version spans 14½ inches across and is shot at from a range of 30yd (*kinteki*). A larger version for what is considered long-distance shooting (*enteki*) measures 5 feet across and is shot at from 65yd. One arrow has missed the target, suggestive of the Japanese aesthetic principle of *wabi-sabi*, which acknowledges that imperfection is inherent in all things. (Photograph by Tim Macmillan)

(E) *Kin mato*. This gold target is shot at only on special occasions. Measuring just 3½ inches, it appears as a tiny speck at the standard distance of 30yd. By tradition, it represented a general's wrist. The samurai code of honour dictated that people should only kill those of their own station. However, inferior infantry archers might aim at a general's wrist without fear of breaching the code. Although honour codes were taken very seriously, it is doubtful that this level of nicety would survive the heat of battle. (Photograph by Tim Macmillan)

(F) *Hoshi mato* – also known as the star target. This has a black spot against a white background and is used mostly for ceremonial archery. Like the *kasumi mato*, it measures 14½ inches across. (Photograph by Tim Macmillan) archer needed to be mobile on the battlefield, perhaps standing unevenly in rocky terrain and in many instances kneeling to minimize his size as a target. Another difference is that from art we can see that the samurai drew his bow to an anchor point that was in line with the shoulder, not just beneath the ear as in *kyūdō*. In battle he would dispense with rigid formalities and he would shoot with speed and purpose. However, the mechanics and the flow of the nocking, draw and release would have been broadly similar, albeit faster.

THE SECOND ARROW

One noticeable aspect in *kyūdō* is that the archer holds a second arrow in his/her string-hand. The arrow on the string is called the *haya* and the second arrow, held with the ring and little fingers, is known as the *otoya*. In formal *kyūdō*, after shooting the first arrow, the archer kneels to nock the second. Obviously this would be too ponderous a procedure for use on the battlefield, but the concept and ability to hold one, or even more, arrows in the string-hand whilst shooting suggests that this may have been a rapid-nocking technique employed by the samurai. As discussed in the composite bow section pages 205–7, many cultures have techniques for burst-shooting, which include holding additional arrows in either the bow-hand or the string-hand. From these positions an arrow can be fitted to the string far more speedily than can be done when drawing it from a quiver.

INFANTRY ARCHERS – THE RISE OF THE *ASHIGARU*

Foot soldiers from the lower stations of society first began to serve in samurai retinues in the late 13th century to assist in repelling Mongol invasions; many of these were archers. However, the first mention of the term *ashigaru*, which is what these light troops came to be called, was in the 14th century. According to the *Taiheiki*, 800 *shashu no ashigaru* (*ashigaru* shooters) fought for the Sasaki clan at the battle of Shijo Nawate in 1348 (Turnbull 2001: 5). This was a sizeable proportion of their 2,000-strong army. However, it wasn't until the Sengoku period that the *ashigaru* became a major force on the battlefield. The Onin War of 1467–77, which subsequently escalated into the Sengoku (Warring States) era, ushered in profound changes to samurai warfare. During these rancorous civil wars, hungry for manpower, larger armies were recruited, armies that placed a greater emphasis on infantry. *Ashigaru* were then enlisted in the thousands. In some cases, runaway peasants joined these bands for loot and employment, but it is a mistake to think that all *ashigaru* were peasants, just as it is erroneous to think this of English longbowmen. A majority of *ashigaru* were small farmers, tradesmen or merchants who signed up to serve their *daimyō* for relatively short campaigns. There was also a grey area between wealthy land-owning samurai and poorer samurai who were really part-time samurai and part-time farmers – *ji-samurai*. Many of these men exchanged the daily grind of their smallholdings for the camaraderie and adventure of a full-time military life, living in barracks within fortified towns. There were the usual reactionary voices against the shift from traditional samurai warfare, where the horse-archers were in the van and the first to engage the enemy. By their nature, infantry were in the front line and it was shocking to the old guard to have such lowly folk take the first kills. However, the efficacy of the *ashigaru* was irrefutable and they were especially effective in mountainous or forested terrain, ill suited to cavalry, which is where many civil war conflicts took place. The *ashigaru* changed Japanese warfare entirely and brought the *yumi* into the hands of the infantryman. Those who did not shoot were spearmen armed with the *yari*.

Until the late 16th century, it was possible for *ashigaru* to move through the ranks and to become samurai themselves. The most conspicuous example of this was Toyotomi Hideyoshi (1536–98). He was the son of an *ashigaru* and began his own military career as one. However, in 1587, he rose to become the ruler of a newly unified Japan! Ironically, once in power Hideyoshi issued edicts that restricted such status mobility. No longer was it possible for an *ashigaru* to rise above his station.

Before the Portuguese introduced firearms to Japan in 1543, in particular the arquebus, a majority of *ashigaru* were armed with bows. The trend to more and more infantry warfare also led to more and more samurai fighting on foot, not least of all because they had to lead these at times somewhat unruly levies. Gradually the skills of the infantry archer were held in higher esteem. The evidence in art suggests that the lower-status *ashigaru* archers were armed with simple wooden *yumi*s, or perhaps those of the earlier *fusetake* type, having no more than a bamboo backing to a wooden bow. Their distinctive *jingasa* war-hat was broad-brimmed and necessitated them drawing at a distance away from the face. By arming and training the *ashigaru* with bows and with the transition to more and more infantry warfare, Japanese battlefield archery at first resembled that of 14th-century Europe, with massed archers taking up fixed positions, often supported by an equal number of spearmen intermingled in their ranks. Even after the introduction of the arquebus, which was adopted with universal alacrity as the primary arm for the *ashigaru*, archers remained embedded with the gunpowder men. The slow-loading arquebus could not compete with the *yumi* for rapid and reliable shooting in a pressed situation. In the *Zōhyō Monogatari* (written *c*.1657–84) advice is given to:

> Stand one archer in the space between two matchlock men, to cover the arquebuses reloading. An arrow can be loosed in between the two matchlockmen firing, thus covering the reloading interval. (Quoted in Turnbull 2005: 129)

An *ashigaru* arrow-bearer from the *Zōhyō Monogatari*. He carries a box of 100 arrows. Rapid shooting tactics – *sashiya* – expended a great deal of ammunition, and resupply was crucial. (Japan Archive/Stephen Turnbull)

The arquebus required considerably less training than the bow, which was its chief advantage. As with all bows, shooting the *yumi* effectively required constant practice. In time, new ways and new tactics were developed for highly trained and strictly drilled corps of infantry archers, both *ashigaru* and samurai. In part these owed something to the tactics developed by the squads of arquebusiers.

SATSUMA HEKI-RYŪ

The civil wars of the 15th and 16th centuries had given more and more employment to infantry archers, and many new schools, focused on infantry archery, emerged. Chief among them was the Heki-ryū and its many offshoots. In the Heki-ryū system of *koshiya kumiyumi* (battlefield archery), still practised today by a few select schools, archers adopt a variety of kneeling and crouching stances, thus minimising their exposure as targets.

For the basic kneeling stance, the archer begins by sitting on the heel of his leading leg (the left) but with his right leg tucked in close to the body, foot flat to the ground. As he draws the bow, the archer repositions to shoot. He opens out by stepping to his

(**A**) Practitioners of the Satsuma Heki-ryū demonstrating *koshiya* (battlefield archery). The foreground figure shows the kneeling posture at full draw. Note the string is held away from the face, which is necessary when shooting whilst wearing a helmet with a wide neck guard. (Image courtesy of the Satsuma Heki-ryū)

(**B**) In this detail, the second-rank archer demonstrates the method of supporting his weight on his elbow whilst fitting an arrow to the bowstring. He presents a minimal target, yet by simply drawing in his right leg, he can assume the shooting position exhibited by the archer in the front row. (Image courtesy of the Satsuma Heki-ryū)

(**C**) The archers, outstretching their right legs and putting their weight onto their left forearms, are crouching in a semi-prone position while they take arrows from their quivers and nock them to the string. It is a drill that reduces their size as targets on the battlefield. (Image courtesy of the Satsuma Heki-ryū)

(**D**) In a rhythmic advance, during which, after each shot, the rear rank steps through the front rank to take up the forward position, the archers have reached the target line and are shooting at extreme close range. The targets represent the typical type of shields that were used by entrenched archers. (Image courtesy of the Satsuma Heki-ryū) right with his right foot and rising on his left leg to assume a vertical kneel. In this position, the knee of his right leg is directly above its heel. It is a dynamic motion that assists with the drawing of heavier bows. The right leg was stepped back close to the body during nocking, allowing the archer to sit back on his left haunch and so return to being both a narrower and lower target. When shooting from a static position, the nocking speed could be enhanced by taking a handful of arrows and resting them, tips on the ground, against the inner thigh of the right leg. Unlike horse-archers, who raise their arms above the head to draw, the infantry archer seeks to remain as small as possible and so comes to the half-draw with his arms down and then raises the bow from below into full draw.

Regiments of infantry archers operated in disciplined, well-drilled formations. Files were spaced apart so that there was a bow-length between each man. This gap not only allowed the rank behind to shoot simultaneously, it also allowed them to advance between the files when ordered. When advancing on the enemy, the ranks operated in the following manner. After the front rank had shot and had begun to nock, the rank behind stood to move through the gaps and so become the front rank. Minimizing height by assuming a relatively low squat, the footwork resembled that of a 'fencing step', with the left foot leading each pace and the right foot collecting behind it but never passing it. Most elaborate of these procedures was the ability to nock whilst lying face down and semi-prone. In order to accomplish this, the archer extended his right leg, throwing it diagonally behind him, whilst folding his left leg completely. He stabilized by pushing his bow-arm forward and resting on his elbow. The bow was thus held horizontally in front of the archer, which explains the necessity of the files being so widely spaced. In this position, he could easily retrieve an arrow from the quiver on his back and slip it under the bow and onto the string before returning to a kneeling posture to shoot.

For archers moving forward in open ground, the battlefield was not always a bi-directional entity. Squadrons of cavalry especially could sweep around at any angle, and the further forward the archers advanced the more vulnerable they became. Kneeling archers were equally capable of changing the direction of their shots as their standing counterparts. It is a swift matter to spin either 90 or 180 degrees on the fulcrum of the left knee. The open order of the two-rank chequerboard formation allowed for archers, particularly those at the ends of a formation, to be facing in opposite directions in the event of being surrounded. It was a most versatile system.

SHIELDS

Prior to the dynamic, fast, and flowing tactics of the Heki-ryū style of advance, infantry archers were more static. They needed protection both against the sweep of a cavalry attack and also against the arrows of the enemy. On the battlefield they used tall, rectangular, wooden shields (*tate*) that, by means of a hinged prop, were free-standing. Although similar to the pavise of the European crossbowmen, *tate* were characteristically narrow. The *yumi*-bowman needed only minimal screening; he didn't have to bend over to span his weapon in the manner of the crossbowman. Having a narrow shield made it less weighty and more portable. Ranks of infantry archers could edge forwards when necessary. It was common for *kaidate* (shield walls) to be formed for both defensive and offensive tactics. These were sometimes staggered several rows deep, causing significant obstacles to enemy manoeuvres with cavalry. Such a sophisticated use of shield walls required good battlefield communications, as well as well-drilled and well-disciplined troops.

At some point during the Kamakura period it became usual to display a clan *mon* (heraldic device) on the shields. Before then, we see markings but no actual heraldry. Almost universal were black bands on the shields; these possibly served as a means of unit identification. There are also references to various inscriptions in black ink, such as prayers and poetic exhortations to bravery. For siege warfare, much larger, significantly wider shields were used. The equivalent to the European mantlet, these gave protection to several archers, who could cluster behind. Free-standing shields, of either pavise or mantlet dimensions, were used universally by archers on the battlefield and in sieges. Samurai armies also employed *sakamogi* extensively. These were barricades, made either with brushwood, sharpened stakes or thorny branches. All provided good vantage points for the archer.

Despite the fact that a shield was a principal defence against arrows in both Europe and the Middle East, there were no circumstances in which a Japanese soldier or samurai carried a shield on his arm. For the samurai, this function was catered for by *sode*. These were large rectangular panels of lamellar armour suspended from the shoulders. They gave a flexible, energy-absorbing first layer of defence against missiles and protected much of the upper body. Moreover, *sode* left both hands free for riding and shooting a bow. In rare circumstances, there are tales of samurai being able to deflect arrows with either a sword, staff or *naginata*. It is a skill called *yadome,* though the reality must be taken with a pinch of salt.

TAJIMA THE ARROW-CUTTER

During the first battle of Uji (1180), a retreating body of warrior monks sympathetic to the Minamoto cause tore up the planking of a bridge over the river Uji in order to stall the Taira pursuit.

> Then Gochin no Tajima, throwing away the sheath of his long *naginata*, strode forth alone onto the bridge, whereupon the Heike [Taira] straightaway shot at him fast and furious. Tajima, not at all perturbed, ducking to avoid the higher ones and leaping up over those that flew low, cut through those that flew straight with his whirring *naginata*, so that even the enemy looked on in admiration. (*Heike Monogatari*, quoted in Turnbull 2005: 256)

SIEGE: ESCALADE AND SORTIE

In this scene from the Gempei War, Minamoto forces attempt to assault a Taira stronghold. Taira archers (red banners) send arcing shots from the parapet surrounding the gatehouse, giving cover to a sortie of samurai horse-archers, who gallop out through the gates, bows at the ready. Other Taira archers on the gatehouse parapet shoot enfilading arrows at Minamoto troops (white banners) attempting to scale the wall. Simple wooden stockades like this were typical of the many hundreds of fortresses that were erected during the conflict. Within were living quarters, stables and, most importantly, a well. There is insufficient evidence that the iconic *mon* of the Taira (a butterfly) or that of the Minamoto (a gentian) had yet come into use, but the distinguishing red and white banners were certainly extant.

Prior to the age of gunpowder, skilled archers were essential for holding an enemy back from the walls. They were equally useful to the attackers, who sought to pick off these defenders with marksman accuracy. Minamoto archers shelter behind their wooden mantlets (large, static shields), waiting for the opportune moment to take a shot.

The mounted samurai are making a sortie to launch a direct attack on the enemy's command. As well as guarding the open gates with archers above, crossbowmen stand behind the pillars with their weapons spanned, ready to shoot at anyone who approaches. As a final defence are troops armed with the *naginata*. Many more of these stand ready in the guardhouse.

THE JAPANESE YUMI

The leaping and ducking sounds a fanciful foreshadowing of such exploits in present-day Japanese martial-arts films. However, the high-speed windmill effect attainable by an adept wielder of a *naginata* might well be capable of deflecting a number of arrows. There have been instances of stunt performers cutting arrows, shot from very lightweight bows, in flight. Moreover, some martial arts schools record *yadome no jutsu* (the art of arrow-cutting) as once being part of their historical curriculum. The *Maniwa Nen-ryū* does at least acknowledge that this is an advanced technique! Nevertheless, its viability on the battlefield, especially against heavyweight, fast bows, is highly questionable.

INFANTRY ARCHERS AT THE BARRICADES

After the battle, an army of the Taira clan attacked the monks who were by now ensconced at the Buddhist temple of Miidera. Both sides used the bow. The monks, about 1,000 in number, built a makeshift barricade from hastily felled trees. Manning the defences, they repelled repeated attacks from the Taira's samurai horse-archers who rode at them time and time again.

> At the Hour of the Hare they began to draw their bows and the battle continued the whole day, until when evening came three hundred of the monks and their men had fallen. (*Heike Monogatari*, quoted in Turnbull 2005: 257)

Gojin no Tajima at the first battle of Uji (1180) fending off arrows with his *naginata*. The art of cutting or deflecting arrows with a weapon is called *yadome no jutsu*. (Woodblock print, author's collection. Photograph by Kim Hawkins)

It is an age-old principle that infantry archers facing cavalry can only operate if they have a strong defensive position, be that pot-holes, sharpened stakes or, as in this case, a bulwark of timber – a *sakamogi*. Even so, the monks took considerable casualties during the assault, which lasted from dawn until dusk. Disdaining to treat the monks with the chivalrous respect they would afford fellow samurai, the Taira broke through the barriers at nightfall and set fire to the monastery.

There is an almost identical account of the Taira attack on the monastery at Nara in the same year.

> At Nara, about seven thousand monks, young and old without distinction, put on their armour and took up their position at Narasaka and Hannyaji, digging ditches across the road and making breastworks and palisades … the monks fought on foot while the imperial army fought on horseback, and as they kept riding up for the attack, the ranks of Nara were thinned and they began to give ground, so that by nightfall, after fighting from early morning, both their positions were broken through. (*Heike Monogatari*, quoted in Turnbull 2005: 258)

Once again, the Taira resorted to fire. They ignited a conflagration, which, fanned by a strong wind, raged with savage destruction and in which 3,500 people died.

INCENDIARY ARROWS

Given that the vast majority of Japanese fortifications were wooden stockades, encircling wooden buildings, fire was a potent weapon for siege warfare. One recipe

CEREMONIAL ARCHERY AT COURT

It was during the Heian period that the New Year event, known as *jarai*, was held on the 17th day of the first month. During the 9th century this became known as *kokka no daiji* – 'the great national event of state'. However, under the aegis of Minamoto no Yoritomo, the ritual was moved to the fourth day of the year and became known as the Omato-shiki. To this day New Year shooting events, known as *yumihajime*, attract thousands of participants throughout Japan. Archery is living legacy.

In the *momote-shiki* ritual, 10 archers, each with 20 arrows, maintain a constant rate of rhythmic shooting, one after the other, giving the effect of rain falling. It is performed as a prayer at coming-of-age ceremonies.

Similar solemnity is afforded to *hikime* ceremonies. These purification rituals are conducted at the opening of shrines, dōjōs or civic buildings, at five months after pregnancy and as a general exorcism against illness or dire happenings. *Hikime* is the name of the extremely large bulbous arrowhead used in these ceremonies. It is also the Japanese word for a toad, which these arrowheads are considered to resemble. Unlike the shrill pitch of the *kaburaya*, the *hikime* produces a deeper note, which has a haunting, flute-like quality to it. It drives bad spirits away.

TOP LEFT Sachio Kamagata of the Ogasawara-ryū holding the *jindo-hikime* that was used for the ceremony to open the Redwood Kyudojo in California. This is the first time that an Ogasawara *hikime* ceremony has been performed outside Japan. (Kim Hawkins)

LEFT Kiyomoto Ogasawara shooting a *hikime* arrow at the ceremony to inaugurate the Redwood Kyudojo, California in 2016. In attendance are: Kiyomoto Ogasawara (master), Sunaguchi Yoshinori (*kaizoe* – master's assistant), Tim Macmillan (*kaizoe* – sword-holder) and Paul Murphy (*kaizoe* – bow-holder). A net was set up in front of the target area to catch the blunt *hikime*. The first shot was across the *yamichi* and into this net, purifying the grounds. Next, to purify the structures of the kyūdōjō, kiyomoto-sensei moved to behind the main two-storey building and shot a wonderful arcing *hikime* arrow over the roof, its soft, ethereal note seeming to hang in the air long after it had faded in the distance. (Kim Hawkins) for incendiary arrows included saltpetre, ash and sulphur (Cummins & Minami: 108). I suspect that the 'ash' referred to here is a mistranslation for charred wood (ie charcoal). If so, then this is the recipe for gunpowder. An alternative recipe included the addition of camphor, presumably the resin from the camphor tree. For the 'night-attack celestial incendiary arrow', the following was required: saltpetre, sulphur, borneol (a type of herb), old sake spirits and a decoction of moxa (derived from mugwort). Strangest of all was the recipe for the 'Tengu goblin incendiary arrow', which called for the addition of mouse-droppings to the usual gunpowder mix (Cummins & Minami: 108). Notwithstanding the curiosity of the mouse-droppings, similarities between these recipes and those for incendiary arrows in Europe are striking. Both cultures use resin, saltpetre, sulphur, charcoal and alcohol (brandy in Europe, sake in Japan).

Dōsha

Men who staked their lives and, more importantly, their reputations on their skill with the bow in battle spent many hours practising at targets. It had always been so. Their quest was not only for accuracy but also for distance and endurance. These attributes were the focus of a particular type of competition that evolved in the early 17th century. *Dōsha* (hall shooting) is a classification of sport archery that derived from the great shooting contests at Sanjūsangendō temple. These competitions necessitated the shooting of military strength bows with the objectives of distance, endurance and rate of shooting. Similar contests were also held in Edo, first in the Asakusa district and subsequently, after a fire destroyed the hall in 1698, under the eaves of the Tomioka Hachiman shrine. Other popular venues for distance shooting were in the Aozuka district of Kyoto, near the Gion shrine in Yosaka and one in Kiyomizudera. Some had longer ranges than others but the première event was at Sanjūsangendō.

SANJŪSANGENDŌ

In an effort to keep the samurai tradition of strong archery alive, an annual shooting challenge was established in 1606. It was called the *toshiya* (passing arrows) competition, also known as the *dosha*. It took place on the boardwalk veranda of the Buddhist temple of Sanjūsangendō in Kyoto. Archers shot from a kneeling position in order to mitigate the difficulty of reaching a target at a distance of 131yd, despite the obstacle of a low overhanging roof. Clearly bows of considerable power were required in order to maintain a sufficiently low trajectory. However, simply hitting the target was not the essence of the challenge – it was to be able to do so repeatedly over a sustained period.

The inspiration for the contest was a samurai by the name of Asaoka Heibei, who was famed for shooting 51 arrows in rapid succession, each hitting the target. Over time, the *toshiya* evolved into four events. In the *hiyakui* (100 shots), each competitor shot 100 arrows and the winner was the one with the most hits. Similarly, the *seni* (1,000 shots) was competed for in the same way, with each archer shooting 1,000 arrows. Endurance as well as accuracy was central to the spirit of *toshiya*. In the *hiyakazu* (number of arrows in a day) contest, which was for boys who had not yet celebrated their coming of age, shooting was relentless for 12 hours. According to a sign at the shrine, at the event in 1774, a 13-year-old shot 11,715 arrows, with nearly all hitting the target. Men who competed in the *ōyakazu* (great many arrows) event required even greater endurance. They had to shoot as many arrows as possible over a 24-hour period. In 1686, Wasa Daihachirō set the record by shooting 13,053 arrows, of which 8,133 hit the target. There is a story that at one point he rested and an onlooker rebuked him for his pause. Then seeing that his bow-hand was swollen, the onlooker cut it to relieve the pressure. Daihachirō was able to resume his efforts, apparently with even greater accuracy. The onlooker, so the story goes, was none other than Hoshino Kanzaemon, the previous record holder (Sinclaire 2001: 125). The *toshiya* was discontinued in 1861. However, a derivative exhibition shoot, under the name Ōmato Taiki (Festival of the Great Target) continues to be held at the shrine on the second Sunday in January. It attracts around 2,000 archers and large crowds of onlookers. Preceded by a sacred Buddhist ceremony, lines of archers (both male and female) take turns on the shooting line. The veranda is no longer used but instead acts as a backdrop, while archers shoot at conventional targets ranged at 66yd.

TOP LEFT The archery competition at Sanjūsangendō temple from a woodblock print of the early 18th century. The open-sided veranda made this an ideal venue for spectators and, as this print shows, it was a festive occasion, with Kyoto society turning out to witness these impressive feats of archery. Note the conspicuous girth of the bows. (Library of Congress)

ABOVE Detail of a wooden roof beam at Sanjūsangendō temple in Kyoto. It was removed during restoration work in 2007. The porcupine of arrowshafts embedded into the beam is an indication of the challenge faced over the centuries by archers struggling to find the right trajectory to reach the distant target beneath the low roof. (Andy king50/Wikimedia Commons/CC BY-SA 2.5)

LEFT Court ladies, or courtesans, amusing themselves with an indoor archery game. They are shooting tiny bows, much shorter than a *hankyū* and very short blunt arrows. Presumably they are aiming at either knock-down targets or bells or gongs. Arrows from similar sets traded as antiques have a quarter-inch wrapping of fish-skin around the nocks, offering a secure grip for the pinch grip. (Image courtesy of Arthur Credland)

A JAPANESE ARCHERY HOUSE IN JEDDO.

An archery house in Jeddo from an 1882 edition of the *Graphic* (a British weekly illustrated newspaper). Here geishas are entertaining a foreigner. Although such diversions might seem frivolous to a military man, they speak to the enduring legacy of archery in the Japanese imagination. (Image courtesy of Arthur Credland)

Decline

As the centuries of peace passed and the bow was no longer required in warfare, there was an inevitable decline in the number of people who could shoot to the old military standards. Nevertheless, the importance of archery to Japanese society was ingrained and the reverence for the bow remained, as did a myriad of ceremonial rituals. Alongside this was an increase in 'archery games' enjoyed at all levels of society. During the latter years of the Edo period, indoor archery became an increasingly popular pastime. It was conducted in the environs of temples and shrines and it was also run commercially in the amusement areas of large towns, often in the red-light districts where it went hand-in-hand with other recreations. Notwithstanding these associations, archery games were also enjoyed in refined court circles and in the houses of wealthy *daimyō*s. It is for indoor archery that a much shorter version of the *yumi* was developed – the *hankyū*.

Currently popular with the older generation in Japan, *shihan mato* is an indoor shooting game that uses the *hankyū* (half-length *yumi*) together with exceptionally long arrows. Competitors shoot sitting on their heels. The *hankyū* may be more manageable for the frail in these circumstances, but it is not essential in order to shoot with this posture – that can be achieved with a full-sized *yumi*. It is because it is a bow of low power, which suits it to indoor recreational use. Such bows had no serious military application.

IMPACT: THE STING OF THE SAMURAI
Range

Recalling an attack by a Chinese army on the building foundations of Ulsan Castle in 1597, the *Zōhyō Monogatari* gave the following words to the young commander Yoshimi Taizo, who commanded his *ashigaru* to 'draw the enemy near and shoot in such a way that the arrows are not ineffective' (quoted in Turnbull 2005: 131). In an earlier passage it stated that:

> When the enemy are a distance away it is important not to shoot arrows from the quiver. The *ko gashira* [lieutenant of archers] who is in command will take charge of the matter and will take charge of the shooting of arrows when the enemy are closer. The decision about the effective shooting distance is a difficult one to make. (Quoted in Turnbull 2005: 130)

The issue of effective range for archery is one that has been discussed in the longbow, composite bow and crossbow chapters of this book. It is fundamental to understanding the impact of battlefield archery and it is a question that is grossly distorted by the arcing arrowstorms of popular culture. In all previous instances, I have argued that long range shooting, though at times possible, has the potential to waste arrow supplies and be less effective than the hard hit of close range shots. These same precepts seem to be given equal weight by the author of the *Zōhyō Monogatari*.

GREAT FEATS

Perhaps the greatest recorded archery feat of all time is attributed to Nasu no Yoichi, a warrior and renowned archer in the service of the Minamoto clan. During the battle of Yashima in 1185 a Taira warship sailed into sight, bearing a red-lacquered fan at the top of its mast. Minamoto no Yoshitsune, the Minamoto commander, who was standing by the shore, summoned Yoichi and ordered him to shoot down the fan.

The *Heike Monogatari* provides considerable detail about the young man. He was only 20 years old and he wore an armour laced with light green silk cords over a deep blue battle robe, edged with red and gold brocade. The arrow that he used was a turnip-headed arrow, carved from stag horn, and the shaft was fletched with hawk's wing feathers. Nasu no Yoichi:

> mounted a fine black horse with a lacquered, shell inlaid saddle and a tasselled crupper. Holding his bow firmly, he gripped the reins and rode towards the sea … The fan was too far off to take a shot from the beach, so he rode about one tan further into the water … The target still seemed very distant … As the boat rolled and pitched, the fan atop the pole flapped in the wind … The Heike [Taira] had ranged their ships in a long line to watch the spectacle. On land the Genji [Minamoto] lined up their horses neck to neck in anticipation. (Quoted in Hurst 1998: 113)

Yoichi prayed to the gods that he would hit his mark, vowing, if he missed, to break his bow and to kill himself. After these devotions, the wind subsided and he took his shot.

> Small man though he was, his arrow measured twelve hand breadths and three fingers, and his bow was strong. The whirring sound of the arrow reverberated as it flew straight

A 19th century woodblock print of Nasu no Yoichi riding into the waves to shoot at the fan hoisted on the mast of one of the Taira ships during the battle of Yashima (1185). He not only had to deal with his proud steed plunging in the turbulent surf and to shoot at a great distance, he also had to hit a very small target that was constantly and erratically moving. (Denman Waldo Ross Collection, Boston Museum of Fine Arts)

to its mark. It struck the fan close to the rivet. The arrow fell into the sea but the fan flew up into the air. It fluttered and dipped in the spring winds and then suddenly dropped into the water. When the red fan, gleaming in the rays of the setting sun, bobbed up and down on the white crests of the waves, the Heike offshore praised Yoichi by beating on the gunwales of their boats, and the Genji on the shore applauded him by rattling their quivers. (Quoted in Hurst 1998: 113)

In the *Taiheiki* (a late 14th-century chronicle), Ogasawara Magoroku, who was defending against a surprise attack on his stronghold, opened the shutters on a window and with an arrow fitted to his string called down a challenge to the attackers. Then he shot:

with a singing sound the arrow flew away that measured twelve hands and the breadth of three fingers. Its arrowhead hit square in the middle of the foremost rider's helmet and drove through clearly to the first neck plate, so that he fell headlong from his horse. (Quoted in Hurst 1998: 120)

Both the shooting of a distant fan and such spectacular penetration of armour would suggest bows of immense draw-weight, not to mention that both stories extol the fact that their heroes shot especially long arrows – meaning perhaps that they had an especially long draw. It was a common theme.

Minamoto no Tametomo (1139–1170) 'surpassed other men in ability, his spirit was intrepid to the end, and he was a powerful drawer of a strong bow, a virtuoso at fitting and shooting arrows fast … and the length of his draw was the best in the world' (Hurst 1998: 112). Tametomo was renowned for his size and strength and it took five men to string his bow (Sinclaire 2001: 121). The feats achieved with this 5-man bow were the stuff of legend. During the Hōgen War (1156) he allegedly shot two men clean through with a single arrow (Sinclaire 2001: 121). Upon his subsequent capture, the Taira severed the sinew on his bow-arm before exiling him to the island of Oshima. Sixteen years later, he had rebuilt his strength and as a squadron of Taira ships approached the shore of his island, Tametomo sank one of them by holing it with an arrow below the waterline. Rather than be captured again, he committed suicide. Unfortunately, the consensus amongst modern scholars is that the tale is a fiction, though Tametomo was a real person, famed as a great archer, and it is probable he shot a powerful bow. The point of the legend's reiteration here is that irrespective of whether or not the story is correct in every detail, the idea that an arrow could drive through the planking of a ship presumably had plausibility. What is more difficult to determine is the draw-weight of bows in general use.

DRAW-WEIGHTS

In Japan, the measure of a bow's strength was recorded by stating the number of men required to string it; thus Tametomo in the story above had a 5-man bow. Different cultures had different means of representing the power of the bow (see page 211) and it is impossible to translate these ideas precisely into a draw-weight measured in pounds that we would understand today. In practice, a man who could shoot a particular bow was in all probability able to string it on his own, but his bow was considered to be five times stronger than the average. Hypothetically, I propose that the average draw-weight of a '1-man bow' was 40lb. That is what reasonably strong people without sustained training for powerful bows can manage. Most Yabusame riders today shoot bows in the 25lb–30lb range. With a 40lb baseline, then the spectrum of Japanese 'man-strength' bows from 2 to 5 fits well with what we see in other warrior archer cultures. A 2-man bow would be 80lb, at the respectable lower end for a war bow, and a 5-man bow, like that of Tametomo, would be 200lb. We know that this is at the upper limit, which only a very rare individual can manage. We also know that such individuals do exist. Joe Gibbs of the English War Bow Society shoots a 200lb longbow.

It may have been possible for a 200lb bow to send an arrow that would punch through a ship's timbers and to sink it. Many of the landing-craft type ships used at the time were relatively lightly built. We know for certain that elite archers can manage bows of that draw-weight. The story of Tametomo sinking a ship may or may not be true, but it is certainly not absurd.

Clearly the draw-weight of a bow has an effect on its 'impact'. However, it is a mistake to think extremely heavy bows are always desirable, especially for the horse-archer, who has the ability to ride relatively close to his target. It is also a far greater challenge to shoot a heavy bow from the saddle than it is on foot. Other factors must also be taken into consideration, such as the extent to which being 'over-bowed' compromises an archer's shooting form or fatigues him in battle. There has always been bravado about shooting big bows, but there is a story in the *Heike Monogatari* about Minamoto no Yoshitsune that is most revealing. At the battle of Yashima (1185) he was fighting on horseback in the shallows when his bow was torn from his grasp by a grappling hook. Yoshitsune plunged beneath the surf to search for it. His retainers were appalled, thinking that no bow, no mere artifact, could be worth his life. Yoshitsune explained:

A 19th century drawing of Minamoto no Tametomo, an archer of legendary strength. The standard metric for draw-weight was expressed in the notional number of men required to string a particular bow. Tametomo had a 5-man bow, possibly equivalent to 200lb. (Wikimedia Commons/Public Domain)

It was not because I begrudged the loss of the bow. If it were one that took two or three men to bend, a bow like that of my uncle Tametomo, then I would gladly let it fall into the hands of the enemy. But if a weak one like mine were taken by them, they would laugh at it and say, 'Is this the bow of Yoshitsune, the commander-in-chief of the Genji?' That would be unbearable. I had to recover it even at the risk of my life. (Quoted in Hurst 1998: 115)

Yoshitsune's confession that he shot a weak bow is telling. At this period, honourable samurai fought on horseback and with the bow, shooting at other honourable samurai. It would have been possible for Yoshitsune to have acquitted himself honourably with a 1-man strength bow, a 40lb bow. Such a bow was perfectly capable of shooting accurately at ranges of 40yd and more. Longer ranges are unlikely to have been employed by the horse-archer. A 40lb bow had the potential to fell a horse, and at the very least to land arrow-strikes on an enemy. If that enemy wore armour, then the hits would be unlikely to have mortal consequences, but a man armed with a 40lb bow could be seen to be fighting honourably in the traditional manner. He could display skill and valour in front of his peers. Of course Yoshitsune's bow may well have been more than 40lb, perhaps a useful 50lb or even 60lb; it just didn't qualify as a 2-man bow.

FIGHTING PORCUPINES

Musashibo Benkei (1155–89) was a giant of a man, renowned for his strength, who achieved lasting fame for the manner of his death amidst a storm of arrows. Benkei, a warrior monk (*sōhei*), was the steadfastly loyal retainer of Minamoto no Yoshitsune. In 1189 he fought a heroic last stand at the battle of Koromogawa. His master, sensing defeat, had withdrawn into the stronghold. Benkei stood guard at the bridge. In time, as facts migrated into legend, the story was told that Benkei killed more than 300 enemy soldiers who crossed the bridge to fight him. Too afraid to face him in close combat, the remainder of the enemy strategized to kill him with archery. When the battle was over they observed that Benkei was still standing. The great giant, riddled with arrows and dripping with blood, stood there stock-still and defiant. It was only after a horseman struck him as he galloped by that Benkei finally fell. According to the story, he was already dead but had remained on his feet and at his post. This heroic incident is referred to in Japanese folklore as 'The Standing Death of Benkei' (Turnbull 2016: 93). Although the tale has undoubtedly been exaggerated, the image of the warrior being able to withstand multiple arrow wounds before succumbing to death is a common theme in Japanese history.

The *Azuma Kagami* (a 13th-century chronicle) gives the following account of an incident during the Shōkyū War (1221):

Their court warrior made a stand, raining arrows on the Easterners from behind their shields … As Hatano Goro Yoshishige stepped out he was hit in the right eye. His senses reeled but he was able to shoot an answering arrow. (Quoted in Turnbull 1998: 122)

Here is a story that reminds us of the importance of the shield in archery warfare. It also highlights two recurring themes in both the art and literature of samurai warfare – the idea that a warrior could, and should, fight on after being struck by an arrow, and the concept that he should shoot 'an answering arrow'. It is a common image in the art of the period to see a great number of arrows just penetrating armour by their tips but hanging harmlessly, perhaps struck by shafts from no more than a 1-man bow.

An even grittier tale, or rather series of tales, concerning a samurai's apparent immunity to the effects of an arrow strike appeared first in a report of the siege of Kanezawa Castle (1086–89). It concerned the heroism of Kamakura Kagemasa. The account was recorded in the *Hōgen Monogatari* (*The Tale of the Hōgen*), written around 1320 but describing events from the Hōgen rebellion in 1156. Two of Kagemasa's descendants, announcing their ancestral pedigree to the enemy, as was the custom, recalled Kagemasa's legendary fighting spirit:

> Kamakura Gongoro Kagemasa, at the age of sixteen, charged in the van of the battle, and while he had his left eye shot out and stuck to the first neck plate of his helmet by Toriumi Saburo, he took that enemy with his answering arrow. We are his descendents, Oba Heita Kageyoshi and his brother Saburo Kagechika. (Quoted in Turnbull 2006: 51)

Following this feat, a fellow samurai attempted to extract the arrow. In order to steady the victim's head while he pulled, he stepped on Kagemasa's face. Kagemasa reacted angrily to such a violation of a samurai's honour and sprang to his feet, attacking his would-be saviour with his sword. Passions abated and the arrowhead was removed (Turnbull 2006: 50).

A century after the original action and some 30 years after its telling by the brothers, another descendent of Kagemasa, one Kajiwara Kagetoki, retold the tale – with some embellishment! Whilst boasting his ancestral provenance prior to the battle of Ichinotani (1184), he reported the incident as follows:

> I am Kajiwara Heizō Kagetoki, who is descended in the fifth generation from Kamakura Gongoro Kagemasa, a renowned eastern warrior who was a match for ten thousand other men. When he was sixteen he rode in the vanguard of Hachimantarō Yoshiie at the siege of Kanazawa in Dewa. He received an arrow in his left eye through his helmet, but pulled it out and with it killed the archer who loosed it. (Quoted in Turnbull 2006: 51)

The garnish that he avenged himself with the same arrow that shot him challenges credulity, and the evident exaggeration in these tales inclines us to dismiss all such claims. However, beneath the hyperbole, it would seem that there might be a grain of truth to the general idea that arrows, even those that had penetrated armour, were not necessarily fatal or even entirely debilitating to an enraged and courageous samurai.

Horses were perhaps less resilient. After his declaration during the Hōgen rebellion, Kageyoshi was struck in the thigh by an arrow. It went right through and penetrated his horse sufficiently deeply that it brought the animal down. (Turnbull 2006: 51). If such a story is true, then it speaks

Detail from a copy of the picture scroll from the Gosannen War, depicting Kamakura Kagemasa receiving an arrow in the eye. Note that the original, by Hidanokami Korehisa, was painted in 1347, roughly 260 years after the incident. Whilst the written accounts describe the arrow entering the left eye, it is represented here in his right eye. The artist has portrayed the shaft penetrating at an angle and to a depth suggesting that it has passed through the side of the eye-socket and embedded in the helmet. That it is possible to survive such a gruesome injury is evidenced by the well-documented account of the successful surgery undertaken by John Bradmore to extract an arrowhead from the eye of Prince Henry (later Henry V), an injury he sustained at the battle of Shrewsbury (1403). (Japan Archive/Stephen Turnbull)

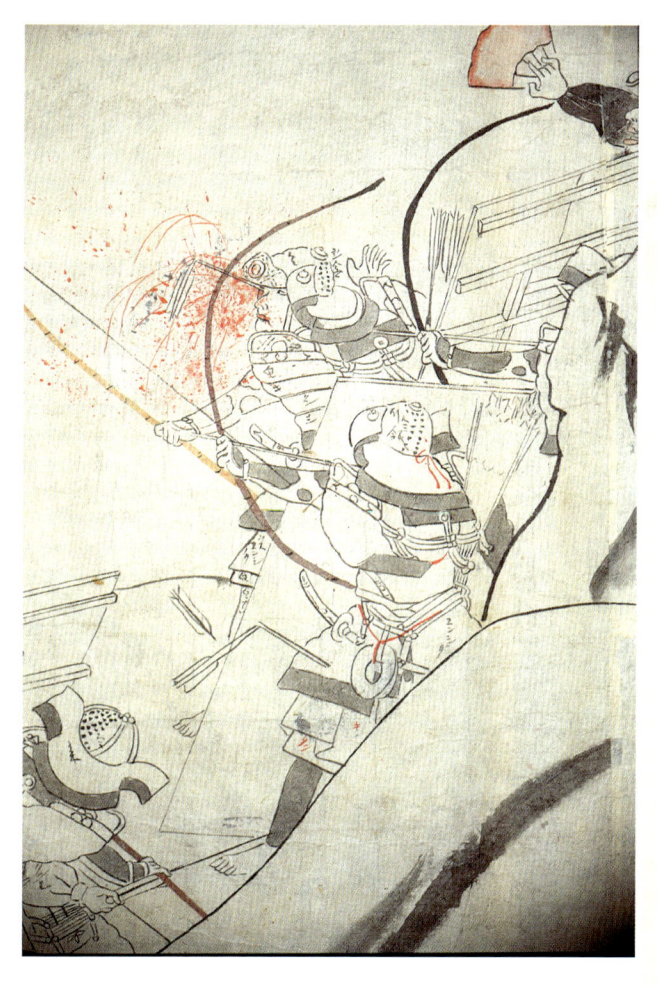

to bows of tremendous power. Weaving a path between the two stories, we may consider a difference between close-range, direct shots from a powerful bow and either distance shots or ricochet arrows from medium-strength bows. With a multitude of arrows raining in all directions on a turbulent battlefield, many may be struck by deflected shafts. It is otherwise difficult to reconcile arrow strikes that can drop a horse with the images in art of samurai having multiple arrows sticking out of their armour. At the battle of Ichinotani (1184), Kumagai Naozane's horse was shot from under him. Rising to his feet, he pulled several other arrows from his armour. Then he drew his sword and set about fighting on foot (Turnbull 2016: 71). This tale exemplifies the common theme of the pin-cushioned samurai, who seemingly has numerous shafts sticking out of his armour but who has received relatively little harm.

Armour

I am not aware of any thorough, empirical testing of authentically constructed Japanese armour against war arrows shot from military strength bows. From the anecdotal evidence of the tales, it would appear that samurai armour was reasonably effective against arrow strikes. This is what might be expected, since the whole point of armour is that it is reasonable proof against the weapons of the day. As with European armour, it will fail on occasion but it must generally have been good at its job. Certainly that is the circumstantial evidence from art and the chronicles.

Woodblock print by Utagawa Kuniyoshi (1798–1861). It depicts Ishikawa Sadatomo at the battle of Shizugatake (1531). His blade is chipped, he has lost his helmet and he has been pierced by seven arrows. These have pinioned him in the leg, the side and the back. Some have penetrated his armour to a significant depth. Although bleeding and mortally wounded, he fights on. In this and numerous other similar prints, it is common to see warriors pierced with multiple arrows whilst still fighting courageously. (Kim Hawkins)

Samurai armour, like all armour, was developing constantly and there are many different styles. It is a complex subject, which there is not space to consider fully here. However, it is essential to have some understanding of the armour that battlefield archery was up against. What follows is a generalized overview of just some of the key elements. It is of necessity incomplete, but hopefully it suggests the extraordinary ingenuity of design that prior to the Edo period was predominantly required to defend against arrows.

Ō YOROI

The iconic samurai armour, worn from the Heian period to the end of the Muromachi period, is known as the *ō yoroi*, which means 'great armour'. It was designed both to defend against arrows and to offer the necessary range of motion to the horse-archer. An outwardly similar armour remained in use during the Edo period, though it had to adapt to the arrival of firearms, which was done by introducing a heavier, solid plate cuirass.

Prior to that, the cuirass or *dō* was of lamellar construction, made from overlapping plates of iron, lacquered against the climate and laced together. Despite its many variations, the *dō* changed little in essence. It was a springy, box-like cage that offered good protection to the vital organs within the chest and belly, combining elements of a glancing surface with enough rigidity to give separation from the body within and enough flexibility to yield when struck and so absorb the energy of a hit.

Worn beneath the *dō* was a shirt called a *shitagi*. This was often augmented with a short jacket called a *wakibiki*, made of either mail or brigandine construction sewn within a fabric covering. The *wakibiki* could be worn either beneath the *dō* or over it. It protected the shoulders, shoulder-blades and pectorals, extending from high on the neck to no lower than the sternum. When mounted, the stomach receives a certain amount of additional protection from the front of the saddle and also from the horse's neck. When fighting on foot, a longer mail-lined jacket called a *manchira* could be worn. These items of secondary armour are very important to note. When arrows are seen protruding from armour, it does not follow automatically that they have reached the body within.

A 19th-century depiction of a 14th-century samurai. He wears colourful *ō yoroi* armour. His feet are fully in his stirrups, unlike in the *tachisukashi* style of riding used for *yabusame*. The extremely broad and long neck-guard (*shikoro*) of his *kabuto* helmet offers good protection to his neck from arrows that may be shot from the side or behind. Horse-archers by their very nature ride up to the enemy and then turn away to regroup, so defences to the back are especially important. Note how the *kari-ebira* quiver spreads a fan of arrows in layers across his back. This would be very effective in slowing arrows before they struck the metal of the cuirass. Perhaps most conspicuous of all are the great *sode* that hang from his shoulders. These flexible plates cover a great deal of his torso and would be useful arrow-stoppers before the main armour was even threatened. Similarly, a skirt of *kusazuri* plates, which hang from a belt, give protection to the hips and thighs. (Library of Congress)

BELOW RIGHT A faithful painting of the famous 12th-century Japanese National Treasure *aka-ito-odoshi dō-maru-gusoku* (red-laced *dō-maru* style armour) housed in the Oyamatsumi shrine in Ehime Prefecture, Japan. This armour is said to have been worn by none other than Minamoto no Yoshitsune. It shows the armour style when battlefield archery, especially horse archery, was at its zenith and is conspicuous for the amount of coverage given by suspended plates. These hanging panels offered significant protection against arrows. Although faded, the detachable, painted leather covering for the breastplate is evident. It is called the *tsurubashiri-gawa* (the bowstring running leather) and its principal function was to ensure that the bowstring did not catch on the lacing of the *dō* beneath. A secondary function was that it gave yet another layer of resistance to an arrow strike. To penetrate the *dō* an arrow must pass through this outer leather, then through a matrix of cords of tightly braided silk or leather, inside and out, then through the overlapping iron plates and finally through a leather lining before finally pricking the undershirt. (Image courtesy of Trevor Absolon, samurai armour author and authenticator)

FAR RIGHT A copy of a *kabuto* from around 1300. The domed skull is reinforced with gilded strips that have been secured with large dome-headed rivets. Note the width of the neck guard (*shikoro*), necessitating a wide anchor-point for the archer. This flare of the *shikoro* also creates significant distance between the thickly laced overlapping plates and the neck. Even if an arrow pierced it, it has the space to slow significantly before reaching the mail-reinforced, high-necked under-jacket. The elaborate horned crest (*kuwagata dai*) is in the form of an *oni* (ogre or demon) head with glass eyes. (© Royal Armouries)

The *dō* was at the heart of a Japanese set of armour, but it was surrounded by an ingenious curtain of hanging defences. These had movement and absorbed the shock of arrowstrikes in the same way that archery backstop netting, by yielding on impact, slows an arrow. Large shoulder plates called *ōsode* and a girdle of multiple panels called the *kusazuri* were assembled using scales made from either rawhide or iron, sometimes with alternating layers of each. Whether of metal or rawhide, each lame was lacquered. There was always a trade-off between the greater protection offered by iron, which was also more expensive, and the lighter weight of rawhide. The entire assembly of a great armour, sometimes numbering over 2,000 individual pieces, was laced together with colourful cords, made from either braided silk or from doeskin. These cords, which passed both behind and over the surface of the armour plates, could be arranged in a variety of patterns and colour combinations. In the original publication of *The Longbow* in 2013, I concentrated solely on the longbow's use by English armies and by English navies, for it is in their service that it made its most conspicuous impact. Moreover, a greater focus was been given to its use in the campaigns of Edward III (r. 1327–77). I consider this to be the longbow's apotheosis and a source of many good examples of its versatility. However, in this extended volume I have been able to examine it a little in a broader context and acknowledge its wider use in other armies. They also acted as a first bastion of defence. Lacing can be cut, lacing can be pierced – relatively easily – but in so doing energy is absorbed and severing just one or two laces had little effect on the integrity of the overall armour. Most importantly, the lacing system created a highly flexible defence, one that not only gave freedom of movement to the warrior but also one that moved, twisted, bounced and otherwise absorbed energy when arrows hit.

A further consequence of complex lacing was that arrows inevitably became snagged in the mesh. This might explain so many accounts and images of samurai pin-cushioned with numerous shafts. In many ways, having multiple arrows sticking into one's armour must have become a badge of honour, indicating that one had been in the thick of the fighting. There was nonetheless blood. Arrows did get through on occasion, and the protections for the arms and legs were less thorough than for the head and torso. The *kote* (sleeves) were made of fabric, often a silk brocade, which incorporated various combinations of quilting, mail and small plates. Shin-guards, called *suneate*, were made of plate. However, priority was given to leaving arms and legs relatively unencumbered so that the samurai could ride his horse and shoot his

ABOVE LEFT A pile of *nerigawa kozane* (rawhide scales) of the type used in the construction of some Japanese armour. They have been cut from a larger sheet of very thick rawhide, punched with holes and filed smooth. Before they can be laced into an armour assembly, they have to be protected from the wet climate with lacquer. (Courtesy of Robert Soanes © Katchushi Armour Studio)

ABOVE RIGHT An Edo-period *mempo* (face mask). *Me-no-shita-men* is the generic name for all manner of face mask designs. They were intended to give some protection to the face but mostly to be psychologically intimidating. They were made variously of lacquered iron or leather. Real hair was often used for moustaches or beards. Worn over a silk scarf called a *fukusa*, they could be hot and stuffy. Face coverings like this didn't start to develop until the latter part of the 15th century. They sit close to the face and are of relatively thin gauge. It is doubtful that they offered any significant protection against arrows. They are, nevertheless, splendid. (© Royal Armouries)

bow with élan. Arrows that breached the curtain defences of the *ōsode* and *kusazuri* might draw blood, but wounds to the arms and legs were seldom mortal.

The iron helmet (*kabuto*) was domed and robust, giving good protection against downward sword-cuts and all but the most powerfully shot arrows. Most distinctively, it had a broad, flared neck-guard called a *shikoro*. When this had a long tail, as some styles did, not only the back and the sides of the neck were protected, but also a portion of the upper back. It was made from multiple lames of either iron or rawhide and held together with lacing. Most vulnerable of all to archery was the face. Many tales recount facial injuries. To defend against this, some samurai wore a form of anthropomorphic visor called variously a *mempo* or a *mengu*. This could be beaten out of metal but was usually of lacquered leather. A *mempo* incorporated the nose and extended to under the chin. Other variations gave greater or lesser coverage. All had visages of great ferocity and were adorned with whiskers made from real hair.

Although the *kabuto* was a well-made and well-designed piece of armour, there were instances of it being penetrated. During an attack on the monks of Fujishima in 1338, an arrow struck and felled Nitta Yoshisada's horse. Pinned beneath his fallen steed, Yoshisada was a sitting duck and a second arrow penetrated his *kabuto* and entered his forehead. According to legend Yoshisada survived the wound, but feeling disgraced he drew his sword and managed to decapitate himself. Of equal interest to the account of an arrow penetrating a helmet is the reference to his horse being shot. In all archery warfare, horses, which present large, soft targets, constitute the highest casualty rates. The *Zōhyō Monogatari* advises 'when the enemy advance in a dense mass, divide up into right and left sections and shoot. In the case of a mounted enemy shoot at the horses' (quoted in Turnbull 2005: 130).

ASHIGARU ARMOUR

During the Warring States period, enormous quantities of armour had to be procured for the ever-growing armies of *ashigaru*. Much was scavenged from the fallen on the battlefield, and there was also tremendous mass production of munition-grade cuirasses and helmets. Less expensive armour, called a *tatami gusoku* (folding armour),

THE *HORO*

The *horo* was a type of cape made from densely woven silk that attached to a samurai's back. It ballooned behind him when galloping on a horse and acted as a first defence against arrows. *Horos* were worn by the *tsukai-ban*, a rank of elite samurai that were the equivalent to aides-de-camp. Since their duties often involved them acting as messengers, these were samurai who might have to cross enemy lines and so be caught up in a chase. The *horo* was also worn by some elite cavalry squads. In 1568 Oda Nobunaga established two units of Horse Guards (*o uma mawari–shū*). These were handpicked samurai known as the 'Black Horo Guards' and the 'Red Horo Guards'. His successor, Toyotomi Hideyoshi, increased the numbers of these units, having 'Yellow Horo Guards', 'Red Horo Guards' and 'Great Horo Guards', the latter wearing extra large *horos* of nearly 5 feet in diameter (Turnbull 2008: 13).

In later centuries, when the *horo* was used solely for ceremonial parade and as an identifier of the *tsukai-ban* rank, it was laid over a wickerwork frame. This gave the illusion of it billowing, even when the rider was at a standstill. Of course, with the fabric taut over the frame, it would not have been able to serve its original protective function. The *horo*'s ability to slow incoming arrows depended on the cloth being loose.

For a television documentary some years ago, the author tested the effectiveness of a *horo*. One was set up in front of a wind machine with sufficient power to make it billow. A small target of ballistic gel was placed between the *horo* and the wind machine. The author then shot at the *horo* several times with a 65lb *yumi*, using sharp points. In most cases, upon striking the *horo*, the arrow collapsed the 'balloon' but, having exhausted most of its energy by this action, it was repelled as the *horo* instantly billowed out. The machine provided constant wind energy, as would be generated by a galloping horse. Mostly, arrows with a bodkin-style point were repelled entirely, punched out as if they had bounced on a trampoline. Those that did puncture the *horo* were snagged by twisting silk enveloping them and quickly lost energy before lightly hitting the target behind. Ensnared in the silk, they then dropped and hung limply. A sharp broad-headed arrow had more success; it cut through the silk. However, by the time it reached the ballistic gel behind, it barely made a mark. Overall the *horo* achieved an approximately 70 per cent success rate, either rebuffing shots entirely or slowing them to strike with inconsequential impact. Note that the *horo* was only an additional first line of defence. The real security came from the armour worn beneath it. By way of further investigation, the author wore a *horo* and, with his horse's rump well protected by a thick caparison, was shot at with rubber blunts. Both the author and his assailant (Andrew Bodley) were mounted and both horses ran exceedingly fast. The way the *horo* behaved in this exercise was of note. It fluttered erratically, its central *mon* dancing wildly in all directions. An archer needs a point of aim and this constantly changing mark made the work of the pursuer significantly harder. Even so, numerous hits were landed and, as might be expected with blunt-head arrows, the *horo* repelled every one.

Evidently only those of high-status were entitled to wear the *horo*. George Cameron Stone, in the encyclopaedic glossary of arms that he compiled in 1934, reported, reassuringly, that 'when you are killed on the battlefield the enemy will understand, as they recognize the *horo*, that the dead was not a common person, and so your corpse will be well-treated' (Stone 1961: 300). However, this comforting thought is soon chased away, as he goes on to say, 'when you have killed an enemy who wears the *horo*, wrap his head which you cut off in a piece of his *horo*' (Stone 1961: 300).

THE *HORO* (OPPOSITE)

In this scene from the latter part of the Sengoku period, a messenger of the Takeda clan carrying their distinctive centipede design on his *sashimono* banner and wearing a *horo*, is pursued by samurai of the rival Uesugi. The fleeing messenger may appear to be at the end of his luck, but the intriguing arrow-stopping properties (as tested by the author) of the billowing silk *horo* offer him a chance of survival. The fluttering fabric means the Takeda *mon* in the centre of the *horo* will shift constantly, confusing the eye of those taking aim, while the ballooning and the give of the silk fabric serve to deplete the arrows of energy before they can pass through to strike the rider's armour.

THE JAPANESE YUMI

was constructed from small plates fixed to a shirt of mail. It was doubtless less effective as a defence against arrows than was the *ō yoroi*, but the *ashigaru* fought on foot and usually had the additional protection of large wooden shields.

CONCLUSION

The gradual switch to massed infantry '*ashigaru* warfare' after *c.* 1350 and the subsequent introduction of the arquebus in 1543 changed the Japanese battlefield beyond recognition. Nevertheless, the bow was held in such high esteem that it did not become obsolete; its role was reduced and adapted, but it remained a relevant military arm. During the halcyon days of the horse-archer, when the bow was the signature weapon of the elite, it is most probable that they shot bows of military weight comparable to those of other cultures, that is to say within a range of 60–120lb for the cavalry archer and up to 200lb for a man on the ground. However, it is worth reminding ourselves that at the height of the *yumi*'s supremacy on the battlefield, it was of a significantly simpler construction than that used today. From the 9th to the 14th centuries, the samurai used the basic *fusetake* and *sanmaeuchi* forms. These were not quite as efficient at delivering energy as the later forms, which had more sophisticated lamination assemblies. Similarly, the *ashigaru* mostly used a more basic form of the *yumi*. Moreover, the *ashigaru* may not have developed the ability to shoot very heavy bows in the same way as an elite 12th-century samurai, who had trained to do so since childhood. In summary, this means that we cannot talk about the military effectiveness of the *yumi* as if it were a single weapon, used in only one way by troops of equivalent skill and strength. Despite the similarity in profile over the centuries, *yumi*s manifested in a number of different forms and were used by several different classes of warrior, as well as for sporting, hunting and ceremonial. In all cases, the *yumi* has bequeathed a rich and enduring legacy.

In this illustration from the *Zōhyō Monogatari*, a wounded *ashigaru* is about to receive field surgery to remove the arrow from his eye. It is a further indication both of the prevalence of facial wounds from arrows and also of the optimism that they can be survived. The method of extraction is self-evidently basic and would have required considerable Stoicism to endure. (Japan Archive/Stephen Turnbull)

EPILOGUE

There is an old adage that books are never finished; one simply stops writing. Moreover the limitations of space mean that only so much can be included in any one volume. At the outset I had entertained the notion that, as well as expanding the catalogue of composite bows, I would be able to include something on early wooden longbows, together with a few comments on various native bows from Africa and the Americas. I should have liked to have written about Viking archery, about the composite bows of the Franks and about the palm-wood bows of Central and South America that tormented the Conquistadors, with their 5-feet-long arrows – the overhang allowed them to thread the front of the arrow through jungle undergrowth or branches for a concealed shot. Regrettably such aspirations had to be set aside as more and more information about the subjects under primary consideration vied for attention. Mostly though, I had intended to frame the bows under discussion in the wider context of their pre-historic origins.

Archaeology continues to unearth fresh evidence and the investigation of early bows remains both ongoing and fascinating. In 2012 three bows constructed of yew wood were discovered at La Draga in Banyoles, Spain. They have been dated to around 5,400 BC. In 1990 a magnificent yew longbow was found at 'Rotten Bottom' in the Moffat Hills in Scotland. It dates to 5,200 BC. A year later the yew longbow of 'Ötzi the Iceman' was revealed in the Alps, dating to around 3,200 BC. These joined previous discoveries, the Meare Heath Bow, made of yew, from Somerset in England (2,690 BC) and, oldest of all, the Holmegaard bows, made of elm, from Denmark (c. 7,000 BC), as superb examples of Neolithic bows. Although all were primarily hunting bows, rock art indicates that such bows were also used in battle. In recent years there have been yet newer finds as the glacial ice melts in the high mountains of Norway. In Oppland, bows and arrows in extraordinary condition, dating to between 4,000 and 1,500 BC, have been released from the glacial deep-freezer. Of course the joy we have in seeing such exquisite ancient objects revealed in such pristine glory is tempered by the sadness of knowing why the ice is lifting the veil on her secrets – they are poignant gifts from a dying planet.

Cave painting from Morella la Vella, Spain. It depicts archers in battle and dates to around 6,000 BC. (Locutus Borg/Wikimedia Commons/Public Domain)

Man's relationship with the bow is an ancient one. In 2010, stone arrowheads were excavated from a sediment layer in the Sibudu Cave in South Africa. They are calculated to be 64,000 years old. Mankind has been using the technology of bows and arrows for at least that long. Together with the sling and the atlatl, the bow enabled mankind to exceed the reach of his biology – to strike further than he could throw. It was pivotal to his development. In historical terms, it has been the merest blink of an eye since we stopped using bows as mainstream weapons. They are in our DNA. Those who still shoot bows know their magic; it is a spell and a power that endures.

ACKNOWLEDGEMENTS

THE LONGBOW

My thanks to my good friends Dr Tobias Capwell and Gordon Summers, who read some portions of the draft text and gave invaluable feedback. I owe an age-old debt of gratitude to Robert Hardy, whose groundbreaking work on the subject in his 1972 BBC documentary 'The History of the Longbow' started me on what has become a lifelong interest. His subsequent writings on the subject have been an inspiration, as have the scholarly writings of so many others, whose researches I have drawn on for this book. I am grateful also to Dr Alan Williams for his guidance in setting up the deceleration tests in 2003. I am equally grateful to Dr Matthew Pain, who organized the blunt-trauma impact tests in 2011. I am indebted to Ian Coote, Joe Gibbs, Mark Stretton and Gary Symonds, members of the English War Bow Society, who have allowed me to photograph them shooting their great warbows, who have participated in archery experiments for some of my television projects and who have been very generous with their time in answering my questions. My gratitude also extends to Mick Manns, fletcher, and Hector Cole, arrowsmith, who have both shared their extensive knowledge with me. The bowyer Chris Boyton has been a constant source of information over many years. I thank him for that and for the two longbows that he made for me. They delight me every time I shoot them. Thank you also to the numerous people and institutions who have provided me with photographs: their names are credited alongside the images. Mostly, however, I wish to thank all those many friends with whom I have spent countless pleasurable hours 'bow in hand' and who share with me a passion for this ancient weapon – I have learned much from you all. However, the opinions expressed in this work are entirely my own and not necessarily the views of those who have been kind enough to give me their time and advice in its preparation.

THE COMPOSITE BOW

I owe an old debt of gratitude to Edward McEwen, who first introduced me to the enchantment of composite bows. A scholar and a maker of fine bows, Ted was also a practising horse-archer long before it became the phenomenon it is today. He has been an inspiration. As the long-serving editor of the *Journal of the Society of Archer-Antiquaries* he promoted the academic study of everything pertaining to archery, but in particular to that of the composite bow.

Of equal inspiration and assistance has been Lukas Novotny, a composite bowyer and horse-archer of distinction. I thank him for allowing me to spend time at his workshop, photographing him building bows, for the magnificent bows he has made for me and for everything he has taught me about horse-archery and the composite bow in general. He is always very generous with his knowledge.

Robert Molineaux belongs to a new generation of archer-antiquary scholars and is also a fine maker of composite bows. I am deeply indebted to him for creating the line drawings that populate the typology in the composite bow chapter and also for his erudite input.

Justin Ma and Peter Dekker, eminent scholars in the field, deserve special mention. They have been unstinting in sharing their encyclopaedic knowledge and in reading sections of the text. Thanks are also due to Stephen Selby, Adam Karpowicz, Wendy Hodgkinson, David Joseph Wright, Gökmen Altinkulp, Cemal Hünal, Jaap Koppedrayer, Han Zhang and Annette Bächstädt who have all helped in various ways.

My sincere thanks also go to Nathalie Guion and Hilary Merrill at the Sonoma Coastal EquesTraining Center, who welcomed me warmly when I proposed the idea of a horse-archery club – the California Centaurs.

THE CROSSBOW

For this chapter, I owe a particular debt of gratitude to my friend David Joseph Wright, who not only provided me with many splendid line drawings to illustrate the text but was also a constant sounding-board throughout the writing process. Leo Todeschini of Tod's Stuff and Andreas Bichler have also made singular contributions. Both of these gentlemen have provided me with wonderful photographs of the magnificent replicas that they have made and also shared with me their deep knowledge of the subject in patient correspondence. Similarly, I have plundered the brains of a long list of friends, much brighter than I. Among them are Tobias Capwell, John Waller, Lukas Novotny, Chris Boyton, Hector Cole MBE, Ralph Moffat, Alan Williams, Mark Hatch, Peter Dekker, Justin Ma and Stephen Selby. I thank them all. Relatively little literature on the crossbow exists in English. It has been studied more widely in Europe. Of particular note is Holger Richter's *Die Hornbogenarmbrust* (Ludwigshafen, 2017), which although not quoted from directly in this work, has been a source of much inspiration.

THE JAPANESE *YUMI*

Firstly I must extend my profound gratitude to Kiyomoto Ogasawara of the Ogasawara-ryū for his generous assistance in supplying photographs. Similarly my thanks are owed to the esteemed *yumi*-maker Keitarō Yokoyama, who also provided me with splendid images. Both were also kind enough to answer some of my questions. I owe an immeasurable debt to Tim Macmillan, who not only aided me with correspondence to Japan and with some photographs of his own but who has shared so much of his passion for and knowledge of Japanese archery. I received singular assistance from Jaap Koppedrayer, a Dutchman who lives in Georgia USA and makes the most excellent *yumi*s. He was extraordinarily generous with his time and knowledge, giving me much advice and providing me with many images. Many thanks also to Earl Hartman for his kindness in contacting the Satsuma Heki-ryū and the latter for their generous contribution of photographs. Advice, assistance and images were also forthcoming from Maria Peterson, Andrew Bodley, Paul Martin, Trevor Absolon and Stephen Turnbull. My thanks to them all and of course my deepest gratitude goes to my wife, not only for her superb photography throughout this book but also for her patient and unflagging support.

BIBLIOGRAPHY

THE LONGBOW
Primary sources

CCR Ed II = 'Close Rolls, Edward II: May 1323', *Calendar of Close Rolls, Edward II: Vol. 3: 1318–1323* (1895), 711–13.

CCR Ed III 1363 = 'Close Rolls, Edward III: June 1363', *Calendar of Close Rolls, Edward III: Vol. 11: 1360–1364* (1909), 528–37.

CCR Ed III 1369 = 'Close Rolls, Edward III: October 1369', *Calendar of Close Rolls, Edward III: Vol. 13: 1369–1374* (1911), 109–14.

Cecil = 'Cecil Papers: 1562–1597', *Calendar of the Cecil Papers in Hatfield House, Vol. 23: Addenda, 1562–1605* (1973), 1–10.

CSPCA = 'America and West Indies: Addenda 1582', *Calendar of State Papers Colonial, America and West Indies, Vol. 9: 1675–1676 and Addenda 1574–1674* (1893), 9–17.

CSPDEA = 'Addenda, Queen Elizabeth – Volume 14: September 1569', *Calendar of State Papers Domestic: Elizabeth, Addenda, 1566–79* (1871), 81–84.

Decretals = 'Decretals of Gregory IX with gloss of Bernard of Parma', Royal MS 10 E IV, *c.* 1300– *c.* 1340, British Library.

GC = 'Gregory's Chronicle: 1368–1402', *The Historical Collections of a Citizen of London in the Fifteenth Century* (1876), 88–103.

LCCW = *London Consistory Court Wills 1492–1547: London Record Society 3* (1967).

LPFD = 'Henry VIII: May 1542, 1–10', *Letters and Papers, Foreign and Domestic, Henry VIII, Vol. 17: 1542* (1900), 168–86.

Memorials = 'Memorials: 1371', *Memorials of London and London Life: In the 13th, 14th and 15th Centuries* (1868), 347–61.

PRME = 'Henry V: October 1416', *Parliament Rolls of Medieval England*.

Published works

Anonymous, trans. K. Crossley-Holland (1973). *Beowulf.* London: The Folio Society.

Anonymous, trans. G.W. Kramer & Klaus Leibnitz (2001). 'The Firework Book: Gunpowder in Medieval Germany', *The Journal of the Arms & Armour Society* 17.1 (March 2001), 1–88.

Ascham, Roger (1968). *Toxophilus: The Schole, Or Partitions, of Shooting*. Wakefield: S. R. Publishers Ltd. Originally published in 1545.

Ayton, Andrew & Preston, Sir Philip (2005). *The Battle of Crécy, 1346*. Woodbridge: The Boydell Press.

Barber, Richard (1997). *Life and Campaigns of the Black Prince*. Woodbridge: The Boydell Press.

Barker, Juliet (2005). *Agincourt*. London: Little, Brown.

Bartlett, Clive (1995). *English Longbowman 1330–1515*. London: Osprey Publishing.

Blair, Claude (1972). *Medieval Armour*. London: B. T. Batsford Ltd.

Bradbury, Jim (1985). *The Medieval Archer*. Woodbridge: The Boydell Press.

Bradbury, Jim (1992). *The Medieval Siege*. Woodbridge: The Boydell Press.

Breiding, Dirk (2000). 'Horse Armor in Europe', *Heilbrunn Timeline of Art History*, the Metropolitan Museum of Art at http://www.metmuseum.org/toah/hd/hors/hd_hors.htm> (accessed 14 November 2012).

Cambrensis, Giraldus (1894). *The Historical Works of Giraldus Cambrensis – The Itinerary through Wales* (trans. Sir Richard Hoare). London: George Bell & Sons.

Chaucer, Geoffrey (1981). *The Canterbury Tales*. New York, NY: Bantam Dell.

Cole, Hubert (1976). *The Black Prince*. London: Purnell Book Services Ltd.

Cummins, John (2003). *The Art of Medieval Hunting: the Hound and the Hawk*. Edison, NJ: Castle Books.

Curry, Anne (2009). *The Battle of Agincourt: Sources and Interpretations*. Woodbridge: The Boydell Press.

DeVries, Kelly (1992). *Medieval Military Technology*. Toronto: University of Toronto Press.

Dyer, Christopher (1998). *Standards of Living in the Later Middle Ages*. Cambridge: Cambridge University Press.

Edge, David & Paddock, John (1988). *Arms and Armour of the Medieval Knight*. London: Guild Publishing.

Fiorato, V., Boylston, A. & Knusel, C., eds (2000). *Blood Red Roses*. Oxford: Oxbow Books.

Franklin, Benjamin, ed. Jared Sparks (1882). *The Works of Benjamin Franklin, vol. VIII*. London: Benjamin Franklin Sievens.

Froissart, Jean, trans. Lord Berners, ed. G. C. Macaulay (1904). *The Chronicles of Froissart*. London: Macmillan & Co.

Gairdner, James, ed. (1986). *The Paston Letters (Vol. 2)*. Stroud: Alan Sutton.

Hardy, Robert (1992). *Longbow: A Social and Military History*. Sparkford: Patrick Stephens Ltd.

Heath, E. G. (1971). *The Grey Goose Wing*. London: Osprey Publishing.

Hildred, Alexzandra (2011). *Weapons of Warre: The Armaments of the Mary Rose*. Portsmouth: The Mary Rose Trust.

Keen, Maurice, ed. (1999). *Medieval Warfare*. Oxford: Oxford University Press.

Konstam, Angus (2011). *The Great Expedition – Sir Francis Drake on the Spanish Main 1585–86*. Oxford: Osprey Publishing.

Latimer, Hugh (1832). *Latimer's Sermons*. Library of the Old English Prose Writers, Vol. VII. Boston, MA: Hilliard, Gray.

Mason, R. O. (1970). *Pro Aris et Focis*. London: Tabard Press (originally published 1798).

Megson, Barbara (1993). *Such Goodly Company*. London: The Worshipful Company of Bowyers.

Nadolski, Andrzej & Lewandowski, Marcin (1990). *Broń strzelcza, Uzbrojenie w Polsce średniowiecznej 1350-1450*. Łódź.

Nicolle, David (2000). *Crécy 1346*. Oxford: Osprey Publishing.

Nicolle, David (2011). *The Great Chevauchée – John of Gaunt's Raid on France 1373*. Oxford: Osprey Publishing.

Nuttall, Zelia, ed. (1914). *New Light on Drake: A Collection of Documents Relating to his Voyage of Circumnavigation 1577–1580*. London: The Hakluyt Society.

Parks, George R. (1954). *The English Traveler to Italy*. Rome: Edizione di Storia e Letteratura.

Paterson, W. F. (1990). *A Guide to the Crossbow*. London: Society of Archer-Antiquaries.

Payne-Gallwey, Sir Ralph (1981). *The Crossbow*. London: Holland Press.

Pickering, Danby, ed. (1762). *The Statutes at Large: From the First Year of K. Hen. V to the 22d Year of King Edw. IV. Inclusive, Vol. II*. Cambridge: Joseph Bentham.

Powicke, Michael (1962). *Military Obligation in Medieval England*. Oxford: Oxford University Press.

Riesch, Holger (1995). 'Archery in Renaissance Germany', *Journal of The Society of Archer-Antiquaries*, Vol. 38.

Richardson, Thom & Beabey, Mark (1997). 'Hardened Leather Armour', *Royal Armouries Yearbook 2*, 46–52.

Rogers, Clifford (2000). *War Cruel and Sharp: English Strategy under Edward III, 1327–1360*. Woodbridge: The Boydell Press.

Rogers, Clifford (2010). *The Wars of Edward III: Sources and Interpretations*. Woodbridge: The Boydell Press.

Rule, Margaret (1982). *The Mary Rose: The Excavation and Raising of Henry VIII's Flagship*. London: Conway Maritime Publishing.

Seward, Desmond (1999). *The Hundred Years War: The English in France 1337–1453*. Harmondsworth: Penguin Books.

Smythe, Sir John (1964). *Certain Discourses Military*. Washington, DC: Folger Shakespeare Library (originally published 1590).

Soar, Hugh (2009). *The Crooked Stick: A History of the Longbow*. Yardley, PA: Westholme.

Soar, Hugh, Gibbs, Joseph, Jury, Christopher & Stretton, Mark (2010). *Secrets of the English War Bow*. Yardley, PA: Westholme.

Strickland, Matthew & Hardy, Robert (2005). *The Great Warbow*. Stroud: Sutton Publishing.

Vale, Malcolm (2016). *Henry V, The Conscience of a King*. New Haven: Yale University Press.

Wadge, Richard (2009). *Arrowstorm*. Stroud: The History Press.

Waller, Jonathan & Waller, John (2010). 'The Personal Carriage of Arrows from Hastings to the Mary Rose', *Royal Armouries Journal*, Vol. 7 No. 2, 155–177.

Walsh, Margaret & Williamson, Allen (2006). 'Royal Financial Records Concerning Payments for Twenty-Seven Contingents in the Portion of Joan of Arc's Army Which Arrived at Orléans on 4 May 1429'. Historical Academy for Joan of Arc Studies.

Williams, Alan (2003). *The Knight and the Blast Furnace*. Leiden: Brill.

Television shows

Weapons That Made Britain – Longbow (2004). Lion Television for Channel 4, UK.

Going Medieval (2012). Lion Television for H2 Channel, USA.

THE COMPOSITE BOW

Barnes, Jonathan, ed. (1995). *The Complete Works of Aristotle Volume Two.* Princeton University Press.

CSPF = 'Elizabeth: July 1582, 21–25', in Calendar of State Papers Foreign, Elizabeth, Vol. 16, May–December 1582, ed. Arthur John Butler: 170–88. http://www.british-history.ac.uk/cal-state-papers/foreign/vol16/pp170-188 (accessed 2 May 2015).

Dekker, Peter (2012). 'A Practical Guide to Manchu Military Archery', in *Journal of Chinese Martial Studies*, 2012, Issue 6: 80–173.

Dennis, George, trans. & ed. (1985). *Three Byzantine Military Treatises.* Cambridge, MA: Harvard UP.

Dennis, George, trans. & ed. (2010). *The Taktika of Leo VI.* Cambridge, MA: Harvard UP.

Elliott, Mark (2001). *The Manchu Way.* Redwood City, CA: Stanford UP.

Elmy, D. (1969). 'Steel Bows in India', in *Journal of The Society of Archer-Antiquaries*, Vol. 12.

Faris, N.A. & Elmer, R.P. (1945). *Arab Archery.* Princeton, NJ: Princeton UP.

Heath, E.G. (1971). *The Grey Goose Wing.* London: Osprey Publishing.

Herodotus, trans. A.D. Godley (2013). *Complete Works.* Hastings: Delphi Classics.

Jankovich, Miklos (1971). *They Rode Into Europe.* London: Harrap.

Khorasani, Dr Manouchehr Moshtagh (2013). *Persian Archery and Swordsmanship.* Frankfurt-am-Main: Niloufar Books.

Klopsteg, Paul (1987). *Turkish Archery and the Composite Bow.* Manchester: Simon Archery Foundation, The Manchester Museum.

Komnene, Anna, trans. E.R.A. Sewter (2009). *The Alexiad.* Harmondsworth: Penguin.

Koppedrayer, Kay (2002). *Kay's Thumbring Book.* Ontario: Blue Vase Press.

Latham, J.D. & Paterson, W.F. (1970). *Saracen Archery.* London: The Holland Press.

Liao Wanzhen, trans. Stephen Selby (1999). 'Whistling arrows and arrows whistles'. Asian Traditional Archery Research Network. http://www.atarn.org/chinese/whistle/whistle.htm (accessed 12 September 2015).

Marcellinus, Ammianus, trans. W. Hamilton (1986). *The Later Roman Empire.* Harmondsworth: Penguin.

Morse, Edward Sylvester (1885). *Ancient and Modern Methods of Arrow Release.* Nabu Public Domain Reprint from Bulletin of the Essex Institute, Vol. Xvii. Oct–Dec 1885.

Nicolle, David (1994). *Saracen Faris.* London: Osprey Publishing.

Nicolle, David (2001). 'A Mamluk Training Manual', in *Osprey Military Journal*, 2001, Issue 3/5: 42–49.

Nicolle, David (2002). *A Companion to Medieval Arms and Armour.* Woodbridge: The Boydell Press.

Öztopçu, Kurtuluş, trans. (1986). *A 14th Century Mamluk-Kipchak Military Treatise: Münyetü'l-Ġuzāt.* http://www.scribd.com/doc/114356754/Munyatu-l-Guzat#scribd (accessed 21 August 2015).

Pant, G.N. (1978). *Indian Archery.* Delhi: Agam Kal Prakashan.

Paterson, W.F. (1984). *Encyclopaedia of Archery.* London: Robert Hale Ltd.

Pritchard, J.B. (1969). *Ancient Near Eastern Texts Relating to the Old Testament.* Princeton, NJ: Princeton UP.

Pritchard, J.B. (2011). *The Ancient Near East – An Anthology of Texts and Pictures.* Princeton, NJ: Princeton UP.

Procopius, trans. H.B. Dewing (2007). *History of the Wars: The Persian War.* New York, NY: Cosimo.

Ray, Purnima, trans. (2014). *Vasistha's Dhanurveda Samhita.* Yokohama: JP Publishing House.

Selby, Stephen (2000). *Chinese Archery.* Hong Kong. Hong Kong University Press.

Selby, Stephen & Karpowicz, Adam (2010). 'Scythian Bow from Xinjang', in *Journal of the Society of Archer Antiquaries*, Vol. 53: 94–102.

Smail, R.C. (1995). *Crusading Warfare 1097–1193.* Cambridge: Cambridge University Press.

Stone, George Cameron (1961). *A Glossary of the Construction, Decoration, and Use of Arms and Armor in All Countries and in All Times.* New York, NY: Jack Brussel. Reprint of 1934 edition.

Tian, Jie & Ma, Justin (2015). *The Way of Archery: A 1637 Chinese Military Training Manual.* Atglen, PA: Schiffer Publishing.

Thompson, Maurice (1878). *The Witchery of Archery.* New York, NY: Charles Scribner's Sons.

Turnbull, Stephen (2003). *Mongol Warrior 1200–1350.* Oxford: Osprey Publishing.

Verbruggen, J.F. (1997). *The Art of Warfare in Western Europe during the Middle Ages.* Woodbridge: The Boydell Press.

Williams, Derek (1998). *Romans and Barbarians.* New York: St. Martin's Press.

THE CROSSBOW

Primary sources

Cal Pat = *Calendar of Patent Rolls, Edward III, 1345–1348*.

CCR Ed I 1277 = 'Close Rolls, Edward I: March 1277', in *Calendar of Close Rolls, Edward I: Vol. 1, 1272–1279*, ed. H.C. Maxwell Lyte (1900), 373–75.

CCR Ed I 1278 = 'Close Rolls, Edward I: January 1278', in *Calendar of Close Rolls, Edward I: Vol. 1, 1272–1279*, ed. H.C. Maxwell Lyte (1900), 435–40.

CCR Ed I 1284 = 'Close Rolls, Edward I: December 1284', in *Calendar of Close Rolls, Edward I: Vol. 2, 1279–1288*, ed. H.C. Maxwell Lyte (1902), 307–09.

CCR Ed I 1288 = 'Close Rolls, Edward I: April 1288', in *Calendar of Close Rolls, Edward I: Vol. 2, 1279–1288*, ed. H.C. Maxwell Lyte (1902), 502–04.

CCR Ed I 1293 = 'Close Rolls, Edward I: October 1293', in *Calendar of Close Rolls, Edward I: Vol. 3, 1288–1296*, ed. H.C. Maxwell Lyte (1904), 303–05.

CCR Ed II = 'Close Rolls, Edward II: August 1326', in *Calendar of Close Rolls, Edward II: Vol. 4, 1323–1327*, ed. H.C. Maxwell Lyte (1898), 638–43.

CCR Ed III = 'Close Rolls, Edward III: September 1328', in *Calendar of Close Rolls, Edward III: Vol. 1, 1327–1330*, ed. H.C. Maxwell Lyte (1896), 413–14.

CCR Rich II = 'Close Rolls, Richard II: July 1390', in *Calendar of Close Rolls, Richard II: Vol. 4, 1389–1392*, ed. H.C. Maxwell Lyte (1922), 274–83.

CSPD Eliz I = *Calendar of State Papers Domestic: Elizabeth, 1581–1590*, ed. Robert Lemon (1865), 520–29.

LPB = 'London Port Book, 1567–8: Nos 500–599 (May–June 1568)', in *The Port and Trade of Early Elizabethan London: Documents*, ed. Brian Dietz (1972), 79–97.

LPFD Hen VIII 3 = *Letters and Papers, Foreign and Domestic, Henry VIII, Vol. 3, 1519–1523*, ed. J.S. Brewer (1867), 345–55.

LPFD Hen VIII 14 = *Letters and Papers, Foreign and Domestic, Henry VIII, Vol. 14 Part 1, January–July 1539*, ed. James Gairdner & R.H. Brodie (1894), 330–48.

LPFD Hen VIII 18 = *Letters and Papers, Foreign and Domestic, Henry VIII, Vol. 18 Part 1, January–July 1543*, ed. James Gairdner & R.H. Brodie (1901), 114–34.

THCN = *An Essay Towards A Topographical History of the County of Norfolk, Vol. 6* (1807).

Published sources

Alm, Joseph, trans. H. Bartlett Wells, ed. G.M. Wilson (1994). *European Crossbows: A Survey*. London: The Royal Armouries.

Andrade, Tonio (2016). *The Gunpowder Age*. Princeton, NJ: Princeton University Press.

Bell, Adrian R., Curry, Anne, King, Andy & Simpkin, David (2013). *The Soldier in Later Medieval England*. Oxford: Oxford University Press.

Blackmore, Howard L. (1971). *Hunting Weapons*. London: Barrie & Jenkins.

Bradbury, Jim (1985). *The Medieval Archer*. Woodbridge: The Boydell Press.

Bradbury, Jim (1992). *The Medieval Siege*. Woodbridge: The Boydell Press.

Breiding, Dirk H. (2013). *A Deadly Art*. New York, NY: The Metropolitan Museum of Art.

Caius, Johannes (2005). *Of Englishe Dogges*. Alcester: Vintage Dog Books. First published in 1576.

Carpenter, D.A. (1996). *The Reign of Henry III*. London: The Hambledon Press.

Crombie, Laura (2016). *Archery and Crossbow Guilds in Medieval Flanders*. Woodbridge: The Boydell Press.

ffoulkes, Charles (1912). *The Armourer and his Craft*. London. Methuen.

Hyland, Anne (1993). *Training the Roman Cavalry*. London: Grange Books.

Komnene, Anna, trans. E.R.A. Sewter (2009). *The Alexiad*. Harmondsworth: Penguin.

Latham, J.D. & Paterson, W.F. (1970). *Saracen Archery*. London: The Holland Press.

Liebel, Jean, trans. Juliet Vale (1998). *Springalds and Great Crossbows*. Leeds: The Royal Armouries.

Paterson, W.F. (1990). *A Guide to the Crossbow*. London: Society of Archer-Antiquaries.

Payne-Gallwey, Sir Ralph (1981). *The Crossbow*. London: The Holland Press. Reprint of the 1903 edition.

Pizan, Christine de, trans. Sumner Willard (1999). *The Book of Deeds of Arms and of Chivalry*. University Park, PA: Penn State University Press.

Powicke, F.M. (1960). *The Loss of Normandy 1189–1204*. Manchester: Manchester University Press.

Powicke, Michael (1962). *Military Obligation in Medieval England*. Oxford: Oxford University Press.

Richardson, Thom (2016). *The Tower Armoury in the Fourteenth Century*. Leeds: The Royal Armouries.

Selby, Stephen (2000). *Chinese Archery*. Hong Kong: Hong Kong University Press.
Selby, Stephen, (2003). *Archery Traditions of Asia*. Hong Kong: Hong Kong Museum of Coastal Defence.
Sensfelder, Jens (2016). *Jahrblatt der Interessengemeinschaft Historische Armbrust*. Norderstedt: Books on Demand.
Smail, R.C. (1995). *Crusading Warfare 1097–1193*. Cambridge: Cambridge University Press.
Smythe, Sir John (1964). *Certain Discourses Military*. Washington, DC: Folger Shakespeare Library. Originally published in 1590.
Storey, Randall (1998). 'The Tower of London and the garderobe armorum', in *Royal Armouries Yearbook 3*. Leeds: The Royal Armouries.
Strickland, Matthew & Hardy, Robert (2005). *The Great Warbow*. Stroud: Sutton Publishing.
Turnbull, Stephen (2001). *Siege Weapons of the Far East (1)*. New Vanguard 43. Oxford: Osprey Publishing.
Tyerman, Christopher (1988). *England and the Crusades*. Chicago, IL: University of Chicago Press.
Wadge, Richard (2007). *Arrowstorm*. Stroud: The History Press.
Wendover, Roger of, trans. J.A. Giles (1849). *Flores Historiarum*. London: H.G. Bohn.
Williams, Alan (2003). *The Knight and the Blast Furnace*. Leiden: Brill.
Wilson, Guy M. (2007). 'What's in a Name? One-Foot and Two-Foot Crossbows', in Robert D. Smith, ed., *ICOMAM 50: Papers on Arms and Military History 1957–2007*. Leeds: ICOMAM: 300–25.

THE JAPANESE *YUMI*

Aston, W.G. (2008). *Nihongi Volume 1: Chronicles of Japan from the Earliest Times to AD 697*. New York: Cosimo Classics. First published in 1896.
Cummins, Antony & Minami, Yoshie (2013). *The Book of the Ninja*. London: Duncan Baird.
Grayson, C.E. (1963). 'Shaho Sambu Sho', *Journal of the Society of Archer-Antiquaries*, Vol. 6.
Guttman, Allen & Thompson, Lee (2001). *Japanese Sports: A History*. Honolulu: University of Hawai'i Press.
Hoff, Feliks (2002). *Kyudo: The Way of the Bow*. Boston, MA: Shambhala Publications.
Hurst, G. Cameron III (1998). *Armed Martial Arts of Japan*. New Haven, CT and London: Yale University Press.
Ikegami, Eiko (1995). *The Taming of the Samurai: Honorific Individualism and the Making of Modern Japan*. Cambridge, MA: Harvard University Press.
Newman, Jesse, C. (2016). *History of Kyudo and Iaido in Early Japan*. Bloomington, IN: AuthorHouse.
Ogasawara, Kiyotada & Ogasawara, Kiyomoto (2014). *About the Ogasawara-ryū*. Kindle Edition, Amazon Digital Services.
Onuma, Hideharu & DeProspero, Dan and Jackie (1993). *Kyudo: The Essence and Practice of Japanese Archery*. Tokyo: Kodansha International.
Sinclaire, Clive (2001). *Samurai: The Weapons and Spirit of the Japanese Warrior*. Guildford, CT: The Lyons Press.
Turnbull, Stephen (1977). *Samurai: A Military History*. Oxford: Osprey Publishing.
Turnbull, Stephen (1998). *The Samurai Sourcebook*. London: Arms and Armour Press.
Turnbull, Stephen, (2001). *Ashigaru*. Oxford: Osprey Publishing.
Turnbull, Stephen (2005). *Warriors of Medieval Japan*. Oxford: Osprey Publishing.
Turnbull, Stephen (2006). *Samurai: The World of the Warrior*. Oxford: Osprey Publishing.
Turnbull, Stephen (2008). *Samurai Armies 1467–1649*. Oxford: Osprey Publishing.
Turnbull, Stephen (2016). *The Gempei War*. Oxford: Osprey Publishing.

INDEX

Note: page locators in bold refer to illustrations, captions and plates.

1448 Statutes of the Armuriers Fourbisseurs d'Angers 154
abrish (arrow) 210

Abu Simbel drawing 191
Accles and Pollock 180
Achaemenid bow, the 164
Acre, siege of 153, 213
Adrianople, siege of 213
adzutsu-ebira (Japanese closed quiver) 253
Agincourt, battle of 18, 23, 27, 44, 63, 74, 80, 82
Agni Purana (poem) 179
aka-ito-odoshi do-maru-gusoku (red-laced *do-maru* style armour) 292
al-Bunduqdari, Baybars 213
al-Mas'udi 232
al-Tarsusi, Murda ibn Ali 101, 111, 206
al-Yūnanī, Taybughā al-Ashrafī al-Baklamishī 104, 130–131, 146, 175, 184, 193, 194, 204, 205, 212–213, 215
Albigensian Crusade, the 138–139
aligning the skeleton 207
Aljubarrota, battle of 62
Alm, Josef 100, 102, 113, 119–120
Altinkulp, Gökmen 195
ambidextrous archery 200, 201
ambler (palfrey), the 51
ambling gait, the 51, 192
Ambroise 126
Amenhotep II, Pharaoh 185–188, 230
American Revolutionary War, the 87
amgakji ('female' thumb ring) 187, 187
angle of strike and armour penetration 82–83, 86
angles of shot from a horse 201, 201, 202–204, 204–205, 264, 268
angular bow, the 163, 163, 164, 185, 185, 191
Annals of Sima Qian (book) 212
Anthony the Great Bastard of Burgundy 145
ap-Gwilym, David 103
Arab Archery (treatise) 174, 181, 187, 201, 205–206, 208, 212, 215, 216
arbalist (crossbowman), the 91
Arblaster, Robert 103
archaeological finds 125, 162, 168, 182–183, 218, 218, 219, 223, 297
  see also Mary Rose (warship) excavation, the
archer in battle, the 80–81, 82, 86
archer in feudal Japan, the 234
archer's paradox 82, 182
archer's stance 46, 74
archer's wristguard 182–183
Archery Manual of Li Chengfen, The (manual) 200
arcuballista (Roman crossbow) 30
arcuballistarii (crossbowmen) 97, 98
Aristophanes 222
Armagnac–Burgundian Civil War, the 74
armaments required to defend against a siege 137–138
armour development 11, 13–19, 15, 16, 17, 18, 19, 23
  see also samurai armour
armour penetration
  by arrows 13, 30–31, 32, 82–86, 85, 226, 228–230, 250, 289, 290, 290, 292, 293, 294–295
  by crossbow bolts 153–155
armour proofing 154
armour weight 13
arquebus, the 61, 66, 76, 275, 296
Arrian 130

arrow bag 47, 48, 647
arrow construction 24–25, 26
arrow-loops and slits 50–53, 51, 53
arrow selection for armour penetration 228–230
arrow selection on the battlefield 31, 32, 231
arrow shafts 215, 223, 250–251
arrow supply 23–26, 46–47, 81–82
arrow types 28, 29, 48, 61, 68, 139–142, 157, 158, 212–213, 228–229, 250, 280–282
arrowhead construction 27–30, 28–29, 30
arrowhead styles 11, 30, 30, 83, 297
  barbed arrowheads 214
  bodkins 15, 18, 25, 28, 29, 31, 31, 32, 38, 48, 85, 214, 228, 251, 252, 294
  broadheads 31, 32, 48, 250, 251, 252
  crescent arrowheads 68, 68, 214
  karimata (forked arrowhead) 252, 259
  lozenge-shaped arrowhead 214
  ornamental arrowheads 251–253, 252
  swallowtail arrowhead 32
  swept-out swallowtail arrowhead 32
  tanged arrowheads 214, 253
  trilobate arrowhead 214, 222
  Westminster Type 16 arrowhead 31, 32, 48
arrowstorm, the 80–81, 82
Ars tactica (manual) 130
Arsuf, battle of 126, 226, 230
Asano Masachika 258
Asaoka Heibei 282
Ascham, Roger 26, 27, 36, 37, 40, 158
ashibumi posture, the 272–274
ashigaru 274–275, 275, 285, 296, 296
ashigaru armour 294–296
Ashikaga Takauji, Shōgun 264
Ashton, Graham 237
Ashurbanipal, King (Assyria) 183, 207
aspen and arrow construction 24, 26
Assize of Arms (1242) 41
Assyrian wall-relief 190, 206
Assyrians, the 158, 163, 182, 183, 185, 185, 190, 191, 201, 206, 207
Aston, W.G. 258
asymmetric bow design 237–238
asymmetric Hun bow, the 167, 167
ATARN (Asian Traditional Archery Research Network) 233
Ateas, King 222
Athens and Scythian archery 221–222
'Auld Alliance', the 70
Ayton, Andrew 42
Azdamur, Viceroy of Tripoli 194
Azuma Kagami (chronicle) 261, 288
azusa-yumi (cherry birch) 238

backstrap tendons 171, 174
bag-type incendiary arrow 28, 29
baldric, the 111, 118, 221
baleen 103, 104, 105, 106, 125, 250
balestrino (small crossbow) 121
ballistae (artillery) 97
bamboo arrows 250
bamboo-strip construction method, the 124, 238–239, 239, 240, 242
Bannockburn, battle of 62, 129
bascinets 18
bash (angled static tip) 159
Basilius, Peter 90
battle dress 41, 43, 43–44, 70, 130, 234–235, 256, 263, 290–293, 291, 292, 293

battle formations 36, **42**, 47, **58**, 60, 84, **126**, **130**, 233, **277**
Baugé, battle of 71
Bayeux Tapestry, the 206, 211, **211**, 216–217
beech and composite crossbows 107
Beever, Jason 218, **218**
Bel, Jean le 58, 59
Bellifortis (book) **145**
belt-and-claw system, the **110**, 111, **111**, 114, **130**, **134–135**, 147
Bening, Simon **143**
Benkei Musashibo 288
Beowulf (poem) 10
Berkhamsted bow, the **103**
Berne Historical Museum 114
Bible, the 200
Bichler, Andreas **89**, **143**, **147**, 150, **151**, **152**
Bin, Sun 124
'bird-striker' curve *(toriuchi)* 249
birun, the **215**
Black Death, the 41
Black Prince, the 41, **42**, 139
Blanchard, Alan 134
blindfold shooting 208
bloomery hearth process, the 16
BLS (British Longbow Society) 10
blunt-force tests 84–86, **85**, 152
blunts 37, 38, **38**, 50, **102**, **145**, **222**, **294**
boarding actions in naval archery 64, **65**, 66–67
boarskin quiver **147**
bolt penetration of armour 150
bolt-shooting rate 112, **119**, 122
bone laths 211
Book of Hours (book) **143**
boomerang shot, the 201
Border Reivers, the 121
Boroughbridge, battle of 62
Bosworth, battle of 61
Bouvier, Gilles le 110
bow-and-pike fighting combination 87
bow care and maintenance 44–46
bow construction 19–22, **21**, 71, **172**, 172–173, **173**
bow-hand carriage 206
bow-hand ring, the 183, **183**
bow selection and tactical impact 231
Boxer Rebellion, the 95
Boyton, Chris **75**, 101
bracing height **164**, **215**
Bradmore, John **289**
'brazing' of arrowheads 30, **30**
breastplates 14, 16, **16**, 130, 149, **292**
  see also plate armour
Breton, William le 126
bridle (cord loop), the 91, **115**
brigandine, the **9**, 15, **17**, **41**, 44
Brussels Guild, the 142
building materials 20–22, **21**
bulbous nocks **215**
Burgundy, house of 73–74, 102
Burrell Collection, Glasgow Museum, 13–14
busha (military archery) 257

Cadzand, battle of **66**
Caenin, siege of 73
cage-type incendiary arrow **28**, **29**
Cambrensis, Giraldus (Gerald of Wales) 20, 78
Canterbury Tales (book) 42
care and maintenance 175–176
Carrhae, battle of 204
catalpa wood 238, **238–239**
cataphracts (heavy armoured cavalry) **202–204**
cave painting, Morella la Vella, Spain **297**
CCR Ed II (Close Rolls of Edward II), the 91
centenaries **42**, **45**
CFPs (custom force plates) 84–85
chariot-archers **185**, 185–190, **188–189**
chariot platform **190**
chariots and the crossbow 122
Charles, Comte de Clermont 63
Charles I, King 33, 87
Charles the Bold 75
Charles V, Emperor 77

Charles VII, King (France) 70, **70**, 71, 72, 73, 74
Chaucer, Geoffrey 42
Checksfield, Nicholas **232**
chess piece of an armoured horse 19, **19**
chevauchée (horseback raid) **48–49**, 48–50, **51**, 54, 81
Chinese archery 226–227, **227**, **228–229**
Chinese composite bow 238
Chinese crossbows **92**, 92–96, **93**, **94**, **95**, **96**, 122–124, **123**, 148–149, **153**
chivalry 90
Chongdou, Cheng 124
Choson Dynasty, the 168
chronicles 20, 44, **45**, 58, 59, 69, 73, 78, 82, 110, 125, 134, 147, 230, 257–258, 286
Chroniques (book) 82
chu ko nu (Chinese repeating crossbow) **94**, 94–96, **95**
cinnabar red 223
city state conflicts in Italy, the 69
close-range fighting 53
closed quiver, the 217
clout (cloth) shooting 38–39
coat-of-plates armour 15–17, **16**, **41**
Cocherel, battle of **62**
codification of Japanese archery practices 245, 257, 261–262
Coeur de Lion, Richard (the Lionheart) **126**
Cole, Hector 30, 109, **146**, 149
Comanche, the 191
Compagnie d'Ordonnance, the 72–73
companies of archers 42
composite bows 10, 101, 104, **105**, 105–107, **107**, 150, 156–176, **161**, **171**, **172**, 184, 190, 193, 211, 212, **213**, 216, 217–219, **218**, **219**, 226, **227**, 233, 237
  and recurve composite bows 159, 161, **211**
composite lath, the **92**, 94, 95, 97, **105**, **106**, 107, 112, **116–117**, 119, **134–135**, **139–141**, **152**, 155, 156–158, **157**
composite materials in medieval armour 15
compulsory bow ownership and the yeoman class 41
conditioning box, the **172**, 175
Constantinople Guild of archers 210–211
Constantinople military tattoo 198
Constantinople *ok meidan* 210
constrictor knots 47, **47**
Coote, Ian **20**, **22**, **52**, 78
copper-fletched quarrels 146
cord-and-pulley system, the 113, **113**, **116–117**
coronel-headed bolts **143**
correlation between power of a bow and rate of shooting 231
cost of arrows, the 26
Coton, Tom 19–20
court ladies **283**
courtepy, the 43–44
coustille (long knife/short sword), the 72
cranequin (rack), the 91, 101, 111, 112, 114–115, **115**, **116–117**, **130**, **138**, 152, 153, 155
Crécy, battle of **9**, 15, **18**, 19, 23, 27, 42, 44, **51**, 54–60, **55**, **56–57**, **62**, 81–82, **82**, 83, 103, **136**
Crimean Tatar bow, the 166, **167**, **227**
criminals in military service 42, 43
crossbow, the 10, 16, 34, 44, 50, 54, 55, 62, 88–116, **89**, **108**, 126–134, **145**, 148–152, 155
  see also European medieval crossbows; Genoese mercenary crossbowmen
crossbow at sea, the 146–147
crossbow bolts **144**, 146, **147**
crossbow fraternities 73, 142–145, **143**
crossbow quiver 146
crossbowmen in France after the battle of Agincourt 129–133
crucible steel 178
Crusades, the 88, 126, **126–127**, 128, **128**, 137, 138–139, 205, 230, 231–232
cuir-bouilli (hard leather) 14, 19
Cyrus the Great 164

daikyū (longer Japanese bow) 249
d'Arc, Jeanne (Joan of Arc) 71, **72**, 139
Das Feuerwerkbuch (book) **28**, **138**
database of medieval soldiery 129–133
David II, King (Scotland) 62

de Beauchamp, William, Earl of Warwick 128, 129
de Clare, Richard (Strongbow) 10–11
de Cordebof, John 129
de Grailly, Sir Jean III **42**
de la Pole, William 1st Duke of Suffolk **51**
de Lannor, Gilbert 22
de Malemort, William and John **148, 149**
De nobilitatibus, sapientiis, et prudentiis regum (manual) **116**
De re militaris (manual) 97
de Snetesham, Thomas 147
de Stanegate, William **147**
Decretals of Gregory IX, the **64**
Deeds of Henry V, The (chronicle) 23
deer-hide glues 240
defences against cavalry 280
deflex bow-limbs 159, **162**, 241
Dekker, Peter **157**
design of the longbow 12
Dhanurveda Samhita (manual) 200, 207, **214**
Diaz, Blasco 137
Die Weisskunig (book) 76, 77
Dijon, defence of 151
Dikshitar, V.R. 180
distance shooting 39–40, 78–79, 209–212, **227**
Dlugosz, Jan 22
dō (samurai cuirass) 290, 292
dogfish skin **107**
dokatu (ceremonial bell) 237
dōsha (hall shooting) contest 282–283, **283**
Douglas, Sir William 71
Drake, Sir Francis 67, 68
Drake/Hawkins West Indies voyage, the 67, 68
draw length 10, 23, 33, 97, 218, 237
draw-weight 158
    of Chinese bows **92, 95**, 226–227, **227**
    of composite bows 159, **163**, 169–170, 179, 194, 195, **207, 213**, 218
    of crossbows **92, 95**, 97, 99, 101–102, 104, 108, **108**, 111, 112, 113, **116–117**, 149, 150, **151**, 152
    of Japanese bows 184, **287**, 287–288
    of medieval European longbows 11, **20**, 22–23, 37, 39–40, **46**, 55, **74**, 85
drawing arrows in battle 47–48, 81, 82
Duplin Moor, battle of 62
Dürer, Albrecht **130**
dysentery ('the bloody flux') 44
Dzungar Khanate, the 168

earth butts 33, **34–35, 36**, 37, **102**
ebira (Japanese quiver) 253
Edo period, the 245, 284, 290
Edward I, King 11, 19, 41, 128, **148, 149**
Edward II, King 41
Edward III, King 11, 19, 20, 26, 27, 33, 34, 36, 37, 41, 42, 43, 48, **51**, 54, 64, 65, 81, 103, **116**, 292
Edward IV, King 20, 33, 43, **63, 75**
Effendi, Mahmud 209
Egyptian–Hittite chariot battle **188–189**
Egyptian scale armour **228**
elevation shooting **52**, 78
Elizabeth I, Queen (England) 39, 46, **145**
Elmer, Dr Robert 179
Elmy, Douglas 179
Encyclopaedia of Archery 158
English archers 11, 36, 40–43, 54–60, **62–63**, 69, 76
equipment selection for certain outcomes 226–227, 231
Erpingham, Sir Thomas 80
escalades 50–52, 53, **53, 66**
estramaçon, the 154
European medieval crossbows **93**, 99–106, **100, 101, 102, 105**, 125–126, 153
    see also crossbow, the
EWBS (English War Bow Society) 13, **20**, 22, **22**, 25, 52
    see also Coote, Ian; Gibbs, Joe; Stretton, Mark; Symonds, Gary

Falkirk, battle of **62**
false string, the 91
Fastolf, Sir John 133
Fechtbuch (manual) **131**
Ferguson, James 72

feudal power in England 40–41
Fey, Godemar du 54
ffoulkes, Charles 146
Fifth Crusade, the 128
Finsbury Fields **34, 39**
fish-glues 174, 240
Flanders and crossbow manufacture 110
fletchings 24–**25, 48**, 78, **144**, 146, **149, 183, 215, 250**
flexible armour 16, 86
flight arrows 209–210, **210**
flight-shooting 39–40, 78–79, 209–212, **227**
Flodden, battle of **63**, 87
Flores historiarum (chronicle) 134
'flu-flu' arrow 10
forecastle, the 63, **66–67**
foreign crossbowmen under the English crown 128
foreshafts **215**, 223, **223**
forest laws 37–38
Forest of Dean, the **148, 149**
forging of arrowheads 30
Formigny, battle of **63**, 73
Francis I, King (France) 134
francs-archers (free archers) 73
Franklin, Benjamin 87
Franks, the 211
fraternities *see* crossbow fraternities; longbow fraternities
Frederick II, Emperor 147
Free Companies of archers 69
French longbow archery 72–73
French royal line tensions 73–74
Froissart, Jean **82**, 83
fukinsei (asymmetry) in the *yumi* 237
'full-proof' armour 16
Furusiyaa Art Foundation Collection, the 177
furusiyya track, the 194–195, 199
fusetake (bamboo construction style) **239**, 296

gaffle (bending lever), the 113–114, **114**
Galloway, Richard **75**
gambeson (aketon), the 15, 44, **232**
Gamboa, Pedro Samiento de 68
Gao, Ying **168**, 175, 184, 205, 206, **207**, 227
Garde Écossaise, the **70**, 70–71
gastraphetes (slider mechanism) 96–97, **97**, 98
gauge of steel and armour proofing 154
Gempei War, the 236, **246–248, 266–267, 278–279**
Genoese mercenary crossbowmen 55, 58, 59, 64, **66–67**, 82, **136**
geometry of a composite bow 159–161, **160**
German archers 75–77
German crossbows 111
Gibbs, Joe **20, 21**, 22, 41, **46**, 54, 78, 84, **227**, 287
Gilbert, Sir Humphrey 68
Gishi Wajin-den (book) 237
glues 161–162, **170, 171, 172**, 174, 230, 240, 241, **244**
Gochin no Tajima 278, **280**
Go-Daigo, Emperor 261
goat's foot lever *see* gaffle (bending lever), the
gohonhigo (bamboo construction style) **239**
Going Medieval (TV programme) 84
golf 71
gorytos, the **217, 218**, 219–220, **220**, 221, **221**
Gosannen War, the **289**
gourd-shooting 193–194, **194, 196, 208**
Grant, Gen Ulysses S. 262, 266
great-crossbow, the **116**, 116–120, **119, 120, 138**, 138–142, **139–141**, 150–151, **151**
great feats 285–290, **286**
Greek crossbows 96–97, **97**
guerrilla warfare by Welsh archers 11
Guin Tushu Jicheng (encyclopaedia) 95
Guinegatte, battle of 73
gunpowder **28**, 155, 212, 282

Halidon Hill, battle of **62**
hamon (band of steel) 251
Han Dynasty, the 93, 148–149, **212**
hankyū (shorter *yumi* half-bow) 249, 284
Hanmer, Anthony 39
Harborne, William 198, 200
Hardrada, Harald 211
Harfleur, siege of 73

haridai (shaping bench) **243**
harrow formation **42**
hasamimono (everyday objects *kasagake* course) 265
hassetsu (stages of shooting an arrow) 272
Hastings, battle of 211
'hat-shooting' mythology and *kasagake* 262–264
Hausbücher (housebooks) **130**
Hawkins, Sir John 66, 68
Hawkwood, Sir John 69, 75–76
Hayashi Riman 250
haze (wax-wood) 239–240, **241**
Heaumers Company of London 154
heavy war bodkin **31**
Heian period, the 124, 248, 255, **281**
Heike Monogatari (manual) 285, 287
Heki Danjō Masatsugu 271
Heki-ryū (school) 271–272, 275
helmets **9, 18, 41, 132, 292**, 293
Heneage, Sir Thomas 46
henon bamboo 240
Henry I, King 90, 133
Henry III, King 41, 128, 137, **148**
Henry IV, King 30, **62**
Henry V, King 26, 44, **62, 102**, 134, 289
Henry VII, King 33, 61
Henry VIII, King 26, 33, 39, 91, 145, 146, 153, 212
'herecon' battle formation (*hérisson* – hedgehog), the 42, **58, 70**
Herodotus **162**, 219
Heron of Alexandria 96, **97**
Herrigal, Eugene 257
Hidanokami Korehisa **289**
hikime (ceremonial whistling arrow) **256, 281**
hilal kuram Turkish bow, the 164, **165**
hinoki (Japanese cedar wood) **260**
'hip curve' *(koshinari)* 249
History of the Northern Peoples (book) 152
Hiuchi, siege of 269
hiyakazu (number of arrows in a day) contest 282
hoardings **53**
hobilars **42, 51**
Hof, Feliks 245
Hōgen War, the 286, 289
Holegaard bows, the 297
Homildon Hill, battle of **62**
Honourable Artillery Company, the 145
Horikawa, Emperor 248
horn blunt **222**
horn-bows 106, 161, **170**
horo (cape) **294**, **295**
horse-archer, the 42, 43, 48, **48–49, 50, 51**, 190–207, **191, 192, 194, 196–197, 202–204**, 211, 217, **220**, 225, 228, 231, 232
 see also samurai horse-archer, the
horse-armour 19, **19**, 59, **188**, 232
horse-whip 222
hosha (Japanese ground archery) 271
hoshi mato (star target) **273**
Hoshino Kanzaemon 283
Howard, Lord Adm Thomas 20
Huang, Qin Shi 122
Hubert, Jean 71
Hun composite bow, the 76, 211, 237
Hundred Years' War (1337–1453) 11, 19, 23, **42**, 44, 53, 54–60, 64, 72, 73
Hungarian closed quiver **216**
hunting crossbows 91, **155**
hwajeon incendiary arrow 212
hyakuban (100-shot *kasagake* course) 265
Hyksos, the **163**, 183

Ibn Shaddād 226, 230
ice-skating Manchu archers **208**
Icelandic horses **51**
Ichinotani, battle of 290
ikki uchi (Japanese ritual mounted single combat) 269
Imjin War, the 96
impact forces **85**, 85–86
in-hand shooting 205–206
incendiary arrows **28–29, 48**, 61, 68, 139–142, 212–213, **228–229**, 280–282
incendiary bolt **138, 139–141**
indentures 43

Indian Archery (book) 176
Indo-Persian bow, the 166, **166**
indoor archery as a pastime 284, **284**
infantry archers 207–208, 211, **220**, 227, **228–229**, 231, 237, 274–277, **275, 276**, 280, 285, 296, **296**
Innocent VI, Pope 119
insect repellents **25**
intelligence messages by crossbow 137
interior castle stonework **51**
interlocking grain 100
inuōmono (dog-shooting) **264**, 264–268
Inuōmono Mokuabumi (treatise) 264
invitational crossbow shooting matches 145
Ishikawa Sadatomo **290**

jack, the 15, 44
Jaffa, siege of 126, **126–127**
Jahan, Shah 177
Jāme al-Hadāyat fi Elm al-Romāyat (treatise) 208
James the Conqueror, King of Aragon 138–139, 153
James VI, King (Scotland) 72
Japan Society, the 253
Japanese hemp and resin strings **244**
Japanese isolation 236
Japanese *kyūdō* archers 184
jarmaki, the **204**, 204–205
Jauderell, Roger **45**
Jauderell, William **45**
jazerant (*kazaghand* – armoured coat) 230, **232**
ji (halberds) 122
ji-samurai 274
Jimmu, Emperor 238, 262
Jinchuan wars, the **228–229**
John, King 128, 134
John the Fearless 74
Journal of the House of Commons, The 33
Journal of the Society of Archer-Antiquaries, The 237
julbah, the 215

kabbadeh (training chain and bow) 180, **180**
kaburaya (turnip-head whistling arrow) **259, 266**, 269, 281
kabuto (helmet) **292**, 293
kabza (grip) **159**
Kagetoki Kajiwara 289
kalkan (shield) 195
Kamagata Sachio **281**
Kamakura Kagemasa 289, **289**
Kamakura Shōgunate, the 261
Kanezawa Castle, siege of 289
Kani, Mustafa 164, **173**, 174, 210
kari-ebira quiver 253–255, **255, 256**, 259, **266–267, 291**
Karpowicz, Adam 162, **163**, 227
kasagake (ancient mounted target shooting) 262, **264, 265**
kasan-gezi (angled join) **159, 165**
kasanbash (angled join) **159, 172**
kasumi mato (targets) **273**
katana (Japanese sword) 236
Kawanakajima, battle of **268**
kenjutsu (the art of the sword) 234
kepade (Turkish bow), the 164
Keys, John **145**
Keyser, Konrad **145**
Khan, Genghis 192
khatrah (follow-through) 184
kin mato (gold target) **273**
King-at-Arms, Berry 73
kisha (Japanese horse-archery) 257–258, **268**
kishagake (gloves) **256**
kishagasa (hat) **263**
Kitab-ı Makbûl der-Hâl-i Huyûl (manual) 195, **196**, 200
Klamath Valley Native American bow **161**
kneeling archers 237, **273**, 275–277, **276**
kokasagake (short range *kasagake* course) 265
Komnene, Anna 88, 102, **102**, 149, 226, 227, 232
Koppedrayer, Jaap **215**, 239–240, 241
Korean bow **157**, 168, **168**
Korean horse-archery 200
Koromogawa, battle of 288
koshiya kumiyumi (battlefield archery) 275, **276**
Krak des Chevaliers (castle) 138
kuji kasagake (by lots *kasagake* course) 265

kulak (leather insert) 187, **187**
Kul'Oba burial mound, Ukraine 218, **218, 219**
Kumagai Naozane **234–235**, 290
kura (saddles) **256, 263**
Kurikara, battle of **266–267**
kusajishi (horse-archery event) 258
kusazuri (armour panels) **291**, 292
kusune (resin-oil mixture) 244
Kyriell, Sir Thomas **63**
kyūba no michi (the way of the bow and the horse) 234, 257
kyūdō (the way of the bow) 236, 245, 248, **256, 260,** 271–274
kyūjutsu (the art of archery) 234, 271

lacquering and binding the *yumi* 245
lacquering of arrow-shafts and quivers 250, **252, 254**
Ladislaus Jagiello, King (Poland) 20, 22
lamellar armour **230**, 278
laminated lath, the 104
lances 69
lances fournies 72, 73
land endowments for crossbowmen 126, 129
Landsknechte, the 76
Langland, William 43
latchet, the **120,** 120–121
lath, the 91, 92, 94, **94, 96,** 104, 107, **108,** 118, 119, **124, 128, 143**
Latimer, Hugh 37
le Areblaster, William 129
le Baker, Geoffrey 14, 59, 64, 147
Le Livre de Chasse (book) 46
leather thumb-tabs 182–183
Lee, Gen Charles 87
leg tendons **171,** 174
length of Japanese *yumi* 248–249
Leo VI, Emperor 232
Liang, Zhuge 94
Liebel, Jean 116, 118, 120, 147, 151
lightweight longbows 10
Lincoln, siege of 134–137
linden and shield construction **136**
livery arrows 78, 85
lock, the 91, 92, 93, **93,** 99
long draw, the 22
long-needle bodkin arrowhead **32**
longbow, the 8–13, 19–24, **20, 21,** 33, 40, **50,** 53, 54, 55–61, 66, 68, **75,** 75–87, 101, **148,** 151, 158, 159, **227,** 292
Longbow, The (book) 11, 292
longbow fraternities 73
looting and plundering 43, **45, 48–49,** 50
Lor, Raymond de 133
Loshult gun, the 58
Louis, VIII, King (France) 134–137
Louis IX, King (France) 128
Louis XI, King (France) 73
Luttrell, Sir Geoffrey 37
Luttrell Psalter, the **36, 37, 37,** 111, **111**

Ma, Justin **207**
Macmillan, Tim **263, 281**
madake bamboo **240**
Maes Moydog, battle of 128–129
Magna Carta, the 128
Magnus, Claus 152
Magyar/Hun bow, the 167, **167,** 174
mail 14–15, **15**
Maling, battle of 124
manchira (mail-lined jacket) 291
Manchu era, the 226
Manchu infantry archers **228–229**
Manchu plum-needle arrow, the 207, **214**
Manchu quiver **216**
Manchu track, the 199–200
Mancini, Dominic 15
Maniwa Nen-ryū, (manual) 280
maple as a building material 170, **170**
Marcellinus, Ammianus 213
Marignano, battle of 134
Marshall, William 128, 137
Martin of Nazareth 126

Martyrdom of Saint Sebastian, The (painting) 113
maruki-yumi, the 238, **238–239**
Mary Rose (warship) excavation, the 12, 20, 22, 26, **28, 48,** 61
Mason, R.O. 87
massed ranks of archers 36, 84
materials used in composite bows 170–174, **171, 172**
materials used in *yumi* 238–240, **239, 240, 241**
Maximilian I, Emperor 76–77, **130**
McEwen, Edward **215**
Meare Heath bow, the 297
medieval hood, the 43–44
medieval knights 11
medieval longbows 10–11, 12
mempo (face mask) 293, **293**
Metropolitan Museum of Art, New York 99, 114, 121, 182
Miao, the 124
Milemete, Walter de **116**
military context of bows, the 6, 11, 13
military manuals 97, **116, 130, 131,** 194, 195, 196, 200, 206, **210,** 217, 232, 285, 287
Minamoto no Tametomo 286–287, **287**
Minamoto no Yoritomo, Shōgun 261, 262
Minamoto no Yoshiari 261
Minamoto no Yoshinaka **248, 266,** 269, **278–279**
Minamoto no Yoshitsune 285, 287–288, **292**
Ming bow, the 168, **169**
Ming Dynasty, the 93, **124,** 168, 186
Miyoshi Kiyotsura 125
Mizushima, battle of **246–248**
modern steel bows 180–181
mogu (Korean hunting-related contest) 200, 266
mokuba (wooden horse) **256, 263**
Moleyns, Robert 10
Mongolian bow, the 168, **168**
Monstrelet, Enguerrand de 44, 60, 80
Montfort, Simon de 138
Morizumi Suwa 261
Morse, Edward **182**
mounted archers *see* horse-archer, the
mounted crossbowmen **130–131,** 133–134
Mughal crab bow 157, **166,** 166
mulberry wood 239–240
multiple-bolt, single-bow siege crossbow **96**
Münyetü'l-Guzat (treatise) 194, **196,** 206, **210**
Murad II, Sultan **194**
Murphy, Paul **281**
museum exhibits 12, 13–14, 19, 91, 99, 108, 114, 121, 150, **152,** 155, 177, 196, **204, 205,** 206
Museum of the Han Dynasty, the **30**
mushamma (waxed linen) **198**

naginata (pole weapon blade) **278,** 280
namisun (regular *yumi* bow) 248
naraca (iron arrow) **213**
Nasu no Yoichi 285–286, **286**
Nationalmuseet, Copenhagen 12
Native American archery 191
naval archery 40, **40,** 61–68, **65, 66–67, 68,** 146–147
Naval Research Advisory Committee report (2007) 13
navek (arrow-guide) **213**
Neade, William 87
Neolithic Period, the 12
nerigawa kozane (rawhide scales) **293**
Neville's Cross, battle of **62**
New Year ceremonial events **281**
nigiri (grip) 245
Nihāyat al-suʾl wa l-umniyya fī taʿlīm aʿmal al-furūsiyya (manual) 217
Nihon Shoki (chronicle) 257–258
Nikephoros II Phokas, Emperor 232
Nikkō Tōshōgū shrine 261, **263**
Nitta Yoshisada 293
nobi (long *yumi* bow) 248
nockless arrow, the **215**
nocks **215, 221,** 241, **244,** 250, 274, 277
node placement **242**
non-contact and contact recurve bows **160**
noriyumi (betting-bow) competitions 271
Norman invasion of Ireland, the 10–11
North American composite bows **161,** 161–162
Novotny, Lukas 164, **164, 165, 181, 182, 185, 198**

Novotny bow, the **106**
Nydam longbows, the 12

Obusuma Saburō 268
Obusuma Saburō Ekotoba (narrative scroll) 268
Oda Nobunaga 294
Of Englishe Dogges (book) **145**
Ogasawara Kiyomoto **258, 260, 281**
Ogasawara Magoroku **286**
Ogasawara Mochinaga 266
Ogasawara Nagakiyo **261**
Ogasawara-ryū (school) 261–262, **263,** 271, 272, **281**
Ogasawara Sadamune 264
Ogilvy, Sir Patrick 71
ok meydani (arrow places/shooting ground) **196–197,** 199, 210
olive wood and bow construction 101
Ōmato Taiki (Festival of the Great Target) 283
On Marvellous Things Heard (book) 223
one-foot crossbow *(arbalistae ad unum pedem),* the **118**
one-piece plates 16
Onin War, the 274
Orléans, relief of 71
ornamentation 89, 100, **107, 114,** 115, **136, 143, 147, 152, 155,** 156–158, 177, **177, 178,** 187, **198**
'Ortie' (great-crossbow) 146
Oshia, Prince 257–258
osier wickerwork 139
Othée, battle of 74
Ottoman horse-archery 193–198, **196–197**
Ottoman military treatises 130–131
Ottoman track, the 195–196, **196–197,** 199, 210
Ottoman war bow **157**
Ötzi (Stone Age hunter) 12, 297
'overdraw' 210
overlapping scales of hardened leather as armour **228,** 230
Ovid 224
ō yoroi (samurai armour) 290
ōyakazu (great many arrows) event 282–283
ōyumi (Japanese crossbow) 124–125, **125**

Pain, Dr Matthew 84
palanquin bow *(kago hankyū)* 250, **250**
Pant, G.N. 176
papal bans on the crossbow 88, 90
Paris, Matthew 134
Paris, siege of **72,** 139
Parthian horse-archers **202–204,** 225
Parthian horseman carving **206**
Parthian saddle **225**
Parthian shot, the 201, **201, 202–204,** 262
Paskyn, John 133
Paston, John 10
Paston, Margaret 10
Patay, battle of **63**
Paterson, W.F. 91, 114, **118,** 152, 158, 176, 253
patten-making 26–27
pavise (mantlet), the 53, **53, 136,** 139
pay
 for archers 41, **41, 42,** 43, **45,** 73
 for crossbowmen 126–128, 129, **132,** 133–134
Payne-Gallwey, Sir Ralph 103, **118, 136,** 150
Peasants' Revolt (1831), the 36
peherer (runner) 188, 190
penetration testing 82–86, **85**
Percy, Sir Harry **62**
Perry, Cmdr Matthew 236
Peter the Saracen 126
Peterson, Maria **273**
Philip II Augustus, King (France) 126, 133
Philip of Macedon 222
Philip the Fair 145
Philip the Good 74, 75
Philip VI, King (France) 19, 54
Phoenician finger-tips **182**
Phylarchus 220
Pian del Carpine, Giovanni da 228–230
'piecing' and arrow repair 27, **27**
Piers Ploughman (poem) 43
pila (javelins) **202–204**
Pinkie Cleugh, battle of 39, **63,** 87

Pizan, Christine de 137, 139, 146, **148**
pizane (mail standard) 15
plate armour 86, 129, **132,** 149, 151, **154, 209,** 230, **230,** 286, 289, 290, **291,** 292, **292**
 see also breastplates
poison arrows 216, 223, 224
Poitiers, battle of 27, **42, 45,** 60, **62**
Pollaiuolo, Antonion del 113
Polo, Marco 228
popinjay shooting 40, **40, 143,** 145
power-stroke, the 91, 92, **92, 93,** 101–102
practice of archery by royal decree, the 33, **34–35,** 34–36, 37, 38–39, **39,** 71
practice of drawing 164
precision bronze casting 122
'prickshaft,' the 38, 39
'princess curve' *(himezori)* **242,** 249
Pro Aris et Focis (book) 87
Procopius 226
production costs 155
protection and armour 230–231
 see also armour proofing
punishment for manufacture of sub-standard arrows 81
puta (leather bag target) 208, **209**

qabaq (gourd), the 193–194, **194, 196,** 208
Qi, Jiguang 205, 206
Qing arrow **158**
Qing bow, the **157, 160, 169,** 169–170
Qing Dynasty, the 94, 95, **123, 157,** 168, 169, 186, 187, 199, **228**
Qing military examinations, the 207–208
quarrels **31,** 91, **144,** 146, **146,** 147, **148–149**
Queen Mary Psalter, the **100**
quenching 149
quill, the **24,** 94, **143, 183, 215**
quivers **146, 147, 216,** 216–217, **217,** 219, **221,** 250, **252,** 253–255, **254, 255, 256,** 259, **266–267, 291**

range and arrow force 79, 80
range and effectiveness in battle 285, 289–290
range of the crossbow 150–151, 152–153
rapid nocking 205
rate of deceleration, the 79, 151–152
rationing of flights to distant targets 53, 81, 82
rattan binding 245, **256**
razor-nock arrow, the **215**
recruitment and mobilization 41–42, 43, **45,** 48, 129
recurve composite bows 159, 161, **211**
recurved longbows 6, **75, 82,** 160
Redwood Kyudojo, California **273, 281**
reflex bow-limbs 159, **162,** 241
reflex laths 107
reisha (ceremonial archery) 257
Renata, Apella 137
rendering shot arrows unusable 213
replacements for breakages 46
replica blunts **37, 38**
retrieval and repair of arrows 27, **27**
rice-glues 240
Richard I, King 90, 126, **128**
Richard III, King 20, 61
Richemont, Arthur de 73
Richerus (Richer of Reims) 125
rikugei (accomplishments) of a gentleman 257
'rising peg' system, the **100**
riveting (stitching) plates 15–16
Robin of York **120**
rocket arrows 212
Roger of Wendover 134, 137
Rogers, Clifford 26
rolling nut, the 98, **98,** 99, **99**
Roman crossbows 97–99, **98**
Romance of Wu an Yue (book) 122–123
rongyu (Chinese mounted infantryman) 122, **123**
Rothwell, William 104
Rotwyler, Michel **131**
Rouen, siege of 134
Royal Collection, Sandringham House 177
royal pardons 42, 43
Royal Toxophilite Society, the 209
Ruckarmbrust (German 'back' crossbow) 111

kulak (leather insert) 187, **187**
Kul'Oba burial mound, Ukraine 218, **218, 219**
Kumagai Naozane **234–235**, 290
kura (saddles) **256, 263**
Kurikara, battle of **266–267**
kusajishi (horse-archery event) 258
kusazuri (armour panels) **291**, 292
kusune (resin-oil mixture) 244
Kyriell, Sir Thomas 63
kyūba no michi (the way of the bow and the horse) 234, 257
kyūdō (the way of the bow) 236, 245, 248, **256, 260,** 271–274
kyūjutsu (the art of archery) 234, 271

lacquering and binding the *yumi* 245
lacquering of arrow-shafts and quivers 250, **252, 254**
Ladislaus Jagiello, King (Poland) 20, 22
lamellar armour **230**, 278
laminated lath, the 104
lances 69
lances fournies 72, 73
land endowments for crossbowmen 126, 129
Landsknechte, the 76
Langland, William 43
latchet, the **120**, 120–121
lath, the 91, 92, 94, **94, 96,** 104, 107, **108,** 118, 119, **124, 128, 143**
Latimer, Hugh 37
le Areblaster, William 129
le Baker, Geoffrey 14, 59, 64, 147
Le Livre de Chasse (book) 46
leather thumb-tabs 182–183
Lee, Gen Charles 87
leg tendons **171,** 174
length of Japanese *yumi* 248–249
Leo VI, Emperor 232
Liang, Zhuge 94
Liebel, Jean 116, 118, 120, 147, 151
lightweight longbows 10
Lincoln, siege of 134–137
linden and shield construction **136**
livery arrows 78, 85
lock, the 91, 92, 93, **93,** 99
long draw, the 22
long-needle bodkin arrowhead 32
longbow, the 8–13, 19–24, **20, 21,** 33, 40, **50,** 53, 54, 55–61, 66, 68, **75,** 75–87, 101, **148,** 151, 158, 159, **227,** 292
Longbow, The (book) 11, 292
longbow fraternities 73
looting and plundering 43, **45, 48–49,** 50
Lor, Raymond de 133
Loshult gun, the 58
Louis, VIII, King (France) 134–137
Louis IX, King (France) 128
Louis XI, King (France) 73
Luttrell, Sir Geoffrey 37
Luttrell Psalter, the **36,** 37, **37,** 111, **111**

Ma, Justin **207**
Macmillan, Tim **263,** 281
madake bamboo **240**
Maes Moydog, battle of 128–129
Magna Carta, the 128
Magnus, Claus 152
Magyar/Hun bow, the 167, **167,** 174
mail 14–15, **15**
Maling, battle of 124
manchira (mail-lined jacket) 291
Manchu era, the 226
Manchu infantry archers **228–229**
Manchu plum-needle arrow, the 207, **214**
Manchu quiver **216**
Manchu track, the 199–200
Mancini, Dominic 15
Maniwa Nen-ryū, (manual) 280
maple as a building material 170, **170**
Marcellinus, Ammianus 213
Marignano, battle of 134
Marshall, William 128, 137
Martin of Nazareth 126

Martyrdom of Saint Sebastian, The (painting) 113
maruki-yumi, the 238, **238–239**
Mary Rose (warship) excavation, the 12, 20, 22, 26, **28, 48,** 61
Mason, R.O. 87
massed ranks of archers 36, 84
materials used in composite bows 170–174, **171, 172**
materials used in *yumi* 238–240, **239, 240, 241**
Maximilian I, Emperor 76–77, **130**
McEwen, Edward **215**
Meare Heath bow, the **297**
medieval hood, the 43–44
medieval knights 11
medieval longbows 10–11, 12
mempo (face mask) 293, **293**
Metropolitan Museum of Art, New York 99, 114, 121, 182
Miao, the **124**
Milemete, Walter de **116**
military context of bows, the 6, 11, 13
military manuals 97, **116, 130, 131,** 194, 195, 196, 200, 206, **210,** 217, 232, 285, 287
Minamoto no Tametomo 286–287, **287**
Minamoto no Yoritomo, Shōgun 261, 262
Minamoto no Yoshiari 261
Minamoto no Yoshinaka **248, 266,** 269, **278–279**
Minamoto no Yoshitsune 285, 287–288, **292**
Ming bow, the 168, **169**
Ming Dynasty, the 93, **124,** 168, 186
Miyoshi Kiyotsura 125
Mizushima, battle of **246–248**
modern steel bows 180–181
mogu (Korean hunting-related contest) 200, 266
mokuba (wooden horse) **256, 263**
Moleyns, Robert 10
Mongolian bow, the **168,** 168
Monstrelet, Enguerrand de 44, 60, 80
Montfort, Simon de 138
Morizumi Suwa 261
Morse, Edward **182**
mounted archers *see* horse-archer, the
mounted crossbowmen **130–131,** 133–134
Mughal crab bow 157, **166**
mulberry wood 239–240
multiple-bolt, single-bow siege crossbow **96**
Münyetü'l-Guzat (treatise) 194, **196,** 206, **210**
Murad II, Sultan **194**
Murphy, Paul 281
museum exhibits 12, 13–14, 19, 91, 99, 108, 114, 121, 150, **152,** 155, 177, 196, **204, 205,** 206
Museum of the Han Dynasty, the **30**
mushamma (waxed linen) **198**

naginata (pole weapon blade) **278,** 280
namisun (regular *yumi* bow) 248
naraca (iron arrow) **213**
Nasu no Yoichi 285–286, **286**
Nationalmuseet, Copenhagen 12
Native American archery 191
naval archery 40, **40,** 61–68, **65, 66–67, 68,** 146–147
Naval Research Advisory Committee report (2007) 13
navek (arrow-guide) **213**
Neade, William 87
Neolithic Period, the 12
nerigawa kozane (rawhide scales) 293
Neville's Cross, battle of **62**
New Year ceremonial events 281
nigiri (grip) 245
Nihāyat al-suʾl wa l-umniyya fi taʿlīm aʿmal al-furūsiyya (manual) 217
Nihon Shoki (chronicle) 257–258
Nikephoros II Phokas, Emperor 232
Nikkō Tōshōgū shrine 261, **263**
Nitta Yoshisada 293
nobi (long *yumi* bow) 248
nockless arrow, the **215**
nocks **215, 221,** 241, **244,** 250, 274, 277
node placement **242**
non-contact and contact recurve bows 160
noriyumi (betting-bow) competitions 271
Norman invasion of Ireland, the 10–11
North American composite bows **161,** 161–162
Novotny, Lukas 164, **164, 165, 181, 182, 185, 198**

Novotny bow, the **106**
Nydam longbows, the 12

Obusuma Saburō 268
Obusuma Saburō Ekotoba (narrative scroll) 268
Oda Nobunaga 294
Of Englishe Dogges (book) **145**
Ogasawara Kiyomoto **258, 260, 281**
Ogasawara Magoroku 286
Ogasawara Mochinaga 266
Ogasawara Nagakiyo 261
Ogasawara-ryū (school) 261–262, **263**, 271, 272, **281**
Ogasawara Sadamune 264
Ogilvy, Sir Patrick 71
ok meydani (arrow places/shooting ground) **196–197**, 199, 210
olive wood and bow construction 101
Ōmato Taiki (Festival of the Great Target) 283
On Marvellous Things Heard (book) 223
one-foot crossbow *(arbalistae ad unum pedem),* the **118**
one-piece plates 16
Onin War, the 274
Orléans, relief of 71
ornamentation **89**, 100, **107, 114,** 115, **136, 143, 147, 152, 155,** 156–158, 177, **177, 178,** 187, **198**
'Ortie' (great-crossbow) 146
Oshia, Prince 257–258
osier wickerwork 139
Othée, battle of 74
Ottoman horse-archery 193–198, **196–197**
Ottoman military treatises **130–131**
Ottoman track, the 195–196, **196–197,** 199, 210
Ottoman war bow **157**
Ötzi (Stone Age hunter) 12, 297
'overdraw' **210**
overlapping scales of hardened leather as armour **228**, 230
Ovid 224
ō yoroi (samurai armour) 290
ōyakazu (great many arrows) event 282–283
ōyumi (Japanese crossbow) 124–125, **125**

Pain, Dr Matthew 84
palanquin bow *(kago-hankyū)* 250, **250**
Pant, G.N. 176
papal bans on the crossbow 88, 90
Paris, Matthew 134
Paris, siege of **72**, 139
Parthian horse-archers **202–204**, 225
Parthian horseman carving **206**
Parthian saddle **225**
Parthian shot, the 201, **201, 202–204**, 262
Paskyn, John 133
Paston, John 10
Paston, Margaret 10
Patay, battle of **63**
Paterson, W.F. 91, 114, **118,** 152, 158, 176, 253
patten-making 26–27
pavise (mantlet), the 53, **53, 136,** 139
pay
    for archers 41, **41, 42,** 43, **45,** 73
    for crossbowmen 126–128, 129, **132,** 133–134
Payne-Gallwey, Sir Ralph 103, **118, 136,** 150
Peasants' Revolt (1831), the 36
peherer (runner) 188, 190
penetration testing 82–86, **85**
Percy, Sir Harry **62**
Perry, Cmdr Matthew 236
Peter the Saracen 126
Peterson, Maria **273**
Philip II Augustus, King (France) 126, 133
Philip of Macedon 222
Philip the Fair 145
Philip the Good 74, 75
Philip VI, King (France) 19, 54
Phoenician finger-tips **182**
Phylarchus 220
Pian del Carpine, Giovanni da 228–230
'piecing' and arrow repair 27, **27**
Piers Ploughman (poem) 43
pila (javelins) **202–204**
Pinkie Cleugh, battle of 39, **63**, 87

Pizan, Christine de 137, 139, 146, **148**
pizane (mail standard) **15**
plate armour 86, 129, **132,** 149, 151, **154, 209,** 230, **230,** 286, 289, 290, **291,** 292, **292**
    see also breastplates
poison arrows 216, 223, 224
Poitiers, battle of 27, **42, 45,** 60, **62**
Pollaiuolo, Antonion del 113
Polo, Marco 228
popinjay shooting 40, **40, 143,** 145
power-stroke, the 91, 92, **92, 93,** 101–102
practice of archery by royal decree, the 33, **34–35,** 34–36, 37, 38–39, **39,** 71
practice of drawing 164
precision bronze casting 122
'prickshaft,' the 38, 39
'princess curve' *(himezori)* **242,** 249
Pro Aris et Focis (book) 87
Procopius 226
production costs 155
protection and armour 230–231
    see also armour proofing
punishment for manufacture of sub-standard arrows 81
puta (leather bag target) 208, **209**

qabaq (gourd), the 193–194, **194, 196,** 208
Qi, Jiguang 205, 206
Qing arrow **158**
Qing bow, the **157, 160, 169,** 169–170
Qing Dynasty, the 94, 95, **123, 157,** 168, 169, 186, 187, 199, **228**
Qing military examinations, the 207–208
quarrels **31,** 91, **144,** 146, **146,** 147, **148–149**
Queen Mary Psalter, the **100**
quenching 149
quill, the **24,** 94, **143, 183, 215**
quivers **146, 147, 216,** 216–217, **217,** 219, **221,** 250, **252,** 253–255, **254, 255, 256,** 259, **266–267, 291**

range and arrow force 79, 80
range and effectiveness in battle 285, 289–290
range of the crossbow 150–151, 152–153
rapid nocking 205
rate of deceleration, the 79, 151–152
rationing of flights to distant targets 53, 81, 82
rattan binding 245, **256**
razor-nock arrow, the **215**
recruitment and mobilization 41–42, 43, **45,** 48, 129
recurve composite bows 159, 161, **211**
recurved longbows 6, **75, 82,** 160
Redwood Kyudojo, California **273, 281**
reflex bow-limbs 159, **162,** 241
reflex laths 107
reisha (ceremonial archery) 257
Renata, Apella 137
rendering shot arrows unusable 213
replacements for breakages 46
replica blunts **37, 38**
retrieval and repair of arrows 27, **27**
rice-glues 240
Richard I, King 90, 126, **128**
Richard III, King 20, 61
Richemont, Arthur de 73
Richerus (Richer of Reims) 125
rikugei (accomplishments) of a gentleman 257
'rising peg' system, the **100**
riveting (stitching) plates 15–16
Robin of York **120**
rocket arrows 212
Roger of Wendover 134, 137
Rogers, Clifford 26
rolling nut, the 98, **98, 99, 99**
Roman crossbows 97–99, **98**
Romance of Wu an Yue (book) 122–123
rongyu (Chinese mounted infantryman) 122, **123**
Rothwell, William 104
Rotwyler, Michel **131**
Rouen, siege of 134
Royal Collection, Sandringham House 177
royal pardons 42, 43
Royal Toxophilite Society, the 209
Ruckarmbrust (German 'back' crossbow) 111

Russell, Simon 103
rust 109
ryūha (schools of archery) 257, 261–262, **263**, 271, 272, **281**

saddle-pads 191, **224**, 224–225
safety cords **109**
sagittarii (regular archers) 97
Saint Sebastian archery guild, Lille 142
sakamogi (barricades) 278
sakoku (isolation of Japan) 236
sal (bending section) 159, **165**
Saladin 101, **126**, 206
sallet-style helmet **9**, **41**
'Sampson belt,' the 113
samurai, the **256**, 274, 288–289, **294–295**
 and armour 290–293, **291**, **292**, **293**
samurai horse-archer, the 234–236, **235**, 268–270, **278–279**, 288, **291**
 see also horse-archer, the
Sanbonhigo (bamboo construction style) **239**
Sanjūsangendō temple competition, Kyoto 255, 282, **283**
Sanmaeuchi (bamboo construction style) **239**
sanmaeuchi style of *yumi* 296
Saracen Archery (book) 181–182
Sarmatians, the **221**, 224
sashiya (rapid-shooting tactics) **275**
Sassanian draw, the **182**
Sassanian shooting glove, the 183, **184**
Satsuma Heki-ryū, the **276**
Sauveuses, Sir Guillaume de 60
Schweizerischen Museum, Zurich 150, **151**, **152**
Scottish archers 11, 54, 69, 70–72
Scottish decrees on longbow archers 71
screw (vice), the **115**, 115–116, **120**
Scythian archery 217–225, **220**, **221**, **224**
Scythian arrrowheads **222**, 222–223
Scythian bow, the **162**, 162–163, **163**, 218, **218**, 237
Scythian saddle **224**, 224–225
second arrow in the hand **273**, 274
Second Crusade, the 137
Secret History of the Mongols, The (book) 192
Selby, Stephen 93–94, 162, **163**
Selim III, Sultan 209
Seljuq Empire, the 192
'semi-proof' armour 16
Sengoku (Warring States) era, the 274
Senior, Steve **98**
Senwosret I, Pharaoh 183
Seventh Crusade, the 128
Shaho Sambu Sho (book) 238, 258, 269
shields 13–14, 277–278, 288
shigeto-yumi (lacquered bow with rattan binding) 245
Shihodake (bamboo construction style) **239**
Shijo Nawate, battle of 274
shiko-ebira (Japanese open quiver) 253, **254**
shikoro (neck guard) **292**, 293
Shinto ceremony in *yabusame* 259
shitagi (shirt) **291**
shitanaga abumi (Japanese stirrup) **263**
Shizugatake, battle of **290**
Shōkyū War, the 288
shooting at the marks **34–35**, 38–39, **39**
shooting contests 282–283
shooting guilds 142
shooting in elevation ('shooting underhand') **52**, 78
shooting on horseback **130–131**, 158, 185–188, 190–191
shooting rates 81, 82
shooting techniques **181**, 181–184, **182**, **183**, 185
shoulder-quivers 216–217
Shrewsbury, battle of **52**, **62**, **289**
Shushin-ron (treatise) 261, 262
Siberian ibex, the 162
Sibudu Cave, South Africa 297
sieges and the crossbow **134–135**, 134–139, **148**, 153
signalling through arrows 269
silk bowstrings 176
silk pom-poms on steel laths **109**, **155**
silver ring 187, **187**
sinew backing 161, **161**, 165, **171**, **173**
sipur, the 210, **210**, **213**
siyahs 159–161, **160**, 167, 211, **227**

Sluys, battle of 64–66, **66–67**, 147
'small curve' (*konari*) 249
Smart, William and John 42
Smythe, Sir John 10, 44, 78–79, **130**, **131**
snakeskin **107**
Soar, Hugh 80
sode (armour panels) 278, **291**
sōhei (warrior monk) 288
solid thumb-ring, the **186**, 186–187, **187**
Song Dynasty, the **96**
Southgrove Farm archaeological dig 98
spanning 91, 93, 97, **98**, 101–102, **102**, 105, 110–113, **111**, **112**, **113**, **116–117**, **118**, 120, **124**, **128**, **130–131**, **138**, 155
spanning stands (*hancepes*) 119, **119**, 151
specialist crossbowmen 126–134
'spine' of an arrow-shaft 250
sport and horse-archery 233
spur ring 186, **186**
St Briavels Castle, Gloucestershire, England 148
stacking 159
staghorn and relief carving 100
Statute 33 of Henry VIII 33
statute on distance shooting (1542) 39
Statutes of the Armourers of Paris (1451), the 16
steam-bent wood 107, 238
steel-lathed crossbows 108, 108–110, **109**, **116–117**, 119, 150, 152, 155, 180–181
steel production 110, 178, **178**, **179**
 and armour 16, 109
steel recurve bows of India **176**, 176–181, **177**
steeled arrowheads 30
Steigreifarmbrust (German stirrup crossbow) 111
Stepenova, Dr Elena 224–225
steppe pony, the 192
Stewart, John, Earl of Buchan 70–71
stirrup, the **110**, 110–111, **118**, **128**, **130**
stirrups for horse-archers 191–193, **225**, **263**
Stone, George Cameron 226, 294
stone arrowheads 297
stonebow, the 90
straight-limbed bow 160
'strength bows' 169, 170
Stretton, Mark 13, **25**, **28**, **29**, 68, 81, 83, 84
stringing the bow 174, 241–243, **243**
sugakji ('male' thumb-ring) 187, **187**
Sunaguchi Yoshinori **281**
suneate (shin-guards) 292
superstition and custom in Japanese bow-making 245–248
supply arrows in battle 46–47
swordsmiths 251
Symonds, Gary **52**

tachisukashi (riding style) 260–261, **291**
tactical aims of archers 231–233, 285
Tai bai yin jing (military manual) 124
Taiheiki (chronicle) 286
Taira no Atsumori **234–235**
Taira samurai **246–248**, 261, **266**, 269, 278, **278–279**, 280, 286–287
Taktika (book) 232
Tale of Aquat, The 170
Talhoffer, Hans **131**
tamahagane (Japanese steel) 251
tanabata (7-shot *kasagake* course) 265
Tanentonne, Peter de 126
Tang, Jingchuan 184
Tang Dynasty, the 124, **230**
targets in *kyūdō* **273**
tashin (bowyer's scraper) 172
tate (Japanese shields) 277
Taybughā *see* al-Yūnanī, Taybughā al-Ashrafī al-Baklamishī
tekne kuram Turkish bow, the 164, **165**
tempering 30, 179
Tenchōchikyū no Shiki (the ceremony of heaven and earth) 259
tendyek (tensioning tool) 172
Tengu goblin incendiary arrow 282
tepeliks 174, **174**, 175
terms for feudal service 129
Terracotta Army, the 93, 123
territorial militia of archers in France 73

tests of crossbow bolt speeds 55
testudo (tortoise) battle formation **202–204**
Tewkesbury, battle of **63**
textile armour 15, 31, **84**
Third Crusade, the 126, **126–127**
Thomas of Split, Archdeacon 192
Thompson, Maurice 210
three-finger draw shooting technique, the 182
thumb-draw shooting technique, the 181–182, **182**, 221, 255
thumb-ring, the 183–184, **186,** 186–187, **187,** 200, **207,** 221, **221**
thumb-tab, the 182–183, **183**
tiller (stock), the 91, 100–101, **102, 103, 108,** 112, **125, 131,** 175
Todeschini, Leo **97, 98,** 99, **99, 109, 111,** 113, **120, 121**
togari-ya (pointed arrows) **252**
tōkasagake (single-shot *kasagake* course) 265
Tokugawa Iemitsu 236
Tokugawa Ieyasu 236
tombstone in Landesmuseum, Mainz **205**
tomo (arm-guard) 255–256
topography selection on the battlefield 53, 58–59, 86
toshiya (passing arrows) competition 282–283
Tournai, siege of (1340) 50
Tower Armoury, the 146, **148**
Tower of London, the 115
Towton, battle of 30, **30,** 60–61, **63**
Toxophilus (book) 26, 158
Toyotomi Hideyoshi 236
training 38–39, 122, 194–200, **196–197,** 207–208, 227, 257, 258, **263,** 264, **270,** 272, 275–277, **276,** 282
Treaty of Brétigny, the 34
trebuchet barrages 213
trigger, the **100**
Tsagaan Khad Mongolian bow, the **168**
tsubo-abumi (Japanese stirrup) **263**
tsukai-ban (rank of samurai) **294–295**
tsumari (short *yumi* bow) 248
tsuru (shooting string) **244**
tsurubashiri-gawa (the bowstring running leather) **292**
Tsurugaoka Hachiman shrine 261
tulughma (horse-flanking manoeuvres) 232
tuning the bow 175
Turkish bow, the 164–165, **165, 217**
Turkish targets **209**
Turkoman/Arab horse, the 192
Turpin the *arbilistarius* 126
Tusard, Gerard **130,** 133
two-finger salute, the **45**
two-foot crossbow (*arbalistae ad duos pedes*), the **118**

Uesugi samurai **294–295**
Uji, battle of 278–280, **280**
UK Defence Academy, Shrivenham 151
Ulrich V of Württemberg, Count **89**
Umetada, Motoshige **252**
Umetada Myōju 251
urushi (lacquer) 245
Utagawa Kuniyoshi **290**
Utagawa Yoshikazu **268**
utsubo-ebira (elaborate closed quiver) 253

Valencia, siege of 153
valet de guerre 72
Varangians, the 211
Vasistha 200, 207, 208, **210, 213**
Vegetius 97, 137
Vergil, Polydore 61
Verneuil, battle of 53, **63,** 71
Villani, Filippo 69
Vinci, Leonardo da 119
vintenars **42, 45, 48–49**
viretons (vires) 146, 154
Vishnudharmottara Purana (poem) 179
volley-shooting 79–80, 124, 147

Wadge, Richard 43
wakibiki (short jacket) 291
Wallace Collection, the **18,** 79, **108, 115, 155,** 177

Wallop, Sir John 153–154
Walsingham, Thomas 82, 150
War in Ancient India (book) 180
waraji (rice straw pad) **244**
warbows and the recreational longbow 10
Warring States Papers, The 148–149
Warring States period in China, the 92, 94, 95, 186
Wars of Scottish Independence (1296–1357) 11
Wars of the Roses (1455–85) 11, 27, 43, 60–61, **63**
Wasa Daihachirō 283
water buffalo horn 106, **170,** 174
Wavrin, Jean de 44, **45**
waxing of crossbow strings 44, **136**
Way of Archery, The (book) 168, 175, **207**
Weapons That Made Britain – Longbow (TV programme) 55, 79
Wedyngton, Rychardus (Dick Whittington) 36
Welsh archers 11, 78
wet-weather clothing 43–44
Wheatley, Mark 38
whistling arrows **212, 256, 259, 266,** 269
'White Company', the 69
William, Duke 211
William II Rufus, King 88–89, 125
William of Alberney 134
William of Poitiers 125
William of Tyre 205
Williams, Dr Alan 79
Willoughby, Lord 133
Wilson, Guy 102
windlass, the 101, 112, **112, 116–117, 118,** 138, 139–141, **143,** 154, 155
wood for arrows 24, 26–27
woodcut of *samurai* **234–235**
wooden bow-staves 104–105
wooden crossbows 102–104, **103,** 106–107, **128**
wooden laths 101, **102, 134–135,** 150
wootz 178–179, **179**
wych elm and bow construction 20, 107
Wynkeley, Richard 83

Xiongnu, the 191

yabusame (Japanese mounted archery exhibitions) 256, **256,** 258, 258–259, 260–262, **263, 264,** 291
yadome (deflecting arrows) 278, 280, **280**
yadome no jutsu (the art of arrow-cutting) 280
Yashima, battle of 285, **286,** 287–288
Yayoi period, the 237
yew and bow construction 20, **21, 74,** 78, 101, 102, 103, 107, 119, 120
Yin, Chen 122–123
Yohonhigo (bamboo construction style) **239**
Yokoyama Keitarō **241,** 242
Yoshida Shigekata 271
Yoshida Shigemasa 271
You, Du 124
Ystoria Mongalorum (book) 228
yugake (shooting glove) 255, **256**
yugaeri (bow rotation) **260,** 272
yumi (Japanese bow) 158, 234–236, **236, 237,** 237–249, **239, 240, 241, 242–243, 244, 256,** 275, 296
yumigata-kyōseiki (shaping blocks) 241, **244**
yumihajime (New Year shooting event) **281**
yumiya no michi (the way of the bow and arrow) 234
Yūryaku, Emperor 257–258

Zen Buddhism 257
Zhou Dynasty, the 185, 187
Zhuge Nu (Chinese crossbow) 94–95
Zi, Mo 96
Zie, Étienne 199, 207–208
Zōhyō Monogatari (manual) 275, 285, 293, **296**
zoorkhaneh training routine 180